MAN AND SOCIETY

CONTRIBUTORS TO THIS VOLUME

ELIO D. MONACHESI
University of Minnesota

J. O. HERTZLER
University of Nebraska

WILSON D. WALLIS
University of Minnesota

HERBERT BLUMER
University of Chicago

HOWARD P. LONGSTAFF
University of Minnesota

GEORGE B. VOLD
University of Minnesota

LAWRENCE D. STEEFEL
University of Minnesota

RICHARD A. HARTSHORNE
University of Minnesota

EVRON M. KIRKPATRICK
University of Minnesota

JOSEPH R. STARR
University of Minnesota

EMERSON P. SCHMIDT
University of Minnesota

RICHARD L. KOZELKA
University of Minnesota

MARY J. SHAW
University of Minnesota

MAN AND SOCIETY

A SUBSTANTIVE INTRODUCTION
TO THE SOCIAL SCIENCES

EDITED BY

EMERSON P. SCHMIDT
UNIVERSITY OF MINNESOTA

NEW YORK
PRENTICE-HALL, INC.
1937

268553

Preface

OWING to the growth of the separate disciplines and to the breadth of materials in the social sciences, few people have a clear conception of the scope, purpose, and content of the whole field. In order to introduce the student in his first or second year to all the social sciences, an increasing number of colleges have introduced orientation courses, in which several weeks are devoted to each of the major disciplines.

This book had its origin in the difficulty of securing adequate materials for such a course in which several of the contributors have participated. At the University of Minnesota an outline syllabus directing the student to scores of books has been used, on the theory that there is merit in an examination of the work and viewpoints of many authors. But for extension students and for many colleges this procedure is impossible. A need exists for a single book that will survey the field of the social sciences but that will preserve the advantage of presenting the work and viewpoints of a number of authors.

The aim of the present volume has been to acquaint the reader with the core of knowledge in each of the social sciences. Because space limitations prevent an exhaustive treatment of the various subjects, a selected bibliography is provided at the end of each chapter for those who wish to devote more time to any of the topics. This introduction to the spirit, the methods, and the subject matter of each of the social sciences should prove educationally valuable to the student and should provide, to some extent, vocational guidance early in his college career.

The editor wishes to thank the contributors for their prompt and whole-hearted coöperation in compiling this work. Many of them have read and criticized chapters prepared by their colleagues. In addition, thanks should be given to Eugen Altschul, Bruce D. Mudgett, D. G. Paterson, J. W. Stehman, Arthur R. Upgren, and Dale Yoder, each of whom has criticized one or more of the chapters and made many helpful suggestions.

EMERSON P. SCHMIDT

Editor

Contents

CHAPTER   PAGE

I. SOCIOLOGY AND CULTURE, *Elio D. Monachesi* 1

Introduction 1
The nature of group behavior 5
Definition of Sociology 7
Sociology as a Science 9
Sociology and the other sciences 13
The methods of sociology 18
The Nature of Human Groups 24
Primary groups 24
Secondary groups 25
The Nature of Culture 29
The culture trait 30
The culture complex and pattern 32
Folkways, Mores, and Institutions 37
Social Change 41
Differential rates of change in parts of cultures.... 45
Maladjustment and the Individual 50
The Value of Sociology 52

II. SOCIAL INSTITUTIONS, *J. O. Hertzler* 55

A Birdseye View of Social Institutions 57
The Causes of Institutions 58
The Range of Social Institutions 59
The Functions of Institutions 60
The satisfaction of human needs 61
The mechanisms of community existence 61
The instruments of social control 62
Attributes or "Type Parts" of Institutions 63
The underlying idea 64
A complex of folkways, mores, and customs 64
Codes 65
Standardized habits 65
Associations or organizations 66
Physical extensions or property 66

CHAPTER PAGE

II. SOCIAL INSTITUTIONS *(Cont.)*

The Main Groups of Institutions in Modern Society.. 67
Economic institutions 68
Matrimonial and domestic institutions............ 70
Political institutions 73
Educational and scientific institutions............ 76
Communicative institutions 78
Religious institutions 79
The æsthetic and expressional institutions........ 80
Recreational institutions....................... 81
Health institutions 82
The Overlapping and the Interrelationship of Insti-
tutions 84
Institutions and Social Change................... 85
Institutions do change......................... 85
Culture contact and institutional change.......... 87
The relative inflexibility of institutions........... 89

III. SOCIAL ANTHROPOLOGY, *Wilson D. Wallis*........ 92

The Field of Anthropology...................... 92
Some Phases of Anthropology.................... 94
Social Groupings 98
The household circle 101
The camp 102
Ceremonial grouping 103
Comradeship 104
Social orientation of personality................. 105
Age 107
Social functions of dress and ornament........... 110
The medicineman 113
Initiation ceremonies 116
Status of the child............................ 120
Separation of the sexes........................ 128
Freedom and compulsion in marriage............. 131
Kinship 136
Joking relationships 136
Opinion 138
Chieftainship 141
In Conclusion 142

CHAPTER   PAGE
IV. SOCIAL PSYCHOLOGY, *Herbert Blumer* 144

Introduction 144
Original Nature 147
The Nature of the Group Setting................. 154
Development of Social Conduct................... 160
Human Nature 166
Social Interaction 169
Personality 175
Motivation 184
The Study of Conduct and Personality........... 186
The Present Status of Social Psychology......... 196

V. PSYCHOLOGY AND SOME OF ITS APPLICATIONS, *Howard P. Longstaff* 199

Part I—General Psychology....................... 199
The Subject Matter of Psychology................ 199
Scientific Psychology vs. Popular Opinion.......... 201
Native Behavior 203
Emotions 205
How Original Behavior Is Modified............... 206
Learning 208
Conditioned Responses 209
Insight 211
Transfer of training.......................... 211
The effect of age on learning................. 212
Improving one's learning...................... 213
Factors Affecting Memory....................... 215
Motivation—Why We Learn..................... 216
Complexes 220
Rationalization 221
Personality 224
Part II—Applied Psychology...................... 231
Differential Psychology 231
The Law of Normal Distribution................. 232
Continuity of Variation......................... 234
Intelligence 235
The Binet Test................................ 235
Is intelligence native or acquired?.............. 238
Constancy of the I. Q......................... 239
Racial and nationality differences.............. 240

CHAPTER   PAGE
    V. PSYCHOLOGY AND SOME OF ITS APPLICATIONS
        (Cont.)
        Family histories 242
        Immediate ancestry 243
        Native Intelligence: Its Implications.............. 245
        Vocational Guidance 246
        Selection of Personnel.......................... 249
        The Psychology of Advertising.................... 249
          The application of the scientific attitude to adver-
            tising 249
          Applying psychological content in advertising..... 250
          Psychological techniques applied to advertising.... 252
        Psychology in Law............................. 254

   VI. MODERN CRIMINOLOGY, George B. Vold.......... 257
        The Problem of Crime and Its Definition........... 257
        The Amount and Cost of Crime................... 259
        Traits and Characteristics of Apprehended Criminals 265
        Environment and Crime......................... 272
        The Machinery of Justice........................ 277
          The police 277
          The prosecutor 282
          The judge 283
        What Should Be Done with Criminals?............ 286
          Changing penal philosophy..................... 286
          Institutional treatment of offenders.............. 289
          The indeterminate sentence, probation, and parole 292
          What does the present penal system accomplish?... 296
        Crime Prevention 298
          Helping the near-delinquent.................... 299
          Mobilizing existing community resources.......... 300
          Reducing community and general social disorgani-
            zation 301
          Eliminating the defectives..................... 302

  VII. HISTORY, Lawrence D. Steefel.................. 305
        What Is History?.............................. 305
        The Scope of History........................... 306
        How We Can Know About the Past................ 309
        Why We Want to Know About the Past............ 313

CHAPTER   PAGE
VIII. HUMAN GEOGRAPHY, *Richard A. Hartshorne*..... 323

The Nature and Purpose of Geography............ 323
Definition of geography........................ 324
General Principles of Land Utilization.............. 327
Regional contrasts in land use.................. 327
Regional land use reflects the comparative value of
resources 327
Summary of the major forms of settlement and land
use 329
World Survey of Agricultural Land Use............ 330
Lands of little or no development................ 330
The cultivated lands........................... 342
The Effect of Commerce on Regional Differentiation.. 354
Changes in transportation...................... 354
Bases of inter-regional trade................... 356
Importance of relative location................. 357
Regions of Industrial Urbanism................... 359
Factors underlying industrial location........... 359
The principal industrial areas.................. 365
Divisions of Human Geography.................. 373
Relations to Other Social Sciences................ 375
Significance of regional differentiation........... 375
Man and nature............................... 377

IX. ELEMENTS OF POLITICAL SCIENCE, *Evron M. Kirkpatrick* 380

Political Science: The Scope and Character of the
Present Study 380
The State as a Concept of Political Science........ 385
Sovereignty of the State....................... 389
Government—The Machinery of the State.......... 391
Law as a Concept of Political Science............. 393
Political Theory 398
Attempts to Classify States..................... 402
The Impossibility of Classifying States............ 403
Classification of Governments................... 404
Monarchy, aristocracy, and democracy........... 406
Unitary and federal systems................... 407
Parliamentary and presidential governments...... 410
Autocratic and democratic governments.......... 412

CHAPTER   PAGE
IX. ELEMENTS OF POLITICAL SCIENCE *(Cont.)*

The Constitution as the Basis of Government....... 428
The Study of International Relations.............. 429
  The future of international relations.............. 431
  Difficulty of achieving world coöperation......... 433
  Progress in international organization............ 437
  International law 438
  The League of Nations.......................... 439
  The International Labor Organization............ 440
  The Permanent Court of International Justice.... 440
  Other agencies of world organization............ 441
Conclusions 442

X. POPULAR PARTICIPATION IN GOVERNMENT, *Joseph
   R. Starr* 444

Self-Government in the Modern World............. 444
The Meaning of Citizenship...................... 446
  The rights and privileges of citizens.............. 448
  The duties and obligations of citizens............ 451
The Modes of Popular Participation in Government.. 452
  Public officeholding 452
  Voting 457
  The initiative, the referendum, and the recall...... 465
The Electoral Process........................... 469
  Nomination procedures 469
  The electoral campaign 477
  The election proper 483
The Individual Private Citizen and Public Policy... 484
The Organization of Popular Participation in Govern-
  ment 485
  The political party 485
  Other social groups............................ 493
The Improvement of the Modes of Popular Partici-
  pation in Government...................... 496

XI. THE MACHINERY OF GOVERNMENT, *Joseph R. Starr* 500

The Need for Political Organization............... 500
The Constitution 501
The Separation of Powers....................... 503

CHAPTER | PAGE

XI. THE MACHINERY OF GOVERNMENT *(Cont.)*

The Legislative Branch 510
Structure 510
The election of legislative bodies................. 513
The organization of legislative bodies............ 516
The Executive Branch........................... 518
Structure 518
The powers of the executive branch.............. 521
Functions of the Legislative Branch............... 524
Relations between the legislative and executive
branches 527
The Administration 535
The Judicial Branch 540

XII. THE ECONOMICS OF PRICE, *Emerson P. Schmidt*... 545

Production 548
The Entrepreneur in Production................... 550
Exchange Value 557
Regime of Price 560
Market Price 562
Normal or Long-Term Price...................... 573
Constant-cost industries 576
Decreasing-cost industries 577
Monopoly Economics 579
Application of Economic Theory.................. 582
Production under constant, increasing, and decreas-
ing cost 586
Prison production is relatively small............. 588
Conclusion 591

XIII. THE DISTRIBUTION OF INCOME, *Emerson P. Schmidt* 592

Income Defined 592
Wealth Defined 593
The Distribution of Wealth...................... 594
Functional and Personal Distribution of Income..... 598
Personal distribution of income................. 599
The factors of production...................... 603
The Marginal Productivity of Labor.............. 605
The Supply of Labor............................ 610

CHAPTER · PAGE

XIII. THE DISTRIBUTION OF INCOME *(Cont.)*

Causes of Inequalities............................ 614
The Correction of Inequalities..................... 623
    Eliminating monopolies 626
    Taxation 630
    Education 632

XIV. ECONOMIC SECURITY, *Emerson P. Schmidt*........ 636

Introduction 636
Workmen's Compensation 637
Health Insurance 640
    The British Columbia system of health insurance.. 644
    Criticisms of public medicine.................... 648
Old-Age Security 649
    Voluntary private industrial schemes............. 652
    Labor-union schemes 655
    Old-age retirement systems of public employees... 656
    State old-age aid before 1935................... 658
    Old-age assistance under federal-state laws....... 660
    Compulsory retirement pensions................. 661
    Constitutionality 667
Unemployment 668
    Types of unemployment........................ 668
    The extent of unemployment................... 669
    Seasonal unemployment 672
    Cyclical unemployment 673
    Who pays for the social security program?........ 687
Conclusion 696

XV. CAUSAL RELATIONSHIPS AND THEIR MEASUREMENT, *Richard L. Kozelka*........................ 698

Why? The Search for Causes...................... 698
The Development of Explanations................. 700
    Supernatural causes 700
    Natural causes 701
Natural Causes and the Scientific Method.......... 704
    The scientific attitude........................ 704
    Fundamental stages in the scientific method....... 706
How Much? The Statistical Measurement of Causes.. 725

CHAPTER PAGE

XV. CAUSAL RELATIONSHIPS AND THEIR MEASUREMENT
(Cont.)

Methods of Analyzing Masses of Data.............. 729
The central value—the average................. 729
The measure of dispersion 736
The measure of correlation 738
Index numbers and ratios...................... 742
Dangers of Statistical Indigestion................. 748

XVI. SOCIAL VALUATION, *Mary J. Shaw*.............. 752

Introduction 752
Value judgments and value terms.............. 753
Value judgments based on preference........... 754
Judgments of value in the social sciences......... 755
Critical Reflection in the Study of Social Values...... 759
Origin of reflection in social conflict.............. 759
Analysis of meaning—a first step in solving conflicts 765
Instrumental and final values................... 770
Freedom as a Social Value...................... 774
Limitations upon the meaning of freedom......... 774
Freedom of speech............................ 778
Conclusion 785

INDEX 787

CHAPTER I

Sociology and Culture

ELIO D. MONACHESI

University of Minnesota

INTRODUCTION

MANY people have read or seen Marc Connelly's now famous fable, "The Green Pastures." [1] Without attempting to evaluate the artistry or beauty of this creation, we find that it gives us dramatically significant illustrative material in the realm of sociological phenomena. Although many of the situations in this play are symbolic and for some may seem vague and even without meaning, "The Green Pastures" unfolds before us a universal phenomenon that sociologists have called "ethnocentrism." [2] Neither the story nor the Biblical history of mankind is the main interest of "The Green Pastures" to sociologists; the focal point of their attention is the manner in which a certain portion of our population, the so-called backward Negro of our Southern States, anthropomorphizes and interprets the teachings of the Bible. Cultural anthropologists have pointed out that mankind the world over demonstrates an interest in and participates in practices that are defined as religious. Whether the existent belief is in one all-powerful God or in a group of gods, the mechanism under-

---

[1] Connelly, Marc, *The Green Pastures* (Farrar & Rinehart, New York, 1929).
[2] Sumner, William Graham, *Folkways*, pp. 13–15 (Ginn & Company, Boston, 1906).

1

lying these practices appears to be the same. What is of importance to sociologists are the various beliefs and interpretations that mankind places upon these religious experiences. Myths regarding man's origin are many and varied. Similarly, there are differences in the purposes that are attached to man's life on earth, and this diversity extends to the status of man after death.

Many people believe in some kind of an existence after death. This existence may take place in a "heaven" or in a "happy hunting ground." Usually this sought-after place is the antithesis of what people consider undesirable and unsatisfactory on earth. Heaven, or whatever it is called, is a state which the individual has come to regard and to believe desirable. In "The Green Pastures," heaven is pictured as a place where the activities of the individual are centered around a perpetual fish-fry, an abundance of ten-cent cigars, and rhythm. For the majority of Southern rural Negroes these are the elements constituting a desirable and happy existence. Their experiences and their contacts with the world of reality direct their thinking, especially their wishful thinking, into such fanciful realms.

Unless we are sophisticated to the point of scoffing at naïvete, there is another sociological lesson to be derived from "The Green Pastures." Man in general seems to pattern God and the hosts of heaven as personalities much like himself. Thus in "The Green Pastures" God becomes "de Lawd," wearing the frock of a Southern Negro preacher, using the Southern Negro dialect, and behaving in general as a venerated, respected, negro minister. He is conceived in terms of the experiences and within the limits of the horizons of the people who create Him. To be sure, this is the God of the superstitious and highly emotional Negro of the Old South. Nevertheless, the sociological principle of ethnocentrism, or cultural conditioning, is to be found there. By ethnocentrism we mean the habit of looking at other people, their behavior, and their products in terms of one's own behavior, experience, and products. People tend to place themselves and their activities in the center of the universe and rate other peoples' acts and expressions in terms of the amount of similarity arising from the comparison. The greater the degree of similarity, the more the likelihood of their acceptance.

Persons, also, in general are apt to engage in fanciful creations in terms of their experiences. The phenomenon of ethnocentrism with its emphasis upon a person's own experiences and ways of going about the activities of life gives that person a point of departure for excursions into the lives of people outside his own circle of acquaintances. In general, unless factors have modified the individual's attitudes (to be discussed later), the tendency will be to place one's own behavior and one's own group above all others. In other words, we all feel more or less superior about what we do and what we possess, and tend to evaluate others by our own standards.

What, in our experiences and habits, makes us react in this way? What makes the Southern rural Negro think of Heaven as a continuous fish-fry? What makes the Sicilian immigrant pin a five-dollar bill on a standard whose center is covered with the image of his patron saint on a particular Sunday morning? Why is this Sunday specifically designated as the occasion for escorting that saint, to the tune of a brass band, up and down the streets of a "little Italy"? Why, for instance, are we ready and do we consider it the manly thing to take up arms and kill in defense of our country, but not in defense of our fraternity or sorority? Why, if we come from old Bostonian homes, are we apt to consider afternoon tea a laudatory custom and an expression of refinement? Why do we think that the practice of the *couvade,* among some of the tribes of British Guiana, is barbaric, or at least, superstitious?

Many answers have been given to these and to similar questions. Often the answer is based on the commonly employed and little understood term, "human nature." Thus, it is explained, one does not kill his parents because it is not "human nature" to do so; or, one refrains from breaking some of the mandates of the moral code because it is not "human nature" to do so. The answers in another category have been based on the acceptance of a psychological theory—the belief in numerous "forces," "drives," and "instincts," or a few specific ones. These are supposed to provide the source of human behavior as well as to direct it. An individual may instinctively kill another when questions of honor are involved. The newspapers now and again announce in the column of an enthusiastic but unwary sports writer that the hero of the hour plays football "instinctively." Or the trapped heroine of a novel is driven by her finer instincts to fight off the villain with his insidious and ulterior motives. Again, who has not heard that "gentlemen are born, not made"?

Still another category of answers depends on the concept "race." The Italian sings and whistles tunes from the grand operas because he is an Italian. The Jew is a shrewd business man because he is a Jew. The Negro is lazy and full of rhythm because he is a Negro. These are common enough explanations even though they explain nothing and in the process misuse the term "race."

If we are to attempt a satisfactory answer to these questions, it is necessary first to analyze what it is we are attempting to do. To be sure, we are trying to explain the "why" of human behavior, but in explaining it we must first of all know something about the individual whose behavior we are attempting to explain.

The nature of group behavior

To most of us it is obvious that the individual's behavior varies from group to group. It may be said that groups of people set the stage for the individual's behavior. It is also obvious that the individual acts differently when he is alone and without contact with others. The behavior of the individual at a church service, where attention and reverence is required, is certainly different from the behavior of that same individual at a dance given by his fraternity to celebrate the exploits of the football team. Yet in both of these instances the individual remains physically the same. His inherited talents, mental and physical, remain constant. *What has happened is that the setting has been changed.* The individual has been removed from one setting and placed in another, and it is because of these different settings that the individual's behavior has changed. Each setting calls for a definite type of behavior on the part of the individual, if he is to get along satisfactorily with others. There are exceptions, but on the whole it is true that most of us behave in accordance with the pattern prescribed by the setting.

An examination of the setting will show that it is usually made up of other people, specific patterns of behavior, and values. The behavior patterns set down what can and what cannot be done by the individuals. They define what is acceptable from us in a specified situation, and what is not. Thus the traditional position of the lowly pledge of a fraternity in comparison with that of the initiated member is really a matter of prescription. Each part has been defined beforehand and each individual is expected to play his part in accordance with its definition. The goal of such behavior, that is, the playing of one's part according to its definition, is acceptance. We attach significance to our behavior because it obtains for us the approval of others, and by playing the game according to the rules we succeed in adjusting ourselves to others who also play according to the same rules. These rules are nothing more than specific behavior patterns identified with each of the groups to which we belong or with which we come in contact, and which, in effect, make each group different from other groups in so far as behavior is concerned. These behavior patterns become identified with values for the individuals who belong to the groups. There develops, therefore, an emotional attachment on the part of the individual for these patterns. Any deviation from them is frowned upon and arouses resentment and antagonism. These find their expression in a variety of ways, ranging from the heaping of ridicule on the deviator to his complete removal from the group. Thus, the individual who behaves boorishly at a dinner party, who dares not eat in accordance with the dictates of polite society, will be ridiculed and snubbed, and will probably not be invited again. On the other hand, the person caught taking silver is removed and placed in a public institution.

All of these are illustrations of how the behavior of the individual varies from situation to situation, and these situations must be thought of in terms of other persons, whose approval or disapproval attaches significance to this behavior. It is this behavior of the individual and the forms it assumes in various groups that constitute the field of *sociology*. The sociologists' main purpose is to understand the individual's relation to groups, how he is affected by them, and how he in turn affects the groups.

DEFINITION OF SOCIOLOGY

There have been numerous definitions of *sociology*. An examination of them will show that although they differ, they nevertheless possess a basic uniformity. All are primarily concerned with, among other things, man's behavior in groups. Man's behavior in groups is different from his behavior in isolation, and it has not been adequately or satisfactorily explained by any of the other numerous disciplines that make up that activity to which has been given the name "science." The focal point of the sociologist is social relationships, interaction, the relation of one individual to others, or the reciprocal modification of persons in contact with one another.

It is of small concern, from the standpoint of sociology, to know that Italy's population is about forty-three million. To know this is of little assistance in understanding the relations that exist between the rural Sicilian and the suave member of the professional class in Milan. Nor does it help us to understand how the average Italian feels about Mussolini's dictatorship, or how he feels about having to draw in his belt another notch in order to make possible, as he is told, another Roman Empire. The mere enumeration of members of a particular group yields little beyond the fact that such and such a number constitutes some particular group.

However, the individuals who are counted together produce something through being associated. They are related to one another in a definite manner, and this relationship causes a phenomenon that is not only over and above each of them, but also affects their behavior toward one another. That a definite number of men meet together at stated intervals in a definite room has little sociological significance. What is of importance and interest to the sociologist is what happens in the course of that meeting. What rela-

tions are developed between the individual men? To what
extent do these relations affect the relations that these individuals have with other persons who do not belong to the
immediate grouping under consideration?

An illustration may serve to make this clear. We are all
familiar with groups of businessmen who make it more or
less of a habit to meet at weekly luncheons. The specific
purposes of these numerous organizations vary in detail, but
it has been said that fellowship is the one purpose characteristic of most of these groups. Formality is dispensed
with, and the conversation and activities in which they
engage are usually conducive to an atmosphere of congen-
iality. This is *interaction* and its product. It is not important, except for census purposes, to note that organization
A has its meeting on Thursday noon and that it has a
membership of seventy-five. It is, however, of importance
that this organization brings seventy-five men together and
that these men interact with one another. They exchange
ideas, comment on the trend of business, express optimism
regarding national affairs, recount with appropriate eye
winks and smirks the latest gossip and scandal, and make
or seek opportunities to sell goods or services. It is probable, too, that resolutions are passed condemning or prais-
ing the action of some public official, and often a speaker is
invited to address the members on questions of national,
international, and economic import.

Thus the members are informed and instructed. When
the meeting is finally adjourned, each member has been
exposed to new ideas, which he takes with him. In some
instances these ideas will affect his relations with other
people with whom he has contacts. His own prejudices
may have been reinforced, or new prejudices may have
taken root. He may come out of the meeting feeling that

the only salvation for the country is in an immediate return to the political philosophy of Thomas Jefferson, or of Alexander Hamilton, and he may be convinced more than ever that the "isms" of modern times are un-American and destructive. His relations with his employees may possibly be affected, and even his future support of an educational institution may depend on its inclination to teach in accordance with his own economic philosophy. In other words, the interaction set in motion at a Thursday noon meeting of seventy-five businessmen may have produced effects upon these men that in turn affect their contacts with others. These effects are the products of their association.

The interaction phenomenon is not restricted to businessmen's luncheon clubs. The individual's behavior cannot be adequately explained or understood without reference to all the groups to which he belongs or with which he comes in contact. It is from these that he receives his ideas, his outlook on life, and his behavior patterns. *The science of sociology, then, is the study of groups and the products of group interaction, the role the individual plays in their creation and how he in turn is affected by them.* It seeks to discover and to explain constant uniformities in the structure and growth of groups, and in the reciprocal influence of groups and the individuals that comprise them.

SOCIOLOGY AS A SCIENCE

There has been considerable controversy over the right of sociologists to call their work a science, and some have questioned the wisdom of maintaining a separate discipline called sociology, believing that sociology merely duplicates the work of the other disciplines that deal with man in a less efficient fashion.

There are possibly two chief reasons for this attitude. In

the first place, it has been brought about by the attempts of some sociologists to merge, in their enthusiasm and zeal for reform, *what is* with *what ought to be*. In other words, they have attempted to be scientists as well as reformers, and this duality of purpose has been frowned upon. In the second place, those that deny the need of sociology, and its scientific character, use the term *science* in a restricted sense.

If by science we mean the formulation of laws that make it possible to predict and consequently to control phenomena, then sociology and the other social sciences have had comparatively little to offer.[3] There is nothing in the field of the social sciences that corresponds to the law of gravity. The precision found in the neat and compact formulae of chemistry is lacking in the social sciences. But is this the only criterion by which a study can be judged a science? Is science exclusively the formulation of laws? If we examine science and what has come to be regarded as scientific, we note that science is more a matter of a frame of mind and a method (technique) than of specific results. The results are varied, but in obtaining these results the individual has been dominated by a certain logically consistent frame of mind, and has used legitimate methods upon which men have agreed. These methods have made it possible to observe and classify phenomena, and when other individuals use these same methods and data they will arrive at the same results. The "frame of mind" is one of intellectual integrity, in which the individual willingly follows wherever the data may lead him. He must be willing to modify or to change completely his hypothesis as the facts, as he finds them, require. In his researches, also, he must use methods

   [3] Piper, Raymond F., and Ward, Paul W., *The Fields and Methods of Knowledge,* pp. 134–139 (Alfred A. Knopf, New York, 1929).

by which others can go over the same ground and arrive at the same conclusions. This describes what some people call science. The emphasis of science is on method rather than on results. From this point of view there is unity in all science—a unity that is derived from methods and the frame of mind of the scientific investigator. Sociologists and social scientists are, or at least they should be, dominated by these considerations. The fact that they have been unable to arrive at laws or formulae regarding human social relations arising out of group life that are comparable to the laws and formulae of chemistry, for instance, does not preclude the possibility of such achievement.

Some difficulties stand in the way of the sociologist that do not beset the researcher in the natural sciences, and these difficulties will probably exist for some time to come. No one is especially concerned at present about the moral aspects of the microbe that may be the source of influenza, but many people would be immediately agitated by the statement of a social scientist whose researches lead to the conclusion that a number of vested interests in the community are associated with a large portion of the juvenile delinquency, if not responsible for it. Such a conclusion would create much discussion and would perhaps heap abuse upon the one making it, if it were backed up with data that specifically pointed to these vested interests. He would, of course, be undermining the *status quo* out of which not a few individuals in the community are making more than a comfortable living. Whenever one's living is involved, criticism is apt to cause an emotional explosion. The relations of men towards one another always involve their emotions. Men are accustomed to regard what they do and how they do it as sacred and unquestionable. This is the first difficulty that faces the researcher in social science, and it is one that for the most part has been gradually eliminated from the field of natural science. But the natural sciences met with obstacles. One need only remember the difficulties that were experienced by Giordano Bruno, Galileo, Harvey, Darwin, and Pasteur (to mention a few of them) to see how the natural scientist met with resistance and abuse when his results questioned the entrenched interests, beliefs, and creeds.

There is also another difficulty that makes the work of the social scientist different from that of the natural scientist. The social scientist deals with people and their interaction, while the natural scientist is more or less concerned with phenomena outside of the human field. No one will object to the union of hydrogen and oxygen. It is impossible, however, to regiment or control persons for purposes of scientific experiments. Our laws, morals, and so-called good taste limit what we can learn about human beings. It is a relatively simple thing to trace the nervous system of a human corpse, but it is impossible to place a human being in complete isolation from childhood to adulthood for scientific purposes. Human rights must be respected, and the knowledge regarding human beings in association with one another must be limited by these rights.

In passing it might be well to mention another difficulty experienced by the social scientist that operates to a minimum for the natural scientist. We have referred above to the scientist's frame of mind, which plays an important role in scientific investigation. An individual's past experiences, his prejudices, and his values have little opportunity to make themselves felt in the results obtained by the natural scientist. What he thinks about the sanctity of monogamy, whether he believes in high tariffs or free trade, or whether he votes Republican or Democratic can hardly affect the results of his experiments in physics. The only thing that can effect them is his own intellectual integrity. There is nothing moral or immoral about the fact that "at a constant temperature the volume of a given quantity of any gas varies inversely as the pressure to which the gas is subjected." On the other hand, these same considerations may to some extent color the findings of a social scientist. They may succeed unconsciously in coloring his conclusions or directing them in a particular way or channel, since he is attempting to study these very same phenomena. The social scientist first of all has the task of divesting himself of his own conditioning, because the things he is studying are so intimately connected with his own values and emotions. These may, without intention on his part, lead him to ignore some of the relations between fragments of data. This situation will continue to exist, to some extent, as long as the social scientist can make limited use of experiments in the social field. As long as we attach moral significance to parts of our behavior, facts about this part of our behavior will continue to have moral significance.

Sociology and the other sciences

For purposes of discussion, the disciplines which have made man their object of study may be divided into two general categories: those that have restricted themselves to the study of man as an organism, and those that have been concerned with man as a social animal interacting with other men and producing, by means of interaction, a social system. The first category includes disciplines such as biology, biochemistry, physical anthropology, and usually psychology,[4] while disciplines such as economics, political

---

[4] There are phases of psychology that may be placed in the second category.

science, cultural anthropology, the new history, and sociology are placed in the second category. The first category of disciplines has looked at man as part of the animal kingdom and has attempted to obtain knowledge regarding his physical make-up, his evolution, and his inheritance. Briefly, these sciences attempt to tell us, as Kimball Young puts it, the "how" of man's behavior.[5] Their generalizations are applicable to man as a whole. Thus the laws of heredity operate regardless of whether a person is a Methodist or a Catholic. These sciences are concerned with man, his relation to the physical world and its effect upon him. Psychology, too, is concerned with the "how" of behavior. In its attempt to obtain knowledge regarding the nature of the conscious and the unconscious, of the sensations and feelings, the perceptions, the instincts or drives, the reflexes, and original nature, it too is attempting to formulate laws or concepts that are applicable to mankind as a whole. Psychology, like biology, is concerned with the nature of the mechanisms of human behavior, and as such furnishes us with the knowledge of the basis of our social life, which is rooted in our biological and psychological make-up.

The disciplines in the second category have not been basically concerned with the biological and psychological mechanisms of human behavior, but have centered their attention upon the products of this behavior and how these products have affected man, the creator. They attempt to understand the "why" of behavior. An understanding of the way in which an individual acquires habits, although it is interesting and useful, does not complete the picture by any means. It does not tell us why a number of our people

[5] Young, Kimball, *Social Psychology,* pp. 233–234 (F. S. Crofts & Company, New York, 1930).

collect stamps while members of a primitive tribe collect human heads. This type of behavior, to be sure, has its foundation in our biological and psychological mechanisms, but in order to know what we collect and why, it is necessary to turn our attention to another field. This is the field of the social sciences. The part that these disciplines really play, then, is to attempt to complete the picture of the human being by studying man in his various relations with other men, and the results of these relations.

This discussion is intended to introduce the reader to a consideration of the relation between sociology and the other social sciences. An examination of the fields covered by the various social sciences shows that their points of departure are different. The economist is concerned with man's activities connected with the production and distribution of goods and services. To him the problems of food, clothing and shelter, buying and selling, methods of trade and exchange, and similar activities hold the center of the stage. The political scientist is chiefly concerned with the nature of the state and the government, their forms and interrelations, and their functions, expressed in laws, codes, and sovereignty. The problems connected with the state and its agents are the center of attention for the political scientist. The cultural or social anthropologist devotes his attention to the social life and practices of primitive and pre-literate peoples.[6] He views and studies the totality of their social relations. The "old" historian laid his major emphasis on recounting what happened, in terms of biographies, battles, and dates. The "new" historian, in contrast, is not content with recording specific events but also attempts to study the interplay of the events that have

---

[6] Wallis, Wilson D., *An Introduction to Anthropology*, Chapter I (Harper & Brothers, New York).

shared in the creation of civilization. Even here, however, we note a considerable amount of division of labor in that there are specialists among the historians—some deal with economic history, others with political history, and others with still different phases of past events.

With the various tasks performed by these disciplines, is man completely studied? There are many aspects of man's life that are not made the interest of the forementioned sciences. The ones that are the concern of sociology are those aspects of life that are termed social; those patterns of life that exist because men belong to groups constitute the focal point of sociology. No economic or political relations are ever purely economic or political. They are made possible by group activity and coöperation. The family thus has many economic phases, but it is more than an economic unit. The state, too, may touch upon and does enter into many phases of group life, but those phases are not intelligible alone in terms of the structure and function of the state. To know that in the United States, for example, governmental powers are divided into three branches does not explain to us why our Supreme Court has twice called Federal laws regulating child labor unconstitutional. The economic philosophy of the majority of the members of the Supreme Court, which they acquired in a particular setting, has created within these men a resistance to certain specific kinds of changes.

Even though sociologists have at times limited their researches to social relations that are non-economic and non-political, it does not follow that social relations that are not political or economic make up the field of sociology. Man is no mere sum of economic, political, familial, recreational, religious, artistic, literary, scientific, and military activity. All of these separate activities are interrelated, and they are abstracted from their configuration and treated separately as a matter of convenience, because by so doing we can analyze them and learn about them more easily. Yet in order to understand them fully, they need also to be studied in their interrelation, and this is the task of sociology. This does not mean that sociology is a synthesizing science; it does not stand as the queen of the social sciences. It seeks to discover formulae or generalizations that cut across all human association, and in so doing it must and does rely upon the other social sciences. Thus the sociologist has long pointed out the differences between rural and urban populations in so far as the types of human activity are involved. These two populations differ in their economic pursuits, which are of interest to the economists, but associated with these activities are others. The two groups differ, to mention a few points, in family stability, standards of living, mores, folkways, resistance to and acceptance of inventions.[7] Out of these differences come two types of individuals—the urban and the rural. These differences are usually constant and recurring. Sociology is thus concerned with the forms of group interaction. For instance, when activity A is found to be associated with activity B and C, these, interpenetrating one another, give rise to individual M. Sociology is not concerned primarily with the study of the phases of social behavior that have been ignored by other disciplines, although this might have been true at one period in the development of sociology.[8] Sociology goes beyond this and attempts to understand and describe that which is constant in all human association, as

[7] Sorokin, P. A., and Zimmerman, C. C., *Principles of Rural-Urban Sociology* (Henry Holt & Company, New York, 1929).

[8] Phelps, Harold A., *Principles and Laws of Sociology,* Chapter I (John Wiley & Sons, New York, 1936).

well as to point out the nature of the processes involved in this association.

The methods of sociology

Science without method is not possible. Science must, like most other human labors, use techniques that make it possible to handle the elements of specific problems. Sociology has little claim upon methods (techniques) that are solely its own; it has always used methods that have been employed by other scientists. Perhaps the inability to devise methods of its own may be in part responsible for the paucity of its results.

A considerable amount of attention has been devoted by writers in the field of sociology to the question of method, and numerous lists of methods have been offered, which usually include the historical, comparative, case-study, statistical, and experimental methods. All of these have been employed by sociologists in the study of social relations.

The historical method has been used in what is termed the "genetic approach to social phenomena." The method consists in looking back into the events and processes that have contributed to the creation of specific institutions, movements, and group behavior patterns, in any particular civilization. Any effective study and understanding of Nazi Germany would have to depend upon the historical method. Modern Germany stands apart from the past events but is rooted in them, and its characteristics are determined to a considerable degree by these historical precedents.

The comparative method in many respects resembles and supplements the historical method in that it also looks back into the past for developments that seem to have contributed to specific human relationships. The comparative method, however, goes beyond the historical method in that

it attempts to draw generalizations about human social relationships by drawing inferences from comparisons. Thus
it has been possible to learn about constant recurring relationships in urban and rural civilization by studying past
relationships and comparing them with present rural-urban
relationships. The comparative method reveals similarities
in social developments which can be formulated into generalizations, and by its use the projection of present trends
into the future is made possible. If we know that in the
past D and E have always contributed to the creation of F,
the presence of D and E in a problem under consideration
should make possible the prediction of the probable appearance of F in the future.

The study of interrelations and their patterns is made
possible by the case-study method. This method has generally been restricted to the study of specific instances or
occurrences. An analysis of the factors contributing to a
specific event or pattern of behavior will give insight into
similar patterns of behavior or events. The case-study
method dissects a problem into its elements and brings into
relief the interrelationships of these elements and their
development. Such a method has been particularly useful
in the study of factors involved in individual behavior.
Remarkable illustrations of its use and results are found in
studies of delinquents.[9] A complete analysis of the individual is made, from which generalizations are formed.
This method need not be restricted to the study of individual behavior; it can also be used in the analysis of social
movements, institutions, and so forth.

---

[9] Shaw, Clifford, *The Jack Roller* (University of Chicago Press, Chicago,
1930).

Shaw, Clifford, *The Natural History of a Delinquent Career* (University
of Chicago Press, Chicago, 1931).

Although the statistical method is usually discussed as a separate and distinct method, it really represents the logical supplement of the case-study method. Most people think that the statistical method involves merely enumeration and construction of statistical tables. There is more to it than this. Measurement and the mathematical treatment of data, in order that generalizations may be formulated, are important phases of this method. Measurement depends upon the discovery of units expressed quantitatively. Sociologists have been concerned with this problem, as well as with the construction of scales for measuring social phenomena.[10] The statistical method has been used in studying portions of our population in order to compare the characteristics of one class with those of another. Illustrations of this use are extensive in the field of criminology. Instances of poverty, bad housing, unsupervised recreation, broken homes, unemployment, school problems, and many others, singly or in combination, have at one time or another been correlated with delinquent behavior as measured either by court appearances or by convictions to correctional institutions. Another sociological field in which statistics as a method have played an outstanding role is in the measurement of attitudes and social distance (the degree of understanding and sympathy existing between two or more persons). Social status and social patterns have also been

[10] Thurstone, L. L., "Attitudes Can Be Measured," *American Journal of Sociology*, 33: 529–554, Jan., 1928.

Droba, D. D., "Methods Used for Measuring Public Opinion," *American Journal of Sociology*, 37: 410–423, Nov., 1931.

Kirkpatrick, Clifford, "Assumptions and Methods in Attitude Measurement," *American Sociological Review*, 1: 75–88, Feb., 1936.

Chapin, F. Stuart, "A Quantitative Scale for Rating the Home and Social Environment of Middle Class Families in an Urban Community," *Journal of Educational Psychology*, 19: 99–111, 1928.

analyzed by the use of statistics,[11] and this method has also been used to predict future relationships in the social field.

There has been a great deal of abuse of statistics in sociology. Now and then unreliable data have been poured into mathematical formulae, dressed up in mathematical symbols, and passed off as scientific. The statistical manipulation of data does not change the nature of the data. Little good can come from applying refined statistical methods to data that do not lend themselves to such treatment. Some so-called social scientists are too easily carried away by the semblance of respectability that mathematics gives their research work, and are apt to make generalizations that are worthless. A knowledge of when to use statistical methods is just as important as knowing how to use them. The investigator must be thoroughly familiar with the trustworthiness of his sources. In addition, he must be absolutely sure that his data are truly representative of the phenomenon under study.

In sociology it is impossible to examine every manifestation of a particular relationship, since economy and practical difficulties stand in the way of such procedure. Consequently, it is often necessary to take a sample of the data. There is nothing new about the method of sampling. It is used day in and day out by most individuals. The cook who wants to taste the results of his mixture does not eat the contents of the pot, but rather takes a spoonful or two of the contents and, provided the various ingredients are thoroughly mixed, he gets from his sample a knowledge regarding the whole. Grain inspectors do not attempt to examine

---

[11] For a discussion of the results obtained by the use of statistics in sociology, see Chapin, F. S., "Some Results of Statistics in Sociology," Chapter XVII of Bernard, L. L., (editor), *The Fields and Methods of Sociology* (Farrar & Rinehart, New York, 1934).

every grain of a shipment—a small portion of it will serve this purpose. Provided that no one has so planned that the inspector gets only the best of the lot in his sample, he will be able to get a fairly accurate estimate of the grade of the shipment. Again, in buying a basket of fruit it is often necessary to look underneath the top layer. Much of the same thing is necessary in sociology. One must be certain that the portion of the field he has chosen for investigation is truly representative of the whole, otherwise any generalizations derived from such a study are not applicable to the whole of the field. Faulty generalizations made from an inadequate sample have often been made in sociology. In the field of crime, much has been written about the part that mental deficiency plays in criminal behavior. Some have suggested a causal relationship between feeblemindedness and criminality. Studies do indicate that the population of correctional institutions is made up of a greater proportion of feebleminded individuals than is present in the law-abiding citizenry. But before this conclusion can be accepted, there are several questions that must be answered: Do the people who get caught, convicted, and incarcerated actually represent the whole criminal population? Are the people whose scores make up the standard for comparison truly representative of the law-abiding population?

The experimental method has had limited usage in sociology, owing to the inability to carry on experiments among human beings. It is impossible for the sociologists to take a bit of society and subject it to analysis in the laboratory, and to control and vary the conditions of the experiment. Nevertheless, there have been studies in which the experimental method was employed.[12] Furthermore, if the soci-

[12] See Lundberg, George A., *Social Research,* pp. 37–45 (Longmans, Green & Company, New York, 1920).

ologist is aware of what goes on around him, he will see a number of fascinating experiments in living, some of which are truly gigantic, such as Fascism in Italy and Germany and Communism in Russia. To be sure, the sociologist can do little to vary and control the conditions of these experiments; he can, however, learn a great deal from observing them.[13]

Much of what goes under the name "New Deal" in American attempts at business recovery is also of the experimental character. The Roosevelt program offers many unusual opportunities to the sociologist for observing the beginning of social experiments. What the ultimate effects of these activities on American life will be may never be known, because of conditions which may destroy many of these experiments before they are actually under way. There is, however, a possibility that some of the experiments may reach completion and thus offer an opportunity to the sociologist to observe and record the modification in human living brought about by them.

The above discussion of methods does not pretend to be exhaustive.[14] Only those methods that have had general use have been considered. Methods are tools, and the specific task at hand determines the method chosen. The use of one does not preclude the use of others in understanding a particular problem; often a problem must be attacked by the use of several methods in combination.[15]

---

[13] In this connection it is appropriate to point out that Italy's present population policy has given Professor Corrado Gini, of the University of Rome, ample opportunity to put to test his theories regarding the rise and decay of nations. Much of what is known as Fascist demography is at his disposal for use in proving or disproving his theories.

See Gini, Corrado, "The Cyclical Rise and Fall of Population," in *Population* (University of Chicago Press, Chicago, 1930).

[14] For a more complete analysis of the problem of measurement and method in the social sciences, see Chapter XV.

[15] See Lundberg, G. A., *op. cit.*, Chapter IV.

THE NATURE OF HUMAN GROUPS

Before attempting an analysis of group behavior it is well to examine the nature and varieties of groups to which individuals belong.

Primary groups

Looking at groups as a whole, it is possible to discern two general types. On the one hand, the individual belongs to such groups as the family, the fraternity, and the play group; on the other hand, the individual may be a member of a religious denomination, a political party, and the sophomore class of a university. The purposes of these groups differ and so does the membership, but the groups also differ in the kinds of relations that are created by the interaction of the members. In the first type of groups the interaction is usually of a face-to-face variety, personal and intimate. Life in these groups is to a considerable degree permeated by sentimentality and loyalty to other persons belonging to the group. Mutual aid and coöperation are outstanding characteristics of these groups. They mark the first development, in the child, of a conditioning to other persons, and furnish for the child his first contact with fundamentals of social life. They constitute the most important cogs in the socializing process and are the depositaries of those traits which are usually referred to as human. These they give to the newborn individual, and he, in response to these traits, gradually becomes a person. In this sense then, these groups may be spoken of as primary.[16] They constitute the first steps in the building of human beings, and how well these groups perform this function determines to no small extent

---

[16] Cooley, Charles H., *Social Organization*, p. 27 (Charles Scribner's Sons, New York, 1922).

what sort of a person the individual will ultimately be. In them the individual first gains knowledge regarding what is acceptable and what is not acceptable in the way of behavior. This also involves acceptable ways of thinking about situations. The activities of an infant have no significance for him at the beginning. They acquire significance only as the group places approval or disapproval on them. Thus the group sets up for him a series of definitions regarding situations. He learns what is expected of him, under specified conditions, and what he can expect from others. This process is a gradual one, to which much is contributed by his primary groups.

Secondary groups

In contrast to the primary groups, the secondary groups usually are marked by less intimate, non-face-to-face relations. The type of interaction involved in most secondary groups lacks in personal elements. In most cases such interaction involves little in the way of sentiment and is removed from the day-to-day activity of the individual. Secondary groups involve the relations of human beings wherein personal contact and personal give-and-take relations are at a minimum. We need only contrast the interaction taking place within a family with that taking place within a national consumers' union to see how these two groups differ from one another. There are, however, other groups which stand in an intermediate position. The difference is one of degree, and these two categories of groups tend to merge into another. Even though a political party is a secondary group, a local ward committee of that party is, for the individual member, a primary group. Thus there are groups which, if taken in their entirety, are secondary, and if broken down into their components, become primary.

Groups, although characterized by coöperation and loyalty within their membership, are often antagonistic and
opposed to one another. They engender in their members
a *we-group* or *in-group* feeling in contrast to an *other-group*
or *out-group* feeling for individuals belonging to other
groups. This is a common, well-known attitude which can
be summed up in the sentence: "We belong and you do
not." Here, too, the amount and intensity of these feelings
vary from group to group and are generally dependent upon
the similarities between groups. The greater the divergence
in aims and purposes, the more intense is the feeling of
antagonism and resentment between groups. Thus the out-
group feeling of fraternity A for fraternity B will not be
as intense as the out-group feeling of fraternity A for a
non-fraternity group. The antagonism of a group of striking workers towards an employer group is usually intense
and often leads to violence. Many will recall our feelings
for the Allies in contrast to our feelings for the Germans.
The names we applied to each are expressions of these
feelings. Such group loyalties are universal and probably
as old as man himself. We cannot be in constant association with other men and not have these feelings develop.
They, with other factors, may be thought of as a connective
tissue that holds the individual members of the group together. Most groups, with the exception of mobs, crowds,
and audiences, are more or less permanent in character.
They manifest solidarity. The individual belonging to them
acquires position or status with reference to other persons.
The acquisition of status, which is derived from membership in the group, as well as the ways in which the group
promotes ease and satisfaction in living, are factors that
determine the permanency of the group. As long as a group

furnishes the individual with certain satisfactions, it is serving a purpose that binds the individual to it.

College fraternities are usually old and well established, and yet they have a considerable membership turnover. Some members are graduated; others fail to return to school. A stream of new individuals is constantly flowing into the fraternity. In order to get new members the group must prove that life within a fraternity is better than life without one. One of the important points that is made by the "rushers" to the prospective "pledge" is the fact that by belonging to the fraternity the individual will have obtained congenial friends. The matter of prestige to be obtained by membership in the fraternity is another point that is often made. The individual is shown the number of trophies won by the fraternity. He is impressed with the number of Varsity football players who belong. Nor is the fact overlooked that a certain United States senator is a member. In other words, the fraternity holds up to the individual a series of attractions that bid for his acceptance. These attractions are usually in terms of satisfaction that can be obtained only by joining a fraternity, and particularly that fraternity. After the individual has accepted the invitation to join the group, the serious work of moulding him begins. The group transmits to him its ideals, its behavior patterns, and its values. It is no secret that some fraternities go so far as to dictate what the individual may wear and with whom he may seek relaxation. He is forced to look at things and to do things as the group wants, and in this fashion the group is perpetuated. The group has life and solidarity which is separate and distinct from that of the individuals composing it, and it forces these individuals to conform to a prescribed behavior.

To be sure, the life of the group itself is subjected to

modifications that arise from its individuals. This is a reciprocal action. It would be inconceivable otherwise. New members have been conditioned by other groups and are already equipped with definite behavior patterns and ideas. In the process of becoming conditioned to the behavior and ideals of the new group, the previous conditioning must be modified, but in the modification it can change to a degree the ideas of the transmitting group. Out of this process may arise a new pattern of behavior which combines the elements of the two conditioning processes.

Most groups of today are the products of the cross fertilization of the products of past groups. An unusually good illustration of this is to be found in the Constitution of the United States. With the exception of the amendments that have been passed since the first ten, the document is exactly as it was when first written and adopted by the original thirteen colonies. This product of a group of individuals living in the latter part of the eighteenth century, when it took months to cross the Atlantic, in a civilization mostly rural in character, is still functioning, even though life has been greatly changed. Most of the men responsible for the framing of our Constitution would perhaps be amazed if they could see what is being done under the document that they created. The expansion in the meaning of the Constitution has been the result of attempts to meet needs arising out of the changing aspects of our civilization. Out of the impact between a political philosophy of the eighteenth century and the social order of the nineteenth and twentieth centuries has come the present interpretation of the Constitution. Thus a group product of one era, through a process of change, is transformed to a group product of an entirely different era.

THE NATURE OF CULTURE

It is to these products of group interaction that the name *culture* has been given. This culture permeates and circumscribes our lives from the moment of birth to the grave. In fact, it prescribes what is to be done with our bodies after death, as well as the thoughts we have regarding our future after death. An examination of one's self in a mirror will easily reveal the nature of culture and why it is regarded as the product of individuals acting together in groups. A man dressed for the street will see in the mirror evidence that his hair is cut short, his face is clean shaven, he has a shirt with a collar neatly arranged with a tie. He probably has a suit consisting of vest, coat, and trousers. His coat has lapels with notches and one button hole. Several buttons adorn the end of his coat sleeves. He wears shoes, probably oxfords, and socks. If one were to ask this same individual why he dresses the way he does, why his hair is cut as it is, the answer would probably be, "Because others do so." From this answer comes insight into the nature of culture. It is man-made, and it constitutes the mode of life of men; so tightly does it hold us in its grasp that we seldom question the "why" of it. Yet it is this phenomenon that to the greatest possible degree determines for us how and when we shall behave. It fills our heads with thoughts; it provides us with our morals, our likes and dislikes, our ambitions, and our hopes. In short, "Culture or civilization, taken in its wide ethnographic sense, is that complex whole which includes knowledge, belief, art, morals, law, custom, and any other capabilities and habits acquired by man as a member of society." [17] We should note in particular that

---

[17] Tylor, Edward B., *Primitive Culture,* Vol. I, p. 1 (John Murray, London, 1913, Fifth Edition).

culture consists of habits and capabilities acquired by man as a member of society. This is a group phenomenon, behavior that is group inspired.

The culture trait

To study any phenomenon it is necessary to break it up into its elements. By so doing it is possible to analyze the interrelations between units and to arrive at the nature of their configuration. The search for and the finding of a unit is part of the task of any study. In the study of culture the unit is known as the *trait*. The study of the culture of any people would necessitate the breaking up of that culture into its constituent traits. The concept "trait," however, is not rigid but permits a great deal of elasticity in its use. The nature of culture itself to some extent is also responsible for this. An automobile, for example, can be considered as a trait in our culture, and if one were making a study of our culture, it would be proper to list it as a trait. On examination, however, it will be noted that an automobile is made up of several parts or traits. Furthermore, connected with the material object to which the name automobile is given is the use to which it is put. This is just as much a part of our culture as the actual automobile. Therefore if one were to be particularly meticulous in his study of our culture, he would have to list the parts of the automobile as well as its uses. The choice of what is to be used as traits depends upon practical considerations. Regardless of whether the automobile is considered as a trait or reduced to wheels, axles, pistons, and all the other components, it is obvious that each trait has connected with it knowledge pertaining to its use. This knowledge is not the object itself, but it involves the ideas about the object. It will also be noted that many of our culture traits are not objects but ideas regarding life and our relations to others and to the world. They are expressed by word of mouth or in written form. These are non-material culture traits. Our regard for our flag, the contempt of some of us for non-American "isms," are examples of non-material elements in our culture. Culture traits are either material or non-material.

The inability to think of the automobile or of any tool apart from its use indicates that culture traits tend to combine with one another. There are objects that have been found whose use is a matter of speculation, but in a study of modern culture this is a rare thing. Traits do not exist in isolation; they are interrelated, and to understand the culture of any people it is necessary to see traits in relation to others. An examination of our own culture will show that we are a hand-shaking people, but the mere listing of this trait leaves a great deal to be desired in understanding this manner of behavior. Connected with the overt behavior is a series of other traits. Hand-shaking is connected with our concepts of friendship; it is part of the ceremony of sealing bargains. The actual meaning of a trait, its position in the whole of culture, depends upon the way it is associated with other traits, and the study of traits is never complete unless these configurations are examined.

In addition to this tendency to combine with one another, traits have an evolution of their own and cannot be understood except as they are considered in their historical setting. Most of what we do and think would not be intelligible from the standpoint of a scientific analysis if the background of our culture were not known. The individual is seldom aware of the history of his culture and of his behavior. Perhaps the occasions are few wherein it becomes necessary for him to know his own cultural background.

Yet this is a necessary part of a scientific study of culture. The traits of a culture are constantly being modified so that they assume from time to time different meanings and different usages. To understand why they are as they are at any given moment is possible only by use of the historical method.

A third characteristic of culture traits is mobility. Traits through the agency of man may spread from one area to another. Man in his migrations over the surface of the earth takes his culture with him, and the contacts between people often result in the exchange of culture traits. Modern means of communication have considerably accelerated this exchange of culture traits and their cross-fertilization. This tendency of traits to spread has diversified cultures and has enriched each one with contributions from all parts of the world.

The culture complex and pattern

The tendency of traits to combine with one another results in the formation of culture complexes. As has been pointed out above, the mere overt act of handshaking carries with it several meanings for the individual. The central or chief trait is the hand clasp, around which are clustered other traits. A culture complex is the clustering of traits around a central or core trait. These clustering traits may be either material or non-material, or a combination of both. Culture complexes, since they are made up of culture traits, have the same characteristics as traits. They, too, tend to combine with one another, to spread from area to area, and they also have a unique history of their own. Cultures are combinations of culture complexes or adhesions of complexes. In our American culture professional baseball may be considered a culture trait, but the mere act of the nine men on each team being distributed in a prescribed manner at intervals over a field, and going through prescribed activity under the watchful eyes of two or more umpires, is only a phase of our baseball complex. It is the central or core trait of this configuration; connected with it are a series of other American cultural traits. Huge stadia have been built with grandstands, boxes, and bleachers. Intense rivalries have developed that sometimes lead to near riots. Ladies' day is another feature of the game. The ever-present peanut, cigar, soda-pop, and hot-dog vendor is also another necessary part of it. The spring training build-up, with its horde of star "hold-outs"; the usual temperamental outbursts of Dizzy Dean and Wesley Ferrell; the exorbitant salaries of star sluggers; the Sunday and holiday double-header; the comeback try of Lefty Grove and others; the "daffiness boys" of Brooklyn and the "Gas House Gang" of St. Louis; all lead up to the gigantic climax called the World Series. These and many other traits are parts of the complex called professional baseball. This complex is associated with still many other complexes in American culture. The salaries that big-league stars receive for their efforts cuts across the American sense of value that pays a school teacher in some states of the Union the magnificent sum of thirty-five dollars per month. Even American advertising activities are linked up with baseball. Big-league stars are asked, for a price, to endorse foods, cigarettes, and other products. The base-ball complex gives an insight into a frame of mind that makes an athlete a hero and ignores the efforts of a struggling music composer. The same complex reveals to some extent our interests, in that newspapers, while giving an insignificant amount of space to international affairs, give on the average about two complete pages per issue to news about sports in general in which professional baseball occupies a conspicuous place. Out of the mere fact that eighteen men are playing a game arises a variety of behavior which is associated with numerous other complexes of American culture. This is how culture is built. It is a configuration of a variety of complexes that are functionally related to one another, and give meaning and purpose to the lives of the individuals stimulated by them.

Culture complexes are not distributed at random over the surface of the earth, but tend to be localized within more or less restricted geographical areas. Out of the localization of culture complexes has developed the culture-area concept. When the sociologist speaks of the culture area, he means the territory over which a distinct culture prevails. There is a considerable number of illustrations of this concept derived from primitive cultures, but our own society presents an especially interesting one in the delinquency areas. The fact that certain areas of cities contribute a greater number of juvenile delinquents and adult criminals than other areas of the city is not a recent finding. Cesare Lombroso recognized this interesting fact, but only in recent years has a thorough study of this phenomenon been made. Clifford Shaw of Chicago has been particularly active in this field.[18] He and his associates have studied the areas of Chicago, first from the standpoint of the differences in the number of juvenile delinquents that come from these areas, and then from the standpoint of the characteristics of these areas that might be responsible for the different delinquency rates.

---

[18] Shaw, Clifford, *Delinquency Areas* (University of Chicago Press, Chicago, 1929).

Shaw, Clifford, and McKay, H. D., *Social Factors in Delinquency, Report on the Causes of Crime,* Vol. II (National Commission on Law Observance and Enforcement, Government Printing Office, Washington, 1931).

For purposes of comparison Chicago was divided into areas which contained five hundred boys between the ages of ten and sixteen years. This was necessary in order to have comparable units for analysis. The study dealt with boys only. Three series of data were used to indicate the distribution of delinquency in each area. It should be remembered that these series are by no means measures of the actual amount of delinquency in any area, as many delinquents are never caught, and what leads to the juvenile court, probation office, or contact with the police differs from area to area.[19] The series served to show the variations from area to area of the amount of delinquency of males between ten and sixteen years of age in (1) 9,243 alleged delinquent cases dealt with by the police and probation officers in 1926; (2) 8,141 alleged delinquent cases appearing before the juvenile court in the period 1917–1923; and (3) 2,596 delinquent cases committed to correctional institutions during the period 1917–1923.

The addresses of these boys were spotted on the map of Chicago, and it was noted that the dots tended to cluster at certain points. The next phase of the study was to examine the characteristics of these areas in which juvenile delinquents were concentrated, and it was found that these areas differed from other areas in many ways. Proximity to industrial and commercial areas was one characteristic. Industry and commerce are probably not in themselves responsible for the high rate of delinquency, but they set a series of other factors in motion that are usually associated with high rates. We all know that areas adjoining the location of commerce and industry lose their desirability for residential purposes. People with means soon move out

---

[19] Robison, Sophia M., *Can Delinquency Be Measured?* (Columbia University Press, New York, 1936).

of them. The owners of this property are faced with the problem of continuing to derive some income from it, but also look forward to the day when commerce and industry will buy it. Rents are reduced, and in consequence little is done to keep the property in repair. These areas then attract the lowest income groups. Thus they select the under-privileged and those who are most apt to become economically dependent. In most American cities these people are the Negroes and the recently arrived immigrants. The unattractiveness of the environment, physical as well as social, makes the individual want to move out as quickly as possible; consequently these areas are also marked by a high rate of mobility with an attendant succession of cultural groups. These factors, low economic status and mobility, undermine the efficiency of the usual neighborhood organizations. The church, the various social clubs, and parent-teacher associations are usually ineffective in expressing neighborhood opinion and desires. There is little collective effort. Most of the organizations in these areas come from without in the form of charity or social work. There is then little neighborhood control over the individual, and the area becomes the hangout of adult offenders and gangs. There is free contact between the juvenile delinquent and the adult offender, and often the young boy attempts to model himself after the "big shot" of the area. These factors provide a positive influence for the concentration within these areas of juvenile delinquents, or at least the concentration within them of individuals whose conduct leads to the juvenile court or to contact with the police and probation officers. Lawlessness may be traditional, and the growing boy may find that his prestige and status depend upon his criminal activity.

These, then, are the general characteristics of a delinquency area, providing a set of behavior patterns for the individual and giving him experiences and values which are different from those found in areas of low delinquency. These areas take on a culture in which the daily life of the individuals is built around a configuration that leads many of them to the juvenile court and correctional institutions. Such areas also provide them with experiences that make them respond differently to many of the things that those who have been reared in areas of little delinquency, with their spacious lawns, fine homes, and clean streets, hold in high esteem.

In describing the delinquency area it will be noted that what was actually done was to describe the distribution over Chicago of a number of characteristics. If one were to superimpose maps of these distributions, configurations of complexes would appear. It is in this fashion that culture areas are derived that present a clustering of culture complexes.

The configurations derived from the clustering of complexes are designated as culture patterns. Each configuration may be looked upon as a pattern, and the pattern is the way or manner in which complexes are functionally related to one another. Cultures are distinguishable from one another by their respective patterns.[20]

FOLKWAYS, MORES, AND INSTITUTIONS

If this discussion were to go no further, it might be implied that culture was an entity apart and distinct from the individuals who utilize it. Even though culture can be analyzed, to understand a given culture it must be considered in rela-

---

[20] For a detailed discussion of culture traits, complexes, areas, and patterns, see Wissler, Clark, *Man and Culture*, Chapters IV and V (Thomas Y. Crowell Company, New York, 1923).

tion to the person who lives in it and makes use of it. For the individual, culture consists of behavior patterns, material objects, ideas, and attitudes—personal acquisitions that are socially or group determined and inspired. Culture acts in the capacity of a regulator of human behavior, which promotes orderliness in human society. This orderliness is a universal characteristic of human association, making possible the efficient achievement of the ends of human association. Though the attention of many individuals is now and then attracted to the unusual, reflection will show that the unusual is only sporadic in human society. If this were not so, chaos and disorder would eventually destroy society. One need only to recall the horrors and chaos accompanying war and revolution. The 1936 Revolution in Spain is an adequate illustration. The individual was no longer able to predict the behavior of others, constituted authority disappeared, and commerce and industry were checked. There was no more orderliness in society.[21] The universal fact that persons respond similarly to the same stimulus underlies the regularity in human association. It is group behavior—the behavior of individuals which is prescribed by the groups to which they belong. According to William Graham Sumner [22] this behavior falls into two categories: *folkways* and *mores*. The differences between these two categories of behavior centers around, for the most part, the degree of compulsion on the individual that is associated with each.

Man's first task is to live, and in order to make this possible, it has been necessary to devise methods by which a livelihood can be achieved efficiently. Out of this necessity

---

21 Sorokin, Pitirim A., *The Sociology of Revolution* (J. B. Lippincott Company, Philadelphia, 1924).
22 Sumner, William Graham, *op. cit.*, pp. 1–118.

have grown the folkways. They are the manner in which men achieve desired ends. A successful method of obtaining game, of crossing a stream, of keeping the evil spirits from one's hut, of pacifying the gods, developed by the individual through a process of interaction with his fellow men, becomes the method of the group. Out of the individual's behavior that succeeds in mastering or controlling his environment arise group behavior patterns. In present society the same process is continually going on. The newborn child learns from his elders how to get along in the world. They begin to transmit the folkways to the child very early in his life, so that by the time he ventures forth from the family group and comes in contact with individuals from other groups he has at his disposal the rudiments of socially acceptable behavior. Part of the socialization process is the acquisition of the folkways by the individual.

As groups continue to function, many of the folkways gradually become more compulsive in character. Attitudes of right and wrong become associated with particular ways of doing things. Group welfare becomes an issue, and folkways become mores. They are still ways of doing, but now they have become the *only* acceptable ways of doing, because any other course of action is deemed detrimental to the group. The group makes its displeasure felt when the mores are not observed by ostracizing the individual or, in some cases, by completely removing him from the group. In the case of mores the group demands conformity and punishes infringements, while in the case of folkways nonadherence may not result in expressed or overt group disapproval. It is part of the mores of our society to appear in the street fully clothed. Nudism is not tolerated, and anyone rash enough to test the compulsiveness of this behavior pattern will encounter serious difficulties. On the

other hand, it is a folkway for men to wear collars
and neckties, but non-adherence to this way of dressing,
although subjecting the individual to some discomfort,
does not lead to any serious difficulty. People may raise an
eyebrow, they may look inquisitively and show by their
facial expression that they question the taste or intelligence
of the individual who does not conform, but they seldom
go beyond that.

The fact that mores carry with them forcible adherence
does not necessarily mean that all laws are mores. There
are many laws that are not mores, and consequently their
enforcement suffers. The failure of the Eighteenth Amendment and of the Volstead Act is a case in point. Laws that
are not part of the mores of a people are seldom effectively
enforced. Ways of thinking about things, people, and the
world have arisen in connection with ways of doing or
behaving. Action and thought are related to the extent
that what the individual thinks about is determined by his
experiences with things and people. This constitutes the
frame of mind of the individual, into which is stored his
experiences or conditioning. To this frame of mind are
attached the tendencies of the individual to act in a specific manner, which are usually referred to as attitudes.[23]
Each of us is disposed, because of our past interaction with
others and with things, to act in a particular manner under
specified conditions. The attitudes set the stage of our
behavior; they provide the scenery and the background.
The individual who has been reared in a strict Protestant

---

[23] For an unusually penetrating discussion of attitudes see:
Kirkpatrick, Clifford, "Assumptions and Methods in Attitude Measure-
ment," *American Sociological Review,* Vol. I, No. 1, Feb., 1936, pp. 75–88.
Kirkpatrick, Clifford, and Stone, Sarah, "Attitude Measurement and the
Comparison of Generations," *Journal of Applied Psychology,* Vol. XIX,
No. 5, Oct., 1935, pp. 564–582.

home usually resents and feels antagonism for the Catholic. His behavior toward Catholics is set by his conditioning. For expediency, attitudes and behavior are often contradictory. Many of us are placed in situations where it is better to act in a particular manner even though we may think differently. When one's bread depends upon adherence, hypocrisy may become a virtue.

Culture, then, consists of objects, behavior patterns that are either folkways or mores, and attitudes or the mental counterpart of behavior. These elements keep the individual in line and determine his behavior. In combination they create social institutions, which in turn create the social order. Social institutions are nucleated patterns of behavior and cultural objects—the products of interaction. In all institutions are to be found material culture traits that have either utility or symbolic value in addition to prescribed attitudes and ways of behaving for the individuals who come under their influence. Institutions arise out of the needs of men, and they are the methods that have been developed to meet these needs. They are socially transmitted in that they are preserved and passed on from generation to generation.[24]

SOCIAL CHANGE

For purposes of analysis in this discussion, it is necessary to arrest culture in its movement. Culture, however, is not static but is essentially dynamic. New traits are added, and those already existent are modified from time to time. This change in culture is derived from two sources: invention, and borrowing or diffusion. From the standpoint of the totality of culture in the entire world, invention is the only

[24] See Chapter II, "Social Institutions."

source of culture change, but if viewed from the several existent culture areas, diffusion is another source of such change.

To most individuals, inventions are usually associated with the names of the individuals who have made them. Edison is associated with the phonograph, Newton with calculus, Marconi with wireless telegraphy, Fulton with the steamboat, Whitney with the cotton gin, Bell with the telephone, and the Wrights with the aeroplane. To be sure, these men did the inventing, but this is only part of the story. Their work and creation was made possible by the culture in which they lived and worked. The inventor functions in a given culture. It is the culture that furnishes the inventor with the necessary tools and materials with which he creates. Inventions do not just happen, but rather are episodes in the accumulation of culture. Men of ability far above the average are able to make inventions, but unless the culture provides them with the necessary tools and materials they can accomplish little. Inventions are culturally determined. They are not isolated instances of the individual's creative ability; rather, they are the products of a process that involves cultural factors that stimulate the inventive or creative talents of the individual. It seems probable that the development of culture up to a certain point makes some inventions inevitable. That this may be the case is supported by the fact that persons independently of one another have made the same invention. William Ogburn, in his *Social Change*,[25] presents a list of 148 inventions and discoveries made by two or more persons independently and virtually simultaneously, in many cases. This list suggests that the culture in which these persons

[25] Pp. 90–102 (Viking Press, New York, 1924).

lived had set the stage for the new creation or discovery. Undoubtedly a list of inventions and discoveries which were made only once could be prepared, but this would not necessarily preclude the cultural determinism of inventions because it is unlikely that an individual will continue to labor on a particular thing if he knows that someone else has already created what he himself seeks to create. Modern means of communication tend to make duplicate inventions less likely than in times past.

Cultural determinism is present not only in inventions and discoveries but also in diffusion. When people come in contact with one another, the amount that they borrow from each other is determined by their culture. What they can use is to a considerable degree determined by their life activities. Their culture pattern exerts a selective influence over the borrowing process. The extent to which the new traits seem adaptable to a culture facilitates or impedes the borrowing process. Traits that do not readily fit into the existent culture pattern will usually be rejected. They are said to be untimely. Many traits from Soviet Russia, with their communistic characteristics, would receive no welcome from a definitely capitalistic society; nor would polytheism be accepted by a long-established monotheistic society. The present culture patterns of both Germany and Italy would resist any trait-complex that was contaminated with liberalism or democracy. The difficulties encountered by Christian missionaries in their attempts to impart to the "savages" the true and only method of salvation is another illustration of the selective influence of the culture pattern over what will be accepted. Long-standing life patterns which have had value and reverence attached to them by groups seldom give way easily to new patterns of behavior and thinking. This fact is sometimes overlooked by reformers in their zeal and enthusiasm. The forcible imposition by one group upon another group of new trait-complexes has often resulted in complete disruption of the life cycles of the group imposed upon. Little regard for what others consider valuable and significant has been displayed by so-called civilized groups in their endeavors to give to the unfortunate primitive man the fruits and wonders of civilization. Italy's, or rather Mussolini's, raid on Ethiopia is a good illustration of this disregard.

But we need not seek examples from contacts between nations to illustrate this phenomenon; there is an ample supply within our own culture. Social workers at times display no respect or regard for the values of their clients, but go merrily on imposing their standards and values upon individuals who may have, because of their position in life, no use for them. Patriotic groups now and again do the same thing. Political parties are notorious in these attempts. In fact, there are few groups that do not feel that their particular way of thinking and doing is the best and only way.

Diffusion may be either organized or unorganized. Traits and trait-complexes sometimes spread without any effort being made to spread them. Two people in their contact with one another may borrow each other's trait-complexes without a preconceived plan of diffusion. Trait-complexes are thus borrowed and assimilated without plans for the process. In organized diffusion a conscious effort is made to spread trait-complexes by the use of well-planned drives to bring about its achievement. The conquests of one group by another is often followed by a program aiming at the revision of the conquered group's culture. Migrations sometimes bring about the same result. Education is sometimes used, as well as propaganda in its variety of forms. Advertising, another method of spreading culture, has become increasingly prominent in modern society because of the unusual facilities offered by the modern means of communication. The radio and newspaper are particularly useful in organized diffusion.

Differential rates of change in parts of cultures

An invention or a borrowed trait-complex affects only a part of culture at the outset. It may call for a change in only one way of doing or behaving. Not all parts of culture undergo change simultaneously. The impact of the new on the old at first makes itself felt on one part of the culture pattern, but gradually, or in some instances suddenly, other parts of the pattern begin to feel the dislocation and, unless accommodations are made, maladjustment will occur. The differential in the rate of change in parts of cultures is at the basis of culture maladjustment. The delay, or the time ensuing between the appearance of a maladjustment and its elimination, is called the period of *lag*.[26] Culture lags, or periods of culture maladjustment, are inevitable wherever and whenever culture changes. Needed changes may bring with them a number of new problems, which at times offset the good derived from the change itself.

Our culture is full of examples of culture lags. Maladjustments have developed in consequence of changes in parts of our culture that have not been followed by corresponding changes in other parts. The major portion of change occurs in our material culture [27]; and change in the non-material culture lags considerably behind. We are

[26] Ogburn, W. F., *op. cit.*, pp. 200–268.
[27] *Ibid.*

ready to adopt new mechanical devices, but we are not ready to change our philosophies, our mores regarding human relations. New gadgets for refrigerators are easily accepted, but new methods of treating criminals are resisted. America is particularly susceptible to inventions that increase the efficiency of the machine, but is resistant to plans and programs alleged to increase efficiency in human relations. As a consequence, we handle twentieth-century machines while we think about one another, in many respects, in terms of neolithic philosophies. Qualitative differences between races have never been substantially proved, yet we continue to discriminate as if there were no doubt that the white man is superior to the colored man. The frontier has disappeared, rural economy is being replaced by metropolitan economy, yet some persons continue to think and act in terms of "rugged individualism," a philosophy of the eighteenth and nineteenth centuries whose realization depends on the existence of vast and undeveloped natural resources.

At the basis of all social problems are culture lags. These problems are the result of differences in the rate of change in culture. The maladjustments create confusion and inject uncertainties in the relations of individual to individual, individual to the group, and group to group. The orderly and efficient attainment of the purposes of life is thus hampered. Life in society is made efficient to the extent to which it is possible to predict what people will do under specific conditions. Heterogeneity in definitions of situations can result only in heterogeneity of behavior. Behavior patterns and attitudes developed out of conditions prevailing at any one time may not be at all adequate when these conditions no longer prevail, and their retention may involve considerable hardship for some of the members of society.

It has long been known that in our society the administration of criminal justice is weak and inadequate, in many respects. State crime commissions, a Federal crime commission, criminologists, lawyers, and police officials have all suggested the need for revising much of the machinery whose task is to prevent crime as well as to treat those who commit it. Many who are responsible for numerous crimes seem to escape treatment or punishment, under the present set-up. Al Capone, the notorious gangster of Chicago and its vicinity, was able to evade successfully the law many years and is now serving a sentence because of income tax evasion on an income that was derived from unlawful activity. The frequent inability of authorities to convict guilty individuals is in part due to the existence of loopholes and technicalities in our legal system. Everything must be done in accordance with the law, and any deviation may be used to evade the law. These technicalities, well known to those in the legal profession, have had an honorable history. The original intention behind most of them was to protect the individual from arbitrary and unwarranted use of authority by the agents of government. The accused individual has a number of rights that must be respected. He must be indicted in a specific manner, and this indictment may not be in error, even grammatically. The crime of which the individual is accused must be exactly stated. If he kills another with a knife and the indictment states that he killed with a gun, then the indictment was insufficient. His trial must be conducted with due regard for rules of evidence, and he must be allowed the privilege of counsel. Several other privileges are granted him. Any breach of these rules is sufficient

to result in a new trial or in freedom for the accused.[28] At
a time when individuals could be spirited away at the will
of an executive, these protections were undoubtedly necessary. In a civilization predominantly agricultural and
characterized by primary group relations, these bulwarks
thrown around the individual against government could
work as they were intended to work. But with changes in
culture, with the development of a machine complex, with
a shift from primary to secondary group relations, these
rights play into the hands of those who prey on society.
Possibly the time has come to change our concepts pertaining to the relations between the individual and government
so that society may adequately suppress those that would
destroy it.

Scientific discoveries have gradually made the re-inter-
pretation of man's place and purpose in the universe
necessary. The telescope has projected the human mind
out into the vastness of space and has minimized the importance of the earth in the scheme of things. Life upon earth
has acquired a new significance. Scientific discoveries have
caused a great deal of confusion regarding the appropriate-
ness of some theological concepts. The resistance of some
people to necessary modifications in their theology has created maladjustment. Science has changed some parts of
our culture while other parts have remained unchanged.
The conflict between science and religion remains an open
issue, necessitating for some the complete divorcement of
science and religion, an anomaly in a world in which science
has come to play such an important role.

It is probably unnecessary to cite any more illustrations

---

[28] For an interesting discussion of technicalities in operation, see Kava-
nagh, Marcus, *The Criminal and His Allies* (Bobbs-Merrill Company,
Indianapolis, 1928).

of culture lags.   The reader can, if he is interested, find
numerous others.   Several words of caution are needed, however: Culture lags and maladjustments in culture are relative, and it depends upon the individual whether they
constitute lags.   Some persons gain from the existence of
every lag.   The fact that the existence of slums seems to be
associated with high delinquency rates may make little difference to persons owning these properties, and a change
may be unwelcome to the delinquent himself, who has
known nothing else.   When culture lags arise, a situation
is created in which many persons have much to gain by
the maintenance of the status quo.   Adjustment for them
is maladjustment for others.[29]   This is one of the reasons
why lags persist even though their existence is known.
Society is made up of groups with different purposes; what
is desirable for one group may be undesirable for another.
But through the various devices of propaganda, education,
and use of wealth, it is possible to gain control of the
machinery through which change may be initiated, and
to block anything that tends toward the modification of
conditions.

The heterogeneity of society is, then, one factor in
culture inertia, and there are several others deserving of
mention.   Even though lags are known to exist, it is often
impossible to devise or create means to reduce them.   Inventions are dependent on culture, and even though necessity may stimulate effort, this does not necessarily result in
an invention.   Also, people often believe that it is better
to suffer and to get along with things as they are rather than
to venture into the new and unknown.   And then there is
the factor of habit.   The new usually involves the reorgan-

[29] Wallis, Wilson D., "The Concept of Lag," *Sociology and Social Research,* 19: 403–405, May-June, 1935.

ization of parts of our lives. This reorganization entails
thinking and attempts at readjustment. The introduction
of new traits may run counter to the tradition of the group,
especially when there exists in one culture an antagonism
for things that come from another.[30] Deviations from the
accepted way seldom meet with approval, and all of these
factors make for resistance to change.

MALADJUSTMENT AND THE INDIVIDUAL

Culture maladjustment and conflicts in culture may be
studied as entities. It is, however, necessary to relate them
to individual behavior, since it is through the individual's
behavior that they find expression. The displacement of
the old by the new, in culture, means readaptation on the
part of the individual, and unless he has developed techniques for solving problems, unless he has plasticity in his
personality, he may find himself with a scheme of life unable to bring about satisfactory adjustment. The contact
of cultures, because of the mobility of people, often results
in conflict. When different ways of doing and thinking
compete with one another without resulting in disaster to
the individual, it may arouse suspicion in the minds of
many regarding the efficacy of any one method. How can
one be sure that his way is the only way?

There is little possibility of *personal disorganization*
developing in a homogeneous culture. In isolated and
unaccessible places one seldom finds the social problems
that are characteristic of places that are in the midst of constant contacts. The impact of cultures produces situations
in which the life pattern of the individual is full of contradictions; he is personally disorganized; he has no consistent

---

[30] Ogburn, W. F., *op. cit.*, pp. 145–196.

way of adjusting to life. He may come from a family in which the father is considered the master of the lives and destinies of its members; he may belong to a church that places emphasis on honesty and obedience; he may belong to a boys' gang that raids downtown department stores; he may go to a school that teaches that each individual is born free and equal; he may be working after school in a store under an individual who has no concern for human rights and freedom; as he grows up, he may marry a woman who has been reared in an entirely different environment, with different standards and patterns of behavior. In all of this one may wonder what is right and what is wrong.[31]

The lot of the sons and daughters of some immigrants is a difficult one. They stand in a marginal position, unable to accept the culture of their parents because it is inadequate for their lives, and yet they are unacceptable to many of the representatives of American culture. This might explain the undue proportion of criminals among the first generation native born. Such culture conflict seems productive of human suffering in varying degrees. The transmission to the individual of contradictory behavior patterns reflecting contradictions in the culture will inevitably make the problem of adjustment more difficult. It is probable that with an ever-increasing culture and with development of more efficient means of communication, conflicts in culture and the difficulties of adjustment will also increase. As more and more traits are added to a culture, the possibility of newer increments is increased. Unless much more effort is given to attempting changes in the non-mate-

---

[31] For an excellent discussion of a phase of confusion in our culture see Kirkpatrick, Clifford, "The Measurement of Ethical Inconsistency in Marriage," *The International Journal of Ethics,* Vol. XLVI, No. 4, July 1936, pp. 444–460.

rial sphere of human activity, it may become progressively difficult for men to live together in the future.

The meeting of that which is new with that which is old is usually followed by conflict or opposition. In fact, part of the social process of interaction is made up of opposition. Opposition of culture takes place when individuals from different cultures come in contact. The other phase of interaction is coöperation. Conflict alone, without coöperation, would ultimately lead to destruction. Through these two processes society is created. Opposition may be in the form of conflict that aims at the destruction of opponents, or in the form of competition. Resolving opposition is made possible through accommodation—that is, arriving at a working plan wherein the identities of opposing elements are reconciled. The fusion of cultures on the other hand is called assimilation. Both processes are basic to social life. For example, Catholics live side by side with Protestants. Both retain their specific identity, but for mutual benefit they assume a degree of tolerance toward one another that permits them to follow their religious inclinations without interference. American culture itself is an illustration of assimilation. It is made up of contributions of many cultures, all of which have been fused together. The methods of solving problems of opposition depend upon the nature of the culture involved. Cultures in which a spirit of change prevails will be more ready to accommodate or assimilate the new. Ethnocentrism, with its emphasis upon one's own group, determines how new traits will be received and the manner in which they will be employed.

THE VALUE OF SOCIOLOGY

This summary is an attempt to give the reader some of the outstanding problems involved in human association.

Such introductions have limited value. They serve to initiate an acquaintance; knowledge and understanding, however, depend on more than an acquaintance. It is necessary to handle problems, to pursue the facts to wherever they lead, to become intimate with the phenomena under consideration.

Since we live in a culture in which the desirability of human activity is determined by the results, it does not seem presumptuous to discuss the value of sociology. Knowing why we behave as we do should make us more tolerant of the behavior of other people. The despised savage and his seemingly peculiar behavior represent a process of interaction. He, also, is a product of his culture, which for him has meaning and value. It consists of the folkways and mores of his group. It will be possible to evaluate races only when and if cultural differences are totally eliminated from the response of the individual to stimulus. Until then we must admit that we, as white people in America, are discriminating against the colored people because we live in a culture that elicits such behavior. An understanding of the origins of our prejudices and attitudes may make us more willing to give others, who do not see eye to eye with us, the benefit of doubt.

At present a great deal of discussion centers around a planned society. Anything that approaches an effective plan must depend upon accurate information about past plans and how they have worked. Discoveries of constant elements in past human association may insure the success of plans for the future. The researches of sociology and of the other social sciences are necessary to a critical understanding of plans. Much of the waste and inefficiency in human effort can be eliminated if proposed programs are viewed through the light of experience. To know what has happened in the past, if conditions remain the same, should give clues to what we can expect of the future. Knowing what we can expect from the future may make possible the more careful and thoughtful formulation of plans.

BIBLIOGRAPHY

Sumner, William Graham, *Folkways* (Ginn & Company, Boston, 1906).

Ogburn, William F., *Social Change* (Viking Press, New York, 1924).

Wallis, Wilson D., *Introduction to Sociology* (F. S. Crofts & Company, New York, 1928).

Wallis, Wilson D., and Willey, Malcolm M., *Readings in Sociology* (F. S. Crofts & Company, New York, 1933).

Lowie, Robert H., *Culture and Ethnology* (Douglas C. McMurtrie, New York, 1917).

Wissler, Clark, *Man and Culture* (Thomas Y. Crowell Company, New York, 1923).

Chapin, F. Stuart, *Cultural Change* (D. Appleton-Century Company, New York, 1928).

Lundberg, George A., *Social Research* (Longmans, Green & Company, New York, 1929).

Recent Social Trends in the United States (Report of the President's research committee on social trends, McGraw-Hill Book Company, New York, 1933).

Chapin, F. Stuart, *Contemporary American Institutions* (Harper & Brothers, New York, 1935).

Sorokin, Pitirim A., *Contemporary Sociological Theories* (Harper & Brothers, New York, 1928).

Encyclopaedia of the Social Sciences,[1] (The Macmillan Company, New York, 1933–1934).

---

[1] This work is indispensable in the study of the social sciences. Virtually every term, phrase, and idea in the social sciences is discussed by competent scholars.

CHAPTER II

Social Institutions

J. O. HERTZLER

University of Nebraska

THE TERM "social institutions" is widely used in our
everyday speech and in the popular press, as well as in
the abundant literature of the social sciences and history.
In fact, since Plato it has been a common term in all literature dealing with the life of men in groups. At various
strategic times, as for example in the eighteenth century in
western Europe, or in the United States in the last half-
century, it has been a subject of absorbing interest and wide
discussion among social thinkers and practitioners. This
extensive usage seems to point to some fundamental and
continuous aspect of social life to which the term refers.

While we live in a world of automobiles, mechanisms
which we know to be extremely complicated and relatively
efficient, we really have very little understanding of them.
Their occasional repair and yearly improvements we leave
to specialists. To be sure, most of us know how to drive
cars, and that you have to keep them supplied with water,
oil, and gasoline, and we know that these are put in here
and there, although we rarely do this ourselves. We know
that the engine knocks, that the gears scrape, that the body
squeaks, and that the tires blow out. We also know that
various fundamental principles of physics are involved in
their operation; we can usually distinguish makes and
models; we can tell when an automobile is not working

55

right. But how many of us are familiar with all the different parts of an automobile? How many of us can do our own repairs when something goes wrong? And yet practically all of us use automobiles.

Our knowledge of social institutions is also woefully lacking in profundity and comprehensiveness. We are conscious of human society as something that exists, and that functions in certain ways, but we have little understanding of its component mechanisms and processes. To be sure, we follow necessary routine procedures, although we usually do not know why we do so, and we can distinguish some of the major institutions by name, although their specific nature and function are quite vague. We are more or less aware that some of them are functioning much more effectively than others at the present time. We know that all of us are somehow connected with them, and that they are of cardinal importance in any social system. Beyond this we are confused and largely ignorant, although we admit that we are curious. With a few notable exceptions, even among experts, the term "social institutions" has been used without any noticeable precision or universality of meaning, and without any great degree of consistency. This is an unfortunate, perhaps even a dangerous situation in connection with a concept of such obvious importance.

It is the purpose of this chapter to make a brief but comprehensive analysis of social institutions in the light of the best recent data and conclusions, setting forth their place in the social system, their function, their nature and content, their main groupings or fields, and certain problems connected with their continuous efficacy and with the effects upon them of social change.[1]

---

[1] For parts of this chapter the writer has drawn upon previously published works of his that treat the subject of social institutions. Special

A BIRDSEYE VIEW OF SOCIAL INSTITUTIONS

That societies are organized and continuous is due to necessity. Among mankind there is an infinite number of individual natural, acquired, and imagined wants for which satisfaction is sought. But the individuals do not live in a vacuum. Their wants, in the great majority of cases, must be satisfied in competition or in conflict with some persons and in coöperation with others. This produces an even greater array of social needs that must be met systematically and effectively by providing various appropriate social activities or functions. Thus a society is an aggregation of human beings taking the form of a vast and complicated mechanism functioning to satisfy, more or less imperfectly, these individual wants and these social needs. Within this great mechanism all individuals are organized to a greater or lesser degree, formally or informally, both consciously or unconsciously, depending on the nature of the activity, into varied, innumerable, and sometimes inconsistent or conflicting functional interrelationships. All of these functional interrelationships break down into clusters of social usages, which are deemed to be either desirable or necessary, and are maintained and usually enforced by various degrees and amounts of group pressure. These usages in turn consist, concretely, of more or less uniform, standardized, repeated, and permanent forms of behavior, and of the social and material aids necessary to satisfy the real or imagined wants and needs. Some of these standardized forms of behavior are quite inconsequential as far as objectives fundamental

acknowledgment is made of permission granted by the McGraw-Hill Book Company, holders of the copyrights, for the use of certain materials from his *Social Institutions,* New York, 1929, and also a chapter by him in E. B. Reuter (editor), *Race and Culture Contacts* (McGraw-Hill Book Company, New York, 1934).

to general well-being or group efficacy are concerned; others
are actual obstacles; still others satisfy minor wants and
needs, while the greater portion constitute those great clusters of major regulative devices whereby civilizations function, flourish, and endure for centuries.   These usages are
the social institutions.

THE CAUSES OF INSTITUTIONS

Among the various human groupings that constitute any
human society, whether it be primitive, ancient, or modern,
human nature always expresses itself through wants, urges,
and various other typical forms of expression; various problems arise in connection with successfully living together;
various individual and social operations must be carried
on; order must be maintained and activities and forces must
be regulated; necessary tasks must be performed.   Definite
agencies must exist to satisfy these inescapable human
concerns in a uniform, standardized manner.

Among all peoples there is a considerable array of natural,
acquired, or imagined wants, urges, interests, and desires,
some of them most imperative in their nature.   Some of
these grow out of organic needs and instinctive drives and
are bound up with individual survival, such as the want of
food, shelter, sex gratification, association, security, and
health.   Others are of a more derivative nature and are
related to self-gratification and self-expression.   These must
be satisfied in a socially acceptable manner.

Furthermore, certain social needs are practically permanent and have undoubtedly existed since the first
human groupings—needs for providing, organizing, ordering, regulating, forbidding, safeguarding, standardizing, and
enforcing various social activities, as functions directly or
indirectly related to group survival and well-being.   These

needs have always given rise to appropriate organized and standardized means of dealing with them. It has always been necessary to suppress the killing of fellow group members, except in certain special circumstances; it has been necessary for the members of a given group to satisfy their wants for food and other basic necessities without running afoul of each other; it has always been necessary to maintain order and to provide some protection against external aggression; it has been necessary for all groups to regulate, to some extent, the relations and intercourse of the sexes, and the relations of the generations, if the groups are to survive; it has always been necessary to transmit from generation to generation the social heritage of the group, especially the knowledge that has to do with individual and group survival; it has always been necessary to have some philosophy and some standard procedures for dealing with the supernatural.

We might say, by way of summary, that social institutions are caused by the need of satisfying the compelling demands of individual and social life.

THE RANGE OF SOCIAL INSTITUTIONS

The range of institutions is wide, since the needs and interests which call them forth are not all equally pressing, critical, or permanent. Some institutions exist simply because they are accepted or tolerated by part of the group, and do not concern or seriously interfere with the rest of the group. In many cases these are merely survivalistic forms as, for example, polygamy in eleventh-century Japan, which was confined only to the upper classes, or some of the institutions of chivalry still in effect today. Other fairly well-established institutions are not the results of the general needs of the whole group, but rather are imposed on the whole society by the group or groups in control, and are maintained and exalted by various cleverly spread superstitions and fictions until they are at least tacitly accepted, such as the caste system of India or certain phases of capitalism. Still others result from a desire to satisfy some passing whim, or grow out of the aberrations and eccentricities of a particular age, notably many of the institutions of a revolutionary or dictatorial régime. Again, emergencies such as natural catastrophes or depressions create special situations which must be met by institutional devices. Many of the procedures of the Hoover administration and the "New Deal" fall in this category. Also, in every society there is always an informal body of usage, such as the common law, literary criticism, or present-day athletics, which governs certain phases of human interest and activity.

Above all this, however, is the great block of more or less permanent and universal formal regulative institutions, the props of social order, the agencies through which the various essential forms of social control are exercised. Among these are the institutions of production, distribution, and consumption of economic resources and products among all peoples, the matrimonial and domestic institutions, those related to government, education, communication, health, religion, recreation, and group morale. In an examination as limited in extent as this must be, we will have to confine ourselves largely to the institutions that are of major significance in any social order.

THE FUNCTIONS OF INSTITUTIONS

The functions of institutions do not set forth distinctly different activities; they may be considered merely as different ways of looking at social institutions from the point of view of the major social services they render. The basic institutions perform all of the functions described below at the same time.

The satisfaction of human needs

Social institutions are essentially the procedures and agencies whereby the various fundamental needs discussed above are satisfied. All of these needs involve human beings in various innumerable relationships, which must be regularized in the interests of general order and must be coöperative and organized, if they are to be sufficiently efficient and economical of human energy. A great number of varied social institutions, many of which are to be discussed below, are the means whereby these fundamental needs are cared for. In addition, every minor social need is crowded into an institutional mold. If any established and well-observed institutional form or procedure has endured beyond a generation, there is good reason to believe that it is or was at some time bound up with a basic need of the particular group. In general, most institutions are more or less permanent and universal means of satisfying the common and basic needs of human beings in their respective natural and social environment.

The mechanisms of community existence

This point is another phase of the preceding one. The jobs of ordering, regulating, and standardizing the conduct and relationships of individuals and groups constitute the operative phases of any community's existence. A community is what its social institutions make it. Take away its institutions and it is simply an inchoate and disorderly mass of functionless and meaningless human animals. In fact, if any considerable number of basic institutions is weakened or eradicated, the structure and the scheme of functioning of the community are destroyed. · Consider what any village would be like if suddenly all economic activities ceased, if all means of transportation became useless, if the rules and laws governing the relations of the sexes and of parents and children were abandoned, if the schools and churches closed permanently, if all law-making and law-enforcing agencies ceased to function, and if the knowledge and use of all forms of communication, including language and writing, disappeared. Social institutions are the machinery which carries on all the activities that are necessary to the proper functioning of a community.

The instruments of social control

Even the provision of the minimum essentials for individual and social well-being requires a people among whom peaceful and ordered coöperative pursuits and habits have become the common thing. A society in which we find strong antagonism of interests, injustice, lack of coöperation, inefficiency, or disorder is weak, and usually is disintegrating. Apart from actual anti-social habits and viewpoints, it is easy for us to be ignorant of our obligations to each other (especially in complex societies where the relationships are so largely impersonal), to be shortsighted or incapable of comprehending the effects of our acts, or to act only with reference to ourselves. Every society, to insure itself against the absence or breakdown of the behavior necessary to produce orderly social life, is controlled by agencies, which the great bulk of the citizens supports enthusiastically, because they see that without them disaster would occur. These agencies are chiefly social institutions in one form or another. They produce common viewpoints and behavior in individuals and groups, and through their approval by the community, they compel obedience to all the necessary social rules and procedures, and punish disobedience in various ways. Through the common will expressed by means of institutions the community exercises authority and compulsion in order to provide order, peace, security, freedom, self-expression, and general well-being.

ATTRIBUTES OR "TYPE PARTS" OF INSTITUTIONS

An institution, like any other mechanism with complicated functions to perform, is not a simple thing. The carburetor of an automobile consists of tangible parts of steel, aluminum, brass, and possibly cork, working together according to known laws of physics, and as the result of deliberate design. An institution consists of human beings, and it works in and through human beings, each one of whom is a unique, ever-changing biological and social creature, playing a multitude of social roles continuously. Moreover, the dominant institutions are largely matters of informal growth and accretion, with varying but, on the whole, a rather insignificant number of specially or deliberately designed elements. Most of them have "jest growed." Institutions are so much a part of ourselves that it is hard to observe them objectively. Therefore, the problem of taking them apart and revealing them in terms of their typical constituent parts or attributes is not easy. Every institution, however, tends to have an assemblage of elements and characteristics appropriate for the functions it is called upon to perform, and the social scientists are pretty well agreed on certain elements that are almost universally present in all major regulative institutions.

The underlying idea

An institution is fostered by and has at its core some idea or belief, more or less consciously held by the members of the group, regarding the specific need, function, and purpose of the organized behavior. Basic in the underlying ideas is the notion of some specific form of order in the social life which is felt to be necessary. Thus the essence of law is a concept of ordered relationships of human beings and things, by means of definite rules and prescribed punishment; inherent in the institution of property is a conception of order regarding the use or possession of things and creatures; in all educational institutions is the idea that in the properly ordered relations of the generations, knowledge and experience need to be systematically imparted. This is what Cooley had in mind when he stated that "an institution is simply a definite and established phase of the public mind." Even behind the most temporary and insignificant institutions there is an implied or expressed idea of social purpose.

A complex of folkways, mores, and customs

The relative proportion of each of these varies widely with given institutions. It is by means of these that the concept or idea underlying the institutions first objectifies itself. They are the forms which the regularized patterns of group behavior take. Thus the family evidences itself by acting in certain ways that have general utility, that are looked upon as essentially right, and that are in the form of customary procedures that have come down from the past, many of which take the form of ceremonies and rituals.

Codes

Practically all institutions, in order to produce a certain minimum standard of action necessary to enable the necessary functions to be performed, include some sort of rules or laws, more or less definitely understood, which must be followed by all persons connected with or involved in the necessary usage. These codes embody the modes of action that have always served the ends desired. They are more or less specific expressions of that which is demanded, sanctioned, and disapproved in the various fields of social behavior.

Thus, states have their constitutions, the enactments of their legislative bodies, their treaties with foreign countries, their court decisions, their administrative rules, as well as a vast array of unwritten rules and implications governing the informal relationships of members of each state. Underlying the family are not only the various legal statutes governing its formation, perpetuation, and dissolution, but also a set of unwritten demands governing the relations of husband and wife, of parents and children. All religious and ethical institutions have written and implied requirements that are inherently related to the underlying idea.

Standardized habits

Viewing the action of the individuals involved in the interrelationships which necessitated the regularizing of behavior, we find that it consists of those learned, stable, repeated, and reciprocal ways of acting which we designate as habits. The institutional stimuli produce more or less uniform responses or reactions, or systems thereof, in the individuals of each generation as they come upon the scene. In brief, our daily behavior as individuals, in a social world

consisting largely of institutions, consists of habits. Our
daily behavior as citizens of the community, as fathers, as
children in a family, as teachers or pupils in schools, as
employers or employees, as property owners or renters,
as soldiers, as policemen, as churchmembers, as mechanics,
as businessmen, or in any other roles that we play in life,
is largely a matter of habits.

Associations or organizations

Most institutions, in fulfilling their necessary functions,
operate through a certain number of definite associations or
organizations. An association is a body or group of human
beings, united and organized for some common and specific
purpose or end, and having appropriate methods and agents
of functioning, especially administrative machinery. Frequently an institution will have the nominal or actual character of an association. The association is thus the
objective and perceptible machine of the institution, the
chief structural element, through which the underlying idea
is carried into action. The political parties, the bureaus
and departments, the legislative bodies, the courts, and the
police systems are associations through which the functions
of government express themselves; the schools, colleges
and universities, with their teaching staffs, administrative
boards, and student organizations, are associations through
which the educational function is carried on; corporations,
boards of trade, boards of directors, sales staffs, trade unions,
personnel bureaus, and so on are associations carrying on
industry and commerce.

Physical extensions or property

In order to function properly some institutions need certain physical equipment, such as the homestead and private

furniture, offices and buildings, apparatus for communication and transportation, machinery, laboratories, church edifices and altars, factories, stores, capitol buildings and court houses, filing equipment and typewriters, jails and penitentiaries, art galleries, and so on. These constitute the material or physical body of the institutions.

THE MAIN GROUPS OF INSTITUTIONS IN MODERN SOCIETY

An exhaustive enumeration of social institutions is impossible, because they are as numerous as the wants, needs, and interests which they fulfill, and range from those institutions which are relatively insignificant to those that are vitally important to group well-being and efficiency, and from those purely local to those which are worldwide. Nor is it our purpose to offer a classification of institutions; no classification is entirely satisfactory, since each and every principle of division would do violence to some institutions.

Our purpose is merely to call attention to the institutions that operate in the different major or pivotal fields of contemporary social life. We cannot, within the confines of a single chapter, go into the extensive anthropological and historical findings regarding the forms which institutions have taken in other eras and civilizations.[2] These fields, as set forth below, conform roughly to the types of regulatory needs of human beings in groups. The combined institutions in a particular field constitute what we call an "order," that is, a segment of the functional activities that are essential in any society. However, even such a division of the subject, for purposes of examination and analysis, is more or less arbitrary.

---

[2] See Chapter III, "Social Anthropology."

Economic institutions

The need of providing for the production and distribution of food, shelter, clothing, and other necessary equipment and services, and of determining the nature, content, and limits of consumption of things and services, is functionally met by a great battery of economic institutions. These institutions in some combination are basic to the satisfaction of all other needs. If the wherewithal of material existence is not met, there can be neither individual nor social life. In modern societies economic institutions have become doubly important because there are so many services, commodities, and even luxuries that give satisfactions above the mere subsistence level, which are deemed indispensable for the whole population. Furthermore, the growth, widespread diffusion, and increasing interdependence of modern peoples have necessitated the development of vast and complicated institutions of distribution and consumption which barely existed in earlier societies. Today more human interests, energies, and procedures center around the economic aspect of life than around any other.[3]

Although economic institutions have always been socially organized and have always involved coöperation on a greater or lesser scale, in modern times they have become, of necessity, parts of an economic order or system in which standard ideas, principles, codes, techniques, and a host of common organizational forms prevail over great international areas of the earth. Common practices of an economic nature have a more universal acceptance at present than those of any other institutional field.

The most significant economic institutions, with their

---

[3] See Chapters XII. XIII, and XIV for an analysis of the operations of some of the economic institutions.

functions, follow: *Property* is the economico-legal institution that establishes the possession and use rights regarding various types of corporeal and non-corporeal things, as between persons, families, and larger groups, and the social responsibilities that accompany these rights. *Contract* is the economico-legal institution which standardizes and enforces agreements as to the exchange of property or services. *Production* is the institution concerned with the various processes whereby the materials for human use are made available, or whereby human energies, abilities, and skills are made available in the way of paid services that satisfy human and social needs. *Distribution* refers to those institutionalized ways whereby the products and proceeds of production are divided, not only among the factors of production, but also among the population as a whole; it includes most of the economic institutions discussed below. *Market* is the buying and selling institution, and *exchanges* are various organized ways of carrying on this function. *Money,* as a medium of exchange and a standard of value, and *credit,* as a routinized form of deferred payment in sales or loan contracts, are indispensable aids to exchange in modern society. *Interest* is the system of payment for loaned funds, whether these are used in production, distribution, or consumption. *Banks* are the various institutions carrying on financial and credit transactions of all kinds for industry and for the public at large. The various *transportation* institutions give commodities place utility and facilitate both the economic and non-economic movements of persons and things. *Labor organizations* are institutional means whereby workers organize in order to assure themselves a degree of security and recognition in the contemporary industrial system. *Consumption* institutions determine the use of finished products and of services in the satisfaction of individual or group needs and interests, emphasizing especially standards and scales of living.

Matrimonial and domestic institutions

The two chief institutions in this field are marriage and the family. While these are closely related, so close in fact that many people view them as an indivisible unit, they are nevertheless two distinct institutions. While most marriages eventually resolve themselves into families, there seems to be a growing tendency for marriages to remain merely marriages. Also, there are families of a sort, though not completely sanctioned ones, which have not been preceded by formal marriage.

Marriage rests basically upon certain biological and psychological characteristics of human beings. Mankind consists of two sexes, drawn together at times by powerful sexual urges, which result in mating, and in turn may result in offspring. Furthermore, the sexes are complementary to each other; they enjoy together the most completely satisfying associations, and are forced to coöperate with each other in every group. Marriage, in the first place, is a means of regulating, canalizing, and stabilizing sexual intercourse, for among all peoples sex has been found to be too tumultuous an instinct to be left uncontrolled. As such it is purely a *social* arrangement, for mating and reproduction can occur without it. While society holds cohabitation allowable and even desirable, it has at all times required it to be more or less exclusive and permanent, and according to definite rules. In a complex modern society, sexual relationships, like all others, seem to require more and more discipline. Furthermore, increasing attention is being paid to physical competence and health for marriage. In the second place, marriage provides a typical functional relationship between two personalities which, in Western civilization, should be complementary and compatible. Significant in this respect are mutually acceptable habits, ideals, and attitudes, common or adjustable cultural backgrounds, common purposes, and mutual stimulation and reinforcement. Usually the purely sexual aspect of marriage recedes in importance, in time, and companionship and partnership and the sense of personal completeness and fulfillment in this relationship become more important. This element becomes doubly important if the marriage merges into a family, because it determines the nature of the cultural environment of the children. The integration of personality is receiving increasing attention as a factor in modern marriage. In the third place, marriage quite universally is the manner of establishing not only a new social unit in society, but also a new economic one. It involves the ownership and use of property, obligations of maintenance, and competence as earners and disbursers of income. While marriage usually involves all three of these needs, a considerable number of second marriages and of marriages occurring late in life may consist mainly of the last two.

Attached to marriage are betrothal, or the formal disclosure of intention to marry, and divorce, the legitimized procedure in dissolving what is deemed by one or both parties to be an unsatisfactory marriage contract.

The family is the fulfillment of marriage. Its primary purpose is to serve as society's institution for its own self-perpetuation, for it produces, disciplines, protects, and provides for the care and maintenance of offspring. Also, it still is the main agency for providing the oncoming generation with its social heritage, that is, giving it its fundamental conditioning in the form of attitudes and habits, and of making it capable of participating fully in adult life. In brief, the family is the portal through which human beings enter life, both physical and social. Since the family is so important, society insists that it follow some approved pattern and that the parents primarily, and the community secondarily, be made definitely responsible for the maintenance of minimum standards and efficiency of function. A time comes in every family when offspring must also be prepared to assume certain more or less standard responsibilities toward parents and toward each other. Marriage standardizes and fixes the mutual functions and obligations of the husband-wife relationship; the family does this in American society for the relationships between father and mother, parents and children, and siblings.

The family thus is a standardized interrelated group consisting of a man and a woman and their children—a typical association of sexes and ages. As such it is a society in miniature, since it possesses all of the essential relationships and most of the essential functions of the larger social organizations. As a particular social unit it is a means whereby every individual is assigned a definite place in society by which his or her social relations to the rest of society are determined.

The normal modern family has lost many functions which the family of past times itself conducted; the schools have taken over most of the educational responsibilities, many of the recreational and some of the health and nurture responsibilities; factories of various kinds have taken over most of the tasks of the preparation of food, clothing, and other necessities; churches have assumed much responsibility for ethical and religious training and instruction; trade, technical, commercial, and professional schools of all kinds, trade unions, and many other organizations and institutions have undertaken the task of providing the child and young person with the necessary training and skill essential to gaining a livelihood. Various tasks of a recreational, instructional, or nurturing nature have been assumed by such organizations as nursery schools, Boy Scouts, Girl Scouts, playgrounds, and social centers. The stupendous social changes of the last century and a half are responsible for this decline of functions, or rather, they have made it necessary that these other institutions take over complicated functions which the family could no longer competently perform. But the family still needs to function as the primary agency in the maintenance, protection, and disciplining of the child; in the incubation of moral and religious traditions and practices, of manners, social attitudes, and economic habits; and in the formulation of individual ideals, aims, and incentives.

Political institutions

Political institutions serve a variety of related functions. Outstanding among these functions are the insurance of ordered relationships of all kinds within the group between its members, the establishment of rules of group living conducive to general well-being, and their enforcement; also the insurance of life, liberty, rights, peace, justice, and the pursuit of all socially acceptable individual and minor group interests and ends. They guarantee security of life, person, and property; they protect against external aggression. They also supplement, maintain, and even produce, at times, various other institutions essential to group amity, health, or prosperity in a changing world. In brief, political institutions consist of all the means of maintaining order and security in and among human groups. In all groups that are larger and more heterogeneous than the family, the

necessary activities and relations are too complex and mani-
fold and too far-reaching in their effects to be left to the
spontaneous regulation of individuals, however well inten-
tioned they may be. Without political institutions, general
anarchism, chaos, and inability to survive would prevail.

The state is the chief of all the political institutions. It
is, in fact, a system of institutions by means of which are
carried on (1) executive or administrative functions; (2)
legislative functions, whereby representatives of the people
enact the common will into law, which in turn establishes
new administrative functions, new political obligations, and
new rules of social behavior; and (3) judicial functions,
among which are the interpretation of laws, the adjudica-
tion of disputes, and the determination of guilt in the case
of illegal conduct. The state consists of a great array of
constituent sub-institutions, prominent among which are
the administrative systems, whether they be of a democratic
or dictatorial nature, various kinds of chief executives and
cabinets, legislatures, with varying degrees of power, constitutions, unwritten or written, the law, the courts, jury
systems, political parties, the police, the military, and the
innumerable institutions of divisional and local government.

Since the state reflects the will of its citizens, it has broad
authority and great effectiveness as an enforcing agency.
Therefore it is frequently called upon to enforce the minimal requirements of behavior in other institutional fields;
in fact, it has some administrative supervision over practically all other social institutions in the community. For
example, various economic activities must be guaranteed,
enforced, regulated, or prohibited by the state; the marriage and family requirements are placed in its charge;
religious rights and freedom are a matter of state provision;

minimal moral standards in the various expressional fields are established by the state.

In the modern state, while the prohibitive, restrictive, and regulative functions have increased, the positive and constructive activities and agencies have multiplied at an even greater rate. It has become the agency through which groups carry on various general purposes that private individuals, families, neighborhoods, and even states (subdivisions of the sovereign state) cannot carry on by themselves. Thus the modern state does not only provide for the observance of new types of contracts, for the protection of new forms of property and new conceptions of human and group rights, for the regulation of social classes, and the control of large, powerful corporations and combinations thereof. It protects public health; provides, supervises, and endows education; administers relief, provides care for the defective and aged, and carries on many other forms of social service. It carries on public industries and utilities, owns public lands, provides public recreation (national, state, and municipal parks, golf courses, stadia, and so on). Occasionally it makes provision for art and music, and carries on a multiplicity of other similar functions. The state is continually invading new social provinces and administering them in behalf of the general welfare; there seem to be no limits to its range. It is not only the final authority in social control, but is becoming the general agent for providing a growing mass of services and utilities that cannot be successfully run privately or locally.

International interdependencies of all kinds have recently increased in number, and international conflict has become more universally disastrous. In consequence, a great number of *international* political institutions have developed to facilitate and order international relations. Among these are expanded diplomatic and consular offices, international conferences, the League of Nations, the International Labor Office, and the Permanent Court of International Justice.

Educational and scientific institutions

Much education in all stages of culture, including our own, is informal, that is, it is acquired by suggestion and contact, and by participation in the everyday procedures of the family, the neighborhood, and the community. But such an education is not sufficiently comprehensive, selective, and systematic to meet the needs of the individual or the group in any society above the most primitive level. Practically all societies meet their educational needs with an array of formal, specialized institutions. This is necessitated by the magnitude of the problem of instruction and training.

The function of education is to prepare the individual for full and successful participation in the life of his group, as an occupant, citizen, and member of a maintenance group. Even meeting the minimal requirements for such a life in a modern society is a sizable order. In the first place, there is such a vast and ever-increasing amount of basic experience and knowledge, much of which is indispensable for every member of the community if he is to live efficiently. This must be imparted to each successive generation. Secondly, due to the complexity of life, certain minimal social standards must be inculcated, and certain general social habits must be developed. Thirdly, it is necessary to give the group members a measure of preparation for livelihood, usually consisting of occupational skills and professional proficiencies. Beyond these lies a fourth objective—to bring, ultimately, all grades and types of individuals to the point of maximum individual achievement consistent with social usefulness—to put life at its highest human level.

The chief educational institution is the school. Its purpose is the deliberate and systematic instruction of all youth along the necessary lines, so that we need not depend upon the well-intentioned but partial, spasmodic, and often irresponsible and unsocial instruction that is received in the family, or on the hit-or-miss, unbalanced information received through the broader social contacts. The school carries on its task by means of a specially trained personnel. It uses definite and previously established principles, methods, and programs, with the aid of special plant and equipment. The school accomplishes its work more efficiently, and with greater economy of money and effort, than any other agency. As such the school has become the primary agency for inculcating practically all of the necessary institutional lore and procedures. In its higher reaches, in the colleges and universities, the school functions not only to conserve and transmit the social heritage, but also as an agency for its expansion and enrichment. Colleges and universities thus become a combination of educational and scientific institutions.

Schools of all kinds, ranging from the kindergarten to the most advanced forms, are provided both by semi-private groups and by the state. Those sponsored by both groups follow pretty much a common pattern at each educational level, though most of the innovation and experimentation occurs in the semi-private organizations. In this country the proportion of education obtained in the public institutions is increasing.

Educational tasks are also carried on by private and public, semi-formal and formal organizations and associations, such as libraries, university extensions, correspondence schools, and home study courses arranged by mail and by radio, discussion groups and forums, museums and galleries, lecture courses, lyceums and chautauquas, the press, and the radio, in many of its activities.

Scientific institutions are closely allied with educational institutions. They are systematic agencies for analyzing, by appropriate means, all the various kinds of phenomena that concern man. This they do by discovering facts and relations between facts, and by classifying and stating their findings in some standard way so that they are universally usable. Such knowledge and methods enable men to control, more or less, some of these various phenomena in the interests of human well-being. They also provide, to some extent, the power of predicting effects of significance to man and of determining existing causes and trends. Research is the organized technique of science for the discovery and propagation of knowledge. Science becomes the means of improving practically all institutions. Scientific functions of an organized and systematic nature are actually being carried on by the various departments of the colleges and universities, with their scientific standards, trained staffs, and special equipment; by the research bureaus, institutes, and foundations, usually semi-public in nature; and by various local, national, and international scientific societies.

Educational and scientific institutions are the chief bulwarks of modern societies against retrogression.

Communicative institutions

Language is one of the primary factors in the achievement of humanness, for it makes possible thought, which is one of man's basic characteristics. Without this chief tool —language—thought would be without articulation and expression, hence probably non-existent. Any society, if it is to be well knit, to be capable of meeting its regular functions, and to endure for any length of time, must have means whereby wants, needs, desires, ideas, discoveries, and knowledge of all other cultural achievements may be communicated from man to man, from place to place, and from time to time. The basic communicative institutions, language and writing, which has grown out of it, serve these functions. As such they are fundamental to the operation of practically all of the other social institutions.

Both language and writing are standardized cultural products. Language consists of sounds, deliberately produced, that have a standard specific and arbitrary meaning throughout a given cultural area. These various sounds are used in combination to convey wishes, desires, and ideas. When these sounds are translated into standardized graphic figures or letters, we have writing. Writing makes the expressed ideas not only more permanent, but also transmissible in time and space.

In recent times the scope of language and writing have been vastly increased by mechanical extensions which, however, are only improvements of the basic institutions. Among these mechanical extensions are the printing press and all its developments, the telephone, the radio, and the telegraph, both with and without wires, and the postal systems, which utilize all the modern forms of transportation. Some of these inventions have themselves become the core of new institutions, such as the postal service and various public utilities.

Religious institutions

For the great majority of the people of any group, religion has a form which is definitely institutional. It consists of those widely acceptable beliefs and those symbolic and organizational forms whereby satisfactory relations are thought to be formed with the intangible, incomprehensible, and uncontrollable aspects of the larger environment. Men, as more or less closely organized bodies of believers, seek to obtain for themselves a sense of security in dealing with the mysteries of life and the hereafter. The great religious systems are all comprehensive attempts to combine in institutional forms the ideas, beliefs, customs, codes, organizations, and material aids that will, at least in a measure, satisfy these basic and almost universal needs.

Among us the chief and most all-inclusive religious institution is the church, which consists of theologies and creeds, bodies of organizational law, religious orders, administrative personnel, both ecclesiastical and lay, specialized religious instructors and leaders, ceremonials, rituals, and symbolisms, hymns, prayers and incantations, shrines, cathedrals, and other places of worship, not to mention various tangential features of an educational and recreational nature more or less related to the religious function. The church is both a definite association of men and an institutional device for maintaining and perpetuating the beliefs, ideas, and practices of the people of a given religious persuasion. Through its codes and organizations it is an important factor in regulating a large number of other social relationships in which its members are participants.

The æsthetic and expressional institutions

Man's need of giving vent to his various expressional abilities and urges is almost as great as his craving for food or sex gratification. These expressional urges, usually vastly stimulated by association with his fellows, take the form of an intense desire to express emotions or beauty in its various objective forms, a desire to express thought with appropriate dignity or majesty, a desire to express movement rhythmically, or the desire to enjoy and appreciate beautiful things. The systematization and standardization of the expressional forms, which is necessary for their transmission and their mutual comprehension, and the groupings of interests and persons around them, has led to their institutionalization. Especially significant are the institutions, in various forms, concerned with the production and appreciation of beauty and thought, that are grouped around the arts of painting, sculpture, music, the drama, the dance, poetry, literature, and architecture.[4] These institutions include the canons of the respective arts, the schools of art, the associations of artists and lay admirers, the great museums for purposes of instruction, display, and discussion, and various other generally known features.

Recreational institutions

Recreation is as old as mankind, but institutions that are deliberately organized to provide recreation for both young and old are a very recent addition to the battery of indispensable social institutions. They have become necessary because of the congestion, impersonality, and increased tempo of modern life; the confinement, speed, and excessive routinization of modern occupations, with their enervating and debilitating effects; the shrinking of the physical home; and the loss of many opportunities for pleasurable free activity, coöperation, and association, which were once available in smaller, close-knit communities.

Through various organized and more or less standardized

---

[4] For the underlying psychological and sociological reasons for the institutionalization of expressional urges, see Hertzler, J. O., *Social Institutions*, pp. 63–64 (McGraw-Hill Book Company, New York, 1929).

private, semi-public, and public agencies, provision is today
being made for satisfying the needs for pleasurable physical
activity, for the release of surplus energies, and the stimulation of various interests and abilities, artistic and otherwise,
for the enjoyment of nature, for protected but stimulating
competition and rivalry, for feeding starving emotions and
thwarted rhythmic responses, and, in general, for adding
relaxation, zest, stimulation, sheer fun, and happy play to
life. It has been discovered that the craving for recreation
cannot be repressed without causing numerous individual
and social ills; hence the widespread efforts to provide adequate satisfaction.

Among the institutions and sub-institutions that render
these functions with varying degrees of proficiency in American life are gymnasia and playgrounds; private, municipal,
state, and national parks, each conducted by the appropriate park service; private and public golf courses, swimming
pools, and bathing beaches; dance halls and dancing clubs;
community centers, country clubs, athletic clubs, lodges,
clubs for playing various games, bowling alleys, libraries,
and reading clubs; singing, debating, and orchestral societies; garden clubs, bird clubs, the Boy Scouts, the Campfire
Girls, the national Y.M.C.A. and Y.W.C.A., and theaters
of all kinds. These and others have become established
phases of our social life. They meet basic needs, but like
many institutions in other fields, they have not all become
regularized in the interests of general well-being.

Health institutions

In times past also these institutions had only rudimentary
counterparts, which were usually bound up with institutions in other fields. In modern complex societies health
has come to be a matter of general social concern, owing to

such factors as the new knowledge regarding the nature and transmission of disease, the increasing communicability of contagious diseases due to the greater crowding and mobility of populations; the cost to the community and nation of various physical and mental diseases and disabilities, in terms of both dollars and national vitality and efficiency; the relationships between ill-health and accident, poverty and dependency; the knowledge of the effects, in terms of ill-health and low individual efficiency, of bad housing, lack of sanitation, failure to quarantine, excessive fatigue, occupational poisoning, and other unhealthful living and working conditions. Health, in brief, has come to be a problem beyond the grasp of the individual or the family; we have arrived at the point where its prevention and control must be managed in an institutionalized manner.[5]

The health institutions are both semi-public and public. They exist as health centers, sanitaria, and hospitals for all types of physical and mental cases; municipal, state, and federal departments of health, dispensaries, nursing organizations, and services; clinics for general medical diagnosis and treatment, as well as those which provide various special health services—pediatric, dental, psychiatric, nutrition, eye and ear, venereal, and contraceptive. They also assume the form of associations such as the National Tuberculosis Association, the Red Cross, and the Mental Hygiene Association. They include the medical professions, especially in their organized forms, and medical social service organizations.

Owing to the crucial significance of modern health institutions—our bulwarks against epidemics and general physical and mental deterioration—they, of necessity, must

---

[5] See Chapter XIV for a discussion of socialized medicine.

become more standardized, specialized, and coöperative, and more socially focused.

THE OVERLAPPING AND THE INTERRELA-
TIONSHIP OF INSTITUTIONS

From the preceding sections of this chapter, the reader might get the idea that each institution is a clear-cut entity, operating independently in a single field of social functioning and regulation. This is far from the actual situation. We divided them into fields simply for purposes of analysis. Actually, they all function at the same time as agencies of a vast complex whole. There is much overlapping of the institutions in different fields; for example, marriage falls predominantly in the domestic field, but it is also an economic institution, since it involves property and financial arrangements. The family is an educational and recreational, as well as a domestic institution. Property is both an economic and a legal institution, and contract functions in several fields. Most other institutions operate in two or more fields.

Similarly, while particular institutions perform one or more distinctive functions, they are all merely coöperating aids in one great interrelated organic whole. Each is inextricably bound up with others, because human behavior is varied and multiform. The family is bound up with the school, religion, the state, and various institutions of production and consumption, to mention only a few. Marriage is unavoidably related to civil and religious institutions. Education involves families, the state, and several economic, scientific, health, and recreational institutions. The church is dependent upon business corporations and advertising agencies. All institutions try to make use of the newspaper in the conduct of their affairs.

Institutional interdependence is also extended through the fact that institutions possess many members in common. An individual at any given time in his own behavior functions along a variety of lines, and conforms to numerous more or less uniform institutional requirements. At a given time he may be a citizen, a parent, a pupil, a teacher, a scientist, a member of a profession, a member of a church, an etcher, a member of a country club, a member of several fraternal orders, a member of the National Guard, a participant in various public or semi-public recreational undertakings, and a willing conformist to various public health requirements.

INSTITUTIONS AND SOCIAL CHANGE

Institutions do change

Institutions are never completely static, in a state of equilibrium. They do change more or less with changing trends in culture and social organization. As one social era passes into another and the major habits of life change, the specific expressions of individual and social needs also change. Institutions must change their content and function, or eventually give way to others better adapted to the times. Systems of economic production succeed each other as population, resources, and conditions of transportation change; autocratic systems of government give way to democratic forms, and these may in turn revert to dictatorships; independent local stores give way before chain systems, with their economies in buying, advertising, and management; mayors and aldermen in our city governments surrender functions to trained and specialized city managers as municipal administration becomes more complex and technical, and as public functions and expenses multiply; companionates are taking the place of families in our cities, where life is impersonal, where children are a luxury, and where women must frequently earn their own living; churches cease to be merely prayer-meeting and Sunday affairs and assume seven-days-a-week programs, involving recreational and educational as well as religious activities.

In the last century an unusual number of occurrences have forced institutions to change. Notable among these have been the rapidly changing nature of our technology since the Industrial Revolution, the large scale of our contemporary social relationships, the multiplicity of our mental contacts due to the rapidly advancing means of communication and transportation; the constantly changing ratios of population to resources and production; the conflict of classes; the rapidly increasing inventions; the extensive and varied stimulation of urban life; and the extension and acceptance of science in daily life. These have produced unheard of changes in the home, the relation of the sexes, the workshop, religion, legislation, education, government, and almost every other set of institutions.

Another reason for change is the fact that institutions are composed of persons, and persons die off in time to be replaced by others who will be different to some extent. Hence, the personnel is continually changing, and because of this the functioning is affected. Some of the institutions are intelligently controlled and administered in the interests of general well-being, and are continually being adapted to new purposes. The old institution is pruned and rebuilt and, if it is healthy and sound at the core and has not been maimed by too much pruning, it will function efficaciously among the new conditions.

The changes that go on in the institutions of a group are never harmonious or parallel, however; some are dis-

integrating at the same time that others are just emerging
from pre-institutional or sub-institutional forms, while still
others are undergoing reconstruction. Furthermore, the
changes, whether for better or worse, are occurring at various rates of speed. In no society is the institutional equipment ever in a state of perfect repair, adjustment, or
efficiency; in fact, the general efficiency may be said to be
about that of a five-year-old automobile.

Culture contact and institutional change

In the preceding paragraphs, institutional change that is
largely the result of spontaneous forces and factors within
the culture was discussed. Possibly even exceeding these
internal conditions, as dynamic factors today, are the contacts with other cultures and races. These are caused by
disparate economic conditions, commercial penetration, religious proselyting, travel, international alliances for military purposes, the development of international radio
communication, and innumerable other factors. Compact,
homogeneous, isolated groups have almost disappeared, and
the most intemperate nationalistic efforts can never restore
them. The contact of peoples and cultures results in the
impact of the institutions of the contacting societies upon
each other and, though serious clash and dislocation do not
always occur, mutual modification unavoidably does. Today some sort of institutional adjustment necessitated by
culture contact, usually on a fairly large scale, is going on
among practically every people. Below are a few propositions presenting the more important and frequently recurring possibilities.

1. Cultural contact greatly accelerates and complicates
the processes of change continually occurring in institutions.

2. When cultures meet there is unavoidably some mixing, as well as substitution and selection, of institutional

elements; in fact, the only way to prevent cultures from mixing is to keep them from touching, or to exterminate one of them instantly.

3. The contact of alien cultures usually disturbs the institutional balance of both or all of the cultures involved and often creates a serious state of social disorganization.

4. The long-run tendency is toward some kind of equilibrium; this, in fact, must occur if the society is to endure, because the institutions are its functional mechanisms and its chief agents of social control.

5. If there is a dissolution of institutions, in most cases it is gradual and piecemeal, owing to the emotional attachments, the values, and the ingrained individual and racial habits which people have in connection with them.

6. The breakdown of old institutional elements and the building up of new or revised ones is not a mass movement; it occurs in the individuals of the respective cultures. First, a few embrace a new element, then more, until finally a uniform behavior pattern exists.

7. In the process of borrowing, the institutional elements selected are not always best or most appropriate from the point of view of an efficient culture.

8. When institutions meet, usually the superficial and overt aspects—the techniques, and material constructs—change first, while the underlying ideas, values, and attitudes are more slowly modified.

9. In most cases the institutions bound up with primary group interests and relations resist change longer than those involved in secondary group relations.[6]

---

[6] These propositions have been adapted from a paper by the present writer entitled "Culture Contact and Institutional Change" appearing in Reuter, E. B., (editor), *Race and Culture Contacts*, pp. 48–56 (McGraw-Hill Book Company, New York, 1934).

The relative inflexibility of institutions

While institutions do change, the most notable feature of their changing is the fact that, in the great majority of the cases, the changes are belated and usually inadequate; they do not come in a clear-cut way, but are carried into effect grudgingly, half-heartedly, and often disguised by fictions of various sorts. It seems to be in the very nature of institutions to outlive their usefulness. Few spontaneously terminate their existence when their work is done; they tend to persist even though the need which called them into existence has disappeared, or has so changed as to demand wholly different adjustments. At the same time, outgrown and useless institutions emphasize authority and precedent, scorn innovations, and function dogmatically. They thus become social fossils—depositories of archaic attitudes, beliefs, ideas, codes, and habits.

This must not be construed to mean that an institution is bad or useless or full of survivals simply because it is old, nor does it mean that the only good institutions are new ones. There are some very ancient institutions which still efficiently serve their appropriate functions. But this is exceptional; institutions that have any history at all are pretty sure to show some leftovers or "survivances."

Why do institutions hang on, or persist in a particular form, after they have lost their usefulness, or after they have outlived their age? They do this for several reasons. Institutions are structures, parts of the social organization of any people; hence they must be reasonably stable and rigid. This results in a tendency to crystallization. They are products of the past, having grown out of group habits of long standing and of high efficacy—originally, at least. They are control agents with conserving functions, serving as bulwarks against confusion and disorder. Old men usually are in charge of institutions, and they are invariably conservative and resistant to change. The essential conservatism of the masses themselves results in an opposition to change of anything that is bound up with self-preservation. Many institutions have a protected position, and hence survive beyond their time. Institutions engender loyalty and pride, which promote their longevity. Finally, new institutions, like all other cultural devices, have to be made out of old materials.

The result of this is that old features and functions which are no longer of use continue to be maintained at a cost of energy and with a personnel which may be, and usually is, sadly needed elsewhere. Men become victims of their ancestors' machines; they have with them a false sense of security, which is caused by rigidity, routine, overstandardization, and overorganization, and which is enjoyed at the cost of progress and more flexible, better-adapted institutions. The institution's measures of value are sought in the past rather than in the present.

But it is only the high functional value of institutions that entitles them to respect, support, and the authoritative position that they hold in social life; they are not ends to be held in reverence, but expedient means. Hence they should be kept adaptable—capable of abandoning the outgrown and useless elements, but not so plastic as to be without strength. The best institution is one that is rigid enough to control and stabilize, but modifiable enough to change as soon as the need clearly points to a modification of form and content. To insure these qualities requires that all institutions be subjected to continual scrutiny by an alert and informed public that is willing and able to make such modifications in its own ideas, attitudes, codes, and behavior as the situation requires. After all, the institutions emanate from human beings, and are part of them. Consequently, institutions are no more efficient or progressive than the majority of men allows them to be.

BIBLIOGRAPHY

Hertzler, J. O., *Social Institutions* (McGraw-Hill Book Company, New York, 1929).

Reuter, E. B., (editor), *Race and Culture Contacts*, pp. 48–56 (McGraw-Hill Book Company, New York, 1934).

Hamilton, Walton H., "Institution," *Encyclopaedia of the Social Sciences*, Vol. 8, pp. 84–89 (The Macmillan Company, New York, 1932).

Ballard, L. V., *Social Institutions* (D. Appleton-Century Company, New York, 1936).

Dawson, C. A., and Gettys, W. E., *An Introduction to Sociology*, pp. 66–118 (Ronald Press Company, New York, 1935).

Chapin, F. Stuart, *Contemporary American Institutions* (Harper & Brothers, New York, 1935).

Judd, C. H., *The Psychology of Social Institutions* (The Macmillan Company, New York, 1926).

MacIver, R. M., *Community: A Sociological Study*, pp. 153–165 (The Macmillan Company, New York, 1924).

CHAPTER III
Social Anthropology

WILSON D. WALLIS

University of Minnesota

THE FIELD OF ANTHROPOLOGY

ANTHROPOLOGY is, literally, the science of man. In practice, however, the field is more limited. Many sciences deal with man; for example, medicine, human anatomy, history, sociology, economics, political science, psychology. Anthropology overlaps all of these. Its distinctive field, which is entered only incidentally by other disciplines, is the realm of preliterate cultures. These fall under two great divisions: (1) prehistoric, and (2) contemporary preliterate cultures, "contemporary" referring to the period of initial European contact. The prehistoric includes the known span of human existence prior to written records, that is, prior to approximately five thousand years ago. Contemporary preliterate cultures include the aboriginal New World, Africa (except the northern fringe and Egypt), and all of the remainder of the Old World except the European area and the South, Central, and East Asiatic areas in which historical civilizations have flourished, notably India, Persia, China, Korea, Japan, and the outposts of these civilizations. Oceania, including two of the largest islands in the world, was inhabited by preliterate peoples. In both the Old World and the New there were several thousand tribes. The anthropologist, therefore, has no dearth of potential material. His troubles are

created by the multiplicity of the cultures which he studies
and by the wealth of information about them. Even so,
we constantly regret the meagerness of our information.
During the last four hundred years preliterate peoples have
been dying off, owing to outright extermination or to disintegrating effects of European contacts. The last Tas-
manian died a half-century ago; the last Beothuck, of
Newfoundland, a century ago; most of the Indians east of
the Mississippi had been killed or driven away before the
ethnologist arrived. Other large portions of the world are
ethnographically unknown, notably the interior of New
Guinea and most of the great area drained by the Amazon
and Orinoco Rivers. Each year hundreds of trained workers
are engaged in studying various phases of preliterate life,
including language, folklore, customs, and material culture;
more than a score of journals are devoted to recording these
observations; and each year hundreds of new books describe
native life and customs. Even so, irrecoverable items of
native life are disappearing more rapidly than they are
being recorded.

It is difficult for people to believe that those who talk, act,
think, and live in very different fashion from themselves
can be quite as human as they. The greater the difference,
the more emphatic this difficulty. Primitive peoples take a
similar attitude, which often is so deeply rooted that they
are unconscious of it. Thus the Eskimo call themselves
Inuit, which means "People," or "Human Beings," and refer
to Indians as "Children of a Louse's Egg." Neighboring
tribes call the Hopi *Moki,* which means "Cowards," whereas
their name for themselves, Hopi, means "Men." Bushmen
call themselves Khoi-khoi, which means "Men of Men," or,
as we say, "We the People." The name which many Australian tribes apply to themselves means "Men." Generally

speaking, preliterate people have about the same measure
of contempt for us as we have for them, each group being
ignorant of the language, ways of life, ethical standards,
pleasures, trials, and hardships of the other. Civilization
has brought preliterate peoples little for which they can be
grateful. Diseases, death, and theft of lands are the amplest
behests of civilization to preliterate folk.

By studying these types of preliterate civilization we
learn about man, and read a fuller story of human civilization than conventional history offers; also, acquaintance
with others is one of the best ways of learning about ourselves. Those who are immersed in their own civilization
do not understand it, for they have no perspective of it.

To understand one's civilization one must stand apart
from it. A historian can do this, for he can view present-
day civilization from the standpoint of the civilization of
Rome, Greece, or medieval Europe; or American civilization from the standpoint of English, French, or German
civilization. The study of preliterate cultures takes us out
of the sphere of European cultures and their backgrounds,
the early historical Mediterranean civilizations, and gives
us a wider perspective of our civilization. If one wishes to
know about human life in the large, one cannot remain
ignorant of preliterate cultures. Preliterates are bone of
our bone, flesh of our flesh. Their civilizations, however
much they differ from our civilization, have much in common with it, for in any culture there are certain persistent
"human" problems with which man must cope.

SOME PHASES OF ANTHROPOLOGY

Anthropology embraces much more than the strictly
social side of preliterate life. It deals with the physical
traits of men, and with their group or racial variations. It

deals with the vast stretch of the prehistoric, giving us accounts of stone implements and early metal work. It deals, also, with the material side of contemporary pre-literate culture—the technology, which includes the devices utilized by preliterate man, such as canoes, hunting and fighting weapons, dwellings, and the range of his economic activities. These matters cannot be included in the present brief survey, which is limited to phases of social life.

Early students of culture recognized stratifications of cultures, lower and higher stages of civilization: a hunting and fishing stage, a pastoral stage, a stage of agriculture. Peoples who made pottery were differentiated, by culture level, from peoples ignorant of this art. There is some justification for such classifications.

Similarities, however, often hide a great variety of differences, so that, for most purposes, it is misleading rather than enlightening to classify peoples in this manner. Thus Eskimo and Australians are hunting and fishing peoples; but in almost every respect their cultures and manner of life are as dissimilar as those of any two peoples could be. Aside from the use of the spear-thrower, there is almost nothing in common in the devices used in hunting and fishing, or in the methods employed in taking game. Also, their social and political life differs in almost every respect. Again, Plains Indians live by hunting and, with some exceptions, are non-agricultural. Yet they have almost nothing specific in common with either Australians or Eskimo. Similarly, the Northern Iroquois of northern New York State practice agriculture, and so do Pueblo tribes of the Southwest of the United States. Yet little else do they have in common. Toda, of India, keep buffaloes, and Masai, of East Africa, are a cattle-keeping people; yet otherwise these two groups are culturally almost as far

apart as any two groups that could be selected. Economic
stratifications, moreover, are not mutually exclusive. Thus
Iroquois, although agricultural, depend largely on fish and
game for food. Village Plains Indians, on the Upper Mis-
souri River, hunt the buffalo almost as much as do other
Plains tribes; yet they live in permanent abodes and practice agriculture, as do Iroquois. Most Woodland Indians,
east of the Mississippi, are agricultural; yet all depend in
varying degree on fish and game, and so are hunters and
fishers as well as agriculturists.

A culture area is characterized by its civilization. Culture includes all the forms of life or achievement that are
characteristic of the group and are not mere individual
traits or peculiarities. In our civilization such things as
radios, churches, elections, war, football, are examples of
culture traits. Eskimo culture traits include snow-houses,
harpoons, skin-covered boats, shamanism, seasonal ceremonies and visits. A tribe is within a culture area, for it
has many culture traits of adjacent tribes. The culture
area is geographic, in the sense that a political entity, a
nation, for example, is geographic, yet has non-geographic
characteristics. Some culture areas, like nations, have natural boundaries, whereas the boundaries of some culture
areas have no distinctive geographic features. Thus Eskimo
constitute a culture area. Though they extend along the
Arctic circle from northeastern Greenland, across North
America, to eastern Siberia, throughout this stretch of territory they have the same culture, with only local differences. Most of North, Central and South America can be
divided into culture areas. Attempts to divide Africa into
culture areas have not been so successful, but some of its
culture areas are easily recognized. Oceania comprises the
culture areas of Australia-Tasmania; Polynesia, from New

Zealand to Easter Island and Hawaii; Melanesia, from New Guinea north and east; and Micronesia, including Yap, the Carolines, the Marianas, and other islands. Culture areas have considerable stability, barring outside interference from intrusive peoples—notably, ubiquitous Europeans. Eskimo culture has remained much the same for at least the last three hundred years. Some American tribes live today much as they lived four hundred years ago. There is comparable persistence of culture in many isolated portions of the civilized world, especially in mountainous regions. Culture stability, however, is only relative. All cultures are constantly modified, though some features may change very slowly.

Forces which initiate change come sometimes from within the tribe, or from within the culture area, and sometimes from outside the culture area. Culture traits spread from one area to another; and thus culture change is induced by introduced traits. Plains Indians, for example, did not domesticate the horse, but secured it from tribes that had obtained it from the Spanish. Culture areas, then, are not watertight compartments; culture traits seep from one area into another.

In most instances there is reason to believe that when a culture trait is present over a wide area, it has spread from a single source. Thus agriculture probably had only one origin in the New World and spread from this place of origin, presumably Mexico, to tribes hundreds of miles away, moving gradually from one tribe to another, and eventually penetrating a large portion of the tillable area of the New World. Similarly the use of the wheel, unknown in the aboriginal New World, has spread from one place of origin. Practically every modern device has spread from a single place of origin.

SOCIAL GROUPINGS[1]

Everywhere men live in a social group. "A No Man's land is like a barnacle which misses its way and finds nothing to adhere to. There is no possibility of independent existence." Even when the possibility of independent existence is present, the opportunity seldom is embraced.

Man may complain of his fellows, but he prefers a complaining social life to an uncomplaining nonsocial Robinson Crusoe one. In many cases man could live alone if he would; but he will not. The potential advantages of social life are fairly obvious. Lowie's statement regarding the Crow Indians will apply, with appropriate modifications, to almost every group:

> The single human being is a mere worm at the mercy of the elements. A man may be a champion marksman, but when there is no game to shoot he falls back on the pemmican his wife has stored against that very emergency; and even in the chase he is most efficient when he hunts in company. Robes and leggings are made by wives or kinswomen; his arrows are made for him by a skilled craftsman. He seeks renown but his chances, as a lonely raider, for achieving fame are small. He must join a well-organized party.
>
> It meant everything to be able to face life not alone but with a comrade, shielded by one's family and clan, in the bosom of one's club. That is why the kinless man was an outcast and byword of shame, the target for the brutality of sadistic tribesmen, forced to throw himself on the mercy of benign supernaturals.[2]

In living together, men develop community or social solidarity, which is increased by many common interests and activities. The eating of food together establishes a social

---

[1] In this chapter many primitive culture traits and culture complexes will be discussed. The student is urged to make a list of parallel traits in our own civilization. Opposite each such modern trait, place the primitive counterpart, noting in each case the page where the latter is found.

[2] Lowie, Robert H., *The Crow Indians,* p. 329 (Farrar & Rinehart, New York, 1935).

tie. Procuring and utilizing food increases social solidarity, for competition within the tribe is practically always friendly. In many areas, moreover, game must be shared with one's fellows; in some tribes there are detailed regulations for its distribution in family or clan. Religion is another cementing tie. There are no religious schisms in a preliterate group, and the bond of a shared supernaturalism draws the members of the group together. So strong a bond is language that one ethnologist defined the tribe in Australia as a group of people who speak the same dialect. In other parts of the preliterate world such a group does not always constitute a tribe; but we may say, conversely, that in a given tribe there is a common language. Tribes which speak the same language are friendly. The word Dakota, for example, means "Ally," or "Friend."

Dakota did not fight those who spoke their language. In the Plains area of North America when a band encountered another the common question was, "What language do you speak?" If members of the encountered group spoke the same language as the challenger, they were accepted as friendly; if they spoke a different language, they were regarded as hostile. These were usually valid judgments.

The crises of life, such as birth, death, and marriage, strengthen social bonds. Birth is a matter of importance not merely to the infant and its family, but also to every member of the group. Many tribes, therefore, have ceremonies designed to induct the newborn child into the mysteries of social life and assure him a welcome on earth, where he has come to initiate his career among those who will henceforth be his fellows, with whom he will share a common life. When death removes a member of the group, the loss is a matter of general concern. Marriage establishes a new tie which, because it affects the relations of those immediately concerned, likewise affects their relations with others. Any great crisis is usually a matter of group concern. War, a crisis of the highest order, a threat to group existence, demands measures that strengthen social solidarity. When the group is threatened, individual differences are submerged in unified purposes. The phenomenon has a counterpart in civilized nations, whose members unite, if ever, during war. Defensive measures in other calamities, such as drought, earthquake, and terrifying eclipse, may strengthen social solidarity. Solidarity is strengthened by ceremonial performance, song, dance, art, and mythology. Usually the song and the dance are peculiar to a tribe. One is reminded of class and college songs, processions, and pep fests, which foster class or college spirit, or inspire the team.

The art and mythology of a tribe are seldom precisely duplicated in any other tribe. Each, in effect, is a language of communication. Art and mythology communicate common ideas, appreciations, ideals, proprieties, and concepts. To live in a group and participate in its various forms of thought, life, and activities, is to become like one's fellows in all fundamental respects. Thus the group attains a solidarity which holds its members together; and, largely because of accommodation to group pattern, life has more meaning and satisfaction than it would have for those individuals in any other group. Hence, in savagery as in civilization, "in order to live a life answering to the social nature and instincts of man, it is necessary to replace the individualistic or atomistic conception of society, and view it as a moral unit of individuals coöperating towards a common end. This end must always directly or indirectly include the common good, for no other ends are worthwhile or morally lawful unless they harmonize with the purpose of all human existence, which is the attainment of the good

life. . . . A true society is an organic fellowship in which
the actions of any single member affect in some way the
well-being of the whole, in which the well-being of the
whole suffers as soon as single members suffer in regard to
the common requirements of the good life. Such a conception of human society necessarily includes a common set
of laws or moral ideals in terms of which all members will
strive to maintain the common good." [3]

The household circle

The most intimate group to which an individual belongs
is the household circle. The household or family circle is
a social grouping, usually with definite allocation of place.
Thus in the hunting areas of North America the father
commonly sits opposite the entrance to the dwelling, and
definite places in the abode are assigned wife, daughters,
and sons, respectively. Among Lenge, of Portuguese West
Africa, if there is only one hut for a man and his two wives,
the first wife and her children sleep to the right of the
doorway, the second wife to the left of the doorway. Among
Maori, of New Zealand, the place of honor in the house is
under a window. Slaves are allotted the corner to the left
(as one enters the house). In the Yakut (Siberia) house
the bench opposite the door, usually on the southern wall,
is reserved for honored guests. The master of the house,
and his married sons and their children, sit on the right
side; grown girls occupy the left side. Less honored guests
occupy the lower ends of the right and left sides, nearest the
door. Among Kazaks (Central Asia) the seat of honor is
opposite the door of the *yurt*, or hut.

[3] Michel, Dom Virgil, "Ideals of Reconstruction," in *The Social Question*,
Vol. VI, p. 23 (Wanderer Printing Co., St. Paul, Minnesota, 1936).

The camp

Each local group of the Arunta (Central Australia) has a definite arrangement of its main permanent central camp, in which a certain place is assigned each constituent marriage class. In the Choritja local group, for example,

The camp is divided into four main parts like sectors of a circle. The northern is occupied by the camps of the Ungalla and Umbitchana men, and eastern by those of the Appungerta and Panunga; the southern by those of the Unkaria and Bultara, and the western by those of the Purula and Kumara. The individual or family camps and *mia-mias* are dotted over the ground occupied by its section of the tribe, but each of the main four divisions has its *Ungunja*, the common meeting-place of the men of that division and a primitive form of men's club house. Thus, Ungalla and Umbitchana have their *Ungunja*, Appungerta and Panunga theirs, and so on. These *Ungunjas* are on the outer margin of the main camp. Each division has its *Lukwurra*, the common meeting-place of the women, and primitive form of a women's club-house. These *Lukwurras* are on the inside of the main camp.

The *Ungunja* is strictly tabu to women, the *Lukwurra* to men, and the rules and restrictions in regard to visiting different camps are very definite and strict. Any man may visit any *Ungunja* at any time, but he must go in a certain direction. For example, an Ungalla man wishing to visit the Bultara-Uknaria *Ungunja* goes round by the western margin to the south; to visit the same *Ungunja* an Umbitchana man must go around in the opposite direction. The members of two sections, occupying one division of the main camp, walk in opposite directions. A man may visit all *Ungunjas*, but, to the men of any one section, the actual camping grounds of certain other sections are tabu or *Ekeirinja;* he may not enter any part of them except the *Ungunja,* and this only from the outside.[4]

Similarly, the camps which women may visit are clearly defined. Men walk on the outside of the general camping ground; women walk on the inside.

[4] Spencer, Baldwin, and Gillen, F. J., *The Arunta, A Stone Age People,* Vol. II, pp. 501–503 (The Macmillan Company, London, 1927). By permission.

Ceremonial grouping

Spatial grouping according to social distinctions is likely to be pronounced on ceremonial occasions. In the *Kashim* or *Kazgee* of the Bering Strait Eskimo, a ceremonial chamber and meeting-room, "the sleeping place, near the oil lamp which burns at the back of the room opposite the summer entrance, is the place of honor, where the wise old men sit with the shamans and best hunters. The place near the entrance on the front side of the room is allotted to worthless men who are poor and contribute nothing to the general welfare of the community, also to orphan boys and friendless persons. . . . All guests whom it is desired to honor are given seats on the side of the *Kashim* where the old men of the village sit. If that side of the *Kashim* chances to be fully occupied, some of the men make room for their guests." [5]

The new groupings formed at Ontong Java (Polynesia) for ceremonial purposes greatly strengthen the larger tribal bond. "In each of these new groups the members had to coöperate, although at other times perhaps they rarely saw one another." This coöperation served to remind them that the more permanent groups were not all-important, and that they themselves were in a measure bound to people who had similar rights to their own. Several of the ceremonies seem to have had as a main or subsidiary function the creation of a general atmosphere of goodwill in which old hostilities died and new ones could not spring up. No ceremony was more effective to this end than the feasts, though the food was eaten in the privacy of the household. The dances at tribal ceremonies "increased the general good-

---

[5] Nelson, E. W., "The Eskimo about Bering Strait," 18th *Annual Report of the Bureau of American Ethnology*, pp. 286–287, 1889.

will. The rhythmic exercise created a sense of individual well-being and put the performers into harmony." [6] To the performers, the Orokaiva (New Guinea) ballet brings "aesthetic satisfaction, camaraderie, and heightened self-esteem." [7]

Comradeship

Tanaina (Alaska) have two kinds of partnership or comradeship. There is the *slu tsin,* or "not for work" partner, and the *sel ten,* or hunting partner. The former relationship is formed only by wealthy men and involves men of different moieties. The two men who wish to enter into such partnership exchange presents of considerable value, such as a skin sloop or a sea-otter parka. They conduct diplomatic relations between the moieties. One is host and protector of the other while the latter is a visitor in the former's moiety. A man has only one *slu tsin.* The *sel ten* partnership is formed mainly for hunting purposes. For this purpose a man may choose a member of either moiety, or even more than one man. A member of such a partnership gives his partner the game which he has killed, a small part of which is returned to the donor. Members of such a partnership are close friends, and do not fight one another in intermoiety contests. Frequently they function as intermediaries between moieties when one moiety demands blood revenge from the other. Among Sandra, of Central Africa, two men become blood brothers by eating two coffee beans smeared with blood from incisions in their abdomens.

   [6] Hogbin, H. Ian, *Law and Order in Polynesia; A Study of Primitive Legal Institutions,* p. 207 (Harcourt, Brace & Company, New York, 1934).
   [7] Williams, F. E., *Orokaiva Society,* p. 258 (Oxford University Press, London, 1930).

This establishes a bond between themselves and their clans. The bond of friendship endures as long as the two men live.

In Dahomey there is, among both sexes, an institutional-ized best-friend relationship, and even a second and third best, who substitute in that order. The best friend is chosen where one will. In him one reposes confidence, nar-rates thoughts and actions without compunction or hind-rance, confesses problems, secrets, and even crimes and moral lapses. The respective best friends assist the man and woman who are planning an elopement. If a man com-mits a crime and flees the country, his best friend is seized and tortured; indeed, he surrenders himself willfully to this fate. When a man dies, his best friend announces, in the house of the deceased, the son chosen by the deceased as heir. This choice may be unknown to the family and may, indeed, contravene their expectation. The best-friend bond "assumes complete confidence between friends. It entails lack of reservation in the recounting of a man's actions and beliefs, and makes for an association where a person may speak his mind without equivocation, where he may discuss his problems with the certainty that there will be no ulterior motivation in the answers of his friend, and where he may share his dreams without fear of ridicule or indignity." [8]

Social orientation of personality

Social life creates and constitutes a unique dimension which influences the individual at every important moment of life. The group provides the atmosphere in which he lives and in which his life attains meaning. Personality is in large part the product of its forces. The activities of the

---

[8] Herskovits, Melville J., "The Best Friend in Dahomey," in *Negro*, edited by Nancy Cunard (Wishart & Company, London, 1934).

individual are so thoroughly oriented in a social world of which he is a creative part as well as a product that one can understand the individual only through knowledge of his social orientation. In both preliterate culture and civilization, the social forces which impinge upon the individual ramify into every department of life.

Economic status is seldom as important in preliterate culture as in civilization, for economic differences are less marked in the former than in the latter. This is especially true of the simpler cultures in which there are no important economic inequalities. In many areas, however, there is a differential in economic status, and some men have special economic privileges. In Melanesia and the greater part of Polynesia social privilege is closely bound up with economic status.

In some parts of Africa there are three clearly marked economic classes, embodying a definite stratification of the population—royalty and nobility, common people, and slaves. Usually economic status carries over into the next world. There are comparable economic distinctions in the higher aboriginal cultures of the New World.

In Cairo, a century ago, the servant who led the donkey on which his driver sat called out to those who were in the way, using a different appellation for each of the following classes of individuals: Turks, old or middle-aged Moslem natives, young men, boys, green-turbaned descendants of the Prophet, females of the middle class, poor females. "A woman of the lower class, however old she may be, the servant must call 'girl,' or 'daughter,' or probably she will not move out of the way." [9]

---

[9] Lane, Edward W., *The Manners and Customs of the Modern Egyptians,* p. 144 (Everyman's Library, London, n. d.).

Age

In most cultures considerable importance attaches to age—

> For age is opportunity no less
> Than Youth, tho' in another dress.

The ancient Greek refers to the "deeds of the young, the counsels of the middle-aged, and prayers of the aged," [10] and advises, "Respect the words of your elders." [11] Attic Greek recognizes four distinct stages in the life of a male: *pais, ephebos, aner, geron.* These are principally age distinctions, but denote also the social status of the individual. Those who are no longer able to perform their tribal functions cease to be men and women, *andres* and *gunaikes;* the ex-man is a *geron,* the ex-woman, a *graus.* The respect apportioned them depends upon their social usefulness. When new emergencies arise, people go to the *Gerontes,* the "Old Men of the Tribe," the repositories of tradition. Their advice is *Presbiston,* which means both "oldest" and "best"; whereas, "young men are always being foolish." Indeed, it may be necessary to consult those who are still older, namely the deceased ancestors, the heroes, the Chthonian people who rest in their sacred tombs.

Arunta, of Central Australia, have for males fifteen terms for age and social status and for females, eleven. This plethora contrasts with the five status terms for males in ancient Rome, which denote age status from boyhood to old age bordering on infirmity.

In Australia age and social influence are frequently almost synonymous. The right to live may be denied the newborn child, though ordinarily a few days of mundane

---

[10] Hesiod, *Fragment,* 19.
[11] *Homeric Hymns, To Hermes.*

existence is a lease on life. When, however, hunger is gnawing hard, the infant may be killed in order that its elders
may live. There, as in European civilization, the young
are the victims of many taboos and injunctions from which
their elders are exempt. In Western Victoria they may not
paint their faces or heads in time of mourning, and must
lacerate their brows and wail loudly in earnest indication of
grief. The lad may not eat female opossum, for this
makes him peevish and discontented; in some tribes the
female quadruped of every species is tabu to him. If he
eats magpie lark, his hair will turn prematurely white. The
Narrinyeri boy who eats wallaby will rapidly grow grey;
sore legs will result from eating the fish which they call
tyiri. Many kinship terms connote relative age. There is
no word for brother, but there are terms that mean, respectively, a brother older, and a brother younger, than the
speaker. Many kinship distinctions have social significance,
for many duties and privileges of the aborigines are correlated with age. Among Deiri, senior male *Piraurus* (a group
of men having marital rights with a group of women) take
precedence over junior male *Piraurus,* it being also the duty
and pleasure of the senior *Pirauru* to take the wife of an
absent *clau* (husband) and protect her during the latter's
absence. In the Urabunna tribe the relationship of *Piraun-
garu* between a man and a woman can be established only
with the sanction of the old men of the group, the initiative
in the matter being taken by the older brothers of the
would-be husband. In Queensland many old men have the
youngest and best-looking wives; a young man is fortunate
to secure even an old woman. In the Gregory district old
men claim the first marital privileges, and often practically
monopolize the women of their marriage class. Kurnai old
men practically monopolize the women. Wailwun old men

secure young girls as wives; young men secure only old women.

There are physical evidences of the social progression accompanying age. In some tribes of southeastern Australia, age is indicated by extent or style of scarification; five marks indicate an adult. On the Herbert River, boys under a certain age are not decorated. When they have attained a certain number of years they receive a few cross-stripes on chest and stomach. The number of stripes is gradually increased until the youths are fullgrown.

There is much truth in John Millar's observation that "as in all barbarous countries old men are distinguished by their great experience and wisdom; they are upon this account universally respected, and commonly attain superior influence and authority." [12] Treatment of the aged is, however, of various sorts; and underlying motives likewise are various.

Maya honor and revere parents above all others, and respect their elders, whom they do not contradict, beyond remarking, if they do not agree with what is said, "So says my elder"—implying that were this not the case, the speaker would express a different opinion. Among the Diegueño of Southern California, in initiation ceremonies the old men execute the large sand-paintings and instruct the novices in their meaning—much as old men do in Central Australia.

In New Caledonia teeth or skulls of old women are placed in the yam plantations to ensure a good crop, for they possess *mana*. Natives of Bowditch Island select an old man as a ruler; a young man, they say, is a poor ruler. At Vate, New Hebrides, the aged are buried alive at their own

---

[12] Millar, John *Observations Concerning the Distinction of Ranks in Society,* p. 108 (London, 1773).

request. It is a disgrace to the family if an aged chief is not buried alive. Accordingly, when an old man feels sick and infirm and thinks he is dying, he tells his children and friends to make preparations for his burial.

A younger Chinyanja (Central Africa) addresses an old man by the respectful title *Bambo,* which is comparable with our Sir. "Respect the elders; they are our fathers," is an Ewe (West Africa) proverb. Respect for the aged is an established principle among Dahomeans. Among Nama Hottentots, age distinction is reflected in kinship terms, political authority, and the grouping of huts. The position of the huts records the relative seniority of the master occupant. On the extreme right, facing the center, are the huts of the clan chief and his descendants. Immediately to the left are the huts of the next oldest clan "brothers," then those of others, in order of age. The family cluster of huts likewise reflects the age status of master occupants. To the right, as one enters the circle, stands the hut of the oldest son, then the huts of the others in order of age of the sons. They treat the aged with respect and affection, and make ample provisions for their needs. However, in cases of extreme poverty, or when the aged person is suspected of witchcraft, he or she may be placed in a small hut, supplied with provisions, and abandoned when the group moves to another locality.

Social functions of dress and adornment

Our magistrates (says Pascal) are well aware of this mystery of dress. Their scarlet robes, the ermine in which they administer justice, the *fleur-de-lis,* and all their august apparatus are most necessary; if the doctors had not their mules, if the lawyers had not their square caps, and their robes four times too wide, they would never have duped the world, which cannot resist so authoritative appearance.

We cannot even see an advocate in his long robe and with his cap on his head without an enhanced opinion of his ability.[13]

And Swift remarks:

If one of them be trimmed up with a gold chain, and a red gown, and a white rod, and a great horse, it is called a Lord-Mayor; if certain ermines and furs be placed in a certain position, we style them a judge, and so an apt conjunction of brown and black satin we similarly entitle a Bishop.[14]

In every tribe some demon is whispering, "Strephon have a taste!" Individual tastes, however, are socially controlled, and distinctions in costume are largely matters of social differentiation, tags of social status. The Biblical injunction that women shall not array themselves like men has been heeded in every culture. In More's *Utopia* a difference in costume distinguishes the sexes, also the married and the unmarried, though "the fashion never alters." At Roebuck Bay, Australia, men wear a girdle in the form of a large pendant oyster shell artistically etched and colored; women wear scarcely more clothing but always cover the breasts. Sex, like age, frequently is indicated by kind or amount of scarification. In Central Australia waist girdles are worn only by men, chest bands principally by women; and men and women wear distinctive neck and waistbands. The style of the male headband differs from that which graces native ladies. Among Mara and Anula, on the Gulf of Carpentaria, men and women have differential types of aprons, or pubic tassels. At Kimberly, northwestern Australia, males wear a distinctive garb of opossum fur and a cord of human hair. On important occasions sex differentiation in adornment is consistently observed. At Dierie cannibal feasts, men who have participated in similar feasts smear

---

[13] Pascal, Blaise, *Pensées.*
[14] Swift, Jonathan, *A Tale of a Tub,* Section II.

themselves with charcoal and fat and make a black ring
around their mouths; women paint, in addition, two white
stripes on the arms. Men who have not indulged in such a
feast are painted with white clay. In northwest central
Queensland blood feathering is used in the costumes that
males don for the dances, but not in the costumes of females.
Women do not wear the singed leaves, which are the decoration of the men. The Dalebura decoration of the emu-
feather fly flap was a luxury of head ornament enjoyed,
among those attending the corroboree, only by men. Adornment varies with social personality and emphasizes it.
Among Narrinyeri, girdles of emu feathers are worn only
by young unmarried girls, who, until they bear a child, wear
a fringed apron. If a woman bears no child, the apron is
taken from her and burned by the husband when the wife
is asleep. In some tribes of New South Wales unmarried
girls wear a waistband of twisted opossum hair with a pendant apron of opossum hair.

Age also is indicated by dress and adornment. Throughout Australia young children go nude. In the Central tribes,
only when the infant reaches childhood is it adorned with
a headband. On the Bogan river young females wear a
distinctive apron of emu feathers. Narrinyeri boys may not
cut or comb the hair from the time they are about ten years
of age until they pass through the rites which admit them
to the tribal status of men. The length of the pubic tassel
worn by the Dierie indicates the age of the wearer. Old
men have the distinctive privilege of wearing a circlet or
coronet of emu feathers. Until a girl is married, she wears
a small apron made from opossum or kangaroo hide, cut
into strips which hang a few inches from the waist. After
marriage it is left off. "This is truly savage."

In the great Dierie council, composed of distinguished

men, warriors, orators, and heads of totems, each man wears on his head a circlet of feathers. For any special activity or the performance of any unusual feat or ceremony, where more than usual respect is paid an individual or more than usual demands are made upon him, a distinctive garb is essential to the new social orientation. The messengers or ambassadors which tribes at the McLeay and Nambucca Rivers, New South Wales, send to invite other tribes to the initiation ceremonies are distinguished by headbands "colored with very pale yellow ochre, instead of the usual deep red, whilst their hair is drawn up and crowned by the high topknots of grass, resembling nodding plumes." In western Victoria messengers are painted in accordance with the nature of the information which they carry. If the information concerns an important assembly, a corroboree, a marriage, or a fight, red and white stripes are painted across the cheeks and nose. If the message is about a death, their heads, faces, hands, arms up to the elbows, and feet and legs up to the knees are painted with white clay. Thus the appearance of the messenger conveys the nature of the news; and the decoration is an index to information as well as to social function. On grand occasions, South Australian tribes decorate with feathers of emu, pelican, cockatoo, and with red and white ochre, or leaves of the gum tree. The inward change accompanying such celebrations demands an appropriate outward manifestation.

The medicineman

In Central Australia, when a man aspires to become a medicineman he goes alone to the mouth of a cave which the natives regard with superstitious dread. Here, anticipating a new life, he lies down to sleep—and to awake as a medicineman. In the Boulia district, North Queensland,

the candidate who desires to become a medicineman leaves
the camp for three or four days, subsists on bushes, and
thus starves himself, and ensures dreams. Strange thoughts
and hallucinations become deeply imprinted on his mind.
The dream experience initiates him into a new field of
activity. In Arunta, Unmatjera, and Binbinga tribes,
medicinemen are made by spirits. Anula medicinemen
have concourse with friendly spirits that dwell in the sky.
Specialization in the functions of medicinemen brings further differentiation of personality. Among Kurnai and
Warramunga there are two kinds of medicinemen: (1) di-
viners, bards, or seers, and (2) chanters. Both kinds receive
revelations, principally from spirits of the dead who communicate to them the appropriate rites, oral formulas, and
manual dexterity, and, in the case of the *nulla-nullung,* the
materials of their craft and the techniques. Arunta have
three types of medicinemen, only one of which initiates new
members. Members of one group of Arunta medicinemen
are initiated by *Iruntarinia* (ancestral spirits), members of
another, by *Oruncha* spirits. Australian medicinemen are
exalted above the common run, and transition from the
status of common mortal to that of the exalted position of
medicineman involves radical change of personality. The
would-be medicineman withdraws into solitude in the forest
or the desert, undertakes rigorous observances, fasting, and
privations—perhaps, for him, violent intellectual feats—
designed to launch him on a new career with a new personality corresponding to his new functions. A common experience in the process is the feeling that the personality is
changed, that the individual dies and is reborn. In the
Kombingberry the personality of the medicineman must be
renewed periodically; the medicinemen go regularly in a

body to the mountains, where they conduct numerous ceremonies, endure privations, and fast several days.

So complete is the change of personality that Arunta,
Binbinga, and Warramunga medicinemen believe their viscera are changed when they enter upon the career of medicineman. After the period of transition there is a time
of proof, of education complicated by numerous tabus
which must be scrupulously observed by the medicineman
before he can practice his profession. He must show that
he has attained the new personality adapted to his new
functions. In New South Wales, men who sleep on the
grave of a deceased person are henceforth free from dread
of apparitions. The spirit of the deceased visits the sleeper,
seizes him by the throat, cuts him open, removes his intes-
tines, replaces them, and sews up the wound. If a man
can thus brave the solemnity of the company of the dead,
he is henceforth a medicineman of acknowledged merit.
Physical discomforts pave the way to the desired psychic
transformation. When Warramunga medicinemen are
being made, the candidates may not rest, but must stand
or walk about until, exhausted and dazed, they scarcely
know what is happening. They may not drink or eat. In
this stupified condition they are *ungalinni*. Their sides are
cut open, their viscera are removed, and a new set is
inserted. Thus medicineman personality is made and
remade. "Those indeed who can encounter these seeming
perils are esteemed proper persons to become *Car-rah-dys*"
(medicinemen). Personality is enhanced, thanks to contact
with the supernatural. "The so-called medicineman is a
leader, perhaps even the typical leader of primitive society;
and just because he is, by reason of his calling, addicted
to privacy and aloofness, he certainly tends to be more
individual, more of a 'character,' than the general run of

his fellows. The sociologist will point to the force of custom and tradition, as coloring the whole experience, even
when at its most subjective and dreamlike. But each
according to his bent must work out these things for
himself." [15]

Initiation ceremonies

In Australian society the initation ceremonies through
which the lads are inducted into tribal life are soul-stirring
experiences. The intention of the ceremonies, a teleology
of which the natives usually are aware, is twofold: to effect
a momentous change in the boy's life, and to arouse in
him a lively sense of the nature and importance of the
lessons then taught him. Whether deliberately aimed at
or not, this result is realized.

The lad's association with his mother and the other
women is broken off, and he leaves their camp never to
return; henceforth he must remain in the ranks of the men.
The new life is an almost total separation from the old;
the break could not be more complete. The boy is suddenly carried off from the camp and hurried away amid
great excitement, especially upon the part of the women, to
the initiation ground, where much that ensues is novel and
impressive. The ceremonies are frequently interrupted
with long delays, during which the boy must stay out in the
bush, eating little, and seldom speaking or being spoken to.
The main object of this partial seclusion is to impress him
with the fact that he is about to enter the ranks of men,
break with his old life, and begin a new one. He has no
precise knowledge of what is in store for him. The conviction that something out of the ordinary, something mysteri-

---

[15] Marett, R. R., *Anthropology* (Henry Holt & Company, New York,
1932).

ous, is about to happen to him, emphasizes the importance of complying with tribal rules, of respecting the old men, and of realizing his new status in tribal life. Throughout the ritualistic part of the ceremonies, all that the novice sees and hears is new, surrounded with an air of sanctity or mystic significance, designed, whether consciously or not, to impress him and thus to launch him more effectively upon his new career. As part of the initiation ceremonies the lad is taken out hunting. During this time he must undergo on behalf of the old men many of the self-denials which should characterize his new life. Before the close of the ceremony he throws his boomerang in the direction of the place where his *Alcheringa* (ancestress) is supposed to have lived, thus indicating departure from her camp and authority to the camp and authority of the men. Tribal fathers and elder brothers tell him that in the future he must not play with the women and girls or camp with them, as has been his wont, but must live in the camp of the men.

Up to this time he has gone with the women to secure vegetable food and small animals, such as lizards and rats; now he accompanies the men in the hunt for larger game. He looks forward to the time when he will be admitted to all the secrets of the tribe and acquire a place in the social life with the rights and privileges that belong to the older men; for until he has been initiated he is not entitled to the rights and privileges that pertain to the older men. "A boy, about sixteen years of age, who had not yet been initiated, was kept isolated from the camp, while a younger boy, about eleven years old, was permitted to take part in the proceedings." On one occasion, when the bull-roarer was sounded, an old man was driven off with the women and children because, never having been initiated, he was not in the ranks of men.

In Sparta, age distinctions sharper and more numerous
than in Athens centered in the great initiation ceremonies
of the *Iranes,* or full-grown youths, to the goddess Orthia
(Bortheia). "These initiation ceremonies," according to
Sir Gilbert Murray, "are called *Teletai,* 'completions'; they
mark the great 'rite of transition' from the immature,
charming, but half-useless thing which we call boy or girl to
the *teleios aner,* the full member of the tribe as fighter or
counsellor, or to the *teleia guna,* the full wife and mother."

Frequently the new social status acquired through initiation ceremonies is indicated by ornaments that only initiated youths may wear. In the North Central tribes of
Australia, before the fire ceremony and the three-day period
during which no one speaks to the novice and he to no
one, the youth returns to the camp with all the ornaments
worn by a man—forehead band, arm strings, pendants, and
so on—and provided with shield and spear-thrower. These
befit and proclaim the new social personality. The new
personality is further indicated by change of name. Sometimes the lad receives a secret name, and, in some southeastern tribes, a personal totem or guardian animal. In
the Wakelbura tribe the uninitiated youth is called *Walba;*
after initiation he is *Kaula.* He then receives a new personal name, and his former name is not mentioned again.
In this tribe the ceremonies of initiation extend over a
period of several years. Upon completion of a stage of
the ceremonies the youth receives a new name. Some
young men acquire as many as four successive names, which
usually denote personal qualities or accomplishments, for
example, Quick Sight, Courage, Good Fighter, Skillful
Medicineman. Initiation ceremonies bring also specific
food privileges. The uninitiated boy may eat only female
animals; male animals must be brought to the camp and

given to the aged and those who have large families. When
the lad has passed through one phase of the initiation ceremony he may eat honey; after passing through another
phase he may eat the male of some specified animal, perhaps the "paddymelon"; after passing through another
phase he may eat the male of the opossum; and so on, until
his initiation is complete, when he may eat anything.

In the Dieri only the young man who has been made a
Kulpi is considered a "complete man." The *Kulpi* take
precedence over other men, and most matters of tribal
welfare are entrusted to them.

They hold the most important positions and have much
influence in the government of the tribe. When the head-
man complimented a *Kulpi* on the satisfactory manner in
which he had accomplished a mission entrusted to him, it
was customary to refer to him as a *Kulpi*. Only *Kulpi*
are sent on special missions to other tribes. A non-*Kulpi*
would not have as much influence as a *Kulpi*. Others often
express regret that they are not *Kulpi*, and envy the superior
position of those who are thus distinguished. *Kulpi* take
precedence at grand corroborees, where they are the leading
dancers and "masters of ceremonies" generally.

In civilization no single factor has such potency in influencing personality, social or psychological, as these Australian initiation ceremonies. We move gradually rather
than abruptly from one status to another, our old life merging by almost imperceptible changes into the new. "We
live in slow, quiet times, and nothing ever happens to mark
the years as they go by, one after the other, and all the
same." In Australia pre-adolescent life is suddenly ruled
out of conversation. In order that the new life may be
rooted in itself, the pre-adolescent life is not referred to
after the initiation ceremonies.

In South Australia a mystic vocabulary is inculcated, known only to those who have passed through the prescribed course of instruction. The initiated learn, in addition to the general nomenclature with which women and children are familiar, secret names for each man, woman, animal, plant, locality, and hunting-ground. Of necessity a psychological change accompanies this abrupt social change. A new psychological as well as a new social self is developed.

The change must be keenly realized in the warm vital experience of the boy—a transition that is abrupt, brutal, and, if undesignedly formative, none the less effective. Euhalayi say that a fully initiated man can sing a charm which will make a porcupine relax its grip and be taken captive without trouble. In the social realm, too, he can carry out a program denied those who have not acquired this status. He is launched upon his career abruptly and with potent suggestions which can make the social order relax its grip on him when he confronts it with the knowledge and prestige of a fully initiated man. The plea,

> Oh, that a man would arise in me,
> That the man I am might cease to be,

need not, for the primitive Australian, be in vain.

Status of the child

Eskimo parents are fond of their children, and treat them kindly. They never beat them and rarely scold them. Eskimo children are dutiful; they obey parents and take care of them in their old age. A Central Eskimo story relates the punishment by drowning of men who inordinately teased and tormented a boy. Greenland Eskimo infants who because of the death of their mother are likely to die of starvation are killed. A child murdered under other circumstances changes into an evil spirit and exacts vengeance. A common motive in Eskimo traditions is the vengeance of orphans upon those who maltreat them. If there is no grown-up son to act as family provider in case of death of the father, the latter's property goes to the nearest relative, who adopts the children of the deceased as his foster children. Greenland Eskimo children may not eat young rough-seals, eggs, entrails, heart, lungs, liver, narwhale, small animals such as hare and ptarmigan or meat cooked in pots containing one of these forbidden delicacies. Such food may be partaken of only when the youth has captured an animal of the species in question. Children suffer from the tendency of sin to attach itself to those in proximity to the evildoer. This danger applies especially to children whose parents have committed a sin, for the sin attaches to the child, particularly a sin committed by the mother. When the *angakok* (medicineman) comes to treat a sick child he immediately inquires whether the mother has transgressed a tabu. If the mother confesses that she has broken a tabu, the attachment leaves the child's soul, and the child recovers. Should people eat of a seal from which the mother of a newborn child has partaken, the child's soul may become so light that it flies out of its body.

In no tribe is the status of children the same as that of adults. In most tribes the only training given children is by way of example. They are almost never physically punished. Ridicule and praise are sufficient restraint and incentive. Cree parents, for example, are fond of their children and indulge them. The father does not punish them.[16] "If the mother, more hasty in her temper, sometimes bestows a blow or two on a troublesome child, her heart is instantly softened by the roar which follows, and she mingles her tears with those which streak the smoky face of her darling." Iroquois do not humiliate their children by severe or disgraceful punishments. For a month after the jimson-weed ceremony, Diegueño boys who are passing through the initiation ceremonies are fed only a little acorn or sage-weed mush, and wear tight "hunger-belts" of tule. The time is spent in bathing, body-painting, and dancing. At the expiration of a month they are deloused, the belts are removed, and a foot race is held. During the ensuing month they are fed all the acorn mush they desire, and during the first half of each night are instructed in dancing. At the puberty initiation into the Chungichnish cult, the heads of the boys are carefully freed from lice, so that they will never again be troubled by these parasites. Diegueño have elaborate (separate) puberty ceremonies for boys and girls.

A Pima story relates the punishment which a woman visited upon two bright grandchildren who had quarreled and, in the course of the melée, had upset the water in which food was being cooked. After a whipping, they ran away, and the efforts of the old woman to catch them failed. But the moral of the tale is not clear. Often myths are appealed to as a means of keeping children in restraint. Disobedient Takelma children are frightened by cries from the rolling skulls of dead people, which kill all in their path. Takelma believe there is a people who consist of mere skulls, and children who disobey are threatened by the cry

---

[16] Material quoted on this page and on pages following is taken from the *Handbook of American Indians* (Government Printing Office, Washington, D. C., 1907, 1910), and the *An. Ref. Bureau Amer. Ethn.*

of "Ximu! Ximu!" ("Skull! Skull!"). Wasco send boys to fish after dark to get the spirit of *Itcixyan,* who lives in the water and helps people.

A Wishram boy trains at the cascades. "He looks for strength; he travels over all kinds of land and mountains. He takes a command with him; he who trains him gives him a command. Whatever the trainer commands, that he must do for him before he lets him go. If he sends him off, he carries rocks for strength. Wherever the trainer directs him to carry them, there he carries them; he piles up as many rocks as he tells him to. If he carries that many, then he fulfils that command of his. If he falls short, the trainer sends him off again next day in the evening; he must fulfil his order before he is released. An inspector, a certain person appointed just for those things, looks after the work of those who are training. This one command is also for strength. He goes out at night, he goes to make twisted wood-ropes out of a grove of oak saplings. He, the trainer, gives the order; the inspector goes to see how many wood-ropes the boy makes. If he reports to the trainer that he has done as many as he had apportioned, the one that trains is released. If not he must try again." Paiute boys may not eat the jack-rabbits which they have killed.

During the *Powamu* ceremony at Oraibi, a Hopi pueblo, the hair of children not yet initiated into one of the religious organizations is cut. The hair of the boy is cut very short, a lock, however, being left over each ear and above the forehead. Very small boys wear only the forehead lock; and girls retain merely a small strip of hair around the forehead.

Careful attention is given to the training of the Menomini child. "It is taught especially to respect the aged and to revere the powers of nature. 'Never speak ill of anything you see; it may be a *manitou*,' is an old proverb. When a lad has reached the age of six, his physical training begins in earnest. In the fall, when the weather is sharp, the little fellow is sent to bathe in the icy water before eating (as frequently among tribes in the Northwest). Sometimes in the winter he has to run down naked to the river and plunge through a hole in the ice, returning bare, so that his parents may see that he has obeyed their instructions, when, as likely as not, they order him to run around briskly for a while to toughen him. After they think he has had enough, they call him in before the fire and tell him why he was made to suffer in this way. In a less violent way girls receive the same treatment. These tests are kept up until just before the children are fifteen, when they receive their severest trials. About this age they are taught to go without food for two or three days at a time in preparation for the crisis of their lives, the dream fast. They are denied soup or salt at all times, as it is firmly believed that broth is a food only for old or sick persons and will therefore weaken a healthy one, and that salt shrivels the tendons and dries up the juices of the body. Children are required to sleep doubled up so that their tendons will not be stretched, because if this happens they are likely to be doubled up in old age."

Menomini children under eight years of age are not struck. Older children when naughty are whipped with a pack strap. "Pulling a child's ears makes it scrofulous; striking it about the head makes it deaf and foolish. 'Only white men are capable of such barbarities.' Small children are scolded or a little water is thrown in their faces to wash away their troubles. Babies who cry at night are ducked and older little ones are frightened by being told that the owl will steal them, or are shown an image to frighten them and make them stop their noise."

The Teton Dakota ceremony "Transfer of Character" is held prior to the naming of an infant. "Should the infant be a boy, a brave and good-tempered man, chosen beforehand, takes the infant in his arms and breathes into his mouth, thereby communicating his own disposition to the infant, who will grow up to be a brave and good-natured man. It is thought that such an infant will not cry as much as infants that have not been thus favored. Should the infant be a girl, it is put into the arms of a good woman, who breathes into its mouth." A Teton Dakota child's future is known by the company which its infancy keeps.

At the Ponco ceremony known as "Turning the Child" a lock of hair is cut from the boy's head and a name which belongs to the boy's gens, that is, his kinship division, is bestowed upon him. The ceremony is held in the spring, in a tipi.

When about eight years of age, the Omaha boy must ascend a bluff and remain there fasting and praying during the day, that the spirits may visit him and make him a great man. The "Turning the Child" ceremony is held when the boy (or girl) has reached the age at which he can move about unaided, and can direct his steps. He is then sent into the "midst of the winds," into the element essential to life and health. His feet are placed on a stone, emblem of long life upon earth and of wisdom derived from age. "The 'flames,' typical of the life-giving power, were invoked to give their aid toward insuring the capacity for a long, fruitful, and successful life within the tribe. Through this ceremony the child passed out of that stage in its life wherein it was hardly distinguished from all other living forms into its place as distinctively a human being, a mem-

ber of its birth gens, and through this to a recognized place
in the tribe. As it went forth its baby name was thrown
away, its feet were clad in new mocassins made after the
manner of the tribe, and its *nikie* name was proclaimed
to all nature and to the assembled people." When mocassins are made for the young child a hole is cut in the middle
of the sole, so that if a spirit messenger from the post-
mortem realm should come for it, the child may say, "I
cannot go on a journey; my mocassins are worn out."
Similarly among the Oto a small hole is cut in each of the
first mocassins made for the child. When relatives come
to see the child they examine the mocassins, saying, when
they observe the holes, "Why, he (or she) has worn out
the mocassins; he has travelled over the earth!" This is
a wish that the child may live long. The new whole mocassins put on the child at the close of the ceremony that
introduces it into the tribe constitute an assurance that it
is prepared for the journey of life, and that the journey
will be a long one. The ceremony of "Turning the Child"
is held in the spring after the first thunder of the season
has been heard. When the grass is well up and the birds
are singing, particularly the meadow lark, the tribal herald
proclaims that the time for these ceremonies is at hand. A
tipi is set up, sanctified, and the keeper of the rites, who
belongs to the sub-gens of the child, prepares for his duties,
and enters the tipi. The young are given numerous injunctions in the form of pithy sayings called forth by the
appropriate occasion.

Thus if a boy uses his knife when cutting up meat—an
impropriety—the old men say, "Your knife eats too much
meat; you should bite the meat." Using a knife for such
purpose makes one lazy; a person should rely on his own
resources, and, so training himself, be prepared for any

emergency. If a lad helps himself to food in a kettle returned by a borrower, the old men say, "If you eat what is brought home in the kettle, your arrows will twist when you shoot"; meaning, the youth who thinks first of himself and forgets the old will never prosper; nothing will "go straight" for him. Sometimes after an attack on a camp, the men bring an arm, leg, or head from the battleground and induce the boys to strike or step on the mutilated portion of the dead enemy, as though striking *coup,* that is, taking war honors. Familiarizing the youth with scenes of war stimulates desire to perform valorous acts.

Eight days after the birth of an Omaha child the medicineman is sent for. He stands by the entrance to the tipi in which the child lies, raises his hand to the sky, and intones in loud ringing voice the following invocation:

Ho! Ye Sun, Moon, Stars, all ye that move in the heavens,
    I bid you hear me!
Into your midst has come a new life.
    Consent ye, I implore!
Make its path smooth, that it may reach the brow of the first hill!

—and so on, until its pathway through life has been made sure. Among the Osage when a child is born the medicineman is sent for. He recites to the infant the story of Creation, and of the animals which move on the earth. After he has pressed a finger on the mother's nipple, then on the lips of the child, the latter may take nourishment. Before it drinks water, he or another medicineman is summoned. Again the account of Creation is recited, and the origin of water is related. A similar ceremony is performed before the child eats solid food.

When a war party takes a captive, one who has lost a child or has no children may adopt the captive to fill the vacant place. After the ceremony of adoption the person becomes an Osage, in all respects as one born into the tribe, and is subject to the duties and requirements of the family into which he has entered by a ceremonial new birth. The drama of adoption represents the death of the captive not only to the people of his place of birth, but also to his entire past life, and his rebirth into the family of the Osage who have saved him and "made him to live" by adopting him. A Winnebago father's advice to his son includes the following injunction: "Never overdo anything. The war-bundle bearers practice in the same way as the professional medicineman. The carrying of the war-bundle makes a weakling of nobody, but makes one strong. Those who carry the war-bundle will not be killed; the spirits will see to that. If an Indian who is held in great honor falls ill, and you cure him, the people will consider you a medicineman, and they will greet you with the ceremonial greeting. Not anything of a social standing will you obtain unless you do this. When an honored Indian is about to die, it is incumbent upon you to show your skill. . . . Now be careful in heeding the warning enjoined by your father." In many Siouian tribes, which have age qualifications for membership in societies, there are separate organizations for young boys. In the Oglala they mimic the men. Mimic hunting parties are frequent. Boy associations fight mimic battles with one another. The lads use small bows, and sometimes a contestant is unintentionally killed in the fray.

Separation of the sexes

Sex dichotomizes almost every phase of preliterate social life. In aboriginal Australia men live apart from women; respective participation in tribal ceremonies is contrasting; privileges within the domestic circle differ; freedoms in the choice of a mate are contrasting.

Australian women are rigidly excluded from ceremonial and tribal activities; esoteric knowledge is not for them; the information they receive is deception. Their life is with the children; their occupation is the less exciting hunt for the smaller food animals. The Australian woman lives in a psychic atmosphere markedly different from that in which the male is nurtured. Hence the conditions under which the personality develops depend upon the sex of the individual. Women may take an active part in certain phases of social life while rigidly excluded from other phases. In Dahomey an army of some three thousand women was stationed in the royal palaces. Several hundreds of these were trained in the use of arms under a female general and subordinate officers and went through their evolutions with as much expertness as male soldiers. Yet the remainder of their sex profited little. Yoruba women are subjected to much discrimination, both religious and social. They are excluded from the men's esoteric rites. The bull-roarer, known as Oro, or the voice of Oro, is used in the men's sacred rites. Restrictions which apply to Australian women apply with equal force to Yoruba women. No woman may see the bull-roarer and live. All women, under penalty of death, must say they believe Oro a powerful Orisha, or god, and act in accordance with that belief. When his voice is heard they must shut themselves in their houses and refrain from looking out, the penalty for disregard of this injunction being death. A woman who, in the presence of a man, places herself in the entrance to one of the Oro groves, practically commits suicide. If during the dark hours of the night when Oro's voice is heard, a man turns a woman out of the house, a thing not unknown, or if he persuades a woman ignorant of the nature of the place to enter one of these groves, she is killed. Oro puts in an appearance somewhere nearly every night, and it is uncertain when and where he will show himself. A female who values her life remains at home between the hours of dusk and dawn, for any woman who sees Oro will be given to him—that is, will be killed. Should a man reveal the secret of Oro to a woman, and this fact become known to officers of the society, she and he will be put to death; though a woman who knows the secret is safe if she pretends ignorance and does not divulge her knowledge.

The separation of the sexes and the sex discrimination found in Australia and Dahomey characterize the Toda. Toda women have distinctive hairdress but do not vary the coiffure to the same extent as do men. Tatooing is practiced only by women. The oldest girl in a family wears three locks similar to those worn by boys; if, however, she has a brother older than herself, she wears only two front locks. The hairdress of boys does not vary with relative age status in the family. Within the household, separation of the sexes is observed. The floor of the house is divided into two parts by a line passing through the hole in the floor in which the women pound the grain. To the portion near the door, called *Kikuter,* dairy activities are restricted. The portion behind the pounding-hole is assigned to female occupants. The sacred is tabu to women. No part of the sacred dairy ritual or dairy premises is accessible to them, nor may they have anything to do with the sacred buffalo. This restriction extends even to the paths along which the sacred buffalo travel; these may be traversed by men and boys, but not by women or girls. Within the village is a path to the dairy which is traversed by the dairyman, and another which is taken by women who go to the dairy for buttermilk. Women may not go to the dairy or to other places connected with it except at appointed times when they receive buttermilk from the dairyman; and then they must stand at a designated spot.

In Tahiti and the Marquesas temples are tabu to women. In Tahiti, where women are allowed to approach or enter them on special occasions, a piece of white cloth is spread on the ground or floor. On this they must stand or walk, so that they will not pollute holy ground.

Freedom and compulsion in marriage

It is a commonplace that in savagery the wife is frequently a purchasable object. The Siberian Gilyak, for example, pays for his wife with boats, dogs, cauldrons, kettles, spears, or other useful objects. Many writers consider such transactions indications of the degradation of woman. Yet to the native, even to the native woman, purchase may not detract in the least from her dignity. Purchase of a bride is not a mere mercenary transaction, but fancy and choice have an influence among preliterate folk, as among European peoples.

A Wyandot who seeks a wife consults with the mother of the coveted girl, sometimes directly, sometimes through the agency of his mother. The mother of the girl consults the women councilors of the gens, to obtain their consent, and the young people usually accept their decision. Sometimes, in such matters, the women councilors consult with the men.

Often the widow belongs to relatives of her late husband, who have a conditional, or even unconditional, right to her. Among the Chippewa the brother of the deceased usually takes the widow as wife—a practice, known as *levirate,* prescribed, under certain circumstances, in the Mosaic code. He must do so at the grave of her husband, which the widow walks over by way of effecting her release. She may go to her husband's brother, who in that event must support her. An Alaska Eskimo widow may refuse to take a second husband, and may persist indefinitely in her widowhood.

The preliterate damsel may require certain qualities in her suitor, for lack of which he may be rejected. On one occasion a Montagnais girl refused to appear at the prepared marriage ceremony because her would-be husband could not even call a loon. "I heard him yesterday, and he frightened the bird. Let him find another wife." If the girl's parents have been completely won over to the match, then her resistance is of no avail. The Naskopi suitor seeks consent of the girl's parents or nearest relatives, and by offering tempting presents, usually wins his case. If the girl will not comply with the wishes of relatives who desire to give her up, they inform the prospective husband that they cannot turn her heart. Soon thereafter she is taken forcibly to the tent of her suitor, or to that of his father. A Blackfoot myth relates a summons of the men by the women, the latter having decided to choose suitable husbands. The men responded with seemly alacrity, befitting so noble an occasion as risk of being chosen as a husband, and lined up for inspection in a row before the women's camp. But in North America it was only in the realm of mythology that women—professedly—openly exercised the choice of mate; and we know of no other similar mythological reference in the New World.

Among the Eskimo of Smith Sound, Greenland, betrothals are frequently made by the respective parents. Often the bride is carried off by force, her resistance probably pretended rather than genuine. If there has been no betrothal in infancy, parents do not influence the girl in her choice of a husband, and receive no presents from him.

Among Hudson Bay Eskimo unborn children sometimes

are betrothed; and usually those so betrothed marry when grown. Generally the parents or, if they are dead, the brothers and sisters of the girl have a deciding voice in her matrimonial arrangements. But the girl may have a strong preference and insist upon her choice of mate even when realization appears remote. Sometimes the consent of the girl is asked. If she looks upon the match with disfavor she may enlist the sympathy of her mother. In that event the affair is postponed to a more favorable opportunity or until the unwelcome suitor becomes disgusted with her and takes another maid.

If the only obstacle is the refusal of the girl, she soon disappears mysteriously with a female friend who sympathizes with her, and with whom she stays away from camp for two or three nights. Shortly thereafter she is abducted by her lover and is kept away from the village until he has subjected her to his will. But the course of Eskimo love runs not always smoothly. In one instance an unwilling bride was tied in a snow-house for two weeks and not allowed to go outside. In another two or three weeks she left her husband, who admitted that she had pulled nearly all the hair from his head; he also exhibited numerous bruises from her well-directed blows.

"Medicines," that is, objects with magical properties, assist in capturing an unwilling lover or sweetheart. Perhaps they are used by men more frequently than by women, as appears to be the case in the Plains area of North America, where they are prevalent. Women, however, use such medicines and spells. A love medicine used by the Yana girl is accompanied by the following incantation: *"Suliva!* May you think about me to yourself! May you turn back to look! Would that I might stand before his face!" and so on.

In southeastern Asia and outlying islands maids have considerable independence. A Cham girl invites the man to marry. Among the Karens, of Burma, if a girl's parents compel her to marry the man she does not love, she may hang herself; wives sometimes hang themselves because of jealousy, and sometimes out of chagrin, because they are subjected to deprecatory comparisons. A favorite threat of wife or daughter, when not allowed to have her own way, is that she will hang herself. A Dyak is not a pleasing suitor until he has taken heads—a common requirement in the Malaysian area, and in parts of the Philippines.

The Maori, despite the fact that girls often are betrothed in infancy, have a proverb: "As a fish selects the hook which pleases it best out of a great number, so also a woman chooses one man out of many."

Infant betrothals, a practice in many areas, sometimes occur among the Witoto, of Colombia, though usually a marriage is arranged at the initiative of the young man. On Hudson Island the girl is betrothed when very young. In New Caledonia she is betrothed at birth, and at about the age of seven or eight she goes to the house of her fiancé, in whose family she lives until of marriageable age. On Hurd Island, the girl who is about to choose a husband sits in the lower room of the house; over her head are let down, through chinks in the floor of the upper room, two or three coconut leaflets, the ends of which are held by her suitors. She pulls one and asks, "Whose is this?" If the reply is not to her liking, she pulls another, and another, until she hears the voice of him whom she prefers; whereupon the leaf is pulled down. The rejected suitors slink away, and leave the lovers alone. Of old, say Samoans, the women courted the men. Among Garos, of India, all proposals of marriage must emanate from the lady's side. Infringement of this custom can be atoned for only by liberal presents of beer to her relations from friends of the bridegroom. He pretends unwillingness and runs away, but is caught and subjected to ablution, and then taken, in spite of resistance and the counterfeited grief and lamentations of his parents, to the bride's house. Batak girls may be sold into marriage before birth, especially if the expectant father is in debt and hard pressed for ready money. "Child betrothals," they say, "save the virtue of young girls for their future husbands."

Prescriptions in preliterate society with regard to marriage are usually described as detailed and rigid. Marriage regulations are represented as applying with a persistence and pervasiveness foreign to our culture, limiting personal choice in artificial and invariant manner. Custom, however, is sometimes overridden. Examples of departure by savages from marriage customs are numerous. Betrothal by parents and payment of a dowry to the bride's father by the bridegroom's people is the acknowledged procedure among the Roro-speaking people of British New Guinea. When the proffered bride price is refused, elopements frequently occur, and then a post-nuptial price is paid to mollify the feelings of the unwilling father-in-law. Similarly, among Southern Massim, though marriage within the clan was forbidden by tribal law, if a girl were particularly amorous of a certain man of the prohibited clan she might have her way in spite of tribal law. Among Northern Massim polygamy is "allowed" only in the case of chiefs and those in the direct line of descent. In the Trobriands, however, wealthy commoners, who have magical powers to boot, frequently take more than one wife, and no one dares challenge them. Thus in the choice of a mate custom is often flouted.

Kinship

We trace descent of name through the father, and reckon kinship on either father's or mother's side. Some peoples trace descent of name and property through the mother, to the exclusion of the father. This system is known as matrilineal descent. Possibly there are survivals of it in the literature of medieval and later Europe, in which a preponderant position is assigned the mother's brother, who in many respects assumes a paternal attitude toward his sister's child. There is possibly a survival of the former importance of the mother's brother in the belief found among Egyptian Arabs to the effect that innate virtues are inherited through the mother, rather than through the father, and that most men resemble, in both good and evil qualities, the maternal uncle.

In their kinship systems many peoples make distinctions that are not observed by us, particularly the distinction of maternal or paternal relationship, and connotations of age relative to the speaker or to some third person. Thus in Chinese there are separate terms for maternal and paternal grandparent; for example, one's father's father is *Tsu Fu,* one's mother's father is *Wai Tsu Fu.* A father's older brother is *Pai Fu,* a father's younger brother is *Shu Fu.* There are five terms for uncle, depending upon whether he is father's older brother, father's younger brother, husband of father's sister, mother's brother, or husband of mother's sister. Similarly, there are five terms for kinds of aunts.

Joking relationships

Among several peoples there are institutionalized joking relationships. These are special privileges of banter, often

passing into obscene and insulting remarks which are, however, always permissible between those who enjoy this relationship and who take no umbrage when the privileged
person indulges in them. Indeed, they are expected of the
joking relative. Such joking relationships exist among
many Siouian tribes, for example, Winnebago and Crow.
They are found also among Shawnee and Creek, among
whom they involve clanship. Thus among Shawnee only
members of linked clans joke with one another. Among
Nama Hottentot there are joking relationships between
cross-cousins of opposite sex, that is, children of brother
and sister. The privileges include horse-play and sexual
intimacy. Among Oraon, of India, the joking relationship
applies between a man and his sister's husband, or his wife's
sister, riddles playing a part in the ribaldry. Among Batak,
of Sumatra, a younger brother may speak in joking fashion
to the wife of his older brother. In case of the death of the
older brother, she becomes his wife. Those cross-cousins
between whom marriage is proper and permitted speak to
one another without the usual restraints and exchange
jokes, riddles, and songs, which contain plays on words
comparable with our puns.

Thus in these tribes those who might marry one another
have the joking relationship, whereas there is no ceremonial avoidance or joking relationship between individuals
of the same sex. This fact suggests that the joking relationship is an outlet for the feelings of restraint and self-
consciousness when individuals of marriageable relationship
meet, an outflow of pent-up emotion which, in most cultures, is hidden under modesty, avoidance, or studied
unconcern. In Dobu a man has a joking relationship with
his father's sister and with her daughter, with whom he also
has marriageable relationship. Among Manus, Admiralty

Islands, a joking relationship exists between a man and
those who are descendents through the female line of his
father's mother. A man jests with his father's mother, and
behaves uproariously with his father's sister and her daughter. "He twits his father's sister on her conjugal relations,
he threatens to strip her daughter naked in her presence, he
handles the breasts and even on occasion, if these persons are
not conspicuously older than he, may mock-handle the pubes
of the father's sister and of the father's sister's daughter. He
tells lies to these women, whatever their age relative to his
age, and he plays practical jokes upon them. He always
makes obscene references when he meets them if there is no
quarrel at the moment between him and them." The joking relationship applies to male cousins who are descendants
of brother and sister. "Only tragic happenings disturb
their joking attitudes." Confession of sex sin and obscene
joking liberties are associated as kin functions.[17] The institution of joking relationships exists also in Australia.

Opinion

Opinion is an important agency in the regulation of social
life at any culture level. "Set shame of other men's contempt in your hearts," says Homer. Hector confesses to
"very sore shame of the Trojans and Trojan dames with
trailing robes, if like a coward I shrink away from battle."
Phoinix says: "Some immortal stayed my anger, bringing
to my mind the people's voice and all the reproaches of men,
lest I should be called a father-slayer amid the Achaians."[18]
Students of human nature have long recognized this compulsory phase of opinion. "For the Actions of men proceed

---

[17] Fortune, Reo F., *Manus Religion*, p. 86 (American Philosophical
Society, Philadelphia, 1935). See also pp. 168, 187.
[18] *Iliad*, Books VI, IX, XV.

from their Opinions, and in the well governing of Opinions, consisteth the well governing of men's Actions," declares Thomas Hobbes (*Leviathan*). "Government is founded in opinion," is the dictum of David Hume (*Essays*); and William Godwin refers to the "omnipotence of opinion." [19] Pepys speaks of going to see a riding, in Greenwich, "for a man, the constable of the town, whose wife beat him." The reference is to "an ancient custom in Berkshire, when a man had beaten his wife, for the neighbors to parade in front of his house, for the purpose of serenading him with kettles, and horns, and hard bells, and every species of 'rough music,' by which name the ceremony was designated." [20]

> Nothing in poverty so ill is borne
> As its exposing men to grinning scorn.[21]

Samuel Johnson refers to opinion as "very necessary to keep society together. What is it but opinion, by which we have a respect for authority, that prevents us, who are the rabble, from rising up and pulling down you who are gentlemen from your places, and saying, 'We will be gentlemen in our turn'?" [22] Admiral Byrd remarks, regarding life in Little America, Antarctica, during the long winter: "If any particular quality of the conversation stands out in memory, it is the power of ridicule. Ridicule is a crushing force anywhere; in a crowded existence, such as a polar shack, it carries a sting that penetrates and destroys." [23] Jules Janin's

---

[19] *Enquiry Concerning Political Justice,* Preface (London, 1798).

[20] Pepys, Samuel, *Diary,* date of June 10, 1667. Notes by Richard Lord Braybrooke, Vol. II, p. 252 (Everyman's Library, London, 1923).

[21] Oldham. Quoted in James Boswell's *Life of Samuel Johnson,* Vol. I, p. 82 (London, 1927).

[22] *Ibid.,* Vol. I, pp. 439–440.

[23] Byrd. Richard E., *Little America,* p. 223 (G. P. Putnam's Sons, New York, 1930).

dictum applies to savagery as well as to civilization: "Slander stabs more keenly than steel; it crushes with greater certainty than a pistol bullet." [24]

Jenness remarks upon the amenability of the Copper Eskimo to the moods of those about him. "The Copper Eskimo . . . follows the multitude, agrees to whatever is said, and reflects the emotions of those around him. Whenever we laughed the Eskimos laughed, and when we smiled they smiled. If a man, overwhelmed by grief, gave vent to his feelings and wept aloud, the natives around him nearly always wept also. Any individualist . . . therefore is fairly certain to become a man of note and influence. The easy merging of one man's will in another's makes for the 'tolerance' of Eskimo society, wherein each person may do what he wishes without any interference from the rest. It partly accounts, too, for the ease with which these natives are dominated by Europeans, their pliant natures yielding readily to the aggressiveness of the outsider." [25] A powerful motive among the Creek was, for the able, social esteem, and, for sluggards, fear of ridicule. Two Ashanti proverbs testify to the power of opinion: "When it is the unanimous wish of a people that you dress your hair in a certain way, you are compelled to do so". "When the united people want to kill you, then the chief kills you." In Papuan society scoffing is a dangerous enterprise; "disdainful remarks are never forgotten. The number of persons with whom one comes into contact is not considerable, and daily life becomes monotonous in that it offers few possibilities for diversion. Insults thus grow deep roots and are cherished

[24] Quoted in John G. Mulligen's *The History of Duelling,* Vol. I, p. 300 (London, 1841).
[25] Jenness, Diamond, *The Life of the Copper Eskimos,* p. 232 (Department of Mines and Fisheries, Ottawa, 1922).

for years." [26] Among Tasmanians ridicule was a weapon for
social control. A man who had violated tribal custom must
perch on the low limb of a tree while his assembled fellows
jeered him. When a Druse of the Jebel, Syria, shows
cowardice in battle, the host at the next meeting around the
coffee-fire deliberately spills coffee on the offender's robe.
This is equivalent to a death sentence. The coward must
see to it that he does not come out of the next battle alive.
It is dangerous to flout opinion. Few men, savage or
civilized, have the courage to do so.

Chieftainship

Among the Tanaina of Cook Inlet, Alaska, at least at the
Lower Inlet, there are a first chief and a second chief. The
first chief, the *Tuyok,* is a man of wealth who plays the
part of guardian patriarch. He is always in the village,
watches over the well-being of the villagers, sees to it that
the sick are well attended, that women whose husbands are
out hunting are provided with wood and water. He also
receives visitors to the village. Fellow villagers describe the
Tuyok as a father who looks after his children. He pays for
the burial of a man who has no relatives, adopts orphans,
and attends the performances of the shamans. "The *Tuyok*
belongs to the village; men belong to outside work." The
second chief, the *Jakacik,* is often out of the village and is
the leader in war and hunt. He must be well versed in
crafts and arts, and capable of judging the winds and tides.
The office is not hereditary; only one who has shown evidence of ability to perform the duties pertaining to the
office is elected to it. Among Shawnee, a chief should

[26] Thurnwald, Richard, "Adventures of a Tribe in New Guinea (the
Tjimundo)," in *Essays Presented to C. G. Seligman,* p. 356 (Kegan Paul,
Trench, and Truebner, London, 1934).

belong to the Rabbit group, although membership in it is
not absolutely essential, for this group has a peaceful name.
A chief who is to lead a war party must first lay aside the
office of civil chief.

IN CONCLUSION

Savages are but civilized men without the trappings
of the many superficial acquisitions of civilization which
tend to hide the underlying essential similarities. Human
nature is human the world over; and life in society imposes
similar though by no means identical duties and restraints.
Age, sex, and economic pursuit are everywhere important.
Similar psychological factors play a part in all societies,
"primitive" or "civilized." Our own civilization has a
counterpart or parallel for nearly every primitive culture
trait or complex.

BIBLIOGRAPHY

Goldenweiser, Alexander A., *Anthropology: An Introduction to Primitive Culture* (F. S. Crofts & Company, New York, 1937).
Kroeber, Alfred L., *Anthropology* (Harcourt, Brace & Company, New York, 1932).
Linton, Ralph, *The Study of Man* (D. Appleton-Century Company, New York, 1936).
Lowie, Robert H., *An Introduction to Cultural Anthropology* (Farrar & Rinehart, New York, 1934).
Lowie, Robert H., *Primitive Society* (Boni & Liveright, New York, 1920).
Marett, Robert R., *Anthropology* (Henry Holt & Company, New York, 1912).
Marett, Robert R., *The Sacraments of Simple Folk* (Oxford University Press, London, 1933).
Murdock, George P., *Our Primitive Contemporaries* (The Macmillan Company, New York, 1934).
Radin, Paul, *Social Anthropology* (McGraw-Hill Book Company, New York, 1932).

Radin, Paul, *Story of the American Indian* (Liveright Publishing Corp., New York, 1927).

Wallis, Wilson D., *An Introduction to Anthropology* (Harper & Brothers, New York, 1926).

Wissler, Clark, *An Introduction to Social Anthropology* (Henry Holt & Company, New York, 1932).

Wissler, Clark, *The American Indian* (Oxford University Press, London, 1922).

Hastings, James, *Encyclopaedia of Religion and Ethics* (Charles Scribner's Sons, New York, 1908–1927).

Encyclopaedia of the Social Sciences (The Macmillan Company, New York, 1930–1935).

Handbook of American Indians (Government Printing Office, Washington, D. C., 1907, 1910).

CHAPTER IV

Social Psychology

HERBERT BLUMER

University of Chicago

INTRODUCTION

SOCIAL psychology is one of the youngest divisions of
social science. It was first recognized with its present
name toward the end of the past century; the first text
carrying the title "Social Psychology" appeared in the early
part of the present century; and it is only during the last
two decades that courses in the subject have been included
generally in academic curricula. Despite its recency the
subject has attracted the interest of a large number of
scholars, writers, and research workers, so that today its
literature is extensive, its theories are many, and its points
of view are very diverse. During its brief history it has
undergone considerable change as well as development.
Even at the present time it is responding to the introduction of new points of view which are altering its subject
matter, its problems, and its methods of investigation.
This has caused it to be marked by considerable diversity
and lack of agreement. To understand the field of social
psychology it is necessary to recognize this divergency in
viewpoint and interest.

At the beginning of the present century, when social
psychology was first emerging as a recognizable field of
study, it was preoccupied with the problem of the nature
of the "group mind." Due to a number of philosophical

and historical developments, the belief had arisen that human groups could be conceived as possessing "minds" or "souls" like those that individuals were supposed to have. Ideas, beliefs, hopes, dreams, and wishes were attributed to groups as over and above individuals. Many felt that the main task of social psychology was to study group minds. This interest was reinforced by the emergence, especially in France, of a psychology of crowds.[1] The crowd was said to possess a character and mentality of its own, which could not be understood by studying individuals, since as individuals became parts of crowds or mobs they lost their own conscious personality and were fused into a new and higher mental structure. Under the influence of such beliefs social psychology became essentially a group psychology, with special interest in the minds of crowds.

In the development undergone by social psychology during the last three decades there has been a considerable decline in interest in studying the group mind and the crowd mind. While crowds and different types of groups still interest social psychologists, they are rarely viewed as possessing "minds," whose analysis is felt to be the primary scientific task. Indeed, the conception of a group mind, or a collective mind, has evoked abundant criticism on the ground that it is a metaphysical view that can not be verified. As a result of this criticism and as a result of the difficulty of making any empirical analysis in terms of "group-mindedness," this view has largely disappeared from present-day social psychology. Further, there has been a tendency to relegate to a place of minor importance the many forms of collective behavior that had formerly intrigued the students of group and crowd minds. Mobs,

---

[1] See especially LeBon, Gustav, *The Crowd* (G. Allen & Unwin, London, 1903).

crowds, manias, social contagion, social epidemics, panics, stampedes, fashion, strikes, riots, mass behavior, agitation, and revolutions—such groups and types of collective behavior may gain some consideration at the hands of present-day social psychologists, but it is usually only a secondary consideration. The tendency is to entrust these problems to the newly emerging study of *collective behavior,* where they are treated alongside of such problems as social unrest, public opinion, propaganda, social movements, literary and nationalistic revivals, reform movements, myths, and legends.

Today, the interest of social psychology is focused largely on the *social development of the individual.* It is now generally agreed that every human being grows up inside of some form of group life, that in this development he is subject to the stimulation and influence of his associates, and that his conduct, his character, his personality, and his mental organization are formed inside of this association with his fellows. The central task is that of studying how the individual develops socially as a result of participating in group life. As we shall see, different ways have been proposed for studying this problem. Moreover, this central problem has many phases that are given markedly different emphasis by different social psychologists. Yet it represents the interest shared by all students who are recognized today as social psychologists.

Social psychology is particularly subject to the importation of theories and points of view from surrounding sciences and disciplines. The very nature of its central problem has placed it between the older and more recognized fields of psychology and sociology, and has invited the borrowing of the theories of both. Any general theory that gains any vogue in these two fields is rather certain to be applied to the field of social psychology. This means that the general theoretical disputes in psychology and sociology are transferred to social psychology, where, furthermore, are to be found the theoretical contentions as they exist between psychology and sociology. Likewise, social psychology reveals the presence of theories and points of view which have come from philosophy, psychiatry, anthropology, and other social sciences. This general situation has meant that on its theoretical side social psychology is likely to be marked by disagreement and by eclecticism, that is, the fitting together of parts of different theories.

ORIGINAL NATURE

To study the central problem of the social development of the individual it is necessary to consider the nature of the equipment with which the human infant begins life. There is some conspicuous difference between the views held by different groups of social psychologists regarding original nature. One of these views, the doctrine of instincts, was very prominent in social psychology up to a decade ago [2]; today it has very much less support. We shall begin by discussing it.

The view that human behavior can be explained in terms of instincts arose as a consequence of the development of the theory of organic evolution. The theory of organic evolution developed by Charles Darwin and his followers bridged the chasm which previously had been thought to separate human beings from animals. Human beings now came to be regarded as merely a higher type of animal, linked to the rest of the biological kingdom. Once this

---

[2] See McDougall, William, *Social Psychology* (John W. Luce & Company, Boston, 1924).

new view of human beings was formed, it was inevitable
that students should seek to explain human behavior by
principles that had been found satisfactory in explaining
animal behavior. Previously, it had been customary to
explain the behavior of animals in terms of instincts, and
this type of explanation was felt to be quite successful. It
now became the practice of many psychologists to explain
the conduct of human beings and the life of human groups
by the doctrine of instincts.

The doctrine of instincts may be thought of as a pre-
deterministic view of original nature, since this original
nature is used to explain social behavior. The view pre-
supposes that human beings, like other forms of animal
life, are born into the world with a biological make-up
which pre-determines them to certain kinds of behavior
under requisite circumstances. Instincts are regarded as
the factors in the original or biological nature that lead to
these different kinds of behavior. Thus the seeking of food
is ascribed to a hunger instinct, the seeking of a mate to
a sex instinct, fighting to a pugnacious instinct, the solicit-
ous care of an infant by its mother to a maternal instinct,
and the seeking of companionship and association to a
gregarious instinct. Since this view is widely current in
the popular thought of today, other illustrations will occur
to anyone. Generally, it has been believed by those who
hold this view that all significant forms of human conduct
were to be explained by an appropriate instinct or combination of instincts. The task was to identify the proper
instinct or instincts felt to be responsible for the given kind
of human conduct. Instincts were thought to give individuals their basic motives and desires and, consequently,
their interests and goals in life. Furthermore, since human

institutions, such as the family, religion, education, and recreation, were recognized as being made up of individual actions, they were, in turn, believed to rest on instincts. The actual development of the child into an adult was explained, on one hand, as a maturation of certain of his instincts, and, on the other hand, as the redirection of his instincts into new forms of behavior.

While many instinct psychologists declared that instincts could be modified and could undergo change, logically, their whole approach has been a form of biological determinism. Since instincts were recognized as innate or inborn, to explain behavior solely by instincts meant really to declare that the biological make-up determines this behavior. In practice, as soon as the instinct psychologist succeeded in identifying the appropriate instinct in any given instance of human behavior in which he was interested (such as the sex and parental instincts in the case of marriage) there was no further need for explanation. To carry the explanation further one would have to account for the existence of the instinct or instincts, and to do this would lead one to a different problem—the study of the biological evolution of the human species. In practice, then, the interpretation or explanation of human conduct took the form of designating the instincts that were believed to be responsible for that conduct.

Criticisms which have been directed against the instinct doctrine during the last two decades have greatly lessened the prestige which it formerly had in social psychology. The criticisms have been of different kinds. One significant criticism is that the instinct psychologists show very marked disagreement among themselves as to what they mean by an instinct, and as to the specific instincts which they attrib-

ute to human beings.[3] The definitions which are given for
the concept of instinct vary from the view that the instinct
is a very specific, fixed form of behavior (as in the nest
building of the robin) to the view that an instinct is a vague,
general urge. The number of instincts supposedly possessed by human beings ranges from one or two up to
several hundreds. The critics have argued that if instincts
were present in human beings they should be capable of
being identified, and that, if they could be identified, this
should lead to agreement as to their character and number.
The absence of this agreement is believed to point suspi-
ciously to the absence of instincts. A second major criticism
has been that the study of human infants does not reveal
a biological nature that is made up of a small number of
definite elements such as the instinct doctrine assumes.
Human infants are found to have a complex, diversified,
but unsystematized repertoire of actions, bespeaking a
similar biological nature. This picture of the original
nature of human beings, which is arrived at through empirical study, is presented as being strikingly at variance
with the picture which is postulated by the instinct doctrine. A third criticism calls attention to the great variability of human conduct that is found to exist between
people who belong to different cultures (such as the settling
of quarrels among certain Eskimo groups by the two opponents singing songs at one another, in contrast to our
practice of fisticuffs between two embittered school boys).
It is declared that this variability forces one to explain
human behavior in terms other than instincts, since instincts, by definition, are common to human beings and,
consequently, cannot be used to explain differences between

---

[3] See Bernard, L. L., *Instinct: A Study in Social Psychology* (Henry
Holt & Company, New York, 1924).

them. These critics point out that the heuristic value of the concept of instincts is that it permits one to generalize his observations of one member of a species to other members of that species. Thus, the observation of beavers building a dam may lead one to attribute to them an instinct to build dams; since instincts by definition are possessed by all the members of the given species, one can declare in this instance that other beavers who have not been observed have this instinct and will engage in the same dam-building activity that has been observed. The variability of human behavior is held to be a severe obstacle to such generalizing; consequently, the concept of instincts loses all of its heuristic value as applied to human beings.

Ultimately the question as to whether human beings have instincts turns on the matter of definition. However, the criticisms which have been made of the doctrine have succeeded in bringing the problem of original nature into the open and have seriously challenged the simple deterministic view of original nature which is implied in the instinct view.

A second way of viewing original nature that is widely current today in social psychology is to regard the human infant as possessing varied, complex, but unsystematized sets of reflexes. These reflexes represent the original ways in which the infant responds to the stimuli in its environment. The reflex is a definite and specific kind of behavior which can be observed and studied in an experimental fashion. Many of these reflexes, such as the grasping reflex, have been identified; the human child has hundreds of them. Many are complicated and some, like chewing and swallowing, fit together in fairly elaborate patterns of behavior. It is generally recognized, however, that there is very little organization between the reflexes possessed by

the human infant; hence, it can do practically nothing in
the way of complicated behavior, in contrast with older
children or with adults. The development of such behavior
necessarily means that these original reflexes have to
undergo redirection, change, and especially organization
into new patterns of conduct. The equipment of reflexes
possessed at birth, while very important as the basis for
the formation of subsequent behavior in the child, consequently is not viewed as predetermining that formation.
It is especially in this respect that this view of original
nature differs markedly from that represented by the doctrine of instincts. Other features of this view are (a) that
it is not hypothetical but is confined to what is actually
observable in the infant, and (b) that its attention is
directed toward the small units or segments of the infant's
behavior (this, of course, is what the reflex represents) and
not toward the general character of the infant's behavior.
This view of original nature is identified with what can be
termed the stimulus-response approach in social psychology. Later we shall consider how, in accordance with this
approach, original nature is viewed as developing into social
conduct and into personality.

There is a third important view of original nature, in
present-day social psychology, that also fits into a special
major approach which we shall have occasion to consider
at some length. According to this view the human infant
comes into the world with an unformed, unorganized, and
amorphous nature. This is shown by its pronounced helplessness, by its inability to carry out concerted actions, and
by its thorough dependence on older human beings for the
satisfaction of its needs and, so, for survival. Its general
behavior is random and unorganized. It is felt that this

signifies a similar vague and unorganized state of the child's impulses and feelings. The infant is recognized to be very active, and consequently, to have impulses (such as the thirst impulse) which occasion it distress and consequently stir it into activity. These impulses, however, are regarded as being plastic and unchannelized, that is, as not being directed toward any specific goal. The infant has no idea or image of "what it wants," but merely experiences discomfort and distress under the influence of an impulse. This impulse gains expression in its emotional behavior and random activity. According to this view, the development of the infant into childhood and adulthood is fundamentally a matter of forming organized or concerted activity in place of its previous random activity, and of channelizing its impulses and giving them goals or objectives. This view, then, like the previous one, recognizes original nature to be important, but not determinative of its subsequent development. It emphasizes the active nature of the child, the plasticity of this nature, and the importance of the unformed impulse. It is substantially the view taken by the group of social psychologists who may be conveniently labeled "symbolic interactionists."

Of these three views of the original nature of human beings, the last two are those most frequently held in present-day social psychology. The last two views are not in conflict with each other, but they emphasize different attributes of the infant's behavior and nature. However, as we shall see, each gives rise to a different way of treating and interpreting the main problems of social psychology. A knowledge of original nature is merely a prerequisite to the more important concerns of social psychology. One must have such knowledge in order to consider intelligently the problem of how the human infant is influenced and affected by the groups, such as its family, in which it grows up.

THE NATURE OF THE GROUP SETTING

If it is important for social psychology to understand the nature with which the infant begins its life in society, it is equally important to know something in general about the nature of human group life. Every human infant is born into a human group. Its survival during the early stages of infancy depends on aid, protection, and care at the hands of some older human beings, whether its parents or others. In this sense, the group is prior to the child. It becomes important, consequently, to consider the nature of human groups in order to understand the influence of the group setting on the social development of the child. This topic, like that of original nature, is subject to different representations; it is necessary to consider the more important of these views as to the nature of social life among human beings.

We shall begin with the view of "cultural determinism." Just as the instinct doctrine represents an extreme view of original nature, so cultural determinism represents an extreme view of group life. It is extreme in the sense that it regards group life as the determining influence in the development of the child, and, consequently, thinks of original nature as being of minor or of no importance. Cultural determinism views the life of human groups as consisting of a body of customs and traditions, conventions, institutions, and ways of behaving which have been accumulated in the course of the group's historical experience. These ways of living are impressed on children born and reared in any given group; they are viewed as existing prior to individuals who acquire them and, consequently, it is believed that they cannot be explained by referring to these individuals. In this sense, culture transcends individuals— it is "super-organic"—that is, it has a character, a history, and a method of development of its own which cannot be explained by referring to the make-up or experience of separate human beings. Thus, it is contended, no one of us has created the language which he speaks, the moral code which he follows, the system of laws which he must obey, the economic system in which he must work, the body of rights and privileges which he enjoys, and the set of obligations which he must observe. These organized forms of group life come to the individual from the outside and, consequently, cannot be accounted for by the characteristics and attributes of individuals.

Indeed, just the opposite is held to be true by cultural determinists. Their belief is that the growth and social development of the individual comes about by his taking over the ways of living of his group. His own behavior and conduct must be understood as an expression of these cultural patterns. His language, his food diet, his religious practices and beliefs, his moral code, his forms of play and recreation, his economic activities and ambitions, his political interests and beliefs, his prejudices, his type of courtship and married life—all these are regarded as manifestations of the cultural patterns of his group or groups. This molding influence of culture is clear in our external behavior; we speak the language of our group, use its monetary system, employ its forms of greeting, participate in its ceremonies and ritual, and in general follow its customs and conventions. However, the cultural determinists believe that the influence of culture extends far beyond these external forms of behavior. They believe that it shapes our tastes and appetites, our desires and wishes, our hopes and ambitions, our inclinations and aversions, our attitudes, and our thoughts and values.

This effort to explain the inner life and psychic activities of the individual in terms of the cultural patterns of the group is the most interesting work being done at present by cultural determinists in the field of social psychology. It is being carried on especially by a group of French scholars. Most conspicuous among them is Lucien Levy-Bruhl [4] who has sought to prove that not only *what* people think is shaped by culture (this group uses the term "collective representations") but also, and more important, *how* they think. His studies of primitive people lead him to believe that their logic and forms of thinking are different from our own because of their different collective ideas. Our logic is governed by the law of contradiction; that of the primitives by the law of participation. Thus, our logic would not permit us to say that an individual can be in two different places at the same time, yet such thinking is quite possible under the logic of primitive people. The African chieftain who requests that no damage be done to the photograph which has been taken of him in order that he not be harmed or suffer illness is giving expression to this primitive logic, or as Levy-Bruhl would say, to pre-logical thinking. The chieftain "participates" in the photograph; to damage it would be to injure him. Halbwachs, another French scholar, has sought to show that memory, which has always been regarded as peculiarly individual, is shaped and organized in the individual by the collective memories of the group, and that the process of recalling a memory by the individual is a social process, made possible only by

---

[4] Levy-Bruhl, L.. *How Natives Think* (G. Allen & Unwin, London, 1926).

reason of the fact that the individual uses the ideas or collective representations of his group.[5] Blondel has sought to explain the affective and emotional life of individuals in terms of collective representations or cultural patterns.[6] Other French social psychologists have made similar studies and interpretations of other phases of the individual's mental life.

The approach of cultural determinism is usually regarded by social psychologists as extreme. While it may explain what is common to the conduct of people who belong to the same cultural group, it is pointed out that it does not account for the important differences that prevail between such people. In general, it views the individual as a passive recipient of the cultural patterns of his group, and ignores the contributions which he may give to his own conduct. It pays little attention to original nature, sees no problem in social development, and belittles the possibilities of human beings having unique lines of experience. While the approach of cultural determinism is interesting, it is not entirely in accord with the main current of social psychological thought.

A more widely held view of the nature of human group life is that generally taken by those social psychologists who have been referred to as employing the stimulus-response approach. While they recognize that human groups possess culture, in the form of customs, traditions, folkways, mores, conventions, and institutions, their belief is that these are really constituted by sets of individual habits. A group merely consists of a number of individuals;

[5] Halbwachs, M., *Les Cadres sociaux de la mémoire* (F. Alcan, Paris, 1925).

[6] Blondel, C., *L'Introduction à la psychologie collective* (A. Colin, Paris, 1928).

its so-called ways of behavior are regarded as being merely
what is either common or uniform to the individuals who
compose the group. The various forms of culture or ways
of group activity are not thought, then, to exist as real and
separate things with a life of their own. They are thought
to be combinations of the activities of separate individuals.
The individual, alone, is real; the group is merely a convenient way of referring to a collection of individuals.
According to this view, the group setting in which the child
is born and reared consists of separate individuals, such as
father, mother, brothers, sisters, neighbors, playmates, relatives, and so on. Each of these individuals has his own
habits and ways of acting, between which there may be
uniformity or common characteristics, such as that all of
them speak the same language, or wear clothing. These
separate individual ways of behaving, taken together, constitute the social milieu of the child, or stated otherwise,
they comprise the social stimuli to which the child is subject.

A third view of human group life is that held by those
social psychologists whom we have termed the symbolic
interactionists. They, also, recognize that the life of human
groups presents itself in the form of a body of customs,
traditions, institutions, and so on, but they do not regard
these forms of culture as consisting merely of so many different individual ways of acting. Instead, they believe
that these forms of culture consist of *common symbols*,
which are mutually shared and possessed by the members
of the groups. Individual ways of acting are alike because
these individuals are guiding their behavior by a symbol
which they share in common. Thus, individuals wear clothing, in accordance with the custom of their group, because
each of them shares the *common understanding* that he is
supposed to wear clothing. In the same way, any custom,

folkway, or way of acting common to a group of individuals is traceable back to their possession of a common symbol or understanding.

This view deserves a little further elaboration. Group life is believed to consist of coöperative behavior. Thus, for illustration, in a university classroom the students and instructor have to coöperate in order for the class to exist as a group. The students listen while the instructor talks. If the students and instructor all talked at once or paid no attention to each other there would be no class, as we understand it in our culture. Their activities are adjusted to each other so as to give rise to orderly coöperation. One might say that this occurs because of our customs and traditions of classroom behavior. More accurately one can say that it is due to the fact that students and teacher have a common understanding or common expectation as to what they are to do. Thus the students understand they are to take certain seats and listen to the instructor; they expect this of one another. They also expect the instructor to talk to them instead of, let us say, going to sleep in his chair; he shares their understanding of what he is to do. The coöperative activity in the situation arises from and is made possible by the sharing of common symbols, understandings, or expectations.

According to this view, then, the group setting into which the child is born is made up of coöperative forms of activity that prevail because the people in the group possess a set of common symbols or understandings. What is important in the setting or milieu of the child is not primarily the activities of the individuals around it, but the symbols and understandings that guide these activities. The child's social environment, in this sense, is symbolic. This, then, is the view of the symbolic interactionists.

A knowledge of original nature and of the group setting will now permit us to approach the central problem of the social development of conduct. To a large extent our task here is to show the interplay between the original nature and the group setting, since it is in this interplay that social development occurs. This consideration makes it unnecessary to treat any further the view of biological determinism, as in the case of the instinct doctrine, and the view of cultural determinism, since each regards one or the other of the two factors of original nature and the group setting as unimportant. This leaves us with two views of original nature and two of group life, representing the approach of the stimulus-response social psychologists and of the symbolic interactionists. These are the two dominant views in modern social psychology; our subsequent discussion will consist largely of following the thread of each of them in treating the general problem of social development in its different ramifications.

DEVELOPMENT OF SOCIAL CONDUCT

Our discussion may begin with the way in which the formation of the child's conduct is regarded by those social psychologists who work primarily with the stimulus-response formula. As we have seen they view the original nature of the infant as consisting essentially of an elaborate equipment of reflexes which are, however, lacking in organization or systematic character. The group setting consists of individuals who engage in separate activities between which, however, there are common and uniform features. These activities and the individuals who manifest them constitute the social stimuli to which the child is subject in the course of its development. The task is to explain how the original reflexes of the infant become formed and organized, under the influence of the social stimuli, into habits or patterns of conduct.

To explain this development of the original ways of responding into new forms of behavior under the influence of social stimuli, use is made of two schemes. One is the widely current notion of the conditioning of responses. This scheme is associated with the classical experiments of Pavlov, the Russian physiologist, on the salivary secretions of dogs. It was found that if a neutral and innocuous stimulus (such as the sounding of a buzzer) were presented to the dog immediately before being fed with meat, after a few repetitions this neutral stimulus by itself would cause the dog to secrete saliva, a response which it previously did not call forth. The conditioning of responses is a mechanism, then, by which responses are transferred to new stimuli; it is a primary explanation used by many social psychologists to account for the changing of human behavior or the development of conduct. However, the conditioning of responses means merely that an already established response is called forth by a new stimulus; it does not explain how new responses appear. To fill this gap, the adherents of the stimulus-response approach usually evoke some theory of habit formation according to which pre-existing forms of response become integrated or fit into a new pattern of conduct. Thus, it is believed that in association with other human beings one's own responses are called out by the stimulation of others and in this process become woven into new patterns of behavior.

This mechanism of habit formation and that of the conditioning of responses are offered to explain how the individual develops his conduct through his association with other people. It is through them that the child is supposed to acquire a language, to adopt the customs of its group,

to learn how to act like others, and to form its own social
habits. Since, according to the scheme, all of these forms
of behavior are in the nature of responses, we should note,
again, the nature of the social stimuli to which they are
made. These stimuli are necessarily things that can influence the sense organs of the individual; hence, they are the
specific kinds of human behavior that the individual may
observe around him, what he may hear, or, as in the case
of substitute stimuli, what he may read. The presentation
of such forms of behavior to the individual, especially to
the child, may be reinforced by gestures of approval and
disapproval, by words of praise or blame, by threats, by
exhortation, by encouragement, by censure, by prohibition,
and so forth. It is felt that it is these gestures, especially,
which constitute the social stimuli in response to which the
individual forms his social behavior.

On the whole, the effort to explain the development of
social conduct by the conditioning of responses and the
mechanism of habit formation has not been especially illuminating or fruitful. It has usually been merely the trans-
lation of descriptive accounts of such conduct into the terms
and principles of the stimulus-response scheme. Thus one
might seek to account for the development of habits and
attitudes of delinquency among certain boys living in the
slum areas of our large American cities. In terms of the
stimulus-response scheme, this has usually meant the isolation of the social stimuli, in such areas, in response to which
delinquent behavior is formed—such stimuli as the congested living in such areas, the lack of effective parental
control, association with bad companions, and the prestige
attached by the boys to skillful stealing. The development
of delinquent responses to such "stimuli" would then be
accounted for in terms of "conditioning" or in terms of

some theory of habit formation. An interpretation of this type usually tells one little that he did not know prior to the interpretation. The deficiency of this general interpretation of social conduct in terms of the stimulus-response scheme arises undoubtedly because of the difficulty of determining the exact stimulus to which a given form of behavior is a response. Since ordinarily, as in the case of delinquency, the number of stimuli in the situation to which one might respond are very many, the selection of some of them as being the incitants to the given behavior being studied is rather arbitrary, in the absence of any experimental control. The social psychologist usually selects as the social stimuli those features of the situation which impress him as being important, but in doing so he tells us little that could not have been gained without the notions of stimulus and response. The declaration that the formation of the given behavior, such as delinquency, has occurred by "conditioning" or by a certain type of habit formation seldom says anything more than that such formation of behavior has occurred. As we shall see, it is rather with respect to other problems that the stimulus-response approach seems to have value as a scheme of study and interpretation.

A more satisfactory explanation of the formation of social conduct in the individual through his association with others seems to be offered by the symbolic interactionists. As we have seen, they view the human infant as an immature organism, having a great deal of activity that is prompted by impulses, which, however, are vague in character. The actual behavior of the child is random and unorganized. The social setting of the child, as in the case of its family life, is represented by organized ways of acting which exist because the members possess common expectations as to how they should act. The task here is to explain how the

interplay between the organized forms of group life and
the unorganized behavior and impulses of the child leads
to the formation of organized social conduct on its part.
The explanation that is offered to this problem is in terms
of the *satisfactions* that are given to the impulses, and in
terms of the *"definitions"* that are given to the behavior.
A few words should make this clear. The associates of the
infant respond to its impulsive activity by giving certain
satisfactions that are prescribed by the culture or the common expectations of the group. Thus, to take a classical
example, the infant has a thirst impulse which it expresses
in a diffuse way by its crying and by agitated and random
behavior. In our culture the parents or attendants of the
infant give it water to drink since among us this is the kind
of liquid which one is expected to use to satisfy thirst. In
this way, the impulse is given the particular kind of satisfaction that our culture prescribes; elsewhere in the world
the satisfaction that is given may be quite different. In
certain parts of France the infant is given a weak solution
of wine to drink, since this is what is expected; in different
regions in China tea would be used to satisfy the thirst
of the child. Through the given form of satisfaction the
impulse becomes organized, that is, directed toward a goal,
instead of being merely an expression of distress. Thus,
through the repetition of the given satisfaction, the thirst
impulse develops into a *wish* for water in our infants, into
a wish for wine in the case of certain French infants, and
into a wish for tea among some of the Chinese infants. In
these instances, the impulse has been formed into a wish
by becoming organized around an image of the requisite
satisfaction. When re-experienced now, the thirst impulse
comes under the guidance and direction of the image. The
impulse now has a goal or object—something which it

formerly did not have. The behavior, instead of merely being a random expression of distress, becomes directed toward the object of satisfaction. In this way it is believed that the vague impulses of the infant become organized and its random behavior channelized.

The other mechanism of importance is known as the "definition of the situation." This refers to the indication that is given to the individual as to how he is expected to act in a situation, or what view he is to take of it. Thus, the mother's words, "No, no," is one way in which a given situation is defined for the child. A slogan such as, "A real man acts this way," is another illustration of defining a situation. References to a given line of conduct as dangerous, unseemly, improper, or desirable are further "definitions." Gestures of disgust, approval, interest, doubt, and so forth likewise form ways of defining the situation. A "definition of a situation," then, is the means by which the attitudes and views of the group are conveyed to the individual. In getting the group's definition of a situation, the individual is able to act like others and, in doing so, to acquire a new form of social behavior. Stated otherwise, it is through the "defining of the situation" that the individual takes over the expectations and understandings of his group. This gives him a set of symbols which serve to direct his behavior; this body of symbols or meanings represents the activities that make up his social conduct.

Satisfaction and definitions represent the ways in which the members of the group respond to the ongoing activity of the child. It is through them that the child develops objects and objectives, and acquires a set of schemes or rules which it uses to guide its behavior in its social relationships. It is important to note that this process of satisfaction and definition is not confined to the social development of the child; this process is the primary way, also, by which changes in social behavior occur among adults. As we shall see later, it is possible for the individual under certain circumstances to "define situations" in his own way without direct dependence on the responses of other human beings.

This discussion of the development of social conduct, whether conceived in terms of the stimulus-response formula or in terms of symbols or expectations, points to the influential role of culture. The formation of organized ways of acting in the individual represents to a large extent the ordering of his activities by the cultural patterns of the group. Each individual tends to reflect in his own habits and thoughts the customs and traditions of his group. In this sense, we must think of a large part of his conduct as being cultural, and of his developed nature as being largely cultural. It is this cultural nature of the individual which enables us to understand the wide diversities in behavior that prevail among different peoples, as among, let us say, an Eskimo tribe, a Bantu tribe in Africa, a Chinese village in central China, the nobility in 17th-century France, and an élite group in New York today. The members of these different groups have had their conduct formed inside of the peculiar cultural patterns of their respective groups.

HUMAN NATURE

In addition to the cultural nature, which the individual forms in his interaction with other human beings, it is important to note another aspect which has been termed "human nature," in the narrow sense of the term. We are indebted to Professor C. H. Cooley for the most illuminating treatment of this topic. Cooley regards human nature in the following way:

By human nature we may understand those sentiments and impulses that are human in being superior to those of lower animals, and also in the sense that they belong to mankind at large, and not to any particular race or time. It means, particularly, sympathy and the innumerable sentiments into which sympathy enters, such as love, resentment, ambition, vanity, hero-worship, and the feeling of social right and wrong.[7]

In this statement Cooley thinks of "sympathy" not in the sense of pity or compassion, but instead as the unique human ability to project oneself imaginatively into the position of another and to experience vicariously his feelings and state of mind. In watching a tight-rope walker who appears as if he were about to fall, one may himself experience uneasiness and a feeling of loss of his own equilibrium, even though he be seated comfortably and securely in a chair. One may share the embarrassment and dismay of a high school girl who has forgotten her lines in a play. Or, one may realize that he is an object of envious attention, which, of course, is tantamount to viewing himself through the eyes of his observers. Sympathy refers, then, to the human ability to put oneself imaginatively into the role of other human beings. Sentiments, such as those which Cooley mentions, are founded on the trait of sympathy. To be genuinely vain, for instance, one must look on oneself as an eulogistic or praiseworthy object, from the point of view of some person or group of persons. In this sense, sentiments are peculiar to human beings.

Cooley regards the formation of human sentiments, as well as the cultivation of sympathy, to be results of the social experience which the individual has in primary groups. Some primary groups are the family, play groups,

[7] Cooley, C. H., *Social Organization*, p. 28 (Charles Scribner's Sons, New York, 1912). See also by same author, *Human Nature and the Social Order* (Charles Scribner's Sons, New York, 1902).

sets of companions, rural neighborhoods, fraternities, and
so on, wherein the individuals maintain intimate and personal relations with one another. The persons who form a
primary group live in one another's experience; what affects
one of them, such as an injury, is a matter of direct and
deep personal concern to the others. The child is born and
reared in such primary groups; by participating in their
life, it is inducted in the intimacy and personal relations
that prevail. It is led to take, imaginatively, the roles of
its fellow members in these primary groups, and to incor-
porate into itself the sentiments that prevail among them.
In this way it becomes human.

Primary groups, as Cooley points out, are universal among
mankind. Among all peoples, regardless of race, degree of
civilization, or form of culture, are to be found these small
groups having a common psychological structure in the form
of intimate, personal, and sentimental relations. Since they
exist in all peoples, and since everywhere they have the
same psychological make-up, it follows that all normal
human infants will develop a *common* human nature as
a result of life in such groups. Everywhere they will
develop the same general set of sentiments, such as those
Cooley has mentioned. In the light of this analysis we
can understand more clearly that people everywhere share
in a common nature—a nature which is not innate but
which develops socially through primary-group association.

The implication of our discussion is that the child,
through its association with others, develops a cultural
nature and a human nature. Culturally, it will be like the
people of its own group but very different from people who
have different cultures. In terms of human nature, it will be
very much like people everywhere. This raises an interesting question as to the relation between culture and human

nature. In general, culture can be thought to set the ways in which human nature may express itself. Thus, while all people can be insulted and resent insults, the ways in which they can be insulted and the forms of resentment will be largely determined by the patterns of culture. Further, one may think of culture as a covering which overlays human nature and tends to screen it from easy observation. When people of different cultures meet, their attention is caught by one another's cultural behavior (such as forms of dress, kind of language, forms of greeting, customs, conventions, and so on) because such behavior is visible, strange, and frequently shocking. They are led, consequently, to regard each other as strange, alien, queer, and uncultured. Since others do not act and look like one's own kind, it is rather inevitable that one is led to regard them as being not quite human. Indeed, this is likely to be the common experience of people on meeting those whose cultural behavior is significantly different from their own. To the extent, however, that one can penetrate through this cloak of culture, and enter intimately into the personal and primary-group life of these people, one becomes aware of their sentiments or their human traits; in other words, one finds them to be human and like the members of one's own group.

SOCIAL INTERACTION

Throughout the discussion of the formation of social conduct in its two aspects of cultural nature and human nature, references have been made to the interaction that goes on between human beings. It is important that we now consider more closely the nature of this interaction and the more important forms that it takes. In the discussion of this topic we are compelled again to consider the divergent treatment of this topic as it exists between the stimulus-response social psychologists and the symbolic interactionists.

The treatment in terms of the stimulus-response conception is relatively simple. It should be prefaced by a short statement concerning the fundamental nature of the stimulus-response scheme. In a rigid sense, this scheme is based on a neurological conception according to which the human being is merely a responding organism. All activity of the individual is recognized to consist of muscular movements; muscular movements, moreover, are recognized to occur because of innervation by currents of nervous flux. Such currents are merely transmitted by, or conducted through, the pathways of the nervous system; they arise at sensory nerve endings, or receptor organs, as a result of stimulations that take place at these points. According to this view the individual is merely an organism responding to stimuli, with the nervous system being merely a set of conductors. Behavior represents responses to stimuli; the development of new behavior represents the establishment of new responses to stimuli. In accordance with this view, all conduct comes inside of the stimulus-response formula.

In applying this scheme to the association of human beings, we observe that each constitutes a source of stimulation to the others; each in turn is a responding organism to the others. The stimuli are anything done or said that excites a receptor organ, thereby throwing into play the neurological mechanism leading to response. Thus, interaction between human beings consists of an elaborate process of stimulation and response, which may make use of any or all of the sense organs, and of any or all of the sets of muscles of the individual. Any movement of an individual, any gesture that he makes, any sound which he

utters, any feature or aspect of his appearance, becomes a
stimulus if it happens to excite some receptor organ of
another individual. The response comes in the form of any
muscular movement that follows upon the excitation of a
receptor organ. In the association of human beings the
interplay of stimuli and responses clearly becomes very
elaborate. The ways in which stimulation may occur are
multitudinous, and the kinds of responses correspondingly
many, but the process (in the form of a nervous excitation
and a muscular response) always remains the same. Some
authors have endeavored to analyze this stimulus-response
scheme of interaction into differentiated elements. Usually, this has led to formal classifications, such as arranging
stimuli into visual, olfactory, auditory categories, and the
like, and arranging responses in terms of the different systems of the musculature which are brought into play. Such
analytical attempts seem to yield little of value. On the
whole the approach to social interaction in terms of the
stimulus-response conception has not thrown much light on
the nature of social interaction, probably because of the
basic physiological character of this conception.

The symbolic interactionists view social interaction as
primarily a communicative process in which people share
experience, rather than a mere play back and forth of stimulation and response. They hold that a person responds
not to what another individual says or does, but to the
meaning of what he says or does. Their view, consequently,
might be regarded as inserting a middle term of interpretation into the stimulus-response couplet so that it becomes
stimulus-interpretation-response. What is chiefly important is that the interaction is believed by them to be carried on by symbols or meanings. Thus A acts; B perceives
this action and seeks to ascertain its meaning, that is, seeks

to ascertain A's intention; B responds according to what
meaning or interpretation he has attached to A's act; in
turn, A responds according to the meaning which he sees
in B's response. One might think of social interaction as
a shuttling process and liken it to a game of tennis, with
the understanding that each of the participants is responding to what he judges to be the meaning or intention of
the other person's actions. Since each participant responds
on this basis, he must, in some sense, be viewing this action
from the point of view of the person who is engaging in
the action. In this way, he comes to share this individual's
perspective. This is what is meant by the statement that
human interaction involves the sharing of experience, and
is not merely a series of adjustive responses.

In the early days of social psychology the belief was very
common that all social interaction was in the form of imitation or suggestion, or of the combination of the two. It
is now recognized that the great bulk of interaction is in
the nature of divergent responses which individuals make
to one another. Sometimes one's response to the action
of another may resemble that action; more likely it will
represent a different kind of behavior. This suggests that
it is under only special conditions that social interaction
takes the form of imitation. Likewise, the circumstances
under which interaction takes the form of suggestion are
also limited. While imitation and suggestion have a much
more limited scope than was previously thought, they
remain two very important forms of interaction that deserve
our consideration.

The nature of imitation has been treated very satisfactorily by Ellsworth Faris in an article on "The Concept of
Imitation." [8] Construing imitation broadly as a reproduc-

[8] *American Journal of Sociology*, 1926, Vol. 32, pp. 367–378.

tion of a copy, that is, doing essentially what one observes another doing, Faris is led to recognize three kinds, each of which requires a different type of explanation. The first can be identified as quick, unwitting imitation, an illustration of which is the contagion of yawning, or flight in a panic, or imitative behavior in a mob. Such imitative action requires that the individual be already strongly disposed to act in a certain way; under such circumstances the sight of another person acting in that way releases one's own act, without one's intentions and usually without one's awareness. Thus, if one feels fatigued and bored in a lecture room, he is already prepared to yawn; and the sight of another person yawning serves to release his own impulse to yawn. In this kind of imitation it is clear that there is no interpretative process involved; the imitation follows directly and automatically upon the perception of the given form of action.

A second form of imitation can be thought of as being gradual and unwitting in character. It is best illustrated by the acquisition of a dialect. One who resides for a considerable period of time in a community whose speech is marked by a different dialect is very likely to undergo a change in his own pronunciation, in the direction of the dialect. Such a change occurs, ordinarily, without awareness and, frequently, contrary to an individual's desire not to change his manner of speech. Such imitation can be explained, Faris declares, by a rather subtle process of imagination. If a person, who is in contact with those employing the different dialect, is led to re-enact in his own mind the scenes in which such people have spoken to him (as he might in recalling some discussion he has had with them), he will have a definite tendency to speak to himself as they had spoken to him. In having an image of

them speaking to him, he will be essentially talking to himself as they had spoken to him.   Thus, unwittingly and
inaudibly, he is using their dialect.   Through the repetition
of such imaginative rehearsals of the talking of others he
tends increasingly to speak in the manner in which they
speak.   This type of imitation is not confined to the acquisition of dialects; through it one may also acquire gestures,
mannerisms, kinds of posture and carriage, and even attitudes and values.   This gradual unwitting imitation, as
in the case of the quick unwitting imitation, shows the
absence of any interpretation of what one imitates.

The third kind of imitation recognized by Faris is conscious or intentional imitation, as in the case of the copying
of a fashion.   Here the imitation occurs because of a conscious desire to act in accordance with the copy of behavior
which is presented.   This given behavior is interpreted by
the individual in such a way that he intentionally seeks
to copy what he sees.   This form of imitation is the most
common of the three kinds.   It is clearly an instance of
the symbolic interaction that has been discussed previously.

Suggestion is a form of social interaction that has
intrigued students of human behavior for a long time.   The
theories of suggestion are legion, and the differences between
them are usually quite significant.   Practically all agree
that the operation of suggestion involves the disappearance
of the critical interpretation that one ordinarily employs
on hearing requests and commands.   The conditions under
which the normal critical faculties disappear and the manner of their disappearance is made partially clear to us by
the knowledge of hypnosis.   In the hypnotic situation
(where suggestion is most pronounced) the subject has had
his range of attention narrowed down until it is largely
confined to the hypnotist.   The subject seems to become

immune to stimulations to which he would ordinarily be receptive. One might say that the subject has become *preoccupied* with the hypnotist, so that he is acutely and sensitively responsive to him but to no one else. Some writers refer to this by saying that the subject is *in rapport* with the hypnotist. In this condition of hypnosis the subject has seemingly lost his ability to invoke different images and to play them over against one another, as we do in ordinarily critical reflection; instead, he appears to be under the control of a small, restricted set of images. These few remarks are sufficient to indicate that an individual becomes suggestible when he gets thoroughly *in rapport* with others, or when he becomes thoroughly preoccupied with them, so that he loses his ability to call forth different kinds of images which might permit him to remain in a detached and critical position. In ordinary social life one may enter into different degrees of *rapport* with his associates, depending on the situation, and show a corresponding variation in suggestibility. As a process, suggestion represents a divergence from the usual interpretative activity that characterizes social interaction; it is only at certain points and under certain conditions that it displaces the usual form of interpretative interaction.

PERSONALITY

No single topic is given more attention in contemporary social psychology than that of personality. Social psychology is frequently defined as the study of personality. Sometimes, also, some particular element of personality, such as attitudes, is singled out for major consideration. We shall consider the treatment that is usually devoted in social psychology to the nature of personality and its composition.

In our earlier remarks, some discussion was given to the development of social conduct in the child. Our interest was devoted primarily to the forms of behavior which are built up in the interaction with one's fellows. One can and must think of these forms of behavior as having their counterpart in the appearance of an organization in the individual. To acquire or to develop new ways of action is to form a different personal organization; the more profound and extensive are the changes in one's forms of conduct, the more altered and changed is the individual himself. Personality can be regarded as the personal or social organization which is formed by the individual as he develops social conduct. One writer refers to personality as the "social man";[9] this expresses the same idea. Personality represents the organization of tendencies to act that are developed by an individual in the course of his interaction with others. This usage, it should be noted, differs from a widespread popular conception, wherein personality is identified with the kind of impression that one makes on others.

In accordance with this general way in which personality is viewed in social psychology, different kinds of personality would be represented by such socially formed individuals as a real-estate salesman, a frontiersman, a primitive witch-doctor, a slave, a slave holder, a Chinese peasant, a sophisticated and urbane aristocrat, and a father in a patriarchal family. In these illustrations the respective personalities stand forth vividly as definite social types. It should be clearly understood, however, that every one of us has a personality in exactly the same sense, even though it be not as definitely delineated and marked. Each

---

[9] Allport, Floyd, *Social Psychology* (Houghton Mifflin Company, Boston, 1924).

one of us, in other words, has a whole body of social actions built up as a result of contact and association with the members of the different groups in which we have lived. The tendencies to these actions, as they become organized and fit into patterns, constitute our respective personalities.

This matter can be understood a little more clearly, perhaps, through a consideration of the tendencies to social action. It is the general practice among social psychologists to explain such tendencies by the concept of attitudes. An attitude represents the way in which one tends to act toward a given object or situation. Some writers refer to it as the *set* of the organism toward a given type of behavior; others, as a sort of condensation of a pattern of conduct, which exists as a readiness to carry out this pattern of conduct. What is important to note is that an attitude does stand for the form of behavior that one would engage in, were he actually to act toward the object of the attitude. In this sense, some attitudes may be very precise and others more general, depending on how definite and precise would be the behavior in which one would engage. Standing for forms of conduct, our attitudes would exist for all objects and situations toward which we are prepared to act: mothers, friends, policemen, insurance agents, teachers, ministers, schools, the law, churches, political parties, races, and so forth. Each of us has an extensive set of attitudes corresponding to individuals, peoples, groups, institutions, and situations that are objects to us. It is the constellation or organization of these attitudes in the case of each of us that constitutes our respective personalities. It should be stressed again that these attitudes stand for forms of social conduct. The personality, consequently, represents the organization of our social conduct. In the course of our association with others as we come to develop new forms of social conduct, correspondingly we develop new attitudes. As these attitudes fall into new patterns of organization, we change our personalities.

Our consideration of personality and its formation from the stimulus-response view will be brief, since the treatment is ordinarily quite simple. An attitude is viewed as a tendency to respond in a certain way. Since the stimulus-response scheme is fundamentally a neurological scheme, the attitude is regarded as a neurological set, that is, a series of nervous pathways prepared to innervate certain muscle systems. The personality is the organization of attitudes, so it in turn might be regarded as a sort of master set of the nervous system. The problem arises as to how the attitudes fall into a larger pattern of organization. The explanation of this problem is given in the two mechanisms of conditioning of responses and habit formation that we have previously discussed. Particularly the latter, since it is presumed to lead to a process of integration of separate, discrete sets of habits and reflexes, is employed to account for the formation of personality.

An additional explanation is made in terms of "thinking," since the process of thinking is a means whereby the individual can by himself, so to speak, devise new ways of behavior and form — correspondingly, new attitudes. Through the process of thinking, also, habits of conduct and corresponding attitudes may become organized in larger patterns. The importance of thinking makes it advisable for us to give it some specific treatment in terms of the stimulus-response approach. Thinking is regarded as essentially an internal process of acting through the use of language symbols or by use of verbalization. The word or language symbol is viewed as a substitute stimulus, that is, it refers to some object in the environment to which response might be made. Thus, through the use of the language symbol one may respond incipiently or actually as one would to the object which is symbolized. Through the use of this scheme it is felt that one can explain thinking in terms of the stimulus-response formula. When one thinks, he is silently talking to himself and responding to his own talk; and just as he may develop new ways of action in response to the social stimulation of others, so he may do likewise in responding to the language that he addresses to himself. From this point of view thinking represents the internalization of a process of interaction, made possible by the fact that words serve as substitute stimuli. More specifically, it can be thought of as the internalization of the process of habit formation. Indeed, in terms of solving problems, thinking is regarded as an interior trial-and-error procedure generically like that in which a rat might engage in seeking to work its way out of a puzzle maze. In this process of thought the individual is capable of forming new habits, and consequently his activity therein is subject to the same mechanisms of conditioning and habit formation that have been previously considered. Since one's own habits and attitudes are likely to be among the stimuli to which one is responding in the act of thinking, larger integrations of forms of behavior are likely to be built up. Thus thinking becomes a significant way in which the individual may develop, as well as alter, his attitudes and his personality.

The treatment of personality by the symbolic interactionists requires a more elaborate consideration. We can begin with a brief account of attitudes. The attitude is regarded not so much as a neurological set, but as a general readiness to act according to the *meaning* or value of an

object. It can be thought of as corresponding to this value.
One author, indeed, speaks of it as the subjective aspect
of a value, and of the value as the objective aspect of the
attitude.[10] The point is that our attitudes toward objects
such as individuals, groups, peoples, practices, and institutions are determined by the meanings that such objects
have for us. The attitude arises, consequently, through
the process by which such objects are defined for us.

The most important of these objects is the individual's
own self. It is through the development of a self that the
individual forms a personality or gives organization to
his attitudes. This topic is usually given no consideration
in the stimulus-response approach, but in the view of the
symbolic interactionists it acquires a position of central
importance.

The most illuminating treatment of the self has been
given by George H. Mead.[11] In referring to a human being
as having a self, Mead simply means that such a person
may act socially toward himself, just as he may act socially
toward others. An individual may praise, blame, criticize,
or encourage himself; he may become disgusted with himself, and may seek to punish himself, just as he might be
able to act in any one of these ways toward someone else.
What this means is that a human being may become the
object of his own actions. How does an individual become
an object to himself? And what is the significance of his
having a self? These are the two questions we wish to
consider. Their answers will cast much light upon the
nature and formation of personality.

---

[10] Thomas, W. I., *The Polish Peasant in Europe and America* (Alfred A.
Knopf, New York, 1927).

[11] Mead, G. H., *Mind, Self, and Society* (University of Chicago Press,
Chicago, 1934).

The growth of the self in the child, Mead points out, passes through three stages. The first stage, appearing usually during the second year of the child's life, is marked by meaningless imitative acts. The small child who has seen its parents read newspapers may hold a newspaper before it and move its head from side to side. It does not get the meaning of this act; the newspaper may be upside down, and besides, the child cannot read anyway. However, this otherwise useless imitative behavior is significant—it implies that the child is beginning to take the roles of those around it, that is, to put itself in the position of others and to act like them.

In the second stage—the play stage, which appears later in childhood—this role-taking becomes very evident, and, furthermore, it becomes meaningful. We are familiar with the behavior of children as they engage in play-acting— "playing mother," "playing nurse," "playing teacher," "playing janitor," and so forth. Here the child puts itself in the role of the given person and acts in accordance with the part. What is of central importance to such play-acting is that it places the child in the position where it is able to act back toward itself. Thus, in "playing mother" the child can act toward itself in ways in which its mother is accustomed to act toward it. The child may talk to itself as the mother does, addressing itself by its proper name and making commands to itself. It is apparently in this play stage that the child first begins to form a self, that is, to direct social activity toward itself; and it is important to note that it does so by taking the parts or roles of other people. This latter point has great significance, because it means that the *particular* ways in which it does act toward itself are set by the customary actions of those whose roles the child takes. A more vivid way of stating the point is to say that the child views itself in terms of the way in which it is viewed by those whose roles it takes; its conception of itself is formed out of the way in which it is regarded by others. We shall have occasion to stress this point again shortly.

In the play state, strictly speaking, the child forms a number of separate and discrete objects of itself, depending on the different roles from which it acts towards itself. This is shown in the fickleness and inconsistency with which we are familiar in the case of small children, as contrasted with the consistency of adults. This sets the problem of how a unified self is established—a self which remains more or less constant from one situation to another. Mead explains that the development of a unified self, a conception of oneself that remains the same, is a result of experience such as is had in participating in games. In the game situation, the participant has to take the roles of a number of people simultaneously. We may illustrate this with the game of baseball. On a given play, a player expects each of the other members on the team to carry out a given action. In adjusting himself he anticipates what each is going to do. In this sense he takes a number of roles in his imagination at the same time.

Mead points out further that this role-taking ability, as it is developed in the game situation, permits the individual to take the role of the group, that is, what is common to a number of different individuals. He speaks of this as taking the role of the "generalized other." One may then act toward oneself from the position of the "generalized other," and consequently guide one's actions in terms of the expectations of this generalized other. One does this, for example, when he governs his conduct by some moral conception or maxim. He is really talking to himself and acting toward himself from the standpoint of the generalized other, which can be thought of as representing the group. A young man may seek to act in all situations like a gentleman; accordingly, he governs his conduct from the standpoint of this role, reminding himself, urging himself, cautioning himself, as the case may be, in accordance with the demands and expectations of this role. It should be clear that in taking a generalized role, the individual is able to stabilize his conduct, that is to say, keep it essentially consistent from situation to situation. Correspondingly, in response to such a generalized role, the individual is able to integrate his attitudes or to develop an organized self.

It has been indicated that the individual derives his conception of himself largely from the way in which he is conceived by others. This point shows, especially, how closely our personalities are formed by the kind of positions which we occupy in our various groups. Toward each social position (teacher, dean, graduate student, minister, mother, doctor, and so forth) people have certain common attitudes; they expect a certain kind of conduct and behavior from people in these status-positions. Consequently, one who occupies such a position is aware of these expectations and is cognizant of the way in which he is viewed by people because he does have such a status. To maintain this position his conduct must conform to these expectations, and it is inevitable that he views himself largely in accord with the public attitude toward his role. In this way his conception of himself reflects the attitudes of others and the social organization that is sustained by these attitudes.

What is implied by this treatment is that the individual undergoes a change in personality as he develops a new conception of himself. Viewing himself differently, he places new expectations on his conduct and guides this conduct by these new rules or demands. To have a new conception of oneself means, in accordance with Mead's view, that the individual has a new generalized other, which, in turn, is to be recognized as representing a common or abstract group role. Tracing backward this relationship, one may say that an individual changes his personality by getting a new social position; in this new status, he becomes cognizant of the new way in which he is viewed by society; a generalized other is formed corresponding to these views and expectations held by the group; the presence of this generalized other means that he has a new conception of himself, and his conduct and tendencies to action are organized in accordance with this conception of himself.

From what has been said, one can see the intimate way in which the personalities of people are connected with the nature of social life in their respective groups. Whether personality be viewed in the formal way proposed by the stimulus-response adherents, or in the more subtle manner suggested by the symbolic interactionists, it shows clearly the impression of group life. Since it represents patterns of action which have developed under the influence, guidance, and pressure of one's associates, it can be recognized as being genuinely social.

MOTIVATION

One problem pertaining to social conduct and personality to which a short discussion should be devoted is that of motivation. Many people have sought persistently to learn if human conduct could be explained by a few fundamental motives, and many have proposed a wide diversity of schemes. Some reference has already been made to one of the more pronounced efforts to reduce social behavior to a simple set of motives, in our discussion of the doctrine of instincts. The loss of interest in the instinct approach has not lessened the concern of many social psychologists with the problem of fundamental motivation. Some, borrowing from the studies on animal behavior, have been led to speak of "drives" as the source of human motivation, and to regard simple sets of these drives as the basic human motives. One author, Allport, has proposed an ingenious scheme which would permit fundamental motives to be placed inside of the original reflex equipment of the child.[12] He has singled out six of the original reflexes of the human infant which he considers basic, or, as he terms them, "prepotent." These reflexes are starting and withdrawing, rejecting, struggling, hunger reactions, sensitive-zone reactions, and sex reactions. Around each of these prepotent reflexes important habit systems are organized, such as concealment, modesty, pugnacity, aggressiveness, passivity, constructiveness, and rivalry. The prepotent reflexes, as well as the habit systems formed on them, represent ways in which individuals are peculiarly responsive to stimuli. Because of this sensitivity to stimuli, and readiness to respond, the prepotent reflexes acquire a character which makes them act as motives.

The scheme which seems to have attracted the widest attention among social psychologists is that known as Thomas' four wishes. In his work *The Polish Peasant in Europe and America* Thomas has suggested that social conduct might be an expression of one or another of four fundamental wishes. These wishes are for response, recog-

---

[12] Allport, F. H., *Social Psychology* (Houghton Mifflin Company, Boston, 1924).

nition, new experience, and security. Every human being, declares Thomas, has a fundamental desire for a certain amount of kindness, sympathy, and affectionate attention; each seeks a place of distinction and importance in the eyes of his fellows; each searches for a certain degree of novelty, new stimulation, and unaccustomed experience; and, finally, each wishes a place in life that yields him safety and security. While these wishes, according to Thomas, vary in degree of intensity, from person to person, they are universal among all human beings. Types of personality arise according to which of the four is dominant in the make-up of the individual; thus people in whom the wish for security is dominant are likely to be staid, conservative, and Philistine. Thomas believes that if all four wishes are adequately satisfied, the individual is well adjusted, that if one or more are not adequately satisfied, the individual is maladjusted. The reorganization of conduct and personality can be effected by playing upon these four wishes and by satisfying them.

No scheme of motivation proposed so far has been so useful, either theoretically or practically, as to gain general acceptance among social psychologists. Some writers, indeed, believe that it is impossible to reduce human conduct to a simple set of motives. While the problem of motivation persists, it generally is given only minor consideration in social psychology.

THE STUDY OF CONDUCT AND PERSONALITY

Much of the interest of social psychologists is taken up by research. A great deal of work is being devoted to the investigation of social behavior and to the study of personality. It is in this area that theoretical differences become pronounced, since different points of view dictate what kind of problems are to be selected for study, and what methods are to be employed in the investigation. This is particularly true in the case of the stimulus-response point of view and that of the symbolic interactionists—the two most important approaches in contemporary social psychology. The theoretical differences between these two views cover the most significant controversy in social psychology, and this controversy becomes most vivid when the problem of how to conduct social psychological research arises. We shall consider the research approach of each group and the nature of its investigations.

The stimulus-response formula leads inevitably to the focusing of attention on a limited span or unit of conduct. Since the human being is regarded as a *responding* organism, the immediate task is that of ascertaining the stimulus to which the response has been made. Or, if one starts with a given stimulus, one's interest is in knowing what will be the response that is made to it. In either event, one is concerned with bringing behavior inside of the stimulus-response couplet, so that the behavior is bounded, so to speak, on one side by a stimulus, and on the other by a response. The stimulus-response couplet becomes the unit of observation. Actual conduct, as we see it in the case of people as they engage in their ordinary forms of living, is believed to represent a highly complicated series and texture of such stimulus-response sequences. The application of the stimulus-response scheme to its research study becomes exceedingly difficult because of the profuseness of stimuli and responses in this conduct. To use the stimulus-response approach effectively one must be in a position to detect accurately what are the stimulus and the response that are in relation to one another. The stimulus-response approach favors the study of human behavior under conditions that afford a reasonable certainty of being able to isolate the respective stimulus and response.

It is for this reason that the stimulus-response approach has not lent itself readily to the general observation and study of human conduct. Instead, it favors specific study and observation of behavior under limited conditions, wherein stimuli and responses can be detected with assurance. It is easy to see how this approach would encourage investigation of human behavior under essentially laboratory conditions, wherein one has stimuli under control and where, consequently, one can determine with reasonable certitude the responses that are made to a specific stimulus. Our attention will be given first to these experimental studies as they are being carried on in the field of social psychology.

Most of this experimental work is devoted to the study of how the ability of an individual to perform some task is influenced by the presence of other human beings. This is believed to throw light on the larger problem of how one is influenced by living in a group. This experimental work has been nicely summarized by Dashiell in an article on "Experimental Studies on the Influence of Social Situations on the Behavior of Individual Human Adults." [13] He finds that the experimental work covers seven kinds of group situations to which individuals may be subject.

It is easy to see that (1) these group members may play the role merely of *passive audience* for the subject; (2) they may be *working alongside* him but not with any particular reference to him; (3) they may be *contestants* against him in that work; (4) they may verbally seek to affect his work with *remarks about him* or what he is doing;

---

[13] In the *Handbook of Social Psychology,* edited by Carl Murchison (Oxford University Press, London, 1935).

(5) they may coöperate with him by *interchange of ideas*; (6) they may be his sole source of information thus forcing him to rely upon *rumor* or hearsay; (7) in all these situations their influence upon him may be due to sheer numbers or *majority* or to personal *prestige*. Each of these describes a relationship common enough in daily life so that any findings obtained would have promise of wider social application.[14]

The other important method of doing experimental work is to subject individuals to some definite stimulation, for the purpose of observing the changes that take place in their attitudes, views, or opinions. One of Thurstone's studies will serve as an example. He tested a number of high school students to ascertain their attitudes toward the German people. Then he showed half of this number a motion picture which depicted German soldiers and citizens in an unfavorable light. Finally, he retested the students, using those who had not seen the picture as a control group. He ascribed the differential change in attitude among those who had seen the picture to the influence of this picture.

In addition to this interest in experimentation, the stimulus-response approach lends itself especially to the use of devices of investigation such as questionnaires, schedules, and tests. The items on such forms are seemingly in the nature of definite stimuli; the responses are given easily in the form of checked and categorical replies. A great deal of use is being made of such devices in contemporary research in social psychology, especially in the study of attitudes. Questionnaires have been devised in large numbers to ascertain the attitudes of people on such topics as race, nationality, war and militarism, religion, and fascism. This interest in identifying attitudes through the use of

[14] *Ibid.*, p. 1099.

questionnaires has turned, in response to certain scientific concerns, to the task of measuring such attitudes. Several devices for measuring attitudes have been proposed, of which the most interesting and ingenious are those prepared by L. L. Thurstone.[15]

From these remarks, one can infer that the stimulus-response approach favors, distinctly, the use of research methods that are "objective" and that permit measurement and quantification. The reasons for this are quite apparent. As we have already seen, the stimulus-response scheme is fundamentally neurological; in accordance with it, the inner processes that intervene between stimulation (which always takes place at some receptor organ) and response occur in the nervous system, as a rather elaborate transmission of currents of excitation. Strictly speaking, in this scheme there is no place for the insertion of so-called mental or psychic experiences. (This explains in part why the stimulus-response scheme is so congenial to what is known as the "behavioristic" approach, which abjures concern with "mental" phenomena and limits itself to what can be observed.) With the checking off of inner experiences to neural processes, interest in observation becomes focused primarily upon the responses. These are presented in forms that are observable either directly or indirectly and, consequently, satisfy the scientific rule of being open to public verification. Generally speaking, the stimulus-response scheme requires that both the stimulus and the response be observed; hence it readily lends itself to the "objective" approach.

The tie-up with the interest in measurement and quantification is obvious. First, one should note that there is a widespread belief among many social scientists that the

---

[15] Thurstone, L. L., "The Measurement of Social Attitudes," *Journal of Abnormal and Social Psychology*, 1931, Vol. 26, pp. 249–269.

formation of their disciplines into genuine sciences requires the introduction of measurement and quantitative procedures, such as mark the physical and natural sciences. Many social psychologists have taken this view with respect to their study. The kinds of data and subject matter that are delimited by the stimulus-response approach, because of their "objective character," suggest the possibility of quantitative treatment. It is from this angle that one should largely view such research devices as questionnaires, schedules, tests, and scoring sheets; they are devices of an objective and quantitative nature.

These remarks should make clear the general way in which the stimulus-response approach views the investigation of human behavior. The character of the approach tends to commit its adherents to a research procedure wherein the behavior to be studied is narrowed down until it comes within the span of the stimulus-response couplet; a procedure which permits one to identify both the stimulus and response; and a procedure which enables one to describe objectively and handle quantitatively what is being observed. From this point of view one can understand the direction taken by much research in social psychology, and the nature of this research.

The line of research implied in the view of symbolic interaction proceeds in a different direction. Its nature is shaped by the way in which this scheme views human behavior. The difference can be stated rather tersely: the stimulus-response approach is interested in *reaction*; the symbolic interaction view in *action*. There is involved here more than a play on words. That the stimulus-response scheme is concerned with response is evident. Some discussion will be necessary to make clear what is meant by the opposing notion of "action." We have already seen, in our discussion of original nature, the interest taken in "impulses" by the symbolic approach. By beginning with this concept we can fill out what is meant by action. The view is that activity begins with an inner impulse rather than with an external stimulus, and that this activity may undergo quite a course of development before coming to overt or external expression. Thus, to give one example, a bank cashier who embezzles some money may have been thinking of committing such an act for months before actually doing so. According to the symbolic-interactionist view, all of the meditating, thinking, day dreaming, planning, and imaginative playing with temptation that might go on in such a case constitute part of the actual act of the embezzlement. In this sense, action may have a covert or inner career before coming to external or overt expression. It should be noted that the stimulus-response view limits its concern to essentially this overt or external aspect.

Another way of stating this point is to declare that the symbolic interactionists accept the *act* as the unit of study, and not the stimulus-response couplet. The "act" includes the complete span of action, such as we have in mind when we say that an individual is carrying out an act. Its initial point is set by the experiencing of an impulse; its terminal point by the reaching of an objective or goal that gives satisfaction or consummation to the impulse.

Fuller attention must be given to the act, its course of development, and the forms which it may take in this development. The experiencing of an impulse, since it stands for tension and discomfort, stirs the organism into activity. This activity is random and merely "explosive" unless it comes under the guidance of an image. In the usual course of an act, the impulse tends to call up images of what offers some possibility of satisfying the impulse.

This gives rise, on one hand, to a wish (an impulse accompanied by an image of its satisfaction) and, on the other hand, to a goal or objective. This goal may be immediate, as in the case of food when one is hungry, or remote, as in the case of an ambition to complete a college education. The career of the act in moving toward its goal may be quite checkered; the act may be balked, frustrated, hindered, encouraged, or aided, and much of this may happen before the act gains any overt expression. This means that the act may have a very elaborate and rich inner development. Experiences of anxiety, fear, apprehension, hope, eagerness, gratification, dismay, and so forth, may characterize the act during its inner stages. In the face of frustration, the act may work itself into a variety of imaginative processes, such as day dreaming, analyzing, deliberating, and planning. These are all forms that it may take before coming to external expression.

When it is viewed in this way, we can understand the importance which is attached to the life of inner experience. It is during the inner phase that the act is likely to gain its richest development, undergo its greatest transformation, and acquire the form that it will show when it is expressed. The external or overt phase of the act, by comparison, seems to be of less importance in this respect. Further, in terms of the formation of attitudes and the organization of personality, this inner career of action is of paramount significance.

One would expect that starting from such a view, actual study and research would use methods and techniques that aim to penetrate into the area of inner experience. Such is the case. We find that much use is made, in social psychology, of such devices as the life history, the interview,

the autobiography, the case method, diaries, and letters.[16]
These devices are employed for three purposes. First, to
gain a picture of the inner and private experiences of the
individual that seem to constitute the background for the
emergence and existence of a given form of conduct. Thus
the account given by a delinquent of his life history is held
to reveal the texture of personal happenings, which presumably has given rise to, and which sustains, his delinquency. Second, to show the nature of the individual's
subjective slant on life—the world as he views it, the values
and meanings which different objects have for him, the
"definitions" with which he seems to meet situations, his
stock of attitudes, and the way in which he views himself.
Third, to throw light on the life and operation of the
imaginative processes: fantasying, evading, planning, deciding, and the different ways in which, in his imagination,
he meet difficulties, frustrations, and problematic situations.

The difference between the line of research in accordance
with the stimulus-response formula and that following out
the view of symbolic interaction is apparent. The issue
involved is a center of much controversy; pointed criticisms
are made of each view by the advocates of the other.

The basic criticism usually made of the experimental
approach, and of the objective, quantitative approach in
the form of questionnaires, schedules, and tests, is that
they fail to catch the "meanings" which mediate and
determine the way in which individuals respond to objects
and situations. The items on a questionnaire, on a schedule, and on a test may be clear and precise; and, the individual may answer in the categorical and definite way that

---

[16] The outstanding instance is the *Polish Peasant in Europe and America*
by W. I. Thomas and Florian Znaniecki (Alfred A. Knopf, New York,
1927).

is needed for the quantitative treatment of the responses. But the point is made that the responses to these items do not tell what is the meaning of these items to the individual; hence, the investigator is not in a position to state what are the individual's attitudes or to know what would be his likely behavior if he were actually to act toward the objects to which the items refer. Similarly, it is charged that, in the experimental studies, there is a failure to consider the way in which the subject views the experimental situation; were he to revalue this situation, his responses would be very different. These criticisms, of course, are true projections of the fundamental view which symbolic interactionists have of human conduct, namely, that people act toward objects and situations in terms of what these objects and situations mean to them. Consequently, to understand their conduct, one must view the objects and situations through their eyes, so to speak. It is believed that the objective stimulus-response approach errs on this fundamental point, since the investigator or the experimentor regards the stimulus in terms of what it means to him, and not in terms of what it means to the subject. This being so, one is not in a position to evaluate the response, and consequently unable to form a proper judgment of the subject's personal organization and his tendencies to act.

On their side, the advocates of the objective and experimental approaches criticize the manner of research procedure of the symbolic interactionists as being subjective and unsuited to the development of scientific knowledge. To endeavor to understand conduct in terms of the "meaning" of objects to the acting individual merely leads the investigator to read his own feelings and ideas into such conduct. This is viewed as a dangerous procedure; the investigator ceases to be an impartial and detached observer but introduces his own subjective experiences, his likes and dislikes, into the interpretation of the conduct and the situation being studied. Such an approach is contrary to the character of scientific investigation. The charge is made, further, that the information that is gathered through the use of life histories, free interviews, and so forth, is so variable and unique in character that the task of comparing it is very difficult, and of generalizing accurately on the basis of it, virtually impossible. Scientific knowledge requires a body of basic data which are precise, data on which competent observers will agree, data which can be easily compared for purposes of generalization, and data which lend themselves to quantitative treatment. Such data, it is declared, are not forthcoming from the kind of investigations followed by the symbolic interactionists.

So far the basic issue between these two divergent approaches has not been settled, nor have the differences been reconciled. Some social psychologists have declared that the two approaches are supplementary, and that the presumed issue between the two is fictitious. This, however, is just an instance of the eclecticism which is so pronounced in social psychology. The issue remains, and theoretical interpretations as well as research continue to bifurcate along the two lines represented by the stimulus-response approach and the symbolic interactionist approach.

THE PRESENT STATUS OF SOCIAL PSYCHOLOGY

At the beginning of our treatment reference was made to the fact that the field of social psychology is particularly subject to the importation of theories from adjoining sciences, disciplines, and fields of study. One sees this today in the presence of social psychology, of psychoanalytic theories, psychiatric theories, Gestalt psychology, behaviorism, configurationalism from the field of philosophy, theories of genetics, endocrinological views (views relating to the importance of glands), theories of physiological types, and other views. It would have been too lengthy a task to have presented these views in addition to those to which we have given first consideration. It is sufficient to note that they have added to the theoretical confusion that prevails in social psychology.

This host of views that are pressing for consideration has meant that most of what is written in social psychology is exceedingly eclectic. Authors in general and textbook writers in particular choose, according to their fancy and discretion, views and theories from a variety of fields, and apply them to topics of social psychological interest. This makes the average treatment conglomerate and confusing, even though it may be superficially satisfying. It unfortunately sets social psychology to the task of trying to bring divergent views and notions together into a not too strained harmony, rather than the task of seeking empirical solutions of problems. Social psychology becomes a synthesis of imported theories instead of an analysis of its fundamental problems.

The problems of social psychology are genuine. The central one of the development of social conduct and the formation of a social organization in the individual is inescapable. Only the first steps have been taken toward the solution of these problems.

BIBLIOGRAPHY

Murphy, Gardner, and Murphy, Lois, *Experimental Social Psychology* (Harper & Brothers, New York, 1931).
Thomas, W. I., and Znaniecki, Florian, *The Polish Peasant in Europe and America* (Alfred A. Knopf, New York, 1927).

Young, Kimball, *Social Psychology* (F. S. Crofts & Company, New York, 1930).

Dewey, John, *Human Nature and Conduct* (Modern Library, New York, 1922).

Karpf, F. B., *American Social Psychology* (McGraw-Hill Book Company, New York, 1932).

McDougall, William, *An Introduction to Social Psychology* (John W. Luce & Company, Boston, 1908).

Mead, George H., *Mind, Self, and Society* (University of Chicago Press, Chicago, 1934).

Allport, F. H., *Social Psychology* (Houghton Mifflin Company, Boston, 1924).

Bernard, L. L., *Introduction to Social Psychology* (Henry Holt & Company, New York, 1926).

Cooley, C. H., *Human Nature and the Social Order* (Charles Scribner's Sons, New York, 1922).

CHAPTER V
Psychology and Some of Its Applications

HOWARD P. LONGSTAFF

University of Minnesota

PART I—GENERAL PSYCHOLOGY[1]

THE SUBJECT MATTER OF PSYCHOLOGY

THE scientific study of human behavior is called psychology and, like all other sciences, it deals only with observable, measurable, or demonstrable facts or phenomena. Psychology does not teach that mind is some mysterious force or power that directs our activities; it does teach, however, that the proper study of man is man's behavior.

Practically the only way we have of knowing and understanding a person is through his behavior. By "behavior" the psychologist means all the actions, reactions, and speech of a person that are definitely observable and subject to study. Thus, the people we feel we know least about are either those who act and talk least, or those whose actions and speech we have least opportunity to observe. On the other hand, we feel that we know most about those people who behave most, those who act and talk most. What is the difference between a very dear friend and a stranger?

---

[1] The reader who wishes a more comprehensive treatment of general psychology will find the following reference an exceptionally well-written and interesting treatise on this subject:

Robinson, Edward S., *Man as Psychology Sees Him* (The Macmillan Company, New York, 1932).

In the case of the stranger we have not had an opportunity to observe his behavior; on the other hand, in the case of the friend, we have seen him act a great deal. As a result, we have learned to know what he will do in various situations. We have learned what will please him, what will make him angry, sorry, disgusted, and so forth. We have also learned what he can and cannot do. We say that John is a good student, and that Henry is a poor one. How do we know? We have observed their behavior in the school situation. How do we know that our friend William becomes angry easily? Because we have observed his emotional behavior for many years. We learn to know our fellow men through their behavior. That is the reason why people are interested in analyzing man's behavior, classifying it, and studying its causes and results.

One of the basic hypotheses of psychology is this: *every act has a cause.* These causes are stimuli, and the acts which result from the stimuli are responses. Thus, modern scientific psychology is sometimes called "stimulus-response psychology." The stimuli are actually energy changes in the individual's environment, or within himself, that cause the individual to respond. Suppose that while you are reading these words someone fires a gun behind you. What is the result? You jump or start, probably drop this book, and look around. Let us analyze this situation briefly. The explosion of the powder in the gun was a sudden change in energy which in turn set up sound waves in the air. These sound waves were also changes in energy. They entered your ear, where they stimulated the auditory nerve, and the result was a nerve impulse which flowed along the nerve to the brain, where it stimulated other nerves leading to the muscles in your legs and arms. When the nerve impulses reached these muscles they aroused them to action in such a way as to cause you to jump and to drop the book. The whole sequence was a purely natural, mechanical process. We need not think of any mysterious forces or powers, because the physicists, the neurologists, and the physiologists have already demonstrated, under rigorous scientific conditions, that the processes involved in the above example actually do happen. Thus it becomes evident that our study of psychology should be the study of the stimuli that affect us and the responses that they arouse.

SCIENTIFIC PSYCHOLOGY VS. POPULAR OPINION

Nearly everyone is interested in human behavior, yet not everyone is a psychologist in the true sense of the word. The major difference between the psychologist's interest in human behavior and that of the layman lies in the way the problem of behavior is approached. The man in the street states that one of his fellow men has a pleasing personality, or that another is crazy, or that still a third is feeble-minded. It is true that in all these instances he is interpreting human behavior, but he makes little or no attempt to define personality, insanity, or feeble-mindedness, and if he does, his definitions are couched in vague and indefinite terms. He has not carefully isolated for study these various phenomena of behavior. He has not made long and meticulous observations of behavior under specific sets of conditions. He has not systematically varied these conditions and noted the changes which resulted from such variations. He has not made careful measurements. He has not checked and rechecked the responses that his fellow men make to specific situations, in order to determine whether the behavior is typical or exceptional. In other words, he has not made use of the scientific method.

The psychologist attempts to do what most men neglect to do. He analyzes behavior bit by bit, isolating, observing, measuring, checking, and verifying. His attitude is the critical, impartial, cold attitude of the scientist. This attitude is well illustrated by the story of the traveling man and the scientist occupying the same seat in a railroad train. Noticing a flock of sheep feeding on the hillside, and wishing to strike up a conversation, the traveling man said to the scientist, "I see that those sheep have just been sheared." The scientist replied, "Yes, on this side." The traveling man was ready to assume that because one side of the sheep was sheared, the other side was also sheared. He generalized concerning a whole situation from data covering only part of it. The scientist based his conclusions only upon the facts he had at hand. In this instance the scientist might have gone further and advanced what is known as an hypothesis, which is merely a big word for guess. He could have replied somewhat as follows: "It has been my experience that when sheep are sheared, they are sheared on both sides of the body; therefore, the chances are good that both sides of these sheep are sheared, although I cannot make a definite statement that such is the case without *verification.*" For the scientist, only that exists which can be proved to exist. The best process of verification is the scientific method. This method is the best yet devised by man for the discovery of truth, and if we are seeking the truth about why we behave as we do, then the application of the scientific method to the problem should result in the most truthful answer.

Most men find the scientific method difficult to subscribe to because it necessitates withholding judgment until the facts are at hand. Few people can go about with their minds an eternal question mark. They want an answer, even though it is not thoroughly proved. They would rather have a false belief than no belief at all. Another common characteristic that makes the scientific attitude frequently distasteful is the insistence that beliefs fit in with desires. One of man's greatest weaknesses is his proneness to accept as true that which he wishes to be true. This weakness is especially prominent in the field of psychology, because psychology deals with that which is dearest and closest to man—his own behavior. Few men will admit that they do not understand their own actions.

There is a rough historical relationship between the development of the various sciences and their closeness to man's behavior. The first sciences have been those farthest removed from man's everyday activities. Astronomy is one of the oldest sciences because it deals with the stars, which are remote from our own experiences. Chemistry comes next —then biology and physiology. Psychology is the youngest of the experimental sciences. Its youth is primarily due to man's inability to look at his own behavior critically and impartially.

Let us turn now to a more direct examination of some of the problems dealt with in modern psychology. It will be impossible to give a comprehensive picture of this science in the space allotted in this book, but we can at least present enough material to give the student some idea of its content and methods.

NATIVE BEHAVIOR

The first section of this chapter will be confined to a general discussion of the development of certain behavior patterns. Development being our major interest, let us start with the newborn infant. Examination of such an individual reveals a number of types of behavior already in existence. First, we note such activities as sucking, sneezing, grasping, crying, and breathing. These types of behavior seem quite definitely established and relatively fixed, and we call them reflexes. The reflexes are fairly well organized at birth, and are modified but little as we grow older; consequently they contribute little to the development of new behavior as time goes on.

We find also a second type of behavior, which consists of movements of the limbs and body. This type is more variable and unstable than the first. On the surface most of these movements appear to be useless, and they rarely occur twice in the same manner. They are random movements. We observe still another, a third type of behavior, which seems to involve the whole organism. If we prick the infant with a pin, nearly every part of his body will respond. The infant will cry, kick, and slash. If we suddenly cause a loud rasping sound to be made, we find him behaving in much the same manner. This third type of behavior, resulting from disturbing or painful conditions, gives rise to the mental states that we call *emotions*.

Obviously the newborn infant's repertoire of behavior seems limited, and we are impressed with the general picture of helplessness. Yet, this meager behavior composes much of the raw material from which our complex adult behavior is fashioned.

Language, for example, which plays such an important part in our lives, develops out of the cries, wails, and strange sounds uttered by the infant. So it is with most of our other behavior; it has sprung from the feeble activity that was ours in infancy.

EMOTIONS

The rudimentary emotional behavior noted above is destined to play a tremendous role in adult life. As a matter of fact, the emotions are probably as important as, if not more important than, any branch of human behavior. They furnish the tone of life and determine whether or not life is worth living. To appreciate the part they play in your own existence, try to imagine what life would be like without them. Imagine receiving a telegram stating that you had just inherited a million dollars, yet having that telegram mean nothing more to you than a statement of fact. Without emotion, that is all it would be. There would be no elation, no joy, no excitement—merely an awareness of the fact. Imagine an existence devoid of sorrow, happiness, or elation. It would be an uninteresting existence, to say the least. These complex adult emotional states evolve from the rudimentary emotions of the child.

An experiment conducted by Dr. J. B. Watson threw considerable light upon the nature of the primitive emotional behavior of the infant. He took a newborn infant in the laboratory and made careful observations of its responses to various stimuli. He discovered that the infant was capable of making three emotional responses. He suggested that for purposes of classification these be labeled *fear, rage,* and *love.* He further discovered that only a very limited number of stimuli would arouse these types of behavior. Pain, loud sounds, sudden withdrawal of support, and a quick push as the infant was dropping off to sleep were the only adequate stimuli for fear responses. Restraint of movements seemed the only adequate stimulus to rage; while patting, stroking, and turning the infant upon its stomach were the stimuli which aroused the pleasant, happy-appearing behavior which he called love. From this limited repertoire of responses, and the relatively few stimuli which arouse them, develops the complex emotional life which the adult experiences.

So much, then, for the three elementary types of behavior, which are modified and elaborated into the infinitely complex behavior of adult life. Remember that these three basic types are *reflexes, random activity,* and elementary *emotions.* How are these developed and modified as we grow older?

HOW ORIGINAL BEHAVIOR IS MODIFIED

First, the three basic types of behavior are strengthened through exercise. That is, one of the simplest ways in which modification of behavior occurs is through behavior itself; as the infant behaves, this very process tends to strengthen the structures involved. Second, there is a change that results from growth and which is called *maturation.* In this process the conductivity of certain neural pathways is altered by the growth of an insulating sheath. For instance, walking is in part dependent upon the growth and hardening of the bones in the limbs, as well as the growth and strengthening of the muscles.

In addition to changes which occur in the nervous system, the bones, and the muscles as a result of maturation, there are changes, resulting from growth, in another very important group of structures known as the glands of internal secretion, or the endocrine glands. These glands are: the thyroids (located in the neck), the adrenals (just above the kidneys), the sex glands (the ovaries in the female and the testes in the male), and the pituitary (located just under the brain). These glands secrete chemical substances called hormones into the bloodstream, which conducts them to various parts of the body where their presence causes tremendous changes in behavior.

The secretion of the thyroid influences the chemical activity of the body. If this gland under-secretes, the individual's activity becomes lazy and sluggish. If there is a deficiency in the secretion of this gland from birth, the individual is both mentally and physically retarded. An over-secretion of this gland results in over-activity. The individual becomes nervous, jumpy, high-strung, and easily fatigued. The hormone secreted by the sex glands gives rise to our secondary sex characteristics—the deep voice and broad shoulders of the male, the high voice and other typically feminine characteristics of the female. Malfunctioning of these glands may lead the individual toward the development of the characteristics of the opposite sex. The pituitary is closely allied with physical growth. Under-secretion of this gland leads to midgetism, while over-secretion leads to giantism. The adrenal glands are closely related to emotional stability, over-secretion leading to agitation and a general worked-up state of the body.

Recent experiments have indicated that the endocrine glands, the thyroids, the adrenals, the sex glands, and the pituitary glands not only exercise individual effects, but are so closely related that when one gets out of balance it tends to disturb the total glandular balance of the body. It is also known that the relative importance of these glands changes with age. The pituitary becomes less important as the individual grows older, whereas the importance of the sex glands is increased with age. Thus it is apparent that these glands produce alterations in the individual's character, and that as these changes occur, his feelings also change, with the net result that the individual, for all practical purposes, is actually a different person.

Finally, there are social implications involved in the changes produced by maturation which, in turn, influence the individual's behavior. As the individual grows older and larger the attitude of his parents and fellow beings toward him changes, and with this change in attitude come marked changes in his behavior.

Returning again to the newborn infant, we observe his helplessness, his utter inability to adapt himself to the world about him. We have pointed out that he becomes more adapted as the result of maturation. But maturation does little more than to extend the potentiality of the individual. Structures change to some extent; new organs become functional; but if maturation afforded the only changes in behavior, the individual would never be more than a crudely functioning machine.

LEARNING

Up to this point we have indicated bases, raw materials to be processed; and we have stated that these are changed by exercising and maturation. Let us next examine another factor in behavior evolution, the factor of learning. We can probably best understand learning by examining some examples of it. Learning has been studied with both human beings and animals as subjects. Many people have criticized animal psychology by insisting that animals are devoid of understanding and that what applies to animals will not apply to men. This criticism is not wholly without merit, yet psychologists have discovered that not all human learning involves understanding. The average person understands very little, if anything, about his motor skills. The champion golfer probably knows very little about the actual nerve-muscle relationship involved in hitting a golf ball. To bring this closer home, try to describe walking; do you really understand how you balance yourself, how the weight is shifted from movement to movement? The truth is obvious; you *do not understand*—you just walk. Learning, then, is far more primitive than understanding. Even the simplest forms of animal life can learn. Earthworms have been taught, by means of a simple T maze, to turn to the right rather than to the left. What is the significance of this argument? Merely this: If we wish to understand how our original behavior is modified, we must study the processes involved in its modification. And, we know that in many types of animal and human learning the processes involved are quite similar. Thus, since we can much more conveniently use animals as subjects than human beings, psychologists feel justified in doing so.

CONDITIONED RESPONSES

The eminent Russian physiologist and neurologist Ivan Pavlov, using dogs as subjects, made a tremendously important discovery about learning. He found that a stimulus that would not arouse behavior acquired the power to do so if it was presented at the same time that an adequate stimulus was given. This experiment is known as the conditioned-reflex experiment. Briefly, it was conducted as follows:

Pavlov observed that when meat was given to a dog there was an increase in the amount of saliva secreted in the dog's mouth. (Meat was an adequate stimulus.) He also observed that ringing a bell in no way affected the amount of saliva secreted. (The bell was an inadequate stimulus.) But, if the bell was rung at the same time that the meat was given to the dog, and this process was repeated several times, the sound of the bell alone would eventually cause an increase in the amount of saliva secreted.

This is one of the important ways in which our own behavior is modified, and the number of stimuli which will arouse it increased. Thousands of inadequate stimuli, which have no effect upon the newborn infant, will cause responses in an adult. These stimuli arouse behavior because they have been associated with adequate stimuli, which *would* arouse behavior. Pavlov and others also discovered that once a stimulus acquires the ability to arouse behavior, it in turn can condition other stimuli. Thus, in Pavlov's experiment, a light was made to produce an increase in the flow of saliva after it had been presented to the dog frequently along with the established adequate stimulus of the bell. When an inadequate stimulus becomes an adequate one, we speak of it as a *substitute stimulus*.

Students of Pavlov, in Russia, and others have repeated Pavlov's experiments, using children as subjects. Instead of measuring directly the increase in flow of saliva by inserting a tube into the jaw, as Pavlov did with his dogs, they counted the number of swallowing movements. These investigators discovered the same mechanism at work in human subjects that was found in the dogs. Mateer also found a relationship between intelligence and the capacity to form a conditioned reflex, thus indicating a relationship between learning that does not involve understanding and learning that does. Students of learning have discovered, in addition to substitute stimuli, a process known as a substitute response. In the substitute-stimulus process a new stimulus arouses an old response. In the substitute-response process a new response is made to an old stimulus. For example, the child responds to an anger stimulus by kicking, crying, and scratching, while an adult responds to the same stimulus by cursing, by merely doing nothing, or by planning a means of revenge.

But not all the changes in behavior can be attributed to the processes involved in the substitute-stimulus or the substitute-response mechanisms, although at one time there was a group of psychologists who claimed that such was the case.

Insight

Ruger, of Columbia University, performed an interesting experiment which indicated still another type of learning. Using human beings as subjects, and mechanical puzzles as the learning material, he found a type of learning which he attributed to *insight,* that is, "seeing the point." In the conditioned reflex experiment the changes come about gradually, just as they do in learning to swim, to write on a typewriter, or to pitch a curve in baseball. But in Ruger's experiments he found learning appearing suddenly. The first time his subjects tried to solve the mechanical puzzles they made a great many mistakes. They tried first one thing, then another, until finally they solved the puzzle. The second attempt involved fewer mistakes because the subjects remembered the approximate position of the pieces of the puzzle just before it was solved, and they attempted to get them in this position again. With the second or third solution most of the subjects "caught on" to the trick involved in the puzzle, and from then on they made few or no mistakes. In other words, *understanding* was of major importance in this type of learning.

Transfer of training

Still other aspects of learning are worth our consideration. One of these deals with the *transfer of training.* Psychologists once believed that the mind was made up of various faculties, such as the faculties of reasoning and memory.

It was held that these faculties were more or less separate categories; that is, if one did any reasoning at all, no matter what the material he was reasoning about, his ability to reason about all things would be improved. This belief formed the basis of a very widely held theory of education known as *formal discipline*. Educators who held this theory contended that all students should study mathematics, because since a student had to reason in mathematics, he would thus strengthen his reasoning ability as a whole, and this strength would be transferred to all situations requiring reasoning. Psychologists have learned, however, that the mind is not made up of separate faculties, and that practice in mathematical reasoning is helpful in other situations only insofar as identical or common units are found in both situations. For example, when students are set to memorizing series of six digits, they make rapid progress in the amount of learning they accomplish in a given time interval. When they are then set to learning ten digits they are much more efficient than students who have not practiced memorizing the six digits. This superiority is the result of the transfer of the methods they developed in memorizing the six digits, or in other words the transfer of elements which were identical in the two processes. If, however, these same students are set to memorizing poetry, they are no better memorizers than students who have not practiced memorizing numbers, because there are no identical elements involved in learning digits and poetry.

The effect of age on learning

Another interesting discovery is that ease in learning changes with age. Up to the age of about twenty-two, skill in learning improves each year; but from that time on there is a gradual decline. There was a considerable disagreement among psychologists as to whether this decline represented a real organic deficiency or whether it was merely a decline in the desire to learn. Most psychologists would agree today that in general the decline is probably a reduction of desire rather than a reduction of ability, although we must remember that exceptions to this do occur. By the time one is twenty-two years old he has learned enough to compete fairly successfully in the world in which he lives. He has learned about as much as he really wants to know; consequently, he does not try as hard to learn as he formerly tried, and the result is slightly poorer learning.

Improving one's learning

These discoveries concerning how we learn are probably not as important, however, as the discovery of the facts concerning the best ways to learn. It has been discovered that learning is an active process. The more aware, the more attentive the subject is, the better he will learn. The student who sits down and reads a book passively, hoping that what he reads will stick in his mind, is doomed to disappointment. Probably the best contrast to such a method of study is the following: The attentive, alert student reads the assignment through rapidly in order to get a general idea of it. He then goes back to the beginning and studies each paragraph intensively, seeking to discover each point the author makes. After studying the first paragraph, he looks away from the book and attempts to recite the important points noted in study thus far. He then checks his recitation against the text to see if he remembers all of these important points. Then he goes on to the next paragraph and repeats the process; but, in addition, he tries to discover how the points made in the preceding paragraph are related to those in the present one. This procedure he repeats until

he completes the whole assignment. The student then
goes back to see if he can recite to himself the important
points made in the whole assignment, and to see if he can
point out the relationships between these important points.
A device which will facilitate this work is to underline the
important points as one goes along. This has proved to be
a very effective and efficient method of learning. But there
is more to learning than merely getting the material in mind
so it can be recited. There is the additional problem of
keeping it there—remembering it. Ebbinghaus discovered
that about seventy-two per cent of barely learned material
is forgotten within the first twenty-four hours. To over-
come forgetting one must systematically review what one
has learned. The first review should occur no later than
a week after the original learning. The second review may
come about a month after learning; the third from two to
three months later, and so on. Only by such a schedule of
periodic reviews can the student expect to hold in mind
what he has learned.

Motor or muscular learning is not so easily forgotten as
informational learning. This is probably due to the fact
that since motor learning is a slower process than informational learning, we actually spend more time at it. Also,
in motor learning each learning period is a review period
during which we put into effect all that we have learned
previously, whereas in informational learning we are frequently acquiring new facts without adequately utilizing
and reviewing the old. From the cradle to the grave, man
is constantly learning and forgetting. Since forgetting plays
nearly as large a part in life as learning, let us glance hastily
at some of the factors involved in this process and the
conditions that modify it.

FACTORS AFFECTING MEMORY

It has been discovered that there is a close relationship between thoroughness of learning and speed of forgetting. Barely learned material is forgotten nearly as soon as it is learned. On the other hand, material which has been over-learned, such as swimming, playing a musical instrument, or reciting the multiplication tables, is rarely completely forgotten even though such learning is not used for a long period of time. With a short period of practice most of it soon returns.

A second factor affecting memory is the use of the material learned. Without use learned material is forgotten, just as a muscle atrophies through disuse. A third factor has to do with our *acceptance* and *rejection* reactions. Knowledge which coincides with our beliefs and gives us pleasure we accept as true. Such knowledge we find relatively easy to remember. Knowledge which is distasteful to us, which makes us uncomfortable, is frequently rejected, or forced out of our consciousness—or, as Hart expresses it, dissociated. Actually this material is not really forgotten but is forced out of the focus of our attention and into that portion of our mind which Freud calls the unconscious. As an example of what is meant by "wishful" forgetting, consider the student who sits up half the night studying for an examination which he is nearly certain he will fail. As he retires, he carefully winds his alarm clock and places it close to his head so that he will be sure to awaken in time for the examination. But the next morning he doesn't awaken until long after the examination has started. Upon examining the clock, he discovers that he forgot to turn on the alarm switch the evening before. Such forgetting ranges from forgetting the name of someone we do not like to the profound state known as total amnesia, in which a person forgets the past completely and does not even remember his own name.

There are many factors involved in our rejection behavior. The most important factor is probably the habits one forms in facing the problems of life. The person who faces his problems squarely and attacks them in a straightforward manner will probably be little bothered by dissociation. But on the other hand, the person who tries to dodge his responsibilities, to solve his problems by feigning illness, or by claiming others have it in for him, is very likely to suffer from dissociation. These facts have a very practical application. If we wish to avoid serious mental difficulties we should strive to build up habits of facing our problems squarely. We should admit defeat when defeat is inevitable and forget about excusing ourselves for our shortcomings. Only by this straightforward facing of life's problems can we expect to develop normal, well-adjusted personalities, for every time we dodge reality we are adding a unit to our store of mental instability, and, what is even worse, we are making it easier to add another unit of instability in the near future. Thus, apparently harmless little acts of "kidding" ourselves or dodging small responsibilities may lead eventually to a complete breakdown of all the mental development, modifications, and changes that have taken so many years to acquire.

MOTIVATION — WHY WE LEARN

We have pointed out some of the ways in which the help-less, unadjusted infant becomes adapted to his environment. We might well ask at this point why he did adjust. Why do we learn? Why do we work? Why do we strive to develop and improve ourselves? In fact, why do we do anything? The very basis of psychology is the attempt to answer the slang question, "How do we get that way?" We are not content to know that we have grown taller, that our glands have changed, that we have experienced conditioned reflexes. We want to know the motive that lay behind John Jones' running for senator, what motive prompted Bill Smith to work hard enough to make Phi Beta Kappa, and so on. When we ask the man in the street why he performs any given act, he responds quickly with a superficial answer which he sincerely believes to be true, but which may be only very remotely related to the real motive actuating his behavior. This problem of motives is of great importance.

Little was done about motives in psychology until Sigmund Freud cast a bombshell into the psychologists' encampments. Undoubtedly Freud was too radical, as well as too narrow, in his views. His major tenet was that the sole motivating force in life is sex. Back of every act we perform lies the driving principle of the sex urge. Obviously, Freudian teachings do not afford an adequate explanation of all the motive forces in human life. But it is generally agreed that Freud's teachings started the ball rolling, and that much of our present interest in motives is due to his focusing our attention upon this problem. He contended that behind all human behavior were to be found undercurrents of motives, and that beneath many of our acts which on the surface appear trivial lie forces of tremendous proportions.

He illustrated his theory by interpreting dreams. All dreams, he held, had two aspects, one the *obvious,* the other the *hidden* or latent. By the former he meant the content of dreams as noted by the dreamer; by the latter he meant the deep-seated motives, desires, and impulses of the subject. Let us analyze a dream and see what we find:

A college girl, a person who has been very highly thought of by her parents and relatives and around whom much of the typical family interest has revolved, returns home from college for a short vacation. Her older married sister is also visiting at home with her recently born infant. The baby is now the center of attention. Everyone is talking about the baby and paying attention to it, where previously our subject had occupied the center of the stage. The younger daughter has the following dream. Her sister drops her infant, which she has been carrying in her arms, and the fall kills it. Instead of being sorry, the members of the family in the dream find this extremely funny, and they all laugh uproariously.

Here we see expressed in a dream the deep undercurrent of jealousy aroused in the younger daughter by the infant. She was undoubtedly unaware that she had such a feeling; and if she had been asked if she would like to see the infant killed, she would have responded with a horrified "No!" Yet actually beneath her consciousness there was lurking this deep hurt, aroused by the infant's usurping the center of the stage, which she had previously occupied.

Freud made a great deal of the fact that people have very little understanding of their own motives. We all possess a great many fears and desires which we will not admit even to ourselves; and because we do not admit them, we think we do not have them. In this respect we are much like the ostrich, which hides its head in the sand and thinks it is completely concealed. It is common to hear bachelors talk loud and long of the advantages of bachelorhood. As a matter of fact this abnormal willingness to point out the advantages of single blessedness is a good indicator of the hidden desire to be married and have a home. Of course, we cannot generalize and say that all bachelors want to get married. Actually there are wide individual differences in the insight people have into their own motives. But psychologists who have studied this question are fairly well agreed that we all have a large body of unconscious motives which materially influence our behavior. To prove this, we have only to watch ourselves fully and to analyze our own behavior for a day or so to find a situation where we overtly express reason after reason for doing or not doing something, when actually the reasons we are giving are not true ones at all. Usually in such situations we don't want to give the real reason, and we often talk ourselves into believing that the superficial reasons we are giving are the true ones.

Such behavior is not necessarily an indication that one is becoming seriously neurotic. As a matter of fact, there is no reason why we should analyze all our behavior carefully and know every real reason for everything we do. The danger lies in building up habits of dodging the serious problems of life by giving superficial reasons for not meeting them squarely. If you find you cannot bear to be around people who have red hair or who wear glasses, there is a very great likelihood that a deep-seated motive is connected with some past experience that is coloring your behavior to an unnecessary degree. And there is a real reason for trying to find out the basis of such behavior.

On the other hand, it is not correct to assume that all our motives are either sharply understood or unconscious. Actually, many of them are in a middle group where they are about half conscious and half unconscious. We must think of our motives as ranging from the completely unconscious to the completely conscious, with the majority of them somewhere between these two extremes. Neither are all our motives of our own personal making; many are the result of our social heritage. Because we have grown up in a society which frowns upon it, we do not practice polygamy. The reasons for our adherence to monogamy are probably not the result of careful analysis, but are really the parroting of things we have been brought up to believe. Political beliefs are notoriously illogical, but we have been taught to believe certain principles. We have been steeped in a party bias, and whenever a political question arises, we immediately measure it by the tenets of whatever party we belong to. We accept the bias of the party uncritically, *unconsciously,* and we do our reasoning from that point on.

COMPLEXES

Let us see how these motives arise. The basis of most of them, we shall find, is emotional experiences. Any experience or group of experiences that have aroused us emotionally is very likely to have left its mark. We call such marks complexes.

We can learn much of what is meant by the word "complex" by examining behavior that involves a complex. An individual takes up golf. He enjoys the game immensely, often too much for the good of his work or the attention he pays to his family. He finds it such a pleasant sport that he wants to play all the time, and when he isn't playing, he wants to talk about it or to think about it. Commonly, he is called a "golf bug." Technically he has developed a golf complex, which is *a series of ideas which have become emotionally toned.* Let us consider another example given by the British psychologist Bernard Hart.[2] A former Sunday school teacher became a confirmed

[2] Hart, Bernard, *The Psychology of Insanity* (The Macmillan Company, New York, 1928).

atheist. He gave as his reason a careful study of the literature of religion. It was true that he had made a very intensive study of the subject and that he could converse in a highly enlightened manner on the whole topic. But Hart found after a careful psychological examination of the patient that a fellow Sunday school teacher had eloped with the girl to whom the first was engaged. In this case the complex was being indirectly expressed by repudiating the beliefs which had been the principal bond between the two Sunday school teachers.

These two examples show us two quite different ways in which behavior can be influenced by complexes. The behavior of the golfer was directly influenced by the golf, and we might say that the complex was expressing itself directly. In the case of the Sunday school teacher, the complex was expressing itself indirectly.

RATIONALIZATION

Frequently in behavior where our emotions are involved, we are loath to admit that the emotions are the real motivators. We feel the need to believe that we are acting rationally. We hate to admit even to ourselves that our emotions are the causes of our behavior; hence we tend to substitute an apparently logical process. This process of substituting reasons that seem rational for behavior that is really motivated by our emotions is called rationalization. The case of the Sunday school teacher cited above is an excellent example of this mechanism.

It is surprising how much of our behavior is really determined by our complexes while they are hidden from ourselves by the mechanism of rationalization.

There is a close relationship between the intensity of the emotion and the influence complexes exert upon our behavior. The stronger the emotion, the greater the influence of the complex upon our activities. In general, complexes affect our actions by facilitating ideas and situations which are in harmony with them, and by inhibiting those not in harmony. Thus it is evident that complexes are thoroughly natural processes resulting from experiences which arouse our emotions. They influence our thinking and behavior in a perfectly natural and explicable manner. Consider the golfer mentioned above. Before he took up golf, the fields, hills, and valleys may have had little interest for him; but now he sees every pasture as a potential fairway, every stream and puddle as a possible water hazard. His behavior is definitely altered by the existence of his complex, is as definitely influenced as though he were actually propelled by some machine.

Thus we see that when a person talks himself into going to the theater by stating that he is too tired to study, that he will feel more like working after relaxing for an hour or two while watching a play, he is rationalizing; and the real motive for going to the theater is not that which he is giving. The mechanisms of complexes and rationalization so frequently distort and hide our real motives that we must consider with some degree of suspicion all apparent motives. We cannot be certain that because a person thinks he knows why he is behaving in a certain manner that that is his real motive; and usually the more certain the individual is, especially if he becomes emotional in his insistence that he knows why he is behaving thus, the better the chances are that he does not know, and the motive actually behind his behavior is a complex. A good test to apply to our own behavior is to consider the emotional component of any activity we perform. Whenever the emotional tone which accompanies one of our acts is high, whenever we feel exceptionally well pleased with ourselves, whenever the result of our reasoning seems irrefutable—whenever these symptoms occur, look for a complex. The better you feel, the greater the possibility of a complex being operative. Results arrived at as a result of reason are not emotionally toned. Reason is cold and hard, and conclusions arrived at as a result of its use are obvious because they are substantiated by fact. Pure truth is devoid of emotion.

We see then that in addition to maturation and learning, our emotions also play a very important role in altering our original behavior. Much of our behavior is motivated by our emotions. Not, as Freud claimed, only by sex, but by all the emotions we are capable of experiencing. Consciously and directly we seek to do what will give us pleasure, and to avoid what will cause us pain. If some of our search for pleasure seems socially unjustifiable, we rationalize to make it compatible. If still other experiences are so painful, distasteful, or incompatible that we will not even admit them to ourselves, then they are expressed indirectly by means of dreams or, in highly modified form, by building elaborate rationalizations. In any event, the emotions furnish the basis for our motives.

Up to this point we have been considering the individual by examining his component parts, rather than by considering him as a whole. We have pointed out a few of the ways in which this equipment is enlarged, some of the ways in which it is modified, and we have dealt briefly with motives or the forces responsible for some of the changes that take place.

PERSONALITY

Let us now consider the individual as a whole. The topic in psychology which considers the individual as a going concern is personality. Personality has been variously defined by different writers, but for our purpose a modification of Dr. J. B. Watson's definition seems best to suit the purpose. Let us consider personality as *an individual's total assets and liabilities, both actual and potential*.

To look at personality in this broad sense we must again start with the individual at birth. He is born into a particular environment; and at birth he has a certain physiological and neural equipment. Both the equipment and the environment possess certain qualities. Some of these qualities are assets and some are liabilities, actual and potential. This mechanism and environment are constantly interacting; as a result of this interaction both are influenced and changed. Neither the individual nor the environment is ever completely free of the influence of the other; the individual and his environment are never in a state of balance. Both are constantly changing. Neither an individual nor his environment is ever twice the same. Thus an individual at any one moment is the result of what he had to start with plus what he has lived through. Your personality as you read this is the result of the constant interaction between yourself and your environment from the time of your conception down to this present moment. Thus it is obvious that your personality is a highly complex subject, and that it will continue to become even more complex. It is disturbing to some that we can never completely understand personality because it will not stand still long enough to be thoroughly investigated. If it were possible within the next twenty-four hours to make a complete analysis of yourself up the present moment, you still would not have a complete picture, because of the changes which had occurred during the twenty-four hour period devoted to the analysis. It may seem to the reader by this time that the topic is hopeless and that we may as well forget it. But such is not the case. The fact that we can never have complete understanding does not mean that we cannot discover much of value.

Let us consider some of the more important factors that may be responsible for one's personality. One of our first considerations will be that of health, for without doubt this is an important factor in determining our feelings and actions. When one is ill he is not the same person he would be if he were well. It is a common occurrence to hear a person state that he "feels like a new man" since he had his appendix removed or some ailment cured. As a matter of fact, he is a new person. He feels differently and he behaves differently; his whole pattern of reactions is altered by the removal of a source of infection which was sapping his physical energy and poisoning his body.

Illness is important in another way, because of the effect it has upon the behavior of the invalid's relatives and associates. When a person is ill he usually receives much more attention, care, and sympathy than when he is in normal health. To many this additional consideration is so pleasant that they wish it to continue. Thus the individual who appears to enjoy ill health, who is constantly complaining about how bad he feels, and who is constantly trying new medicines is often doing so because of the added attention and sympathy he receives.

The glands of internal secretion, which we have mentioned previously, are also of considerable importance in influencing our personalities. Most is known at present concerning the thyroid gland. Its over-secretion leads to an increase of bodily activity, nervousness, and irritability, while under-secretion may cause a normally hard-working, energetic person to become a fat, lazy loafer. The other glands, in all probability, directly or indirectly influence behavior to a sufficient degree to bring about noticeable changes in it. Students of personality are following endocrinological research with much interest.

Physical appearances are also of great importance in personality, both directly and indirectly. Since our personalities are in a way reflections of what others think of us, our appearances are naturally important. It has been found that, frequently, leaders are above the average in height. This does not mean that large people have more intelligence, but it does mean that people select as their leaders individuals who look the part. This may be a hang-over from earlier times when one of the major prerequisites of leadership was physical prowess.

There is another important side of physique which operates not only with leaders, but to some extent with all of us, especially those with unusual physiques either good or bad. This is the indirect importance of physique. The youngest child in a family may soon learn that he cannot hope to compete with his older brothers physically, and quite frequently the bigger brother gets considerable pleasure out of making this fact painfully apparent. To compensate for his physical inferiority, the child develops traits of craftiness, or works harder in school in order to appear superior mentally. The homely child may soon discover that he is not wanted for his looks; hence he compensates by building habits of being so pleasant and agreeable that people like him in spite of his looks. When such habits are developed, few serious problems arise; but there is another type of habit that may be developed. The child may build up habits of avoiding social contacts, and may resort more and more to his own company. He may build elaborate air castles in which he pictures himself as very large and handsome, or a great hero acclaimed by the crowds. A moderate amount of such behavior is indulged in by most persons, but they have enough social contacts to keep it from becoming serious. But where the habit grows and the individual spends more and more of his time engaging in his own dreams and fantasies, it develops into a serious mental condition which is very difficult to deal with. Many inmates of our insane hospitals suffer from this disorder. These are by no means the only types of maladjustments that may result from physical inferiority, but they are sufficient to indicate the influence of a poor physique on personality.

Not only does a poor physique influence personality; a beautiful physique may just as easily give rise to personality problems. The handsome young man who is constantly being reminded by members of the opposite sex of his beauty may develop into a perfect snob, and may expect the adoration of his male associates. He may build such unsocial and snobbish habits that they more than counteract his physical attractiveness. As a result he may become extremely unpopular. This may in turn give rise to serious conflict, and lead to habits of self-pity and day dreams and their serious consequences. It should be apparent from the above that physique, with its contingent characteristics of disease and glandular balance, is of considerable importance in shaping our personalities. However, although these factors are important, they do not constitute the complete basis of personality; they may be over-stressed simply because they are definite, observable characteristics. Probably our habits and our attitudes are of far more importance than physical characteristics. These habits and attitudes reflect how well we have been able to adjust our behavior to the demands of our environment, and it is really this factor of *adjustment* which lies at the bottom of the whole problem.

Let us observe briefly what is meant by adjustment. The infant is born into his environment with certain biological needs already established. He must have food, water, shelter, and protection. All of these must come from his environment. At first these are all supplied him with little or no effort on his part, but as the child grows older his demands upon the environment also grow. He not only wants food, but certain kinds of food; not only liquids, but certain kinds of liquids. Paralleling the growth of the individual's demands upon his environment are demands made by the environment upon the individual. The inevitable result of these mutual demands is *conflict*. The child eventually makes a demand on his environment which the environment cannot fulfill; he soon discovers that he cannot have all of his desires satisfied without effort. He also learns that demands are being made of him which he must meet or expend considerable energy to avoid. In other words, the child soon finds out that the world is not a "basket of roses," and that the universe is not operating for his sole benefit. Constantly he meets obstacles which block his path; and very frequently obstacles come to meet him. All of such obstacles which he meets call for adjustment, and therein lies the tale of personality. As a matter of fact, personality is really the result of one endless series of adjustments.

A fourth factor of personality is intelligence. A person of limited intelligence is very apt to be hampered in making an adequate adjustment, because he doesn't recognize problems when he meets them. One of the tasks to be performed in one type of intelligence test is to fit variously shaped blocks into a board, which has correspondingly shaped holes cut in it. The low-grade moron, for example, may spend a long time in trying to get a circular block to fit a square hole; he just does not recognize the problem. The same is true in many life situations. He is very likely to possess little in the way of understanding and sympathy; since he cannot imagine himself in another's place, he does not really see what is going on around him. We find the same phenomenon at a slightly higher level. The retarded boy in school will be physically much larger and older than his classmates, yet these smaller and younger children will constantly put him to shame intellectually. He cannot adjust himself to this problem normally because he hasn't the mental equipment. The result is that he adjusts in the only way he can—by bullying the little boys on the playground, where his physical superiority counts, or by dodging the whole unpleasant situation by staying away from school. In either event he is becoming a social problem. Psychologists have discovered that segregating these mentally deficient pupils and adapting the curriculum to their abilities frequently leads to their becoming interested, coöperative, hard-working students.

It should not be assumed, however, that high intelligence will always be an asset. The person of superior intelligence sees more things in life to desire; consequently he has more adjustments to make. In a general way the most integrated personality is that of an individual whose desires and attainments are relatively equal. William James gave the following formula for self-esteem:

$$\text{Self-esteem} = \frac{\text{Success}}{\text{Pretensions}}$$

If we pretend more than we accomplish, we cannot have a

good opinion of ourselves. Likewise, we will be dissatisfied if we are not rewarded for our accomplishments. The greatest danger both to our personality and to our own mental health is the likelihood of our not adjusting our conflicts in a normal, rational manner. When we dodge reality and solve our problems by resorting to day dreams, by feigning illness, or by making excuses, we are building habits whose only outcome will be maladjustment. Thus our major problem in personality is to take a careful inventory of our assets and liabilities, and, using this as a basis, to strive to attain that which is attainable for us, and forget that which is beyond our reach. In so doing we should not develop the attitude of the fox who said he did not care for grapes anyway, because they were sour. Rather, we should admit that there are many desirable things in the world that are beyond our power to attain. Thus we will not spoil the success and happiness that can be ours.

PART II — APPLIED PSYCHOLOGY

DIFFERENTIAL PSYCHOLOGY

When Wilhelm Wündt opened the first psychological laboratory in Germany, in 1879, he was primarily interested in discovering general laws of behavior common to mankind as a whole, and most of the work he and his students did was directed toward this end.   Soon after the laboratory was established a young American, James McKeen Cattell, came to study under Wündt.   Cattell quickly observed that, while the subjects as a group performed in more or less the same manner, occasionally there would be an exception when a subject behaved differently from the others.   These exceptions interested Cattell so greatly that he set up an experiment to discover why they occurred.   Displeased with this idea, Dr. Wündt forbade Cattell the use of the laboratory for such studies.   But Cattell then conducted his experiments at his lodging, and later induced Wündt to accept these research results for his doctor's thesis.   When he returned to America Cattell continued his work on individual differences and stimulated an extensive amount of research on the topic.

Today the study of individual differences is one of the leading divisions of psychology, and the results of studies in this field afford one of the most important sources of knowledge concerning our everyday activity.   Present-day education is based largely on concepts laid down by students of individual differences.   The psychological testing movement, which is playing an ever-increasing role in industry, business, vocational guidance, and personal selection, is derived from the researches of the differential psychologists. The prevention of accidents, the licensing of automobile drivers, and the scientific detection of crime are all heavily indebted to the psychology of individual differences for inspiration and technique. As a matter of fact, wherever psychology is used in a practical way, we find contributions made by the differential psychologists.

THE LAW OF NORMAL DISTRIBUTION

We commonly hear it stated that in America everyone is born free and equal. Psychologists, examining this

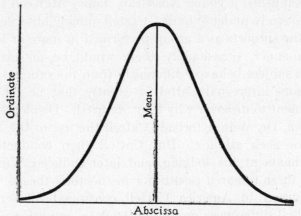

Figure 1. The Curve of Normal Distribution

hypothesis, have found no scientific evidence to support it, but instead have built up a tremendous number of facts which indicate that no two individuals are alike or equal in any sense of the words. Obviously we are not all equal in weight, height, health, or physical structure. We are not equal in economic competition; if we were there would be fewer labor disputes, relief cases, and class struggles. We are not equal politically—the illiterate slum dweller, bullied by a ward boss, is not as free as the educated and independent citizen when he goes to the polls to vote. Psychology has failed to discover any way in which we *are* equal, but has found that in all measurable human characteristics individuals differ, and that their differences tend to follow a comparatively stable pattern.

The curve reproduced in Figure 1, which is called *the curve of normal distribution,* illustrates this pattern. If a sufficiently large number of people are tested on any measurable human characteristic and the results are plotted in

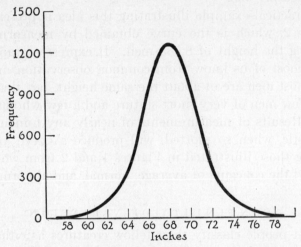

Figure 2. Distribution of Height of 8,585 Men

such a way that the measurements are recorded on the base line or abscissa, and the number of individuals obtaining each measure are recorded on the perpendicular axis or ordinate, a figure closely approximating that in Figure 1 will be obtained.

The normal curve flattens out at the extremes, indicating that relatively few individuals are found who possess an extremely large or small amount of the characteristic under consideration. As we move from the extremes toward the middle we find the curve rapidly increasing in height. This indicates that a larger and larger number of the people measured obtain similar scores. At the middle is found the maximum height, signifying that the greatest number of people possessing the characteristic under consideration have it to a degree about half way between the extremes of the group. In other words, most of the people are fairly similar in their possession of a given trait. They are "average persons."

A practical example illustrating this idea is presented in Figure 2, which is the curve obtained by measuring and plotting the height of 8,585 men. It expresses graphically what most of us know from common observation, namely, that most men are of about the same height, but that there are a few men of very short stature and a few who are very tall. Results of measurements of nearly any human characteristic, when so plotted, will produce a curve approximating those illustrated in Figures 1 and 2 from which are derived the concepts of average, normal, and abnormal.

CONTINUITY OF VARIATION

Most people classify their fellow creatures as either possessing or not possessing various characteristics. When considering insanity, for example, most men regard their associates as either sane or insane. As a matter of fact, this idea is woefully untrue, for insanity is a matter of the degree or amount of certain behavior patterns that an individual possesses. All men have insane characteristics, but some people possess these traits to a greater extent than other people.

The most seriously insane individuals are confined to asylums, but outside the hospitals are many cases which, though not violent, are definitely abnormal. Still other people are not regarded as being decidedly abnormal but are thought to be merely peculiar. Men differ, then, not by large jumps or sudden gaps but by continuous small degrees. We cannot justifiably pigeonhole individuals into types but must interest ourselves in establishing norms or measures that characterize the largest number of people, and then determine how far any particular person varies from these norms. Only for convenience in analysis do we rate people as idiots, morons, normal, and so forth.

INTELLIGENCE

In the field of mental measurement the idea of continuity of variation has been extensively used. Cattell and his students attacked the problems of measuring intelligence at the turn of the century. Starting with the assumption that intelligence was composed of many elements such as speed of reaction, perception, and coördination, they tested a large number of college students to discover the extent to which each subject possessed these traits. The scores on the various elements were combined into composite measures for each of the subjects, and this composite score was supposed to be a measure of the subject's intelligence. But when these scores were compared with school grades, which were known to require intelligence to attain, no relationship was apparent, and so the hypothesis of measuring intelligence by measuring its elements had to be discarded.

The Binet Test

Alfred Binet, a French psychologist, approached the problem from an entirely different point of view. He contended that a number of short tasks requiring varying degrees of intelligence to perform should be selected, and that each subject's intelligence would be indicated by the number of these problems he could solve. Binet devised a test comprised of fifty-four of such tasks, varying from easy to quite difficult ones. A large number of children from three to twelve years old were divided into ten groups according to their age levels. To standardize the test, Binet measured the performance of each age group. In this manner, Binet discovered the level of difficulty each age group could master. The child's attainment on the test was called his mental age. If a child could perform the tasks usually accomplished by six-year-old children he was said to have a mental age of six years, or if his performance coincided with that of the average ten year old, he was given a mental age of ten. This procedure has proved very useful in psychology; it is simple and easily understood, and its logic is sound.

In 1916, eleven years after Binet's test was first published, Lewis M. Terman, a psychologist at Stanford University, revised, lengthened, and improved Binet's scale. The revised edition measured mental age from the three- to the eighteen-year level, and in addition to the use of mental age as a scoring device Terman adopted another method of scoring known as the Intelligence Quotient or I.Q., which had been worked out by Professor Stern, a German investigator. The I.Q. is the ratio between the mental age (M.A.) and the chronological age (C.A.) and is expressed by the formula $I.Q. = \dfrac{M.A.}{C.A.}$ This method of recording test results was a decided improvement over the use of the M.A. alone, because the mental age indicates how far a person has advanced mentally but fails to show if he is bright or stupid. When an individual's mental age is compared to his chronological age, however, it is immediately apparent whether the student is average, retarded, or superior. If he is actually ten years old and has an M.A. of ten, he is average, but if he is chronologically five years old and has a mental age of ten, he is a very superior child, for he knows as much at five as the average child knows at ten. Conversely, if his C.A. is ten and his M.A. is five, he is a very dull child, for he has progressed only half as far mentally as the average child of his age. When the M.A. and C.A. are equal, we get an intelligence quotient of 1.00. In practice, the decimal

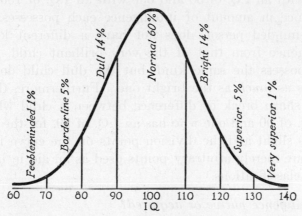

Figure 3. Distribution of I.Q.'s in a Normal Group

point is dropped and we speak of this I.Q. as being 100. If the M.A. is ten and the C.A. is five, the I.Q. is 200; if the M.A. is five and the C.A. is ten, the I.Q. is 50.

When the I.Q.'s of a large number of children selected at random are plotted, a curve similar to that reproduced in Figure 3 is obtained.[3] It is evident from this curve that the majority of children have I.Q.'s between 90 and 110, and this is considered an average group. About 14 per cent have I.Q.'s between 80 and 90, while a similar number fall

---

[3] This figure is taken from Garrett, H. E., *Great Experiments in Psychology* (D. Appleton-Century Company, New York, 1930).

between 110 and 120. A smaller group, 5 per cent, occur between 70 and 80, and the same number are located between 120 and 130. Finally about 1 per cent is found at each extreme, that is, below 70 and above 130. These latter groups represent the very dull and the very bright, respectively.

At this point it is important to keep in mind the theory of continuity of variation. The only difference between the child with an I.Q. of 50 and one with an I.Q. of 150 is the difference in amount of intelligence each possesses. The feeble-minded person does not have a different kind of intelligence from that of the very brilliant child. They both possess the same kind, but the dull child does not possess as *much* as the bright one. Furthermore, there is not a sharp break or difference between a child who has an I.Q. of 90 and one who has an I.Q. of 89, for the difference is slight and the division points on the curve in Figure 3 are merely arbitrary points used as an aid in making rough classifications.

Is intelligence native or acquired?

The question of whether intelligence is native or acquired has long been a controversial point among psychologists and between some psychologists and sociologists. Many psychologists contend that intelligence is a native trait and that, barring diseases of the nervous system, environmental forces alter an individual's intelligence very little. On the other hand, many sociologists and a minority of psychologists hold that environment can materially influence intelligence. The writer adheres to the opinion that intelligence is relatively impervious to environmental influence, and this opinion is based upon a mass of experimental work which has never been successfully refuted.

Constancy of the I.Q.

Supporting this hypothesis is the evidence that deals with the constancy of the I.Q. Terman and his students, as well as other experimenters, have shown that the I.Q. changes little from year to year. For example, they have found that children who have an I.Q. of 115 when they are five years of age have about the same I.Q. when they are ten, twelve, and fifteen years old. This indicates that environment and experience have relatively little influence on intelligence.

Frank Freeman of the University of Chicago, Barbara Burks of Stanford University, and Alice Leahy of the University of Minnesota each conducted a major study of the influence of environment on the intelligence of foster children. The problem involved was to learn what influence the environment of a foster home exerted upon the intelligence of adopted children. Freeman found that in a few cases the I.Q. of adopted children was raised as much as twenty-five points by their new environment, although for the group as a whole the I.Q. was changed only about five points, which is about equal to the error involved in the test itself. He also found that the intelligence of the foster children was more like the intelligence of the foster parents than would be expected if the environment had no effect. On the basis of the results, Freeman concluded that intelligence was materially influenced by environment.

This conclusion is open to serious criticism. As was pointed out, the average change in I.Q. found by Freeman was little more than would be expected due to the error involved in the testing instruments themselves. The correlation between foster parents and foster children, while higher than would be expected by chance, was still very low. Probably the most serious criticism of Freeman's study is the lack of control of the factor of selective placement.   By selective placement is meant the condition of superior foster parents selecting superior children for adoption and inferior parents selecting inferior children.   If this factor were operating, one would certainly expect the existence of a definite relationship between foster parents and foster children.   The children used as subjects in Freeman's study ranged in age at the time of adoption from six months to eighteen years.   By the time a child is a year or two old it is possible for an intelligent person to get some idea of the child's intellectual ability, and this fact would result in selective placement.   It is also common knowledge that orphanages and similar institutions do everything in their power to match foster children with foster parents; consequently it is nearly a certainty that selective placement affected Freeman's results.

In the Burks and Leahy studies these selective factors were controlled, and little support was found for Freeman's conclusions.   Miss Leahy conducted her experiment after the Burks and Freeman researches had been completed and after much controversy had raged over them.   Knowing the weaknesses in both studies, she controlled her investigation adequately, so it is open to none of the criticisms levelled at the other two.   Her results indicate nearly conclusively that environment plays very little part, if any, in intelligence.

Racial and nationality differences

Studies of racial groups that show that races differ from one another afford a second line of evidence indicating that intelligence is native.   According to the results of both language and non-language tests, Southern Negroes are decidedly lower in intelligence than American whites.   Between other races and nationality groups there are found to be similar differences in intellect. Those who believe intelligence to be acquired argue that such differences are the result of opportunity rather than of heredity, but under experimental investigation these arguments fail to stand up. Using as subjects one group of full-blooded Negroes, a second group three-fourths Negro and one-fourth white, a third group about one-half Negro and one-half white, and a fourth group of people who had only a small amount of Negro blood, Ferguson conducted an experiment in which he found that the first group scored only 64 per cent as high as full-blooded whites, while the second group scored 70 per cent as high. The third group scored 82 per cent as much, and the fourth group scored 96 per cent as much as full-blooded whites. From these results it is apparent that the more similar the Negro's heredity is to that of the white man, the more similar the Negro is to the Caucasian in intelligence. Joseph Peterson likewise performed several experiments to determine the reason for the differences between Negroes and whites, and his conclusions agree with those of Ferguson. Hunter and Garth likewise found a definite relationship between degree of white blood and intelligence in their extensive studies of American Indians.

During the World War large numbers of Negro recruits were tested and found to be definitely inferior to white soldiers. This does not mean, however, that all Negroes are inferior to whites. Some of the Negroes tested just as high as any white soldier did, which indicates that overlapping occurs. On the average, however, Negroes as a group are less intelligent than white people. Similar results obtained in many other experiments indicate that there are racial differences in intelligence which appear to be due to heredity.

Family histories

Family histories add more evidence to the case for native intelligence, and none is more illustrative of the point than the history of the Kallikak family. Kallikak is, of course, the fictitious name of a real family. Martin Kallikak, who came from an intelligent family, was a soldier in the Revolutionary War. During his service in the army he met a feeble-minded barmaid who bore him a son. Like his mother, the child was very inferior in intelligence, and when he grew up he married a girl whose mentality was as low as his. Their many children were likewise feeble-minded and married equally inferior mates. When this study was conducted six generations had descended from the union of Martin Kallikak and the barmaid, and of the four hundred and eighty descendants nearly all were undesirable citizens. One hundred and forty-three were feeble-minded, thirty-three were prostitutes, twenty-four were chronic alcoholics, thirty-six were illegitimate, three were criminals, eighty-three were such physical weaklings that they died in infancy, three were epileptics, and eight were keepers of brothels.

After the War Martin Kallikak married a woman of high intelligence, and from this marriage there have been four hundred and ninety-six descendants, of whom practically all have been a credit to society. Among them are doctors, governors, lawyers, and many individuals of high standing in their communities. This second line of Kallikaks has served and enriched society, while the first line has cost the public thousands of dollars to care for their weak minds and bodies and to restrain their criminal and unsocial tendencies.

The history of the Edwards family furnishes ample evidence of the results of good heredity. Richard Edwards was a great lawyer who married an intelligent woman of excellent lineage. The descendants of this pair have been as illustrious as the members of the first line of Kallikaks have been infamous. Among the Edwards descendants are found one hundred clergymen, two hundred and sixty-five college graduates, sixty-five college professors, twelve college presidents, sixty doctors, sixty prominent authors, one hundred lawyers, thirty judges, eighty public officers, three congressmen, two senators, one vice-president, two presidents of the United States and the wife of a third president, one chief justice of the Supreme Court, one general in the army, and seventy-five army officers. Since these people lived in different times, chronologically, and in many different places, it seems absurd to suggest that environment was solely responsible for this display of genius. Therefore it would seem that the source of much of such superiority must be in the germ plasm, and that heredity, rather than environment, must lie behind the achievements of the Edwards family.

Immediate ancestry

When immediate ancestry or family resemblance is studied, more evidence that intelligence is native is apparent. Biologists and laymen readily admit that biological characteristics such as facial appearance or hair and eye color are inherited, and that in these traits members of a family resemble each other more than they resemble unrelated people. It is natural to assume that intelligence should follow the same tendencies if it, too, is inherited.

In order to express similarity between two traits or characteristics a mathematical statement called the coefficient of correlation is commonly used. This coefficient ranges from .00, which indicates no relationship, to 1.00 which denotes perfect similarity.[4]

Scientific experiments have shown that brothers and sisters are related in physical characteristics to the extent represented by a coefficient of correlation of .50. When the biological traits of all twins selected at random are measured the correlation is around .75. Fraternal twins, which are the result of two eggs being fertilized by two sperms, correlate about .50 on biological traits. Such a correlation between fraternal twins would be expected because their heredity is no more similar than that of other brothers and sisters. The correlation between the biological characteristics of identical twins is approximately .90, however. This high correlation is due to the similar heredity possessed by identical twins, which are the result of one egg being fertilized by one sperm.

If intelligence is inherited there should be the same intellectual relationship among related individuals as there is biological relationship. Many experiments have shown that approximately the same correlations do exist. Intellectually brothers and sisters and fraternal twins correlate around .50. All twins correlate about .75, and identical twins correlate .90 and above.

What stronger proof that intelligence is inherited could one ask for than to find intelligence following the same laws as biological heredity? This, with the evidence provided by racial differences, by actual family histories, and by the experiments on the constancy of the I.Q., explains why so many psychologists strongly contend that intelligence is native.

---

[4] See pp. 739–742.

NATIVE INTELLIGENCE: ITS IMPLICATIONS

Knowing whether intelligence is the result of nature or of nurture is of great value in dealing with the problems of mentality. If environment were the most important factor in determining intellect, then, obviously, feeble-mindedness and other mental defects could be cured by changing the environment. Since environment cannot work miracles, since a dull child is bound to become a dull adult and a brilliant child is destined to become a brilliant adult, the problem of intelligence must be attacked in another way. Today psychologists handle this problem by determining the mental capacity of their subject and then devising courses of education and training which are adapted to the individual's abilities.

The widespread belief that everyone should go to college illustrates how little this method is understood. It is as absurd to tell a class of high school seniors that they should all attend the university as it would be to tell them all to become heavyweight prizefighters. To imagine that the smallest member of that class could hold his own against the world's champion is no more ridiculous than to assume that the dullest member of the class could make passing grades in college. Even though this student spent all his time studying, he would be as doomed to failure as the little fellow in the prizering.

One large Midwestern university conducted a study of its students' attainments over a considerable period of time. Of the entering freshmen it was discovered that twenty-five per cent had only four chances out of a hundred of ever maintaining a C average. Yet with odds that are ninety-six to four against their succeeding, hundreds of such students each year go to college to waste their time in futile study.

Obviously the time has come to reconsider the idea that all men are created equal. Americans who are proud of the idea that any boy born in the United States has the opportunity to become President seldom realize how fallacious this belief is. We must discard such notions that anyone can be what he wants to be, and realize that the important problem is to analyze an individual's abilities and capacities and to direct his course along channels in which he has a greater chance of success.

Nature sets definite limitations beyond which one *cannot* go. However, this does not mean that environment is unimportant. A potential Einstein, born and reared among savages, would never become a great mathematician. Thus it is apparent that one's abilities do not develop independently of one's environment. But the point so frequently overlooked is that environment cannot raise an individual above the limitations laid down by his heredity.

VOCATIONAL GUIDANCE

The division of psychology which deals with the problem of matching an individual's education with his abilities is called vocational guidance. Through the use of many varied tests the vocational-guidance expert studies the total individual. The subject's interest, his abilities, and his personality must all be carefully measured and his health, character, education, and past experience must be considered. Only when all this information has been studied is guidance given. This procedure is illustrated by this actual case handled by the University Testing Bureau at the University of Minnesota and reported in one of the best books on this subject.[5]

Jonathan Schmidt, Case No. 745–2–35 Chemistry 1937

This student was twenty years of age, a sophomore in the School of Chemistry, at the time of first contact with the University Testing Bureau. He was referred to the Bureau by a professor in the School of Chemistry because his grades were getting progressively worse and a check on his vocational choice seemed advisable.

Both of the boy's parents had a grade-school education, the father being a railroad employee. There were six other children in the family, he being second oldest. In high school he participated in athletics and played in the school orchestra. His work experience had been varied—delivery boy, section hand, office boy, and clerk. He characterized himself as friendly, tolerant, reserved, tactful, conscientious, and submissive.

His grades had been mostly C's and D's, with F's in nineteen credit hours of work, for his first five quarters in the School of Chemistry. The only vocational field he had considered was the field of chemistry, and if this choice seemed inadvisable, he had no idea of alternatives. His general ability seemed to be well above average, judging from his percentile score of 87 on the college aptitude test taken when he first entered the university. Now, almost two years later, when he came to the Bureau to check on his vocational choice he was given the Coöperative English Series I Test and received a percentile rating of 47, using Arts College sophomore norms; in the Coöperative Chemistry Test, 85, using norms of those having had one year of high school chemistry; in the Coöperative Algebra Test, 75, using national freshman norms. In order to measure his clerical ability, he was given a clerical aptitude test in which he received percentile ratings of 77 in numbers and 97 in names, using general population norms. On the above achievement tests he rated about average in English, and considering that he had chemistry through qualitative analysis, the rating of 85 would not indicate that he was much superior to the average college sophomore. His background in mathematics seemed fairly good. The results of the clerical aptitude tests indicated that he had superior ability in clerical work. In order to check his vocational interests he was given the Strong's Interest Test. This objective measurement of his interests gave him an A as office clerk, B as personnel manager or specialty

[5] Williamson, E. G., and Darley, J. G., *Student Personnel Work* (McGraw-Hill Book Company, New York, 1937). Quoted with permission of the publishers.

salesman, and B- as Y.M.C.A. physical director or as purchasing agent. This test indicated no technical or scientific interests whatever. From a Health Service report it was learned that the boy was partially color-blind but was otherwise without serious handicaps. It was considered that his difficulty with chemistry might possibly be due to his partial colorblindness, but this would not account for his poor achievement in some of his other courses.

This student's lack of interest was apparently a major factor in his maladjustment. His choice of chemistry was not based upon genuine scientific interests that characterize the successful chemist. On the basis of his interest pattern as revealed by Strong's Test, his mediocre achievement on science and mathematics tests, and his outstanding clerical aptitude, he was advised to go into the School of Business as soon as he could meet the requirements for that school. He would have to maintain better than a B average for two quarters of work in the Arts College if the transfer to the School of Business were to be made by the winter quarter of the following year. This would demand a speedy readjustment. He was, however, very much pleased with the new course outlined to him and quite anxious to have an opportunity to show what he could do. He was urged to come back for interviews at various intervals so that his progress could be noted. After one quarter's work in the Arts College he came back to the Bureau for an interview. He had received grades of A in five credits of work and B's in nine credits of work. In all, he had made up nineteen honor points. He was quite delighted with the improvement in his grades and with his shift in vocational objective.

Over a year after the first contact with the University Testing Bureau, the student was called in for a follow-up interview. He had made up his deficiency of thirty-two honor points in two quarters in the Arts College and had then transferred to the School of Business. He was doing excellent work and keeping his scholastic average above a B rating. He continued to be very well satisfied with his new choice and had made an excellent readjustment both vocationally and scholastically. This is a clear-cut example of a vocationally maladjusted student who was guided into the field of his interests and abilities. By making this transfer from chemistry to business the boy immediately changed from a failing student on probation to a well-satisfied student maintaining a B-plus average.

This case demonstrates the many factors that must be considered in vocational guidance and shows the importance of finding the right field for proper development of abilities.

It should be remembered, however, that the science of vocational guidance is in the developmental stage, and that success cannot be assured in every case.

SELECTION OF PERSONNEL

Somewhat the same procedure as is followed in vocational guidance is used in industry when men are selected for jobs, although in vocational guidance the purpose is to select a job for which an individual is best fitted. In personnel selection the purpose is to select a man, from all those available, who is best suited for a given job. Many of the same tests and analyses are used in both cases.

THE PSYCHOLOGY OF ADVERTISING

Psychology has been applied in advertising, selling, market analysis, law, and in many industrial fields.

In advertising, psychology may be applied by carrying over the scientific attitude, by using *psychological content* or the known facts of behavior, and by adapting to advertising research the techniques used in psychological research.

The application of scientific attitude to advertising

Scientific attitude, as has been explained, is characterized by its insistence upon obtaining facts. The application of scientific method, however, is time-consuming, and for this reason many advertisers have objected to it. What these businessmen save by not applying scientific method, they more than likely lose by wasteful procedures. The director of a large advertising firm recently worked out an advertisement containing what he considered an excellent slogan and an attention-getting contest. At a large cost to the advertiser, a full-page advertisement was run in a number of leading newspapers. An independent research agency made a scientific test of the effectiveness of the advertisement and discovered that the average housewife neither understood the slogan nor was interested in the prize offered in the contest. Had this same test been made before the advertisement was printed in the newspapers, a great deal of money would have been saved. The modern businessman can use scientific method to his profit.

Applying psychological content in advertising

Much of the knowledge psychologists have accumulated concerning man's behavior can be used to determine how people will react to a particular advertisement. Psychologists, for example, have discovered that there are certain factors which determine whether a stimulus will attract attention, and the first requirement of an advertisement is that it be attention-getting. The factors that are involved are intensity, change, repetition, striking quality, definite form, and mental set.

Intensity signifies the strength of the stimulus, and is illustrated by bright colors, which are more quickly noticed than dull ones, and loud noises, which will be heard when weak sounds will not be perceived.

Change and its value as an attention-attracting device is illustrated by the impossibility of passing, without noticing it, an electric sign in which the lights are moving.

Repetition secures attention, because repeated stimuli tend to compel response. One small advertisement on a billboard may go unnoticed, but a dozen copies on the same billboard will attract attention. It is as if the nervous system stored up small stimuli until they assume proportions large enough to cause a response.

Striking quality means uniqueness. A brilliantly colored

advertisement or one with a very unusual design or arrangement is striking because it differs from other advertisements.
This unique quality makes an advertisement stand out and
in that way attract attention.

Definite form means clear-cut, sharply defined stimuli.
A figure that stands out from the background in a photograph, for instance, will attract more attention than a broad,
vague figure that seems to melt into its surroundings.

Mental set is a condition similar to interest. In the fall
we are set to notice fur coats and winter clothing, but in
June these stimuli would have little attention-catching
value.

If an advertisement is to be successful in attracting
attention, it must have one or more of these factors in its
make-up. Poffenberger [6] showed that the number of people
who send in a return coupon is determined by the factors
of attention-getting in the coupon. When he increased
the attention-catching factors in the coupon, the number
returned increased.

Emotions are powerful determiners of behavior and have
an importance in advertising that should not be overlooked.
They represent or are closely associated with all of one's
needs and desires that lie back of buying behavior. A commodity is bought to satisfy a need or desire, so that advertisers must realize that they are selling not a commodity,
but the satisfaction of some human desire. One does not
buy an automobile for itself alone; one buys it because it
will save time getting places, because it makes long trips
and sightseeing possible, and because it satisfies a man's
wish "to keep up with the Joneses." It is purchased
because it satisfies desires.

---

[6] Poffenberger, A. T., *Psychology in Advertising* (McGraw-Hill Book
Company, New York, 1932).

A few of the more important desires are love, hunger, health, the parental desire, the desire for rest and comfort, for self-assertion, and the desire to escape from danger. The advertiser can make his product much more attractive to the consumer by knowing his desires and showing the consumer how the commodity will satisfy these desires.

Belief, feeling, perception, memory, intelligence, association, and suggestion are other types of behavior that must be considered by the advertiser; careful study of them will repay him.

Psychological techniques applied to advertising

The present knowledge of human behavior has been established by the use of research techniques which are not limited in their application to pure science but which may be used in advertising.

Dr. Henry C. Link [7] has pointed out the importance of the advertising theme, which is the vehicle used to associate the need for a commodity with a particular brand of product. The advertiser's prime purpose is to establish his product so firmly in the buyer's mind that when the need for that commodity arises the buyer will immediately think of the advertiser's particular brand. To test how well a theme has done its job of associating need and brand, Link devised the "Triple Associates Method," which provides that a test question be asked of a large number of consumers. A particular brand of soap flakes was advertised by the theme, "Stop those runs in stockings." After the advertisement with this theme had been run once in a leading women's magazine, a large number of housewives

---

[7] Link, H. C., "A New Method of Testing Advertising Effectiveness." *Journal of Applied Psychology,* February, 1934.

were asked the test question, "What commodity advertises, 'Stop those runs in stockings'?" Forty-eight per cent of the housewives responded with the correct brand name. At the same time this successful theme was published, a second theme for a second commodity was printed in five of the leading women's magazines. The second commodity's advertisement had the advantages of color and a more favorable position over the soap-flake advertisement, and yet when the theme for the second was tested by the Triple Associates Method, only about eight per cent of the housewives knew what brand it advertised. It is apparent that themes vary greatly in their effectiveness, and that the Triple Associates Method will show which are successful.

Dr. Daniel Starch [8] explains many scientific methods of investigating advertising problems. One of Starch's techniques, which is used to evaluate the effectiveness of the various elements of an advertisement, he calls the "Laboratory Field Method." Each element, such as theme, illustrations, copy, and borders, is studied separately. For example, if an automobile advertisement were being prepared, about fifteen themes like "carefree service," "comfort on any road," and "low gasoline consumption" would be written, each on a separate card, and the set of cards would be presented to about one hundred potential customers. Each person would then be asked to rate the themes from the one that most aroused his desire to buy to the one that was least effective. An average rating for each theme would then be determined, and the one with the highest score would be used in the advertisement. By the same technique all the other elements in the advertisment can be tested.

The Laboratory Field Method and the Triple Associates

---

[8] Starch, Daniel, *Principles of Advertising* (McGraw-Hill Book Company, New York, 1923).

Method are only two of a large number of scientific techniques for investigating advertisements, but they illustrate that it is possible to build advertisements around facts rather than around opinions.

PSYCHOLOGY IN LAW

Psychologists have long been interested in the accuracy of testimony, or the fidelity of report. In spite of the honesty and sincerity of the witness, psychological experts have found that neither a written nor a verbal report can be accepted as wholly truthful. That even an appreciable per cent of statements made by trained observers is erroneous has been scientifically demonstrated. The inability to report correctly all that happens in a given series of events is due to two factors. First, one does not observe all the events. This is well illustrated by the ability of a good magician to baffle his audience. If the audience observed everything the magician did, everyone would see through his tricks. Second, very few people remember all they observe. Most people think they remember their experiences, but actually there is a considerable amount of "filling in" of forgotten points. This tendency to fill in and round out a story to make it seem logical gives rise to considerable error. In law most of the evidence is given by untrained observers, and this inability to give accurate testimony has considerable significance.[9]

The scientific detection of guilt by the so-called lie detector is another contribution of psychology to law. By the use of this instrument, which is based upon changes in blood pressure and in the rate of respiration, guilt or inno-

---

[9] Münsterberg, Hugo, *On the Witness Stand* (Clark Boardman Company, New York, 1923).

cence can be determined with a high degree of accuracy. Unfortunately a criminal need not consent to the use of the "lie detector," since in doing so he is giving evidence against himself, and furthermore, in most courts evidence obtained with the machine is considered circumstantial and so of questionable value. The lie detector is very useful, however, in police work. When the suspect being tested by it sees he is giving himself away he is likely to confess without any coercion. Clues that lead to concrete evidence also are often uncovered when the machine is used.

Psychology has also been used in studying the confusion involved in trade-name infringements. In determining insanity and intelligence of criminals, psychology has had an important relation to law. Knowledge of child behavior has, of course, been of great value in juvenile-court work.

* * * * *

Only a bird's-eye view of the content and methods of psychology can be treated in this type of book. In the first part of this chapter an attempt was made to cover some of the topics considered in general psychology. But the reader must not assume that these topics are the only ones considered by this science. Many important problems, such as thinking, reasoning, association, suggestion, and others, have not even been touched. Likewise, in the section on applied psychology, the field of medicine, selling, education, art, music, politics, and the like, in which psychology is making increasing contributions, have had to be omitted. The materials which have been included, brief though their discussion has been, are fairly representative and should enable the student to formulate some idea of the content and applicability of psychology.

BIBLIOGRAPHY

General Psychology

Garrett, H. E., *Great Experiments in Psychology* (D. Appleton-Century Company, New York, 1930).

Goodenough, Florence L., *Developmental Psychology* (D. Appleton-Century Company, New York, 1934).

Robinson, Edward S., *Man as Psychology Sees Him* (The Macmillan Company, New York, 1932).

Hoskins, R. G., *The Tides of Life* (W. W. Norton Company, New York, 1933).

Woodworth, R. S., *Psychology, Third Edition* (Henry Holt & Company, New York, 1934).

Applied Psychology

Burtt, H. E., *Employment Psychology* (Houghton Mifflin Company, Boston, 1926).

Burtt, H. E., *Legal Psychology* (Prentice-Hall, Inc., New York, 1931).

Link, H. C., *The New Psychology of Advertising and Selling* (The Macmillan Company, New York, 1932).

Paterson, D. G., *Physique and Intellect* (D. Appleton-Century Company, New York, 1930).

Crane, G., *Psychology Applied* (Northwestern University Press, Evanston, Ill., 1935).

CHAPTER VI
Modern Criminology

GEORGE B. VOLD

University of Minnesota

THE PROBLEM OF CRIME AND ITS DEFINITION

CRIME is a phenomenon as old as society. It is part of the problem of conformity and non-conformity that is raised whenever human beings carry on life in groups and not as isolated individuals. Human society has developed on the basis of life in groups. In the course of time certain ways of behaving have come to be approved as good and essential for the future welfare of the group, and therefore set up as the correct and proper standards of behavior. Other ways of behaving are frowned upon and disapproved of as inimical to group welfare. Individuals who persist in ways that are disapproved of are then considered undesirable and dangerous, and action is taken to compel conformity. The compulsion applied may be informal and unorganized, as happens when an individual violates the accepted standards of good manners and etiquette, or it may be formal and according to prescribed routine, as in the case of law enforcement by the police and other government officers.

Conformity and non-conformity are always relative to the standards of behavior of some group. Conduct which is approved in one group may be viewed as undesirable and dangerous in another. The "causes" of this variant be-

havior, which is called crime, are the same basic factors of
heredity and environment that operate in connection with
all human behavior. The significant differences are those
of social definition; what behavior is considered proper and
worthy of support, what behavior is questionable, and what
behavior is definitely not to be approved—these are the
questions that determine the meaning of the vague terms
"crime," and "criminal behavior."

The criminal is a person whose behavior does not follow
the general pattern approved by law-abiding society—crime
is behavior which does not have the support and approval
of law-abiding people. Law, in general, is the formulation
through political processes of the common principles of
behavior and standards of conduct subscribed to by the
established political majority. Conformity to this common
standard of behavior is the substance of law-abiding behavior; non-conformity is the essence of criminal activity.

Considerable confusion appears in the literature of present-day criminology, due to the frequent assumption that
the causes of crime lie in the individual or in his objective
environment. The control of crime is therefore said to be
affected either by treating a "sick" or "maladjusted" individual or through correcting an anti-social condition in the
environment. The student should keep in mind constantly,
however, that in many cases the "cause" of criminal behavior is identical with that of non-criminal behavior. It is
frequently not a question of behavior at all in the individual
sense, but a clash of codes and conflicting group definitions
of what constitutes approved conduct. Groups and interests, whose codes and definitions are hopelessly diverse, are
in constant conflict, jockeying for position and influence to
secure the assistance and approval of the "state" in making
their particular view the "law" of the political community.

The recent history of prohibition legislation in the United States offers a good illustration of this whole problem. The behavior of the "bootlegger" of prohibition days was essentially the same as that of the liquor dealer of the present post-prohibition period, in that both have sought to supply at a profit to themselves the existing demand for alcoholic drinks. Yet one was a "criminal," the other is a more or less respectable businessman. The difference between the two is not one of behavior, but of community attitude towards the liquor problem. Whether making and selling alcoholic liquors is good business or criminal behavior depends upon which groups or interests dominate the political life of the community so that their views become the "law," and the police power of the state is called upon to compel conformity.

THE AMOUNT AND COST OF CRIME

How much crime is there in the United States? In other countries? How much does it cost? Is crime increasing or decreasing?

These important questions are continually being asked, but no simple or direct answers are possible. No one knows accurately the total amount of crime in any country in the world. Official criminal statistics deal only with certain identifiable aspects of the work of law enforcement, such as the number of offenses reported to the police, or the number of persons arrested, or the number of criminal cases tried in particular courts, or the number of persons received into penal and correctional institutions during any given year, or who are present in such institutions on any given day.

While such statistics give some idea of the extent of the activity of law-enforcement agencies, they cannot be taken as reliable indices of the total amount of crime. Many offenses are never reported; many innocent people are arrested and later released without prosecution; many guilty persons never are apprehended. The great variations from state to state, and country to country, in such matters as the definition of criminal acts, police and court practices, and habits and attitudes of the people toward law and police, all add to the uncertainty and inaccuracy of ordinary criminal statistics. These differences frequently make accurate comparisons quite impossible. Authorities are therefore skeptical of the validity of comparisons between crime rates in different political jurisdictions, or between one country and another.

What do the statistics show, such as they are? Figures indicating the approximate number of prisoners in the United States in 1933 in all types of civil penal institutions have been prepared by the Bureau of the Census and may be summarized in the following simple tabular statement.[1]

Type of Institution	Estimated Total Present on Jan. 1, 1933	Estimated Total Committed during 1933
Federal prisons and camps..............	12,276	8,333
State prisons and reformatories..........	137,721	59,204
County and city jails and workhouses..	51,436	608,484
Institutions for juvenile delinquents.....	32,198	17,967
Totals	233,631	693,988

On the basis of an estimated 1933 population of 125,693,-000, this means that the commitment rate for the year to

[1] *Prisoners: 1933,* p. 1 (United States Department of Commerce, Bureau of the Census, Washington, 1935).

all penal institutions was 552 per 100,000, or one commitment for every 181 persons in the population. These figures obviously do not adequately measure the amount of criminality in the country, since many persons escape arrest and conviction, and since the figures do not take into account those who are arraigned in court and are acquitted, discharged, placed on probation, or given suspended sentences. It should be noted that only about ten per cent of those committed are sent to prisons or reformatories, the "higher institutions of crime."

Another approach may be had through police statistics. For the year 1935, the police of 1,423 cities with a population of 57,222,252 reported as known to them a total of 744,863 offenses.[2] Less than one per cent of this huge number involves the offenses of murder and manslaughter, whereas larceny constitutes over sixty-six per cent. The three offenses, larceny, robbery, and burglary, constitute ninety-five per cent of the total, and the remaining five per cent are distributed as follows: murder, 0.5 per cent; manslaughter, 0.4 per cent; rape, 0.6 per cent; aggravated assault, 3.5 per cent. The most common offense, by far, is that of petty theft, since only twelve per cent of the larcenies reported involved a value of fifty dollars or more, while over twenty-five per cent were for five dollars or less.

These figures, however, do not measure the total number of offenses known to the police. The classification of offenses used in the *Uniform Crime Reports* has been divided into two parts, and the above figures are for the Part I offenses only. Part II includes such offenses as drunkenness, disorderly conduct, prostitution, gambling, and traffic violations, which are not yet reported with suffi-

[2] *Uniform Crime Reports,* Vol. VI, No. 4, p. 6 (Washington, 1935).

cient uniformity or accuracy to warrant tabulation on a national scale. Partial tabulations that have been made indicate, however, that the number of offenses in the Part II group is many times that in the Part I group, probably constituting as much as eighty per cent of the total. On the basis of these figures, it has been estimated that there must be approximately ten million offenses of all kinds that come to the attention of the police each year. That means one offense for every twelve or thirteen persons in the population.

Is crime increasing? Spectacular newspaper presentations of crime news frequently give that impression, but careful statistical analysis does not bear out the fact. It is much more nearly accurate to think of the crime rate in any given state or district as relatively constant, varying

DAILY AVERAGE, OFFENSES KNOWN TO THE POLICE—74 CITIES OVER 100,000 POPULATION, JANUARY THROUGH DECEMBER, 1935

(Total Population: 21,023,312, estimated as of July 1, 1933)

Class of offense	1935	1934	1933	1932	1931
Criminal homicide:					
(a) Murder and non-negligent manslaughter	4.0	4.5	4.9	4.5	4.5
(b) Manslaughter by negligence	2.6	2.6	3.8	3.2	4.2
Rape	4.4	3.8	3.6	3.6	3.5
Robbery	39.0	46.6	54.9	57.0	60.3
Aggravated assault	29.5	30.9	33.2	26.8	30.6
Burglary, breaking and entering	208.2	228.7	240.7	231.9	217.7
Larceny, theft	492.3	498.6	496.8	462.2	454.9
Auto theft	171.0	199.1	215.7	224.5	263.8

only slightly from year to year. Even a major economic and social catastrophe like the depression beginning in 1929 has apparently affected the volume of crime but little. This is well illustrated in the accompanying table. The most apparent as well as significant fact indicated by these figures is the comparatively slight variation from year to year in the daily average number of offenses reported to the police. In the case of robbery and auto theft there has actually been a consistent decrease in the average daily number of offenses during the hard years of the depression.

Crime rates vary greatly from one section of the country to another. Thus the homicide rate, as computed from the Bureau of Vital Statistics reports on the causes of death, for the registration area as a whole for 1933 was approximately nine per 100,000 population, but this ranged from a rate of about one per 100,000 in Maine and North Dakota to twenty-six in Florida. This difference is greater and certainly just as significant as the fact that while the rate for the country as a whole was about nine per 100,000, England and Wales had a rate of less than one per 100,000 population. Why this difference in rates between the two countries? Why should the New England States and the West North Central States have rates not very different from those of England and Wales, while the rest of the country has very much higher rates? Is it due to the presence or absence of the death penalty? Or to the way the laws are enforced?

Much better statistical information on crime than is now available will be necessary before these questions can be answered completely. Some aspects of the problem, however, are clear at the present time. The death penalty, for example, appears to have little or nothing to do with the amount of homicide prevalent in a given state. Life in

Maine is just as secure as in New Hampshire or Vermont, yet these states inflict the death penalty while Maine does not. Conditions in the New England States are such that life is valued highly in the *mores* of the people. Hence there is but little killing in any of the states in this region, regardless of what penalty is prescribed for murder. The same, in general, is true of the West North Central States. This is in contrast to the group of Southern States where homicide rates are high. In this section of the country there are a number of situations in which neighborhood opinion not only condones murder, but also expects it of a man as a matter of "honor." In some sections of this part of the country a man isn't worthy of respect if he doesn't kill anyone who insults his wife, or his mother, or sister,— all, of course, being insults to his own dignity and "honor." Such insults are always forthcoming, or fancied, and the murder rate shows a corresponding increase. Differences in the crime rates of different countries probably reflect similar deep-seated differences in the life values and attitudes of the people rather than the efficacy of any particular penalty, or of any system of law enforcement.[3]

There are no reliable figures on the total cost of crime in dollars and cents. In 1931 the National Commission on Law Observance and Enforcement published a large volume dealing with this question and listing some of the economic costs of crime, but refused to attempt even a guess as to the significant total sum. Others have been less cautious, and "estimates" and "guesses" abound. The usual figures given run from ten to fifteen billions of dollars. Some of the more definite figures include items such as the follow-

---

[3] See Vold, George B., "Can the Death Penalty Prevent Crime," *The Prison Journal*, October, 1932, pp. 3–8 (Pennsylvania Prison Society, 311 South Juniper Street, Philadelphia).

ing [4]: 52 millions of dollars as the cost of the federal system of criminal justice; 52 millions for state prison and penal agencies; 250 millions for state and local criminal justice; 160 millions for private watchmen; 106 millions for insurance against robbery, burglary, and auto theft; 300 millions loss of productive labor of prisoners and law-enforcement officers; and so forth. Regardless of the element of error in such estimates, it is evident that this country spends annually a staggering sum in support of its "crime industry."

TRAITS AND CHARACTERISTICS OF APPREHENDED CRIMINALS

What kind of people are criminals? The most nearly accurate answer is perhaps to say that those who get caught resemble the population from which they come much more closely than they resemble one another. In other words, what peculiarities of race, nationality, religion, education, mental ability or defectiveness, occupation, economic status, and political beliefs characterize the population of any particular locality or community will also characterize the criminals that come from that community. Just how much, or in what specific ways criminals differ from other people in the communities from which they come is very difficult to say, because there is relatively much less information available about the conditions and traits of the general population than is at hand relating to prisoners.

As a class criminals probably differ among themselves as much as the individuals of the law-abiding group. Some are very bright, some very dull, but most of them are merely of average ability; some are exceptionally well educated,

---

[4] These figures have been selected from the report of the National Commission on Law Observance and Enforcement, *The Cost of Crime*, No. 12, June, 1931, Washington, D. C.

others are illiterate, but most of them have about the average education possessed by other average individuals in their age, sex, occupation, race, or nationality group in the general population.

Exceptions from this general rule should be noted. Youth is peculiarly the age of crime. The age groups with highest rates per 100,000 population, both of arrests and of commitments to major penal institutions, are ages nineteen and twenty for both male and female. The average age of persons committed to major penal institutions in 1933 was approximately twenty-six years (26.2 for men; 25.8 for women), while the average age of those arrested in 1935 whose fingerprints were checked by the Federal Bureau of Investigation was 27.6 years. In 1930–1933 the median age of persons killed while committing crimes, in Chicago, was twenty-five years. Yet this youthfulness of the criminal is no new phenomenon. The median age of fifty-two robbers hanged in England during the years 1710–1719 was twenty-six.

This concentration of crime in the young adult years is apparently a phase of the endless quest of the individual for a place in the sun. The first serious test of whether a person is going to conform to the established ways of behavior, or deviate from these ways and receive censure as a non-conformist, comes in the period when the young man or young woman is getting out from under the parental roof and striking out independently. Therefore the "wildness" and "rebellion" of youth is traditional. So also is his criminality—that is, his non-conformity to the behavior incorporated into the criminal law.

Sex is similarly a selective factor. In the general population the distribution of the sexes is approximately equal, that is, there are about equal numbers of males and females.

Among apprehended criminals the distribution is far different. In 1933 twenty times as many males as females, in proportion to total population of each sex, were committed to state and federal prisons and reformatories, while for county and city jails the ratio of commitments was fifteen males to each female. Of persons arrested in 1935 whose fingerprints were checked by the Federal Bureau of Investigation, ninety-three per cent were males.

The selective aspects of such statistics are indicated by the fact that females are arrested in much larger numbers than males for sex offenses, though the sexes are generally involved in equal numbers in such offenses. The difference in rates for the sexes in connection with other offenses is probably due, in similar manner, in large part to social elements such as moral codes, ideas of chivalry, and other conditions of life, and not to any fundamental sex factor as such.

The opinion has been widely held that criminals are a group of defectives, either physically or mentally, or both. This is a plausible explanation of criminality, but one about which there is very scant exact information. The number of prisoners who are lame, deformed, maimed, or otherwise defective is considerable, but there is no comparable information for the same age and sex groups in the general population from which one can determine statistically the relative frequency of such defects in the two groups. It seems reasonable to suppose, however, that since the defective is handicapped in the competitive struggle both for a livelihood and for a mate, he is likely to compensate by attempting to take short cuts to the achievement of money and power. Trickery, deceit, theft, blackmail, and ruthless exploitation of others may result. Such compensation for inferiority is commonplace in all walks of life and by no means peculiar to criminals. How much more frequent it is among criminals than among non-criminals remains to be established.

Mental defectiveness and psychopathy are even more subtly related to criminality than physical defectiveness. In the enthusiasm of the early mental testing movement in the United States, some writers [5] used the terms feeblemindedness and delinquency as synonymous, and the conclusion was general that the great majority of criminals were definitely feebleminded. With the development of more critical research methods, these early conclusions have been considerably modified. A crucial question involved is that of determining the average adult intelligence of the general population. Eminent psychologists are in sharp disagreement not only in the matter of conclusions and interpretations, but also with regard to methods and procedures in testing the intelligence level of adults. The result has been extreme confusion and disagreement in published studies dealing with the intelligence level of criminals. A recent careful study sought to equate the differences in procedures used by different testers and concluded that the ratio of mental deficiency among delinquents and in the general population was about 1.2 to 1.[6] This shows some preponderance of feeblemindedness among criminals but indicates no very great difference in intelligence level between the two groups. What differences there are may be due primarily to the fact that the feebleminded who commit crimes are easier to detect and convict than those of higher intelligence.

[5] Goddard, H. H., *Juvenile Delinquency,* p. 21 (Dodd, Mead & Company, New York, 1921).

[6] Zeleny, L. D., "Feeblemindedness and Criminal Conduct," *American Journal of Sociology,* January, 1933, Vol. 38, pp. 564–578.

Mental disorders of the psychotic (insanity) type have also been pointed to in attempted explanations of criminal behavior. Insanity (psychoses) is not one disease, as the man on the street may assume, but a large number of diseases differing from one another as much as measles from whooping cough. Some of these (paresis) are definite and may be relatively easily diagnosed, others (dementia praecox) are very indefinite and of uncertain diagnosis. Of all admissions to state and federal prisons and reformatories in 1933, 1.6 per cent were diagnosed as psychotic. In some institutions the rate was as high as five per cent, in many others much less. Generally those states that have a well-developed program for the care of their insane show low percentages among those so diagnosed in prison admissions. No good information is available regarding the extent of insanity in the general population, though it is quite probably somewhat less than among prisoners. The point to note is that no large percentage (from one to five) of prison admissions are insane. It should be recalled, also, that many psychotic persons do not become criminal. There is evidently no necessary connection between crime and insanity, though obviously mental derangements of the violent type can easily lead to behavior contrary to law.

Mental derangements of the psychopathic type also play a part in personality disorders and the peculiarities of behavior that may be criminal. Some psychiatrists classify psychopathic personalities into three groups, the egocentric, the inadequate, and the vagabond. The egocentric is characterized by extreme selfishness, defiance of authority, aggressive attitudes of superiority, and a general tendency to self-reference. The inadequate reacts with sulking and a display of dependence and helplessness which may be compensated for by certain gestures of exaggerated superiority. The vagabond type seeks to escape from existing difficulties, either by literally running away or through some substitute escape mechanism such as alcoholism, drug addiction, or other symbolic avenue of escape. Just how or why psychopathic personalities develop has not been adequately determined, but it seems clear that the organization of attitudes represented by this term takes shape early in life and manifests itself in a variety of different situations.

One of several versions of the psychoanalytic theory of how psychopathy enters into criminality may be stated in simple terms. The psychopathic personality is one characterized by mental conflict between adjusted and unadjusted portions of the personality. This conflict in the unconscious mind gives rise to feelings of guilt and a desire for punishment to remove the guilty feeling. The criminal commits the crime in order to be caught and punished. Unconsciously motivated errors leave "clues," so the authorities may apprehend him and administer punishment.[7] The same conflict process may be found in the neurotic, but in such cases remains within the person, and in the absence of injury to others the only "punishment" secured is confinement to a hospital.

The principal objection to such a theory is that it far outruns established facts and related data. The method of diagnosis of psychopathic personality is far from standardized and not very objective. There is a constant tendency to take the fact of criminality as the principal symptom of psychopathy and then to turn around and explain the criminality by the alleged psychopathy.[8] Present statistics

---

[7] For case illustrations see Alexander, Franz, and Healy, William, *Roots of Crime* (Alfred A. Knopf, New York, 1935).

[8] For a good illustration of this see the editorial in *Journal of the American Medical Association,* August 2, 1930, quoted by M. Ploscowe,

on the frequency of occurrence of psychopathic personality in prisons and reformatories are therefore quite unreliable and relatively meaningless. Massachusetts and New York institutions report approximately ten per cent of the commitments to the state penal institutions as suffering from psychopathic personality, while Illinois psychiatrists report seventy-five to eighty-five per cent.[9] This surely indicates a greater difference among psychiatrists and their methods of diagnosis than in the mental conditions of these respective prison populations.

Other personality disorders are also said to play an important part in the production of delinquency and criminality. Especially important are the after effects of encephalitis lethargica, the so-called post-encephalitic personality, and various disorders due to the improper functioning of the endocrine glands. Many individual case studies of criminals seem to show some interrelation between such disorders and specific criminal acts, but as yet no statistical evidence is available regarding the frequency of similar disorders in the general population where no delinquency occurs. In the meantime, endocrinology is developing rapidly as a scientific body of knowledge and in the future may be expected to offer new and more specific bases for the explanation of many kinds of behavior disorders. For the present, however, there is no good knowledge of whether such disorders are more or less frequent among the criminal than among the non-criminal. The assumption is natural that since crime is abnormal social behavior, the criminal must be abnormal mentally or emotionally. It is very probable

Report on Causes of Crime (National Commission on Law Observance and Enforcement, Washington, D. C., No. 13, Vol. I, p. 57).

[9] Sutherland, E. H., *Principles of Criminology*, p. 100 (J. B. Lippincott Company, Philadelphia, 1934).

that such differences and abnormalities may be discovered and isolated, but the only fair conclusion at the present time is that nothing consistently significant has as yet been demonstrated.

The point to note in all this discussion of the characteristics of criminals is that as far as mental and physical traits are concerned, they are very much like everyone else. The peculiarity that makes them criminal is, apparently, not mental or physical defectiveness but a social condition. They are loyal to and identify themselves with people whose way of life differs significantly from that of the law-abiding. In the case of many offenses against property, such as fraud, misrepresentation, and illegal sales, the line between criminality and merely "sharp" business practice is so indefinite that behavior differences between the two are completely indistinguishable. In the field of this kind of crime, it is highly probable that those who are detected and apprehended have less ability, less finesse, and are simply the clumsy and inefficient practitioners. Since the essence of criminality is to be found in the particular social definition given an act, and not in the nature of the individual who commits the act, there is nothing peculiar in the fact that the biological and psychological traits of criminals are largely indistinguishable from those of other people.

ENVIRONMENT AND CRIME

To what extent is the criminal the unfortunate victim of circumstance? Given a background of poverty with its associated vicious accompaniment of exploitation, under-privilege, ignorance, poor homes, poor neighborhoods, and undesirable companions, what chance has the individual to go straight?

In the intelligent discussion of this question the dramatic

dichotomy of whether crime is caused by heredity or environment can not be entertained. Human behavior is always the product of *both* heredity and environment, and since both are *indispensable,* the question of which is the more important becomes futile. The general interrelation is clear. Capacities and abilities, together with their organic structures, are functions of heredity, and as such always *set the limits* beyond which no development can take place. The particular form which these capacities and abilities are to take, and how they are to develop, are primarily functions of the environment. Nature supplies the raw materials, the qualitative substance out of which personality is built; the pattern of approved character and behavior that is developed comes from the surrounding culture, that is, the social environment. In the end product, the human personality as we know it, the two fields of influence are inextricably interwoven.

Environment is no single thing, no simple or uniform set of circumstances. It is rather something acquired or experienced by the individual. Home and neighborhood influences, the pull of companions, and the force of example, poverty, ignorance, vicious surroundings—all these, with many more, affect individuals in a variety of ways. No relationships in this field are either direct or very clear. Many delinquents have come from poor homes, have had uneducated parents, have been surrounded by conditions of poverty and squalor, have associated with bad companions, and so on.[10] Is that the reason why they are delinquent? Not necessarily, for the very same conditions are equally true of many non-delinquents. Since most of the population is in the lower economic income groups, it fol-

[10] See Chapter I, "Sociology and Culture," pp. 34–37.

lows that most delinquents and criminals will likewise come from these groups. Information on the distribution of income in the various classes and groups in the general population is not sufficiently accurate to warrant any general conclusion regarding the specific influence of low income in producing delinquency and crime. Certainly there is no absolute or necessary relation between poverty and crime.

Available factual data throw little light on this question. During the last forty years the money income and the standard of living of the American people have advanced considerably. The level of educational achievement is higher, illiteracy has been greatly reduced, there is probably less child labor, and recreational and cultural facilities are more fully developed than they were in the earlier years, but there has been no corresponding decrease in crime and delinquency. "Improving" the environment in such external ways has apparently had little or no effect on crime or delinquency rates. Moreover, the catastrophe of the recent economic depression, with its ten or twelve millions unemployed, its eighteen or twenty millions on relief, and other millions suffering sharp economic reverses, did not lead to any sudden or great increase in crime in any part of the country. Crime rates have remained surprisingly constant during the whole course of depression and recovery.[11]

The environmental influence in criminality operates in more indirect and subtle ways. A simple illustration will help make this clear. Most people are familiar with the common roadside figure of the young man (frequently a high school or college student) "thumbing" a ride. In Minnesota, as in many other states, there are laws against

---

[11] Vold, George B., "The Amount and Nature of Crime During the Depression," *American Journal of Sociology,* No. 6, May, 1935, Vol. 40, pp. 796–803.

this practice. Anyone who so behaves violates a state law and is therefore guilty of a minor criminal offense. Few, if any, however, of the people who "thumb" rides have any sense of guilt, or any feeling that they are criminals. As long as the immediate intimacy group in which they move expresses no disapproval, the individual is content. It may even be a matter of boasting in the group, something of which the individual is proud. So it happens that an otherwise respectable and upright individual has no feeling of guilt and no hesitancy about violating the law. The man who would be mortified to have his friends see him on the street begging ("Brother, can you spare a dime") has no similar feeling about begging rides from passing automobiles. To him and his group the one is smart and clever, the other "cheap" and reprehensible.

The conduct of the individual is largely guided by the code of behavior of his immediate intimacy group, the group with which he identifies himself and to which he looks for standards of life values and worthwhile behavior. If his group approves, it matters little that the police disapprove, that there may be a law against some particular behavior, that it may be contrary to accepted notions of public welfare. It is the environing group that gives the individual his standards of approved or disapproved behavior, not his equipment of biologically determined physical or mental traits.

The misfortune of the modern world, especially modern America, is that there are so many groups in contact, with different values, different ideas of what is "correct" or approved behavior. These differences are frequently irreconcilable, and the resulting clash of codes, and of individuals who subscribe to different codes, becomes literally a struggle for survival.

Law represents the view of those individuals and groups who are able to compromise minor differences and agree on a general statement of position to be taken. But support of such a generalized statement or "law" always ranges from one extreme to the other. There are those whose views are accurately expressed by the statute and who are wholly satisfied; there is another group who would have preferred a different formulation of the law and are not enthusiastic in support but nevertheless conform; another group may be somewhat hostile but not very active in opposing or resisting the law; and finally there are those in full and determined opposition to it, and who make a virtue of resistance.

It is this situation that brings about the paradox that for every law that is adopted there is simultaneously created a new group of potential law violators. For the same reason, any society which needs a great deal of law to control or regulate its behavior is also likely to have a great deal of crime, that is, violation of law. Law becomes necessary when the influence of custom, of tradition, and of loyalty to group ideals becomes impotent through the clash of endless group differences. The same underlying factors of social disorganization and heterogeneity of groups and behavior codes that lead to a multiplicity of laws, lead also to excessive criminality, that is, violation of these laws. It appears, therefore, that law and crime are two mutually complementary aspects of the same underlying social condition.

Any attempt to determine the influence of environment on criminality must consider this complex pattern of interrelations. The externals of home, school, neighborhood, companions, church membership, income, and recreation become important only as they may be indirect indices of this deeper and more fundamental relationship.

THE MACHINERY OF JUSTICE

The smooth functioning of the machinery of justice requires close coöperation and careful integration of the various more or less independent procedures of apprehension, identification, prosecution, court and legal processes, and disposition and treatment programs. Americans, in general, live on a national scale, move about from state to state, and have business and other interests in more than one state or community. Criminals similarly operate on a national scale, but the machinery of justice, with a few exceptions, is organized on a strictly local and state basis. As the means of communication develop and mobility of population increases, this problem in cultural lag continues to grow in seriousness.

The police

Early American society took its pattern of law-enforcement machinery from the English system of justices of the peace, constables, and sheriffs. Even today a large part of the duties and functions of these officers are a reflection of their traditional background. Colonial cities established a "night watch" consisting of civilians who took their turn in guarding the community and thus supplementing the work of the regular constables of the traditional system. Practically every colony seems to have adopted some such system; Boston establishing its night watch in 1636, and the others as increasing size made the need imperative. As the cities grew, separate "day police" became necessary, and for a period of time there was an impossible system of separate day and night police forces with resulting demoralization and irresponsibility. A unified day-and-night police under single direction was established by New York in 1844 and by Boston in 1854. Similar unification of separate police forces followed rapidly in other American cities.[12]

The police are a much criticized group whose task is far from simple or easy to perform. They are expected to detect and arrest criminals, protect the innocent, help prevent crime, as well as perform a variety of miscellaneous tasks such as supervising traffic, handling crowds, making inspections, and writing reports on special investigations. In all this the police have very few legal rights beyond those possessed by ordinary citizens. A policeman can make a legal arrest without a warrant only if a felony has been committed and if he has reasonable grounds to believe that the man arrested committed the crime. If the act is a misdemeanor he must have a warrant, unless he happened to witness the occurrence. Any citizen has practically that same authority. If a policeman arrests a person illegally, he can be prosecuted for false arrest, as can any other citizen.

The police are expected to enforce the law—all laws—but the statutes of every state include many laws which make criminal a number of acts which prevailing public opinion does not regard as crimes. Good examples are the laws against theatrical performances on Sunday, betting on horse races, playing slot machines, and selling liquor after closing hours. Such laws are to be found on the statute books of many states, yet there is nowhere any strong sentiment in their favor. "Respectable" people violate such laws with impunity and think nothing of it, yet the police are theoretically expected to "enforce the law" with unflagging zeal. The average city has applicable to it approximately 16,000 statutes, federal, state, and city, which may

[12] Fosdick, Raymond B., American Police Systems (D. Appleton-Century Company, New York, 1920).

call for enforcement by the police.[13] Obviously no single
individual—prosecuting attorney, policeman, or judge—
can know all these in any given city, to say nothing of the
comprehension of the ordinary citizen who lives with and
maintains this plethora of laws.

The most common criticisms of police forces in the United
States are that they are blunderingly ineffective, brutal, and
corrupt. The extent to which these criticisms may be justified varies, of course, from one jurisdiction to another.
Inefficiency and ineffectiveness are frequently closely related
to three characteristic shortcomings in the organization of
American police administration: first, that in the selection
of recruits no high standards of individual ability or competence have prevailed; second, that no extensive or systematic training for the job has been provided as a general
rule, either before appointment to the force or afterwards;
third, that most police departments are seriously under-
manned and inadequately equipped. Brutality and corruption are to some extent a reflection of these same factors,
but are more directly related to the existing level of public
morality. Bribery, pressure, special favors, inside information for private profit, "protection," and "graft" are by no
means limited to the police aspects of government.[14]

Efforts that are being made to develop more effective
police systems center in attempts to modify and correct the
above-mentioned conditions. Civil service (such as it is)
now applies to the selection of policemen in practically
every American city of 100,000 or over, but seldom involves
the personnel of the smaller places, rural officers, or the
assistants and deputies of elected officials. The level of
mental ability among American policemen nevertheless is

[13] *Ibid.*, pp. 46-57.
[14] Sutherland, E. H., *op. cit.*, pp. 31-38, 203-212.

notoriously low. If the level of ability possessed by at least ninety per cent of the freshmen in a class-A university is taken as a basis of comparison, over seventy-five per cent of policemen throughout the country fall below that standard.[15] In the selective processes of employment competition, it is evident that the police forces of the country have secured an undue proportion of the incompetent rather than a choice selection of the specially competent.

Why are there so many incompetent policemen? Part of the answer certainly is to be found in the low salaries and unsatisfactory conditions of work that usually prevail. With salary levels only a little above that of unskilled workmen, one should expect to find the ability level also near that of the untrained day laborer. A recent survey of police conditions in Minnesota revealed that outside of the three larger cities, full-time pay for patrolmen ranged between seventy-five and one hundred dollars per month. Including chiefs and other officers, the average annual police salary was around $1500 in the smaller cities and villages, approximately $1950 for the larger cities.[16] Obviously such a low salary schedule will not foster the development of career service made up of competent individuals. The prevailing absence of systematic police training and the common story of inadequate or obsolete equipment reflect other effects of this same drive for what is sometimes called "economy."

The development of police systems on a statewide basis and the extension of power and personnel of the Federal Bureau of Identification of the United States Department

[15] See *Report on Police,* No. 14, June 1931 (National Commission on Law Observance and Enforcement, Washington, D. C.).
[16] See *Survey of Police Training,* Regents Examining Committee, University of Minnesota, 1937.

of Justice are two types of recent change that point the way for further improvement in the efficiency of police administration. By 1932 there was some form of state police in thirty-eight states. There were ten regular uniformed state police systems; twenty-one were highway police, of which nine included general powers over crimes other than traffic; four were state organizations of sheriffs; the rest were governors' reserves.[17]

Opposition to the extension of state police forces has come principally from organized labor, and its fear that such mobile units will be used wherever needed in the state for the purpose of breaking up strikes. Such fear is not without foundation. State police have been so used at times, especially in Pennsylvania, but it must be remembered that municipal and county forces have also been used for this purpose. Labor is beginning to recognize that as a general rule, state police forces are likely to be much more careful and restrained on strike duty than the deputies and "special agents" supplied by private detective agencies, who are generally used to supplement the regular police forces in times of labor troubles involving violence.

Federal agencies are drawn into law enforcement only when the crimes involve specific federal laws, interstate relations, or use of the mails. In the last few years a number of additions have been made to the federal criminal code, notably kidnapping involving the crossing of state lines or the use of the mails (the "Lindbergh law") and the robbery of a national bank. It is this extension of authority which lies back of the increased activity of the operatives of the Federal Bureau of Identification, the "G-men." As soon as these officers had jurisdiction, with their opportunity of

---

[17] Sutherland, E. H., *op. cit.*, p. 215.

crossing state lines without interference and of carrying out a centrally controlled "man hunt," several notorious gangs of kidnappers and bank robbers of the Dillinger type were soon completely broken up and cleaned out. The success of the federal agents in dealing with certain types of criminals is a reflection of the increased efficiency that comes from centralization of administration, careful selection of men, and rigorous training for the work to be done.

The prosecutor

The two principal officials involved in the effective operation of the court system are the prosecutor and the judge. Of the two, the prosecutor is probably the more important since the initiation of criminal proceedings rests primarily with him. He determines whether a particular case shall be prosecuted, what offense to charge and in what degree, whether to accept a plea of guilty to a lesser offense, and so on. He is responsible for the organization and presentation of evidence before the court, and the effectiveness of a "case" frequently varies directly in proportion to the ability and skill of the prosecutor.

In the United States the prosecutor is generally elected, with all that this practice means in the matter of politics and pressure groups. Not only must he be a successful political campaigner, but to be reëlected he must be careful not to offend unduly important groups of voters, such as labor unions, church groups, war veterans, the local Rotary Club, and the chamber of commerce. The most promising suggestion for the correction of this situation is the proposal that the prosecutor be appointed by the governor from a list nominated by the judicial council, subject to removal by the governor on recommendation or hearing by the judicial council, but otherwise holding office for life.

Political pressure would thus be side-tracked and have no direct opportunity to strike at this important office.[18]

In misdemeanor cases prosecution generally starts with the complaint by the victim, or by some witness to the offense who may be willing to appear in court. Frequently the policeman who makes the arrest is also the complaining witness.

In felony cases prosecution is much more complicated. The prosecutor must present at least part of his evidence before the inferior court at the time of arraignment. If the inferior court decides that the evidence is sufficient, the individual is held for the grand jury, or in less serious cases, bound over to the district court for trial. Historically the grand jury originated to protect the citizens against persecution by an over-zealous prosecutor, but as a rule, it has come to function as little more than a rubber stamp for this official. Under the law the grand jury generally has considerable authority to conduct investigations and review the affairs of government. This power has generally been ineffective, due mostly to the absence of skilled investigators on the jury itself and to the lack of funds with which to employ such special personnel.

The judge

Under the system prevailing in most states in the United States, the judge is elected by the voters of a given district for a relatively short term of office, usually from two to six years. In practice this has meant that the dominant political machine has sought to place its candidates on the bench. Making judicial positions appointive, however, does not take them out of politics—it may merely add them to the

---

[18] See discussion in Sutherland, E. H., *op. cit.*, p. 249.

party's patronage system. Since political parties are not dissociated from the underworld of organized crime, either system may place on the bench individuals who are not above the suspicion of having personal or professional interests in the success of various kinds of lucrative "rackets."

Despite the theory of a non-partisan judiciary, there is no simple solution of the problem of politics in the selection of judges, any more than in the case of many other officials not directly on the firing line of party differences. Under the elective system, endorsements by responsible professional groups, like the bar associations and other organizations with a public welfare point of view, help to indicate to the voters who are the competent individuals, but cannot remove the fact of genuine political differences. Many serious students believe that an appointive system, operating in coöperation with wide-awake and active citizens' organizations of a non-partisan character, will best provide for the removal of "politics" from the selection of judges yet insure that the courts will reflect the basic changes taking place in public attitudes on political questions.

The judge traditionally has had two principal functions: to preside over the trial and to impose sentences on those convicted. Into the first go his skill and legal training, as well as his strength of personality. Judges vary greatly in their conduct of a trial. Some interpret their role merely as referee, to see that the lawyers fight fairly; others take a vigorous part in proceedings and exercise considerable control over the whole trial procedure. Most students of the problem are inclined to favor changes in present rules and procedure to increase the control of the judge over the course of an entire investigation, not only in the immediate conduct of a trial.

The judge's function in imposing sentence is one that

has generally been carried out in a traditional manner reflecting the older classical theory of law and criminology. Under this the judge was not expected to determine the sentence in detail; his duty was to impose, like an impersonal machine, the sentence provided in the law. Modern tendencies, however, have modified the law to a considerable extent, permitting wide latitude of choice on the part of the judge in the sentences imposed. This is on the general theory that the treatment accorded a guilty person should be adapted to the particular case. The information brought into a trial gives the judge little basis for exercising intelligent discrimination in passing sentence. A recent New Jersey study revealed that with six judges rotating among the courts and dealing with the same types of cases, wide variations in sentences followed. One judge sentenced fifty-eight per cent of convicted persons to imprisonment, another only thirty-four per cent. One judge placed less than twenty per cent on probation, another over thirty-one per cent, and so on.[19] Similar differences have been pointed out in other places.

Two types of recommendations have developed to correct this problem of sentencing. One is to provide the judge with special information relating to personal history and character from probation department investigators, psychiatrists, and other technical experts, in order that he may be in a position to exercise more intelligent judgment. The other suggestion is to remove entirely the sentencing function from the court and to transfer it to a special commission of experts or some other administrative board. This is on the theory that the extent and type of treatment

[19] See, Gaudet, F. J., Harris, G. S., and St. John, C. W., "Individual Differences in the Sentencing Tendencies of Judges," *Journal of Criminal Law and Criminology*, January, 1933, Vol. 23, pp. 811–818.

needed for a particular person can be determined only as
the course of treatment progresses, and can never
satisfactorily be determined in advance, regardless of
supplementary information supplied the court by advisory
experts.[20]

WHAT SHOULD BE DONE WITH CRIMINALS?

Probably no question relating to present-day penal administration has had more people genuinely puzzled than that
of what to do with the criminal. Many people feel that
our prisons are too comfortable, that the life of the convict is too easy, and that therefore it has little or no effect
in keeping him from repeating his crime or in deterring
others from taking up criminal careers. Others are impressed
with the need for understanding the individual criminal
and the circumstances surrounding the crime, not in order
to punish, but in order to readjust and correct the behavior
disorders that have led the unfortunate persons into crime
and antisocial conduct. These two positions are essentially
irreconcilable, and the supporters of each find it difficult
to understand and hard to sympathize with the views of
the other. A brief review of some aspects of modern
penology will therefore be useful in providing perspective
for an understanding of the underlying problem.

Changing penal philosophy

Under the impact of modern science, thinking about the
causation and control of human behavior has undergone
profound change. During that period of history which was

[20] See discussion in *Report of the Minnesota Crime Commission, 1934,*
pp. 8–13 (printed by Minnesota Law and Order League, Inc., St. Paul,
Minnesota).

marked by the formation of the major national states of Europe, there also developed definite legal codes defining criminal behavior and prescribing punishment as the form of treatment. This was in accordance with the emphasis then placed on man as a rational being, a creature who lived by thinking out the solutions of his problems and by carefully weighing the relative desirability of different possible ways of behaving. Man was conceived of as a free moral agent whose every act was the result of free-will choice. If he chose to do wrong rather than right, he alone was to blame. The object of penal treatment, under such a system of thinking, was to affect the individual's will so that he would choose lawful instead of criminal behavior. The instrument for affecting the will was thought to be fear of punishment. Each crime must therefore carry a penalty providing sufficient punishment so that the individual would fear it so much that the anticipated pleasures of the crime would not attract him. In short, his *fear of punishment* for wrongdoing would lead him to choose lawful behavior.

This general view is what is commonly called "the classical school of criminology" and is associated especially with the writings of Cesare Beccaria [21] (1764). It had its most definite formulation in the French codes of 1791 and 1810, but has appeared in one form or another in the criminal laws of every country affected by European civilization. American criminal law reflects this same philosophy. The criminal act is taken as the unit to be dealt with, and punishments are graduated according to the seriousness of the offense, without reference to the nature of the individual criminal, provided he is sane. The doctrine of "equality

---

[21] Beccaria, Cesare, *Dei delitti e delle pene* (Paris, 1786). (Translated under the title *Crimes and Punishments*.)

before the law" emphasized the rigid application of this rule regardless of the social or economic condition of the offender.

The impact of modern science on thinking about penology comes first with the writings of Cesare Lombroso in 1876.[22] He turned attention from the criminal act to a consideration of the individual. He assumed that crime was like any other event in nature, due entirely to combinations of natural factors, not to the influences of supernatural spirits, not to the operation of a metaphysical entity called the "will." The explanation of criminal behavior was to be found in the nature of the individual himself. With this approach he developed a theory of a recognizable physical criminal type under which the criminal was thought to be a throw-back to earlier animal stages of human development. Crime was to be controlled in the same manner in which man controls other events in nature, that is, by understanding the situation and acting according to whatever "natural laws" apply. This view has been called the "positive" or "scientific" school of criminology, also known as "Lombrosian" or "Italian," from its early distinguished contributor. The object of penology, according to this school, was to protect the general welfare of society. An individual found to possess criminal nature would be put away, either permanently by execution, or through imprisonment until his nature could be changed and he could be trusted with freedom.

These two schools of thought represent fundamental differences in opinion about what should be done with the criminal. The terms "punishment" and "treatment" connote this same difference. Punishment implies the imposi-

---

[22] Lombroso, Cesare, *L'Homme criminel* (Paris, 1895, Second French Edition).

tion on an individual of a prescribed amount of pain or discomfort, the amount determined in advance of application according to existing notions of how serious the offense is thought to be. Treatment implies a diagnosis of the individual's needs and an adjusting of procedure to suit the particular case. Treatment can therefore never be predetermined, cannot be administered *en masse;* it calls, not for equality or similarity of procedure in all cases, but for variations to meet the special conditions of each case. For the legal principle of the same punishment for the same crime, regardless of who the individual may be, the positive school would set up a system of treatment varying with each case, the extent and duration to be determined from the course of the treatment in progress.

Much of the criticism of present-day penal methods reflects the difference in point of view represented by these two schools of thought. To those who believe in punishment, treatment procedures seem "soft," and amount to "coddling"; to those who oppose punishment, it stands as the symbol of medievalism and pre-scientific thinking, the refuge of the ignorant and misinformed.[23]

Institutional treatment of offenders

Prisons and reformatories are the principal institutions of the present for the care of those who commit major crimes. For those guilty of misdemeanors there are the jails and workhouses; special institutions have been developed for juveniles, women, and the insane. The present practice is in striking contrast with that of an earlier day when punishments were direct and personal, some form of bodily abuse such as whipping, burning, or flaying alive;

---

[23] *Cf.* Sutherland, E. H., *Principles of Criminology,* p. 324 ff. (J. B. Lippincott Company, Philadelphia, 1934).

a period when confinement was used only for safe keeping until a court could pronounce judgment and set the exact punishment. In this country today the only ultimate threat in punishment is imprisonment; fines, suspended sentences, probation, and parole all carry the alternative threat of imprisonment and no other form of punishment.

The developments which brought this about seem to have been a reflection of changing public attitudes toward the use of corporal punishment. The ferocity of the earlier punishments was part of the whole attitude of the time. It was an age of calloused indifference to pain and suffering. Children were beaten at home and in school, the wife was subject to similar correction by her husband, the servant by the master, and, in general, the life of the weak and lowly was one of frequent flogging and other physical abuse. With corporal punishment a commonplace, punishments for crime had to be even more spectacular and terrible. Hence the large number of capital offenses with their public hangings or beheadings, whipping to death, burial alive, and other gruesome refinements through the whole horrible list of man's inhumanity to man.[24] What historians call the humanitarian movement was a revulsion against this prevailing cruelty and abuse of the weak and unfortunate. Judges and juries became more and more reluctant to impose the ferocious sentences provided by law, and substituted instead incarceration in existing jails and workhouses, until then used principally for those awaiting trial and for vagrants. Presently, even in the case of serious crimes, imprisonment for long terms, even for life, was substituted for the cruel corporal punishments prescribed by law. This led to the building of more elaborate prisons,

[24] Ives, George, *A History of Penal Methods* (Frederick A. Stokes Company, New York, 1914).

serving the double purpose of better safety and a place where those confined could be made to work for the profit of the community. This is the background of the existing system of state prisons in the United States. Massachusetts built the first such institution in 1805, and by 1824 most states had followed suit. As new states were added, one of the necessary institutions that soon appeared was the state prison.[25]

The early prisons were built largely without consideration for the health or comfort of the inmates. Cells were small, with little light or air, and sanitary facilities were of the most primitive kind possible. This has given way to present-day engineering and architectural features that make the average modern prison about on the level of a workingmen's hotel, from the standpoint of physical comfort. The ordinary inmate confined in the average prison in the United States today leads a reasonably comfortable life from the standpoint of creature comfort. Food is generally wholesome and available in sufficient quantities, but not as a rule served with any regard for the niceties of life. The same is generally true of clothing and cell equipment, bedding and furniture.

The modern prison has developed its present relatively high-class service for taking care of the physical comforts of the inmates without having arrived at any answer to the basic question of what should be done with criminals. The consequence is that it is neither an institution for punishment, in the earlier sense of the word, nor a place where adequate treatment can be provided. As a place of punishment it is too comfortable; as a place for treatment it can only provide routine mass uniformity, instead

[25] Barnes, H. E., *The Evolution of Penology in Pennsylvania* (Bobbs-Merrill Company, Indianapolis, 1927).

of the individualization of programs which good therapeutics requires.

Numerous experiments in prison organization and administration have been tried in recent years, both in this country and abroad. Russia, Belgium, England, Germany, Italy, and Japan have all experimented with the problem of what to do with criminals in a prison. Procedures vary, but in every one of these countries developments point more and more to treatment as the ideal, not punishment. These prisons are run, as far as possible, to find out what the individual needs, what his capacities are, and then to give him training within the institution so that he can hold a job and make other necessary adjustments to his fellow citizens when he is released. This ideal is far from having been generally realized, but developments point in that direction, not to a revival of the theory of punishment as the goal of prison administration for the future.[26]

The indeterminate sentence, probation, and parole

As the purpose of imprisonment has come more and more to be thought of in terms of rehabilitation, several developments have taken place that increase the control of administrative boards, as opposed to the courts, over the length of sentence to be served. Originally the legislature fixed definite penalties for each offense. The tendency has been to modify this so that the legislature sets only maximum

---

[26] For an account of a few of the more recent developments, see the following:

Gillin, John L., *Criminology and Penology,* pp. 340–379 (D. Appleton-Century Company, New York, 1935).

By the same author, *Taming the Criminal* (The Macmillan Company, New York, 1931).

Koerber, Lenka von, *Soviet Russia Fights Crime* (E. P. Dutton & Company, New York, 1935).

and minimum limits, within which some other authority determines the exact sentence to be served. Courts at one time set the exact sentence within the limits placed by the legislature, but the tendency has been for this practice to give way to a system whereby the judge merely imposes the statutory limits (or other limits fixed within those determined by statute), leaving the determination of the exact length of sentence to an administrative body usually called the parole board. This is what is known as an indeterminate-sentence system.

This relaxing of the immediacy of the control of the court over sentences is in keeping with the tendency developing to substitute the ideal of treatment for that of punishment. In theory, under the indeterminate-sentence system, it is possible for the prison authorities to vary the length of sentence of individuals convicted of the same crime in order to adapt it to the needs of the particular individual. The principal agency to put into effect this plan of unequal sentences has been the parole board. Parole boards must determine three important questions for each case: first, whether the individual shall be kept in prison for the full statutory maximum or released after serving a shorter term; second, if the individual is to be released before the expiration of the maximum, at what particular time is such release to be effected; and third, what special conditions should surround the individual subsequent to his early release, in order to insure that he will not again return to a life of crime. If the parole board could really answer these three questions with complete success, the system of individualization of treatment would be far on its way to realization.

A serious difficulty interfering with the successful operation of the parole system has been the fact that parole boards usually have little or no control over the details of prison administration. The prison, therefore, operates under a routine system satisfactory to the prison authorities, while the parole board tends to become merely an agency for fixing the length of sentence. In practice it has little to say about the kinds of sentences that individuals have to serve, and the question of how long or short a time a man stays in prison is important primarily in connection with any changes that may be taking place in his own character and personality. Until the function of releasing individuals from prison can be closely integrated with the program of training supplied in the institution, the two are likely to work at cross purposes, or at best, to become futile through lack of coöperation.

Parole has been extensively criticized as a system of "jail delivery." Newspapers frequently report that a suspected perpetrator of a crime is on parole, and imply that if the parole board had not released this individual there would have been no new crime. The problem, however, is much more complex than the newspaper stories indicate. It must be remembered that practically all prison sentences terminate in the release of the inmate and result in his return to the community. The average length of sentence served is only about two and one-half years. Therefore, whether the parole board releases a man or not, in the majority of cases it would be only a matter of a short time before he would be automatically released by expiration of the sentence. It is a matter of mathematical necessity, unless prisons are to burst from overcrowding, that every year there must be approximately the same number of people released as are received. Parole authorities are therefore confronted with the practical situation that they must release a very large number of individuals every year to make room for new ones who are coming in. The mistake that they may make is in releasing the wrong type of individual. Sometimes they feel compelled to parole inmates, about whose future conduct they are skeptical, to create space for new convicts.

How can a parole board approach the problem of selecting the good risks and rejecting the poor ones in deciding upon whom to parole? That problem has so far been handled only through common-sense judgment on the part of parole boards. That is, they conduct a somewhat superficial examination of the case, call the inmate for a hearing, and study evidence and opinions that they can get on the case. Under this system there is little other than the "hunches" and the experience of parole-board members to guide them in estimating the probable future conduct of a man on parole. It has been demonstrated, however, that this problem can be approached with the methods of science, and that it can lead to what appears to be a much better selection of parolees. A number of research studies [27] have pointed out that it is possible to apply the methods of statistical prediction to this problem and determine with fair accuracy in advance the probable conduct of a person on parole. Serious students of the problem hope that such methods may begin to be applied by administrative bodies

[27] Good illustrations of such studies are:

Burgess, E. W., "Factors Determining Success or Failure on Parole," in *The Indeterminate Sentence and Parole* (Illinois Board of Parole, Chicago, 1928).

Glueck, Sheldon and Eleanor, "Predictability in the Administration of Criminal Justice," in *500 Criminal Careers* (Alfred A. Knopf, New York, 1930).

Vold, George B., *Prediction Methods and Parole* (Sociological Press, Hanover, N. H., 1931).

Monachesi, E. D., *Prediction Factors in Probation* (Sociological Press, Hanover, N. H., 1932).

in control of parole. That seems to be one of the principal fields where modern scientific methods might be more definitely integrated with present-day penal administration.

Probation represents a further development of this same effort to vary penal treatment in accordance with the needs of the individual case. It consists in the substitution for imprisonment of time served under the jurisdiction of a supervising agent. That is, instead of being sentenced to prison a convicted person is required to submit himself to supervision and control by a probation agent, but he is left in the community and generally required to continue his regular work. Or, if he has no job, he is required to find one and stick to it. It is thus a substitute for imprisonment imposed by the court. It really is an alternative sentence. It differs in this respect from parole, which follows a period of incarceration in an institution. Both substitute time served outside of the institution, under supervision, for the customary time served within the institution. The wise selection of probationers, just as of parolees, calls for judgment and full knowledge of the case. In this field, too, it has frequently been true that action has been based primarily on common-sense guesses; and it has been demonstrated that scientific methods could be applied more definitely than they are now being utilized.[28]

What does the present penal system accomplish?

The crucial test of any practice is the pragmatic one of results. Society has found it necessary to protect itself against the criminal. It maintains an elaborate system of law, courts, and institutions. Does the present system

[28] See Monachesi, E. D., *Prediction Factors in Probation* (Sociological Press, Hanover, N. H., 1932).

operate in such a manner that those who have had experience with it return to the law-abiding group and commit no more crime? Has it "cured" the criminal of his non-conforming conduct?

A final answer to these questions is impossible, owing to the nature of the problem. It is impossible to know what the situation would have been had we had some other penal system, or had we used no coercion at all. Criminology, like medicine, is never entirely sure whether the patient recovers because of, or in spite of, the efforts made in his behalf. There is considerable reason, however, for viewing our present penal system with grave concern. At the present time over half of the persons arrested have been previously arrested. From sixty to seventy per cent of those who enter a prison have been either in jail or in prison before. This suggests the inevitable conclusion that the course of penal treatment has not been particularly successful in persuading its subjects not to return to crime. A recent careful study [29] found that out of five hundred individuals released from a reformatory, approximately eighty per cent had returned to careers of crime within five years. If this is at all true of other similar institutions, it would seem that the term "reformatory" is decidedly a misnomer.

It is a growing conviction that the existing penal system is not accomplishing very much, in the rehabilitation of criminals, that leads the serious student to call for a fundamental reconsideration of the whole problem. Penology must be recognized as a field calling for research and scientific methods, for trained experts and impersonal scientists

---

[29] Glueck, Sheldon and Eleanor, *500 Criminal Careers* (Alfred A. Knopf, New York, 1930).

instead of politicians and excitable sentimentalists. A way must be found to make applicable to this field the essential conditions of science, freedom of investigation, and experimentation. Until that is done, little change in the outcome need be expected.

CRIME PREVENTION

The old adage about an ounce of prevention being worth a pound of cure applies with especial force to the field of criminal behavior. Ideas about prevention are likely to reflect the theories held regarding causation. Those who feel that crime is due largely to biological defects of the individual are likely to look to sterilization and eugenics for prevention; those whose explanation of causation is stated in economic terms are likely to think that the way to prevent crime is to modify or overhaul the economic system; and those who conceive of crime as a phenomenon of individual psychology are likely to look to mental hygiene and psychotherapy for prevention.

It is well to realize that there is no one thing that constitutes crime prevention. Prevention is not general but specific. Whatever influences an individual not to follow the pathway of criminal behavior becomes a preventative agent. It may be a job in one case, a friend in another, medical advice in a third, an invitation to a party in a fourth case. Jobs for all, a friendship club for all, or free medical advice for all, would probably not, however, be very useful in crime prevention. The problem is to organize the right group of influences for the particular individual. Without attempting to present an outline of Utopia, the paragraphs that follow will review briefly a few of the efforts at crime prevention that are currently being made.

Helping the near-delinquent

It is clear that a large number of the criminals of tomorrow are the problem children of today. They are misunderstood, antagonistic, rebellious, and almost ready to attack the society which, for some reason, is not taking care of them. Slowly but surely their personalities are developing a definite set of antisocial attitudes which may grow into overt criminal careers. Such children must be made to feel that their lives and their work are important, that they belong, that there is a place for them in the world of worthwhile enterprise. How can this be done? An illustration from the records of a visiting teachers' organization shows what was done in one case.

In a congested part of the city, Lucy, aged eleven, was losing her interest in lessons and coming late to the afternoon sessions, offering as her excuse that "mother was sick," but her classmates whispered that she was talking to boys on the street. The visiting teacher went to the home, and learned from the bed-ridden mother that Lucy had changed since coming under the influence of a playmate and neighbor, Elsie. . . . The visiting teacher saw the necessity of getting acquainted with Elsie, and went to her school. Elsie had an unenviable record for repeating grades, half-day absences and poor conduct. The visiting teacher took this record to her home and questioned the parents. They were aware that Elsie had been left back and that there were days when she had not been at home, as well as absent from school. But they had been unable to find out where she spent her time. The visiting teacher was not content with her explanation that she went "no place," and finally, by careful probing, based on a study of the record card, showing at what date the child began to go wrong, got the information she was seeking. The visiting teacher communicated with the Children's Society, and within a few hours they had put under arrest a man who had been teaching immoral practices to Elsie and a score of her friends. The man was convicted and sent to jail. The visiting teacher took the children under her care and looked out for their recreation and companionship as well as for their lessons. Lucy became at once, when the friendship with Elsie was broken, a better student at school. Her mother lived to see her become again her faithful nurse and housekeeper. . . . Elsie, because her habits of delinquency were stronger, needed careful supervision at school and at home, but the home cooperation was secured, . . . her interest in school was aroused so that she is now making normal progress.[30]

Every community has agencies that are attempting to rehabilitate character. Notable among such groups are the Boy Scouts, the Girl Scouts, the Y.M.C.A. and the Y.W.C.A. groups, the Big Brother and Big Sister organizations, as well as many local neighborhood groups without formal name or organization, which, nevertheless, absorb the child's interests and energies and direct these into socially desirable channels. It must be remembered that the child comes into the world without culture and with no inkling of how he is expected to behave. Every agency and influence that tends to give him a pattern of behavior compatible with that prevailing in the group at large helps prevent delinquency and crime by making of the individual a conformist, not a non-conformist.

Mobilizing existing community resources

Most communities have many agencies that seek to prevent crime, some professional and some non-professional organizations, yet it is a common experience that there is difficulty in getting them to work together. Thus a relief organization works independently of a recreational group, and both the child and his parents experience the disconcerting situation of being parcelled out among many different agencies with no unity underlying the efforts put forth in their behalf. The community needs some form of coördinating agency to act as a central clearing house for handling cases and problems as they develop. Successful effort along this line has been developed in a number of

---

[30] *The Visiting Teacher in the United States,* pp. 44–45 (Public Education Association of the City of New York, 1921).

places, but perhaps the outstanding illustration in the United States is the work of the Los Angeles County Coördinating Council.[31] Effective organization in Los Angeles has been secured through the county probation office. In other communities it has centered in other agencies. The important point is that there is a central agency in the community through which cases needing help are cleared so that the proper agency will be put in contact with the particular individual needing help. No new agencies are created; existing agencies are simply helped to function more efficiently.

Reducing community and general social disorganization

Community life of the present day is characterized by extensive disorganization. People move in and out, have only casual contacts with one another, and do not acquire any feeling of responsibility for maintaining the community as an existing organization. This is likewise true, to a considerable extent, of modern life in general. The moral sanctions and codes of the past have come to have less and less authority in the present. Individuals are living more and more with no feeling of responsibility for their conduct to their neighbors, or to their fellow men in general.

The need for reducing social disorganization is, therefore, widely recognized, but it is not entirely clear just how this is to be accomplished. It is clear that a well-organized and smoothly functioning social order is characterized by individuals who share common ideals and aspirations, whose fundamental needs are satisfied in their social relations,

---

[31] See Scudder, Kenyon J., "The Los Angeles County Coördinating Council Plan," in *Preventing Crime,* edited by Glueck, Sheldon and Eleanor, (McGraw-Hill Book Company, New York, 1936). This book, incidentally, gives an account of twenty-four experiments in crime prevention now in progress in the United States.

whose economic needs are adequately taken care of, and who participate in relations in which individuals trust one another. Efforts to promote these conditions may therefore be taken to be important steps in the move to lessen the prevailing disorganization. Activity that promotes educational development, that broadens the opportunity for each child, that attempts to reduce the paralyzing burden of poverty, and that helps to give each individual a self-respecting position in the world, may be counted as significant in helping to reduce the magnitude of existing social disorganization.

Eliminating the defectives

Most communities have a considerable number of individuals who are definite liabilities because of some fundamental defect. Some are feebleminded, insane, epileptic, or otherwise suffering from incurable disease and therefore permanent wards. All such individuals are seriously handicapped in an effort to find a place in the world, and from this class are recruited a number of criminals. Any far-reaching program of crime prevention must, therefore, seek to eliminate or otherwise care for this group.

Some students of the problem have suggested sterilization of the unfit as the only conclusive solution. Aside from the question of morals and ethics involved, this suggestion raises the important practical difficulty of how to determine who is defective, or what degree of defectiveness to tolerate. In any case, it is clear that some form of permanent care must be provided for this group. In those cases clearly indicating inherited defectiveness, sterilization would seem to be the wise procedure.

The fundamental need in dealing with this group is not difficult to outline. It calls for the early diagnosis of defectiveness and the beginning of specialized care adapted to the particular individual's defect, whether that involves isolation, segregation, sterilization, or merely hospitalization and vocational guidance.

Underlying specific efforts at crime prevention, however, is the perplexing problem of general culture conflict and the differing notions of what is the good life. Until we, as a society, come to hold more homogeneous notions of what behavior is "right" and what behavior is "wrong," we cannot expect to decrease very materially the existing amount of crime, nor prevent the continual recruiting of criminals.

BIBLIOGRAPHY

Gillin, John L., *Taming the Criminal* (The Macmillan Company, New York, 1931).

Gillin, John L., *Criminology and Penology* (D. Appleton-Century Company, New York, 1935).

Glueck, Sheldon and Eleanor, *500 Criminal Careers* (Alfred A. Knopf, New York, 1930).

Glueck, Sheldon and Eleanor, (editors), *Preventing Crime* (McGraw-Hill Book Company, New York, 1936).

Hopkins, E. J., *Our Lawless Police* (Viking Press, New York, 1931).

Koerber, Lenka von, *Soviet Russia Fights Crime* (E. P. Dutton & Company, New York, 1935).

Alexander, Franz, and Healy, William, *Roots of Crime* (Alfred A. Knopf, New York, 1935).

Borchard, E. M., *Convicting the Innocent* (Yale University Press, New Haven, 1932).

Fosdick, Raymond B., *American Police Systems* (D. Appleton-Century Company, New York, 1920).

Fox, L. W., *The Modern English Prison* (G. Routledge & Sons, London, 1934).

Moley, Raymond, *The Tribunes of the People* (Yale University Press, New Haven, 1932).

Nelson, Victor, *Prison Days and Nights* (Little, Brown & Company, Boston, 1933).

Ulman, Joseph H., *A Judge Takes the Stand* (Alfred A. Knopf, New York, 1933).

Zelitch, Judah, *Soviet Administration of Criminal Law* (University of Pennsylvania Press, Philadelphia, 1931).

Pound, Roscoe, *Criminal Justice in America* (Henry Holt & Company, New York, 1930).

Shaw, Clifford R., *The Jack Roller* (University of Chicago Press, Chicago, 1930).

Shaw, Clifford R., *The Natural History of a Delinquent Career* (University of Chicago Press, Chicago, 1931).

Sutherland, E. H., *Principles of Criminology* (J. B. Lippincott Company, Philadelphia, 1934).

CHAPTER VII
History

LAWRENCE D. STEEFEL

University of Minnesota

WHAT IS HISTORY?

THE student who wishes to learn what history is must begin by recalling that the word is used in many different senses. Three of them are of especial importance. The term *history* may mean (1) the past itself, (2) the written record, the narrative or description of the past, or (3) that discipline or branch of study which is concerned with the past. We speak of the statesman who makes history, of the author who writes history, and of the scholar who studies and teaches history. Yet even when this source of confusion has been noted, it is not easy to give a concise and clear definition of history as a subject of study. Most early definitions were too narrow or too subjective; most contemporary ones are so broad that they can hardly be said to define.

This difficulty of definition is due to the poverty of our language, which has one word to denote various things. This word confuses history as a finished product with the raw materials from which it is written, the subject matter of history with its method of work, and the events of the past with the narrative account of them. It is due also to the fact that every age has looked at history from its own point of view and has tended to select from the past, for emphasis in history, those personages, events, and develop-

ments that are of particular interest to it. Each generation, it has been said, recreates history in its own image,
and each generation tends to rewrite history to suit its own
point of view. The progress of political democracy, for
example, was accompanied by increased emphasis on historical study of the life of the masses. The period of exhaus-
tion and recuperation that followed the World War was
marked, naturally enough, by a renewed interest in the
study of similar periods in the past, particularly of the
decades immediately following that other world war which
came to an end in 1815. The period from 1815 to 1848,
which had been regarded as rather dull and unimportant
in the pre-1914 epoch, was seen in the light of post-War
experience to be one of real significance. Let us try, then,
not to find a definition that will explain history at all times
in all places, but to understand it by discussing the scope,
methods, and purposes of historical study.

THE SCOPE OF HISTORY[1]

If we accept as a rough working generalization the statement that history as a subject of study deals with the past,
we are at once faced with the problem of scope. At one
time, it was assumed in the world of western civilization
that the universe was created miraculously in the six-day
period described in the Book of Genesis. The date could
be calculated with reasonable accuracy, and the problem
of the scope of history was an easy one. History began
with Adam and Eve in the Garden of Eden and came down
to the present. At the most, it was a matter of less than

---

[1] Owing to the scope of history and the breadth of its materials, it has
seemed best to include only one chapter on it in this book. This limitation
should not be interpreted as any indication of the importance of the subject
in the Social Sciences. (Editor's note.)

seven thousand years. The records might be scanty, but they gave a consecutive picture of the development of the human race. Today we know that the universe is much older, how old we do not and perhaps never shall know. Geologists believe that the earth is at least one or two billion years old and that man has inhabited it for some 250,000 years. Written records, our most important sources for the knowledge of the past, go back only some five or six thousand years. What now is the scope of history?

In theory, there is no reason why all of this past should not be included under history. Even if we limit our definition a little by saying that history is concerned not with the past as such but only with changes that have occurred in the past, the whole universe and each of its parts has its history. A few men have attempted to write history on this broadest of scales, notably H. G. Wells in his *Outline of History*. In practice, however, most historians have been content to leave many fields that are theoretically history to specialists in other disciplines. The history of the heavenly bodies is normally part of astronomy; the history of the earth's crust, of geology; the history of plants and animals, of palaeontology, botany, and zoölogy; the history of the human body, of biology. "History," as normally understood, means human history, and the controversy over its scope seldom goes beyond that sufficiently broad field.

It will be admitted without question that the scope of history is steadily increasing. Time marches on, and as it does so, it extends history at one end. At the other, the beginning end, history moves back in the time scale as fresh discoveries of records increase our knowledge. But the question remains: With how much of the human past shall the historian concern himself? On this point there have been two mains schools of thought in the past generation.

On the one side are those historians, called by their opponents "old," who emphasize the "traditional" limitation of history to political, religious, and perhaps economic phases of human activity.   The opposing school, which calls itself "new" and, especially in its more extreme statements, exaggerates both its own newness and its opponents' limitations, maintains that every manifestation of human activity is properly part of history.   "In its amplest meaning," wrote James Harvey Robinson in one of the early essays on the "new" history, "history includes every trace and vestige of everything that man has done or thought since first he appeared on the earth.   It may aspire to follow the fate of nations or it may depict the habits of the most obscure individual.   Its sources of information extend from the rude flint hatchets of Chelles to this morning's newspaper.   It is the vague and comprehensive science of past human affairs.   We are within its bounds whether we decipher a mortgage on an Assyrian tile, estimate the value of the Diamond Necklace, or describe the over-short pastry to which Charles V was addicted to his own undoing.   The tragic reflections of Eli's daughter-in-law, when she learned of the discomfiture of her people at Ebenezer, are part of history; so are the provisions of Magna Charta, the origin of the doctrine of transsubstantiation, the fall of Santiago, the difference between a black friar and a white friar, and the certified circulation of the *New York World* on February 1 of the current year.   Each fact has its interest and importance; all have been carefully recorded." [2]   Gradually but surely the view is winning recognition that anything and everything in the human past may be a proper part of history, and the controversy between the "old" and the

[2] Robinson, J. H., *The New History* (The Macmillan Company, New York, 1912). By permission of the publishers.

"new" historians is really not so much on the scope of history as on the relative importance of its component parts. The totality of past human activity is so great that every student of history, "old" or "new," must make a selection of the facts and aspects of history which he will emphasize. His selection will depend on the existence of evidence about them, and his judgment of their interest and significance.

HOW WE CAN KNOW ABOUT THE PAST

Only an infinitesimal part of our knowledge of the past comes from direct observation. The life of an individual is but a tiny fraction of historical time, and his direct knowledge of history is limited to what he himself does, thinks, sees, and hears. For all the rest of history, his knowledge is indirect; it is obtained from the recorded evidence of what others have done, thought, seen, or heard, or else deduced from materials that have survived from the past. Where history as past actuality has left no traces, there can be no history as narrative, and for a large part of man's life on earth, that is the case.

The materials or "sources" from which the historian derives his knowledge of the past are of many kinds. In the days when historians based most of their work on the narratives of others, sources were classified as "primary" or "secondary." Primary sources were those based on more or less direct observation by contemporaries of the events described; secondary sources were those composed from primary sources. This distinction is still used to some extent, but a better method of classification is to divide sources into "tradition" and "remains." By tradition, we mean sources which consciously aim to give information about the past; by remains, those sources which came into existence in the normal course of human activity, which were not intended to convey historical information but from which knowledge of the past can be deduced.

Oral tradition, which after a time is often preserved in writing, is important chiefly for the history of primitive peoples, but arises to a limited extent even in modern times among more advanced civilizations. It includes sagas, ballads, and epics, legends, anecdotes, and proverbs. Usually, the history is so blended with myth that oral tradition is more important for the conclusions about former conditions that may be deduced from it than for the statements of fact that it contains. Written tradition includes inscriptions carved on buildings or monuments, like those recounting the exploits in war and hunting of ancient Assyrian monarchs or the virtues and great deeds of more recent heroes. It includes genealogical notes, such as the tables preserved in the temples of ancient Egypt or the lists of the descendants of the passengers of the *Mayflower*. It includes the annals and chronicles in which the monks of the Middle Ages noted down from time to time the news that came to their ears or the portents that they observed. It includes biography, autobiography, memoirs, diaries, pamphlets, and newspapers. It includes histories in which men have tried to record the truth about their own or about more remote times. Pictorial tradition may include maps of areas, plans of cities, portraits, pictures of scenes or events. Recent developments in photography suggest that pictorial tradition will be of much greater importance for historians in the future than it has been for those in the past. The various types of tradition have this in common, that they are intended to preserve knowledge of the past.

Remains are anything and everything that has survived from the past. They include the fragments of bone, long buried in glacial drift, that prove that men walked the earth before the date of Adam and Eve. They include "kitchen middens," the refuse that enables us to draw conclusions about the diet of primitive man; the bone or flint tools and weapons that show the development of technology among peoples who have left neither oral, written, nor pictorial tradition; the pictures in the caves at Altamira, which show that long before the Egyptians and Greeks there were men who were interested in art. Remains include long-buried cities, brought to light by the spade of the archaeologist; the surgical instruments found at Pompeii; the buildings, roads, boats, bridges, tools—in short, all of the material relics of human activity that dot the earth. Remains include also written documents of many kinds, mortgages, contracts, bills of sale, stamped in cuneiform characters on the bricks and cylinders of Babylonia and Assyria; the day-by-day records of the managers of Egyptian estates; the charters of medieval kings; the laws, court decisions, and administrative papers of the modern states; the accounts and correspondence of businessmen; and others, too numerous to mention. The study and interpretation of these remains is a fascinating business. Sometimes a single discovery will open up a part of history that has been almost unknown; the Rosetta stone, with its inscription in two types of hitherto unreadable Egyptian characters, and in well-known Greek, opened the real study of ancient Egypt. Again, the discovery of the tomb of Tutankhamen, in our own day, brought vividly before our eyes the splendor of the Pharaohs.

These two broad classes of historical evidence are not mutually exclusive. It sometimes happens that a source for one purpose is tradition, and that for another it is remains. Macaulay's *History of England* is classed as tradition in that it narrates a period of history, but it becomes remains for a student of the history of historical writing. In spite of frequent overlapping, the division of sources into these two broad classes serves a practical purpose. Each class is of value in its own way; each involves certain probable errors; and each is subject to special forms of criticism and interpretation.

The methods of criticism and interpretation of historical sources have become in modern times a technical matter of considerable intricacy. They are studied chiefly in advanced courses and are of interest primarily to the professional historian. It is perhaps enough if the elementary student or general reader of history knows that the historian must be constantly on guard against being misled by his sources. Documents are sometimes forged. In the Middle Ages, particularly, even monks seem to have had few scruples about creating titles to real estate. Occasionally documents are forged to fool the historian, or statues of modern manufacture are buried to mislead the archaeologist. An author may deliberately deceive in an attempt to improve his own reputation or to blacken that of an enemy. More often the deception is due less to deliberate distortion of the facts than to national, political, religious, or personal bias. It has even been said that when you find a history written without bias, you can be sure that the author's prejudices coincide with your own. Anyone who reads the accounts of the origins of the World War, or the treatment of the "New Deal" measures in Republican and Democratic newspapers during the presidential campaign of 1936, or the interpretations of Jefferson set forth by the opposing parties, will understand some of the pitfalls that lie in the path of the writer and the reader of history. The historian is trained to criticize his sources, to test them for accuracy, to weigh the available evidence before drawing his conclusions, and to present the results as objectively as possible. But the reader must remember that the historian is human and subject to error. He, like the professional historian, must ask whether or not the writer of history meant to tell the truth, whether or not he was in a position or attitude of mind that would make it possible for him to tell the truth; in short, he must realize that no single book of history can tell the whole truth and nothing but the truth.

Great as are the difficulties in the way of writing history accurately and truthfully, it is going too far to say with Voltaire that "history is simply a fable agreed upon." Historical technique is well enough developed so that wherever there is evidence in existence, the historian can reach, if not absolute truth, at least a very high degree of probability in his statements about the past. The historian asks four main questions of his material when trying to establish historical facts. They are: When? Where? How? and Why? The first three can be answered generally with great accuracy, but our techniques still fail, in many cases, to tell us the reason *why* things happen as they do. We can date events, we can locate them, we can describe them, insofar as we have sources, with scientific accuracy. But we can explain them only by hypothesis, and in that respect history is in much the same position as the other sciences, natural and social.

WHY WE WANT TO KNOW ABOUT THE PAST

There have been and there are many reasons why men have wanted to know about the past, why they have written and read history. To tell a story, to preserve the memory of great men and of great deeds, were among the earliest objects of history. Herodotus, a Greek of the fifth century B.C. who is often called the "father of history," introduced

his work with this sentence: "These are the researches of
Herodotus of Halicarnassus, which he publishes, in the hope
of thereby preserving from decay the remembrance of what
men have done, and of preventing the great and wonderful
actions of the Greeks and the Barbarians from losing their
due meed of glory; and withal to put on record what were
the grounds of their feud." Thucydides, a generation
younger than Herodotus, introduced another element into
the purpose of historical writing. He planned his history
of the Peloponnesian War not only because he expected it
to be interesting but also because he thought it would be
significant. Human nature, he believed, was essentially
unchanging, and so, from the study of history, men might
learn valuable lessons. This idea of history teaching by
example is expressed more definitely by Polybius (second
century B.C.) who wrote, "Had previous chroniclers neglected to speak in praise of History, it might perhaps have
been necessary for me to recommend everyone to choose for
study . . . such treatises as the present, since there is no
more ready corrective of conduct than the knowledge of the
past. But all historians . . . have impressed upon us that
the soundest education and training for a life of active
politics is the study of History, and that the surest and
indeed the only method of learning to bear bravely the
vicissitudes of fortune is to recall the calamities of others."

Among the early Christians, history served another purpose. History set forth the story of God's punishment of
sin and of the curse which the violation of God's command-
ments had brought upon mankind. Orosius, in his *Seven
Books of History Directed Against the Pagans,* aimed to
refute the arguments of those who maintained that the
troubles of their time were due to the abandonment of the
worship of the ancient gods. He brought together, he tells

us, all the examples he could find in the annals of the past "of the most signal horrors of war, pestilence, and famine, of the fearful devastations of earthquakes and inundations, the destruction wrought by fiery eruptions, by lightning and hail, and the awful misery due to crime." [3] If these things had happened in the past, they could hardly be charged to the advent of Christianity. The revival of secular interests in the fourteenth and fifteenth centuries swept away many of the mistaken interpretations of early Christian history and recovered some of the history of antiquity. In the sixteenth century the bitter controversies of Protestants and Catholics again made history an arsenal from which men drew facts to "prove" the truth and justice of their respective points of view.

In the course of the nineteenth century, the idea of the character and purpose of history underwent a fundamental change. Up to that time history was written to entertain, to instruct, to edify, and to prove a thesis. In all its manifestations, however, history was regarded as a branch of literature. While all good historians tried to write truthful history, to write a well-balanced narrative with a pleasing style was considered of the first importance. A reputable but now almost forgotten historian, lecturing at the Collège de France in 1820, told his students that the masterpieces of epic poetry should be the first study of the would-be historian, since it was the poets who had created the art of narrative. From the modern novel, he continued, the student might learn "the method of giving an artistic pose to persons and events, of distributing details, of skilfully carrying on the thread of the narrative, of interrupting it, of resuming it, of sustaining and provoking the curiosity of

[3] From Robinson, J. H., *The New History* (The Macmillan Company, New York, 1912). By permission of the publishers.

the reader." After the poets and novelists, the works of
standard historians should be read with a view of discovering the secrets of their style. . . . When the foundations
of an elegant literary style have been established, the student should re-read the standard works with attention to
the matter rather than the form; for before writing history,
it is necessary to know it.[4] In an early essay, in 1828,
Macaulay declares that "History, at least in its state of
ideal perfection, is a compound of poetry and philosophy."[5]
Today, it is a common but perhaps exaggerated complaint
that the historian pays entirely too little attention to his
style. At any rate the emphasis has changed, for, according
to the *Encyclopaedia of the Social Sciences,* "history as it is
conceived today may blossom into art, may be crowned
with philosophy; but is primarily and necessarily the solid
establishment of facts and the precise exposition of the facts
established . . . in short, the pursuit and the expression
of truth."

In the preface of his first book, published in 1824, Leopold
von Ranke wrote: "History has had assigned to it the task
of judging the past, of instructing the present for the benefit
of ages to come. To such lofty functions this work does
not aspire. Its aim is merely to show what actually
occurred." Ranke's methods of presentation, his application of critical tests to historical sources, and above all, his
introduction of the seminar as a training school for historical scholars, were epoch making. The ideal of his school
was scientific accuracy and objectivity. It was the function
of the historian to discover the facts, to present them, but

---

[4] Robinson, J. H., *The New History,* pp. 27 f. (The Macmillan Company,
New York, 1912). By permission of the publishers.

[5] Essay on "Hallam's Constitutional History," first published in *Edin-
burgh Review,* September, 1828.

to let them speak for themselves. But it was a false hope to assume that the historian could deal with the human past as objectively and scientifically as the chemist with his elements, the astronomer with his stars, or the biologist with his jellyfish. Gradually, it came to be recognized that history might be scientific in its methods but that the works of even the most rigidly scientific historians were conditioned by their personalities and by their environment.

Three influences have been of outstanding importance on the development of historical thought since the early nineteenth century. One was the development of the idea of scientific causation. Historians, too, began to seek cause and effect in their materials. The second influence was the doctrine of evolution established by Darwin in 1859. Historians abandoned the idea of history as a chain of episodes and began to show how the present had evolved from the past. The third influence was the work of Karl Marx. In contrast to thinkers like Hegel who saw in history "the world spirit" realizing itself, Marx based history on materialism. The peculiar characteristics of each age, the customs, the institutions, even the ideas, he taught, are determined by the modes of economic production. History is not the working out of a world spirit; it is the record of class struggle. These influences have produced additional reasons for the study of history. History is still written as literature to amuse and inspire; it is still written to teach and to edify; it is still written as attack or defense in controversy. But it is written also as science, which is its own justification, as an aid to the understanding of the present, and, by followers of Marx, to show the inevitable triumph of the proletariat. The motives of historical study have become more numerous. None of the older ones have completely disappeared, though their relative importance has changed, and it is still impossible even for professional students of history to reach an agreement as to the nature and purposes of history. In its practical results, this disagreement is more valuable than agreement. For, through the clash of conflicting opinions, history moves step by step towards its ideal, the attainment of truth.

Measured in terms of dollars and cents, history appears to have little value except to those who earn their living by teaching or writing it. It has happened that researches by students of Biblical history have resulted incidentally in the discovery of oil wells in the Near East, and investigations in Mexican history have led to the reopening of some rich silver mines.[6] But it can be shown, in a broader sense, that history has both intellectual and material value.

By the general public, history is still regarded primarily as literature. There are thrilling stories to be found in history: the march of the 10,000 Greeks through Asia Minor, about which some of us used to read in Xenophon's *Anabasis* in high school Greek classes; the equally stirring account of the expedition in 1860 of Garibaldi with a thousand men to conquer the Kingdom of Naples for Italy against overwhelming numerical odds, a story told with historic accuracy and literary charm by George Macaulay Trevelyan; the voyages of Columbus to the New World; Admiral Byrd's flights over the South Pole; and thousands of others from all periods of time. History is stranger than fiction, and that it is a true story makes it even more attractive. "Popular" histories, novels based on history, such as the best-seller *Gone With the Wind,* and biographies, advertised as historical but in fact good, bad, or indifferent, have had a wide sale and find eager readers. Hollywood provides

---

[6] Krey, A. C., "History in the Machine Age," in *Minnesota History,* Vol. 14, No. 1, p. 11.

a steady diet of "historical" films; great corporations sponsor radio broadcasts of historical episodes; the newspapers print sequences of historical "strips." It is clear that people want to know about the past.

The study of history satisfies other deeply rooted sentiments in man. Most people are interested in their ancestors and take real pride in discovering—from history—that some of them have done things worth remembering. Men are interested in their localities; they found and support local historical societies to preserve local records and to mark historic spots with tablets that the touring motorist stops to read. Henry Ford, to be sure, has said that "history is bunk," yet he has spent thousands of dollars in building up Greenfield Village, a museum of the history of American life.

Taken somewhat more seriously, as social science rather than literature or "antiquarianism," the study of history helps us to understand the present. Our institutions, our ideas, and our customs are themselves the product of a long history. How can we fully understand the dictators of modern Europe if we do not know the historical background of their rise to power? How can we judge their possible effects upon the world, and so, upon our own lives, without the aid of historical study of past dictators and dictatorships? History, it has been said, repeats itself. This is not strictly true, because the conditions are never wholly the same. Yet there are typical situations that arise from time to time and old problems that seem to return from the past to plague us. An understanding of these problems in the past and the study of the way in which attempts at solution have been made in the past could often be of value in guiding us in the present. Economists have noticed a certain rhythmic cycle in the coming of periods of prosperity and depression. A little more thought of history might have saved the reputation of many a prophet before and after 1929. Another illustration of the way in which the study of history can help men in their approach to current practical problems is to be found in the problem of the abolition of war. If war is the result of vast, almost impersonal forces, it is perhaps futile to hope that treaties, Leagues of Nations, tribunals of arbitration or conciliation, can prevent its recurrence. Instead of wasting time and effort to avert war, we might better prepare to win the next war that is bound to come. If, on the other hand, wars are the product of the mistakes or machinations of small numbers of men, if the causes of war are subject to human control, then we can set about to control them and reduce our taxation for armament. The answer that each one of us will give to this question will depend on his interpretation of the role of the individual personality in the shaping of historical events. But whatever the answer, it must come in large part from history. If we can find out the steps by which past wars have come about, then we can provide a more realistic approach to the question of whether or not there must be a next one. History is the memory of the human race and it serves, or could be made to serve, many of the functions for the community that the individual's memory does for him.

Finally, the study of the past can help us to be "historically minded," that is, to see things in their relationships and in perspective. At different times men have thought and acted in different ways; economic and social conditions have varied; even morality has not always been the same. The study of the past should help us to be tolerant and critical of old ideas and new ones. It is a commonplace of historical observation that the radicals of yesterday are the conservatives of today. Furthermore, many ideas that in past years seemed world-shaking lose their power to arouse men to action or to terrify them to reaction. Far-reaching programs of action often turn out to be much different in development than they were in origin. A knowledge of the ways in which men have acted in the past can be of immediate practical value.

"Historical mindedness" includes an element of humility. We have suggested some of the things that history might help men to do, ways in which a knowledge of the past has served men in the past and might serve again. There are two qualifications on the value of history. The first is that history is not an exact science and that its conclusions cannot be drawn with the sureness and validity with which an engineer decides that a bridge can carry its allotted load of traffic. The second is that the real value of history depends not on history itself, but on the use that is made of it. As the historian surveys the past and the present of the world, he is tempted to conclude by recalling the old cynical aphorism: "The only lesson we learn from history is that we learn nothing from it." This is a challenge to the historian to try ever harder to live up to his ideals, and to those who are not historians, to avoid the mistake of learning nothing, by learning at least something of what the past has to offer.

BIBLIOGRAPHY

Abbott, W. C., "Some 'New' History and Historians," in *Adventures in Reputation* (Harvard University Press, Cambridge, Mass., 1935).
Beard, C. A., "Written History as an Act of Faith," in *American Historical Review*, January, 1934, Vol. 39, pp. 219–229.
Cheyney, E. P., *Law in History, and Other Essays* (Alfred A. Knopf, New York, 1927).

Krey, A. C., "History in the Machine Age," in *Minnesota History*, March, 1933, Vol. 14, pp. 3–29. Reprinted in *The Historical Outlook*, October, 1933, Vol. 24, No. 6, pp. 301–310.

Robinson, J. H., *The New History; Essays Illustrating the Modern Historical Outlook* (The Macmillan Company, New York, 1912).

Salmon, Lucy, *Historical Material* (Oxford University Press, New York, 1933).

Schuyler, R. L., "Law and Accident in History," in *Political Science Quarterly*, 1930, Vol. 45, pp. 273–278.

See especially articles on "History," in the *Encyclopedia Americana*, the *Encyclopædia Britannica*, and *The Encyclopaedia of the Social Sciences*.

CHAPTER VIII
Human Geography
RICHARD HARTSHORNE
University of Minnesota

THE NATURE AND PURPOSE OF GEOGRAPHY

WE ARE all fairly familiar with the geography of the locality in which we live. Its hills and valleys, rivers and lakes, and especially its climatic conditions are well known, even if not in a scientific way. Likewise its cultural landscapes—its fields, woodlots, and farmsteads, and its urban development—are part of our general knowledge. Some may also be familiar with the geography of neighboring regions or even of a few remote ones, but the average person's knowledge of the greater part of the world is only general and often incorrect.

Even within one's own country one can find great contrasts. For example, if we attempt to apply concepts of rural life developed in Minnesota to an area in Mississippi, we will be unable to understand correctly the problems of the latter region. Not only does Mississippi grow different crops; its whole organization of land use, the character and quality of the homes of the land workers, its standards of living, and the racial character of its people are different from those in Minnesota. Also, there are fundamental differences between such a predominantly agricultural region as Minnesota and, say, the industrial area of southern New England, so that the social and political problems, as well

as the economic ones, are very different. In more remote
parts of the world we find even greater differences.

The purpose of studying geography is to gain accurate
familiarity with the world in which we live. This is no
mere academic purpose, since the commercial development
of the past three or four centuries has made the world a
commercial unit in which one part may be affected by conditions in almost any of the others. The dairy farmers of
the central northwest region of the United States are by
no means unaffected by the pasture conditions of Denmark
or New Zealand, since these may have significant effects on
the price of butter in the New York market. The wheat
farmer of the Red River Valley is dependent not merely
on his own soil and climatic conditions; his financial success
or failure may be determined by drought in interior Australia, by grasshoppers in Argentina, or by rains in central
Europe. Nor is this merely a competitive interest. If
factories in western Europe are closed down, our farmers
will find their market for grains, meat, or lard depressed.
The success of Japanese manufacturers in marketing their
products is beneficial to the cotton growers of our South,
and therefore, indirectly, to the industries of the North
which sell to them. An understanding of the conditions
in other lands may, therefore, be of practical value to us in
understanding our own problems.

Definition of geography

The knowledge of one's own region should be put in more
definite, scientific form. In general, science is the organization of objective knowledge into significant classifications
and relationships. In every field, scientists study and measure the different facts and phenomena and the relationships
among them. Geography is the science of the earth's sur-

face; it is concerned with measuring differences in the character of areas, including continents, countries, regions, and localities.

The use of the term "region" in geography corresponds in a sense to the historian's use of the word "period." A region is a continuous area in which the principal geographic features, both cultural and natural, show marked similarity in character and are different from those of neighboring areas. Regions vary greatly in size, from areas as large as our Cotton Belt or the Alpine region in Europe, to the much smaller ones like the southern New England industrial region, or the Blue Grass tobacco region of Kentucky.

The function of geography is to provide a knowledge of the differences in regional character in the different areas of the world, and their relations to each other. The regions of geography are mutually related in a two-dimensional space of latitude and longitude on the surface of the earth. It is, therefore, not enough to study all the regions one after the other; they must be seen in their areal relations to each other as they are on the globe. Maps are the essential medium for this purpose. To an increasing extent modern geography records its findings and demonstrates its conclusions on maps. These maps may include the world as a whole, or just small areas. An increasing number of specific symbols is being used for this purpose Maps are the technical language of geography.

The geographic character of any region is a synthesis of individual characteristics, of which some are solely the product of natural forces and form the "natural landscape," and others result from man's alterations and additions to nature, the "cultural landscape." Geography therefore helps to connect the social sciences and the natural sciences. Its social aspects are included in the various divisions of human geography which will be discussed in this chapter. The divisions of physical geography depend on the various natural sciences.[1] Cartography, the science of mapping, involves both mathematics and astronomy, and is itself used in all other branches of geography. The most important division of physical geography, climatology, depends on meteorology, the physics of the atmosphere. Geology is fundamental to mineral geography and geomorphology, the study of the forms of earth surfaces. Plant and animal geography obviously depend on the biological sciences, as well as on the study of climates and surface forms. Almost all of these branches are necessary for the study of soils, which depends, therefore, on physics, chemistry, geology, mineralology, botany, and zoölogy.

The different aspects of geography cannot be clearly separated in practice. The cultural landscape is built upon the fundamental natural landscape, which is called the *fundament*. The student of the natural features cannot ignore the work of man, since this has been an important factor in modifying soils, stream channels, vegetation, animal life, and even land forms.

All these different divisions of geography are united in the study of particular areas, *regional geography*. Here the purpose is to analyze and synthesize all of the elements that give a region its special character as distinct from other regions: the elements of the natural landscape, of the visible cultural landscape, and also some less tangible aspects of its human development, cultural and political, which, being interwoven with the preceding features, also form a part of the character of the region. Since the earth's

---

[1] The most complete and authoritative reference book for physical geography is Finch, Vernor C., and Trewartha, Glenn T., *Elements of Geography* (McGraw-Hill Book Company, New York, 1936).

surface consists of a well-nigh infinite number of regions, districts, and localities all differing from one another, it presents an inexhaustible field for study. Only those characteristics which extend over large areas comprising many smaller regions can be considered in such a survey as this. Of first importance is the extent to which the face of the earth has been remodelled by the work of man, in his utilization of the land. A world survey of this development will form the major part of this chapter.

GENERAL PRINCIPLES OF LAND UTILIZATION

Regional contrasts in land use

The differences in extent and intensity of land use in different regions may be measured statistically and portrayed by various kinds of maps showing crops, animals, mines, factories, cities, and population. All these maps reflect the great differences in the extent to which the human race is concentrated in certain areas where cleared and cultivated fields, buildings, roads, and streets have almost completely altered the original landscape, while in other areas men are few in number or completely absent, and the original natural landscape remains but little altered by man.

Regional land use reflects the comparative value of resources

Men live for the most part not where climatic, social, or political conditions are the most inviting, but where they can make a living for themselves and their dependents. Natural biological increase has forced men in most regions to utilize all the resources which their technical equipment can make available. When the population presses on the resources, starvation (famines) may ensue unless part of the population can migrate to other areas. Partly for this reason man had settled in practically every habitable part of the world even before the dawn of history.

Before modern times regions of the world varied greatly in their technological knowledge and equipment, but now knowledge of different domestic crops and animals and methods of cultivation has been made known to nearly all parts of the world where it can be applied. Not only did Europeans carrying the plow and domestic animals into North America construct a totally new cultural landscape over most of the continent, but in taking back Indian corn (maize) they caused a major change in the agriculture of southeastern Europe, and the potato made it feasible to cultivate sandy portions of the northern plain of Europe. Few areas of the world remain exempt from contact with what has thus become a universal technical knowledge.

Furthermore, most of the new lands have been affected by this contact for several centuries, so that the development in them is essentially as complete as in similar regions of the Old World. The world of our day has seen the end of the great era of settlement of new lands. Only in the Pampas of Argentina and Uruguay has it been delayed by peculiar social and economic conditions. There are still geographical frontiers, to be sure, on the margins of the dry lands in all the continents, in the "cold lands" of northern North America and Eurasia, and in the hot humid lands of the tropics, but in those regions development does not come from the expansion of older cultures, but from the creation of new techniques.

One major difference remains between the New World and the Old. Although the proportion of land cultivated is as high in Iowa, for example, as anywhere in Europe, the cultivation is much less intensive, and the rural population much less dense. Production per unit of labor in the New World, however, is much higher.

Summary of the major forms of settlement and land use

Three-fourths of the world's surface consists of the seas, in which man can never be at home. Some slight use is made of these bodies of water by people; fish and other forms of sea life are extracted by a small number of coastal peoples, and trade between different land regions takes advantage of the ease of water transport. For the most part, however, the seas remain chiefly of minor interest to man, tending to separate the populated lands.

In the land areas man has developed a great variety of cultural landscapes, which may be grouped in four major classes. First are the unused lands, which have, in fact, no cultural landscape. Second are the areas that man uses so little that the landscapes are largely either unchanged or redeveloped in wild form, and in which human settlements are widely scattered and usually not permanent. Here men live chiefly by fishing and hunting, by gathering forest products, or by grazing domestic animals on the natural grasses. Usually they also grow some domestic crops in small patches of land which, however, may be periodically abandoned.

These two classes of lands, where man has made little or no permanent impression, constitute the greater part of the land area of the world. The other two classes, which man has more or less completely made over, are smaller in area but far more important.

The greater area of these lands consists of the cultivated farmlands, which form the third main group. Here the principal features of the landscape are still formed by the land surface and the vegetation, but in place of the original vegetation are the cultivated fields and meadows, carefully delimited and often fenced off. Roads and houses are generally visible from any point, but not notably concentrated.

Settlements are necessarily small, being either villages from which the workers of the land go out to cultivate, or individual, separate farmsteads.

Towns and cities, the fourth group, present the most striking form of cultural landscape, for in these regions natural vegetation and animal life have been almost completely eliminated. Paved streets and buildings may completely cover the surface of the ground. Aside from the special case of mining towns, the inhabitants of these urban districts do not make their living in any of the "primary" industries, those which develop or exploit the resources of nature. The basic activities which give rise to and support most towns and cities are transportation, trade, and manufacture. Because of the lack of space for land use, and because of the advantage of specialization of labor, the urban dweller produces little for his own consumption. Consequently, the concentration of people at any urban center requires that a large number of persons be engaged in purely local activities, such as making bread or ice cream, operating streetcars or trucks, keeping shops in which the city dwellers secure most of the material requirements. In every city the professional, clerical, and domestic-servant groups constitute an additional large number of people. These various dependent activities probably account for a larger portion of the population of cities than the basic activities.

WORLD SURVEY OF AGRICULTURAL LAND USE

Lands of little or no development

Ice areas. There are two great areas of land permanently covered by snow and ice—the whole of the Antarctic continent, and the interior of Greenland. Both are areas of high altitude in polar regions. In the lowlands of the polar

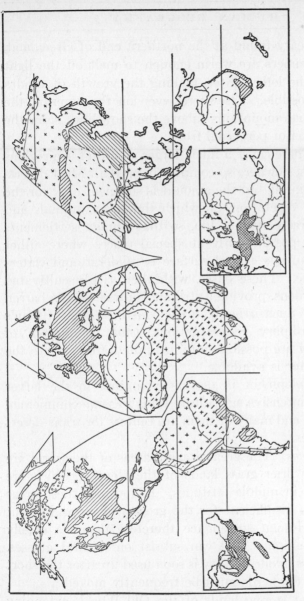

CULTIVATED LANDS

▨ Amerindian
▨ Oriental
▨ Occidental
▨ Plantations

GRAZING AREAS

▨ Nomadic
▨ Commercial

▨ Taiga forests
▨ Tropical forests
▨ Tropical savannahs

☐ Ice areas
☐ Deserts
☐ Tundra

▨ Industria belts
▨ Outlying industrial districts

The Natural and Cultural Landscape of the World.

regions, as Peary found at the northern end of Greenland, the short summers are warm enough to melt off the light snowfall of the long winter, making the growth of tundra vegetation possible. Elsewhere, even on the equator, the summits of high mountains (above the snow line) show the same condition of perpetual frost.

Deserts. These cover a much larger area than ice regions but are almost nowhere so completely barren. Most deserts have some rainfall, but the amount is sufficient only for the most meager vegetation, on which the larger animals and man can scarcely sustain life, so that human settlements are normally possible only at special places where either nature or man has caused surface or underground waters to accumulate. These oases, with their richly cultivated fields and gardens, provide a striking contrast to the barren desert lands. Such irrigated areas constitute one of man's most extraordinary re-adaptations (*not* conquests) of nature. They are possible only in limited areas where the necessary water is available.

Urban development in deserts is limited to the larger oases. Their intensive agriculture leads to some commercial development, and many of them are centers for trans-desert caravan routes.

Grazing areas. The great grazing areas of the world are the distinctly drier grass lands of the steppes, which are found chiefly in middle latitudes. In most of these areas the rainfall is insufficient for the growth of crops without irrigation. Human sustenance therefore depends chiefly on domestic animals that can subsist on natural grasses. Since the grass in one locality is soon used up after the short rainy season, the herds must be frequently moved.

In the great steppe lands of the Old World, extending almost continuously from the Atlantic coast of North Africa across western and central Asia to the borderlands of China, the tribal population migrates with the herds. They depend on these not only for their food, chiefly milk products, but also for most of their clothing, furnishings, and tents. These nomadic movements may be periodic with the rainy season or quite irregular; they may be limited to definite localities, or may, particularly in periods of great distress, extend into neighboring areas. Some "dry farming" is usually practiced in the more favored areas, but crops are uncertain.

By exchange, or by theft, nomads secure some needed supplies from the settled farmers of oases or margins of cultivated lands, but trade thus carried on is small. The total population of nomads is small, but their political importance has been great. Their mode of life and tribal organization, combined with their bitter struggle for existence, have made them a threat to the sedentary populations of neighboring lands for thousands of years, especially before the days of gunpowder.

In contrast to the nomads of the open steppes are the sedentary dwellers of the oases. These irrigated districts are similar to those found in the deserts, both in intensive cultivation and in urban development.

In the steppe lands of the New World, the Americas and Australia, the population is even sparser, though the land utilization may be just as great. Peoples of European origin have developed there a highly commercial form of grazing in which the cattle and sheep are raised not to feed the population, but to provide wool, hides, and meat for the densely populated regions of Europe and eastern North America. In return, the population obtains most of its supplies, including much of its food, by purchase from outside. Except for the sheepherders and cowboys, the rural population is sedentary, living in widely scattered ranch houses.

The areas of this type have a much higher level of culture than all the others of this major group. Their commerce gives rise to urban centers entirely comparable with those of agricultural lands. Indeed, since their cities and towns serve a rural population almost as specialized in production as city dwellers, the proportion of urban to rural population is here higher than in most farming regions. The permanent settlements connected by roads and railroads and the fenced ranches, which are replacing the open range in many areas, form fairly complete though superficial cultural landscapes.

Tundra. In polar areas of low altitude the light snowfall of the long winters quickly melts in the short summer, uncovering the meadows and bogs of the tundra. No month is free from frost, and only dwarf trees can grow. The subsoil is permanently frozen, but in the short summer season (at least one month averaging above 50° F.) the top soil thaws, and grasses and flowers form a rich cover. Agriculture, however, is not practicable. The herding of reindeer by the Lapps and other Arctic tribes of northern Eurasia is a special form of nomadic grazing, due rather to deficient heat than to deficient moisture. In the similar North American tundra, scattered Indian and Eskimo tribes formerly were limited to a precarious livelihood based on hunting and fishing. The introduction of reindeer into Alaska and northern Canada in recent decades has made the greatest change in the utilization of those areas by native peoples. The beginnings of a commercial grazing industry, which might ultimately include musk oxen as well as reindeer, can also be seen in Alaska.

Taiga. South of the tundra in North America and Eurasia are vast areas of *boreal forests,* almost as completely wilderness as the tundra, save on the southern and coastal margins. The forests of evergreen conifers—pines, firs, and larches—stretch for thousand of miles. These constitute the world's greatest resource of commercial timber, but only in recent generations has any important lumbering developed there.

The major handicap of these lands is lack of heat—not, however, the excessively cold winters, colder than on the tundra coasts, nor any lack of hot weather in midsummer, for temperatures over 90° are common; it is the shortness of the growing season, which is from one to three months, that chiefly limits agricultural development. But in addition the conditions of soil and drainage are very unfavorable. The ash-colored soils, *podzols,* developed under the coniferous forest, are infertile, and because most of these areas were covered with ice during the last Glacial Period, the soil is thin and usually mixed with boulders. In valleys and depressions where the soil is deeper, glacial moraines block the drainage, and swamps cover enormous areas. In consequence of all these difficulties, farming is so unsuccessful that even after lumbermen have cleared land there is little incentive to use it for agriculture, whereas on grasslands much farther north, cultivation of wheat may be successful.

Under adverse conditions of soil and drainage, as are found in much of the Great Lakes states, the Adirondacks, and northern New England, the taiga extends far to the south of its normal climatic limits.

Over the greater part of these areas the population is as sparse as in the steppes, if not sparser. Scattered tribes make a meager living by hunting and fishing, with some cultivation of hardy plants such as barley, potatoes, and certain vegetables. Perhaps more important is the commercial hunting for furs. Commercial lumbering is confined to areas accessible to outside markets, that is, along the southern borders, or, as in Sweden, Finland, and Russia, along streams down which logs can be floated to the Baltic or the White Sea, or even to the Arctic Ocean.

It is obvious that there is little opportunity for the growth of urban settlements in either the taiga or tundra lands. The few exceptions, usually small and scattered, result from the development of lumber and its products or from the exploitation of mineral resources.

Tropical forests. Situated near to the equator are regions in which it is always warm or hot and daily rains occur throughout all or most of the year. For the most part, these areas are clothed in the luxuriant vegetation of the evergreen tropical rain forest. One might expect to find there the most productive cultivation of domestic crops, but actually only a small part of these areas is cultivated. Much the greater part of them is a tangle of wild vegetation, and the populations are for the most part sparse, scattered, and backward. This cannot be explained simply on the ground of any inferior character of the "colored" races, for the same races have elsewhere, notably in tropical highlands, achieved great success. Nor is it due to any other single factor, such as the debilitating climate, or the ease of getting along without hard work in lands where nature supplies food abundantly and where clothing and shelter are of little importance.

These factors are no doubt important, but so also are the difficulties of clearing and keeping out the native vegetation from the fields. There is a continual struggle with a multitudinous insect life, which devours crops, domestic animals, and homes of man. Harvested crops cannot be stored successfully in the perpetually hot, humid climate. Above all, tropical diseases may devastate the human population or the domestic animals. Where the latter cannot survive there is little possibility of plowing the soil, the essential process for permanent agriculture. In any case the plow is used but little, because it increases the naturally excessive leaching of soil fertility caused by the heavy tropical rainfall. The relatively infertile soils of the tropics when merely scratched with a pronged stick or hoe become exhausted after a few years of cultivation. Fields must then be abandoned, and new clearings made, often involving the transfer of an entire tribal village. The abandoned clearings become rapidly covered with high brush, which may or may not be replaced by tropical forest. They abound in wild animal life. Hunting in unmarked stretches of forest and brush frequently leads to inter-tribal conflicts. While the men spend their time fishing, hunting, and fighting, the care of the crops is left to the women, along with the work of the household. This is a further reason for the lack of improvement. Small fields are planted with cassava, corn, yams, sugar cane, and perhaps bananas. Much wild honey, wild fruits, and nuts, notably the coconut and palm nut, are found. Livestock is almost or entirely absent, except in the more accessible districts where Eurasian domestic animals, particularly pigs, have been introduced.

In their more primitive condition peoples of these areas had almost no commerce and very little specialization of activities among their members. Over large interior areas this remains true today. There are consequently almost no urban settlements, and political organization hardly extends beyond the primitive tribe. On the other hand, along the coasts and navigable rivers, traders, conquerors, and administrators from Europe, America, China, and Japan have introduced these features. The relatively few cities in which such commerce and administration are concentrated are located chiefly at seaports or on naturally navigable rivers.

Stimulated by these influences, the natives in the interior, while continuing to some degree their former methods of livelihood, spend more time in gathering wild plant and animal products from the forest or the sea—ivory, pearls, wild rubber, coconuts, Brazil nuts, cacao, palm oil, pepper, and other spices.

A later phase, characteristic of the coasts of many of the East Indies and Pacific Islands, is reached when the natives plant and care for trees, to provide a larger and more certain supply for commerce. The more complete revolution in their environment that is brought about through the establishment of plantations will be discussed later.

Tropical savannas. Bordering the tropical forest lands on the north and south are the tropical grasslands, or savannas. Although these are somewhat similar to the steppes of the temperate lands, there are significant differences. The grasses are generally taller but coarser, and therefore less nourishing for domestic animals. Though the rainy season is too short to support forests, it is fairly heavy during that season, and clumps of trees are scattered over the interstream areas, in addition to galleries of trees along the valleys. Considerable areas of this type of fundament in India have long been cultivated and densely populated, but far larger areas in the Sudan, or in the Campos of Brazil, remain essentially unchanged by man. The sparse population makes its living by primitive hoe cultivation similar to that of the tropical forests. In only a few areas, notably in Nigeria, has this led to permanent agriculture and a dense population. In addition to hoe culture, the Sudanese tribes in Africa graze cattle, somewhat after the manner of nomadic peoples of the steppes. In the New World savannas low-breed cattle are raised in semi-wild fashion almost solely for their hides, which form the chief product of export from these areas.

Local areas of little development. In addition to these great zones of slight development, there are local areas of wilderness within even the most highly developed lands. The steep slopes of high mountains, covered with rocky or thin soil, generally can be used only for grazing or lumbering, if at all. Large areas in the Rocky Mountains and in the Scandinavian Alps are completely barren, even below the snow line. In lowland areas climatically suitable for agriculture, adverse soil conditions may limit their use to grazing, as in sandy areas of western Nebraska and in the sand and gravel delta plain of the Rhone, in southern France; or the cut-over forest land may be left to re-grow trees, as in large parts of our Atlantic Coastal Plain from New Jersey to Florida and on the similar plain of northern Germany. Lack of drainage may likewise render larger areas unfit for cultivation, as in the Everglades of Florida and in the great Pripet marshes on the borders of Poland and Russia.

Future trends in these lands. These are the great land areas which man has been unable to bring under subjection. Those who live there do so chiefly by making the most of the wild plant and animal life that nature offers, supplemented, if at all, by most rudimentary and usually transitory cultivation. But the face of the earth is not fixed; within present geologic times, in which climatic and physiographic changes have been but slight, man has radically changed great stretches of the earth, including areas which were thought to be beyond the limits of civilization. What changes, then, can we foresee in these relatively undeveloped lands?

Present indications suggest that not much more is to be

expected from the dry lands. During the closing decades of the past century the settlement of the steppes of North America was stimulated by the widespread belief that "rainfall follows the plough." Pseudo-scientific arguments widely publicized by real estate and political bodies proclaimed that cultivation would gradually bring rain to even the driest desert areas. One ordinary five- or six-year period of more than average precipitation gave credence to this doctrine, until a subsequent period of less precipitation destroyed not only the theory but great numbers of homesteads as well. The most competent climatological studies indicate that there is little that man can do to alter the precipitation in any area. The planting of trees, even forest belts, would have but slight effect on the amount of rainfall.

The development of labor-saving agricultural machinery and the breeding of drought-resistant varieties of grains made possible the great expansion of specialized, extensive grain farming into the steppes. This development of the past generation, however, has already extended beyond the limit of profitability. With the declining birth rate in the great bread-consuming areas of the world, presumably some recession can be expected.

Irrigation may cause the steppe or desert to "blossom like a garden," but such projects are limited in area. Complete development of all irrigable land in western United States by such projects as the Roosevelt Dam in the Salt River district in Arizona, the Boulder Dam, and the Columbia River in Washington, as well as the many smaller ones in the Salt Lake oasis of Utah and elsewhere, would permit cultivation of less than a tenth of the entire arid and semiarid area.

For the most part the dry lands seem to be destined permanently for grazing and, therefore, will necessarily remain sparsely populated. The nomadic areas of the Old World have long since approached their limit of production. A change from the age-old subsistence culture to a modern commercial grazing industry, as is happening under Russian influence in central Asia, may revolutionize the way of living, but will hardly cause any great increase in the population. In the steppe lands of the New World commercial grazing has nearly reached, if not passed, its maximum production in North America, and is probably little short of that limit in South America and Australia. Indeed, grazing may be expected to continue to recede before cultivation in the humid grasslands of the Argentine Pampas and Uruguay. On the other hand, there would appear to be great opportunities for the development of commercial grazing in the savanna lands of South America and Africa, but only if the world demand for leather and meat should increase. The chief handicaps are insect pests and the expense of rail construction for such limited shipments.

The least change in our times has taken place in the northern lands. The results of governmental efforts in Alaska or in northern Russia give little reason to expect any considerable agricultural development. Even according to optimistic predictions (such as Stefansson's) the most that could be expected would be an extensive grazing industry and a small amount of dairy farming.

On the other hand, the humid tropical areas—the tropical forest lands and the more humid parts of the savannas— unquestionably offer great possibilities for development as well as great difficulties. We know that somewhat similar areas in Java and India have been developed by native peoples so that they are among the most productive in the world. A better example is found in Nigeria, where the natives under European guidance have developed a tropical agriculture that supports a population as dense as many farming regions of the United States. It seems fairly clear that development of similar tropical areas in Africa or in the Americas will not depend on immigration, as it did in the temperate lands of the New World, but on the work of the native population itself. In view of the sparse population of most of these areas, particularly in South America, such development will almost certainly be slow.

The cultivated lands

General characteristics. In sharp contrast to the foregoing types of areas are cultivated lands, which man has adapted to his use. Over great areas the natural vegetation, whether grass or forest, has been removed. Man has ploughed the soil and substituted crops of his own choosing. He has replaced much of the indigenous animal life with a few domesticated animals. Necessarily becoming sedentary, he has constructed permanent housing for himself and his animals, which, together with his cultivated fields, forms almost continuous areas of settlement over great distances. The developing interchange of products has caused man to connect the individual settlements by building first dirt or gravel roads, and more recently, paved highways and railroads. This commerce has caused the development of cities, which nearly obliterate the original landscape.

All the agricultural lands are similar in these general ways, but great differences are found in the intensity and specific character of agricultural development. These differences are partly the results of human factors, but to a large extent they are due to differences in the natural conditions of the regions. These conditions, particularly climate, condition the agricultural development so that crops, livestock, and the size and character of the farms in one region may be entirely different from those in neighboring regions inhabited by people of the same race. Such fundamental agricultural differences may in turn lead to major variations in economic, social, and political organization. In the United States, for example, they have resulted in major differences in the racial make-up of the Northern and Southern populations.

The factors that form the natural framework limiting and conditioning the character of agricultural development may be outlined as follows:

THE FUNDAMENT

1. *Climate*
   a. Temperature
      (1) In different seasons, especially in the growing season
      (2) Length of the growing season
   b. Precipitation
      (1) Total amount annually
      (2) Distribution in different seasons, especially in the growing season
      (3) Amount falling as rain, snow, hail, etc.
   c. Hours of sunshine and cloudiness
      (1) Amount of evaporation
   d. Humidity, both absolute and relative
   e. Winds, storms
2. *Soil*
   a. Physical characteristics
      (1) Texture
      (2) Structure
   b. Chemical characteristics
      (1) Organic content
      (2) Content of soluble minerals (for plant food)
   c. Character of soil profile (vertical differences from surface to sub-soil)
3. *Relief* (geometric character of the surface of the ground)
   a. Degree of slope
   b. Regularity
4. *Drainage* (underground)
5. *Wild vegetation* (weeds)
6. *Wild animal life*
   a. Insects
   b. Small animals that destroy crops
   c. Larger animals that may prey on stock
7. *Relative location* (in reference to other regions, particularly consuming regions)

Scientific interpretation of differences in character of development of cultivated lands, as well as any valuable recommendations for changes, requires analyses of these basic factors, including objective measurement and classification. Climatic conditions have long been observed and recorded statistically, but only recently, thanks chiefly to the German scholar Köppen, have the climates of the world been classified by means of objective criteria of temperature and precipitation efficiency. The scientific classification of world soil types was first developed by Russian students before the War, and has been further developed chiefly by Germans and by Americans in our Bureau of Soils. Actual measurements of soils in many areas are still lacking, and the problem is far more complicated than that of climates. Relief can be measured accurately in terms of angle of slope, but this has been done for only a small part of even the cultivated world. Less is definitely known in regard to the other factors listed, except relative location. This last factor is measured not merely in terms of distance, but also in regard to character of intervening space, whether land or sea, mountains or plains.

Probably the most complete study of these factors is being made in detail by the geographers of the Tennessee Valley Authority (Land Utilization Survey). On base maps provided by aerial photography, in numerical symbols representing for the most part actual measurements, are marked the angle of slope, specific conditions of soil, drainage, crops, pasture, woodland, and farmsteads, together with a measure of their productivity. Such a map, together with supplementary information on local climatic differences, relative location, and other factors, can provide us with a fully detailed and organized inventory of the geography of any region.

While the agriculture of a region is conditioned by natural factors, its character is to a great extent also determined by the cultural inheritance of the population. Different peoples have different habits of food consumption, different standards of living, and different techniques of production. Most of the cultivated land of the world is developed under one of three major systems, which originated in three different parts of the world in prehistoric times. The two most important systems developed on or near the continent of Asia, possibly from common origins somewhere in central Asia. The Oriental system, which migrated eastward, has its great development in China, India, Japan, and neighboring lands. The Occidental system developed to maturity in the great river valleys of the Near East, the Tigris-Euphrates and the Nile, and extended westward into Europe. The great European migrations of recent centuries have carried it into far parts of the world. The third system was developed by the Indians in the tropical highlands of America, presumably independently of the two main ones.

Since the sixteenth century, European penetration into tropical regions has resulted in a new, specialized form of agriculture, the plantation system. Finally, irrigation is a special phase of agriculture, common to all three types, in which the grower does not depend primarily on natural rainfall. This form we have already noted in the oases scattered through the great areas of steppe and desert lands.

Amerindian agriculture. The agriculture developed by prehistoric Indian peoples of tropical America is chiefly of historic interest, both as the basis for the pre-Columbian civilizations of America—Mayan, Aztec, and Inca—and for its contribution of a few very important crops to modern world agriculture, particularly corn and potatoes. Throughout the highland region from northern Mexico to Peru the

cultivation of these crops, together with a few crops introduced from Europe, continues as the basis of livelihood for
the greater part of the present population, which remains
predominantly Indian in race and culture.

Oriental agriculture. The best-known feature of Oriental
agriculture is the paddy rice field. Small fields, levelled off
and embanked with mud in order to be alternately flooded
and drained, are intensively cultivated. Plant, animal, and
human manures are applied with great expenditure of labor,
in order to produce the maximum yield of rice per unit of
area. This all-important crop, which is first planted in
seed beds and then transplanted to the fields, is grown on
the same fields year after year indefinitely, and provides
most of the sustenance of the population. Less productive
crops may be grown in the same field in the cooler or drier
season, or on land unfit for rice. Only a small amount of
level land can be used for commercial crops, even in areas
under European control, as in India or Java. That the
exports from the latter areas are nevertheless great is a
reflection of the intensity of land use. Livestock is of minor
importance, except as work animals. The great density of
population necessitates the use of all available land for food
crops rather than for animal feed crops or for pasture.

Three requirements—water, level land, and rich, fine-
textured soil—restrict the areas of paddy rice production
more than those of any other major world crop. In all
hilly regions within the rice lands there is much land that
cannot be used. Only under especially advantageous soil
conditions is it practicable to terrace the rice fields. Consequently, the productive use of land in the rice areas is
limited largely to plains and river valleys, such as the great
flood plains of the Ganges in India and of the Yangtse and
other rivers in central and southern China, and great num-

bers of small delta plains along the coast of the Indian peninsula and the islands of Japan, the Philippines, and Java.

Furthermore, large regions in the Orient have either too short a growing season for rice production or inadequate rainfall for irrigating more than a small amount of river-valley land. Rice production is of little or no importance in the greater part of India and in all of northern China and Manchuria. Some of these regions are nevertheless densely populated. They depend on less restricted crops, such as wheat and barley, various millets and grain sorghums, and, in the northern lands, the soy bean. The intensity of fertilization and cultivation and the minor importance of dairy or meat animals are the general Oriental characteristics of these regions.

In both these types of Oriental areas the intensive and sedentary agriculture has made possible an economic and political organization sufficiently complex to develop urban centers of government, trade, and handicraft. Many of these were great inland cities long before European influences introduced modern commerce and developed the great seaports.

Occidental agriculture. Occidental agriculture likewise shows two major divisions. In the lands around the Mediterranean Sea agricultural production is adjusted to the conditions of the "Mediterranean climate": long, hot, rainless summers and short, mild, rainy winters. Fall-sown wheat and barley are grown for bread; the drought-resistant olive tree supplies fats, and irrigated vineyards yield fruit and drink. On the rough hill and mountain land, which constitutes much of the area, cattle, sheep, and goats are grazed and utilized much after the fashion of the neighboring nomadic peoples. In favored districts irrigation may provide for the production of various tropical and sub-tropical fruits, such as figs, dates, and citrus fruits. With the spread of Europeans into other parts of the world, this type of agriculture has been introduced into the few small areas that have the same type of climate—in southern California, in central Chile, and the southern tip of Africa. In California the development has become highly specialized in the commercial production of fruits and vegetables.

North of the mountain borders of the Mediterranean region the cultural inheritance is much the same. It may have been derived independently from the same sources in the Near East, or brought in from the Mediterranean area. But the northern, humid climate of this region has given a very different character to the agriculture. This is a region of rain at all times, but also of cooler summers, and particularly of colder winters, and predominantly of dense forest cover. These factors retarded the process of land clearing for agriculture. Although wheat, or the closely related rye, is here also the great bread crop, the other characteristic Mediterranean products are largely or entirely eliminated. Livestock both for dairy products and for meat assumes a much greater importance in the farm system. In no other type of agriculture are cattle so important as food producers. Hogs, originally grazed in the forests bordering the small clearings but now fed chiefly from farm crops, provide both meat and fat. Since the stock cannot pasture through the severe winters, except on the Atlantic margins, much of the farmers' fields and work must be devoted to the production of feed crops for these animals rather than of food for himself. Oats, hay, barley, root crops, corn, and potatoes are all used for animal feed and take up more of the land than is cultivated for human foods.

Land handicapped by steep slopes or poor drainage is kept in permanent grass, and is used either for pasture or for hay.

The agricultural lands of Europe, like those of the Far East, developed urban centers of trade, hand manufacturing, and government. With the redevelopment of commerce in the modern period, not merely by coastal and inland navigation but also through the construction of roads, the cities increased greatly in importance. Agriculture became increasingly commercial rather than for the direct sustenance of the rural population. But it was particularly the development of railroads and industrial centers in northwestern Europe during the past century that has made that part of the continent an area in which agriculture is secondary in importance, carried on in large part for the sake of feeding the great urban population. Practically all of northwestern and central Europe is covered with a complete railroad net, so that no farm is more than ten miles from a rail line with which it is connected by hard roads. The industrial revolution has produced here a revolution in agriculture, both by making it primarily commercial and by introducing machinery and commercial fertilizers, even though the crops and animals remain largely the same. During this development in western Europe, most of eastern Europe (the pre-War Russian Empire and the Balkans) and a considerable extent of southern Europe (interior Spain and southern Italy) were largely left out; these areas are still inadequately supplied with railroads and hard roads, and consequently their agriculture remains largely on a subsistence basis. In Russia an attempt is being made to speed up this belated development, under state planning.

The great geographical change of modern times has been the clearance and cultivation by Europeans of a large part of North America, and lesser parts of South America, Australia, and South Africa. These immigrants have carried the northern European grain-and-livestock farming into climatically similar areas. Not only are the people of these neo-European lands of European origin, but also most of their crops, animals, farm systems, and methods of cultivation. In most of these areas the growth of corn (maize) is a major modification, but its principal use for stock feeding is European in character.

Almost from the beginning the agriculture of these new lands has been supplying western Europe. This commercial development made urban centers relatively more important than in the purely agricultural regions of the Old World. Furthermore, industries and railroads developed in eastern North America no later than those in western Europe. In consequence, agriculture in most of the United States and Canada is even more highly commercialized than in Europe. In the new lands developed during the past seventy years railroads have in fact preceded and facilitated cultivation and settlement.

All of these new lands include great stretches of steppe country, which is utilized primarily for grazing. The development of labor-saving machines for cultivation and harvesting, and of drought-resistant varieties of grains, has made it possible to cultivate the more humid portions of the steppes in a specialized form of commercial grain farming. Though the yields per acre are very low, farms of hundreds of thousands of acres can produce great amounts of wheat to be shipped outside. As relatively little is produced for local use, this is one of the most highly commercialized types of farming. It involves a factory system of division of labor, management, and ownership. Large-scale commercial grain farming is now being adopted, under a different economic system, in the similar steppe lands of southeastern Russia. Though these areas are included with the cultivated lands, in their sparse population and scattered points of residence they still resemble the great grazing lands to which they so recently belonged.

The geography of the neo-European lands, similar in its major respects to that of their cultural fatherland in northern Europe, is very different in certain aspects. Individual farms are much larger; cultivation is much less intensive, and consequently production per acre of land is much lower; in place of human labor more and larger machinery is used; per capita consumption, particularly of meats, is higher; houses and barns are larger and better equipped with modern conveniences; in general, the standards of living are higher. Furthermore, rural settlement is chiefly by individual farm houses located on the farms, rather than in the characteristic European farm village from which the farmers go out to their separate fields. The eastern European system of large estates cultivated by peasant workers under the control of an owner or manager is common in the Hispanic American countries but not in northern North America. On the other hand, farm tenancy and frequent shifts of ownership and residence are more common in North America than in Europe.

Plantation agriculture. While European settlers were spreading Occidental agriculture into the temperate lands of the New World, other Europeans were creating the plantation system in restricted portions of the tropical areas, first in America and later in Africa. The plantation system involved the complete destruction of the native economy and widespread clearings of the tropical forest. But the native tribes were not driven out as in the thinly populated temperate areas. Rather they were made, by the slave system, by political pressure, or by economic inducements, to work as manual laborers in the fields, under the control of white managers who were often employed by absentee owners, or even by stock companies. In most of the American areas the natives proved unsatisfactory for this system, and Negro slaves were imported from tropical Africa. Draft animals were brought from Europe (in some areas tropical cattle from India or the grasslands of Africa) and European methods of plowing and cultivation were used to some extent, but not European crops. The native food crops were replaced by special tropical crops such as sugar cane, the produce to be sold in Europe. Much of the food such as flour and fish for the plantation workers was imported from the temperate lands. Economically and socially, the plantation is a factory organized in typical capitalist fashion for the production of one commercial product, nearly all the supplies for the workers being imported from the outside.

This extreme picture is probably now representative of but few plantation areas. Most of them produce at least some food crops, particularly corn, and in a few districts, rice. In some areas marked as plantations on the map on page 331, notably in West Africa, the land is actually owned by the natives, who produce native food crops as well as commercial crops of cacao and palm nuts under European guidance. But in much of tropical America, notably the West Indies, the regular plantation system is most common. To the original list of plantation products, such as sugar cane, cotton, coconuts, and spices, have been added a long list of tropical products that were formerly obtained only by gathering from wild trees or plants. These include coffee, cacao, bananas, hemp, and rubber. The most important products today are sugar cane and rubber. It will be noted from this list that plantation agriculture has contributed but little to the basic food requirements of the urban regions of the world; in fact, it has drawn food supplies away from the more developed temperate lands in exchange for luxury foods and raw materials.

By no means all the plantation areas are shown on the map; many of them are much too small to appear on a world map of this size. The areas of tropical forest and grassland that have been developed for plantation agriculture represent but a small fraction of the total areas available for this type of development. Even within the areas so marked, plantations are usually scattered, separated by great stretches of uncleared land. On many plantations, especially in the West Indies and Central America, continuous production of sugar cane without rotation with other crops soon exhausts the limited soil fertility; old fields are abandoned and new ones cleared.

A distinctive characteristic of plantation areas is the mixture of peoples of different races. The great majority of the population consists of tropical colored peoples, who may be descendants of the original native peoples or of transplanted African Negroes, or, in eastern areas, more or less temporary migrants from India or South China. Economic and political control, however, is almost everywhere in the hands of a relatively small number of people from the temperate lands of Europe, the United States, or Japan, many of whom are but temporary residents in the tropics. In all areas this has resulted in racial mixture. The dominance by the smaller "superior" racial group and the mixture of races present economic, social, and political problems essentially unknown in areas of purely Occidental or Oriental culture.

While the urban development in the plantation districts is in marked contrast to the almost complete lack of cities in neighboring areas of uncleared native culture, it is relatively backward in comparison to that of the more completely developed regions. Urban settlements are limited chiefly to the seaports, where the commercial and political interests of the controlling peoples are concentrated. In the interiors, towns are small and far more primitive, or indeed completely absent.

Two important areas of Occidental agriculture have many aspects of plantation culture. In the Cotton Belt of southeastern United States and in several small districts that raise tobacco, rice, or sugar, single commercial crops predominate. Local food production is inadequate, large plantations are owned by a small class, and labor is performed by landless sharecroppers and farm-laborers, most of whom, except in Texas, are descendants of African Negroes. In contrast to purely plantation areas, far more of the land is used for corn and other crops for human and animal consumption; many small farms are worked by the owners or tenants; cultivation is fairly continuous over large areas; and urban development is more like that of northern United States or Europe, including some industrial as well as commercial developments. In these and other respects the region must be included in the area of Occidental culture.

Much the same is true of the great coffee region of Sao Paulo, in southeastern Brazil, whose principal centers, the port of Rio de Janeiro and the inland city of São Paulo, are typical cities of the modern western culture.

THE EFFECT OF COMMERCE ON REGIONAL DIFFERENTIATION

Changes in transportation

In many of the regions that have been discussed the character of the development was seen to depend on commercial relations with outside regions. This is largely a development of the modern era, in which nearly all parts of the world have been brought into some degree of contact with each other and technological improvement has so greatly decreased the cost of transportation.

In medieval and earlier times, external trade was confined for the most part to valuable luxuries, including precious metals, amber, furs, silk, tea, spices, and a few products of skilled handicraft. The use of the land in any region was, therefore, but little affected by such outside connections. A notable exception is found in the great period of maritime development under the Greeks, and later the Romans, when grain was transported from Sicily, Egypt, and the northern shore of the Black Sea to Athens or Rome, in exchange for olive oil and wine, as well as handicraft products. But, in general, the major commodities of production could not be transported long distances until recent centuries. Following the opening up of the oceans by Columbus and Magellan, ships and navigation methods improved so that it did become practicable to transport most non-perishable goods great distances by sea. For several centuries coastal areas enjoyed a great commercial advantage over inland areas, an advantage offset in small part by the improvement of rivers and the construction of canals and roads. But the expansion of railroads, which followed rapidly after 1830, opened up the interior areas of Europe and North America for greater commerce, both internal and, through the sea-coasts, with other lands. The simultaneous development of steamships, cables, and ship refrigeration was less important in improving ocean shipping. One major difference remains. Coastal areas had only to develop their ports, but in inland areas the far more expensive railroad system had to be constructed. Millions have been known to starve in the interior of China, but not at its ports, even while the grain elevators of America were full of available wheat. Starvation conditions prevailed because the famine areas of China had produced no surpluses to exchange for wheat; but even when American relief organizations were ready to give the wheat, the cost of transporting it into inland areas was prohibitive.

Bases of inter-regional trade

Where modern transportation is available, it is possible to import almost any materials that cannot be produced locally. In mining districts in the Atacama Desert of northern Chile, all the necessary materials, even water, are brought in from outside regions. This example, as well as the more spectacular case of Little America, show that it would be physically possible to maintain even a dense population in any area, no matter how destitute. But in most cases the enormous expenditure of labor and materials necessary to transport all the required commodities makes it quite impracticable to develop these areas.

A region can import the materials it lacks only if it has the resources for producing other surpluses and can find some other region that is unable to produce those materials as cheaply, if at all, and can import them. Whether or not such an exchange will be practicable depends, in addition, on the cost of transporting the articles in comparison with the differences in cost of production in the two regions concerned. For most perishable goods, especially those of low market value, this cost is much too great for widely separated regions. For some commodities this cost may permit some importation but may limit it to only the more intensive needs. For example, Minnesota imports coal for house heating, transportation, and some few manufacturing industries, such as flour mills and bakeries; but for most industries the cost is too great; it is cheaper for the people of Minnesota to import the products of factories located in regions nearer the coal fields.

The goods that a region may import are not limited to those which it cannot possibly produce; it may import many goods that could be produced there but at greater expense of labor and materials than elsewhere, and even others that could perhaps be produced there as readily as in the regions that supply them. In the nineteenth century, farmers in the rougher, wetter, portions of western Europe gave up the production of wheat and rye, and imported them from more fertile regions overseas; now they use their land for oats and barley, and especially grass, to feed livestock, the products of which they sell, using a part of the proceeds to buy flour.

Even when a region has natural advantages for the production of certain goods which can be very widely produced, it may be found more profitable to utilize all the land and labor in specialized production of more restricted products for which that region has particular advantages. For this reason farmers in Iowa, where higher wheat yields are obtainable than in the less humid regions to the west, nevertheless purchase their flour from those *less* productive wheat lands in order to use all their land for the more valuable system of corn, beef, and hog production.

In international trade, however, both of these types of exchange are discouraged by political devices such as tariffs, quotas, and currency derangement, to the economic detriment of all the regions concerned.

Importance of relative location

Although modern transportation facilities have made many regions of the world accessible to each other, the costs of transportation cannot be overlooked. These vary not only with the distance involved, but also with respect to the character of intervening areas. Sea routes, whether trans-marine or coastal, are still cheaper than land routes for most commodities, though not for all. Physical obstacles such as mountains, deserts, and ice areas increase the cost of transportation, in some cases so much as to make trade impracticable.

These elements, distance and the character of the intervening area between one region and any other, constitute the factor of *relative location* of one region with reference to another. Theoretically the relative location of any place may be considered in reference to all places with which it has, or might have, some exchange. As the geographical explorations since 1492 have made the world a commercial unit, this does include potentially all the world, but in practice it is usually of most importance in relation to nearby regions. The areas on either side of the North Atlantic Ocean have developed trade so greatly over all the world that location with reference to one or both of them is also of major importance to most of the regions of the world.

The importance of this factor is frequently overlooked, because modern communication has completely outstripped the movement of material goods. By telephone, telegraph, cable, and wireless we appear to have practically annihilated time and distance, but in the long distance transport of commodities there have been no fundamental changes since the development of the steamship and steam railroad. Thus, a contractor in São Paulo, Brazil, who requires steel plates for the construction of a skyscraper, might place his order in Pittsburgh by telephone in ten minutes. A confirmation of the order might come by plane in a few days;

but the steel, even though it left at the same time, would not arrive for several weeks. Indeed, since the haulage overland from Pittsburgh to the seaboard is still expensive, the Brazilian contractor would probably find it cheaper to place the order in Great Britain, where the steel plants are located at coal fields directly on the coast. On the other hand, if the contractor were thinking of a similar enterprise in Cuzco, in interior Peru, he would find transport costs from the coast across the Andes onto the high plateau so great that he might scarcely even undertake the enterprise.

All these changes, which modern commerce has introduced, do not make the population of a region any less dependent on its natural conditions, including its relative location. The dependence is much less clear and direct, but nonetheless real.

REGIONS OF INDUSTRIAL URBANISM

Factors underlying industrial location

Concentration of modern industry. Commercial activity, handicraft industries, and necessary social and political control led early to the growth of towns and cities in areas of agricultural development. With the evolution of modern manufacturing in factories, in which labor, machines, power, and materials are concentrated, all cities show a development of certain types of "ubiquitous" industries. Machine shops, printing plants, and bakeries must be located close to the consumers of their products, and so are characteristic of all modern cities. In addition, many cities that are primarily commercial may develop particular industries that transform, in minor degree, the raw materials of their tributary regions. Thus, flour mills are important at all the trade centers of wheat-producing areas, packing plants at the centers of livestock raising, lumber or pulp mills at forest centers, and canning factories at fishing ports. Even in the tropical plantation areas, remote from regions of modern industry, one finds sugar mills or vegetable oil factories, as well as at least some industries of the ubiquitous type. In the absence of local resources of water power, coal, or oil, these centers import the relatively small amount of fuel that is needed for their power requirements, but they can hardly develop the great specialized industries such as the metallurgical or textile industries, which require relatively far more power or fuel.

These more specialized industries are concentrated in favored localities.[2] In certain parts of the world they have caused the development of congested urban agglomerations whose populations far exceed those in the intervening rural areas, even though these be highly developed for agriculture. Such regions are classified as distinctively manufacturing in contrast to others where manufacturing, though considerably developed, is less important than agriculture, commerce, or other activities.

The development of these predominantly urban areas is the product of the industrial evolution which began in the eighteenth century. Almost exclusively the work of Occidental culture, both in Europe and America, this development is most marked in two great areas on either side of the North Atlantic Ocean, but has also spread, in lesser degree, into more remote lands, including those of Oriental culture.

Relation to other types of production. These manufacturing areas are not to be thought of as separate from the

---

[2] For detailed discussion of the location of these industries, see Zimmermann, Erich W., *World Resources and Industries* (Harper & Brothers, New York, 1933).

agricultural lands; they are, in fact, included within them, and not by coincidence. Modern manufacturing is closely related to agriculture in at least three important ways: (1) it draws most of its raw materials, food materials for further preparation, textiles, hides, fats, and oils, from farms, ranches, and plantations; (2) the population of the areas of commercial agriculture constitutes an important market for a great number of the products of industry; (3) since the birth rates in cities is commonly too low to maintain them, much less to provide for their increase, the rural areas provide most of the workers for urban industries. O. E. Baker [3] has stated that a major economic contribution of the rural areas of America in the past half-century has been their young people, who were born, raised, and educated at essentially no cost to the cities to which they migrate. On the other hand, this constant movement to the cities has prevented a rapid increase in the density of farm population in northern United States.

The regions of industrial development overlap the areas of richest agriculture, but they do not coincide with them. The location of manufacturing industries depends on other factors as well, notably their relation to mining districts, major trade routes, and commercial centers.

The extraction of minerals is itself a direct cause of urban development, but this is commonly of minor importance since mining activities usually are widely scattered and employ small numbers of people. Far more important is the indirect effect of the close relationship of mining and manufacturing. Most minerals cannot be used by consumers until they have been put through complicated

---

[3] Baker, O. E., "Rural-Urban Migration and the National Welfare," *Annals of the Association of American Geographers,* 1933, pp. 85–87.

processes of manufacture, requiring more labor than the mining itself.

Almost every metal known and many of the non-metallic minerals are used in some kind of manufacturing. A single industry may require a large number of different minerals, but the quantities used are usually so small as to have but a minor effect on the location of the industry. To be sure, the industries directly concerned with the production of particular metals, such as copper, lead, or zinc, cannot ignore this factor. Smelting plants which reduce the mineral ore to the crude metal are in many cases associated directly with the mining activity and may be found in the immediate vicinity of the mines. Since both mining and smelting require the most modern technical equipment, these industrial localities are "oases" of intensive modern technical equipment surrounded by primitive rural landscapes, or untouched and uninhabited wilderness. Such examples are found in Mexico, Peru, the Belgian Congo, western United States, and in the virgin forest of the taiga of northern Canada and Russia.

Iron and coal are used in such large amounts by many industries that they exercise a controlling influence in the location of manufacturing. The equipment of modern industrial civilization is to a large extent built of iron and steel; machines, tools, commercial and manufacturing buildings, and transportation facilities are all made primarily of iron. The amount of iron consumed in the world, all of which requires preparation in factories, is greater than that of all other metals combined.

Even more important is coal. We live in a continuation of the "iron age" which we may call the "coal and iron age." In spite of the development of hydro-electric power in recent decades, most power and heat for industry as well as for rail transportation is still obtained from coal. Only about thirty-five per cent of our electrical energy comes from water power. In many industries the tonnage of coal required for this purpose is greater than that of the raw materials. The metallurgical industries, including those making all kinds of machines, require large amounts of fuel for heating and are commonly found close to coal fields. Large development of one group of industries generally leads to the development of others. One industry may make materials used by another in the processes of production, in machines and tools, or in building equipment. Furthermore, industries necessarily develop cities, and these, with their population dependent entirely on purchased supplies and with their mechanical equipment of streetcars, telephones, and large steel buildings, are much greater consumers of manufactured goods per capita than are the rural areas.

The great commercial centers, such as the great seaports on either side of the North Atlantic or the inland lake and rail centers, develop industries or attract them in great variety. And since most industries collect raw materials from different areas and distribute their products to different regions, proximity to the major trade routes is of great importance. The route between North America and western Europe is the most important of these.

Human factors. Various human factors have also played a part in influencing the location of industries. The act of locating a plant is, of course, a matter of personal decision, which may be more or less accidental. But whether industries thus started will grow and compete successfully with those located in other cities, and especially in other regions, may be determined by the factors previously considered, over which man has but little control. If the location of the region is advantageous, new plants may concentrate at the particular city within it where the industry happens to have started. Examples of this can be seen in the collar and shirt industry of Troy, New York, the rubber industry in Akron, Ohio, and the automobile industry in Detroit.

Certain conditions of human development of a region are necessary before its resources can be developed. Unquestionably the countries of western Europe and the eastern seaboard of the United States had great advantages in this respect in the early period of industrial development. Their scientists made the discoveries upon which invention depends. Their fishing, commercial, and handicraft industries accumulated surplus capital and developed the spirit of enterprise and techniques, both of management and labor. Finally, they had developed that degree of political stability which is essential to the success of so complicated an economic activity as manufacturing.

In contrast to physical conditions, these human conditions are subject to man's control. Some of them have been spread over most of the world. European and American capital has not hesitated to pour into the remote corners of the world, provided only that they were politically stable. With the capital have gone the necessary inventions, machines, management, and to some extent even labor. Skilled labor is generally less mobile, but can be secured by training or immigration. While the established industries of older areas benefit from the "advantage of an early start," those in newer industrial districts, as in Japan, have in fact an advantage of a late start. Unhandicapped by investments in obsolete but not outworn equipment, they can install at the start the most efficient machinery and systems that western industry has been able to develop.

Furthermore, if their labor is less skilled it is far less organized, so that labor costs may be lower.

The principal industrial areas

Major importance of the North Atlantic areas. The Oriental industrial developments and those of the neo-European lands of the Southern Hemisphere are far less important than the two major manufacturing belts on either side of the North Atlantic. The European area, as shown on the map, extends westward from Great Britain and the northeastern corner of Ireland, through northern France and the Rhine countries, across most of Germany, and into central Europe as far as Vienna and the Upper Silesian coal field on the borders of Germany, Poland, and Czechoslovakia. It includes, therefore, important parts of all the states of northwestern and central Europe, except the Irish Free State, the Scandinavian countries, and Hungary. Less important outlying districts, separated from the main belt, are found around the Swedish ports of Göteborg and Stockholm, in the Spanish province of Catalonia, and especially in the cities of the Po Plain of northern Italy. The American belt covers an area nearly as large but not so intensively developed as that of Europe. Stretching along the Atlantic seaboard between Portland, Maine, and Baltimore, it extends westward across the Appalachians as far as the west side of Lake Michigan, and reaches from a line on the north through the lake ports of Toronto, Detroit, and Milwaukee, to the Potomac and Ohio Rivers on the south. It also has outlying districts, particularly around Montreal and St. Louis. A separate region is found in the South Atlantic Piedmont. On the Pacific Coast, manufacturing is still of relatively minor importance in comparison to lumbering, agriculture, and commercial activities.

It is only the major areas, and not all parts of them, that
can be characterized as predominantly urban. The great
number of cities of all sizes, including in many cases a great
variety of factories as well as commercial features, constitutes the more important and dominating element in the
regions. Urbanization stimulates agriculture to more intensive forms of production and more complete use of the land.

In spite of that effect, farms of the two great belts cannot
supply all the food requirements of their urban populations. These regions, together with their outliers, constitute
the greatest consuming markets of the world. Indeed, the
dense populations of these regions consume the bulk of the
manufactured articles that they produce. To a large extent,
therefore, world commerce today consists of the interchange
of goods within the North Atlantic world, and the movement into it of raw materials from all other areas in
exchange for the outward movement of manufactured
products and coal.

In the character of their industrial development these
two major regions are very similar. Both of them are characterized by the great development of the metallurgical and
the textile industries. In particular, the iron and steel
industry is of basic importance in the development of these
manufacturing belts. The primary phase of this industry,
the smelting of iron ore in blast furnaces, is highly concentrated in a relatively few districts. The development of
these districts is based on their location with reference to
that of three things: iron mines, coal mines that produce
coking coal, and consuming markets. But the last, as we
have seen, are particularly important at major commercial
centers of transportation or where other industries are well
developed. Such development, in turn, is considerably
affected by proximity to coal fields. It is primarily for this

reason that it is generally though not always true that "iron moves to coal." More significant is the conclusion that important iron and steel manufacture is found only where coking coal and medium or high-grade iron ore are found within close proximity to each other and not too far from areas suitable for the development of other industries.

The European belt. The juxtaposition of these three factors—coal, ore, and consuming markets—is found in very few areas outside of western Europe and eastern North America. In Great Britain all three factors are found practically coinciding. On the continent of Europe the great region of heavy industry includes the series of coal fields that extends from northern France, across central Belgium, into the Rhineland in Germany, with the richest deposits and greatest developments in the Ruhr, and the Lorraine iron-ore field overlapping from eastern France into Luxemburg. While this region is not, like many of the British districts, immediately on the sea, its coal fields at least are very close to it and are connected with it by the Rhine and other navigable streams and canals across the coastal plain. Therefore other raw materials, including additional iron ore, can readily be secured, and finished products can be shipped over sea routes. For example, the steel industry of this region, as well as that of Great Britain, can draw upon the remote iron mining districts in Spain and Sweden, because of their proximity to the sea and the low cost of transportation by sea.

Within these regions of basic manufacturing are also found a great variety of other industries, some closely related to the iron and steel industry and others, like the textiles, that are dependent on coal and other factors. These other industries are also found at many centers just outside of the basic areas. These centers include the great

ports, notably London and Hamburg, the commercial centers
of rich agricultural development, as in southern Germany,
and the national capitals, London, Paris, Berlin, and Vienna,
which dominate their countries economically and socially as
well as politically. A large number of smaller centers are
located in the low-grade coal and lignite areas of Saxony
and Bohemia, on either side of the mountain border of
Germany and Czechoslovakia.

Finally, in all the highlands in the interior of western
and central Europe, from central France to Bohemia, hydro-
electric power and the heritage of skilled workers from
handicraft days are assets that are utilized in a great variety
of "light industries," which require much skilled work and
small amounts of materials. These activities, originating
in the past in the mountains, have migrated under modern
conditions into the valley towns of the forelands, most notably in the densely populated Alpine foreland of Switzerland.

The American belt. The extraordinary industrial development in America was made possible by the availability
of the world's richest deposits of coal and iron ore. Although
the land distance from the Upper Lakes ore region to the Appalachian coal field is greater than is commonly practicable
for the assembly of the materials for the steel industry, the
cheapness of transportation over the inland seas reduces it
to the equivalent of but two or three hundred miles by land.
The location of all the major districts of heavy industry on
the continent is based on the locations of these two enormous resources and of the principal market for steel products, the highly developed commercial and agricultural areas
of northeastern United States. The various separate but
related districts of heavy industry form together a triangular
area including the Pittsburgh coal field and the south shores
of Lake Erie and of Lake Michigan. Within this area are

found most of the iron and steel industries of the continent, as well as a great variety of other heavy industries associated with them.

The heavy-industry region of the interior provides a large amount of semi-finished products and coal, for the more variegated industrial districts east of the Appalachians. These seaboard districts are highly concentrated at the outlets of the main trade routes from the interior and are particularly dependent on that advantageous position. In southern New England there is also a large number of "light industries" that require skilled workers. Like the similar areas in European highlands, this region lacks coal, but has many water-power sites, and was the earliest center of manufacturing development in the country.

The more recent development of manufacturing in the South Atlantic states has led to the growth of a separate industrial region. This is confined to the Piedmont, between the coastal plain and the mountains, where water power and cheap labor are available. Except for the minor iron-and-steel district based on the mineral resources at Birmingham and cigarette factories near the tobacco fields, the development has been limited primarily to cotton mills, which are dependent on cheap labor costs. Because raw cotton is very cheap to transport and loses little weight in manufacturing, proximity to the cotton fields is of little or no importance.

Other industrial areas. The rapid industrial development of Japan in recent decades has also been limited to a relatively few industries, notably the textiles, cotton and silk manufacture. With inadequate supplies of high-grade coal and practically no iron ore in the island empire, continued governmental support has been necessary to develop an iron-and-steel industry that is still smaller than that of the principality of Luxemburg.

Much stronger foundations for modern industry are to be found in the Soviet Union. The most important district is the Donetz coal basin in the Ukraine, about one hundred miles north of the Sea of Azov. This area includes one of the world's richest coal fields and is but two hundred miles from the important Krivoi Rog iron-mining district. It was developed to some extent before the World War, and is rapidly becoming one of the world's major districts of intensive coal mining and heavy industry. Somewhat similar development, though less important, is taking place in an iron-mining district immediately east of the Urals around Magnitigorsk, while a greater variety of fabricating and textile industries are to be found near the low-grade coal field around Tula, south of Moscow, and at Leningrad, the only Russian port on the Baltic. These widely scattered districts outline a vast triangular area extending from the Black Sea on the south to Leningrad on the Gulf of Finland on the north, and eastward along the northern portion of the Volga to beyond the Urals at Cheliabinsk. As this area is far larger than either of the manufacturing belts of western Europe and North America, it seems doubtful that it will become as intensively urbanized as either of the two older regions. Indeed, the policy of the Soviet government, based both on social and strategic considerations, is to provide for a much wider spread of industrial towns through the rural areas than would be caused by mere economic considerations. A striking example of this is the development of a steel industry in the Kusnetz coal fields, near the mountain border of southern Siberia and Mongolia, southeast of Tomsk.

In Europe of the future, then, we can foresee two major

areas of urban manufacturing development, an older more intensive area in peninsular western Europe, oriented largely with reference to coastal regions and sea routes, and a younger more extensive area in eastern continental Europe, oriented in reference to the vast interior plain. In North America we already have two similar areas—the coastal region from Boston to Baltimore, and the inland region from Pittsburgh to Chicago—as fairly distinct halves of an almost continuous belt. But in this continent the distance separating the two is relatively short, and both depend on three important common factors: the Appalachian coal field between them, the raw iron and steel produced within it, and the trade of the agricultural interior passing through both. In Europe, the nearest points of the two regions are from 750 to 1000 miles apart; they utilize few resources in common; their external trade is along separate routes; most of the intervening area has few resources for the development of manufacturing. Quite aside from the politico-economic separation of the two regions, it seems probable that they will remain geographically separate, so that the future world map will show not two but at least three major areas of industrial urbanism.

Tendencies in growth. Both of the older industrial regions appear to have reached approximately their geographic limits. This appears true as long as manufacturing continues to depend upon those factors which to date have largely influenced its location, notably the areas of coal and iron deposits, of rich agricultural regions, and of sea routes. With the possible exception of some increase in central Poland and in northern Italy, there appears to be little tendency for expansion of the present area in western Europe. In the United States the study of Professor

Garver and his associates,[4] indicates that while ubiquitous types of manufacturing are following the movement of population into such areas as the Southwest and the Pacific Coast, and while the textile industry is continuing its shift to the South Atlantic Piedmont, there appears to be no tendency for the main manufacturing belt to expand notably beyond the limits established in 1900. Adequate resources for a varied manufacturing development are present in southeastern United States, where, it may be noted, important industrial growth would go far to solve the economic problems of the rural population.

In other parts of the world we can expect continued but necessarily limited development. Some development will take place in Japan, and in two or three centers in India, where there are important coal resources and some iron, as well as the enormous market and labor resource of the three hundred million population. This is probable also for small districts around the great commercial cities of the new temperate lands of the Southern Hemisphere, nearly all of which, however, are deficient in coal supplies. Unquestionably the greatest possibility for new development is in China. In addition to vast and richly productive agricultural lands, China has great resources of coal suitably located, but only limited iron ore resources. Development, however, must await the establishment of political stability.

In any case, under present technological conditions, increasing development in new lands will tend to lessen the marked contrast between "industrial countries" and "agricultural countries," which was such a striking characteristic of the world at the beginning of this century. But the areas

---

[4] Garver, Frederic B., Boddy, Francis M., and Nixon, Alvar J., *The Location of Manufactures in the United States, 1899–1929* (University of Minnesota Press, Minneapolis, 1934).

of intensive industrial urbanism will continue to be small in comparison with the world's total agricultural area.

DIVISIONS OF HUMAN GEOGRAPHY

In this brief survey of the earth it is impossible to give due attention to many aspects of human geography. Much of the work of American geographers, for example, has consisted in the study of particular forms of agriculture or manufacturing, either in specific districts, or in terms of their world distribution. These are parts of the division of *economic geography.*

European geographers in recent years have been increasingly interested in the study of settlement forms, including villages (*Siedlungsgeographie* or settlement geography) and towns and cities (*urban geography*). In both cases are included such elements as location and site, the plan or pattern of street and building arrangements, the types of houses and other buildings, the economic character, and the internal functioning or physiology.

Human settlements and forms of land use in any region change with the passage of time. The comparative study of the cultural landscapes of different time periods in the same region constitutes the field of *historical geography.*

Another major division is called *social geography,* in which different regions are studied and compared with respect to such characteristics as health and bodily care, nourishment, clothing, and dwellings, entertainment, education, government, morals, art, and religious life. It is obvious that the aspects first listed will vary in regions differing in climate, soil, production, and relative location. The other characteristics vary also, though the relationships are not so direct and clear. For example, it is only when one knows the basic features of the natural landscape and of economic life of the dry lands of nomadic development that one can understand many of the cultural aspects of the nomads. Examples can be found in their social approval of stealing, the patriarchal tribal government, the artistry of their "Oriental" rugs, and even in many characteristics of their religion. The bible of Mohammedanism, the Koran, is clearly a product and a reflection of life in the dry lands. Such cultural features are just as definitely characteristic of the nomad regions as are rainless skies, parched grass, Bedouin tents, and the rich gardens of the oases.

If a population group has developed a certain unity in its cultural life distinct from that of other groups, particularly in regard to its language or dialect, its folklore and literature, its habits and customs, we may recognize it as a distinct "people" or "folk." In the *geography of peoples*, regional differences between these cultural groups are studied in their relation to such other regional differences as the products they consume and produce, the development and character of their agriculture, their towns and cities, and their types of buildings. A special aspect of this field is the geography of nationalities—cultural groups that have become conscious of their distinction, as groups, which they wish to maintain.

Quite different from the nationalities are those groups who, whether they wish it or not, are distinguished from others on the basis of race, usually as revealed by color. The presence of two or more obviously distinct racial groups in the same area is one of the most significant aspects of the geography of southern United States, South Africa, and most of Hispanic America.

Of all the aspects of social life, other than those directly concerned with land use, none is so closely related to geography as the political organization of the earth into territorial units. The states or countries and their subdivisions —provinces, counties, and townships—are all necessarily defined in terms of area. To be sure, the state is something more than an area—it is both a piece of land and a collection of people—but its underlying and determining criterion is that it is an area of earth's surface. The jurisdiction of a state, unlike that of almost any other social organization, is defined not in terms of the people who are its members, but in terms of its territorial limits. Consequently the character and strength of different states are not only results of the character, inheritance, and training of their populations, and of the form and quality of their governments; they are in large measure bound up in the geography of their areas. *Political geography,* therefore, studies the differences among political areas of the earth, in terms of their size, form, location, boundaries, and external relations; and within each, the relations between the different regions, the connecting routes, and the central capital.

RELATIONS TO OTHER SOCIAL SCIENCES

Significance of regional differentiation

The discussion in this chapter has been oriented to show how a knowledge of geography provides a basis for applying general principles of other social sciences to problems in specific areas of the world. The great differences in fundamental living conditions in the different regions of the world must be taken into account. For example, basic cultural features and institutions, farms, shops, roads, towns, schools, banks, labor unions, and chambers of commerce, which we think of as part of the ordinary everyday life of society, assume a very different character in other parts of the world. Over some wide areas they are essentially unknown.

These differences are not to be thought of purely in terms of a supposed historical sequence. Thus nomadism is often thought of as a necessary stage along the path of civilization preceding sedentary agriculture, whereas in fact most agricultural peoples, including in particular our primitive European ancestors, never went through such a phase. This specialized form of culture has been known to have existed at any time only in grasslands, and never in the forest areas. On the other hand, the absence of that culture in the dry lands of North America in pre-Columbian times did not indicate an inferior cultural stage of the Indians, for in the irrigable districts in our Southwest they had achieved a relatively high degree of agriculture. Our picture of the Plains Indians on horseback dates only from the time when Spanish horses were brought to Mexico and spread throughout the Plains.

Another example can be taken from the field of political science. When the Hispanic American countries secured their independence from Spain, they set up governments modelled after the democratic republic of the United States. It is well known that most of them have worked out very differently, and this fact is often ascribed to a difference between the Latin temperament and ours, or to a supposed degenerating effect of race mixture. But it is not in the more purely Latin countries like Argentina, nor yet in one of great racial mixture, Chile, that dictatorships and revolutions have been the continuously alternating forces in political life. These are more characteristic of the tropical countries of backward economic development and poor transportation conditions, where most of the population is illiterate and there is a marked social division between the small number of economically powerful whites and the great mass of native Indians and mixed peoples.

Man and nature

The natural environment of a region conditions its development, but chiefly in a passive sense. It may render difficult or even prohibit any particular form of human development. It may appear to suggest certain forms, not necessarily the most advantageous ones. But to claim that the fundament in any positive sense determines man's activities in a region is to assume what cannot be scientifically demonstrated. Nevertheless, much geographic work has expended itself on this thesis. Some geographers and various other social scientists as well, following the concept of materialist determinism, have attempted to show that human development was caused by the natural conditions in which it took place.

Suppose we think of various forest peoples suddenly migrating into an area of humid prairie. Some have brought with them crude tools, with which they used to cultivate the forest soil; they find that they are unable to break the heavy sod of the prairie, and so must change their basis of livelihood. If they have also been hunters in the forest they may turn to hunting the grass-eating animals of the prairie, but this will require a change of methods, in which traps and spears will be less useful, the bow and arrow far more so. If they possess the knowledge of domesticating animals, or are able to evolve it, they may tame wild horses, and so greatly improve their hunting ability. In either case, however, by hunting alone they will be able to support but a sparse population. Another group may have brought with them domestic cattle, sheep, and goats, or they might learn from others or evolve among themselves the art of domesticating these animals, if they exist in the wild state. This group might then become nomads, but if commercial possibilities are available they might follow the very different life of cattle and sheep ranchers. Still others might have sufficient technical knowledge and initiative to construct plows with which they could cultivate the soil, and grow all or many of the crops they had grown in the forest, as well as others that they might domesticate from wild vegetation.

Finally, it must not be forgotten that to those who are unable to make any of these adjustments, there remains always the alternative of starvation. And that also happens. Whichever adjustment furnished the most sustenance would lead to the largest population, and this might be expected to drive out the other forms. However, it has not always done so. Sparse numbers of nomadic peoples were able to prevent the growth of agriculture in arable parts of North Africa for many centuries after the collapse of the Roman Empire, and the fertile arable lands of Uruguay are still largely in vast ranches. But in any case, the significant conclusion is that whatever form of life the former forest peoples developed in such a prairie region would be different, in many respects, from their previous mode of existence.

Nature offers the background, the fundamental conditions in which different races of men, with different cultural inheritances and different degrees of ability and initiative, under different times and external circumstances, may develop one or another of many different ways of living, and create different cultural landscapes. But the natural foundation, or fundament, imposes limits in any region. These are not necessarily fixed nor definitely known, but nevertheless they prevent the development of certain types of activities. Furthermore, under a given set of economic and cultural conditions, some of the various uses to which the natural environment of any region may be put are more productive than others, and this is necessarily different in widely differing regions of the world.

This conclusion is in line with the original statement of the purpose of geography—to study and, as far as possible, to interpret the differences between the different regions of the world. The alert student will be constantly on the lookout in studying the other chapters in this book for the effects of such regional differences. These phenomena may belong properly in economics, political science, or sociology, but to interpret them correctly, it is necessary to have a knowledge of the underlying differences in natural conditions and in the actual development of different regions.

BIBLIOGRAPHY

Bowman, Isaiah, *Geography in Relation to the Social Sciences* (Charles Scribner's Sons, New York, 1934).

Vidal de La Blache, P., *Principles of Human Geography* (Henry Holt & Company, New York, 1926).

James, Preston E., *An Outline of Geography* (Ginn & Company, Boston, 1935).

Huntington, Ellsworth, *Human Habitat* (D. Van Nostrand Company, New York, 1927).

Huntington, Ellsworth, and Cushing, Sumner W., *Principles of Human Geography* (John Wiley & Sons, New York, 1934).

Whitbeck, R. H., and Finch, V. C., *Economic Geography* (McGraw-Hill Book Company, New York, 1935).

Bowman, Isaiah, *The New World; Problems in Political Geography.* World Book Company, Yonkers, New York, 1928.

Sauer, Carl, "Recent Developments in Cultural Geography," in *Recent Developments in the Social Sciences* (J. B. Lippincott Company, Philadelphia, 1927).

Hartshorne, Richard, "Recent Developments in Political Geography," *American Political Science Review*, 1935, pp. 785–804, 943–966.

Periodicals: *Annals of the Association of American Geographers; Geographical Review; Economic Geography; Journal of Geography.*

CHAPTER IX

Elements of Political Science

EVRON M. KIRKPATRICK

University of Minnesota

POLITICAL SCIENCE: THE SCOPE AND CHARACTER OF THE PRESENT STUDY

I F AN ordinary individual inspects his own mind, it soon becomes evident that a great part of what goes on there is too intimate, trivial, or senseless to be disclosed. At the same time, he is apt to come to the erroneous conclusion that such a condition is peculiar to himself and that no one else could possibly have thoughts as silly as his own.[1] If, indeed, there could be reproduced before him all of his thoughts, remarks, and actions for one ordinary day, it would be obvious to him how little of what he normally said or thought or did was the result of any really rational consideration of the problems with which he was confronted. It would, without question, annoy him to find how few of these things were the result of a deliberate search for the means of achieving ends.[2]

Nobody supposes that a man falls in love, lights a ciga-

---

[1] For especially interesting comments along this line, see Robinson, J. H., *The Mind in the Making*, Part II (Harper & Brothers, New York, 1921). This book is both an interesting and an informative one for the beginning student as well as for the more mature scholar.

[2] For a consideration of the non-rational aspects of man's actions in the political sphere, see Wallas, Graham, *Human Nature in Politics*, Third Edition (Constable & Company, London, 1920).

rette, talks about the weather, or takes a drink of water only after reasonably intellectual calculations as to the probable results and the best method of achieving such action. Nor does a man give, in most cases, much more attention to his daily relations with the state or its government. He buys a license for his automobile at the command of the state, and when he drives it he obeys traffic rules imposed by that association through its government. He is forced to buy a license in order that he may marry, and when a child is born he must file a birth certificate at the command of the state. He must educate his children and contribute directly or indirectly in the form of taxation for the education of the children of others. He must secure the permission of the state if he wishes a divorce, and he accepts its services in the form of police and fire protection, the supplying of water, and the regulation of the prices he pays for public utility services such as electricity, gas, and telephone. If the state goes to war, he pays the cost, and may be called upon to sacrifice his life for some cause to which he is indifferent. Yet, in all these relationships which the individual has with his government, he exhibits only a minor interest. In other words, the day-to-day activities of man are carried on, to a great extent, without reflection, and this is no less true in his relations with the state and its government than in other fields of human activity. Man seldom questions that which ordinarily passes for true, nor can he be expected to do so and carry on the activities of life. But habitual attitudes and habitual ways of acting must be challenged, for it is by questioning the why and how of daily life that advancement comes. It is one of the purposes of the formal study of the natural and social sciences to question and answer, and to train the ordinary man to do the same; it is in this process of question and answer, in this challenge to the habitual ways of acting and thinking in political affairs, that we find the essence of political science.

Since the times of classical antiquity there has been handed down a considerable body of knowledge which today falls under this categorical term, political science. It is a body of knowledge, systematized and classified, dealing with all matters which involve the origin and history of the state, the organization, activity, and aims of its government, its administrative methods, its functions, its sphere of activity, and even its right to exist. But political science no longer makes an attempt to deal with everything concerning the state. The magnitude and complexity of the modern world make this impossible, and there exists alongside political science a series of related disciplines such as economics, psychology, sociology, history, ethics, and so on, which not only contribute to the student of political science, but in turn make use of the results of his study.[3]

There has come to be, therefore, within the complexities of the modern physical, economic, and social world, a branch of study concerned with observed facts, systematically classified and more or less correlated, and which includes more or less trustworthy methods for the discovery of new truth within its domain. In such a sense political science is a science, although it may be that it can make no claim to the exactness and precision of physical sciences such as physics and chemistry.

The study of any science must begin with definition. The misty curtain which hangs between the crdinary man, and

[3] As to this, see Merriam, C. E., *New Aspects of Politics* (University of Chicago Press, Chicago, 1925); Ogburn, W. F., and Goldenweiser, A., *The Social Sciences and their Interrelations* (Houghton Mifflin Company, Boston, 1927). The second book discusses the relations of anthropology, economics, history, political science, and sociology to each other and to the other formal disciplines.

at times even the scholar, and the understanding of political actualities and ideas is made up of an inadequate understanding of the concepts and terminology with which he comes in contact. The validity of any reasoned conclusions depends upon the consistency with which one uses the language at one's disposal. Certain words have certain meanings; they denote certain things, relations, or operations, and ordinary day-to-day experience does not require great accuracy. In this respect, everyone knows that the language of ordinary conversation is notably vague. It is not adequate for use in a special study. As a result, a distinctive vocabulary must be built up for each of the different sciences, and it is in this respect that the social sciences are handicapped, for, to a greater extent than the natural sciences, they employ the language of every-day conversation.

Words are, after all, intrinsically symbolic, and emotional associations with them often prevent clarity. This is generally true of the social sciences, and particularly true of political science. Words such as democracy, Socialism, liberty, equality, Fascism, and state have powerful emotional connotations. They are frequently used as battle cries, as appeals to the non-rational rather than the rational side of man's nature. This is borne out by the conduct of political campaigns and the political oratory coupled with them, or by the activities of those professional patriots whose campaigns against all those who offend their venerated sentiments are one of the great obstacles to the attainment of truth in political science. Certainly a great proportion of those disputes which arise about the true nature of state, government, law, property, duty, liberty, equality, Fascism, Communism, and democracy would disappear if precise definitions of those words were understood by all.

Artistotle has said that "a definition is a phrase signifying a thing's essence." It is the declaration of the significance of a word or phrase, and logically it aims to unmask the warp and woof of a concept, partly in order to make it definite, and partly in order to provide the possibility of a systematic examination and disentangling of the subject matter with which it deals. This, then, is principally the task of any introduction to an elementary study of any of the formal disciplines—a definition, an unveiling, an interpretation of the principal terminology and concepts of that study. Such a task, however, may be much more difficult than it appears. A survey of some of the most commonly used words reveals so many variations of meaning that one is almost unable to understand what is meant by a particular term unless it is defined as it is used. It has been said that an examination of the different ways in which the term "state" is used would yield as many as two hundred definitions and that perhaps as few as half of these would be in agreement.[4] The situation is not different with respect to other terms, for example, law, sovereignty, government, democracy, Socialism, liberty, and others. Such a situation makes the task of definition and clear thinking an intensely difficult one, and the job of one who would understand is not to memorize the hundreds of definitions that have been given, but to attempt to formulate some general conclusions for oneself and, at the same time, make an effort to understand in the speech and writing of others the meanings which they attribute to the terms they employ.

---

[4] For various definitions of the word *state,* see Garner, J. W., *Political Science and Government,* Chapter IV (American Book Company, New York, 1930); or Wilson, F. G., *Elements of Modern Politics,* Chapter III (McGraw-Hill Book Company, New York and London, 1936).

A complete survey of the elementary principles of political science, of the fundamental concepts and terminology of that study, would include a consideration of the origin and historical development of the things to be considered, both in their actual form in the real world and in their ideal form in the world of ideas. But, if one is to compress a discussion into limits that are at all manageable and readable, a check must be placed upon desires to search out origins and portray the forces and ideas which have played such an important part in earlier centuries and have had so much influence upon the present one.

THE STATE AS A CONCEPT OF POLITICAL SCIENCE

Wherever people live together in groups, wherever individuals dwell in close relationship with one another, certain problems of regulation, of service, and of coördination arise. Streets must be laid out, graded, and repaired; the sick must be cared for; disease must be prevented; protection of life and property against the ravages of fire, theft, and assault must be provided; educational facilities must be created, maintained, and supervised; the demands of industry, agriculture, labor, and other groups must be considered and acted upon; and taxes must be levied and collected for use in taking care of these problems and many others. Life within a community, therefore, calls for the association of people for the purpose of securing a better life. One form of such association is the state.

The state is not a mystical thing, but an association of people living within more or less definite territorial limits, free or nearly free from external control, and possessed of organized machinery for the handling of its problems. This machinery is called government and is, in general, the recipient of habitual obedience. In other words, the state is an association of people just as a church, a lodge, or a trade union is an association of people. It does, however, possess certain constituent elements or attributes which differentiate it from these other associations, and which present certain other problems with which political science must deal. The rules which establish the nature of this society are called laws and have a superiority, in other words are sovereign, over all other rules. The persons who make and enforce the rules are said to be the government, and that portion of the rules which settles the fundamental principles and practices in accordance with which the government operates is called the constitution. These words describe a certain series of relationships in the community, and are only a formal source of reference until supplemented by further discussion.

The state as thus described should not be identified, however, with the community as a whole; the state and society should not be considered as one and the same. There are certain parts of life into which the state should have no thought of entry. It will, as Professor Laski puts it, promote that amount of courtesy between neighbors which is set by the observance of order; but it will not force the Browns of St. Paul to invite the Smiths of Minneapolis to dinner, whatever may be the social aspirations of Mrs. Smith. There are other interests in the community which the state as here conceived is unfitted to control. It has no business to suppress free speech and discussion of public problems; it should not interfere with freedom of teaching in the schools; it can succeed in regulating the religious life of its people only with considerable injury to society; it should be condemned for interfering with free association or unconventional conduct except where the public welfare and the rights of others are at stake. But this is not to say that the state has never been and is not at present considered by many as identical with society, nor is it to say that states have not and do not commonly violate these principles. One has only to look at the extent to which free speech, education, assembly, and individual behavior have been restricted, to be aware of the difference between the moral ideal and actuality. Nor are these violations of principle confined to dictatorial countries, for there is adequate evidence of them in the United States; and it is this constant conflict between ways of viewing the state, both in terms of what it is and what it ought to be, that has caused much of our modern confusion.

Yet, no matter how one looks upon the "shoulds" and "should nots" of political life, no matter what one's attitude may be toward the relation of the state to the activities mentioned above, the state would seem to be more able than other associations to perform many of the functions, and to make the rules governing many of the activities within the modern community. It may be said, therefore, that regardless of how realistic a point of view one may wish to take, regardless of how one looks upon the ethical right or moral duty of the state, ultimate power or sovereignty may be located, as a source of formal and legal reference, in that association.

The above conception is not essentially different from that held by those who view the state from the standpoint of public law. They consider the state in a more abstract sense as an artificial legal person, much as a corporation is an artificial person in the field of private law, and attribute to this legal person ultimate power or sovereignty which is expressed by the government through law.[5]

The state then is an association, but the tendency of men to join together in associations is one of the outstanding characteristics of modern life. There are churches, political parties, trade unions, lodges, clubs, and a legion of other associations, which possess characteristics that are greatly similar to those possessed by the state. They are all organized; they often have a definite territorial basis; in many cases they have treasuries and budgets, own property, have constitutions, statutes, rules of order, and even have some coercive power over their members. What then is the difference between the state and these associations?

In the first place, membership in the state is compulsory, while it is voluntary in other associations. The member is free to withdraw from the state only under very limited conditions. Moreover, the individual can usually be a member of only one state, while he may hold membership in many other associations.

Secondly, the state as it is known today is confined within a definite territory, while other associations may be international in scope. They may cut across national boundaries and include within their membership the citizens of other states.

Thirdly, the state concerns itself with more purposes than voluntary associations ordinarily do. The extent of the interests and activities of the state is broad and general, while that of other associations is limited and particular.

---

[5] For a more detailed explanation of this way of looking at the state, see Willoughby, W. W., *Fundamental Concepts of Public Law,* Chapter IV (The Macmillan Company, New York, 1924).

This is not meant to indicate that the interests of the state coincide with those of society. The concerns of society are the collective total of all of the interests of mankind. In many of these interests the state is relatively unconcerned, and when it so broadens its concerns as to make them identical with those of society, the totalitarian state comes into existence, as in Italy, Germany, and Russia, and the distinction between the state and society is lost.

Fourthly, the state is a permanent and enduring association while other associations may not be. This does not mean that certain other associations such as the Catholic Church do not exhibit qualities of permanence, but that in general the state is permanent while other associations are not. The form of government may change, the location of political power may swing back and forth, but the state as an association continues.

Finally, the state possesses a legal supremacy over other associations which marks it as a thing apart. This does not mean that the state in practice is always supreme, nor does it mean that in the actual exercise of its supremacy it is always morally right, but it does mean that as a distinguishing mark the state possesses this power of legal command and the legal right to use the coercive sanction of force.

SOVEREIGNTY OF THE STATE

It is this last feature of legal supremacy or sovereignty which constitutes one of the most significant features of the state, and any comprehensive discussion of it would lead into most of the aspects of political science. The concept of sovereignty has been given certain distinctive characteristics or attributes, such as absoluteness, permanence, universality, exclusiveness, indivisibility, unity, inalienability, and others.[6] Briefly these have been interpreted to mean that the state is superior to any other association within its jurisdiction, that there can be no legal limit to its power, that its power extends over every person and association within its territory, that this continues as long as the state exists, that this power is a unified thing, that it cannot be divided nor given to others, and so on. While these characteristics convey only an idea of what is meant when sovereignty is spoken of, and while many writers would like to see the use of the word discontinued in both its domestic and international aspects, it does describe, for purposes of formal legal reference, a characteristic of the state.

It must be remembered, however, that in ascribing sovereignty to the state, there is no intention of denying the valuable contribution of those writers who point out that in actuality the state may not be able, in many instances, to enforce its laws, and that the exercise of its power is often morally unjustifiable. That the state may not be able to enforce its laws in all instances and that often the rules are morally unjustifiable is borne out by such historical examples as the effective disobedience of the fugitive-slave laws by the opponents of slavery in the North prior to the Civil War, by the Southern emasculation of the reconstruction amendments in so far as they were meant to protect the Negro, and by the ineffectiveness of "prohibition" in certain sections. In each of these instances the state was unable to enforce its laws effectively, and in each there was a considerable portion of the people who felt the rules were

[6] For a more detailed discussion see Garner, J. W., *Political Science and Government,* Chapter VII (American Book Company, New York, 1930); Willoughby, W. W., *Fundamental Concepts of Public Law,* Chapter VIII (The Macmillan Company, New York, 1924).

morally unjustifiable; yet, there was and is little doubt that the state had the legal power to control these matters. But, though the state does not have a complete monopoly of force and complete supremacy in actuality, it does have a near monopoly of force and a near supremacy in actuality; the degree to which this monopoly and supremacy are possessed vary from state to state in the modern world. Certainly those dictatorial states, Italy, Germany, and Russia, have a greater monopoly of force than the more democratic states such as England, the United States, and France; and some states at some periods do not possess a sufficient amount of this actual power to keep domestic order, for example, the United States between 1861 and 1865.

GOVERNMENT — THE MACHINERY OF THE STATE

The state, however, looked upon as an association, or, from the standpoint of public law, as an artificial legal person, does not act directly, but must have some institutional arrangements or machinery through which to express and enforce its sovereignty. These institutions, this machinery by which the state acts, is called government. Just as other associations such as clubs or churches or trade unions or lodges have their institutional arrangements in the form of a president, a secretary, a treasurer, and committees, so does the state have its institutional arrangements in the form of the executive, the legislatures, the courts, the administrative bodies, and so forth, or government. The government, then, is the agent through which the state acts.

Certain writers, upon viewing the state and government, conclude that for all practical purposes they are identical. They point out that the state orders one not to steal and punishes one for a violation of that order; the state orders the individual to pay taxes and uses coercive means to secure obedience, but these legal rules, these commands of the state, do not come into being, nor are they enforced by some abstract process. They have been willed, they have been created by some man or body of men, and, by some such agency, they will have to be enforced. Legal rules neither express nor enforce themselves. The conclusion then, of some writers, is that if the individual only sees or feels the government and not the state, and if the only contact he has with the will of the state is actually contact with the government or the men who make it up, there can be no real reason to distinguish the two.[7] Nor is there, others say, any value or truth in talking about a government of laws and not of men, for laws are always made by men, interpreted by men, and enforced by men. There can be no government without both laws and men.[8]

There is some validity in such a view, namely, in so far as it makes us aware that the state is not an end in itself, but a means to an end; in so far as it makes us aware that the state is the product of social relations among men and has for its purpose the creation of a better world for the individual to live in; and finally, in so far as it contributes to an understanding that government is always a government of men and that men may err in such a way that they may have to be called to account. Thus, this view has validity just to the extent that it makes it clear that in actual practice it is these men, making up the government, who really express the will and power of the state. Yet,

---

[7] See Coker, F. W., "Pluralistic Theories and the Attack upon State Sovereignty," in Merriam, C. E., Barnes, H. E., and others, *Political Theories: Recent Times,* Chapter III (The Macmillan Company, New York, 1924).

[8] For an illuminating discussion of this point see McBain, H. L., *The Living Constitution,* pp. 1–5 (The Macmillan Company, New York, 1928).

awareness of such facts does not lessen the value, for purposes of formal reference, or for purposes of explaining the fundamentals of public law, of the distinction between the state as an association or juristic person and the government as its agent or machinery. Each of these views supplements the other, each is valuable for its purpose, and each should be understood and used. The danger comes from attempting to supplant one view by the other instead of using one to supplement the other.

LAW AS A CONCEPT OF POLITICAL SCIENCE

The state has been described here as the association of the members of society in such a way as to form a political community. The state is that aspect of society which embodies its political organization for certain common purposes. Yet at any one time, the government of the state is the sovereign organization of the state, that is, at any one time the government possesses in its entirety the sovereign powers of the state, and it is in this sense that the state and government are identified. This does not mean, however, that the government cannot be limited. It is, thus, the government which seeks through its organs to effectuate the purposes of the state in achieving order, and in making possible the good life of the individual, the community, and even the world at large. In order to do this the state lays down certain rules; it expresses its power and its wishes through the government in the form of legal imperatives or law. It makes rules regulating business, providing for the adjustment of disputes between citizens, providing an educational system, requiring licenses to engage in certain professions, laying out streets and highways and providing for their upkeep, protecting life and property, organizing and limiting the government, and doing innumerable other things. Such rules, taken collectively as a system that regulates and orders our conduct and the conduct of our government, are called law.

Law, however, may be divided into separate classes of rules which have a relation to each other and to the collective whole. In this second sense law is made up of various elements varying in manner of statement, in content, and in origin.

There is, in the first place, constitutional law. This is a body of fundamental principles, written or unwritten, which controls the organization and practices of the state itself and the exercise of the powers of its government. The elements which make up this body of constitutional law are the formal written constitution, where one exists, judicial decisions, statutes, administrative rules and orders, and even customs, usages, and conventions.

Secondly, there are laws generally known as statutes which, taken collectively, are called statute law. These laws are merely rules which are written down in a formal manner by the legislative branch of the government, and may or may not be a part of that body of rules known as constitutional law. They are made at a definite time by a definite body, and take a definite place in the legal system.

Thirdly, there is a large body of law which is not statute law, which has grown rather than been made, and which is called common law. It is impossible to point to a definite time when it began or to find a definite person or body of persons by whom it was made. It is not the result of formal action by a part of the government; yet, as far back as the law reports go, in English-speaking countries at least, the judges are found assuming that there is a common law. The statute law assumes the existence of the common law; it is the supplement of the common law and has no meaning except by reference to it. The sources of the common law are the decisions of judges, the works of learned jurists, and the decisions of courts in other countries having a system of law derived from the English.

Fourthly, there is, in Anglo-Saxon countries, another class of law known as equity. The rules of equity are law and not merely expressions of moral judgments as to what is equitable or just. They are the supplement of the common law, and yet in actual practice they produce results contrary to what the common-law rules alone would have produced. Equity fills up the gaps and corrects the abuses of the common law; it is a sort of rival to the common law, offering remedies of a superior character even in those cases in which the common law claims to give relief. To take an example, the common law usually gives only a monetary relief to one who is injured; the common law orders one who injures another to pay damages. If a man makes a contract to buy a horse, but the one from whom it was purchased refuses to deliver it, the common law will only order damages to be paid. Equity meets the problem by ordering the delivery of the horse. It commands the performance of the contract—it forces the man actually to do what he promised.

Fifthly, there is a body of rules or laws which may be called administrative rules and regulations, for want of a better name. They are the result of action by administrative agencies which have been given the power to make rules and regulations for definite purposes and within certain limits which are laid down in statutes. The exercise of this power of administrative officers produces rules of law which have a similar force, and, in many cases, affect the ordinary citizen more directly than the acts of the . legislative body.

Sixthly, there is a type of law known as administrative

law. It is that branch of the law which consists of the rules defining the rights and duties of private individuals and public officials in their dealings with each other, and defining and fixing the procedure by which those rights and duties are enforced.[9] It should be pointed out, however, in order to avoid confusion, that the term is used at times in other senses. It is sometimes held to apply to those rules or orders of an administrative branch of the government which are promulgated with the permission and by authority of the legislature; and, at times, it is held to apply to that special part of public law which describes the nature of the activity of the executive department of the government.[10]

Seventhly, and finally, there is a group of rules commonly called international law. These rules govern the relation of the state to other states, and differ somewhat from the preceding classes in their origin and manner of enforcement. These rules, some writers feel, are not deserving of the title of law at all, or at least only in a very limited sense.[11] The opinion here, however, is that there is an international law composed of those rules which define the behavior of the general body of civilized states in their relations with one another. It is submitted that these rules find their support in precedent and convention and not in vague and ideal doctrines of natural law; that they are possessed of a concrete form amenable to classification and definite arrangement; that in the last analysis the scholar has the material for just as true a study of international law as he has for national or

---

[9] For a more extensive discussion see below, pp. 540–541.

[10] See Keeton, C. W., *The Elementary Principles of Jurisprudence*, p. 202 (A. and C. Black, Ltd., London, 1930).

[11] As to this view, see Willoughby, W. W., *Fundamental Concepts of Public Law*, pp. 282 ff. (The Macmillan Company, New York, 1924). Also, see Garner, J. W., *Political Science and Government*, pp. 190–193 (American Book Company, New York, 1930).

domestic law. Justice Gray has clearly stated a principle established early in our history, namely, the binding force of international law: "International law is part of our law and must be ascertained and administered by the courts of justice of appropriate jurisdiction, as often as questions of right depending upon it are duly presented for their determination." [12]

These rules or principles, which make up the law, are distinguishable from all other rules within the community in that they have behind them the ultimate power of the state. But this must not be taken to mean that they always can be enforced, for there are times when the legal imperatives of the state cannot be enforced—witness the late prohibition law.[13] Nor is this definition or explanation to be taken to mean that these rules are always morally justified. Some men certainly feel that there is no moral justification for rules of the state, or laws, that restrain freedom of speech or association (for example, suppression of the Communist party in some American states), that suppress freedom of teaching (witness the laws by which certain American states have forbidden the teaching of evolution), that interfere with religious freedom, or that provide for capital punishment. Nevertheless, these rules are law, and any other definition deprives the concept of any definiteness or precision upon which to base one's study. This, however, does not deny the value of the contribution of those writers who point out that the laws of the state are often unenforceable and often morally unjustifiable, for such a consideration is a valuable supplement to any consideration of the legal

---

[12] The Paquete Habana, 175 U.S. 677 (1900). See in this connection the material in Haines, C. G., and Haines, B. M., *Principles and Problems of Government,* Third Edition, pp. 595–604 (Harper & Brothers, New York, 1934).

[13] On unenforceable laws, see above, pp. 390–391.

imperatives of the state. Justice and law are often not the same thing. It is urged, therefore, that this conception of law does not deny the validity of those views of law which differ. Law, as are most things in life, is complex. It may be viewed, not as the will of the state, but as that from which the will of the state derives the moral authority that it possesses.[14] The difference is not absolute, but it is a difference in point of view and emphasis. Each view helps to supplement the other, and to provide a more adequate view of the complexities of life. This is, perhaps, an abandonment of precision and simplicity, but life is not simple and precise; it is intricate, complex, and hard to understand. Any real understanding of it comes only from sustained and critical inquiry into its every phase.

POLITICAL THEORY

Wherever one finds an association of individuals with power over other associations and individuals, and making rules and regulations which it commands them to obey, it is only natural that some persons ask themselves how this came to be, what its justification is, whether there are not certain ethical principles which this political association must follow, and what objectives, purposes, or ends it should achieve. It is probably true that in primitive social and political organizations that spontaneously arose to meet the demands of man, there was little speculation about these matters. But it is characteristic of man to examine his surroundings, his beliefs, and his institutions, to question authority and plan for change. The state, being one of the most universal and most powerful of human institutions,

---

[14] See the discussion by Duguit, Krabbe, and Laski in Coker, F. W., *Recent Political Thought,* pp. 533–539 (D. Appleton-Century Company, New York, 1934).

has come in for its fair share of examination, and what is known as political theory or political philosophy has arisen as the outcome of this examination.

At first this speculation may have been inextricably bound up with other concepts, but as man's power of observation and analysis developed, there was built up a continually enlarging domain of political speculation. It usually bears a close relation to the period in which it is expressed, that is, to the political conditions then existent, and it is in its nature essentially relative; it can, in other words, hardly lay claim to the expression of final truths. The chief source of this political theory is the writings of those philosophers who have expressed a definite answer to questions of political speculation relative to their own times. The study of these writings usually begins with a reading of the writers of classical Greece, but may go back into more ancient times. It may, in fact, include a consideration of early Chinese, Hindu, Egyptian, and Hebrew thought. It is worth noting, however, that much political philosophy is unexpressed and must be sought, not in the formal writings of such men as Plato, Aristotle, and others, but in the theory underlying the actual political, economic, and social organization and practices of a period. This, for example, is particularly true of the early Roman period, that is, the period of the Roman Republic and Roman Empire.

The chief problems of political thought have been essentially similar throughout the history of its overt expression. It appears that all political theories move within a given range, and that no new political ideas are possible as long as the state is the product of human nature. All political possibilities have been forecast by the political thinkers of all ages, and no new idea is invented that does not fall within the range of the general political philosophy of the historical world. The form of expression, the structure which surrounds the idea, may vary, but the ideas are essentially the same. It is true, perhaps, that representative government was not known to the classical world, but it comes into the category of the deliberative element which the great thinkers of antiquity, such as Plato and Aristotle, have recognized and discussed. As one noted student of the history of political theory has said, the movement of thought has but come back to the place from which it started twenty-three hundred years ago. This is the lesson to be learned from the study of the history of political speculation, and is, he maintains, no different from the lesson to be learned from the study of the history of all the other varieties of thought by which men have sought the answer to the basic problems with which they are confronted in this world.[15]

Some of the questions to which speculation constantly recurs are questions as to the justification of political authority, that is, as to the very right of the state to exist; as to the proper location of political power within the state, that is, the justification for the existence of particular forms of governmental organization and of the right of any particular person or group of persons to hold the seat of power; as to the proper division between governmental control and individual freedom, that is, the nature of rights against and duties toward the state and government; as to the sphere of economic and social life that properly can be placed under political control, that is, the establishment of some sort of criteria for estimating the extent of the ethical justification of particular political policies and governmental

[15] Dunning, W. A., *Political Theories: From Rousseau to Spencer*, p. 423 (The Macmillan Company, New York, 1922).

functions; and as to the nature of interstate relations and
the amount and type of control necessary between organized independent political communities, that is, a theory of
international relations.[16]

The beginning student may not be able to see much value
in such speculation, and a study of this thought in the past
may seem even less fruitful. There are, however, certain
values in this study which, in reality, makes up one of the
two great branches of political science, the other being the
analytical, descriptive, and comparative study of political
institutions. The political theorist searches for some sort of
final truth within the political sphere, especially in relation
to ethical values. He seeks satisfaction for the demands
which his speculative curiosity makes upon him. It can be
said therefore, that one value in the study of political theory
is the purely intellectual satisfaction that one derives from
it. The inclination at present, it seems, is to underestimate
the very real desire for knowledge which characterizes man,
and the very real satisfaction that he gets from the gratification of that desire. A second value in the study of political
philosophy lies in the close relation between theories and
the actual historical conditions of a period. The study of
political thought is just as essential to an adequate understanding of history as history is to an understanding of
political thought. For example, one cannot hope to understand the development of the American constitutional system without a careful survey of the political thought which
the actual conditions of its development has evoked and
which in turn may have had significant effect upon the
actualities of that historical development. Such is signifi-

---

[16] For a brief résumé of the development of ideas relative to these problems, see Coker, F. W., *Recent Political Thought*, pp. 5–30 (D. Appleton-
Century Company, New York, 1934).

cantly the case with respect to the period in which the constitution was framed and with respect to the period prior to the Civil War. There is, however, another significant value in such a study, and that is in making possible the refutation of false theories. At the same time such a study serves as the basis for the formulation of one's own ideas. The study of political philosophy is the testing ground for the developing mind; it finds the weak spots and proves the strength of that mind. The classics of political theory—and it is essential that the student of political thought know them first hand—offer a real opportunity for developing the immature mind. It is essential that the student be brought into contact with great minds, and given the chance to struggle with them; it is only through such a process that one who wishes to learn can achieve that critical, discriminative, challenging, and skeptical attitude which is so necessary if one is to absorb ideas and develop a habit of personal curiosity and investigation.

ATTEMPTS TO CLASSIFY STATES

The curiosity of man and his desire to systematize and classify knowledge does not stop with an attempt to reach a theoretical explanation, or justification, of the actualities of the world in which he lives. There are, therefore, attempts to simplify the political world by providing classifications for the facts experienced, and this is no less true in the case of states than in other matters.

The differences between states have seemed apparent to many in the past, and the diversity of points of view in looking at the state have led students to attempt classifications. Many of these classifications have followed Aristotle's in pointing to monarchy, aristocracy, and polity or democracy. Monarchy, Aristotle said, is a state in which the ruling power is vested in a single individual; aristocracy is a state in which ruling power is in the hands of a small group; and democracy or polity is a state in which the masses have political power. There have been, of course, all sorts of other classifications of states based upon such criteria as the form, character, or spirit of the government, or based upon the wealth, resources, or strength of the community, and on many other things. Such classifications could be multiplied almost without end, and one could point to theocratic, oligarchic, plutocratic, non-sovereign, land-locked, maritime, and imperialistic states as concrete examples of the forms these classifications take. The categories which these classifications include would be of little value and would be, in the last analysis, classifications of governments instead of states, or classifications based on geographical, topographical, economic, or other considerations not directly related to political science.

THE IMPOSSIBILITY OF CLASSIFYING STATES

Actually, in their real legal and political essentials, all states are identical. It should be recognized that no matter what the organization of their institutional machinery or in what sort of manner their powers be exercised, there is in all states a material sameness of purpose; beneath all the actual or outward appearances, and all the concrete institutional arrangements, there is a real similarity of nature. If all the non-essential elements are left out of the picture, it should be possible to see those elements that appear in all forms of states, whether the governmental organization is presidential or parliamentary, democratic or autocratic, federal or unitary—namely, people, territory, government, association, permanence and sovereignty.[17]   Although this essential identity of states is frequently agreed to, most writers feel that governments can be differentiated and classified in accordance with their form of organization.   In short, it is maintained that governments can be classified. One writer of note, for example, after pointing out that all states are essentially similar—all of them possessing the same sovereign attributes—says that consequently the only method of differentiating them is in accordance with the individualities of their respective governmental organization.[18]

CLASSIFICATION OF GOVERNMENTS

It is true that there are significant similarities and differences among the various forms of governmental organization and that the study of the organization and operation of governments is one of the important fields of political study.   The difficulty with this study, and with the attempts to simplify and to provide labels and pigeonholes for a complex subject matter, is the lack of proper criteria for the simplification and classification of governments.   The difficulty is not lessened by the fact that the political scientist, the historian, the legal scholar, the sociologist, the expert in international law, and other specialists are apt to look upon government from different points of view.   There is no single simple principle according to which all governments of the world can be simplified and classified.   There is no principle which includes all that is wished and excludes all that is not.   In many cases the attempts at classification,

---

[17] For a discussion of these essential elements or attributes of a state, see Garner, J. W., *Political Science and Government,* Chapter V (American Book Company, New York, 1930).

[18] Willoughby, W. W., *An Examination of the Nature of the State,* pp. 351–352 (The Macmillan Company, New York, 1896).   See also Garner, J. W., *Political Science and Government,* pp. 255–256 (American Book Company, New York, 1930).

rather than simplifying the matter for the beginner, actually lead him into a complicated study of comparative government.[19] On the other hand, even though there may be extensive overlapping between forms and institutions of government and even though the principles upon which classifications are based are not exclusive and in some cases are not explanatory without considerable elaboration, there is a value in the classification of governments. Classifications are valuable in helping to make clear to the beginner the fundamentals of governmental structure. This is especially true of those classifications that are broad, possessed of a definite character, and based upon a principle which is commonly agreed to and can be consistently applied. The value of classification of forms of government has led to the devotion of a considerable amount of time to this task, and while many of the older classifications are no longer useful, there are certain classifications that are of considerable merit and are commonly accepted and used by students working in the field of comparative government. Some of the more common classifications are: (1) monarchical, aristocratic, or democratic, based upon the number of persons participating in the government; (2) parliamentary or presidential, based on the relation of the executive to the legislature; (3) unitary or federal, based on the territorial distribution of power; (4) dictatorial or democratic, based on the amount of protection given to individual rights and liberties.

---

[19] For some of the classifications offered, see Wilson, F. G., *Elements of Modern Politics,* Chapters XIII, XIV (McGraw-Hill Book Company, New York, 1936) ; Willoughby, W. W., *Fundamental Concepts of Public Law,* Chapter XIII (The Macmillan Company, New York, 1924) ; Strong, C. F., *Modern Political Constitutions,* Chapter III (G. P. Putnam's Sons, New York, 1930). Note especially the summary on page 73, and the complex tables on pages 354 and 355.

Monarchy, aristocracy, and democracy

One of the oldest classifications, but one of the least useful, is that based upon the number participating in the control of government. It results in the setting up of three types—monarchy, the government of one; artistocracy, the government of the few; democracy, the government of the many. Such a classification is of little value; it tells us nothing distinctive about a government, and it does not fit modern conditions. One might, on such a basis as this, place Italy, Great Britain, and Sweden in the same class, and, while it is true that all are monarchies in the sense of having kings, Italy is a dictatorship, while Great Britain and Sweden are political democracies. It may be pointed out, in addition, that there are practically no states where the system of government leaves power in the hands of only one man, nor are there many where the great mass of the people actually controls the government. It would seem that there is a considerable amount of truth in the contention that, whatever may be the theoretical or legal form of the government, there has never been any government except that of the few. It is significant to note, however, that in modern dictatorial governments, which at least approach one-man rule, there is a great deal of popular participation in the plebiscites that are held. In many of the dictatorial governments there are more people voting in proportion to the population than is the case in the United States. Facts such as these, coupled with the difficulty of distinguishing aristocracy from either of the other forms, make it doubtful whether this classification is, in itself, of any real value.

In the modern world the true opposite of monarchy is republicanism, that is, merely the absence of an hereditary chief of state. Little is gained by trying to contrast monarchy with aristocracy or democracy, as the political writers of former generations did. No aristocracy, in the classical sense, exists at the present time, and it is doubtful whether any ever existed. Many democracies, of course, exist both in Europe and America, but some of them are monarchies and some republics. The worthwhile distinction to make is to contrast democracy with dictatorship, and this is discussed fully later in this chapter.

Unitary and federal systems

A second, more significant classification results in the division of the governments of the world into two classes, unitary and federal. It is a classification commonly agreed upon by students of government, and it is based upon an analysis of the territorial distribution of governmental powers and functions.

A unitary government is one in which the whole power of government is constitutionally placed in the hands of a single central establishment, which in turn delegates power to the political subdivisions of the country. In fact, the very existence of the political subdivisions depends upon the will of the central governmental authority. In a unitary system the central government establishes such areas and institutions, such territorial or political subdivisions as it wishes; and it has the power to alter, modify, or destroy them as it thinks desirable. The governmental systems of Great Britain, France, Italy, Germany, and, in fact, of most of the countries of the world belong to this class.

In the federal system of government the legal form is quite different. Here the essential feature is a distribution of powers and functions between the central government and major political subdivisions. Such distribution of powers is always marked out in a written constitution, and a change in the constitution cannot be made by either the subdivisions or the central government acting alone. The major political subdivisions are not created by the central government, nor is the central government created by the major political subdivisions; both are established by the constitution. Historically, however, it is true that some of the subdivisions of the existing federations were previously in existence and that action initiated by those states later resulted in the constitution establishing the federal system. Such, for example, was the case in this country. The thirteen original states were in existence prior to the federation and participated in the creation of the constitution establishing the federal United States. As a result, the subdivisions do not exist merely at the will of the central authority, nor can their powers or functions be abolished by it alone. In the United States, for example, the constitution specifically delegates certain powers to the central government, and expressly reserves the rest to the major political subdivisions, or "states." Thus the relation of the "states" to the national government is carefully defined; the "states" and the national government have their independent fields of action. One cannot, in theory, encroach upon the field of the other. This, however, is not the only possible arrangement of powers in a federal system. The specifically enumerated powers might be given to the "states" and the remainder left to the central authority. In Canada, the powers of both the central government and the provinces are enumerated in the constitution. Canada furnishes the leading example of this plan, although the enumeration is followed by a clause giving, in the case of the central authority, a general grant of power with respect to matters of national importance, and, in the case of the provinces, a general grant of powers with respect to matters of a local nature.

All the governments of the present day fall into one or the other of the classes described. In view of this fact, the classification as unitary or federal is of considerable significance. It should, however, be pointed out, in order to prevent confusion, that unitary government should not be identified with centralization of powers and functions; nor should federal government be identified too closely with decentralization of powers and functions. It is possible in a unitary system to have a great deal of local self-government, to have a decentralization of power and functions, but such local self-government is under the legal control of the central authority. Such is the case in England; and while the central government may legally, through action by parliament, restrict or abolish the political subdivisions or their powers, in actual practice there is little probability of any drastic changes. In France, on the other hand, there is a unitary government with power highly centralized, both legally and in fact, in the hands of the central authorities, and there is little local autonomy or local self-government. Thus a people can have centralization or decentralization of powers or functions, and, at the same time, have legal control in the hands of the central government.

In a federal system there may also be centralization or decentralization, depending upon the constitutional distribution of powers and upon other factors in the actual operation of the government. The tendency has been, however, toward centralization in both the federal and unitary systems. The significant fact is that in actual operation federal and unitary systems may be much alike. There may be a great deal of decentralization and local autonomy in a unitary system, as in England, or a great deal of centralization, as in France. On the other hand, a federal system may be one with a great deal of centralization of power in the hands of the central authorities, as in the Soviet Union.[20] The conclusion must be that, while the classification as unitary or federal is an important and useful aid in the study of government, some additional information as to the actual operation of the respective governments is necessary for an adequate understanding of them.[21]

Parliamentary and presidential governments

A third classification results in the division of governments into two classes, namely, presidential and parliamentary. It is a classification based upon an analysis of the relation of the executive to the legislature. This relationship has become more important today than ever before because of the increasingly important part the executive is coming to play in the modern world. Not only is the executive coming to play a larger and larger role in the initiation of legislation, but with the increased amount of legislation, especially of a collectivistic type, it is coming to have a greater and greater amount of discretionary power in the execution of law.

Parliamentary government is usually defined as that type of government in which the real executive—cabinet or ministry—is in theory and often in actual practice responsible to the legislature for its policies and acts. The ministry in power, in theory at least, can remain in power only

[20] See Starr, J. R., "The New Constitution of the Soviet Union" in the *American Political Science Review*, December, 1936, Vol. 30, pp. 1143–1152.

[21] For a further discussion of this point, especially with relation to federalism in the United States, see McBain, H. L., *The Living Constitution*, Chapter II (The Macmillan Company, New York, 1928).

so long as it has the support of the legislature; that is, on all important measures it must, upon a test vote, get a majority. If it fails to get such a majority, the ministry is considered to have lost the confidence of the legislature, and must resign or dissolve parliament. The members of the ministry are, as a rule, members of the legislature—in fact, usually members of the majority party. If they are not members, they usually have the privilege of seats in the legislature and have the opportunity to participate in debate, although they do not have the right to vote. Such a system, however, if only formally defined, may be attributed to a number of states in which the actual operation of the government is quite dissimilar. Both England and France have the parliamentary system, but its actual operation is quite different in France from what it is in England, owing to the multiple-party system and other factors.[22]

Presidential government has in general been distinguished from the parliamentary system by the fact that the chief executive is constitutionally independent of the legislature as to tenure, and to a considerable degree as to policies and acts. The members of the administrative branch, that is, the ministers or secretaries who are heads of departments, are appointed by the president, act for him, and are responsible to him, and not to the legislature. These members are not taken from the legislature, and in the United States cannot be members of it, nor can they have seats there. The legislature and executive are independent coördinate departments of the government.

The designation "presidential government" is not very satisfactory because there are governments of Europe which have a president as the head of the state but are parlia-

---

[22] See below, pp. 527–535.

mentary in character. In addition, here again, the formal distinction between the presidential and parliamentary systems serves little purpose unless one goes behind it to determine how the system works in actual practice as well as in legal theory. There are, for example, instances in which the theory of the operation of the presidential system in the United States differs from the parliamentary system in Great Britain, but in which the actual operation of the two governments presents striking similarity.[23] In addition there are striking differences in the way the parliamentary system operates in Great Britain and the way it operates in other countries which have adopted it, and the same is true as between the presidential system in the United States and the presidential system in other places.

Autocratic and democratic governments

There is a further classification which results in a division of governments into two great classes: democratic or popular government, and autocratic or authoritarian. This classification is based upon an analysis of the amount of protection given individual rights and liberties, and has become so significant in the modern world that a somewhat lengthy discussion of it is appropriate.

Autocratic government. The autocratic or authoritarian system is one in which the government is not responsible to the people, in which there is a concentration of the law-making and executive powers in the hands of one group, in which there is an absence of independent parliaments, in which there is no guarantee of individual rights or equality before the law, and in which arbitrary judgments

---

[23] As to this, see McBain, H. L., *The Living Constitution,* Chapter IV (The Macmillan Company, New York, 1928). This is a very readable book and is especially suited to the beginning student.

on the part of the rulers are substituted for rational consideration of cases according to the rule of law. The legality of the actions of the government is subordinated to
political aims, or ends, and the rule of an active minority
or *élite*, consisting of the members of a single party, is substituted for the principle of majority rule. In addition
there is an identification of the single party with the government, and a subordination of the independence of the
judicial branch to the political aims of government.

This autocratic system of government, which has become
a characteristic feature of the modern world, includes
among its adherents governments founded on widely differing social philosophies, namely, those of Fascism and Communism. But, while they differ in some essential aspects,
they have, none the less, close spiritual relationships, and
in many respects their ways of action are very similar.
"Both Fascists and Bolsheviks acquired power through
violence or by threats of violence, and both exalt compulsion as the supreme method of political action. They ridicule democracy and liberalism, regarding these creeds as
superstitions of the ignorant or impractical ideals of the
visionary. They recognize no individual liberties as immune from destruction. They claim a monopoly on the
use of the press and the schools as agencies of propaganda.
They fear free discussion and suppress it ruthlessly. In
both, there is an identification between political party and
government. Both have had aggressive, courageous, skilful,
public-spirited leaders, inspired by the ideal of saving the
people of their country from the injustice or misrule of an
old regime. Both justify their methods of coercion by the
exalted ends they pursue: freedom, comfort, and enlightenment for the Russian masses; unity, power, and prestige for

the Italian nation." [24] Thus it is in social philosophy that they differ primarily, and this aspect of these authoritarian governments deserves brief attention.

Russian Communism. The philosophy of Communism is especially interesting today in view of its attempted application by the Communist party in Russia. It is a branch of the philosophy of Socialism, expounded in the main by the leaders of the Russian Revolution, Lenin, Trotsky, Stalin, and others.[25] Communism is derived from the teachings of Marx, who, through books, pamphlets, and articles written from the early forties to the early seventies of the nineteenth century, founded scientific Socialism upon which many of the later workingmen's movements have rested.[26] The writings of Marx have been, in this respect, like many other great doctrinal writings; they have been given widely varying interpretations by many different groups, each claiming to express the true embodiment of the parent doctrine.

Lenin in his youth became a follower of Marx and clung steadfastly to that faith, and it is true, in general, that the Communists have held to Marx's economic interpretation of history, his notions of the class struggle, the labor theory of value and the surplus-value theory. On the basis of Marx's teachings and their own interpretation of them, the Communists have pronounced the imminent downfall of capitalism and have advocated that the working classes take control of the state and its economic structure. The Communists, that is, the Communists as known through the Russian Communist party and the writings of Russian lead-

[24] Coker, F. W., *Recent Political Thought*, p. 485 (D. Appleton-Century Company, New York, 1934). By permission of the publishers.

[25] *Ibid.*, Chapter VI.

[26] *Ibid.*, Chapter II.

ers, have held to the doctrine that such control can be achieved only by violent revolution, and have urged the workers of the world to seize their respective states by force and use the power of the state to suppress whatever might be left of capitalism. They have insisted on differentiating their program from the program of all other workingmen's groups that have attempted to reconcile opposing classes by alleviating the harshness of the existing differences between them or by attempting to modify the social and economic institutions in a peaceful and gradual way. The Communists claim that through the exercise of the power of the state by the workers, that is, by a dictatorship of the proletariat, classes will be abolished, the economic structure will be reorganized, social and political control will be vested in the whole people as a single producing and consuming class, and the state as hitherto known will disappear.

The Communists follow Marx in severely indicting the capitalist system, but it is not essentially the inadequate production of goods, nor their maldistribution, that calls forth their most severe criticism. It is the inequality of power, which they emphasize as the most destructive evil of capitalistic society. The goal that must be kept in mind, therefore, they say, is equality of social position and of opportunity, not equality of wealth. This, of course, calls for the destruction of the political as well as the economic system of capitalism. The application of this Socialist theory, however, to actual conditions in Russia has been somewhat groping and even opportunistic. There are numerous writings, by competent scholars, describing in detail both this theory and its actual application in Russia. Many of these reports are favorable, many unfavorable, and the average individual can only read and form his judgment on the basis of the understanding thus gained.

There are, however, one or two conclusions that might be ventured here.

First, while the Communist ridicules and denounces the dogmas of capitalism, he holds unreservedly to the theories of Marx and Lenin. In this respect he experiences much the same difficulty in making a reconciliation of Marx and Lenin with current needs that the medieval theologian had in reconciling the dogmas of the Christian Fathers with the expressions of Aristotle. In both cases elaborate rationalizations have been the result. The student of history and political theory should be extremely careful before he adheres unreservedly to any theory; he should always be ready to give sincere consideration to any point of view no matter how it clashes with his own ideas.

Secondly, the present Russian situation is under the cloud of an autocratic heritage from Czarist days, and, even though the new constitutional developments point the way to liberalization and democratization, it is probable that control could not be maintained without a certain measure of dictatorship, and that such will be the case for some time to come.

Thirdly, whatever may be the opinions one holds of the methods used for acquiring and maintaining power, it must be concluded that Socialism has come to stay in Russia, and that tremendous advances have been made in economic, scientific, and cultural matters in that country. It must be further concluded that the coming of Communism is not an impossibility in other countries of the world.

Fascism. As a philosophy of government, Fascism has no doctrinal father as Communism and Socialism have in Marx. There is no manifesto which summarizes and rationalizes Fascism. It has been said that it has no theoretical basis, but that it is wholly practical, wholly empirical.

While there is a certain amount of truth in this view, there are certain doctrinal features of Fascism which may be pointed out. The Fascists deny the validity of liberalism and democracy; they deny that the state exists for the purpose of promoting the welfare of the individuals who make it up. The Fascist looks to the state as the ideal means of promoting action and efficiency, and it is the duty of the citizen to subordinate himself and his claims to the interests and claims of the state. The individual, for the Fascist, has the greatest amount of liberty when he is obeying the commands of the state.

To the Fascist, the state possesses some sort of unity of its own; the state has an organic unity which makes it something more than a collection of living individuals. There is an obligation to the future, and the existence of the state or nation is far more important than the life of its individual members. The state possesses absolute sovereignty; it has both a legal and a moral supremacy. The actions of the state and the immediate interests of the individuals may coincide and they may not, but in either case the state always takes precedence. The ideals of Liberty, Fraternity, and Equality are renounced, and in their place one finds such standards as Responsibility, Discipline, and Hierarchy. The Fascists reject any theory of popular control; they have no confidence in the ability of the people to rule. Government must be in the hands of a few strong men who are able to act, who can get results, who are efficient and resourceful. The best safeguard against strife and discord is the judgment and energy of one man.

The theory of Fascism also furnishes a justification for violence and the building up of a war spirit. It does not feel war to be unjustifiable nor unavoidable; war possesses the value of building up and of testing the virtues of courage, audacity, and virility. Mussolini himself has said: "We are charged with having imposed upon our nation a war discipline. I admit it, and I glory in it." [27] Fascism, in addition, has so exalted the national state as to make war a grave probability in the modern world. It has tended to become militaristic, nationalistic, and imperialistic, to view war as necessary and even desirable, to emphasize the need for the sovereign state and irresistible government, and to apply to the state ethical norms different from those which are applicable to the individual.

Coupled with these notions, one finds in the German variety of Fascism the insistence upon racial purity, upon the value of the Aryan race and its élite form, the Nordic type. The Nazis have found the sharpest contrast between the Aryan type and the Semitic type, and have justified, thereby, their persecution of the Jews.

Many laymen, as well as scholars, are aware of the suppression of liberties in Fascist countries and of the racial persecution in Germany. What both the student and the layman fail to realize, while denouncing these evils of Fascism, is the existence, both in the past and at present, of such offenses in the United States and other so-called democracies. The government of the United States was in operation only a few years before the drastic Alien and Sedition laws were put into force. The most severe penalty was imposed upon David Brown, who was sentenced to two years in jail and was fined $400, for his part in the erection of a "liberty pole" at Dedham, Massachusetts, in October, 1798, with the inscription, "No Stamp Act, no Sedition, no Alien Bills, no Land Tax; downfall to the tyrants of Amer-

---

[27] Mussolini, Benito, *Discorsi del 1925*, p. 189 (Milan, 1926). Quoted in Coker, F. W., *Recent Political Thought*, p. 481 (D. Appleton-Century Company, New York, 1934).

ica, peace and retirement to the President, long live the Vice President and the Minority; may moral virtue be the basis of Civil Government." [28]   It is of interest to mention that in later years Dedham, Massachusetts, was the scene of the Sacco and Vanzetti case.   It is worthwhile to note another significant case, that of Dr. Cooper, who was an editor in Pennsylvania.   He was arrested for the statement that President Adams was incompetent and had as President interfered with the course of justice.   Cooper was tried before Chase, a federal judge, who, as in all such cases, displayed great partisanship.   Cooper offered to prove his charges by summoning Adams and the members of Congress to court, and they refused to appear.   In default of evidence to prove his charges, Dr. Cooper was convicted, fined $400, and sent to prison for six months.[29]   But these acts which "cut perilously near the root of freedom of speech and of the press" have not been the only abuses of governmental power in America.   Slavery, long protected by the government, was an institution for which we can offer no moral justification; and the anti-slavery agitators in the North were endangered by the efforts of the South to bring them within its jurisdiction for punishment. The State of Georgia offered $5000 to anyone who would place William Lloyd Garrison within its jurisdiction, while the *Louisiana Journal* promised $50,000 for the delivery of Arthur Tappan, an anti-slavery man in New York, to the Vigilance Committee.[30]   It is interesting to note that in the case of Garrison,

---

[28] For further details, see Whipple, Leon, *The Story of Civil Liberties in the United States,* pp. 21–27 (Vanguard Press, New York, 1927).

[29] For a full account of the cases under the Sedition Act of 1798, see McMaster, J. B., *History of the People of the United States,* Vol. II, pp. 465 ff. (D. Appleton-Century Company, New York, 1895).

[30] Von Holst, H., *The Constitutional and Political History of the United States,* Vol. II, p. 111 (Callaghan & Company, Chicago, 1888).

a government was offering a reward for the commission of a crime. In addition to these difficulties, everyone knows the story of the troubles of Garrison in Boston and Lovejoy in Illinois.

The World War witnessed further suppression of civil rights, and following the War many states passed sedition laws, that is, criminal-syndicalism laws as they are called in this modern day, and many states outlawed the display of a red flag. It is interesting to note in this connection that on June 26, 1936, Paul Butasch was found guilty of criminal syndicalism in Indiana. He had taken part as a speaker in a student forum of Purdue University at Angola, Indiana, and had spoken in favor of a Farmer Labor party. His student friends rescued him from a severe beating, which had been instigated by businessmen in the audience. When about to leave town in compliance with an order to that effect, he was arrested for advocating the violent overthrow of the government, and sentenced for from one to five years.[31] Furthermore, there has been a revival, in late years, of a widespread violation of workers' rights by vigilantes, private police, labor spies, and even by troops and other government agencies of law enforcement. It was of the situation in California that the Federal Investigating Committee of the National Labor Board could say, "Freedom to assemble and to speak our thoughts and convictions must not be interfered with, especially by those who, as peace officers, are sworn to uphold the law. Force is on their side, but it would be better were that force tempered by justice, legality, understanding, sympathy, and a sense of responsibility. We uncovered sufficient evidence to convince us that in more than one instance the law was

---

[31] *International Juridical Association Monthly Bulletin*, July, 1936, p. **3**.

trampled under foot by representative citizens of Imperial County and by public officials under oath to support the law. . . . The right of free speech and assemblage was denied. Even the federal courts' injunction was jeered at." [32]

It is in the United States, especially in the South, that frequent Negro lynchings and almost complete deprivation of political and civil liberties of Negroes occurs; and it is in the United States that White Guards, Black Legions, Ku Klux Klans, and Silver Shirts have developed—acting in much the same manner as their prototypes, the Black Shirts in Italy and the Brown Shirts in Germany. Nor is this country free of racial and religious prejudice; anti-Jewish feeling is prevalent, and religious prejudice is sufficiently indicated by the 1928 presidential election in which rumors with regard to bringing the Pope to America were circulated and played their part in defeating Alfred E. Smith.

This does not mean that one should not denounce those features of Fascism which one feels to be unjustifiable, but it does mean that the individual should not become so busy shaking his finger at somebody else that he fails to see the dirt on his own hands. Yet, no matter how much the methods or the particular philosophies of the modern authoritarian governments are disapproved, they seem to have become permanent aspects of the modern world in contrast to the democratic type now to be considered.

Democratic government. A government which rests upon the explicit consent of the governed, and one in which the consent is given by an unfettered method, is a democracy. Such a government implies the necessity of free election, free speech, free press, and free association. The govern-

---

[32] National Labor Board Report on the Imperial Valley Situation, Released February 15, 1934.

ment in the democratic community is responsible to the people, and the responsibility must be exercised in a constitutional way, that is, the relations of the government and the governed are subject to established law. The rights of the citizen are guaranteed by independent judges acting in accordance with the general law which has been made by the representatives of the community. The individual is the end, not the state nor the government; the government is merely a tool by which the good life is constructed. Thus, rights are implied in a democracy and lead to a consideration of such qualitative things as liberty and equality, if a true understanding of this form of government is sought.

Actually and traditionally, however, democracy has been defined as a form of government, in terms of its structural and legal content, and not as a social philosophy or way of life. It has been defined in a quantitative sense, that is, in terms of the amount of popular control, and not in a qualitative sense, that is, in terms of the type of that popular control—what it is and what it does. The traditional view has defined democracy as that form of government in which the mass of the people has a controlling right of participation in the exercise of the powers of government. It emphasizes rule by the majority, regardless of the character of that majority. This is probably due to the fact that political science has been and still is interested primarily in the legal and structural sides of government. It has to a considerable extent ignored the ethical and economic aspects of politics.

There is, perhaps, no one definition of democracy which could express all that democracy may imply; it is always the way of looking at things that determines the content which is discovered. A great deal depends upon the individual and the interests he wishes to protect. To the economic individualist democracy may mean a protection of his property and of his economic liberty, while it might mean quite the reverse to the Socialist. Democracy, both as a form of government and as a social philosophy, has meant many different things in the past and means many different things today. It would appear, however, that to define democracy in terms of its qualities, to define it as a social philosophy or a way of life, has become increasingly important. This seems to be especially true in view of the fact that the attack on democracy as a form of government is predominantly in terms of the results of democracy and its effect upon the general social structure. In addition, the form of government is, after all, merely an incidental; it is a means and not an end in the realization of a way of life. The problem of finding a definition of democracy in terms of a general social philosophy, however, cannot be solved to the satisfaction of all. Nevertheless, there are certain general features which seem to stand out. In any consideration of democracy as a way of life, the old qualifications of liberty and equality spring to mind at once.

Liberty. As many would have us think, liberty is not merely absence of or freedom from restraint. Liberty implies restraints, although not all restraints contribute to liberty. The individual does not always feel that he is being deprived of his liberty when commanded to drive his automobile on the right side of the street, nor does he feel that he has lost his liberty when denied the right to pick pockets or to commit murder. It is through such restrictions and regulations that one is secured the opportunity of living the best kind of life; and the opportunity to live the best kind of life, to develop one's personality and individuality, is liberty. The greatest possible liberty does not result from absolute license, but from each individual being able to do what he pleases while interfering to the smallest degree with the rights of others. Thus liberty in society has both its positive and negative aspects. Paradoxical as it may seem, it includes both immunity from interference and subjection to control. Real liberty, however, must be conceived in terms of the individual and the development of his personality. The true test, therefore, of the validity of those limits which society must impose in order to protect and foster liberty, is the degree to which those limitations conform with the actual experience of the individual. Social life cannot exist without rules, but the rules that are made must be based upon the widest possible individual experience, and must in the last analysis depend upon individual judgment. No real liberty can exist where the individual does not possess the power to call the government to account, and liberty has disappeared from the community in which such accountings are not demanded.

These general considerations imply three types of liberty, namely, political, private, and economic. Political liberty is the right to participate in the affairs of government, the right to hold public office, and the right to call the government to account. Such liberty implies the right to an education, as the individual does not possess the means of judging his experience and expressing his views unless such an opportunity is extended. It also implies the necessity of a constant supply of adequate, impartial, and honest news. The individual who does not have an education and a supply of news upon which intelligent action can be based is not at liberty to participate in the affairs of government.

Private liberty is the freedom to choose for oneself in those areas of life which affect mainly the individual making the choice. Freedom of choice in religion is an excellent example. It can be said with regard to liberty in this sphere that any attempt at interference, especially with religious life, has always resulted in injury to society.

Economic liberty is the opportunity to make the earning of one's livelihood of some significance to himself and his personality. To many people this implies such things as the right to a job, the right to a living wage, and the opportunity to have some leisure time. As far back as Aristotle, it was thought that the solution of the problem of citizenship was to deny it to all those not possessed of leisure time. Aristotle was not wrong in his belief that a citizen should have leisure time; a man must have some hours to himself if he is to live a good life. Aristotle's mistake, however, was in his denial that the workers in society could have some leisure time; the problem can be met only by the creation of an economic order which will ensure to the worker economic liberty in the above sense without at the same time hindering the economic development of the world.

Equality. Liberty is not possible where inequality exists. It took Mr. Justice Holmes to point out that freedom of contract could exist only where there was equality of bargaining power. But equality as an aspect of democratic social philosophy does not imply absolute equality for everyone in all things, nor does it imply that all persons were created equal in intelligence, size, or strength. It does imply, however, the absence of special privilege and the presence of adequate opportunity for all. It does not mean identity of treatment, but it does mean that there must be identity of treatment until the minimum requirements for life are satisfied. It does mean that no individual is entitled to sumptuous banquets until the basic hunger of others has been satisfied.

Equality, in the non-legal sense at least, must mean something more than that the poor man and rich man have an equal right to buy a fine dinner, or an equal right to send their sons to Harvard or to Yale, or an equal right to hire competent legal talent when in trouble. Anatole France, in a satirical mood, once said that the law of France treated all men alike, since neither the millionaire nor the beggar could sleep under bridges. It is in the expansion of these concepts, qualities, and ideas of a "way of life" that any real conception of democracy must be sought.[33]

It is not out of place at this point to give some summary of the comparison that has been made between autocratic and democratic government. The democratic government, the popular government, is dominated by the rule of law, while the autocratic government is not. The democratic and free government can only interfere with the subjective rights of citizens on the basis of law, while in the dictatorial government interference can be by an act of authority alone without a legalized procedure. In the authoritarian system the power of government is unlimited; the rights of individuals are granted by the government and extend only so far as the government permits. The democratic, popular government, on the other hand, acting in accordance with the rule of law, can act only on the basis of law. Each organ of the state can act only within and according to the jurisdiction given to it by the constitution, and every act of the government can be controlled by those affected by the act through appeal to courts made up of independent judges. It is also generally true in a democracy that the legislative organs can make only such laws as are general in their application; that is, the law extends to everyone within the

---

[33] For enjoyable reading along this line and for stimulation of thought, any of the essays of H. J. Laski are recommended. See, for example, his "Plea for Equality," in *The Dangers of Obedience and Other Essays* (Harper & Brothers, New York, 1930).

jurisdiction of the state, and the legislator himself is bound by the laws he has made.

An autocratic or dictatorial government, at least of the Fascist type, is a government by a personnel which receives its power from a ruler or dictator who determines his own power; neither he nor the government receives power from the people, nor are they accountable to the people. Democratic or popular government, however, is a government of the people, controlled by the people, and deriving its powers from the people. Dictatorial government is a government in which the first concern is the furtherance of the interests of the state as such, and in which, when a conflict occurs between the interests of the individual and the interests of the state, those of the state take precedence. Rights of the individual are subordinated to obligations or duties toward the state. Democratic government, on the other hand, is a government in which the primary interest is in the individual as an individual, in the development of his personality, in making possible for him a good life. It is a government which gives consideration to the desires of the people, gives them a chance to take a part, gives consideration to the moral side of human life. It takes account of and even emphasizes individual rights and liberties.

The dictatorial state is a totalitarian state; there is no field of life into which the government has no entry. It controls the press, the radio, the churches, the schools, the expression of opinion, the organization of associations, and every other field in which the individual might hope to express his personality. It is a system of government characterized by a strict supervision and regulation of every aspect of internal affairs. A democratic or popular government, however, stands for the highest possible degree of individual liberty. It is a system which stands for the greatest possible promotion of freedom of religion, of thought, of expression, and organization. It is a system which attempts to promote the virtues of liberty and equality, as those virtues must be promoted when any consideration is given to the good life of the individual as an individual. It is not necessarily a government of limited functions; it may perform a tremendous number of functions, but such performance will be based upon a consideration of individual and social welfare.

THE CONSTITUTION AS THE BASIS OF GOVERNMENT

This discussion of the classification of governments has proceeded without any discussion of the fundamental principles according to which a government operates. These fundamental principles are called the constitution.

A constitution, contrary to popular notion, is not merely that narrow body of principles found in a single written document, but includes the whole of the fundamental principles according to which a government operates. A constitution in a broad sense is made up of the formal written document, usually given the name "constitution"; of fundamental laws, often called organic; of judicial and administrative decisions; of customs, usages, and conventions. It should be added that a constitution is not some sacrosanct, God-given thing, but an instrument or tool to be used by the people for the achievement of the common good. Whenever things that are socially desirable conflict with the constitution, the constitution should be changed in such a way that that condition no longer exists. Constitutional power and social desirability may not be the same thing at any given time, but they should be.

Constitutions, no less than governments, have been subject to attempted classifications. The classifications most commonly found are those dividing constitutions into the categories of written and unwritten, rigid and flexible. The classification of constitutions as written or unwritten embodies a distinction which is really a matter of degree. All written constitutions have large unwritten parts, and unwritten constitutions possess large portions that are written. The classification of constitutions as flexible or rigid is one which is dependent upon the process of formal amendment. If the process of formal amendment is identical with the process of passing ordinary laws, then the constitution is said to be flexible. If, on the other hand, the amending process is hedged about with special restrictions which make it more difficult than the ordinary process of legislation, then the constitution is said to be rigid. The resistance of the constitution to change in order to adjust it to new conditions does not depend entirely upon its "rigidity" in this technical sense. A constitution having a difficult process of amendment may, for example, go through a rather easy transformation by judicial interpretation, administrative decision, or just plain customary development. On the other hand, a constitution which may be changed by the ordinary legislative process may go for years without any drastic changes.

THE STUDY OF INTERNATIONAL RELATIONS

Political scientists are interested, not only in the internal affairs and government of the different countries of the world considered as separate entities, but also in the relations of the different countries with one another. Very early in the study of political science, the student finds it necessary to consider the part that individual states and governments play in the world at large. This branch of political science is called the study of international relations.[34]

The fate of civilization depends today, to an extent that it never has before, upon the ability of mankind to regulate in some constructive way the specialized interests of nations, groups, and individuals. Modern developments in the physical sciences have greatly improved the conditions of man's existence. Improved knowledge in all spheres has provided the instrument for the establishment of a material basis of civilization that gives the opportunity of developing the richness of his personality. But these developments are instruments of destruction as well as construction.

The developing agencies of communication and transportation have to a large extent made the world a single unit, an interdependent social and economic whole. Trade routes have no respect for national boundaries, nor are typhoid fever, bubonic plague, smallpox, influenza, unemployment, poverty, prostitution, the drug traffic, or the white slave trade respectful of nationalistic hysteria. These things are affected no more by the lines which mark off one state of the world from another than they are by the lines which mark off subdivisions within a single state. The international character of problems such as these has already made possible some institutionalization of our international relations. At the same time the possibilities of conflict among nations have become greater, and the dangers of conflict almost catastrophic. Another war upon a world-

---

[34] Simonds, F. H., and Emeny, Brooks, *The Great Powers in World Politics* (American Book Company, New York, 1935). This is recommended for beginning students interested in world politics and international relations. More advanced students should read Potter, P. B., *Introduction to the Study of International Organization* (D. Appleton-Century Company, New York, 1928), and Schuman, F. L., *International Politics* (McGraw-Hill Book Company, New York, 1933).

wide scale could easily bring about the destruction of civilization. In future wars there will be no safe place. The largest and even the best-protected cities will constantly be exposed to destruction. The inhabitants will be tortured and killed while they sleep, go about their business, or engage in recreation. Noncombatants as well as combatants will be subject to the horrors of war.

The most imperative need today, therefore, is the development of a constructive program for the maintenance of peace. Unless some wise, constructive, and appropriate program of control is developed, the instruments of progress will become the instruments of destruction. The price of peace is government, and this is true internationally as well as domestically. A system must be developed by which law can be made and enforced on an international scale. Anything less will result in chaos, violence, war, and devastation. They are wishful thinkers who feel that a mere desire for peace, even if it is shared by a majority of the people, will remove the causes for conflict. There must be established an organized world with effective, overriding authority possessed of the means of developing real law on a world-wide scale and of bringing about the orderly regulation of conflict.

The future of international relations

Thus, while the study of international relations has always been of great importance, it has become increasingly so in the twentieth century. Yet, while this is true and promises to be so for some time to come, there is no reason to insist that the study of international relations will always constitute a part of political science. He who can be at all optimistic must see in the future, even if it is a dim and far-distant future, the disappearance of sovereign national states and the organization of a great world state which will keep conflict within orderly channels, just as the present national states go a long way in suppressing violent discord in domestic affairs. It is not to be hoped that all conflict can be removed from the world, for the world must be one of dissension if there is to be progress, but that dissension can be regulated and placed upon a peaceful basis. Violent competition amongst nations must give place to peaceful coöperation amongst peoples.

This problem has a special interest for the student of American institutions because of the close similarity with the situation in this country between 1781 and 1787. The economic and social forces which pushed the states toward closer union and coöperation in that era are comparable to those pushing the world in that direction today. Nor does the analogy end here, for the same forces which were obstacles to the creation of a unified coöperation of the people of America in that day—distrust, suspicion, localism, paid propaganda, and fear of that which is foreign—are of even greater magnitude in the prevention of world coöperation and government now. Such world-wide coöperation must, however, become essentially a coöperation of individual human beings, and not of sovereign nation-states as such. One will search the pages of history in vain for examples of successful leagues or federations, the governments of which were essentially councils of diplomats whose actions were subject to direction and abrogation by constituent state members, and whose commands, when given at all, were given to politically organized bodies claiming sovereign powers and the right to execute or refuse to execute those commands at will. On the contrary, the Achean and Aetolian Leagues in ancient Greece, the present League of Nations, the United States under the Articles of Confederation, and the Swiss Confederation before the war of the Sonderbund are classical examples of failures due largely to the fact that the so-called governments of the leagues or federations had no authority independent of their constituent member states, no power to tax, to regulate economic conditions, or to raise police forces without the unanimous or near-unanimous consent of political bodies with pretensions of sovereignty.

Politically, therefore, the only solution of the present chaotic and near-anarchic world situation appears to be obvious. It is the solution adopted by the United States in 1787, after the failure of its own "League of Nations" had become so apparent; it is the solution suggested by the Swiss Constitution-makers of 1848, when they drastically reorganized the central government after the disastrous War of the Cantons; it is, in short, the organization of some sort of world state based on coöperation of peoples and not of sovereign states. One dare not mention such a project, especially in the United States, without a great deal of trepidation. Traditionally the United States has been less willing to support and maintain even our present feeble international organization than almost any other country. Yet our own political history and organization suggests what seems to many to be the only ultimate remedy for a world chaos caused by the conflict of those swaggering entities which call themselves nation-states.

Difficulty of achieving world coöperation

There has been developing in this century an increasing interest in and knowledge of international control, and a desire to adopt and to advance some form of it. At the same time there has been a traditional opposition to this development based upon certain doctrines or concepts which

are partly psychological in character and which require the
the serious attention of the present-day student.

One of the most significant of these concepts is the
familiar one of nationalism, but only nationalism as conceived of in one of the several meanings which it has come
to have in the modern world. In one sense nationalism
refers to the individual attitude which attributes a real
value to national individuality, and considered in this way
it forms an important part of national movements. In such
a sense it may be a friend and not a foe of international
organization. In addition, there is, in this sense, no sharp
distinction between a genuine patriotism and nationalism.
But there is a second meaning to the term, which connotes
something significantly different. It indicates a national
consciousness so strong that the nation-state is looked upon
as a sacrosanct institution whose decisions are final and not
subject to modification. It implies a disposition to place
an unreasonable, exaggerated, and exclusive emphasis on
the merits of the nation at the expense of all other values.
It so stresses independence that it often has little tolerance
of ideas of common and international welfare. It is a
prejudiced kind of nationalism championed by unpacific
groups and by mass parties, and has the same sort of relationship to national feeling or to national consciousness as
chauvinism does to genuine patriotism.

Nationalism, in this second sense, prepares the minds of
people for war; it holds the national state up as a sacrosanct institution, and where there has been burdensome or
tyrannical action by foreign countries, as in Germany, or
a sense of national shortcoming and inequality, as in Italy,
nationalism breaks out in the most extreme forms. The
racial theories of German Fascism represent a most extrava-
gant expression of nationalism in this second sense. It was

a nationalism of this kind that operated indirectly in bringing on the catastrophe of 1914, and which has been intensified since that time. The states of the world have rushed into a mad race by establishing nationalistic tariffs, armies, schools, and agencies of propaganda. The world-wide depression and the fear of war, coupled with this nationalistic spirit, has driven the world into frenzied attempts to achieve national self-sufficiency. It should be added that this spirit is not confined to capitalist countries, as many would have us believe; in Russia, as well as other countries, there has been support of cultural nationalism coupled with governmental policies tending to promote national solidarity and chauvinism.

The opposition to international coöperation and the danger to world peace comes not only from nationalism but from imperialism as well. Imperialism has been of two sorts: it has meant the organization, expansion, and maintenance of a territorial empire, and it has meant the organization, expansion, and maintenance of a commercial empire. In other words, imperialism has meant not only expansion of sovereignty or territory, but also expansion of trade fostered and protected by political coercion. The period since 1780 has been a period of imperialist expansion. Africa was partitioned mainly after that date, the job being finished by Mussolini in 1936; and certainly it has been in Africa that imperialism has been exhibited in its most outright form.

The world, however, has not rid itself of the imperialist threat to peace and sanity. Germany wants back her Empire, but has little or no chance to get it by consent. Italy is dissatisfied with her position, but room for expansion is limited. Great Britain and France are giving more and more attention to their respective territories, and Japan stands with an eye upon China. Imperialistic expansion, in terms of territory, spheres of influence, or trading and industrial concessions, generates rivalries and hatreds. Imperialism breeds within the minds of men the desires, suspicions, and enmities that lead to war.

Many other concepts as disastrous as these might be discussed were space available; for example, those of the sovereignty, independence, and equality of states. All of them serve to illustrate the difficulties with which our world is faced. It would seem that people are thinking in terms which may have been valid in a world where international relationships were few, but in the twentieth century such conceptions would be ludicrous if they did not result in such tragic consequences. Whether those consequences— war more horrible than any before known, rivaling in destruction the Thirty Years' conflict in Europe, which is said to have caused the death of one third to one half of the German people, disease coming in the wake of conflict, destruction of much of our culture, and moral degeneration —are to be avoided depends partly on the elimination of such forces as those suggested above. That accomplished —and one may honestly doubt if it can be in time to avert catastrophe—international coöperation and organization will become easier, and the possibility of a really significant coöperation of peoples of the world for the purpose of achieving a happier and better existence will be much nearer.

Eventually the state of today, based as it so often is upon a militant, aggressive, and chauvinistic nationalism, may be reduced to a position in the world at large which is more analogous to that of a state in the United States. Chauvinistic nationalism may be exchanged for a genuine patriotism, for a really constructive pride in the community and the contributions it can make to the welfare of all the people of the world. It might be said that the student of the state and of government must feel this to be an inevitable necessity, for if he does indeed believe political authority to be an essential part of good social life, he cannot logically deny its necessity in the world at large. Then, of course, the study of international relations, in its present form at least, will have ceased to exist, for essentially the problem of world coöperation, world organization, or world government would be that of the state and government in general. It seems extremely doubtful to many minds whether international relations can be made more scientific or ethical than they are at present. Indeed, the opinion might be ventured that only in so far as the sovereign nation-state, moved by forces of militant nationalism and imperialism, ceases to exist can we expect a more ethical and scientific political life as a whole; for it is notorious that while domestic political activity is far from ethical, that of world politics has violated every canon of private ethics without scruple. By making the world community identical with some sort of world political organization, not only can violent conflict be eliminated, but also a long step can be taken in the solution of a problem which has puzzled political philosophers for ages, namely, why private ethics have been disregarded by political groups.

Progress in international organization

That many a hard-headed realist will object to this hope of international coöperation and organization on an effective scale as wishful thinking, that in all probability this generation and many more to come will not see it brought to effective realization, that in actuality the world may be plunged into the catastrophe of war before substantial reform is made—all this is frankly admitted. But these facts do not detract from the reality that the many current discussions of international coöperation present fundamental problems and look toward some ultimate solution, even though to many it is an ideal laid up in heaven; nor do they alter the fact that substantial progress has been made, especially since 1914. There has been a predisposition to speak of all plans, of all schemes of international coöperation, as harmless, pleasing, and ideal dreams; but, in actual fact, they have been a steadily growing reality since 1865. The growth of international law and the establishment of the League system are realities and have painted upon the international scene a somewhat different picture than was found there prior to the World War.

International law

There are today over sixty sovereign national states in the world, and though there is a community of interest, there are also collisions between national policies. These collisions have necessitated treaties, conventions, protocols, and even decisions of international tribunals and arbitration commissions, which in turn have come to form an important part of what we call international law. There has been a constant growth of law in the world community, and while there is not, today at least, any agency of successful international enforcement, the rules that have grown up can be recognized as law. In addition, it can be pointed out that our own domestic or national law has evolved from a period in which disputes were settled not by peaceful means but by force, and that even today much of this national law is violated or ignored, though it is still looked upon as law. So it may be that in the international field we are passing from a period of forceful settlement of disputes to a time when an international law with a legislative body having power to make rules, a judiciary having power to interpret them, and an executive having power to enforce them, may be established.

Already there have come into being such institutions as the Hague Tribunal, the Permanent Court of International Justice, the League of Nations, the International Labor Organization, International Administrative Unions, and scores of other special institutions. It is true, of course, that in these cases the agencies set up for the creation of international legislation can only make suggestions and proposals, which the individual nations can accept or reject; and that in the field of international judicial decisions much the same is true. But, backed by world opinion, there is an international law which commands considerable respect and has gone a long way in promoting orderly relations between nations.

The League of Nations

A League of Nations was created after the World War and tacked on to the Treaty of Peace. The League has a constitution in the form of the Covenant, which sets forth its purposes and organizes the machinery by which it acts, namely, the Assembly, the Council, and the Secretariat. The League serves as a meeting place for discussion of world problems, and provides the formal machinery for settling international difficulties in a peaceful manner. It also plays an important part in the removal of the causes of war by the routine administrative and educational services it performs.

As for specific results, while it failed to stop the Japanese conquest of Manchuria in 1931–1933, and failed to stop the Italian conquest of Abyssinia in 1935–1936, it has intervened in several disputes in which it has successfully prevented actual war. It has, in addition, been persistent in its attempts to reduce armaments and to strengthen public opinion against war; and it has, in its less spectacular and more routine work, made great gains in the regulation of opium traffic, research in public health, control of the traffic in women and children, supervision of the mandates, registration of treaties, readjustment of the domestic finances of several members, care for refugees, promotion of intellectual coöperation, research into problems of taxation, trade, and industry, and many other things too numerous to mention.

The International Labor Organization

The Treaty of Versailles provided for this organization along the same general lines as the League. It is made up of an International Labor Conference, the Governing Body, and the International Labor Office, which correspond roughly to the Assembly, Council, and Secretariat of the League. This organization serves as a sort of international clearing house for information on labor problems. It proceeds upon the basis that domestic labor problems have a definite effect upon the world situation, and seeks, therefore, to equalize the labor conditions of production among the member states, to promote health and safety by coöperative action, and to raise the general standard of working conditions and pay.

The Permanent Court of International Justice

The World Court is a continuation of the Hague principle, and the statute for the Court was drawn up in 1920. The Court has a permanent personnel elected by the Council and Assembly of the League. It sits at the Hague in the building erected for the Hague Tribunal and serves as more than a beginning in the attempt to get international disputes settled on a peaceful and legal basis, as domestic conflicts usually are. It is continually gaining in prestige, as many of its judgments and advisory opinions have made it plain that there can be an international court, as differentiated from a mere arbitral commission, and that it can operate upon a practical and useful basis.

The United States is a member of only one of these three institutions, the International Labor Organization, which it joined in 1934. The United States, however, has come to some realization of her interests in world coöperation, and has coöperated to a certain extent with the League. It is only to be hoped that awareness of American moral, commercial, and political interests in the preservation of world peace will lead her to further coöperation.

Other agencies of world organization

In addition to the forms of or institutions for world coöperation mentioned above, there is a legion of others. There are international administrative unions such as the International Telegraphic Union and the Universal Postal Union; there are international unions in Europe such as those for the maintenance of orderly and successful traffic on international rivers, for example, on the Danube and the Rhine [35]; there is a vast amount of unofficial coöperation in the form of conferences or unions which are non-governmental, for example, the International Maritime Committee, the International Chamber of Commerce, and others; there are purely American agencies of coöperation

[35] On November 14, 1936, the German government denounced those provisions of the Treaty of Versailles providing for international control of certain German rivers. See *New York Times,* November 15, 1936.

such as the Pan-American Union, which acts to promote coöperation in many of their common interests among the United States and Central and South America; and finally, there is the consular and diplomatic service that is maintained by each state, and which, with all its faults of formality, rigidity, and secretiveness, plays an important part in world coöperation and the removal of causes of war.[36]

CONCLUSIONS

The present survey, as was pointed out above, is not an attempt to deal with all the conceptions or problems of political science. No doubt many will feel that certain parts should have been expanded and others contracted. It is, however, an attempt to break the way, to introduce the reader to some of the fundamentals, and to arouse in him the desire for a further understanding of these problems. That there are other terms, other concepts, and other problems of vast importance is not denied; and each individual judges their importance on the basis of his own knowledge and experience.

The day has passed when government was a relatively simple affair; its scope and complexity is bewildering even to the scholar at times, but none the less the hope of ours and future generations lies in the training of the ordinary individual in citizenship, in preparing him to make the best use of his own special experience. That this is impossible has not yet been proved; in fact, real political education for the masses has not yet been tried. The hope lies in the development of secondary and adult education and the

[36] For a more detailed description of the organization, functions, and accomplishments of the various agencies mentioned in the preceding pages, see Potter, P. B., and Schuman, F. L., *op. cit.*

continuation of political research in such a way as to approach the attainment of truth. That truth in the social sciences is a high aspiration beset by a bewildering array of obstacles is apparent to all. The reactionaries, the professional patriots, governments, and even university administrators and faculties have at times been so afraid of change, and have placed so much emphasis upon impartiality and suspension of judgment, that there has been danger of losing all real critics, analysts, and reconstructors from our society; and the lofty aspiration for truth may be lost in the realm of a sterile objectivity.

BIBLIOGRAPHY

Coker, F. W., *Recent Political Thought*, Chapters I, II, VI, X–XIII, XVII–XIX (D. Appleton-Century Company, New York, 1934).

Garner, J. W., *Political Science and Government*, Chapters I–XVI (American Book Company, New York, 1932).

Gettell, R. G., *Political Science*, Chapters I–XII, XV, XXI–XXV (Ginn & Company, Boston, 1933).

Haines, C. G., and Haines, B. M., *Principles and Problems of Government*, Third Edition, Chapters I–IV, XIII, XXIII, XXIV (Harper & Brothers, New York, 1934).

Laski, H. J., *A Grammar of Politics*, Chapters I–VI, XI (Yale University Press, New Haven, 1925).

Schuman, F. L., *International Politics: An Introduction to the Western State System* (McGraw-Hill Book Company, New York, 1933).

Willoughby, W. F., *Government of Modern States*, Revised and Enlarged Edition, Chapters I–XI (D. Appleton-Century Company, New York, 1936).

Willoughby, W. W., *Fundamental Concepts of Public Law*, Chapters I, IV–X, XIII, XVI, XVII (The Macmillan Company, New York, 1924).

Willoughby, W. W., and Rogers, Lindsay, *An Introduction to the Problem of Government*, Chapters I–V, XVII, XVIII (Doubleday, Doran & Company, Garden City, N. Y., 1921).

Wilson, F. G., *The Elements of Modern Politics*, Chapters I–IX, XVI, XVII, XXII–XXVI (McGraw-Hill Book Company, New York, 1936).

CHAPTER X

Popular Participation in Government

JOSEPH R. STARR

University of Minnesota

SELF-GOVERNMENT IN THE MODERN WORLD

I N A very simple form of society it is conceivable that each individual might have full charge of his own affairs. Each person might be able to give full expression to his own inclinations without any interference from others. Thus, self-government in a literal sense might be realized in practice, for each individual would govern or control himself in all of his day-to-day activities. This would be possible, however, only in the simplest kind of society, one in which human needs and wants were few in number and differentiation in occupation had not yet developed. Obviously, such conditions do not exist in the modern world. In present-day industrialized society, self-government cannot be realized in this literal sense. Every human being finds his actions and aspirations conditioned by the forces of society, human and material. He must submit to a great number of interferences with what he may fairly regard as his personal, private affairs.

These restraints come from many different agencies, but the agency which is especially important in imposing restraints and in preventing the anarchic exercise of individual will is the state, or, as it is referred to in common speech, the government. Under modern conditions the government impinges more and more upon the individual;

the government concerns itself with an ever-broadening range of human activities and interests. Therefore, if self-government is going to mean anything in the modern world, it will be obvious that the average individual must somehow manage to identify himself with the government. He must somehow become one with the agency which in turn controls him and all his fellows. He will thus be at the same time a controller and one controlled—a governor and a subject.

But how may this be accomplished? How may the citizen both govern and be governed? We are immediately brought face to face with the most difficult problem of political organization. In a small city-state of the ancient world all the citizens could assemble as a council, which meant that there was machinery to permit direct participation in the government by all. In a vast modern state, such as the United States of America, direct participation is impossible except for the select few who at any time hold the important and responsible positions in the government. The great mass of the citizens must be content with much less than this. They must be content to hold small, unimportant, and subordinate positions in the government, to perform minor activities on its behalf, and in general to be satisfied with exerting an indirect influence. In a modern state the mass of the people will ordinarily be subject to the few. It is nevertheless true that the fullest measure of freedom for all depends upon the grant to all of some degree of control over their own destinies. It may also be true, although this has never been demonstrated in a convincing way, that the state needs the abilities and services of the common, average citizen. It is altogether possible that we all might be better governed, if better provision were made to enlist the services of the masses.

The purpose of this chapter is to survey the opportunities and procedures for popular participation in government, and the devices that have been developed for the purpose of making it possible for millions of persons to share in their own government. It is well to realize in advance that the methods to this end that have so far been developed are far from perfect, and that much attention needs to be given to the development of better ones. The first step towards improvement, however, is to gain an understanding of the progress that has been made. It will first be necessary to explain the meaning of citizenship and the duties, obligations, rights, and privileges that belong to citizens.

THE MEANING OF CITIZENSHIP

Citizenship is the condition of a citizen, or a member of the state. All the citizens make up the body politic. All citizens owe allegiance, or obedience, to the government, which is the regularly constituted agency through which the state acts. Persons as a general rule acquire this status of membership in the state by being born into it. Citizenship is thus an involuntary matter, and it is difficult to see how anyone under modern conditions could escape becoming and remaining the citizen of some state. However, the advantages of being a citizen are so overwhelming that only a person of completely anti-social character would wish to avoid membership in a state. A person acquires citizenship by birth according to one of two rules, as determined by the laws of the different countries of the world. One of these is the rule that the place of birth determines the citizenship; the other is that a father transmits his own citizenship to his children. Both of these rules are followed by the United States of America, although the former one is emphasized. Their meaning may be made clearer by a few examples.

A child born in the United States is an American citizen regardless of the nationality of his father, although an exception is made for the children of the diplomatic representatives of foreign countries. Even the American-born children of parents who are themselves ineligible to naturalization are American citizens. On the other hand, a child born abroad, but whose father is an American citizen who has at some time lived in the United States, is an American citizen. In such a case the child may also be claimed as a citizen by the country in which he is born, and his permanent allegiance may not be decided until he becomes twenty-one years of age and takes an oath of loyalty to the country of his choice.

Citizenship may also be acquired by naturalization, a process that involves a change of allegiance from one country to another. Each country by law establishes its own rules to determine the conditions under which it will confer its citizenship upon mature persons, and there is a good deal of variation in the requirements. A candidate for naturalization is always required to make application to the proper authorities, to present evidence of a number of years' residence in the country, and to take an oath of allegiance.[1]

The population of any country includes a number of citizens of foreign countries who are domiciled within its boundaries for business, recreational, or other reasons. These persons are spoken of as resident aliens. Like citizens, they are subject to the laws of the country in which they reside, and owe to it many duties and obligations. Resident aliens enjoy practically the same rights as citizens,

---

[1] See an analysis of the laws of various countries relating to citizenship in Draft Conventions on Nationality, Responsibility of States, and Territorial Waters, pp. 80–113 (Harvard Law School, Cambridge, Mass, 1929).

except that aliens deemed undesirable may be deported, or expelled, from the country. No country except the Soviet Union extends to resident aliens the privilege of participating in the government by voting and holding public office. An unusual situation was created in Germany by the passage of the Nuremberg laws in 1935. These laws express the policy of the Nazi government towards the Jews, and provide that Jews can no longer be German citizens. The Jews, however, are to be treated in many ways like citizens, so it appears that it is the intention of the government to create a new class intermediate between citizens and resident aliens.[2]

The rights and privileges of citizens

In free countries the citizens are guaranteed many rights and liberties which are important factors in the citizens' enjoyment of life and make possible the development of their talents. Probably the most important of these rights is what is called personal liberty, which is the right to move about freely, to follow one's own inclinations, and to engage in any activity not prohibited by law. The right of ownership of property, religious liberty, and the right of equality before the law are also regarded as fundamental. The development of Socialist thought has brought special emphasis upon such rights as the right of all workers to employment or the alternative of maintenance by the state in time of unemployment, the right to rest periods and paid vacations, and the right to assistance in illness and old age. The importance of such rights to the full enjoyment of life by individuals is obvious. The citizen also needs the protection of certain procedural guaranties, such as the right of

[2] *Völkischer Beobachter,* September 16, 1935.

a fair and public trial on all criminal charges and the guaranty that all agencies of the government shall be required to act according to due process of law.

There are certain rights which are essential to effective popular participation in government, such as the right of petition, freedom of speech and of the press, and the rights of assembly and association. These rights are generally classified as civil, or political, rights. They are also called public rights, as distinct from private rights. A regime of rights is absolutely necessary in order to have a healthy political life. Private rights, such as those mentioned in the preceding paragraph, are highly important in order to ensure the free development of the individual; but in order to have self-government by the mass of the people it is especially important that the political rights be preserved. There is a vital difference between democratic governments and the post-war dictatorships of Europe with respect to the guaranty of rights. In a democracy it is desired to open the way for general political activity on the part of the citizens. It may readily be perceived that political activity is an impossibility unless the rights of citizens are maintained. A democratic state must therefore give special attention to the preservation of rights. It must allow the greatest possible freedom to its citizens. Democratic government must in a real sense be free government in order to succeed.

It is characteristic of dictatorships to subordinate the individual in all respects to the social organism. The claims of the state are always considered paramount to the rights of the individual citizens. According to this doctrine the individual citizen has absolutely no rights against the state; and there is no realm of human interests that is recognized as private affairs, as in free countries. It is difficult for the citizen of a free country to realize how completely the dictatorships dominate the lives of the people. The elemental right of life is not protected, for death has been the fate of many of the political opponents of the dictators. Personal liberty is arbitrarily interfered with in many ways, and the mere utterance of criticism is often enough to land an individual in a concentration camp. It has long been supposed that no government could be so autocratic as to control the opinions of its subjects. The unexpressed beliefs of individuals have been considered beyond the reach of the government. In the dictatorships of Europe, however, even this narrow range of private affairs has been effectively invaded by the all-powerful state. The whole populace is so incessantly bombarded with propaganda in the government-owned and censored press, in public meetings, in the streets, and over the radio, that few people can preserve the privacy of their thoughts.[3]

In addition to both private and public rights, effective popular participation in government also depends upon the enjoyment by the citizens of certain political privileges. A privilege is something rather less fundamental than a right. The government is usually under no direct compulsion to grant a privilege, whereas it is required, either by the written constitution or by very firmly established custom, to observe the rights of citizens. One of the most important privileges that citizens can enjoy in free countries is the freedom of access to the agencies of the government. This is provided in a number of ways. In the United States of America, for example, galleries are provided in the meeting places of all legislative bodies for the free use of the public. Individual legislators may be visited by appoint-

[3] Childs, Harwood L. (editor), *Propaganda and Dictatorship* (Princeton University Press, Princeton, N. J., 1936).

ment in the lobbies or corridors, or in the private offices provided at public expense. The public hearings held by legislative committees are open to practically every citizen who wants to express an opinion.[4] Citizens encounter no difficulties in gaining admittance to administrative offices, and even the chief executives of the states and nation are readily approached. An alert staff of news reporters makes it much easier for the average citizen to watch the activities of public officials. The most important political privileges that may be extended to citizens are those of voting for public officers and of eligibility to public office.

The duties and obligations of citizens

In return for all the advantages that the citizen derives from membership in the state, he owes certain reciprocal duties and obligations. The duties and obligations of citizenship include observance of the law, the payment of taxes, and the avoidance of injury to the rights and property of other persons. The obligations of citizenship do not fall equally upon all citizens, but are adjusted to the capacities of different individuals. Adult male citizens are liable to recruitment for service in the army or navy, in emergency corps for the control of conflagrations and floods, and in the sheriff's posse for the pursuit of criminals. Citizens have a duty to assist in preventing crime and in bringing criminals to justice. Many public-spirited citizens fulfill a duty by serving in unpaid, or underpaid, public offices, especially in local government. Most citizens are unaware of the large number of duties and obligations to which they are legally liable, and it is unfortunate that formal notice is not more

[4] Lowell, A. Lawrence, *Public Opinion and Popular Government*, new impression, pp. 249–256 (Longmans, Green & Company, New York, 1921).

often given in the laws so that citizens might be better informed as to what is expected of them. One of the especially significant features of the new constitution of the Soviet Union, effective in 1936, is that it contains an enumeration of the duties and obligations of citizens. Russian citizens are expected to work, to obey the constitution and the laws, to observe labor discipline, to fulfill all social duties honestly, to respect the rules of the Socialist community, and, if liable, to render military service.[5]

THE MODES OF POPULAR PARTICIPATION IN GOVERNMENT

The principal opportunities open to citizens to influence the government are: (1) to hold public office; (2) to vote, including participation in the initiative, the referendum, and the recall; (3) to proceed as an individual to influence the course of public affairs, either by trying to direct the policy of the government or by appealing to public opinion in order to exert an indirect influence upon the policy of the government; and (4) to join an organization, especially a political party, with the idea of bringing concerted pressure to bear upon the government. Each of these modes of popular participation in government will be discussed in turn.

Public officeholding

It is obvious that the most complete mode of participating in government is to become identified with the government as an officeholder. The citizens who at any time hold the public offices make up the government. They are for the time being the government, and have under their direct

---

[5] New Constitution of the Soviet Union, Articles 12, 130.

control all the extensive powers possessed by the modern state. Many citizens are directly connected with the government by holding offices and serving in its employ. No one knows with exactness what proportion of the people is so occupied. The total number of public employees varies greatly from time to time, and from place to place. Under the vast programs of public works undertaken in this and other countries in depression years, the number of public employees was greatly increased over normal times. Their number is greatest in the Soviet Union, where, under the Communist program of almost complete public ownership, the persons employed in practically all the major industries, except agriculture, are employees of the state. Under normal conditions in democratic countries between two and three per cent of the total population are on the public payroll. Since the number of public employees is so large, it would appear that interested citizens have a very good chance to become public officers. The fact is, however, that only a comparatively small number of those on the public payroll really carry much weight in the conduct of government. Most public officers occupy subordinate positions in which their duties and status differ in no material way from those of persons in similar positions in private employment. The mass of public servants are in reality no closer to the government than private citizens are.

All public offices may be thought of as falling into two main divisions—those that are essentially political in character, and those that are essentially nonpolitical. The distinctions between these two groups are not always sharp and clear cut, but it is impossible to have good government under modern conditions without recognizing this classification of public offices. One of the most serious defects of dictatorship as a form of government is that all offices, including the judiciary and the entire civil service, are treated as political in character, and the acme of the spoils system is reached.

The political officers of a government are chosen by political methods; that is, they are elected or appointed on a basis of party affiliation or personal favoritism. They make up the amateur or common-sense element of the government, and are primarily occupied with the authoritative formulation of public policy. The political officers should be responsible to the people who are governed. The nonpolitical officers, on the other hand, are chosen by a nonpolitical method; that is, they are appointed on a basis of merit and professional qualifications for the positions which they fill. They are to a large extent surrounded with guaranties, both legal and customary, which free them from the influence of party politics. They make up the expert and professional element of the government, and are primarily concerned, not with the formulation of public policy, but with its execution or enforcement. The nonpolitical officers should be responsible, not to the people, but to their political superiors.

It will be observed that the distinction between political and nonpolitical offices is not the same as that between elective and appointive offices. On the one hand, in this country many subordinate officers who really have no control over the formulation of the policy of the government are elected on a long ballot; on the other hand, in England and France, with the short ballot many appointive officers, especially the ministers and the highest officials in the permanent civil service, have most important powers over the formulation of policy. It is also true that many important offices in some countries are filled by methods other than election or appointment. For example, the British throne and House of Lords are hereditary, and in the dictatorships of Europe the positions of authority are held by persons who usurped them.

The political officers ordinarily include the members of the legislative bodies and the chief executive and administrative officers, while the nonpolitical officers are found in the judicial branch and the civil service. The judicial branch, while essentially nonpolitical, includes many positions offering to their incumbents the opportunity to play roles of importance in the service of the state. The political officers usually have broad, discretionary powers and frequently exert great influence over the course of public affairs. It is obvious that a citizen, who wishes to participate directly in his government, must aim at one of these superior offices in which broad powers are vested.

It is especially difficult to determine which administrative offices should be treated as political and which as nonpolitical. The numerous administrative officers of a great modern state must be directed and supervised by a group of superior officers who possess broad powers for the purpose. The question is, how many of these offices at the top shall be treated as political in character, and filled by a political method, such as popular election or appointment on the basis of political favoritism? In England the line between political and nonpolitical officers is sharply drawn to separate the ministers, or political heads of the executive departments, from the permanent undersecretaries, that is, the highest-ranking civil servants. Only a few other offices in the administrative branch are treated as political, so that there are in all only a few hundred such offices. The merit system is thus carried far up in the scale of public employment. In the United States of America, however, many thousands of offices are treated as political, and the spoils system is the dominant method of filling administrative positions. Many state and local governments have no merit system at all. The English solution of this problem may be accepted by unthinking persons as right in all respects. It has the disadvantage, however, of placing entirely too many important public officers in the civil service and thus relieving them of responsibility to the people. Under this arrangement there is too much danger of bureaucracy. The American solution of this problem is of course still worse, as it leaves so much opportunity for the distribution of public offices on a spoils basis. The desirable arrangement would be a compromise between the English and the American plans, but one which is much closer to the English than to the American. Instead of leaving only a few hundred offices at the top, as in England, to be regarded as political, a great and populous democracy like the United States should have several thousands. This would give the able citizens more opportunities to participate directly in their government, and the mass of citizens might retain a more direct control over it.

In any case it is essential that the civil service be made attractive as a career, so that a fair proportion of the able young men and women will be inspired to select it as their life work. The civil service must therefore be rendered attractive to such people. There are many aspects of civil-service employment that must be given attention in this connection. Working conditions, hours, salaries, and vacation and retirement allowances must be made exemplary. The civil servants must be freed from entanglements with the political parties. There must be freedom for the civil servants to organize into mutual-benefit associations, and their permanence of tenure during satisfactory service must be protected. But what is probably most important is that able persons in the civil service should have a genuine opportunity for public service. To make this a reality it is clear that many of the offices with general administrative duties and calling for executive abilities should be filled by promotion of persons from the ranks of the civil service. Really able persons will not enter the civil service unless they have some assurance that they may rise in later life to positions of real authority. Nothing is more discouraging to them than to see the higher offices filled by spoils appointees. If able persons have an opportunity to earn promotions to positions commensurate with their abilities, many of them will be content to accept the lower salaries that prevail generally in the public service, and to regard as additional compensation the permanence of tenure, the ideal conditions of work, and the possibilities of public service.

Voting

Voting is the simplest and commonest mode of popular participation in government. It is the one method that is open to almost every adult citizen. The theory is that the people will use their privilege of voting in order to choose public officers who will truly represent them. The people will then be governed by their own representatives. This is considered to be the nearest approach possible, under modern conditions, to self-government. Needless to say, the theory is not always realized in practice. The fact is that voting is very far from being a perfect method of participation in government. For one thing, the opportunities for voting are periodic. A very good method of participation in government would allow for continuous, or at least very frequent, activity on the part of the citizens. For another thing, the voters are limited in their choice to the persons who are put forward as candidates in the election. As everybody knows, the nominations are to a large extent controlled by the political parties, which, to say the least, are imperfect instruments for putting forward the best people as candidates for public office. It is, moreover, true that voting is a poor method of expressing public opinion. In any election many voters cast their ballots indifferently, without a thought of the issues of public policy at stake; many other voters express their choices on the basis of the personalities of the candidates; still others vote in the way they do only because of tradition or habit. In spite of these difficulties, an election might still result in the expression of a definite popular opinion, if only one issue stood out in a clear manner. What actually happens, however, is that there is never just one issue. Elections are always more complicated than that. One issue appeals to one class of voters, and another class is influenced by a different question. The result is that an election rarely, if ever, shows unmistakably what the people are thinking.

Much attention has been given in the development of democratic government to the perfection of the techniques of voting. But it should now be clear that voting is not sufficient in itself for the realization of self-government. Great numbers of voters themselves realize this; they consequently fail to take any interest in elections and neglect to avail themselves of their privilege of voting. Many enthusiasts for democracy apparently thought that all that was needed was to give the vote to everybody, and all the problems of government would promptly be solved. The extension of the suffrage has not proved to be a cure-all. The suffrage nevertheless remains the mainstay of democracy. But under modern conditions the people need other methods besides voting in order to exert a real and continuous influence over their government. The imperfections of voting as a democratic technique are clearly seen in the dictatorships of Europe, where voting has been perverted to serve as a tool of oppression and as a means of securing the submission of the people to autocratic, self-appointed rulers.

Representative institutions were first developed in England, principally in the thirteenth century. From the first the English people were grouped, for purposes of representation in Parliament, into geographical districts, namely, counties and boroughs. It was believed that the people who live near each other have such common interests as to form a community. It was therefore arranged that the local communities which were thought important enough should elect representatives, who would later assemble with the king, the nobles, and many of the chief officials of the Church to form the Parliament, the legislative organ of the country. This idea of a representative parliament was later copied from England by practically all of the civilized countries of the world, and the existence of a representative legislative organ has long been regarded as one of the essentials of popular government.

But for many centuries it was believed, in England and in other countries, that the privilege of voting for the representatives in the legislative organ should be strictly limited to the property owners, preferably to the owners of real property. It was felt that they best understood the needs of the country, and that they were likely to be better educated than their less well-to-do fellows. It also was usual to find the suffrage restricted on religious grounds, on the principle that only the communicants of the cult recognized by the state should be allowed to participate in the government. The breakaway from these undemocratic restrictions of the suffrage came first in the United States of America.

The greater equality that prevailed under frontier conditions in the New World brought about a new realization of
the worth of the common man. However unequal men
might be in abilities, beliefs, or economic status, it was felt
that all should be regarded as equal in at least one respect—
politically. By the end of the eighteenth century several
American states had established a broad democratic suffrage.
In the next century the movement to abandon the old
restrictions proceeded rapidly, especially in the 1820's, so
that by 1830 the general rule was that the suffrage was the
common privilege of all adult male citizens of the white
race. A few restrictions remained, but these were swept
away before the Civil War.

The attempts to establish Negro suffrage in the South
after the Civil War proved unsuccessful. The dominant
whites have by various means circumvented the Fifteenth
Amendment to the federal constitution, which seems to
grant the Negro the suffrage in all states. At first direct
means, such as flogging and intimidation, were employed
to prevent the Negroes from voting. Later more refined
methods were developed. The payment of a poll tax was
made a qualification for voting, and many Negroes are disqualified because they are either unable to make the payment or neglect to do so. Very difficult "literacy tests" have
been imposed and enforced rigorously against the blacks,
but leniently against the whites. The now defunct "grand-
father clauses" were a method of excusing the white people
from the necessity of passing the difficult literacy tests.[6]
More recently the Southern States have concentrated on
devising a method of excluding Negroes from the primary
elections of the Democratic party (in which the real con-

---

[6] Guinn v. United States, 238 U. S. 347 (1915).

tests for control of the state and local governments take place), and the "white primary" now seems to be thoroughly established and has even been sanctioned by the United States Supreme Court.[7]

Manhood suffrage was an implied principle of the French Revolution of 1789, but democratic voting became the regular practice only with the establishment of the Third Republic in 1870. In England the suffrage was extended in a series of Reform Acts, which also more fairly distributed representation in Parliament according to population. These Reform Acts were passed in 1832, 1867, 1884, 1918, and 1928. That of 1867 was the first to extend the vote to any considerable section of the working class, and is therefore properly regarded as the beginning of genuine democracy in England. General manhood suffrage was established only by the Act of 1918, which also introduced limited suffrage for women over the age of thirty years. The limitations upon woman suffrage were removed by the Act of 1928, so that women now vote on exactly the same basis as men in English elections. The establishment of a broad suffrage came later in most of the other countries of the world than in these three great democracies, and of course democratic voting has never been established at all in many places. Woman suffrage is substantially a development of the period since the World War.

The qualifications for voting have become quite standardized in most of the countries of the world, whether they are democracies or dictatorships. Citizenship is a requirement everywhere except in the Soviet Union. The Russian rule is in accord with the Communist principle of the uni-

---

[7] Grovey v. Townsend, 295 U. S. 45 (1935). See also Overaker, Louise, "Direct Primary Legislation, 1934–35," *American Political Science Review*, April. 1936, Vol. XXX, pp. 279–285, at p. 282.

versal brotherhood of all working people, regardless of nationality. The voting age is usually twenty-one years, but it is reduced to eighteen years in the Soviet Union for all people, and in Italy for married men and for widowers with children. The wisdom of reducing the voting age below twenty-one years is, to say the least, open to question. For most persons an enduring interest in politics, if it develops at all, develops rather late in life, so that there is probably a better case for raising the voting age than for reducing it. A residence requirement, usually of less than one year, is found practically everywhere except in the Soviet Union. The most important difference in the residence requirements in the different countries is the date of reference against which the period of residence is calculated. In American states the residence requirement always refers to a period before the election; in European countries having a permanent system of registration of voters, reference is usually made to a fixed date which has arbitrarily been selected for the annual revision of the lists of voters. The American practice would not be well suited to a country in which the dates of the elections are not fixed in advance by law, but may occur at any time determined by the executive. The most important variation in voting qualifications is with respect to women. Women vote on an equality with men in practically all the advanced countries of the world except France, Italy, and Japan.

The positive qualifications for voting are usually accompanied by certain negative provisions, or disqualifications for voting. An individual may satisfy all of the qualifications for voting, but he may nevertheless not vote at all, if he is affected by one of the disqualifications. Classes of persons who are thus commonly disqualified include insane persons, bankrupts, soldiers and sailors in active service, and persons convicted of crime. The disqualification of paupers, as found in the laws of about a dozen American states, does not apply to persons in receipt of relief in time of unemployment. The country with the most extensive disqualifications for voting has been the Soviet Union. For years the Communist rulers of Russia steadfastly excluded from voting all private businessmen and members of professions, the clergymen of all denominations, agents of the old regime, and all persons who had unearned income or who employed other persons for profit. These restrictions were relaxed in 1934, and the new constitution of the Soviet Union, effective in 1936, sweeps away all the disqualifications for voting. The Soviet Union thus has the broadest suffrage of all the countries in the world, for all persons of eighteen years have the voting privilege, irrespective of sex, race or nationality, religion, educational qualifications, residential qualifications, social origin, property status, or past activity.[8]

A broad suffrage, although it is an essential, is not in itself enough to ensure a democratic manner of government. The other essentials of democracy are freedom of choice in elections, a representative legislative organ enjoying real powers, free sources of information about public affairs, and the guaranty of the personal and political rights of the citizens. In the Soviet Union, Germany, and Italy the suffrage qualifications are very liberal; but the dictatorial governments have withdrawn from the people so many other privileges as to make voting a mockery. In each of these countries one political party is recognized as the only legal party. The voters have no other choice than to support the candidates put forward by the dominant parties. They have no practical method for the expression of dis-

[8] New Constitution of the Soviet Union, Articles 135, 136, 137, 138.

approval of their present rulers. Under such circumstances voting is in no sense a means of popular participation in government. On the contrary, elections become merely plebiscites for recording predetermined results.

In addition to all the other qualifications for voting, persons must nearly always be registered as voters, which means that they must have their names inscribed on the list of qualified voters. This was not formerly so. Registration of voters is a very modern device, developed to meet the problems created by the extension of the suffrage and the agglomeration of population in large cities. When there were comparatively few voters it was practical for the officials in charge of elections to determine on election day who were qualified to participate. With a vast electorate, however, this plan would only lead to intense confusion at the polls. In order to facilitate the work of election officials on election day, the law provides for the preparation of lists of the qualified voters in advance of election day. The right of any person to inclusion in the list is determined by the appropriate officials according to the procedure established by law. Any person whose name is omitted from the list is usually given the opportunity to prove, if he can, his right to vote. The systems of compiling the lists of voters, of filing them, and of revising them differ widely from place to place. In American states the system of registration is usually periodic in character, for voters are required to reregister before every election in which they wish to participate. This system, which places a great burden upon the voter, is improved in some places by the provision that a voter, when once registered, remains registered permanently unless he becomes disqualified for some reason provided by law. In European countries the lists of voters remain in effect permanently, and are revised once a year by the proper authorities. The accuracy of any list of voters will of course depend upon the soundness of the information upon which it is based. In American states the law usually fails to provide any method by which the authorities may check up the information given by the voters themselves under oath. Thus almost anyone may be registered who is willing to swear that he has the qualifications for voting. In England the registration officials depend upon the information collected by their own representatives who go about from door to door like census takers. In France, with only male suffrage, the lists of voters can be made up from the information collected for the purpose of administering the compulsory military service law.

The initiative, the referendum, and the recall

In many places the voters have been given the additional privileges of sharing in the legislative process and of recalling public officers before the expiration of their term of office. These opportunities are closely associated with elections, and to many persons they will appear to be only another example of voting. They are, however, the extension of voting to other uses besides that of choosing public officers. The initiative, the referendum, and the recall taken together may therefore be viewed as a separate mode of popular participation in government. They are another way in which the people have a chance of governing themselves and exercising some influence over public affairs. In the exercise of the initiative and the referendum, the electorate becomes temporarily a great amorphous legislative body possessing constituent or legislative powers or both. In the exercise of the recall, each participating voter is in a sense a member of a vast executive council in which the power of removal is vested. These additional privileges are in part designed to correct some of the defects of voting as a method of popular participation in government when it is confined to the choice of public officers. The common object of these three devices is to put the citizens into closer and more continuous contact with their government. They all are modifications of the representative principle in popular government, and are therefore commonly spoken of as devices of direct democracy.

The referendum can be used as a method of letting the voters share in either the constitution-making process or the legislative process. It originated as a method of adopting new constitutions and constitutional amendments. Ever since the State of Massachusetts adopted its constitution by this method in 1780, a favorable popular vote has been necessary in practically all the American states for the approval of a new constitution or a constitutional amendment. A referendum is also necessary in hundreds of American cities for the adoption of a new charter or a charter amendment. The referendum on constitutional questions is uncommon in foreign countries, but it has been adopted by a few, for example, Australia. There is no provision for a popular referendum in the adoption of amendments to the federal constitution of the United States of America; but the election of conventions for the specific purpose of ratifying the Twenty-first Amendment served practically the same purpose as a referendum.

The use of the referendum in deciding legislative questions is less widespread, but it is established by law in a score of American states, in hundreds of American cities, in Switzerland where the plan originated, and in some other foreign countries. In several of the democratic constitutions adopted in Central and Eastern Europe soon after the World War, few of which are now in effect, the referendum on legislative questions was established, especially as a method of resolving conflicts between the two chambers of a parliament. There are two forms of the referendum on legislative questions. In the first place, the legislature may itself order the referendum. The legislature may have a general authorization to test public opinion in this way, or it may be required to submit legislation on certain subjects to the voters. In the second place, the referendum may be brought about as a result of a popular demand expressed in a petition signed by a certain percentage of the electorate as required by law. The referendum is thus in general a method of delaying the effect of a proposed constitution, constitutional amendment, or law until the voters have the chance to express their approval or disapproval.

The initiative is a method whereby the people may propose a constitutional or charter amendment or a law. The initiative of constitutional amendments is established in most American states. The initiative of legislative proposals is, however, less common, being established in only about one third of the American states. The initiative is often linked with the referendum in that an initiated measure, if adopted at all, must usually be adopted by the voters in a referendum. The procedure is begun by the drafting of the proposal by the interested persons. Petitions are then circulated; and, if the percentage of voters required by law affix their signatures, the measure is formally initiated. When the required support for the proposal has been demonstrated by the circulation of petitions, the officer in charge of preparing the ballots is required to submit the proposal to the voters in the next general election. But sometimes the initiated measure goes instead to the legislature. If the legislature enacts it into law, that is the end of the matter; if, however, the legislature rejects the measure initiated by the people, it must be submitted to the voters at the next opportunity.

The recall is a method of disciplining public officers by removing them from office before the expiration of the term for which they were elected. The recall is part of the fundamental law in hundreds of American cities. It is established also in the Soviet Union, and the recall of deputies in the soviets has been a rather common occurrence. In America the recall has been used relatively seldom, but it is an ever-present threat to keep public officers reminded of their responsibilities. The procedure is begun by the circulation of petitions proposing the recall of a particular officer. When the percentage of voters required by law has signed, a special election, known as a recall election, is held in order to determine the question. The form in which the question is submitted to the voters varies from place to place. Sometimes only the question of the recall of the officer is submitted and, if the recall election results in the dismissal of the officer, another election must be held to select his successor. The two questions may be submitted together, and the officer whose dismissal is proposed may even be allowed to run as a candidate to succeed himself.

The devices of direct democracy place new responsibilities upon the voter, and at the same time open up new opportunities for his participation in government. When the voter shares in these activities he really becomes a public officer. The whole electorate becomes a branch of the government, performing functions as important in their way as those performed by the legislative, executive, and judicial branches. Controversy still rages over some aspects of the devices of direct democracy, and it is impossible to foresee the final verdict upon them. At least one thing is already clear: the initiative and referendum on legislative questions have not resulted in the enactment of radical laws designed to overthrow the existing system, as was feared by many a quarter of a century ago. In fact the experiments with direct legislation in many countries have tended to reveal the innate conservatism of the mass of the people. Another result has been to show that the people are less interested in elections that turn solely upon issues of policy than in those in which the personalities of candidates play an important part. The rate of nonvoting is very high with respect to referred measures. The experience with the initiative and referendum under the German democratic constitution of 1919 tended to show that these schemes do not work satisfactorily as part of the national government of a large and populous country.

THE ELECTORAL PROCESS

The electoral process may be defined as the series of activities through which the voters choose from their own number persons to serve as public officers. These activities are grouped in three stages, which follow each other chronologically. The stages of the electoral process are, first, nominations; second, the electoral campaign; and, third, the election itself, or the balloting.

Nomination procedures

The nomination of candidates for election to public office is the first formal stage of elimination in the electoral process. To designate candidates means to narrow the field of choice. It may be assumed that, for every public office of any importance, there are dozens, nay, thousands of persons who would be glad to be the choice of the people. Most of these are eliminated by the honest realization by themselves and their friends that they have no real chance of election. However, there are usually several left who are willing to go to the trouble and expense of making a race. The formal procedures of nomination are necessary in order to keep the number of aspirants to each public office within reasonable bounds. Some people are always willing to believe that the office seeks the man, but more often than not it is actually a case of the man, in fact many men, seeking the office. It has been found as a result of long experience that the process of democratic election works better, and that majority rule is more likely to result, if the number of candidates for public office is restricted in some way. What happens in practice is that a block of voters—usually the members of a political party or some other organization —reach an agreement in advance of the election to unite in the support of a certain person for a particular public office. The person so agreed upon is called the candidate, and the process through which the agreement is reached may be referred to as the nomination procedure.

Many different nomination procedures have been evolved in the different countries of the western world. These procedures are decidedly more elaborate in America than in Europe. Obvious reasons for this difference are that we have a larger area and a larger and more heterogeneous population than any European democracy, but the most important explanation is that we have so many more elective offices. With a large number of elective offices it becomes especially important to limit the number of candidates, for the job of voting is already complicated enough. In the study of nomination procedures it is always important to keep in mind the distinction between the limitations that the law places directly upon the candidates, and those that it places upon the political parties. In this respect there is also a contrast between the United States of America and Europe. In this country the procedures are carefully prescribed by law as affecting both the candidates and the political parties, while in European countries only the candidates are affected and the political parties are left free to make nominations in any way they like.

In the United States of America two important methods of making nominations exist side by side. They are the convention system and the direct primary. The former of these was well developed within the states by 1820, and it was completed with the development of the national conventions of the political parties in the 1830's. The direct primary is a growth of the twentieth century.

In view of the great importance of nominations as a stage of elimination in the choice of public officers, it became obvious during the period when our country was being transformed into a democracy that the making of nominations would have to be brought under popular control. This was easy enough for local offices, for all of the active members of a political party could come together in a mass meeting for the choice of candidates. Such local mass meetings, called caucuses, were very common in our early political history, and they are still the basis of the convention system. More complicated machinery had to be developed for the nomination of candidates for offices in large cities, the counties, the states, and the nation as a whole. In order to create this supplementary machinery the practice arose of having the local caucuses choose delegates to make up the county conventions. The county conventions, in turn, chose delegates to make up the congressional district and state conventions. When the system was fully established, these conventions, in turn, chose the delegates to make up the national convention of the political party. Thus within each political party a pyramidal structure was created: the base of the pyramid being made up of the active party members, meeting in local caucuses; the body, a series of nominating conventions at the different levels of government; and the apex, the national nominating convention. The conventions were created primarily for the purpose of making nominations; but they soon took on other functions —the drafting of the party platform, the election of the permanent party committees, and the arousing of party enthusiasm at the opening of the campaign period. One of the great defects in this complicated structure was that it gave the party members only an indirect control over the naming of the candidates who would carry the party banner in the campaign. Other defects of the system arose in practice, the most serious being that the various conventions fell easily under the control of corrupt machine politicians, or bosses. The bosses did not hesitate to resort to all kinds of trickery in order to control the local caucuses, and through them to dominate the whole series of conventions which rose above the caucuses. In the last quarter of the nineteenth century there was a determined effort on the part of the state legislatures to regulate the holding of caucuses and conventions, in the hope of ensuring popular control over them. Some of the worst abuses were abolished by law, but the best efforts of the legislators did not accomplish the main purpose. One result was, however, to bring the activities of political parties in the making of nominations under legal control. Thenceforth, the conventions were recognized as a legal means of making nominations.

The disappointing experience with the convention system of making nominations led to the enthusiastic adoption by the American states of a new nominating device—the direct primary. When the direct primary is adopted within a state, the political parties are not prohibited from holding caucuses and conventions. The parties often continue to hold their conventions for the special purpose of drafting the party platform. The conventions may even endorse candidates for public office, but the names which will appear on the official election ballot will be those of the candidates chosen directly by the voters in the direct primary. In other words, new legal machinery for the making of nominations is created. Usually the direct primary is established as the legal method of making nominations to all of the elective offices within the state, but sometimes the political parties are permitted to continue to use the convention method for the choice of some candidates. For example, in Indiana the candidates for all state-wide offices are chosen in conventions, and all the others in the direct primary. The direct primary has now been adopted by forty-four states. The convention method survives intact in four states (Rhode Island, Connecticut, Utah, and New Mexico), and of course the choice of candidates for president and vice-president of the United States in the national conventions serves to emphasize the continued importance of this method of making nominations.

The direct primary may be defined as a public election for the purpose of choosing candidates. The primary election is managed by public officers, and is subjected to the same safeguards as the general election. The ballots are prepared at public expense under the supervision of the same officers who have charge of preparing the election ballots. The polls are in charge of boards chosen by the public authorities. The laws to prevent corrupt practices in elections and to preserve the secrecy of the ballot apply in primary elections as in general elections. By all these means the voters are assured of fairness in the all-important matter of choosing candidates.

The direct primary may be either partisan or nonpartisan, depending upon whether the names on the primary ballot appear with or without party designation. In many parts of the country the nominations (and elections also) of all local officers are now on a nonpartisan basis. The nonpartisan idea has also been extended in some states to the nomination and election of judges, and in two states (Minnesota and Nebraska) to the members of the state legislature. The political parties have no formal connection with such nominations and elections, although they may at times play a dominant role behind the scenes. It often happens that a partisan and a nonpartisan primary election are held at the same time and place. When this is the case all the voters, regardless of their party affiliations, are handed the same nonpartisan ballot; but the participation of voters in the partisan primary depends on legal provisions that differ from state to state.

There are two kinds of partisan primaries, namely, the closed primary and the open primary. If a method of testing the party affiliations of voters in the primary is provided, it is called the closed primary; if no such method is provided, it is called the open primary. Four states (Wisconsin, Minnesota, Montana, and Washington) have the open primary and forty states have the closed primary. In the states having the open primary the voters are not required to make any public declaration of their party affiliations. In the polls on primary election day each voter is handed the ballots of all the political parties. He passes into the booth and there chooses the ballot that he wishes to vote. He marks this ballot and leaves all the others blank. The open primary thus makes it possible for a voter to keep his party affiliation secret, in the same way as the guaranty of secrecy in voting makes it possible for him to refuse to reveal the names of the candidates whom he has supported.

In the states having the closed primary two methods have been developed, and are employed by about equal numbers of states, for the purpose of determining the party affiliations of voters. One of these methods is called the enrollment system. Under it the voters are required to declare their party affiliations at the time of registration as voters, and the political party is indicated by a symbol placed after each name in the lists of voters. On primary election day the voter is handed the ballot of the political party in which he is an enrolled member, and there is no possibility of his obtaining the ballot of any other party. The other method is called the challenge system. Under it the voter is required to make a public declaration of his party affiliation by asking for the ballot of a particular political party at the polls on primary election day. If doubt arises as to the truth of the voter's declaration, a "challenge" may be entered by a judge of the election or the representative of a political party. The voter is thereupon required to repeat under oath his declaration of party affiliation. Under both of these methods the object is to ensure that the primary election of a political party shall be "closed" to all persons who are not members of that political party.

In addition to the two dominant methods of making nominations, the convention system and the direct primary, there is a third one of some importance in use in America. This is the petition method. The law provides that a candidate's name will be printed on the official ballot, if he demonstrates that he has sufficient backing by filing with the proper official a petition that has been signed by the required number of voters. This is a very simple method of making nominations. It is established in a few American cities, notably in Boston, and it is also an accompaniment of the direct primary. The direct primary laws usually provide that independent candidates and the candidates of new political parties may be nominated by the petition method. Moreover, minor political parties are usually required to make their nominations by the petition method, so as to save the state the expense of printing many primary election ballots.

In foreign countries the political parties are usually not regulated at all by law with respect to the nomination of candidates. The parties are left free to choose their candidates in any way they like. In some countries—for example, with the better-organized French parties—something resembling the American convention system has been developed for the choice of candidates. In England the choice of the party candidate for the House of Commons is a function of the local association of party members. A nominating committee of about a score of members is appointed, and this committee considers whether there is any local man or woman who would make a good member of Parliament. If they cannot agree upon a local person, a delegation is sent to the national headquarters of the party in London, where additional suggestions are made. When the nominating committee has agreed upon a name, it reports back to the local association, which assembles for the purpose in what is called an "adoption meeting." After selection by the political party the candidate must, in England and in France, comply with certain statutory provisions. In both countries the candidate must appear before the proper official at a stated time and make a formal declaration of candidacy. In England this declaration of candidacy must also be accompanied by, first, a nominating petition signed by ten registered voters; second, the appointment of some individual to be the candidate's election agent or campaign manager; and, third, a deposit of £150 which is returned to him if he polls at least one eighth of the votes cast in the election, but otherwise is forfeited to the public treasury. The last provision is, of course, for the purpose of discouraging frivolous candidacies and publicity seekers.

The electoral campaign

After the candidates are selected the political parties take up the task of acquainting the voters with the qualifications of the candidates and the official policy of the party. Elaborate headquarters are established for the management of the campaign; literature is prepared and distributed; and careful attention is given to all of the methods of publicity, such as the newspapers, the platform, and the radio. This period between the completion of the nominations and the election during which the parties contend for popular support is called, with an analogy to military terminology, the campaign. In the United States of America the campaign lasts several months. There is a mid-summer lull in the campaign after the national conventions have been held in June, but most of the time until the election in early November is occupied with intense efforts to win votes. In foreign countries the campaign is usually much shorter. In England it lasts about three weeks; in France its average length is six weeks. If the campaign were a period during which a serious effort was made to educate the people in public affairs, it could not be too long. But in fact the campaign is a period of intense emotional appeals and excitement, and it should therefore be of short duration.

The desirable arrangement would be to have the political parties carry on quiet, continuous educational activity between campaigns, which could be greatly intensified in a brief campaign. This plan would preserve the spectacular and sporting elements of the game of politics, and would at the same time give due regard to the need of the people for sound information.

There are certain essentials to an effective campaign which every candidate and every political party need. One of these is organization. In a well-ordered political party at least a skeletal organization is maintained in existence at all times. The party has its committees, its clubs, and its headquarters. When the campaign approaches, the peacetime organization of the political party must be recruited to combat strength. Almost every party can command the loyal services of thousands of volunteers. This huge temporary staff is assigned to such tasks as public speaking, canvassing the voters in their homes and in public places, the distribution of literature, and clerical services in the party headquarters. If the party has sufficient financial support, it never relies wholly upon the volunteer services of amateurs, but retains a staff of professional organizers, research workers, publicity men, and clerical employees. The candidates usually have the support of the elaborate campaign organization of a political party, and it is their chief duty to fit into the organization and to contribute their services in public speaking and other ways. A candidate, however, usually needs a personal organization in addition to that of the party. He draws about himself his personal committee of relatives, friends, and political supporters. He often needs, and is required by law in England, to appoint a personal campaign manager. Few candidates are expertly informed in the art of political organization and campaign management. A candidate usually also needs his own headquarters apart from those of the party. Experience has shown that elaborate organization is necessary in order to make much of an impression on the vast electorates found in modern democracies. The lack of such organization is one of the main reasons why independent candidates, who do not have the support of a political party, have such poor chances of election.

Another essential for an effective campaign is a policy, or platform. Both the political party and the candidates must express opinions upon the principal public questions of the time. It is true that they often try their best to side-step the issues and to avoid definite commitments on some matters. But when they do this they usually have to substitute a definite stand on other matters, perhaps of secondary importance. The voters have a way of demanding to know what the political parties and the candidates stand for. The candidate who has no policy at all, or a very vague one, is in a weak position in the contest for votes. The candidate who expects to get the support of a political party must usually make his own platform conform with that of the political party. In the United States of America the political parties have the habit of formulating comprehensive statements of policy in the platforms adopted by the national conventions. The candidates have only to adopt this platform as their own, with perhaps a few modifications to fit local conditions. The issuance of separate platforms by individual candidates is comparatively rare. In England, on the other hand, the political parties avoid comprehensive statements of policy, and the formulation of policy for campaign purposes is for the most part left to the candidates. It is the custom for each candidate to formulate his own platform, which is issued in the form of an "address to the electors." In France each candidate tries to state his own view of political philosophy, which is issued as his "profession of faith."

Probably the most important essential for an effective campaign is sufficient finances. To carry on a political campaign in a large area in which practically every adult citizen has the vote requires the expenditure of enormous sums of money. A political party must somehow collect a fund in order to bear the charges of keeping up its headquarters, paying the salaries of its employees, providing various sorts of materials like printing stock and office supplies, and of expanding its activities in the campaign period. Some of the most serious problems of democracy arise in connection with the collection and expenditure of political funds.

Political parties and candidates in all the countries of the western world receive the greater portion of their funds as voluntary gifts from relatively well-to-do people. Of course this is not true with working-class parties, because they do not have the support of many well-to-do people. Working-class parties must, on the contrary, usually rely upon the small sums contributed by their adherents as membership dues. The British Labor party is perhaps the best example of a major political party which has been financed largely by this means. A political party is unquestionably more secure in its income if it can depend upon large contributors, but the danger is that the receipt of the contribution may place the party under an obligation to the donor. Many proposals have been put forward to relieve the parties of the necessity of relying upon the gifts of a relatively small number of persons, but no plan so far suggested is entirely satisfactory in all respects. The

financing of parties from membership dues would be a fine
solution for the problem, if it did not mean such a precarious
income. The frequently recurring proposal that the political parties be financed by grants from the public treasury
has many objectionable features, among them being the
likelihood that it is contrary to American constitutional
law. The sale of membership certificates, or of the biographies of candidates—plans which have frequently been
tried by American parties—have met with indifferent success. The trouble with all the plans designed to increase
the number of contributors is that the mass of people have
not learned the habit of paying for their politics. They
are not convinced that the political parties have any services
to sell that are worth a price to the common man.

Probably the most likely solution of the problem of campaign financing is for the state to place at the disposal of
candidates some facilities for obtaining publicity for themselves and their programs, and in other ways to assist all
candidates on an equal basis in the conduct of their campaigns.[9] A number of means to this end are in use in different countries, and if all these means could be combined
in one country, much progress might be made towards
equalizing the chances of candidates regardless of the state
of their finances. In England candidates have the right to
use school buildings for the purpose of holding election
meetings.[10] In France the municipalities are required to
furnish billboards upon which the candidates have the right
to affix posters free of charge. In both England and France
all candidates enjoy a limited franking privilege, enabling
them to send one communication to each registered voter

[9] Overacker, Louise, *Money in Elections,* pp. 381–382 (The Macmillan
Company, New York, 1932).
[10] *Ibid.,* p. 219.

without the payment of postal charges. In France the state supervises the printing of the ballots and election circulars of candidates, so as to ensure that the lowest prices are obtained. In many foreign countries the radio is publicly owned or controlled, and political parties and candidates may be allotted time on the air in order to state their proposals. An indirect attack along these lines upon the problem of campaign financing might yield better results than the more direct method of limiting the size of campaign funds.

Political parties and candidates use a variety of methods and techniques in appealing for the support of the voters. They may attempt to appeal to each voter individually, although this usually proves very expensive. Perhaps the simplest method of reaching all the voters individually is to send a form letter or printed leaflet through the mails to each registered voter. Although the cost may be only a few cents per voter, the total cost, especially in large districts, is likely to be prohibitive. Another and probably more effective method of getting into touch with individual voters is to visit them in their homes. This is called canvassing. With large electoral districts and universal suffrage, it is physically impossible for the candidate himself to call upon more than a small fraction of the voters. In England, where canvassing is a favorite method of campaigning, each candidate obtains the assistance of volunteers who go from house to house in his behalf. It is, however, generally much cheaper and more practicable for candidates to appeal to the voters in the mass. This is done either by the use of printed publicity, such as newspaper advertising, billboards, and handbills, or by the use of the spoken word in public addresses in halls, at street corners, or on the radio. Probably the greatest transformation in campaign methods which has ever taken place has followed upon the introduction of the radio. The ease with which it may be used; the personal touch of speaking to the voters in their own homes; the possibility of reaching audiences of unheard-of vastness—these are among the aspects of radio which have made it a major factor in every American campaign since 1924. The radio is less used for political purposes in England, and is only beginning to be used in France; but the dictatorial governments of Europe have exploited it to the fullest extent for political purposes. The radio may have possibilities for political education that are not perceived by anyone at the present time. It should nevertheless be recognized that, together with its great advantages, it has certain disadvantages. For one thing, radio time is very expensive, especially when used on a nation-wide scale. One effect of this is likely to be to increase the strength of the national party machine, for no other agency can collect the funds necessary for its use. The great expense is also likely to lead to the domination of the campaigns by national figures, for the expenditure does not seem worthwhile except for the most outstanding statesmen. The greatest danger is that the radio may be used as a means of addressing a demagogic appeal to all the voters of a nation.

The election proper

To conduct an election in a great modern state is an administrative problem of major proportions. The object is to conduct the election so that everything will be fair and aboveboard, and the people may express their choices without distracting influences. In a word, what is wanted, at least in democratic countries, is free elections. An additional aim of more recent origin is to protect the secrecy of the ballot. In order to realize these aims the state requires a large staff of persons to serve as election judges and clerks. Since elections occur only periodically, no state can afford to retain a permanent staff of election officials. Every time an election comes around the necessity arises of recruiting a vast army of election officials for temporary service. The typical European solution of this problem is to require local-government officials, especially municipal councilmen, to perform this service without extra pay. The American solution is to hire a special staff; but, since the state is not equipped to recruit a large staff in a hurry, the political parties are virtually allowed to nominate the members of election boards. The worst abuses are avoided by the requirement that all boards shall be bipartisan in composition. Neither solution is satisfactory. In both cases the elections are administered by untrained persons. Probably the best solution of this problem would be to have a small permanent staff of experts in election administration who could closely supervise the temporary staff on election day.

THE INDIVIDUAL PRIVATE CITIZEN AND PUBLIC POLICY

In the modern state the average private citizen, apart from the fact that he is also a voter, can rarely have much influence over the course of public affairs so long as he acts only as an individual. However, the opportunities for individual action should not be overlooked as a means of popular participation in government. It all depends upon who the individual is. If he is a close personal friend and confidant of the president of the United States, then he may actually have more voice in the government than any cabinet officer. If he is an elder statesman who is traditionally consulted before important decisions are reached, he may be an important power behind the throne. There are always a few persons in any country who, because of their cleverness or their social or economic status, count for more as individuals than a whole host of ordinary citizens. An able person may by writing books, pamphlets, and articles do much to crystallize public opinion on certain issues. Others, whose abilities lie in the use of the spoken word, may appeal to public opinion from the platform or over the radio. The person who owns a great newspaper, or a chain of newspapers, is obviously in a favored position for the purpose of putting forward his own ideas. The spectacle of the governments of great states consulting the key men in the financial world is another example of individual private citizens taking part in the direction of the government. But it is clear that few individuals are important enough to count for much in the direction of public affairs. The great majority of private citizens must learn to act in concert in order to make their influence felt. Most persons will find it much simpler to give up the notion of participating directly in the government, and content themselves with the next best thing—to join and participate in a political party or other organization whose object is to influence the government. As a member of an organization each citizen will find his own puny strength multiplied by that of the thousands or millions of his fellows.

THE ORGANIZATION OF POPULAR PARTICIPATION IN GOVERNMENT

The political party

Citizens organize themselves in several different ways in order to make their influence felt in the government, but the most important agency for this purpose is the political party. Ideally, a political party is a number of persons grouped together because of their common belief in certain political principles and policies for the purpose of promoting the best interests of the whole nation. As a practical matter, the persons who compose a political party are attracted to it for many other reasons besides their common beliefs, and the party often promotes the interests, not of the whole nation, but merely of the persons who belong to the party. A political party ordinarily consists of two elements —first, the group of more active persons who are recognized as the leaders of the party, and who, if the party is successful in the election, become officers in the government; and, second, the great mass of less active persons who make up the rank and file of the party. Modern political parties are mass organizations, often comprising millions of persons.

The political party, speaking historically, is a comparatively modern phenomenon. The first political parties developed in England in the seventeenth century, but for a long time the English political parties were only small cliques within the governing class. The first political parties with broad membership developed in the United States of America after 1800. In both cases political parties developed as an accompaniment of the extension of rights of self-government to the people—at first to a limited number of people, and then later to the masses. The primary purpose of political parties is to unify the vast number of voters under the democratic form of government, and to enable them to act in a disciplined and orderly manner in seeking to control the government. When the democratic form of government was established in this and other countries, no provision was made in the constitutions and laws for the organization of the electorate. But organization immediately became necessary in order to enable like-minded

persons to act together in the choice of public officers. The
political parties came into existence in response to this
need. They supplement the regular political machinery as
provided by the constitutions and the laws, and they function as a means of transmitting the popular will from the
people to the government. It is doubtful whether democracy would ever have proved a workable system of government without political parties, and it is certain that
democracy could not continue to exist under modern conditions without them.

Political parties may of course be diverted from these
highly desirable ends. It is in the one-party systems of
the European countries subject to dictatorship that the
political party may be observed in a role farthest removed
from its true purpose of promoting popular government.
In each of these countries the political party was used as
an agency to promote a revolution and, after the success of
the revolution, as a means of establishing an autocratic government. The one party, protected in its solitary existence
by the laws and the strong arm of a ruthless government,
is presumed to represent the desires of all the people. It
is really a contradiction in terms to call such an organization a political party, because a party can only be a part
of the nation. One party implies a counterpart, or opposition party. The legal establishment of only one political
party makes it impossible to use the normal means for the
expression of differences of opinion.

The one-party system is wholly bad as a method of realizing popular government. But how many political parties
should exist in a free country? Experience has shown that
several political parties, and sometimes a score or more of
them, are needed to express the various opinions on political questions that develop in a modern industrialized state

when liberty of thought and association are protected. Most of the political parties are, however, of minor importance, and have little chance of gaining the support of any considerable number of voters. It is really a question then of how many major political parties there should be. The English government functioned very successfully for centuries with only two major parties, the Conservative and the Liberal, but the increase in the strength of the Labor party since the World War has raised many doubts as to whether the governmental machine will run as smoothly under a three-party system. In France the democratic form of government has worked quite satisfactorily under the multiple-party system, although the frequent changes in ministry are largely due to the existence of numerous political groups. The general opinion is that the existence of only two major parties makes for the smoothest operation of representative government, but it is clear that the two-party system is a rather rigid mold into which to fit all the different opinion groups which arise under modern conditions. New political philosophies, if they prove to have a broad popular appeal, are certain to break through the two-party system, and will result from time to time in the formation of new parties.

Regardless of the number of political parties existing in a given country, it may be observed that there are comparatively few attitudes about public affairs that lead to coherent political philosophies. Instead of distributing themselves into a large number of groups according to all the possible shades of opinion on political subjects, the voters in a free country tend to cluster in large groups according to the principal points of view that are popular at the time. At the present time there are five outstanding attitudes in politics, each of which has attracted its millions of followers. They are Fascism, Conservatism, Liberalism,

Socialism, and Communism.   In a free country each of these political philosophies is likely to be represented by one or more political parties, and in addition some political parties are likely to try to occupy the middle ground between any two of the principal points of view.   Liberals, Socialists, and Communists all have a habit of breaking up into factions, which may lead to the foundation of many political parties.   Again, the major political parties of a country may not divide at all according to these principal political philosophies.   This is true notably of the United States of America, where the two major parties, the Republican and the Democratic, cannot be distinguished in terms of Liberalism and Conservatism.

It is impossible to summarize these great political philosophies in a few words, and the adherents of any of them would require volumes to express their opinions.   Fascism may be characterized as the belief that the private ownership of property should be preserved at the cost of prohibiting the freedom of action of all individuals.   As practiced in Italy and Germany, Fascism means the glorification of the state, the intense militarization of the whole population, and the thoroughgoing state regulation of economic life. Conservatism is the belief that the existing order should be preserved as far as possible, and that changes and alleged reforms should be adopted only after the most careful deliberation.   Conservative parties in England and other countries are found advocating the protection of the capitalist system and a minimum of state regulation of economic life. Conservatism is an individualist doctrine.   Liberalism is primarily a belief in the desirability of individual freedom. Liberal parties have worked for the extension of the suffrage and the guaranty of individual liberties by the state.   In the economic sphere, liberal parties long advocated freedom from state regulation, but in the twentieth century they have adopted a collectivist doctrine designed to correct the greatest inequalities in the distribution of wealth. Socialism is essentially the belief that the well-being of the mass of mankind can best be promoted by the public ownership and operation of the means of production, exchange, and distribution. There are many different varieties of Socialism, which may be distinguished on two grounds—first, the extent of public ownership believed immediately attainable; and, second, the method advocated for the realization of Socialism. Communism is one of the varieties of Socialism, characterized especially by the beliefs that practically all property should be brought under state ownership, and that this should be accomplished by revolutionary means.

Political parties elect officers and committees, and establish other agencies in order to provide for their own government and to have properly constituted organs which may speak and act in the name of the whole party. All these agencies are spoken of as the organization of the political party. The organization of a political party may be either democratic or hierarchical in form. If democratic, the entire party organization is based upon the membership of the party, which serves as an electorate. In the United States of America much attention has been given to democratic forms in the choice of party officers, committees, and conventions. The convention method of making nominations, which has been described earlier in this chapter, was originally designed as a method of ensuring democratic control within the party organization. The party conventions were, however, often dominated by bosses and small cliques, so that party organization was far from democratic in practice. The direct primary is a later attempt to democratize the organization of the political parties in this country, but the primaries are also often dominated by bosses. American experience has shown that it is very difficult to ensure that the members will have democratic control over the internal management of their political party. In the hierarchical form of party organization the power flows from the top down. The Fascist party of Italy is a good example of this form of organization. Mussolini as the leader of the party appoints the principal officers and committees, and they in turn appoint the subordinate officers and committees.

An especially important branch of the party organization is the bureaucracy, which has practically complete control over the permanent headquarters of the party. The bureaucracy is made up of professional politicians, who become experts in the arts of campaign management and political publicity, and who expect to make their living out of politics. In the United States of America the professional politicians expect to receive their reward by election or appointment to public office; in foreign countries they are usually salaried employees of the party committees. In every country the professional politicians tend to become very powerful, and regularly exercise much influence in the choice of party candidates and in the formulation of party policy.

The general purpose of the party organization is of course to lead the party to victory in the elections. To this end the party has properly constituted organs for the choice of candidates and the management of the campaign. All of the officers, committees, and employees are expected to join in the great tasks of collecting campaign funds and electioneering. Another important function of the party organization is to make an official pronouncement of the policy of the party. This may take the form of the party platform, as in this country, or it may be an election manifesto, as in European countries.

The citizen is never under direct compulsion to join a political party. There is not even in the European dictatorships any tendency to force citizens to join the dominant political party. There are several degrees of association and nonassociation between citizens and political parties. Many citizens like to remain aloof from all political parties, and, as they say, to maintain an independent attitude in politics. Persons who take this attitude are simply depriving themselves of one of the opportunities open to them to participate in politics. Other citizens may choose to attach themselves loosely to a particular party to the extent of regularly voting for the candidates who are put forward in its name. Such people miss the opportunity of participating in the choice of candidates and the other affairs of the party. The closest relationship to the party is that of membership. Political parties are usually anxious to recruit members, and will accept anybody who expresses a general belief in the policy of the party, or who contributes money or services to the party. The Communist party of the Soviet Union, on the contrary, sets up very rigid requirements for entry into its ranks and discourages lukewarm converts from seeking admittance. The person who attaches himself closely to a political party as a member gains many advantages to compensate him for his pledges and services. It may lead to advancement towards elective or appointive office in the state. It means the opportunity to share in the choice of party officers, committees, and delegates to conventions. Above all, party membership opens to the ambitious and public-spirited citizen unlimited opportunities for service to his fellow men and for leadership in the state.[11]

Other social groups

Political parties by no means exhaust the capacity of the people for association and organization. Human beings have an astonishingly wide range of interests. Of course not all human interests require elaborate organization and planning in order to facilitate their expression. It is, for example, easy to enjoy many of the simple pleasures of life in association with one's relatives and friends, without the formation of a club or society. But if one wants to enjoy good music or the drama, or to indulge an interest in games of skill, or to advocate a political reform, then organization becomes necessary. In order to express and enjoy their numberless interests the people group themselves together into an infinite variety of clubs, societies, unions, federations, and associations. Most of these groupings are not even remotely connected with politics, yet a large number of them are the means of expressing political aspirations. Next to the state itself, the political parties are the most important organizations for the realization of political objects. The auxiliary party organizations, consisting of the political clubs and special organizations for young people and women, should probably be ranked next, since they are so closely associated with the political parties and are so closely allied in purpose. All the other social groups may be classified for present purposes into the following divisions: (1) organizations for political purposes that are nonpartisan, that is, that are not political parties; (2) organizations for nonpolitical purposes that have many

---

[11] Davis, John W., *Party Government in the United States* (Princeton University Press, Princeton, N. J., 1929).

political contacts and interests; and, (3) organizations for nonpolitical purposes that have few political contacts and interests.

When social groups other than the political parties undertake to exert an influence upon the political life of the country, they take up activities very similar in many respects to those of the political parties, but with one important exception. Nonpartisan groups never nominate their own candidates for public office. Nonpartisan groups may, and often do, endorse some of the candidates already selected by the political parties, and this action may at times be decisive in the elections. The political parties have almost a complete monopoly of the function of choosing candidates, and it is this fact, above all others, that distinguishes the partisan from the nonpartisan organizations. Another distinction of some importance between the political parties and other groups is the fact that political parties generally try to express opinions upon the whole range of issues which are attracting attention at any given time, while the nonpartisan groups tend to limit themselves to one or a few related issues.

The type of activity which is especially characteristic of the nonpartisan groups, particularly those with an economic basis, is what is called lobbying. In its simplest form lobbying consists of the efforts of individuals and organizations to interview the members of legislative bodies with the idea of convincing them to vote for or against certain proposed laws. The term lobbying is often used in a derogatory sense, with the implication that bribes or promises are given in the course of such interviews. In fact, so many instances of abuses have been brought to light that lobbying has been considered one of the most serious defects of the American system of government. Proposals have therefore been made to abolish the practice of lobbying; but it is readily perceived that this would be impossible to accomplish, because the vast majority of lobbyists are merely exercising their undoubted right to express their opinions on political and economic subjects. It is very similar to the right of petition which is guaranteed in the constitution. A less drastic proposal for dealing with lobbying is to require all lobbyists to register their names, and to reveal the names of the organizations which they represent, and to file a statement of the amount and source of the money spent in the effort to influence legislation. It is now widely recognized that lobbying is a useful adjunct to the work of legislative bodies and other branches of the government. The lobbyists furnish much information to legislative committees and administrative departments, and are always anxious to offer expert advice. Lobbying is in fact a legitimate method of bringing popular demands to the attention of public officers. The prevalence of lobbying in this and other countries [12] shows quite clearly that the people feel that their interests are inadequately represented in the legislative bodies and other branches of the government, and that they demand other means of making known their aspirations. This need has been recognized in many foreign countries by the establishment of special institutions for the representation of economic and other special interest groups.[13] The Economic Council of Germany (now abolished) and the French Na-

---

[12] On lobbying in Great Britain, see Pollock, James K., "Auxiliary and Nonparty Organization in Britain," *Southwestern Political and Social Science Quarterly*, March, 1931, Vol. XI, pp. 393–407; Herring, E. P., "Great Britain Has Lobbies Too," *Virginia Quarterly Review*, July, 1930, Vol. VI, pp. 342–355. Much information concerning the activities of nonpartisan organizations in France will be found in Hayes, C. J. H., *France: A Nation of Patriots* (Columbia University Press, New York, 1930).

[13] Lorwin, Lewis L., *Advisory Economic Councils* (Brookings Institution, Washington, 1931).

tional Economic Council are examples of institutions for this purpose.

Lobbying organizations are not content to try to influence only the legislative bodies. They bring pressure to bear also upon the chief executive officers and the different administrative boards and commissions—especially those which have functions in connection with the regulation of economic life. The lobbyists also try to influence the political parties to adopt favorable attitudes on certain issues, in the hope that through the political parties they may bring about a change in the policy of the government. It is also very common to find lobbying organizations making a direct appeal to the people. The object in doing this is to create a favorable public opinion for the policy advocated by the lobbying organization, and thus to force a change in the policy of the government.

Lobbying is thus another method through which the citizens may participate in public affairs. Like-minded citizens who have a cause to promote, or who would like to see a particular law passed, are entirely within their rights to associate together and to attempt to bring pressure to bear upon the government. Lobbyists should of course always use legal methods in the promotion of their objects. There are plenty of perfectly honest yet effective methods which may be used by organizations of citizens for the purpose of drawing attention to their demands.

THE IMPROVEMENT OF THE MODES OF POPULAR PARTICIPATION IN GOVERNMENT

Democratic government is now faced by the challenge of dictatorship, which has become the dominant form of government on the continent of Europe. There is little in the dictatorial form of government to recommend it to the people who still enjoy their liberty. In the last analysis dictatorship is nothing more than the up-to-date version of the autocratic rule, and autocratic rule has been the curse of the human race throughout the ages. Democracy was the means through which vast multitudes were emancipated from despotic rule, and it would be a great catastrophe if the whole civilized world should again enter into an age of despots.

The development of dictatorship has had at least one good result in that it has aroused a new appreciation of democracy among the people who still enjoy it as a form of government, and it has set them to thinking of how they may protect democracy against the onslaught of dictatorship. There is more appreciation of democracy at the present time, but less tendency to accept it unthinkingly as a perfect system of government. There is a growing realization of the defects of democracy as it has so far been developed. This leads logically to the view that the best method of preserving democracy is to search out its defects, and then to do everything possible to remedy them. Surely the greatest defect of democracy is the failure to draw more than a small fraction of the people into intimate and daily contact with the affairs of government. No serious effort has ever been made to use the abilities of the common people in their own government. Too much emphasis has been placed upon voting as a method of self-government. The mere establishment of a broad suffrage is not enough to make democracy a working system of government. It is, in fact, only the starting point. In addition to voting, the people need other and more effective means of making their influence felt in the daily affairs of government. Some other means to this end, as described in this chapter, have been developed—largely through the ingenuity of the people themselves. The first step in the improvement of democracy is obviously to exploit the existing modes of popular participation to their fullest extent. Above all else, the voters should enter the political parties and make full use of the facilities that such organizations offer for active participation in politics.

Efforts should also be made to improve the existing modes of popular participation. Attention should be given, in the first place, to the wide dissemination of information about public affairs. The need is not primarily for better sources of information about public affairs, since very good sources of information exist in the newspapers, government reports, books, and periodicals. The need is rather to interpret the great amount of accurate information made available by these agencies, and to present it to the voters in a more assimilable form. To educate the people about public affairs is clearly a task of great magnitude. Among the different institutions which might be considered ready and able to undertake this task, the political party stands out as the most likely possibility. The likelihood of an enlightened public opinion in the near future will largely depend upon the ability and the willingness of the political parties to abandon purely propagandist appeals and to make more use of the appeal to reason. Attention should be given, in the second place, to the creation of new opportunities for the discussion of public affairs by the common people. The development of public forums in many American cities opens up many opportunities of this sort. When the establishment of discussion groups on a wide scale is contemplated, the political party again suggests itself as the agency best fitted to undertake the task in the near future.[14]

---

[14] For a study of the progress which has been made in these respects by British political parties, see Starr, Joseph R., "The Summer Schools and Other Educational Activities of British Socialist Groups," *American Political Science Review*, October, 1936, Vol. XXX, pp. 956–974.

BIBLIOGRAPHY

Bruce, Harold R., *American Parties and Politics: History and Role of Political Parties in the United States*, Third Edition, Chapter XIX * (Henry Holt & Company, New York, 1936).

Cole, G. D. H., and Cole, Margaret, *A Guide to Modern Politics*, Book III, Chapter III (Alfred A. Knopf, New York, 1934).

Haines, Charles G., and Haines, Bertha M., *Principles and Problems of Government*, Third Edition, Chapters X,* XI, XII * (Harper & Brothers, New York, 1934).

Ogg, Frederic A., and Ray, P. Orman, *Essentials of American Government*, Second Edition (D. Appleton-Century Company, New York, 1936).

Starr, Joseph R., *Topical Analysis of Comparative European Government* (Ginn & Company, Boston, 1936).

Willoughby, W. F., *Government of Modern States*, Revised and Enlarged Edition, Chapters XVI,* XVII, XXXI,* XXXII * (D. Appleton-Century Company, New York, 1936).

Willoughby, W. W., and Rogers, Lindsay, *An Introduction to the Problem of Government*, Chapters VII,* VIII* (Doubleday, Doran & Company, Garden City, N. Y., 1921).

Wilson, Francis G., *Elements of Modern Politics*, Chapters VIII, IX, X, XI, XII,* XIII,* XVIII (McGraw-Hill Book Company, New York, 1936).

* These chapters will be found particularly helpful.

CHAPTER XI

The Machinery of Government

JOSEPH R. STARR

University of Minnesota

THE NEED FOR POLITICAL ORGANIZATION

WHENEVER a number of people join together in an association for the promotion of a common purpose, it becomes necessary for them to choose officers and committees and to set up other kinds of agencies for the management of the affairs of the whole group. The greater the number of people in the association, the more elaborate must be the organization. It is possible for all the members of a comparatively small organization to deliberate on matters of policy, but it is impractical for all to act together as a committee for carrying into effect the decisions reached. As the membership of the association grows, it becomes increasingly impractical for all the members to deliberate upon the proposals for common action. It also becomes necessary to entrust a few individuals or an inner group of individuals with the main responsibility of managing the affairs of the association, of executing the decisions, and of acting and speaking authoritatively in the name of the whole association.

The state, more than any other association, has need of regularly constituted organs and agencies for the management of its affairs. The state contains a larger number of persons and has a broader range of interests than any other association. For the direction of its interests each state requires a complicated structure of legislative bodies, executive and administrative agencies, and courts of law. This entire structure is known as the government. In this chapter some of the principal branches of the government of modern states will be described and their activities analyzed.

THE CONSTITUTION

The main outlines of government and the distribution of powers within the state are determined in its constitution. The constitution may be defined as the whole body of fundamental rules relating to the structure of government, the distribution of powers among the different agencies of government, and the relations between the government and the citizens. The rules comprising the constitution may be either legal or extralegal in character; if legal, they are enforced in the courts of law; if extralegal, they exist only as custom and are obeyed only because of the force of tradition, and because public opinion is set in favor of their observance. It will be observed that by no means all of the rules in effect within a state are contained within the constitution. In order for a rule to be regarded as part of the constitution it must be, first, fundamental in character, and, second, it must relate to the structure of government, the distribution of powers, or the relations between the government and citizens.

Constitutions are classified in two different ways. In the first place, constitutions are said to be written or unwritten. A written constitution is one that was drafted and promulgated at a certain time in a single document or a few documents, as in the United States and Canada. An unwritten constitution is one that has never been put into definite form, but exists as an agglomeration of rules brought into operation in various ways and at various times, as in Great

Britain. Of course every written constitution accumulates, after a period of time, an accretion of new rules, which for all practical purposes become part of the original document. Thus, all constitutions, whatever may have been their original character, acquire in time many of the characteristics of an unwritten constitution. For this reason many political scientists have tended to minimize the differences between written and unwritten constitutions; but the issuance of a complete constitution in a single document usually creates, in the countries in which it is done, a tradition that is quite different from that of countries having unwritten constitutions.[1] There is so often a tendency to refer back to a written constitution as the authority and guide for later actions. This is especially notable when, as in the United States of America, a supreme court has become the guardian of the constitution and empowered to void other laws that are deemed conflicting with it.

In the second place, constitutions are classified as to whether they are rigid or flexible. If the written constitution contains a clause prescribing a special procedure for the purpose of adding to the original document, or changing the provisions of it, the constitution is said to be rigid. If no special procedure for amendment is prescribed, then the constitution is said to be flexible. An unwritten constitution, and the unwritten portions of written constitutions, are always flexible in this technical sense. Rigid constitutions sometimes prescribe quite elaborate procedures for amendment. The procedure of adopting an amendment usually consists of two parts, proposal and ratification. Amendments to the national constitution of the United States of America may be proposed either by a two-thirds

---

[1] Finer, Herman, *The Theory and Practice of Modern Government*, Vol. I, p. 184 (Methuen & Company, London, 1932).

vote in both houses of Congress or by a special convention summoned by Congress upon the request of two thirds of the states. The second of these alternative methods has never been used. Once proposed, the amendment may be ratified either by the legislatures or special conventions in three fourths of the states. Congress has the power to choose between these two methods of ratification, but the second was never employed until it was prescribed with respect to the Twenty-first Amendment (the repeal amendment) in 1933. Amendments to the national constitution of the Commonwealth of Australia must first be passed by both houses of Parliament, after which they are submitted to the people in a referendum. In the referendum the amendment must be approved, not only by a majority of the voters, but also by a majority of the states. The French constitution prescribes a relatively simple method of amendment of two stages. The two chambers of Parliament, sitting separately, must first resolve that a revision of the constitution is necessary. The passage of this joint resolution has the effect of convening a joint sitting of the two chambers, in which the amendment is proposed as a bill and passed as a new constitutional law. Since the power of amending the French constitution is, for all practical purposes, vested in the authorities that have the power of ordinary legislation, the French constitution is often spoken of as a semiflexible one.

THE SEPARATION OF POWERS

The will of the state, when expressed by the proper authorities in the form of rules, is called law. Much of the law in effect at any given time has been handed down by past generations. The act of formulating the law took place, in many instances, centuries ago. No people, however, can afford to submit themselves completely to the domination of a legal system that has been passed on to them as part of the social heritage. It is always necessary to formulate new law to fill up the gaps in the existing system and to take account of changed conditions. The work of giving expression to the will of the state in the form of new law, or, in other words, of making an authoritative declaration of public policy, is spoken of as the legislative function. In free countries it is believed that the legislative function should for the most part be vested in the representatives of the people who compose the deliberative assemblies that are known as legislative bodies. In order to exercise the function of formulating new law, a legislative body needs to be endowed with sufficient power; that is to say, a legislative body must be granted a share or portion of the sovereign power that belongs in general to the state. The Parliament of Great Britain, consisting of two legislative bodies called the House of Lords and the House of Commons, is in legal theory endowed with all the sovereign power of the state; but Parliament does not attempt to exercise all the power itself, and has delegated large portions of it to other authorities. Legislative bodies, thus endowed by the constitution with all or a part of the sovereign power of the state, make up one of the major powers, or branches, of the government—the legislative branch.

But it is not enough merely to enact laws. They must also be carried into effect and interpreted from time to time with respect to special circumstances. For these purposes the constitution establishes two other major branches of the government—the executive and the judicial. These also need their endowments of the sovereign power in order to carry on their functions. It might be supposed that the three major branches of the government possess among them all the sovereign powers of the state, and this is sometimes true, at least in legal theory. But in some states considerable portions of sovereign power are clearly reserved to other authorities.

It is possible to recognize not merely three major branches of the government, but also two additional ones to make a total of five. The other two divisions of the government that are sometimes recognized as major branches are the administration and the electorate. In the familiar threefold classification of the powers of government the first of these, the administration, is considered part of the executive branch. There are, however, such marked contrasts in the character of work performed by executive and administrative officers that the latter may be considered as composing a separate branch of the government. The executive function in government is properly considered as the work of supervising or managing the day-by-day work of the staffs of employees—in other words, of seeing to it that the laws are enforced. The administrative function, on the other hand, is the work of actually enforcing the laws and carrying into effect the decisions of superior officers. The great importance of the work of the administration cannot be doubted by anyone. It is, however, sometimes supposed that the administration does not have any powers; that, on the contrary, it has only duties and functions. The vast modern development in all countries of administrative agencies which have the power to render decisions and to take actions that profoundly affect the property rights and the daily lives of citizens makes it clear that the administration is a branch of the government that is second to none in power to do good or evil.

The electorate is not usually considered a part of the government at all; but the devolution of important new functions to the voters in connection with the initiative, the referendum, and the recall has served to call attention to the role that it plays in actual government. The exercise of the traditional function of the electorate, that is, the choice of public officers, is essential to the operation of popular government. In view of the great importance of its work, the electorate may properly be recognized as a major branch of the government. Each voter holds a public office, the duties of which are not continuous, but are nevertheless of vital importance. The electorate cannot of course be regarded as a major branch of the government in countries where the voters have been deprived of their functions, or seriously interfered with in the exercise of their functions, as in some of the European dictatorships.

The written constitution often imposes certain limitations upon the whole government and its separate branches. Many prohibitions of this kind are found in both the national and state constitutions of the United States of America, especially in the parts of the constitutions known as the Bills of Rights. These constitutional prohibitions have the effect of reserving to the people a portion of the sovereign power of the state. The government of the United States is thus not endowed with all the sovereign power of the state. Ours is a limited government. The expression of the doctrine of limited government in our constitution was of course intended as a guaranty of the liberty of the people. It is still considered highly desirable that our government should be restricted in authority, but the danger is that the limitations imposed at an early stage in our political history will leave the government too limited in authority to deal with modern problems.[2]

---

[2] For a discussion of the limited powers of the American government, see McBain, Howard L., *The Living Constitution*, pp. 37–41 (The Macmillan Company, New York, 1928).

Some of the most serious problems of government arise in connection with the interrelations among the legislative, executive, and judicial branches. Should these great branches of government be separate from each other as to personnel, and relatively independent of control by each other? It is quite clear that, if these branches were completely independent of each other, carrying on their work in separate watertight compartments, the government could not function at all. Everybody in the government would work at cross purposes, and there would be no harmony of action. The government of the United States of America is said to be one of separation of powers, but the three major branches of government are only partially separated in our system. They are completely separated as to personnel, because no individual can be a member at the same time of two or all three branches.[3] But they are not completely separate as to powers, and they have various kinds of contacts with each other. These relations among the three branches are spoken of as the check-and-balance system. The two fundamental principles of American government—the principles of the separation of powers and of checks and balances—are often thought to be identical. They are, in fact, to a large extent mutually contradictory. If the three branches were completely separate, then they might be said to balance each other. But they are not completely separate. The constitution introduced many checks, or means through which one branch can control another or both of the others. As examples it may be noted that the president's veto power over legislation is a check upon Congress; the Senate's powers to approve appointments and treaties are checks upon the president; and the Supreme

[3] United States Constitution, Article I, Section 6, Paragraph 2.

Court checks both of the other branches through the power of judicial review. The checks, then, are a measure of the incompleteness of the separation of powers. In as far as checks exist, the principle of the separation of powers is invaded.

The differences between the principle of the separation of powers, as exemplified in presidential government, and the opposite principle—the union of powers—as exemplified in parliamentary government, are often dwelt upon. It is easy, however, to magnify the contrast between these principles, and it should be realized that they differ only in degree. For one thing, the administration is regarded in all countries as a subordinate branch, subject to many kinds of direction and control by the other branches of the government. It is never supposed that the administration should be included within the principle of the separation of powers. For another thing, the judicial branch is regarded in all free countries, regardless of whether they adhere generally to the principle of the separation of powers or to that of the union of powers, as a part of the government which should be relatively independent of the legislative and executive branches. An independent judiciary is everywhere considered an essential of free government. Of course the judiciary enjoys varying degrees of independence in different countries. The idea of the separateness of the judicial branch is probably carried the farthest in the United States of America. Here the judiciary is secured in its independence by the grants of power and the guaranties of independence in the national and state constitutions, by the absence of any convenient method of removing judges, and by other devices. The judicial branch of the American government is not merely separate; in fact, it is in many respects ascendant over all the other parts of the government, because the courts serve as the guardians of the constitution and possess the power of judicial review. In England the courts are by no means so independent of the other branches of government. The Lord Chancellor, who is at the same time a member of the cabinet, the presiding officer of the House of Lords, and the chief judge of the national courts, illustrates in his own person a curious union of powers. Moreover, judges may be removed relatively easily by the executive upon the request of both houses of Parliament, although removals are never made for political purposes. In France the Minister of Justice sometimes serves as a judge and at all times possesses extensive powers of supervision over the work of the courts, and an important set of courts—the administrative courts—are treated as part of the executive branch. In the dictatorships of Europe the courts are subjected to political control in various ways, and their independence is completely destroyed. The law codes have been revised, or are in the course of being revised, so as to accord with the dominant political philosophy. The judges are always expected to use their position and powers for the purpose of furthering the interests of the absolutist government. Moreover, the prestige of the regular courts is undermined by the creation of special courts to exercise exclusive jurisdiction over persons charged with political offenses.

When the governments of the different countries of the world (other than the countries under dictatorship) are distinguished as to whether they are examples of the separation or the union of powers, the real differences are found in the relations between the legislative and executive branches. If the legislative and executive branches are distinct as to personnel, and if they have relatively independent powers, then the government is classed as one of separation of powers. The United States of America and some of the Spanish-American republics are the best examples of this form. If the legislative and executive branches are not distinct as to personnel, and if the executive derives its power from the legislative branch, then the government is classed as one of union of powers. Great Britain, France, and the British self-governing dominions are examples of this form.

THE LEGISLATIVE BRANCH

Structure

A legislative body, as found in free countries, may be defined as a deliberative assembly of the representatives of the people, having the primary function of formulating law. The legislative bodies of countries under dictatorships are very similar in structure to those of free countries, but they have to a very considerable extent lost their deliberative character and their legislative function. They are likely to lose their deliberative character because the members are not free to discuss proposed laws or to vote as guided by their consciences. The power to pass laws is to a large extent taken away and vested in the executive branch or in the organs of the dominant political party.

The legislative branch of a modern government may consist of one legislative body, in which case it is called unicameral; or two legislative bodies, in which case it is called bicameral. The bicameral form was originated in England and has been copied widely, and most of the parliaments of the world consist of two houses or chambers. The unicameral form is found in Germany, Finland, Spain, Turkey, and a few other countries, and in all the Canadian provinces except Quebec. In recent years doubts have arisen as to whether bicameralism is well suited to modern conditions, especially in small countries and the political subdivisions of large countries. The adoption in 1934 of the unicameral form for the legislature of the State of Nebraska has aroused much interest in this question.[4] It is well to remember that the bicameral form was continued into modern times for two outstanding reasons. In the first place, the second chamber was considered an effective barrier against too much democracy. A second chamber composed of titled nobles, as in Great Britain, is doubtless best for this purpose; but countries that did not have a nobility tried to gain the same result by fixing longer terms of office for the members of the second chamber, by providing for the continuous existence of the second chamber through the device of partial renewal, by setting up higher age limits for membership in the second chamber, and by many other means. When democracy was widely accepted as a fundamental principle of government, the old argument for second chambers was varied by allegations that the second chamber would serve as a check against ill-considered legislation and would thus prevent the worst excesses of democracy. It is very doubtful that second chambers have served this purpose, and it is easy to find examples when second chambers have been just as hasty, or even more hasty, than the first, or lower, chambers. In the second place, bicameralism was desired in order to make possible two kinds of representation. In order to derive the greatest advantage from bicameralism in this respect it is necessary to render the two chambers really different

---

[4] Lancaster, Lane W., "Nebraska Prunes Her Legislature," *Current History,* January, 1935, Vol. XLI, pp. 434–436; Senning, John P., "Nebraska Provides for a One-House Legislature," *American Political Science Review,* February, 1935, Vol. XXIX, pp. 69–74.

in make-up. One must represent a privileged aristocracy and the other the mass of the people; or one must represent the major political divisions within a federation and the other the mass of the people; or some other method must be found to achieve differences in the composition of the two chambers. In the member states of the American union the only ways found to create differences between the two chambers were to make the upper chamber smaller in membership and to have each member elected from a relatively large district. Many persons justly regard these methods as not sufficient to create real differences, and therefore argue that all the American states should follow the example of Nebraska in adopting the unicameral plan.

It is clear that bicameralism creates serious problems in the modern democratic state, and the simple solution seems to be to abolish all of the second chambers. This, however, will seldom prove easy to accomplish. In England any proposal to abolish the House of Lords, or even to alter its composition or powers, is certain to raise a political controversy of first importance. Few Americans would be willing to abolish the Senate, for it is generally regarded as one of the outstanding successes of the American system of government. In the American states there is likely to be strong opposition to proposals for the abolition of the second chambers. In any case, abolition of the second chamber will always leave the problem of what to put in its place. The people will have to decide whether the unicameral legislature that will be left should be large or small in membership, and whether it should be granted extensive powers or constantly checked by demands from the people for referendums. It seems that Nebraska abolished her House of Representatives rather than her Senate, and it may well be questioned whether the remaining body will prove large enough in membership to represent her people adequately. It would seem to be a mistake to adopt unicameralism only to find that the people are underrepresented, or that popular referendum must be made to substitute for the abolished second chamber.

Bicameralism will thus continue to be the usual form of the legislative branch in many places for some time to come. The chief problem connected with bicameralism has been, and will probably continue to be, the method of breaking deadlocks between the two chambers. One method of doing this is to provide, as in the United States of America, for the appointment of a joint, or conference, committee for the purpose of compromising the differences between the two houses. This method has the great disadvantage of creating what is, for all practical purposes, a third house of Congress. Another solution is to drastically limit the powers of the second chamber and to leave it, as in England under the terms of the Parliament Act of 1911, with only the power to delay legislation for a limited period of time. Other solutions are to provide for a joint sitting of the two bodies to vote on the disputed matter, or to require that both shall be dissolved and an entire new parliament chosen by the people. None of these solutions is entirely satisfactory, and until a better one is devised, each country will doubtless continue to follow its own traditions.

The election of legislative bodies

Some legislative bodies, including the French Senate and the Soviet of Nationalities of the Soviet Union, are indirectly elected. For the direct election of legislative bodies, two plans are in general use. These are the single-member-district plan and the general-ticket plan. A third plan, known variously as functional, economic, or occupational representation, has been followed in the election of some of the legislative bodies in the Soviet Union and, in a limited form, in the choice of the Italian Chamber of Deputies. However, the plan of functional representation has been abandoned altogether in the Soviet Union under the new constitution, and the early abolition of the Italian Chamber of Deputies has been promised by Mussolini on more than one occasion. In the system of functional representation the people are grouped together in economic or occupational constituencies and allowed to select their representatives according to ratios that are intended to reflect the relative importance of each group in the economic life of the whole nation. Functional representation is based upon the theory that economic factors predominate in human relations, and that therefore the people will be better represented, if they are grouped together according to their economic interests.

In both of the usual plans of electing legislative bodies the people are grouped together, for purposes of representation, into geographical units. These plans are based upon the theory that the people who live in the same area have common interests. The single-member-district plan of election, as the name implies, is the method of election in which the whole area to be represented is divided into geographical districts, and one member of the legislative body is elected from each district. Sometimes two members are elected from each district, as in the elections of the United States Senate and a number of American state legislative bodies. This is considered merely a variation of the principal plan. The single-member-district plan may be used for two purposes. In the first place, it is a method of distributing representation according to population. This result can easily be secured by making all of the districts approximately equal in population. The plan is used for this

purpose in choosing the United States House of Representatives, many American state legislative bodies, the
British House of Commons, the French Chamber of Deputies, and many other legislative bodies throughout the
world. In the second place, the single-member-district plan
is a method of providing for the special representation of
certain pre-existing areas, irrespective of their population.
It is used for this purpose in choosing the United States
Senate.

The general-ticket system, also called election-at-large, is
a method of electing legislative bodies in which the districts
are relatively large; at least three members of the legislative
body are elected from each district, and each voter has
as many votes as there are members to be elected. This
method is often used for the election of city councils in
American cities operating under the commission or council-
manager plans of government. The outstanding instance
of the use of the general-ticket system in the United States
is in the election, not of a legislative body, but of the presidential electoral college. In presidential elections each state
is an electoral district, and each political party nominates
as many presidential electors as the state has votes in the
electoral college. The voters almost invariably support the
entire list of one political party, with the result that one list
is elected as a block and all the other lists are defeated. One
party, as we say, "carries the state," and the other parties
get no representation at all. The tendency of the general-
ticket system to result in the complete success of one political party within each district has led to the modification of
this method of election by what is called proportional representation. The chief aim of proportional representation is
to guarantee that each political party shall receive representation in the legislative body as nearly as possible in

proportion to the popular vote cast in support of its candidates. Thus, majority rule will be ensured, and at the same
time each minority of any importance will receive its fair
representation. Scores of different methods of proportional
representation have been proposed, and many of them are
in operation, particularly in European countries.

The organization of legislative bodies

In order to carry on its work smoothly and harmoniously,
a legislative body needs an elaborate organization consisting
of officers and committees. The most important officer of a
legislative body is the presiding officer, who bears the title
of speaker, president, or chairman. Many legislative bodies,
for example, the British House of Lords and the United
States Senate, do not have the power to choose their own
presiding officers, but must accept in that capacity a member of the executive branch. In such cases the presiding
officer does not have very extensive powers of control over
the proceedings of the legislative body. Most legislative
bodies have the right to elect their presiding officers. Such
elections are almost always conducted along party lines, so
that the presiding officer is usually a member of the majority
party or coalition. The Speaker of the British House of
Commons severs all connections with his political party
immediately after his election, and presides over the House
of Commons in an impartial manner. The Speaker of the
American House of Representatives, on the other hand, is
expected to take a prominent part in the affairs of his
political party, and to do everything within his power to
further the interests of his party. Presiding officers usually
have the power of recognition, that is, the power to permit
members to join in the debates; the power to decide disputed questions of parliamentary procedure; and powers

under the statutes and rules to maintain order within the legislative body. In this country the Speaker of the national House of Representatives formerly had the privilege of serving as the chairman of the powerful Committee on Rules and the power of appointing the members of all of the standing committees. These powers were taken away in 1910 and 1911, but they are still possessed by the presiding officers of many state legislatures. The powers of American presiding officers are enhanced by the partisan character of the office. In England, since the Speaker is known to be impartial, it is realized that he may safely be entrusted with vast power. Consequently, he is empowered by the rules to play a large part in limiting the time to be devoted to debate, and by the Parliament Act of 1911 to decide whether a bill is or is not a money bill. Other officers of legislative bodies include the clerk, who has charge of all written records; the sergeant at arms, who has limited power to maintain order; and the chaplain. The legislative body also has a staff of clerical and administrative employees. In some countries an allowance is made to each legislator for the hire of a private secretary.

The most important committees appointed within a legislative body are those called the standing, or permanent, committees because their membership is fixed for a period, usually through the term of office for which the legislative body has been elected. In many American state legislative bodies the standing committees are appointed by the presiding officer, but it is more common to vest the appointing power in a committee or in the political parties. The party or coalition that has a majority of the members in the legislative body is always given control in all of the committees, and it thus has every opportunity to carry its program into law. The powers of standing committees vary greatly from place to place. They play a more prominent part in legislation in the United States of America and France than in England.

The organization of legislative bodies, consisting of officers and committees, as provided by the rules, is usually not considered enough to ensure the dispatch of legislative business; so additional organization is furnished by the political parties. The legislators who belong to a particular party often meet together in what is called in America a caucus. The chief purposes of such meetings are to allow for the discussion of items of legislative business and to agree upon a common line of action in the legislative body. The caucus usually elects leaders, who serve as field-generals of the party forces in the debates, and a number of committees. In this country the most important committee chosen by the caucus is called the steering committee. The steering committee of the majority party has very important powers in connection with determining what items of business shall be allowed to come up for discussion, how much time shall be allowed for such discussion, and the order in which items of business shall be taken up.

THE EXECUTIVE BRANCH

Structure

The executive branch of government may be either unitary or plural in form. The executive branch is said to be unitary when all the executive powers are legally or actually vested in one chief executive officer. This form of the executive branch is found in the national government of the United States and in the dictatorships and other autocracies of Europe. The executive branch is said to be plural, or collegial, when the executive powers are partitioned among several chief executive officers. This form of the executive branch is found in England, France, and the other countries of the world operating under the parliamentary form of government. When a country has the plural form of the executive branch, it usually also has a single chief executive officer who serves as the ceremonial head of the state. For example, in England the king is nominally the head of the state, and of course at an early period in English history was the real head of the state; but nowadays the king has relatively few political functions, and the real chief executive officer is the principal minister, or premier. The premier of England, however, is theoretically only the first among a number of chief executive officers, or ministers, all of whom are supposed to be equal in power. For these reasons England is said to have a plural executive. In a few instances the plural form of the executive branch has been set up without any single officer to serve as the nominal head of the state. This is theoretically the case in the Soviet Union; but the government has been so completely dominated from behind the scenes by one man that the executive branch of the government of the Soviet Union should really be regarded as unitary in form.

After all, the distinction between the unitary and the plural forms of the executive branch is only one of degree. There has probably never been in the history of the world any example of thoroughgoing one-man rule. No government, no matter how dictatorial or autocratic it may be, can be completely dominated by one man. The president, dictator, emperor (or whatever his title may be) must always delegate many affairs to subordinates. This may in fact be required by law. For example, in the national government of the United States the cabinet officers are legally only the agents of the president, but Congress has laid many duties upon the cabinet officers which are performed by them without any direct control by the president. Some executive officers are required to report on the conduct of their offices directly to Congress instead of to the president. In the American states several of the chief executive officers are elected by the people and enjoy powers granted to them by the constitution; consequently they are often quite independent of the governor. Thus our executive branch, which is unitary in form, is in practice often similar to the plural form. On the other hand, the plural form may in practice tend to resemble the unitary form. For example, the premier of England, instead of being the equal of the other ministers, as he is in theory supposed to be, is in fact usually an outstanding party leader with extensive power of control over his colleagues.

The student should be warned that things are not always what they seem to be in the executive branch of government. The chief executive may seem to be the president; but in practice the president is completely overshadowed by the premier, as in France. The chief executive may seem to be the king; but in practice the real head of the government is the dictator, as in Italy. Or the state may seem to have no executive head at all; but inquiry reveals the real head of the state serving nominally as the chief organizer of the dominant political party, as in the Soviet Union. In an American city the chief executive may appear to be the mayor; but again inquiry may reveal that the real head of the city government is the party boss, who directs affairs without holding any public office at all.

Under both the unitary and the plural forms of the executive branch the direction of the day-by-day affairs of government is largely in the hands of the members of the executive advisory council called the cabinet, or the council of ministers. The individual members of the American cabinet are called cabinet officers. Abroad they are generally called ministers. Each minister heads a department of state, or one of the principal divisions into which the administration is divided. The number of ministers varies a good deal from country to country. Every country has ministers of foreign affairs, finance, national defense, internal affairs, trade or commerce, agriculture, the post office, and labor. Other administrative chiefs are admitted to the cabinet when their work is thought of special importance. The whole cabinet is a deliberative body and has as its chief function the determination of the general executive policy. Where the executive branch is unitary in form, the cabinet occupies a subordinate position; it can only give advice to the chief executive, who may reject the advice and follow his own line of policy. Where the executive branch is plural in form, the cabinet is much more than a mere advisory council; it can actually make decisions and carry them into effect.

The powers of the executive branch

The chief executive officers get their powers from the written constitution and the statutes passed by the legislative branch. In addition to these definite grants of power, the chief executive officers derive much of their authority from custom and tradition. In countries having the Anglo-Saxon tradition many of the powers of executive officers, as well as many of the limitations on their powers, are based upon common law. In all the leading countries of the world the powers of the chief executive officers, from whatever source they may be derived, are greatly enhanced by the practices of party government. Ordinarily only party leaders can attain high executive offices; hence most chief executive officers exercise authority both as public officers and as party leaders.

The powers of the executive branch may be classified, according to their nature, as executive, legislative, and judicial powers. If the principle of the separation of powers were applied in a strict and logical way, the executive branch would of course have only executive powers. But no government is organized in this way, so the executive always enjoys a mixture of powers. Among the purely executive powers that are commonly vested in the chief executive officers are the supervision and direction of the administration, the appointment and removal of public officers, control of the armed forces, the conduct of foreign relations, the grant of pardons to persons convicted of crime, the declaration of martial law or of a state of siege, and the supervision of local government. In free countries the chief executive officers do not have the right to exercise these powers in a free and untrammeled way. They are limited in various ways by the law, and checked by the other branches of the government. For example, the United States Senate has the right to approve the appointments and the treaties made by the president. Under the head of legislative powers, it is important to observe that the chief executive officers usually participate directly in the legislative process. In the United States of America the constitution grants to the chief executive the power to veto bills when passed by the legislative branch; but in actuality, largely because of the practices of party government, the chief executive's share in legislation is much greater than the mere negative power to veto bills. In spite of the principle of the separation of powers, our chief executive is expected to assume the leadership in legislation.[5] In countries operating under the parliamentary form of govern-

---

[5] McBain, Howard L., *The Living Constitution*, pp. 114–117 (The Macmillan Company, New York, 1928).

ment, the chief executive officers play a still more important part in legislation. The premier, or all the ministers together, usually have the power to determine when and how long the parliament shall be in session; they have the power to introduce bills into parliament for consideration; they directly assume the leadership of parliament, and if parliament does not accept the proposals that the ministers put forward, the ministers may often retaliate by dissolving parliament and causing a new general election.

In addition to sharing in the work of the legislative branch, the chief executive officers in all countries have an independent legislative power that is called the ordinance-making power. This consists of the power to issue general orders, rules, and regulations that must be obeyed, not only by their subordinates in the administration, but also by the mass of citizens. The executive gets this power for the most part through the delegation of legislative authority by and from the legislative branch. All the parliaments of the world pass many laws that are couched in general terms and contain a provision authorizing the chief executive officers to issue orders and regulations for the purpose of filling up the details in the law. The delegation of legislative authority in this way is becoming more common all the while because of the greater volume and technicality of governmental work. The ordinance-making power of the executive is probably least extensive in the United States of America; it is much broader in England; it is still broader in France and the other free countries of Continental Europe; and it reaches its greatest extent in the dictatorships.

The executive branch of the American government has practically no judicial powers, although many executive officers must here, as in all other countries, coöperate closely with the courts in connection with the prosecution of persons accused of crime, the execution of judicial decisions, and the protection of judicial officers in the performance of their duties. In foreign countries a minister, usually called the Minister of Justice, often has extensive powers to supervise the work of the courts for the purpose of making them function in a businesslike and efficient way. The Minister of Justice even serves occasionally as a judge for the decision of cases of special character.

FUNCTIONS OF THE LEGISLATIVE BRANCH

It is a mistake to suppose that legislative bodies are occupied exclusively in the consideration and passage of new laws. As a matter of fact the legislative branch of government in a free country is expected to perform other important functions besides that of legislation, and these other functions occupy rather more time during the average legislative session than the legislative function. The work which legislative bodies do may be classified into five main divisions, each of which is connected with one of the major functions of the legislative branch. First, there is of course the legislative function. In performing this function legislative bodies discuss and investigate the proposals for new laws, rejecting many of them and passing some as statutes. Second, there is the financial function. In performing this function legislative bodies discuss and finally approve the proposals for raising revenue and for expending public funds. The legislative branch rarely has complete control over the finances of the country. It is usually the duty of certain executive officers to prepare a logical plan for raising and expending public money during the next year or two. This plan is called the budget. It is always considered the duty of the officers in charge of preparing the budget to see to it that the budget is a balanced one; that is to say, the officers should propose to raise at least as much money in revenue as they propose to appropriate for the various activities of the government. After the executive officers have completed the budget they are required to submit it to the legislative branch for discussion and approval. The amount of control that the legislative branch has over financial affairs varies greatly from one country to another. In England, for example, Parliament accepts with little change the budget as submitted by the executive; but in France Parliament gives the budget prolonged and careful scrutiny. The scope of the financial powers of the legislative branch depends in practice upon many factors, such as the form in which the budget is submitted, the amount of time available for the discussion of the budget, and the degree of party discipline prevailing in the legislative branch.

Third, there is the function of controlling the executive branch. The legislative branch, even in countries whose government is organized according to the principle of the separation of powers, is expected to do all that it can to require the chief executive officers to carry out the policies desired by the people. The activities of legislative bodies in the performance of this function will be described later as part of the larger problem of the relations between the legislative and executive branches.

Fourth, there is the constituent function of the legislative branch. In performing this function the legislative branch discusses and passes many laws that are not different in form from ordinary statutes, but are constitutional in nature. The legislative branch also usually plays an important part in the complete or partial revision of the written constitution.

Fifth, there is the electoral function of the legislative branch. Sometimes the legislative branch serves as an electoral college for the choice of important executive officers. Thus the two chambers of the French Parliament meet in a joint sitting for the purpose of electing the president of the Republic. Our national House of Representatives is authorized by the Constitution to elect the president of the United States, if the regular election has not resulted in a majority of the electoral votes for any candidate. These are clear-cut examples of the electoral function; but legislative bodies perform electoral functions informally every day of their sessions, in that it is usually in the give-and-take of legislative debates that reputations are made, marking out certain individuals for advancement to the most important positions in the state. This is especially true of countries operating under the parliamentary form of government, where the legislative branch acts informally as an electoral college for the selection of the premier and the other ministers.

In addition to these five more important functions performed by the whole legislative branch, each chamber of a bicameral legislature has special functions that it performs alone. The British House of Lords is the supreme court of appeals in both civil and criminal cases. The French Senate sits as a court for the trial of persons accused of crimes against the state. The United States Senate serves as an executive council to the extent of approving presidential appointments and treaties made by the president with foreign countries. The lower chamber usually has the right to initiate financial legislation and impeachment proceedings. Under the parliamentary form of government the lower chamber has the exclusive, or nearly exclusive, right to retire the ministers from office.

Relations between the legislative and executive branches

The legislative branch is always considered more representative of the people than the executive branch. This is so chiefly because most legislative bodies, particularly the lower chambers of bicameral legislatures, are directly elected by the people, while chief executive officers are more often than not indirectly elected or appointed. In this country the chief executive is for all practical purposes directly elected by the people, and he may therefore claim to be representative of them. Even in these circumstances, however, the legislative branch seems more representative, because of the greater number of elected representatives which it contains. It is a fundamental principle of free government that the more representative branch should maintain a close watch over the less representative, taking action when necessary to protect the people from too much executive domination. This is an accepted principle no less of presidential government than of parliamentary.

The chief theoretical difference between the presidential and the parliamentary forms of government is that in the former the legislative and executive branches are relatively independent of each other, while in the latter close association between the two is the rule. It is not correct to think of parliamentary government as distinguished by the fact that the legislative branch controls the chief executive officers, because in practice the legislative branch may not be able to make its control a reality. It is important to remember that the chief executive officers also have means of controlling the legislative branch, so that, instead of the legislative branch controlling the chief executive officers, the tables may in practice be turned. The need of harmonious relations between these two great branches of the government, and at the same time of a fair division of authority between them, is very great; and the attainment of these relationships is the most important single problem of modern government. In the daily work of government this problem narrows down to questions of procedure. It is necessary to consider, in the first place, the means and devices that the legislative branch has at its command for use in the attempt to control the chief executive officers, and, in the second place, the means and devices that the chief executive officers have at their command for use in the attempt to control the legislative branch.

Before legislators can take any effective steps towards controlling the chief executive officers they must have much information about what the executive officers have been doing and what they propose to do in the future. Many methods are in common use for obtaining such information. The chief executive often appears before the legislative branch to deliver messages or addresses on the general affairs of government. Such messages usually contain an exposition of the main lines of executive policy. The chief executive officers are required by statute to make periodic reports on the work performed within their respective departments. These reports are published and made available to the members of legislative bodies and to the public generally. In countries with the parliamentary form of government time is set aside during the sessions of the legislative branch during which the legislators may address questions personally to the ministers, for the purpose of gaining information upon specific matters. The nearest parallel to this practice in the United States of America is the voluntary attendance of cabinet officers at the meetings of legislative committees for the purpose of answering questions and for informal discussion.[6] Probably the most effective means that legislative bodies have at their command to obtain information about the activities of executive officers is the investigating committee. Such committees are often appointed by legislative bodies and endowed with the power to require the attendance of witnesses and to examine them under oath, and other powers to facilitate their inquiries. Such committees may of course be used for the investigation of any subject related to legislative work, and not merely the activities of executive officers.

Armed with the necessary information, the legislative branch may proceed with its task of seeing to it that the executive officers act in accordance with public opinion. For this purpose it has numerous procedures at its disposal. First, it may discuss and criticize executive policy in the hope of arousing public opinion. In this way attention may be directed to harmful actions of executive officers, and a demand may arise for a change in executive policy. In most legislative bodies numerous opportunities are provided for such discussion and criticism. In the United States Senate, for example, the extraordinary freedom of debate allows for the frequent criticism of executive policies.[7] Second, the legislative branch may take it upon itself to suggest to the executive officers the line of action or policy that they should follow. Opportunities for informal suggestions of this kind frequently arise in the general debates on executive policy. Legislative bodies may in addition pass formal resolutions instructing executive offi-

---

[6] Luce, Robert, *Legislative Procedure,* p. 220 (Houghton Mifflin Company, Boston, 1922).

[7] Rogers, Lindsay, *The American Senate,* pp. 241–256 (Alfred A. Knopf, New York. 1926).

cers to act in a certain way, but the executive officers are seldom obligated to accept such instructions.

Third, the legislative branch may directly impose its own interpretation of public opinion upon the executive officers and require them to act accordingly. There are two important ways in which this may be done. In the first place, the legislative branch passes many statutes appropriating money for the use of governmental departments and agencies; defining the powers of and imposing duties upon departments, commissions, and other agencies; and generally directing the work of the administration. If such statutes are many in number and detailed in character, they prove to be a very effective means of controlling the executive branch. American legislatures make a practice of passing many statutes of this character, and thus, in spite of the principle of the separation of powers, exercise much control over the executive branch. In foreign countries such statutes are not usually as numerous or as detailed in character. In the second place, some legislative bodies have the right to perform some executive functions, and may when doing so impose their interpretation of public opinion upon the executive officers. Examples of this may be observed in the power of the upper chambers of American national and state legislatures to approve appointments, and in the powers of local legislative bodies in all countries having a thoroughgoing system of local self-government to make appointments and to supervise the local administration.

Fourth, the legislative branch has the right to dismiss chief executive officers from office. In the United States the only method available for this purpose is impeachment. The House of Representatives is authorized by the constitution to bring executive officers to trial before the Senate on criminal charges. The great defect of impeachment as a method of controlling the executive branch is that action can be taken only on the basis of criminal charges; it is therefore not in any sense a method of controlling the policy of the chief executive officers. In countries having the parliamentary form of government there are other possibilities for the removal of the chief executive officers. Since the ministers are expected to take the leadership in legislative work, it is generally assumed that the rejection by parliament of any important part of the legislative proposals put forward by the ministers is a demonstration that parliament no longer has confidence in the ministry, and that it should therefore resign. However, if the partisan majority in parliament is well disciplined, such defeats are unlikely to occur. Moreover, if the ministry is defeated on some part of its legislative program, it is still possible in many cases for it to refuse to resign, on the ground that the rejected matter was not important enough to warrant resignation. Thus the ministry is the judge of its own case. But parliament usually has at its command a means of expressing its own judgment of the importance of the disputed matter in the formal vote of want of confidence. This is a trial of strength between the supporters and the opponents of the ministry, and always results in a clear expression of opinion. In France and other countries of Continental Europe another means of testing the confidence of parliament in the ministry is what is known as the interpellation. This is a formal question addressed to a minister, ostensibly to gain information, but really for the purpose of testing the strength of the ministry, because the minister's answer to the question is always followed by a vote that is understood to be a vote of confidence. In France interpellations may be introduced freely, and this is one of the most important factors in the instability of French ministries.

The chief executive officers, in turn, have at their command numerous methods to control the legislative branch and to counteract the legislative efforts to control them. First, the chief executive officers participate directly in the legislative process. The American chief executive shares directly in legislative work at the end of the process of enacting a new law. He may then veto a proposed new law that has already been approved by both houses, although the legislature may override the veto by repassing the bill with an extraordinary majority. In foreign countries it is more common to find the chief executive officers sharing in legislative work at the beginning and throughout the different stages in the enactment of a new law. That is to say, the chief executive officers have the power of legislative initiative and they sponsor their own bills in parliamentary debates. The ministers are present in person to defend their legislative proposals and to refute the criticisms of their opponents. The American chief executives can suggest subjects for legislative consideration in their messages, and friendly legislators are always willing to introduce the bills sponsored by the executive.

Second, the chief executive officers can use their authority as party leaders to impose their will upon the legislative branch. The effectiveness of this means of control depends of course upon the degree of party discipline established by custom. Party discipline has been highly developed in England, Australia, and a few other countries; it is less effective in the United States of America; and in France and other countries having the group system of politics it is a still less effective force.

Third, the chief executive officers may exercise a good

deal of control over the order of business in the legislative branch. By this means they may to a considerable extent determine the items of legislative business that may be brought up for discussion and action, and which items shall be given precedence over others. In this country the chief executive can exert only indirect pressure for the purpose of determining the order of business in the legislative branch. However, by designating certain bills as those which "must" be passed, and by threatening to call a special session for the consideration of desired legislation, the president may get the desired result. In England the ministers have practically complete control over the order of business in the House of Commons. The ministers not only determine what matters may be brought up for discussion and action, and in what order they shall be brought up, but also they can effectively control the amount of time to be allotted for the discussion of each matter. In France the ministers have by no means so much control over the legislative order of business.

Fourth, the chief executive officers sometimes have extensive control over the sessions, and even the term of office, of the legislative branch. The only practical control of this kind that the American chief executive has is the power to call special sessions. This power may be used to obtain the passage of legislation especially desired by the chief executive. In England the ministers determine when Parliament shall be called into session, and how long it shall remain in session, although these matters are to a large extent settled by custom. What is most important is that the English ministers have the power to cut short the term of office for which the members of the House of Commons are elected, and to cause the election of an entire new House. This act is called dissolution. This is a tremendous power, and far overshadows in effectiveness any of the other means of control—either by ministers over Parliament or by Parliament over the ministers. The threat of dissolution is ever present, and is the most important factor in maintaining a compact majority in support of the ministers. In France the ministers cannot in any circumstances dissolve the Senate, and if they should wish to dissolve the Chamber of Deputies, they would have to get the assent of the Senate. It is generally supposed that the Senate would never give its consent to a dissolution, and this belief together with the unfortunate circumstances following the only instance of dissolution under the present constitution, which occurred in 1877, has practically nullified the provision for dissolutions. As a result the French ministers are deprived of the supreme weapon for controlling Parliament, and this goes far to explain why French ministers are so much weaker before Parliament than English ministers.

The relations between the legislative and executive branches prevailing in any particular country will thus depend to a large extent upon a balance of forces. If the legislative branch has effective means of exercising control, and if at the same time the ministry lacks the prestige of party leadership and such powers as that of dissolution and that of determining the order of legislative business, the result will be, as in France, that the legislative branch is dominant. If the legislative branch has ineffective means of exercising control, and if at the same time the ministers enjoy to the fullest extent the various means of control that have been enumerated, the result will be, as in England, that the executive branch is dominant. One of the most curious results of this balance of forces is that there is decidedly more legislative control over the executive in this country under the presidential form of government than there is in England under the parliamentary form. Theoretical considerations, of course, point to exactly the opposite result.

THE ADMINISTRATION

The administrative branch of government consists of the vast army of public officials, ranging from the political chiefs or department heads at the top down through the various grades of clerks to the common laborers at the bottom, whose general duty is to carry the laws into effect and to perform the multiform tasks of government. There is a good deal of similarity in the structure of the administrative branch from one country to another. An attempt is made in all countries to divide the whole administration into a number of great divisions, called departments of state or ministries. Each department usually has a single administrative head, but, in American state and local governments, boards or commissions are often in charge of some departments, especially those of education and public health. Each department, in turn, is divided into a number of subdivisions, usually called services or bureaus. The theory is that all related services should be grouped together in the same department, so that all persons within a department shall be engaged in a common task. In practice, however, the division of the administration into departments and services is rarely made on a logical basis. Some services are placed in a particular department merely for convenience and not because of any similarity in work. Illogicalities of this sort are very common in the English-speaking world.

In some countries, especially the United States of America, it has proved impossible to fit all the different services into the few great departments. Consequently there has been a tendency to set up these services as separate agencies. The services that are treated in this way are to a large extent those connected with the regulation of economic life, and moreover they are usually the ones for which boards are preferred to a single head, in the interests of providing for more deliberation and less concentration of power. Thus many American units of government have, in addition to the great departments of the administration, a number of independent and semi-independent boards and commissions, such as the Interstate Commerce Commission, the Federal Trade Commission, the Federal Reserve Board, Public Utilities Commissions, and many others. When an administration is organized in this way, with many of its services not brought together into the great departments, it is said to be an unintegrated administration. Americans are probably not prepared to go the whole way and bring about a high degree of integration in the administration, but it is now generally agreed that too many independent establishments have been created and that it would be better to bring these services under a more unified control.

The administrative structures of the various countries of the world differ quite fundamentally with respect to the distribution of power. If the whole administrative system, including the local-government staffs, is brought under the control of the national government, the administration is said to be centralized. Most of the countries with a tradition of Roman law, such as France, have highly centralized administrative systems. On the other hand, if many of the sovereign powers of the state are delegated to the political subdivisions, and if these subdivisions are allowed a good deal of freedom in the administration of their own concerns, the administration is said to be decentralized. The countries with a tradition of Anglo-Saxon law usually have decentralized administrative systems. A decentralized administrative system is an accompaniment of local self-government. If the subordinate administrative officials have little freedom to act on their own responsibility, the administration is said to be concentrated; this is characteristic of the countries with a tradition of Roman law. On the other hand, if the subordinate officers commonly have a substantial amount of discretionary authority, the administration is said to be deconcentrated; this is characteristic of the countries with a tradition of Anglo-Saxon law.

The mass of public servants employed in the administrative branch of the government is commonly known as the civil service. In its broadest meaning this term means all the public servants who are not members of the army and navy. More commonly, however, it is understood that no elected public officers are members of the civil service, and it is also uncommon to consider the most important public officers, such as chief executive officers and judges, as part of the civil service. The term civil service is also more strictly applied in common speech to those public servants who have permanent tenure of office.

There are two ways according to which civil servants are appointed, namely, the spoils system and the merit system. Under the former, public offices are distributed to individuals as rewards for their services to the political party; under the latter, an attempt is made to determine the fitness of all applicants for public employment before they are appointed to office. These two methods of making appointments exist side by side. The spoils system is always used as the method of appointing the highest executive officers, and of filling confidential posts, such as private secretaryships. There is seldom any attempt to extend the merit system in any formal way to the large number of skilled and unskilled laborers that every modern government must employ. The qualifications of applicants for such employment are examined informally by the appointing authority. Appointment to civil-service positions was originally a class privilege, and this meant a particularly bad kind of spoils system. With the growth of political parties in democratic countries the modern spoils system emerged. With the increase in variety and technicality of the tasks of the government, the spoils system has become an undesirable method of recruiting civil servants, with some exceptions, and leads inevitably to a great deal of corruption and inefficiency. The spoils system can wholeheartedly be condemned at the present time as the general method of recruiting the civil service; but it should be remembered that it was an important means of breaking down the aristocratic rule that preceded it.

One of the first steps in establishing the merit system is to classify the different positions into categories, according to the character of the work performed and the qualifications expected of the incumbents. This is necessary in order to plan examinations to test the qualifications of applicants for employment, to establish similar rates of pay for similar work in different departments, and to create a fair system of promotions. The method of classification used in the United States is to set up a rather large number of relatively small classes of positions for which the duties and qualifications of the holders of the positions can be specified in considerable detail. The method of classification used in England is to set up a smaller number of broad classes for which the duties and qualifications are stated only in general terms. These two methods lead to different policies in examining applicants for employment. In this country the examinations are usually specific in character, that is, the examinations are designed to test the qualifications of applicants for the positions sought, and for no others. In England the examinations are often general in character, that is, they test the general abilities and educational attainments of the applicants. A combination of these two methods would probably be the ideal plan.

Another essential step in the establishment of the merit system is the creation of an authority to administer the examinations. The best results are obtained when a separate body, such as a Civil Service Commission, is set up for the purpose and allowed to specialize in the work of examining and certifying the qualifications of applicants for employment. The merit system also requires the establishment, by statute or executive order, of rules to protect civil servants from dismissal for political reasons, to prohibit political activity on the part of civil servants, and in general to regulate recruitment, discipline, promotion, retirement, and dismissal.

The civil servants play an increasingly important part in the government of all countries. Ideally, they furnish the expert element in government.[8] They should be self-effacing, and they should loyally execute the policies agreed upon by their political superiors. The primary duty of civil servants is to furnish facts and advice to guide their political superiors in formulating policy. It is, however, a matter of common knowledge that the expert administrators often do much more than merely give advice. They often make the decisions for themselves and proceed to carry them into effect. This is not necessarily the usurpation of power by civil servants, but is often an inevitable accompaniment of the modern increase in the functions of the state. In fact

[8] Laski, Harold J., "The Limitations of the Expert," *Harper's,* December, 1930, Vol. 162, pp. 101–110.

the greater powers of civil servants under modern conditions is in large degree due to the delegation of powers by the legislature to administrative agencies to issue rules and regulations and to render decisions in special cases. In practice this means that very much detailed legislation is drafted and put into effect by the civil servants, and they have power to render quasi-judicial decisions that profoundly affect the property and daily lives of the citizens. It will do no good to fulminate against these developments as the establishment of "bureaucracy"; they have come to stay. The real problem is to devise means to control the experts, who are so necessary in democratic government, but who should not be allowed to become the rulers, instead of the servants, of the people.

THE JUDICIAL BRANCH

The most important difference in the structure of the courts that may be observed among different countries is that some have only one system of courts and others have two systems of courts, known, respectively, as the ordinary courts and the administrative courts. If these two systems of courts exist side by side, they reflect the distinction between two kinds of law, namely, ordinary and administrative law. Ordinary law, in turn, is divided into criminal and civil law. Criminal law consists of the definitions of criminal offenses and the punishments provided for each. Civil law is the rules established by the state to regulate the relations and business dealings of private citizens with each other. Administrative law is the rules defining the rights and duties of public officials and citizens, respectively, in their dealings with each other, and the procedure according to which these rights and duties are enforced. All countries have administrative law, but only some of the countries having a tradition of Roman law have established a separate system of courts for the enforcement of administrative law. In Anglo-Saxon countries there is only one set of courts, namely, the ordinary courts. There is difference of opinion upon the question of whether or not a separate system of administrative courts is desirable. It is often supposed in Anglo-Saxon countries that administrative courts would adopt a bureaucratic point of view and would not afford proper protection to the individual liberties of citizens.[9] The experience of France, however, has shown beyond a doubt that the individual liberties of citizens are better protected under the dual court system. This result follows, not so much from the mere fact that France has a separate system of administrative courts, but rather from the fundamental principle of French administrative law, to the effect that the state assumes the liability for the wrongs and injuries committed by public officials in the line of duty. This means in practice that French citizens are assured of receiving compensation for the injuries caused by public officials, and in the administrative courts they have a convenient means of enforcing their claims.

The court systems of different countries may also be distinguished as to whether or not they are unified. A court system is said to be unified when provision is made for the direction of judicial work in the interests of efficiency, and when a litigant may get the benefit of any existing legal remedy by applying to any court. In these respects the court systems of most of the countries of Continental Europe and the federal court system of the United States

---

[9] The prejudice against administrative courts in Anglo-Saxon countries is to a large extent attributable to the unfavorable view taken by the late Professor A. V. Dicey in his *Introduction to the Study of the Law of the Constitution,* Eighth Edition (The Macmillan Company, London, 1926).

of America are unified. The court systems of most American states are not unified. The courts may be more completely unified by combining all the courts of similar grade into a single court with separate divisions for specialized judicial work. The English court system was unified in this way by the acts of Parliament passed in 1873 and 1876, and similar plans have been applied to the municipal courts of certain large American cities, notably Chicago and Detroit. A unified court system is preferred by both lawyers and well-informed laymen because it means a simplification of the court structure, a speedier clearing of dockets, and greater convenience and less expense for the litigants.

Each country has a number of grades of courts, which differ in their powers, or jurisdiction. The bottom of the judicial structure is made up of a large number of local courts of limited jurisdiction. Many local courts, especially those in rural areas, are presided over by untrained, or at least not highly trained, justices of the peace. Such courts may deal with criminal cases involving less serious charges, and with civil cases involving relatively small sums of money or amounts of property. Next higher in the judicial hierarchy are found the general trial courts of unlimited jurisdiction. These may try any kind of case, regardless of the seriousness of the criminal charge or the sum of money or the amount of property in dispute. The general trial courts also usually hear cases appealed from the local courts. The next grade of courts is usually the intermediate courts of appeals, and at the top of the judicial structure is found the supreme court of appeals. In the United States and in some other countries having the federal form of government, the structure of the judicial branch is more complicated because of the existence of both federal and state courts. When this is the case, the federal and state courts each have their separate fields of jurisdiction, and the federal courts are superior to the state courts only in matters governed by federal law.

The principal function of the courts is to interpret the law and to apply it to the special cases and disputes that are brought to them for settlement. In addition the courts have certain other important functions. One of these is to exercise judicial review over both legislative and executive acts. The various countries of the world fall into two classes with respect to judicial review of legislative acts. In the United States, Canada, Australia, and a few other countries, the courts have the power to interpret the statutes passed by the national and state legislatures with reference to the written constitution. If the judges consider a statute to be in disagreement with the constitution, they may refuse to enforce the statute. In England, France, the European countries under dictatorship, and in most of the other countries of the world, the power of judicial review does not extend to the statutes passed by the national parliament. In all free countries, however, the courts have the power to review all kinds of subordinate legislation, namely, the orders and decrees issued by executive officers and the ordinances issued by local-government councils. Any act of subordinate legislation may be declared invalid, if it is found to be in disagreement with the higher law contained in the constitution and the statutes passed by the national parliament. In all free countries the courts also have the power to review the acts of executive and administrative officers in order to determine the legality of such acts. If it is found that a public official has exceeded his powers, or has misused his powers, or has unnecessarily injured the person or property of a citizen, the public official can be prosecuted on a criminal charge or made a defendant in a suit for damages. In this way the courts protect the people against the illegal acts of public officials.

Another important function of the courts is to serve as the guardians of the individual liberties of citizens. One way in which they do this, as has already been pointed out, is by exercising the power of judicial review over executive acts. In general, the duty of enforcing the various guaranties of rights found in the constitution, the statutes, and other laws falls primarily upon the courts. The enjoyment of rights by the citizens depends in the last analysis upon the way in which the courts handle the cases of alleged violation of rights. If the courts fairly and fearlessly enforce the law against all persons, the people enjoy real freedom. But if the courts are subservient to the executive branch or to powerful economic or other special interest groups, then the people have no means of preserving their liberty.

BIBLIOGRAPHY

Cole, G. D. H., and Cole, Margaret, *A Guide to Modern Politics* (Alfred A. Knopf, New York, 1934).

Cole, G. D. H., and Cole, Margaret, *The Intelligent Man's Review of Europe Today*, Part IV (Alfred A. Knopf, New York, 1935).

Haines, Charles G., and Haines, Bertha M., *Principles and Problems of Government*, Third Edition, Chapters XIII, XV,* XVI, XVII,* XVIII, XXI, XXII (Harper & Brothers, New York, 1934).

Ogg, Frederic A., and Ray, P. Orman, *Essentials of American Government*, Second Edition (D. Appleton-Century Company, New York, 1936).

Starr, Joseph R., *Topical Analysis of Comparative European Government* (Ginn & Company, Boston, 1936).

Willoughby, W. F., *The Government of Modern States*, Revised and Enlarged Edition, Chapters X, XI, XIV,* XV,* XVIII, XIX, XXI, XXII, XXIII,* XXIV, XXVI,* XXVII, XXVIII, XXIX, XXX (D. Appleton-Century Company, New York, 1936).

Willoughby, W. W., and Rogers, Lindsay, *An Introduction to the Problem of Government*, Chapters V, X, XI, XII,* XIII, XIV, XVI, XVII, XVIII, XXI (Doubleday, Doran & Company, Garden City, N. Y., 1921).

* These chapters will be found particularly helpful.

CHAPTER XII
The Economics of Price

Emerson P. Schmidt

University of Minnesota

EVERYONE is affected by economic conditions. Such terms as price, value, money, wages, and profits are in the vocabulary of all. The economist differs from the layman not in knowing more facts, but in knowing which facts are vital. He knows their relative importance and possesses a clue to what would otherwise be a hopeless labyrinth.

The significance of economics arises out of the fact that human wants are never completely satisfied, and the means of satisfaction are characterized by scarcity. Price changes operate as agencies to bring about an equality between these scarce supplies and limitless desires. High prices stimulate production and check consumption; low prices, by reducing output and encouraging consumption, bring about equilibrium. We can therefore consider economics as the science which deals with social phenomena from the standpoint of price, or value in exchange. It is concerned with the wealth-getting and wealth-using activities of man.

The economist as a scientist is not concerned with human progress and social amelioration. The word "ought" is not in his vocabulary, just as the pure physicist is not concerned with the practical implications of "splitting atoms" or "heavy hydrogen." The chemist may have in mind some human need or profit-making opportunity which will be involved in his research; but the moment he directs his

545

research with such an end in view he is exercising a value-judgment and his research results become "good" in the opinion of some people and "bad" in the opinions of others. Economics has been plagued by much wishful thinking, and many economists have been primarily reformers. This attitude colors their judgment, and explains the differences of viewpoint frequently held by many economic interpreters.

The prime purpose of economics is discovery of facts and relations which grow out of insatiable wants and the scarcity of the means of satisfaction. The economist assumes, as does the natural scientist, that nothing happens by chance. For every event or fact there is a full and adequate cause or causes. If a bank fails, the economist wants to know the steps in the management of the bank which led to the collapse; if a strike occurs, he is interested in relations between management and men which culminated in a termination of production; if wheat prices fall, the economist is convinced that if all the facts were available a satisfactory explanation could be given. Like other scientists, the economist is concerned with the relations between facts so that economic tendencies may be discovered, and that prediction may be made. In the natural sciences many of the facts or data are homogeneous and stable; for example, the chemist has less than one hundred elements with which to deal (excluding isotopes). In economics, and indeed all social sciences, such final units of measurement or composition do not exist. Economic science, however, is in a more fortunate position in this respect than the other social sciences, since demands and supplies can be measured in terms of dollars. Nevertheless, economic facts and events are complex and never recur in exactly the same form or sequence. The economist speaks of numerous laws, such as Gresham's law, the law of diminishing returns, and the law of the proportionality of the factors of production, but hastens to point out that these are essentially statements of economic tendencies rather than strict laws. It is more fruitful to view economics as a technique of analysis than as a body of laws. Change of facts, change of sequence, the human and political factor—all are responsible for the absence of discoverable laws, in the natural-science sense. Thus while economists as such concern themselves with one aspect of human life, they recognize that a complete understanding of any economic phenomenon requires competence in many other social sciences. For example, the cause, conduct, and outcome of a strike can rarely be understood in economic terms alone; common law, statutes, constitution, judiciary, standards of living, social psychology, personalities—all these may be equally important.[1] Nevertheless, a goodly number of broad generalizations, or statements of economic tendencies, are known and seem to apply to nearly all forms of society, whether communist, socialist, or capitalist.[2] It is these to which attention is directed. In this chapter the laws of production and price are outlined and the technique of analysis is displayed.

In order to make his analysis more precise and to reach valid conclusions the economist starts from some rather rigid assumptions. For example, he assumes that when man acts in economic matters he is motivated by the desire for gain; he buys cheap and sells dear; likewise he assumes that freedom of enterprise and free and perfect competition prevail, and that rational action pervades the market-place. Meanwhile the economist recognizes that at times a man

---

[1] The enduring economic treatises give evidence of this broad comprehension. See Adam Smith, *The Wealth of Nations;* John S. Mill, *Principles of Political Economy;* and Alfred Marshall, *Principles of Economics.*

[2] For example, even a communist system must devise a scheme to ration the best seats in the opera hall.

may be motivated by feelings of sympathy, that competition and knowledge may be imperfect, and that much irrational action prevails in economic activity. Nevertheless, the economist concludes that significant analysis must proceed from fairly rigid assumptions. In order to understand realistic phenomena after the basic laws and forces operating in a given situation are understood, proper allowances must be made for the degree to which the actual conditions deviate from the assumptions. Natural and biological science proceeds in the same way. For example, the law of falling bodies states that the velocity of a falling body is not proportional to its weight, yet common sense perception argues that it is proportional; a feather drops more slowly than a brick. The controversy was settled by the experiments of Galileo and others, which showed that the law is true only under specified circumstances, namely, in a vacuum and when the objects start from the same altitude.

In the subsequent analysis of price the basic assumptions of classical economics will be adhered to with such recognition of friction, delays, and imperfect competition as will make the discussion appear realistic and useful.

PRODUCTION

Activities that satisfy human wants and may command a price constitute production. The raising, transporting, processing, and retailing of wheat are all a part of production. Each of these steps, whether it results in a tangible product or a service, is necessary in satisfying the demand of the ultimate consumer. A number of activities, while socially required, may be regarded as either unproductive or as necessary evils. Included within this class are the activities of policemen, firemen, and a vast body of public employees. These individuals perform useful functions by making it possible for others to engage in productive work or by aiding in the preservation of the product of others, but they are not part of the fundamental production system.

In examining the nature of production a distinction must be made between private gain and social production. Winning a wager, stealing, advertising, making fraudulent transactions, launching public or private projects that are never completed, may lead to private gain, but yet not constitute production from a social point of view. In a wager, or in theft, the winner merely takes what the other party loses—there is no net gain. Much advertising matter is informative; it may stimulate wants and cause greater exertion to raise one's standard of living. Out of it may come greater effort, expansion of the scale of output with lower unit costs. Thus advertising may constitute production from the standpoint of society as a whole. However, advertising often merely induces a shift in demand from one seller to another. One producer may put on an advertising campaign which results in decrease in his competitors' sales. His competitors are moved then to launch a similar campaign; thus most students of the problem conclude that much advertising is socially unproductive. When transactions are made through fraudulent means or through one party having imperfect knowledge, the result cannot generally be regarded as socially productive.

Likewise when, for example, a power project or a ship canal is started but is never completed or utilized, the construction may enrich certain private individuals, but the results are not socially productive. Projects launched, completed, and utilized for the production of further goods or services are socially more productive.

To distinguish between socially productive and unproductive labor is not always possible. The dividing line may be obscure; nevertheless this distinction is useful.

THE ENTREPRENEUR IN PRODUCTION

For convenience in analysis, economists divide the factors of production into four classes: land, labor, capital, and entrepreneur. Land includes not only the soil for cultivation but also building sites, waterfalls, mines, and the like, as well as permanent man-made improvements which are virtually as durable as the land itself and are identified closely with the land. Among these improvements are the removal of stones from the soil, drainage, leveling of building sites, and others.

Labor, mental and manual, includes the vast body of skilled and unskilled workmen, clerks, salespeople, and professional classes. Capital refers to man-made instruments of production such as factories and machines, houses, and furniture. Some capital is employed for further production and some, like household furniture, is used for consumption. Unlike land, capital is the result of labor and saving. Some capital is durable and outlasts many uses, while other capital such as coal will be exhausted with one use. Although mines are regarded as land, minerals are defined as capital, but the distinction between capital and land, in general a useful one, is not always easy to make.

By entrepreneur is meant the person or persons who control the business unit. Frequently this person also labors in the shop, as in the tonsorial and retail trade. The business unit may take the form of sole proprietorship, partnership, coöperative, or corporation. Corporation stockholders are legally entrepreneurs, but the great majority of them are inactive, and the entrepreneurial function is actually carried on by a few stockholders. At times stockholders delegate actual management of the business unit to salaried managers who may have complete charge of the routine of the business as well as the making of many important decisions. These managers are, however, not ultimately responsible; they do not shoulder the final financial risks or determine broad business policies, and for that reason cannot be regarded as the entrepreneurs. In addition to taking the ultimate risks of the business the entrepreneurs have as their prime function the coördinating of the other factors of production. This function may be delegated to the salaried managers.

Within limits land, labor, and capital are interchangeable in a business unit. If land rents are high, soil will be cultivated intensively, or tall buildings will be erected,[3] thus utilizing much capital and labor. If capital is relatively expensive more land and labor will tend to be utilized. If labor is scarce and expensive the entrepreneur will tend to substitute capital in the form of large engines, steam shovels, pre-fabricated houses, and so on. Under the pressure of competition every entrepreneur is always on the lookout for cost-reduction techniques. He will tend to expand the employment of each agent of production to the point where it ceases to be profitable, that is, to the margin of profitableness. This process of variation is called the law of the proportionality of the factors of production, or the law of substitution.

The factors of production are available at a price. The forces determining these prices involve the theory of the distribution of income; but here we will take these prices for granted.[4] Usually when more of a factor of production is employed in a given business unit, the return per unit

---

[3] The intensive use of land, however, is the cause of the high rent yields.
[4] See the next chapter.

tends to decline. If a farmer should try to cultivate his one hundred-acre farm alone he might be forced to spread his time over the whole acreage so sparsely that the physical product would be very small. If he should hire a laborer to work with him, thereby doubling the labor on the farm, the physical product probably would not double. A third laborer would add more to the product but possibly would not increase by 50 per cent the output of the two-man combination. If this is the case the farm is being operated under conditions of diminishing marginal returns to labor. The physical law of diminishing returns may be stated thus: In combining various quantities of one factor (labor) with a fixed quantity of another factor (land) increasing one factor will not increase the product in an equal degree. The law of diminishing returns could be illustrated also by assuming a fixed quantity of labor and varying the amount of land utilized. The average output per acre would decline when more acres are associated with a given quantity of labor. This applies not only to land, but also to retailing, to manufacturing, and even to the administration of a university. It expresses a universal tendency, and its significance arises out of the fact that many factors of production are fixed in character by nature, technological considerations, convenience, or custom. Thomas Malthus's pessimistic interpretation of population growth is based on this law. He saw that with a given state of the industrial arts, as population increased on this planet of fixed size, returns per worker must decrease. That is, the standard of living will decline; but this tendency might be offset by more knowledge of production and technological changes.

The businessman is always confronted with the problem of the proper combination of the factors of production. How much of the various types of labor, types of machines and other capital, and land should be associated with himself as entrepreneur in order to effect the best combination? The proportion in which the entrepreneur combines the agents of production will depend fundamentally on the prices he has to pay for each. But his production cost per unit will depend on the amount he produces as well as on what he pays for the factors. If he has a fixed plant which costs him

TABLE I. COST PER UNIT OF OUTPUT

Number of variable agents	Total physical output	Fixed plant and entrepreneur cost	Cost of variable agents *	Total cost
2	200	$1.00	$.20	$1.20
4	500	.40	.16	.56
6	700	.29	.17	.46
8	900	.22	.18	.40
10	1,085	.18	.18	.36
12	1,250	.16	.19	.35
14	1,360	.15	.21	.36

* Labor, seed, fertilizer, and other costs which may be varied.

one hundred dollars a month, and he pays himself one hundred dollars monthly, his total fixed costs are equal to two hundred dollars a month. Suppose he finds he must pay twenty dollars a month for each unit of variable agents (this includes labor, raw materials, and power); he then will attempt to discover the best combination of these agents with his fixed factors. The problem is illustrated in Table I, which should be carefully examined.

A glance at the third column will indicate that the average fixed cost per unit drops continually; it will do so until total output from the plant stops increasing. In the fourth column the average variable costs are shown to fall at first and then rise; they are at the lowest point when four units, or eighty dollars' worth of variables are utilized with the fixed factors. However, the entrepreneur is interested in achieving not the lowest average costs in terms of variable costs, but the lowest total average costs. Even after variable costs begin to rise, fixed costs continue to drop. Total average costs reach their lowest point when twelve units of variables are employed.

A monthly output of 1,250 units costs thirty-five cents per unit. This is the lowest unit cost at which the business concern can operate, and in the long run the price at which the output is sold must at least cover this cost. When an entrepreneur can merely cover his expenses he is said to be marginal. Slight lowering of price or slight rise in costs would make his business unprofitable. He is said to be price-and-cost sensitive. This lowest total unit cost for marginal producers tends by competition to become the prevailing price. But in every business there are many entrepreneurs who are able to combine the agents so effectively or who have special advantages of such a nature that they can produce at lower average costs. These are said to be superior entrepreneurs. They strive to achieve not the lowest average unit costs, but the highest profit combination. The superior entrepreneur will tend to employ the variable agents beyond the point of lowest average unit costs, since the largest profits can be made by him only by expanding production until the marginal costs, that is, the cost added by one more unit of output, equal the selling price of that unit which prevails in the market. Here the total production cost will be somewhat raised, but the higher costs will be more than offset by the larger volume of sales. As long as marginal costs are below selling price, every addition to output will add something to total volume of profits.

In every competitive business, costs vary with the skill of the employer, proximity to market, and other matters. That is, some producers may be marginal (high-cost) producers, and others may be super-marginal, or low-cost producers. For example, on the best Middle West land wheat can be produced for fifty cents a bushel, but in order to satisfy the whole demand for wheat, resort to lower-grade land is necessary; that is, land must be employed on which the cost of production is higher. Although much has been said about the agricultural depression following the four years of the War, many farmers were making substantial profits all through the depression.[5] In the long run the selling price of wheat must be high enough to cover the costs of those farmers who are just kept in production by the demand for wheat. This is what economists mean when they say prices are determined at the margin, or prices are equal to marginal costs. However, even though many farmers cannot cover their costs, that is, they operate at a loss for a number of years, they tend to remain in production, hoping for improved prices, larger yields, or lower costs. After much adverse experience and changes in technique they tend to shift to other products or lose their farms and migrate to cities.[6] Higher prices for wheat may attract farmers to land which was not suited to wheat production under lower prices, and all the previous farmers tend to cultivate their farms more intensively. Another dollar spent on fertilizer, labor, and the like may yield a dollar of wheat or more.

[5] The value of the land is determined by capitalizing these profits at the going rate of interest. For example, if the expected rate of return from land is 5 per cent and the farm produces $1,000 annually over all costs, the farm will tend to sell for $20,000.

[6] If the government makes seed loans, grants farm relief, and forces borrowing rates below the level determined by a free market, sub-marginal producers tend to be kept in business, probably against their own best long-run interests.

In this way shifts in costs, in yields, and in prices of the finished product cause a constant flow of labor and capital into and out of production.

From this analysis it is clear that all businessmen are constantly on the lookout for better combinations of the factors. Obviously the businessman is not in a position to know precisely his average fixed or average variable costs. But if he selects a wrong combination and his competitors guess or estimate more nearly accurately, their costs will be lower, and they will undersell him. This explains to a considerable extent the constant tendency to scrap machinery, to renovate buildings, and to hire and fire employees. Most of such changes are attempts to discover a more effective combination of factors. If machinery becomes unduly expensive, perhaps more direct methods of operation with hand labor will be substituted when old machines wear out. If labor is restless and demands more wages or unduly short hours, the entrepreneur will tend to economize labor and substitute more capital. This is why economists are opposed to artificial forces which fix the prices of land, labor, or capital arbitrarily. If a factor becomes over-priced this tends to discourage its employment. True, all these adjustments take time, and frequently the businessman is not in a position to make adjustments as rapidly as he would like. Nevertheless there are always employers who are on the verge of altering production techniques, and they will take account of prices of factors of production, to arrive at the lowest unit cost if they are marginal producers, or to achieve the highest profit combination if they are superior entrepreneurs. Over a period of time all entrepreneurs adjust themselves to changes in costs in order to effect more satisfactorily balanced proportions among the various factors of production.

EXCHANGE VALUE

The man who attempts to be "jack of all trades" is likely to be master of none; apparently mankind has been aware of this fact not only from the beginning of recorded history but also from the greatest antiquity.[7] Although division of labor and specialization is not a modern phenomenon, it has been carried further in the twentieth century than ever before.[8]

This specialization may take many forms. Ceylon is noted for tea, Cuba for sugar, the United States for motor cars, and Canada for wood pulp.[9] For over one hundred years economists have sung the praises of free international trade on the basis of the advantages of the geographical division of labor. The comparatively high standard of living in the United States is due in part to the fact that this country contains within its boundaries the greatest free-trading market in the world. Within a country, geographical specialization of production takes place. Within a modern city, economic activity is carried on by a host of experts, both great and small, and under free competition each person tends to follow the occupation in which he has the greatest knowledge and ability. Each person pursuing his private interests tends to make a contribution to the other members in society.[10] Although the modern economic system with its elaborate scheme of specialization relies

[7] See Chapter III, "Social Anthropology."

[8] In international specialization of labor, however, we seem to be reverting to more primitive levels.

[9] See Chapter VIII, "Human Geography."

[10] This does not hold for racketeering, which may be defined as the pursuit of economic activity which relies on force, violence, threats, and fear. Producers who rely on appeals to fear by reference to B.O., Halitosis, and the like come dangerously near to being racketeers according to this definition.

on individual self-interest, the system involves a larger coöperation. Henry Ford, following his money-making proclivities, had to rely on the taste, goodwill, and consumer demand of the general public. Production for profit, which is now widely condemned, is a coöperative enterprise in which a vast variety of specialists unite in the production of goods and services for each other.[11] True, coöperation in the humanitarian sense is not intended by the constituent coöperators; rather, it grows out of the pursuit of self-interest.

In 1776 Adam Smith, one of the founders of economic science, said: [12]

As every individual endeavours . . . so to direct (his) industry that its produce may be of the greatest value, every individual necessarily labors to render the annual revenue of the society as great as he can. He generally, indeed, neither intends to promote the public interest, nor knows how much he is promoting it . . . he intends only his own gain, and he is in this, as in many other cases, led by an invisible hand to promote an end that was no part of his intention. . . . By pursuing his own interest he frequently promotes that of society more effectually than when he really intends to promote it. . . . I have never known much good done by those who affected to trade for the public good.

This viewpoint is the acme of rugged individualism; it is the cornerstone on which capitalism has been built for several hundred years. Smith, in other sections of his great work, also urged free competition, and granting that free competition prevailed, he believed that individual self-interest resulted in the greatest "annual revenue for society." [13] All economists recognize that under modern conditions of large-scale industry, monopoly, product differentiation, and trade marks and trade names, where vir-

---

[11] Some of its defects will be discussed later.

[12] *The Wealth of Nations*, 1776.

[13] Smith did not believe in complete laissez faire; he outlined at least four spheres where government activity or control was superior to private endeavor.

tually every manufacturer has at least a degree of control over output and his market, private pursuit of personal gain may not necessarily result in the maximum want satisfaction for the whole of society. This will be discussed subsequently.

When each person or each business concern pursues a restricted sphere of activity, a number of gains are likely to accrue. For example, if the making of shoes is divided into many separate operations, each operation performable by one man, it is possible to substitute machinery for labor owing to the simplification of the operations. It would be difficult to imagine *a* machine which could make *a* shoe, but if shoemaking is divided into a series of successive operations, invention will be stimulated, since it is easier to create a series of machines which can perform the relatively simple successive operations. This permits the classification of tasks and a better fitting of the man to the job.[14] Each man performing a single operation develops a high degree of accuracy and speed. Every piece of capital may be used continually where an elaborate plan of machine technology is installed. In a large shop there is little idle time for man or machine; no steps are wasted; picking up and laying down tools is reduced to a minimum. Compare the neighborhood one-man shoe repair shop with the huge department-store repair shop where each man performs a single operation or a limited number of operations. In short, the division of labor, out of which arises the problem of value and price, makes possible the great physical productivity of society.

Out of private initiative, specialization, and division of

---

[14] Out of this has grown a new branch of science and art, namely personnel administration. See Chapter V, "Psychology and Some of Its Applications."

labor arises the problem of value and price. By value the economist means power in exchange, the quantity of one good which exchanges for a given quantity of other goods. Because of the difficulties of exchanging goods directly for each other, specific commodities have at one time or another been selected to act as measures of value and usually as media of exchange. Thus at one time or another cattle, playing cards, tobacco, beads, and precious metals have been used as measures of value or as media of exchange or both. In the course of history the superiority of gold as both a measure of value and a medium of exchange has been widely recognized. Price, as distinguished from value, reports the exchange relation of goods to money.

REGIME OF PRICE

The capitalist system has frequently been viewed as a planless society. It cannot be denied that it is devoid of any general or central plan according to which specific quantities of goods are produced and specific prices are fixed. There is, however, a plan—a plan controlled by a price mechanism. Bastiat, a noted French economist, upon entering Paris one evening, contemplated the order prevailing in the economic life of the city and remarked, "Imagination is baffled when it tries to appreciate the vast multiplicity of commodities which must enter tomorrow through the barriers in order to preserve the inhabitants from falling a prey to the convulsions of famine, rebellion, and pillage. And yet all sleep at this moment, and their peaceful slumbers are not disturbed for a single instant by the prospect of such a frightful catastrophe."

If one travels to a distant city he is assured of being able to secure what he wants—a porterhouse steak, a pencil, tooth powder, or gasoline for the car. One need not telegraph ahead for these things; they will be there. Under capitalism, enterprising individuals are always on the lookout for profit-making opportunities. Some will run restaurants, others drug stores, and still others filling stations. Laborers are anxious to sell their labor power for a price; capitalists are on the lookout for lending opportunities; material men are trying to sell supplies; the entrepreneur (businessman) gathers labor, money, and supplies, and, combining them in the right proportions at the right time and place, produces commodities or services. All work for a specific result—to get out more than they put in. In this respect the laborer is like the capitalist. The consumer, too, plays an intimate part in this planned society. He is the ultimate arbiter—as influenced by advertising and intriguing displays—of what shall be produced and in what quantities.

The price mechanism regulates production and consumption with basic simplicity. Should a commodity become increasingly scarce, or should a temporary shortage occur, an adjustment in price tends to equate supply and demand. Rising prices discourage consumption; some will not be able to afford the more expensive article; many will buy less of it. At the same time, higher prices may afford more profit-making opportunities, and businessmen will quickly sense the possibilities and tend to increase the supply. When prices are lowered, the buyer may say, "Now is the time to buy." This more or less automatic manipulation of prices up and down, as supplies are smaller or larger, makes it possible so to arrange things that the public can always rely on finding as much as it wishes to buy, and is prepared to pay for, ready and for sale in the shops day by day. It is a very rare experience under capitalism to find that something you wish to buy cannot be had at any price; and as far as thousands of articles are concerned, you may confidently expect that what you want is ready now, to be had without a moment's notice, whether it be a pound of candy or a pair of rubbers. Thus the price system regulates nearly as efficiently in practice as is theoretically possible.

MARKET PRICE

It has been said that if you teach a parrot to say, "Demand and supply determine price," you have made an economist of it. This formula, indeed, contains the core of economics, but it cannot have much significance standing by itself.

Economic terms, even those on every man's lips, have special meanings to the economist. Thus by demand is meant the amount of a good [15] which is taken at a given price, time, and place. By supply is meant the amount of a good offered at a given price, time, and place. A market is usually an area, but frequently the term is used in a more intangible way to designate the forces of supply and demand; that is, we may say, "The market for hogs is weak." A change in demand means that at the former price more or less is taken; if at a higher price the same is taken, this presents an increase in demand, although no more units are sold. When the amount taken at a stable price declines, this is a decrease in demand. However, if the price falls and more is taken, this does not necessarily represent an increase in demand.

If the price of cigars falls from ten cents to nine cents and the same gross dollar sales take place, the demand is said to have an elasticity of one or unity, providing no other

---

[15] Or service; this is implied in *good* or *commodity*.

change has taken place. If such a price decline causes an increase in gross dollar sales, the demand is said to be elastic, that is, the elasticity exceeds unity; if, however, the sales increase in a smaller proportion than the price decreases, the demand is said to be inelastic.

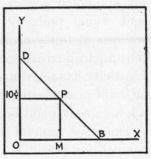

Figure 1.

In the diagram, if price is measured on the Y axis and quantity on the X axis, and if DB represents the demand for the product, then the elasticity may be measured by this equation: Elasticity = PB/PD. Thus if PB is longer than PD, the elasticity is more than one, at the price MP. The demand for salt at the normal price is relatively inelastic—that is, quantity consumed varies little with changes in its price. On the other hand the consumption of perfumes by the poorer classes might change considerably with changes in price. Thus the demand for perfume is elastic. A luxury may be defined as a commodity the demand for which is elastic.

Public utilities, manufacturers of trade-marked products, and taxing bodies are greatly interested in the elasticity of demand. If a tax is levied on a commodity the demand for which is elastic, the tax may raise the price to such a degree that sales decrease materially and do not raise the anticipated tax revenue. Electric utilities charge the domestic consumer about twice as much as the industrial consumer largely because the demand on the part of the former is inelastic and the demand of the latter is elastic. The Department of Agriculture at Washington has made studies of the elasticity of demand for a variety of products, and these studies have been especially significant in framing a policy for restricting output of agricultural products.

The elasticity of demand for most commodities varies at different price levels. For example, at very high prices, say one dollar a pound for pork, a fall in price of 10 per cent would probably not increase consumption greatly, whereas at thirty cents a pound a drop in price of 10 per cent might increase consumption by more than 10 per cent. Elasticity has relevance only for a given price; at a higher or lower price elasticity may be greater or less, although in a few cases it might be virtually the same.

The most general laws of supply and demand under competition are: [16]

I. When at a given price the quantity demanded exceeds supply, the price tends to rise. Conversely, when supply exceeds demand, the price tends to fall.

II. A rise in price tends to decrease purchases and to increase amount offered. Conversely, a fall in price tends to increase purchases and to decrease offering.

III. Price tends to the level at which the quantity demanded and supply are in equilibrium.

These laws are fundamental in economic theory, although in many cases the human factor is of such importance as to obscure and affect the workings of the laws. Their scope is very wide, applying to commodities, services, capital, and labor.

The third law implies a tendency for demand to equal supply. This tendency can be demonstrated by anyone

---

[16] For a more extended analysis, see: Garver, F. B., and Hansen, A. H., *Principles of Economics* (Ginn & Company, Boston, 1928); Davenport, H. J., *Economics of Enterprise* (The Macmillan Company, New York, 1913); Henderson, H. D., *Supply and Demand* (Harcourt, Brace & Company, New York, 1922).

from his experience and observation. With a bumper wheat crop, prices tend to fall; and this also follows from the two preceding laws. If demand is in excess of supply, price will rise. When the price has risen, supply becomes larger, although this takes time in most markets, and consumption decreases. Thus excess of demand diminishes. If any portion of this excess remains, these same forces continue until the entire excess of demand over supply is eliminated. In this way prices regulate production and consumption.

These steps reveal that equilibrium is established and maintained by the agency of price changes, and they enable us to say the most important thing that can be said about the price of anything—that it will tend to be such as will equate demand and supply. These processes reveal also the extreme dependence of both demand and supply upon price. Like three balls in a bowl, if one is moved, one or both of the others tend to move. It is most important to realize this interdependence vividly. In ordinary times the prices of most commodities and services do not change very much, except over a long period of years; the amounts demanded and supplied may therefore seem to maintain a fairly constant level; and we may be tempted to speak of Canada producing so many million tons of wood pulp, or America consuming so many millions of radios per annum, almost as though these quantities were independent of price considerations. But there is no service or commodity produced by man the demand for or supply of which might not be reduced to zero if the price were sufficiently raised or lowered, respectively.

Relations between demand, supply, and price can be elucidated by the following illustrations. At a public auction bidding begins at a low point and competition between the potential buyers gradually forces the price upward until all the bidders are eliminated but one. The pricing process determines who will secure the commodity offered for sale.

Suppose A owns a share of stock in a corporation which he wishes to sell at the highest possible price, but whatever the price, he must sell. X is willing to pay as much as five dollars for the share. The price may be five dollars or anything less. The exact price will be determined by the skill of the traders. But now if X is willing to pay five dollars and Y four, the lower level to which the price can go is four dollars and one cent. But between this point and five dollars there is still room for bargaining to set the price; four dollars and one cent or five dollars may be the final price, or some point between these limits.

Suppose now that four shares are offered for sale by four sellers at whatever they will bring, and that the maximum demand prices are five, four, three, two, and one dollar. The competition among these potential buyers fixes the price at from two dollars as the maximum to anything more than one dollar. When the bidding passes beyond one dollar one buyer drops out, leaving four buyers and four sellers. Since there are only four shares for sale, the price must be high enough to exclude one of the five bidders—that is, above one dollar—and yet low enough to find buyers for the whole supply—not above two dollars. Within these limits bargaining between buyers and sellers fixes the actual market price.

In the above example the shares are for sale at whatever they will bring. Suppose now that each seller has a minimum selling price. One owner will not sell unless he can get one dollar; another unless he can get two dollars; another unless he can get three; and the fourth unless he can get four. Buyers have the same bidding prices as before, but the bidders face entirely changed conditions of supply.

The buyers, each of whom will keep his money unless he can buy at a certain price, now meet sellers each of whom will refuse to trade unless he can get a certain price. Summarized, the situation is as follows:

Demand	Price	Supply
B1 takes 1	$5	
B2 takes 1	4	S1 offers 1
B3 takes 1	3	S2 offers 1
B4 takes 1	2	S3 offers 1
B5 takes 1	1	S4 offers 1

Under these conditions what will the price be? At a price of one dollar, only one share will be for sale; but all the bidders will be disposed to buy. The price must, therefore, be higher than one dollar. At four dollars there will be four sellers and only two buyers. But at three dollars there will be three sellers and three buyers. The price will, therefore, be precisely three dollars, since no one willing to sell at this price fails to sell, and no one willing to pay the price fails to buy. This is stable equilibrium.[17]

These are relatively simple cases. But from the procedures so far developed other illustrations might be worked out. Suppose in a given market the following buyers with their demands prevail:

A will buy 1 share at $30; or 2 at $21; or 3 at $16
B will buy 1 share at $26; or 2 at $20; or 3 at $15
C will buy 1 share at $22; or 2 at $17; or 3 at $12
D will buy 1 share at $18; or 2 at $14; or 3 at $10

---

[17] Here competition determined the precise price; in the previous illustration competition merely set a price range, bargaining fixing the final price. This difference grows out of the assumptions and the data.

The sellers have supplies as follows:

M will sell 1 share at $12; or 2 at $17; or 3 at $20
N will sell 1 share at $ 9; or 2 at $15; or 3 at $18
O will sell 1 share at $ 8; or 2 at $14; or 3 at $17
P will sell 1 share at $10; or 2 at $11; or 3 at $14

Under these circumstances, what will the price be and how many units will exchange hands? How many buyers will go without their wants satisfied? How many sellers will fail to sell? These questions are all answerable with specific solutions.

The best way to answer them is to construct from the above data a supply-and-demand schedule as follows:

Demand	Price	Supply
1	$30	12
2	26	12
3	22	12
4	21	12
5	20	12
6	18	11
7	17	10
8	16	8
9	15	8
10	14	7
10	13	5
11	12	5
11	11	4
12	10	3
12	9	2
12	8	1

By examining the schedule it becomes apparent that the only possible price is sixteen dollars. At this price all buyers who are willing to go this high can buy; all sellers who will sell at this figure or lower can sell. Some of the sellers will not be able to dispose of any or part of their quantities, and some of the buyers will have some or all of their wants unsatisfied.

From such demand-and-supply schedules it is possible to construct demand and supply curves; this is usually done on graph paper in order to facilitate accurate interpretation. In case few buyers and few sellers with small quan-

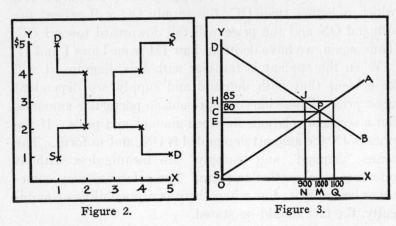

Figure 2.   Figure 3.

tities are involved, as in the second last case, the "curves" will actually be broken lines, as in Figure 2.

However, in most competitive markets such as those for grain and securities, the data are continuous, and every minor change in price brings a new relation between supply and demand. For example, in Figure 3 the demand at eighty cents is 1000 and at eighty-five cents is 900. Likewise supply varies with price. The demand curve (DB) slopes to the right and downward; the supply curve (SA) slopes upward. At the point where the curves intersect demand and supply are in equilibrium; that is, all who are willing to pay that price and higher will have their wants satisfied and all who are willing to supply the product at that or a lower price can dispose of their goods.

It can readily be seen that no other price could be maintained. Suppose the price is OE, or less than OC; then, at this price, ON will be the amount supplied, and OQ the amount demanded. The demand will thus exceed the supply, and the price will tend to rise, i.e., to move upwards toward OC. Similarly if we suppose the price to be OH, which is higher than OC, the supply OQ will exceed the demand ON and the price will fall downward toward OC. Thus, again, we have deduced Law III from Laws I and II.

When the student is familiar with this diagram, it will be evident that both demand and supply are dependent upon price. These curves represent no particular amounts, but a series of relations between amount and price. If the price is JN the amount demanded is ON, and so forth. The terms "demand" and "supply" are meaningless without reference to a particular price. The reference may sometimes be implicit; but when there is a possibility of ambiguity, the fact should be stated.

Demand and supply depend upon price; but they are dependent upon each other, and upon other things as well. Demand depends upon advertising, tastes, habits, and purchasing power; supply depends upon cost of production. None of these factors is constant; all are liable to change. The usual way of describing such changes is to use the expression "increase" or "decrease in demand," and "increase" or "decrease in supply," the same expressions which are commonly employed to describe the consequences of change in price. This identity of language conceals a fundamental distinction between the phenomena described which must be cleared up.

In Figure 4 we revert to demand (DB) and supply (SA) curves, cutting one another at the point P. Suppose that through an advertising campaign or an increase in population there has been an increase in demand. How is this increase represented in the diagram?

The change due to an increase in demand is represented by a new demand curve (in the figure, the dotted curve db), lying at every point above the old demand curve. This correctly indicates that larger quantities will be purchased at the old price. Similarly if we wish to represent a change in the conditions of supply, such as might result, in the case of a commodity, from a tax imposed on its production, we must draw a new supply curve (sa) which, in the case supposed,

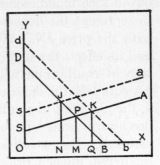

Figure 4.

must lie everywhere above the old supply curve. On the other hand, the decrease or increase in quantity taken or supplied resulting from a change in price is represented simply by shifting of the equilibrium from one point to another on the same curve. The striking pictorial contrast between a movement from one curve to another, and a movement along the same curve, should help to make vivid to our minds the fundamental distinction between a change in the conditions of demand arising from new tastes and higher purchasing power, and a mere change in the amount purchased resulting from an alteration in the price that the sellers ask.

The reader who has grasped this distinction clearly will be able to perceive many instances of the confusion arising out of its neglect in the popular discussions of economic questions which take place. It is common, for instance, for an argument to run something like this: "The effect of an invention on this commodity might seem to be a decrease in price. But a decrease in price will raise the demand; and an increased demand will send the price up again. It is not certain, therefore, that the invention will really lower the price." An examination of the diagram will keep us out of such muddlesome thinking. Let us suppose DB and sa represent the demand and supply before the invention, with the price JN. After the cost-reducing invention has had its effect, the supply curve will be SA. The new position of equilibrium will be given by the point P, where SA cuts DB, the demand curve. Now P lies to the right of J, the old point of equilibrium; hence, since DB must slope downward from left to right, it is clear that if, as it is assumed, the conditions of demand have remained unaltered, the new price MP must be less than the old.

Can we lay down any general propositions or laws as to the effect upon price of an increase or decrease in demand and supply? Another glance at the diagram suggests that we can. An increase in demand is represented in Figure 4 by a movement from DB to db, which cuts the supply curve at K; since the supply curve must always slope upward from left to right, the new price QK must be greater than the old PM. Conversely a decrease in demand is represented by a movement from db to DB, and the new price is seen to be less than the old. We have already seen that a decrease in supply, which is represented by a movement from SA to sa, results in a higher price; and it is the obvious converse that an increase in supply will have the opposite effect. It would seem, then, that we might lay down quite generally that an increase in demand or a decrease in supply will raise the price, while a decrease in demand or an increase in supply will lower it.

NORMAL OR LONG-TERM PRICE

But in analyzing realistic phenomena, caution is necessary. All conclusions as to the effects of causes are necessarily based, implicitly, if not explicitly, upon the assumption "other things being equal." But assumptions of this kind are defensible only when we know that the cause, the effects of which are being studied, will itself produce no change in the "other things." If these "other things" are changing because of any other forces, our reasoning may be wrong or only partially right. For example, in 1934 the Agricultural Adjustment Act of the Roosevelt Administration while in operation was attended by a tremendous increase in hog prices, which was the desired result. Meantime, general business recovery and a serious drought occurred, both of which forces aided the improvement in hog prices. Thus it is difficult to predict economic phenomena and to assign causes with accuracy.

The difficulties of predicting the behavior of prices when new forces make themselves felt may be demonstrated with an illustration. Suppose a cattle plague wipes out the source of meat supply; what will be the effect on the price of fish? [18] The reader might be inclined to say, "The answer is easy; the price will rise most assuredly." The economist will say, "The price will likely rise *at first* if the meat failure is sudden, but after the first effects, the price may be lower than it was before the plague, it may be higher, or it may be the same, depending on a considerable number of conditions."

If the plague is of a serious character, and if after having made itself felt a public proscription prevents any further sales of meat, the price of fish will undoubtedly rise in the

[18] Marshall, Alfred, *Principles of Economics,* Book V (The Macmillan Company, New York, 1920).

market place. A rise of several hundred per cent might occur. Quickly every available boat would be pressed into service and every idle fisherman would be called. Fishermen's wages and earnings would rise. Shortly the supply of fish would increase and the price of fish meat would tend to drop.

If the plague showed signs of continuing, new boats would be ordered; owing to the rise in fishermen's wages more workers would enter this industry. After several weeks or months facilities for fishing would be greatly increased, and the amount of fish meat on the market would expand, and its price would fall. If the business community takes the view that the larger demand for fish is permanent, additional capital would flow into the boat-making and fishing-equipment industries to meet the demand for more facilities.

Suppose the entire stock of cattle is wiped out and the production of beef is banned for the indefinite future; what will be the final price of fish? The answer to this question is not simple. If man is responsible for only a small fraction of the total destruction of fish, as some ichthyologists believe, then the increased demand for fish followed by much enlarged removals from the sea will encounter no increasing resistance in this respect. On the other hand, if the sea is populated with a relatively limited supply of fish, the increased demand will force the fishermen to resort to deep-sea fishing, which is more costly, and to resort to the use of boats with greater draught in order to withstand the waves and storms which prevail farther out from the seacoast. If this latter condition prevails, the fishing industry may be called an *increasing-cost industry*. Similar results would obtain if some of the fishing equipment were made from some rare material, and greater average expenditures were entailed in securing a sufficient supply.

That is, as the demand for the commodity rises, the average cost per unit of the output for the whole industry rises also. Economists have generally believed that the extractive industries, such as mining, fishing, lumbering, and agriculture, are increasing-cost industries. This is due to the fact that here we are dealing with one or more rare agents of production, agents like land, chemical constituents, and mineral deposits, which are either fixed in amount by nature or only very slowly reproducible. To put the matter another way, increasing resistance is encountered to increased production. It is true, of course, that with increase in knowledge through scientific research, new ways may be found for exploiting these natural resources; although fishermen must resort to deeper seas, this disadvantage might be offset by advantageous changes in industrial arts. Nevertheless, the fishing industry would still be regarded as one of *increasing costs*. The problem is: With a given knowledge of fishing and a given state of the industrial arts, does an increase in the demand for fish tend to cause a rise in the price of fish *in the long run?* If the answer is in the affirmative, then the industry is one of increasing cost, even though subsequent discoveries in the art of fishing may actually lower costs.

This principle of increasing cost for the industry as a whole must be clearly distinguished from a mere increase in cost for the individual fisherman that accompanies his expansion of output. Obviously if a given fisherman tried to expand his own output after he had obtained his optimum size, his average costs would rise. The reader will have noticed that neighborhood grocery stores or drug stores all tend to be about the same size. Should a grocer try to enlarge his store he would encounter, sooner or later, rising average costs, and competition with other grocers who have

not expanded to such uneconomic size would tend to force
him out of business unless he has what is known as a spatial
or other monopoly. With a given state of the art of fishing,
if the demand for fish rises, the tendency would be for the
number of fishing concerns to multiply, and there would be
no tendency for the individual fishing concern to increase
in size. In the automobile industry the demand for the
product has greatly expanded since 1910, and enormous
improvements have taken place in the art and technique
of making cars, so that an increase in the size of the individual firm has accompanied the increase in the size of the
total market for the product. This was due to the fact that
the motor industry was in the developmental stage. It
indicates how in actual practice change in demand and
change in technology may develop side by side. Obviously
we cannot be sure that increase in demand will raise prices
in the long run.

Constant-cost industries

Economists have observed that some industries are characterized by constant costs; that is, whether the output for
the industry as a whole is large or small, average cost per
unit remains the same. Should consumption of scissors
double in the next ten years, it is probable that the labor,
raw materials, and other supplies going into the making of
this product would be forthcoming at about the same supply
price. If some costs should drop, such as steel, while others,
such as labor, rise in an equal degree, the net effect on the
final average cost might be zero; in this case we would also
have a constant-cost industry. If the manufacture of automobiles involved the use of a very large part of the output
of some other industry, say the steel industry, then marked
increase in the demand for motor cars might cause a rise

in their price. In the long run, in industries characterized by constant cost, demand for the product has no effect on price, supply considerations alone determining price. In Figure 5, DD represents demand for the product before increase in consumption, and dd is the demand afterward. SS is the average cost for all entrepreneurs in this industry, which is a horizontal line regardless of its distance from the Y axis. Thus whether the demand is OM or ON the cost is five cents, and under competition selling prices are forced down to costs, namely OS or five cents. Economists are of the opinion that the great bulk of industries are characterized by fairly constant costs. That is, a considerable increase

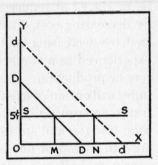

Figure 5.

in demand for any one of many lines of commodities could take place without any increase in cost in the long run. If all industries should expand quickly, demand for scarce natural agents of production would rise, and no doubt increasing costs would be encountered. But since most individual industries consume only a small part of the total output of a given raw material, a considerable increase in output could take place without any rising costs for the finished product.[19]

Decreasing-cost industries

Most individual business firms commonly have unused capacity and could expand output without increasing the

[19] Over a period of several years monetary factors may cause radical price changes, as may business depressions, wars, and other calamities.

size of their plants. Most grocers could handle more trade, most furniture factories could enlarge output somewhat, without enlarging establishments. Because of the large overhead costs in the way of taxes, interest on investment, insurance, and depreciation, all of which may be more or less fixed sums for a given plant, an expanding output can be produced at reduced average costs. If this were meant by decreasing cost, then every concern would be characterized by decreasing cost. But these are merely economies experienced as a result of fuller utilization of the fixed factors of production. Our railway system benefits greatly by fuller utilization of existing facilities. Whether one or many trains are run daily over a given line, the track, right of way, bridges, and stations must be available. If two trains are run intead of one, overhead cost per train will be cut nearly in half and average cost of transportation service would be reduced considerably, although not by one half, for the second train would entail some operating expenses, such as fuel and trainmen's wages.

Thus these economies of fuller utilization are due to the indivisible character of the factors of production. If all the factors of production, engines, rolling stock, right of way, signal systems, depots, and so on could be constructed so that regardless of the volume of business available each factor could be used to its maximum capacity, there would then be no decrease in costs when size increased. Whatever the volume of business, the size of the firm would be precisely determined by current demand. As demand expanded each factor would be increased proportionally and the cost of production per unit would remain as before. Thus indivisible factors in industry, such as steam shovels, engines, machinery, and so on, bring about the so-called economies of large-scale production. To put the matter another way, if the factors of production are infinitely divisible there can be no such phenomenon as decreasing cost for the industry as a whole when output expands.

MONOPOLY ECONOMICS

The foregoing analysis has proceeded on the assumption that in price determination, competition is more prevalent than monopoly; the selling price of a product tends in the long run to be identical with its cost of production, including in costs such profits necessary to attract capital and entrepreneurship. Should the profits temporarily be above this level, additional capital would tend to migrate into this industry, the supply of goods would rise, and the price would fall, bringing profits to zero or virtually so. Conversely, if the industry is operating at a loss the submarginal firms would tend to cease operations, and with decreased supply of goods, price would rise and profits would be established at the minimum figure sufficient to hold remaining producers in production, that is, at cost, as defined above.

This should not be interpreted to imply that cost of production *determines* price; these production costs themselves must be explained, a task left for the next chapter.

Although in the foregoing discussion competition has been assumed, monopoly elements have always been present in the economic system, and seem to be increasingly important. The word *monopoly* comes from a Greek word meaning "single seller," but in modern usage has come to mean a unified control of supply or demand by one or more persons. The English and American common law have been hostile to monopoly. Since 1890 the United States has followed a more or less vigorous policy of stamping out monopolies. Partial or complete monopolies of whiskey, water pipe, steel, farm machinery, oil, tobacco, cash registers, and many other products have been established.[20]

The moderate success of the government in liquidating these monopolies has induced businessmen to seek two other means of achieving profits. (1) Actual combination among competitors being prohibited, the various producers in a given industry have learned to "follow the leader." Instead of each of the producers seeking as large a share of the market as possible by cutting prices, the smaller producers have observed the price tactics of some dominant producer in the field and merely followed his practices. Thus competition is eliminated and an unannounced but tacit agreement assures profits above the competitive level, as in the gasoline business. (2) By product differentiation as evidenced by special trade marks, slogans, fancy wrappers, odorizers, copyrights, window displays, and all the modern techniques of advertising, each producer has endeavored to insulate himself from the rigors of competition. By getting the consumer to "ask for Luckies" and "insist on Gillette Blue Blades," the producer tries to differentiate his product from that of competitors and make the consumer "brand conscious." He acquires partial control of total demand through his knowledge of the laws of psychology and the techniques of advertising, which may be as effective as though he had complete control over the whole supply of a product. Product differentiation and advertising are always evidence of partial or complete monopoly. The reader has probably never heard of a farmer advertising his hogs or his wheat, for hog and wheat production are thoroughly competitive.

---

[20] Ripley, William Z., *Trusts, Pools, and Corporations* (Ginn & Company, Boston, 1905, 1916).

Under monopoly, whether of the older or the newer type
known as product differentiation, restriction of output always takes place; the price is always higher and the profits
usually are larger than under competition.

We have observed how, under competition, selling price
tends to coincide with cost of production. Let us suppose
that in Figure 6 DB represents
the demand curve which a monopolist faces. CC′ represents his
average cost for various possible
scales of output. This curve begins at a high point because with
small output average costs would
be high, due to the presence of
overhead costs; as output rises,
average costs decrease, and reach
a low point at 1000 units of out-

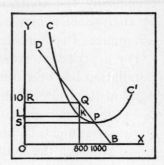

Figure 6.

put. Under competition each producer would tend to
establish a scale of output so as to reach the lowest average
cost per unit. The selling price of the product would tend
to conform with that low point.

The output of the monopolist is restricted to the point
at which, in the light of the demand curve, there will be
maximum profit. That is, he will endeavor to arrive at a
production and price policy under which the unit profit
times output will be a maximum. This will lead to a price
of ten cents, production of 800, and total profits (per unit
of time) of KQRL. Under competition price would be
lower (five cents), output higher, and profits would approach zero. This explains graphically why maximum
production is unattainable under monopoly.

APPLICATION OF ECONOMIC THEORY

Economists use economic theory to understand the forces which determine prices and govern distribution of income, and to develop tools of analysis by means of which problems may be diagnosed and solutions discovered. To illustrate specifically the contribution which economics may make to analysis of a perplexing problem, we will examine the economics of convict-made goods.

For a period in excess of one hundred years the prison population has been turned to productive labor in various parts of the United States. From the beginning this policy has encountered opposition from employers and employees, from governmental labor departments, and other organizations, although the salutary effect of "busy work" and perhaps teaching the prisoners a trade has been recognized. Every state, as well as the federal government, has passed numerous laws controlling the sale of convict-made goods. The United States Commissioner of Labor some years ago reported that "the employers of free labor and their workmen unite in affirming that when *any* convict-made product is placed in competition with the product of free labor the market becomes demoralized, even a small sale affecting prices far out of proportion to the amount of the sale."

The author of one of the best books on labor economics, after recognizing that prison-made goods constitute a part of the total supply of such goods, points out that these goods must affect price just as any supply will influence price. This author then states that if prison-made goods are offered at a greatly reduced price their effect on price is "exaggerated," and that if prison-made goods are sold at the regular competitive price level, they lose most of their objectionable features. A similar attitude is taken generally by writers on labor.

In the light of the best economic doctrine this opposition to convict-made goods does not appear to be sound. The argument rests on the established facts that prisoners typically are paid only nominal wages, that the prison shop is built and equipped by state funds, and therefore "the cost of production," after allowing for lower efficiency, is considerably below competitive costs; finally prison-made goods are nearly always sold "for what they will bring," without sales effort and advertising, which means, as a rule, a price below the competitive level.

The essence of this widespread opposition to convict-made goods simmers down to the view that the practice of selling prison output below the competitive level has a demoralizing effect on external prices. Actually there are three problems involved. Does the production of goods in prison affect external prices? Does the sale of those goods below market quotations affect prices? Does prison production affect employment and profit opportunities outside the prison?

Analysis of price formation does not give substantial support to critics of prison production. Let us assume that only one grade of twine is produced, five per cent within prison and the balance in competitive industry. The prison "entre-preneur," A in the diagram, is the lowest-cost producer, while the other producers range from low- to marginal-cost producers, that is, B to E.[21] DD' is the demand curve for the product, twine; the selling price will be one dollar per unit. The cost of the prison twine is forty cents. Now whether the prison manager sells his twine at forty cents

---

[21] Whether the product is produced in the industry as a whole under constant or increasing cost conditions is ignored here.

or at some other figure up to one dollar cannot have any
influence on the price collected by other producers; the
competitive market price must cover the marginal costs
of E. To put the matter another way, the fact whether
entrepreneur A is a prison-shop manager or merely the most
superior entrepreneur [22] does not alter his price influence.[23]

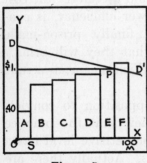

Figure 7.

This analysis does not deny
that prison-made goods affect
price, since they obviously do by
the above assumptions. When a
prison turns to the manufacture
of a specific product, the supply
of the product tends to rise. The
total supply now cannot be sold
at the former price. As shown
by the diagram, if another prison
turned to making twine, the mar-
ginal producer E may become submarginal and drop out.
The price declines somewhat until it coincides with the
cost of producers who formerly were intermarginal, perhaps at D, and who now become marginal. Other producers will reduce output somewhat to make their marginal
costs coincide with the slightly reduced price. Thus there is
no denying that prison-made goods, if produced under low-
cost circumstances, will drive high-cost producers [24] out of
business, forcing their labor and other agents of production
to other uses. But the entrance into the field of production
by any low-cost producer will do the same, and this operates

[22] Lowest-cost producer.
[23] Except that if he were the latter, he would be assumed to be an "economic man" and he would expand production until his marginal costs
equalled one dollar.
[24] Those who are relatively inefficient.

in the interest of consumers; prisons are not unique in this respect.[25] The temporary effect of a prison's turning to the manufacture of a product may be some disturbances. This is far from saying, however, that the practice of prison managers of selling below the market price lowers market price; ordinarily it does not lower price.[26]

One possible argument—that selling far below competitive price levels demoralizes the market because all buyers expect to be able to secure their purchases at this low price and therefore refuse to purchase at the higher prices— depends on the assumption that the buyers expect that this low-priced seller can supply all the demand or a large part of it. This assumption seems highly improbable in the case of prison-made goods, for the supply thrown on the market is usually small in amount and not subject to future increases.[27]

The conclusions to be drawn from the analysis thus far are that where there are entrepreneurial differentials, the entrance of prison production into a field will lower the selling price of the product, eliminating the highest-cost producers, probably, and forcing all external producers to restrict their production somewhat; and the practice of the

[25] No doubt in most prisons true economic cost of production is above the competitive cost. Of the two alternatives, idle prisoners and prisoners employed, there is probably no doubt that the latter is preferable, considering social as well as economic consequence. See Chapter VI, "Modern Criminology."

[26] The above analysis applies to a single-price market. In the immediate environs of a prison it is of course possible that the practice of selling below the competitive price will exclude sales from a distance on account of the transportation factor. One critic of the view herein presented states that when an Illinois prison turned to making barrels, a Chicago factory with $2,000,000 invested was forced out of business. See Chamberlin, Edward, *Theory of Monopolistic Competition*, pp. 62–63, and Appendix D (Harvard University Press, Cambridge, Mass., 1933), for analysis of "spatial monopoly."

[27] See page 589.

prison selling below the external competitive price has no additional demoralizing effect on that price in a given market.

Production under constant, increasing, and decreasing cost

If production is carried on under conditions of constant cost in the industry as a whole, and there are no entrepreneurial differentials, or if a large share of the total product is turned out by producers who are marginal in their entire output, it is difficult to see how prison production can have any permanent effect whatsoever on price. If the industry is in equilibrium and a prison shop manager enters the field, the supply of the product will rise and the price will fall temporarily. The most "sensitive" entrepreneur will retire from the field, and finally equilibrium will be re-established at the old price with somewhat fewer external producers in the field. If entrepreneurial differentials exist and the prison output is sufficiently large to equal the output of the marginal producer or producers, the price will decline so as to conform with the costs of those producers who are now on the margin.

In the case of an increasing-cost industry, if the rare factor [28] is also used by the prison shop in its output, and there are no entrepreneurial differentials, the price collected by external industry is not affected either by the prison turning to this production or by its practice of selling below competitive price level. However, the most "sensitive" external producers will be inclined to retire from the field to make way for the prison production. This may be illustrated by Figure 8. CC′ represents average costs in-

---

[28] There must be some rare factor; otherwise costs would not be increasing with expanding output. See pages 573–576.

creasing as output expands. The distance under BK is the cost of the rare factor which is responsible for the increasing-cost character of the industry. The distance between BK and CC′ represents all other costs which are assumed to be uniform for all producers and for all scales of output. That is, the industry is one of constant cost, except for the rare factor. Thus if the prison must utilize the rare factor, the costs of this factor at the scale OM output will be exactly as though the prison were not in production; the prison manager merely takes the place of some other producer or producers. At the scale of output OM the rare

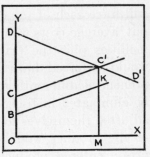

Figure 8.

factor costs MK and all other outlays cost KC′. Since the rare factor for this scale of output remains the same in price whether the prison or some external producer is in production, the entrance of the prison into the field can have no effect on costs or selling price.

If entrepreneurial differentials are found in this increasing-cost industry and the prison enters the field using the rare factor, the marginal producers will retire from the field and all producers will be forced to reduce output somewhat to make their marginal costs coincide with the new reduced price. In this case the entrance of the prison manager will reduce price somewhat, but his practice of selling below the market price will have no additional effect.[29]

---

[29] Since the prison sells below the current market price it is possible that its sales will be to consumers with perfectly inelastic demands or very elastic. Hence the substitution of a prison-shop producer for an external producer may slightly alter the scale or production, depending on what

If the factors of production were perfectly divisible and mobile there could be no such phenomenon as decreasing costs for the industry as a whole.[30] The falling costs which manufacturing commonly experiences are traceable to improved techniques and a fuller utilization of the fixed factors of production. To the extent that prison production will force each of the external producers to reduce his output, average costs would tend to rise; but with the existing facilities plus the prison in operation, the selling prices would be forced down somewhat. In the presence of entrepreneurial differentials, marginal producers would tend to be eliminated in time, and after the remaining plants had adjusted themselves to maximum capacity again, the prices of the product would be slightly lower than before the prison entered production.

Prison production is relatively small

There should be no objection to prisoners being put to useful work; for if they were not criminals they would be a part of the labor supply, and would influence the marginal productivity of labor as a whole. Usually prison production constitutes much less than one per cent of the total production of any given product. In a few instances, such as automobile license plates and twine, the proportion may run higher. Several states have shifted entirely to the state-use system, and the prisons have a monopoly of the making of automobile plates.[31]

---

part of the demand curve the prison happens to satisfy. To analyze the outcome of the various possibilities in this connection would take us too far afield.

[30] Inventions and technical improvements are ignored throughout.

[31] Possibly one of the best ways to reduce the opposition to prison production would be for the state to select one or two commodities and concentrate all production on these. This, coupled with a state-use system, would eliminate much of the criticism.

It is difficult to account for the opposition to convict labor if one examines a few significant facts. For example, the prison labor engaged in productive work in 1932 constituted only ninety-three one-hundredths of one per cent (.93%) of the wage earners engaged in manufacturing in 1929,[32] and only twenty-three thousandths of one per cent (.023%) of all the wage earners in the country, or sixteen thousandths of one per cent (.016%) of all gainfully employed persons.[33] The value of prison-made products constituted only one one-hundredth of one per cent (.01%) of the value of all products of manufacturing. Specifically, in the case of the clothing industry, prison-made clothing, one of the most important items of prison production, constituted less than five one-hundredths of one per cent (.05%) of the total value of clothing produced in ordinary manufacturing, and the figure for textiles was three one-hundredths of one per cent (.03%). No commodity has been found of which prison production amounts to as much as five per cent of the private production in normal times, as the accompanying table indicates. In 1931 when private production had declined drastically, it is true that prison twine amounted to 9.19 per cent of that produced in private industry. Prison production is so small that any serious opposition to it on economic grounds, either from the employers or the employees, seems difficult to understand.

Entirely apart from the foregoing economic analysis, these statistical facts should dispel any belief that prison labor competition is a menace to economic production as a whole. True, in the immediate neighborhood of a prison which concentrates its production on a single product, there are occasional cases where labor and manufacturers may

---

[32] Census of Manufacturers, 1931.
[33] Using 1930 census figures for employment.

have some basis for complaint. But from an economic point of view production is carried on for the benefit of the consumer, and a question may be raised seriously whether even in such cases of localized interest public policy should not be directed for the benefit of society as a whole

RELATIVE IMPORTANCE OF PRISON-MADE PRODUCTS [34]

Item	Prison production as a percentage of private production	
	1931	1929
Twine and rope	9.19	4.78
Brooms	5.85	4.01
Shirts	4.92	3.59
Overalls	1.36	.80
Agricultural implements	.57	.17
Baskets	.03	.02
Brushes	.03	.02
Aprons	.02	.02
All clothing *	.05	.04
All manufacturing *	.02	.01

* Includes output of federal as well as state prisons; the others cover state prisons only.

rather than for some vested interest of labor or capital. Also, the larger the supply coming from prisons, the greater the benefit to consumers as a whole, and laborers, constituting the chief element in the consuming population, are therefore the principal beneficiaries.

Finally, production of goods within prisons increases employment opportunities outside of prisons; this is true because revenue from sales of prison-made goods reduces cost of upkeep of prisons, thereby lowering taxes, and thus

[34] Prison figures are based on *Bureau of Labor Statistics Bulletin 595,* 1932, and those for private industry on *Census of Manufacturers,* 1931. Since the categories of the two sources are not always identical the percentages given must be accepted as only approximately correct.

increasing demand for commodities and capital building. But this effect must be very small.

CONCLUSION

This chapter aims to give the student a glimpse of the character and function of economics. Obviously economics is not primarily a set of laws or rules which can be learned and applied. Rather, economics is a set of tools for analyzing price relationships. If the maximization of physical production is the goal of society, then the economist is in a position to present some advice along this line. He can ascertain where the burden of a tax will fall. He can give an expert opinion on the probable economic consequences of economic reform schemes. Economic laws, however, work through human beings. The element of unpredictability in human behavior prevents economics from becoming an applied science as exact as economists might hope.

BIBLIOGRAPHY

Garver, F. B., and Hansen, A. H., *Principles of Economics* (Ginn & Company, Boston, 1928).

Marshall, Alfred, *Principles of Economics* (The Macmillan Company, New York, 1920).

Henderson, H. D., *Supply and Demand* (Harcourt, Brace & Company, New York, 1922).

Taylor, F. M., *Principles of Economics* (Ronald Press Company, New York, 1921).

Wootton, Barbara F., *Plan or No Plan* (Farrar & Rinehart, New York, 1935).

Davenport, H. J., *Economics of Enterprise* (The Macmillan Company, New York, 1913).

Kiekhofer, William H., *Economic Principles, Problems and Policies* (D. Appleton-Century Company, New York, 1936).

Chamberlin, Edward, *Theory of Monopolistic Competition* (Harvard University Press, Cambridge, Mass., 1933).

CHAPTER XIII

The Distribution of Income

EMERSON P. SCHMIDT

University of Minnesota

INCOME DEFINED

EDWIN CANNAN, an English economist, has said that economics concerns itself with two questions: why we are as well off as we are (production), and why some of us are better off than others (distribution). The first question was discussed in the preceding chapter, and the second will be discussed here.

The term *distribution* means the sharing of wealth and income among people. By wealth is meant the *source* of well-being. By income is meant a flow of services which constitute well-being, nourishment from food, warmth from clothing and houses, transportation from vehicles, and so on. Strictly, a workman's weekly receipts are not income but rather a title or claim to wealth or income. If we designate money receipts, motor cars, and transportation as income, we are led into double and triple counting. Should a student receive a graduation gift of $100 and then purchase a piano for this sum and use the piano for personal enjoyment, this would not constitute an income of $300. Rather the enjoyment alone would be the real income. If a doctor collects $20,000 annually in gross income but has expenses of $8,000 connected with his profession, he would retain only $12,000 net income, which might become the basis for his real income and that of his family. Strictly, his savings out of the $12,000 are not income, and become income only in some subsequent period when these savings are consumed. Should the physician purchase a $15,000 home out of his savings, the home would not be income. If the home has a useful life of fifty years, then one might say that he secured about $1,350 of real income from the house in the first year.[1] Thus real income and consumption may be considered as identical.

Because of the difficulties of measuring income, as defined above, economists are forced to employ a less fundamental definition of income for purposes of analysis, namely, money income. In the case of farmers they must assign a money value to food produced and consumed on the farm. In subsequent pages the word income will, of necessity, be used in the measurable but less satisfactory sense.

WEALTH DEFINED

The term *wealth* is used broadly sometimes to refer to all the sources of well-being in society—food, factories, farms, sunshine, rainfall, and air. Social wealth refers to all these things and forces which enhance our well-being. Public wealth refers to those sources of wealth which are owned by the people collectively, such as schools, highways, post offices, rivers, and in some countries water falls and minerals in the earth. Private wealth refers to the tangible goods and rights that are transferable and limited in quantity.

Clearly the well-being of a nation depends on the character and abundance of all wealth: pure air, pure and abundant water, sunshine, human character and skill, quali-

---

[1] Depreciation of $300; interest on investment at 5 per cent, $750; taxes at 2 per cent, $300, a total of $1,350.

ties of the soil, railroads, factories, farms and food, navigable streams, highways, post offices, and schools. An abundance of these things organized in an efficient way may become the basis of a high income, that is, a high standard of living.

In order to be an economic good, a source of well-being must be both useful and scarce. The economist is interested in the problem of economizing scarce means to meet insatiable ends so that society may secure maximum production. For this reason the economist does not concern himself with sunshine and air; we do not need to economize these.

For centuries society has seen fit to permit the private ownership of economic goods, both for immediate personal satisfaction (houses and clothing) and for productive purposes (farms, factories, and machines). Private ownership of these consumption and production goods predominates in all countries except Russia. Under complete collectivism, distribution might be quite different from what it is under unregulated capitalism. Since private ownership predominates in the United States and elsewhere, the subsequent analysis will be based on this fact, with appropriate recognition of the institutional forces altering the results of distribution.

THE DISTRIBUTION OF WEALTH

No complete census of private wealth has ever been taken, so our knowledge of its distribution is fragmentary, but we do know that the distribution is very unequal. Table I shows the distribution of estates among men over twenty-five years of age who died in Massachusetts in the three periods 1829–1831, 1859–1861, and 1889–1891. The number of people over twenty-five years of age who die in any

one year greatly exceeds the number of estates probated in
any one year, because over one half of the adult males who
die have little or no wealth, and hence there is no estate to

TABLE I. DISTRIBUTION OF THE PROBATED ESTATES
OF MALES IN MASSACHUSETTS [2]

Period	Estimated * proportion of adult males who died leaving no estate to be probated (per cent)	Minimum and maximum limits of class	Percent of total number of estates probated	Percent of total value of estates probated	Average value of all estates probated
1829–1831	52	Under $1,000	47.5	3.5	$4,352
		$1,000 to $5,000	36.6	20.2	
		$5,000 to $25,000	13.6	30.4	
		$25,000 to $100,000	1.9	22.7	
		$100,000 and over	0.4	23.2	
1859–1861	55	Under $1,000	31.7	1.5	8,985
		$1,000 to $5,000	40.9	11.3	
		$5,000 to $25,000	21.6	24.5	
		$25,000 to $100,000	4.3	22.9	
		$100,000 and over	1.5	39.9	
1889–1891	60	Under $1,000	24.6	0.8	13,658
		$1,000 to $5,000	40.9	7.4	
		$5,000 to $25,000	25.9	20.6	
		$25,000 to $100,000	6.2	22.1	
		$100,000 and over	2.3	49.1	

* Estimated from United States census data on population and mortality.

be probated. The distribution of wealth among the deceased males, of course, is not a very accurate criterion of
the distribution among the living, but it will give us some

[2] See the *Twenty-fifth Annual Report of the Massachusetts Bureau of
Labor Statistics.*

conception of the inequality which prevails.[3] In 1890 about 60 per cent of the men over twenty-five years of age who died left no estate to be probated. About 10 per cent left less than $1,000 worth of property; about 16 per cent left between $1,000 and $5,000; about 10 per cent left between $5,000 and $25,000; and less than 6 per cent left over $25,000. Admittedly the inequality is great. However, inequalities in wealth distribution are of less significance than inequalities of income. The Henry Ford family has accumulated a fortune of about three quarters of a billion dollars. The rich are unable and unwilling to consume all their income. The bulk of the Ford money income has been "plowed back" into business research and capital building, making large-scale production possible. Thirty years ago a Ford car cost $2,000 and was greatly inferior to the present $600 car. The Ford fortune and the demand for motor cars create employment for 150,000 workers directly and perhaps another 100,000 workers indirectly in garages, filling stations, and lumber, tire, and steel plants.

In 1908 the average employee of one of the largest tire producers was receiving forty cents an hour. He could buy a small motor-car tire for thirty-five dollars. At that time this tire would run an average of 2,000 miles in its lifetime, making an average cost of one and three-quarters cents per mile. A little calculation indicates that an hour's labor would pay for only twenty-three miles of use of that tire ($\frac{40}{3500 \div 2000} = 23$). Thus to run the car with four tires a distance of twenty-three miles and merely pay for the wear and tear on the tires, the worker had to work for

---

[3] See Garver, F. B., and Hansen, A. H., *Principles of Economics,* pp. 576 ff. (Ginn & Company, Boston, 1928) ; and King, W. I., *Wealth and Income of the People of the United States,* pp. 68 ff. (The Macmillan Company, New York, 1915).

four hours. Obviously few workers owned cars. In 1936 the average wage for all employees of this plant was eighty-eight cents an hour. Had this been the only gain which took place, the laborer would still have had to work one hour to secure fifty miles' of use from a tire, or one hour's work would have yielded enough income to pay for the wear and tear on the four tires over a twelve and one-half mile stretch. However, two other things happened. In 1936 instead of the tire costing thirty-five dollars, it cost eight dollars. Instead of running only 2,000 miles, it would run on the average about 20,000. A calculation will indicate that in 1936 an hour's work would pay for not twenty-three miles of use, but for 2,200 miles ($\frac{88}{800 \div 20,000}$ = 2200)—a ninety-five-fold improvement. Thus under the stress of competition the price was greatly reduced, and the life of the tire was increased by 1,000 per cent. Workers, and tire users generally, benefit from industrialism and accumulated wealth even though the tire factory is owned by one family. These illustrations do not imply that unequal distribution of wealth is of no social significance, but rather that because of the unequal distribution those with little or no wealth may nevertheless enjoy a substantial income or "flow of services," and profit by the accumulation of wealth.

Actually, wealth is widely held. Our six million farms are owned by nearly as many people, more than half of them being free from debt. More than fourteen million families own their own homes. Over twenty million persons own stock in corporations, other millions owning bonds. Nearly fifty million persons own deposits in banks. About one hundred million life insurance policies are in force at present, although the number of persons insured is somewhat less since one person may carry two or more policies. More than twenty million families own motor cars. Similarly the widespread ownership of other wealth, including drug stores, groceries, and other stores, garages, small factories, and household furniture, might be listed. Numerous share-croppers, laborers, and others, however, are virtually propertyless.

To give an accurate picture of the distribution of wealth is impossible with our present state of knowledge. The wealth in the United States is owned by many millions of people; nevertheless, it is considerably concentrated, with about half of the people owning very little, while the other half owns wealth to the value of from one or two thousand dollars to several hundred millions per family.

FUNCTIONAL AND PERSONAL DISTRIBUTION OF INCOME

The problem of distribution may be approached in two ways: (1) What are the forces which determine the sharing of the total income of society among the factors of production, and (2) what forces control the sharing among the persons in society? Regardless of the economic system, whether capitalist or socialist, the functions of laboring, saving, risk-taking, and directing must be performed. If a socialist community desires to increase its standard of living, part of the labor and other resources must be directed toward research and capital building. Meantime those producing food and clothing will have to maintain the others engaged in capital building. Under socialism a certain group will have to be engaged in planning and directing production. If mistakes in capital building occur, as they will inevitably, the whole society will have its standard of living decreased thereby. That is, risks have to be assumed.

Under capitalism the landlord no doubt receives part of his income because of land monopoly, but most of it accrues to him because of his investment in buildings and because he manages the properties. Under socialism similar managers would have to be hired. For these reasons economists are agreed that a mere change in the form of production from private capitalism to state capitalism (socialism) will not transform the distribution of income as fundamentally as is commonly supposed.

True, in so far as landlords or capitalists maintain their standards of living by merely collecting rents and interest without any labor performed, they would, under socialism, be forced to work and thereby become a part of the productive labor supply, enhancing the well-being of society. State officials would have to take their places in allocating land to proper uses and managing properties. Whether the gain obtained by forcing these persons into more active economic functions would be offset by a decrease in the efficiency with which industry is directed and controlled under capitalism cannot be known.

Before turning to an analysis of distribution among the factors, let us examine the sharing among persons and families. Economists agree that a change in the economic system can alter more readily the distribution among persons than among the factors.

Personal distribution of income

The estimated income of the people of the United States in 1929 was about $80,000,000,000. It dropped to half that figure in 1932 and rose in 1936 to over $60,000,000,000.[4]

---

[4] The figures for 1932 and to a smaller extent those for 1936 greatly understate the actual "flow of services." Even at the depth of the depression our houses, motor cars, and many other durable items of wealth con-

These estimates include savings. In the thirty-year period after 1900 our estimated income increased about fourfold, from twenty billions to eighty billions, while the population increased by about 60 per cent. The unit in which we measure our income has greatly depreciated in value during this period (the value of money and the price level are reciprocals of each other) so that the foregoing statistics actually misrepresent reality. In terms of constant values (1913 prices) our income rose from twenty-two billion dollars in 1900 to forty-nine billions in 1929. Allowing for the 60 per cent increase in population during this period, our real income (standard of living) rose by 38 per cent.[5] Thus per capita income rose from $289 in 1900 to $398 in 1929 (in constant values as of 1913). In 1929 the average per capita income of the people was $755 in current dollars of that year. Since nearly all of our data are in current dollars, these figures will be used from this point on, although the student must always keep in mind that the value of money is not constant.

Distribution of income among persons and groups is unequal in many respects. In 1929 per capita income of residents in New York State was $1,365 (the highest), and $261 in South Carolina (the lowest), with the average for the country standing at $755. Among the farmers, California stood the highest with a per capita income of $1,246, and South Carolina lowest with $129, the average for the farm population being $273; these figures all make

tinued to yield their services, although our decreased money incomes prevented us from replacing many goods which were obsolete or considerably depreciated.

[5] Apparently labor has shared this improvement in the same proportion as the whole of society. Professor Dale Yoder concludes that real wages (money wages divided by the cost of living) increased by about 35 per cent from 1900 to 1926. See his *Labor Economics and Labor Problems,* p. 258 (McGraw-Hill Book Company, New York, 1933).

an allowance for commodities and services produced and consumed on the farm, including house rent and food.

In the non-farm population, average per capita income was $908, with the highest, $1,550, in Delaware and the lowest, $412, in South Carolina. In the urban population unequal distribution, both between groups and within groups, is the rule. Great variations prevail between skilled and unskilled workers. Similarly among professional groups and business classes there are inequalities. Within specific trades or professions similar inequalities prevail. For example, the average net income (after allowing for professional expenses) of all doctors in 1929 was over $5,400. But at the bottom of the economic scale about 6,680 physicians had no net income whatsoever in the prosperous year 1929; this constituted about 4 per cent of the profession. Over 50 per cent had incomes of less than $3,800; 25 per cent received only $2,300; and 15 per cent (21,000) received less than $1,500. About 12 per cent received over $10,000, and 2 per cent received over $20,000.

Such inequalities prevail also among attorneys. In 1933 in New York County, New York, about 9 per cent received less than $500, 15 per cent less than $1,000, and the median income was $2,990. About one per cent had incomes in excess of $25,000, some exceeding $100,000.[6]

Because the family is the basic social unit of present society, the distribution of income among families is of more significance than that among individuals. According to some recent estimates, out of some twenty-seven million family units in the United States, about two million or 7.5 per cent had incomes of less than $500 in 1929. Nearly six million families, or over one fifth, had incomes of less than

[6] *The Bar Examiner,* June, 1936, Vol. V, p. 115.

$1,500. Nearly twenty million families, or 71 per cent, had incomes less than $2,500. Only a little over two million families, or 8 per cent, had incomes in excess of $5,000. About 600,000 families, or 2.3 per cent, had incomes in excess of $10,000.[7]

Admittedly inequalities of income are enormous, but not as great as inequalities of wealth. However, the picture in reality is not quite as dark as these figures would indicate. This is true for two reasons: (1) The families with the higher incomes are unable and unwilling to consume all of their annual incomes. These savings go into research, new plant, and stores, and in these ways the capital equipment of society is augmented; under a free competitive system, at least a goodly portion of the advantages of large-scale production, new inventions, and new products work to the benefit of nearly all persons in society. In a socialist society, if progress were desired, a portion of the annual income would also be devoted to new capital building, research, and development of new machines and products. (2) By a process of income and inheritance taxation a large portion of the higher incomes is compulsorily taken from the original recipients. The state, by using these funds to promote education, build libraries and roads, provide police, fire, and health protection, and to conserve natural resources, is contributing to the incomes of the poor. In New York State the federal and state income-tax rates garner 82 per cent of the annual incomes in the highest brackets.

This brief description demonstrates prevalent inequalities of income. Great variations prevail between geographic groups, economic groups, and within trades and professions.

---

[7] Leven, Maurice, et al., America's Capacity to Consume, pp. 55 ff. (Brookings Institution, Washington, 1934).

Inequalities are the rule, rather than the exception. Complete explanation of the causes of these inequalities would lead us into many fields, institutional development, including law and government, economic theory, psychology, and inheritance.

The factors of production

Income earned by groups or individuals usually constitutes reward for contributions to society. The laborer sells his labor power; the capitalist loans his savings; the landlord releases his land for utilization; and the businessman or entrepreneur risks time, labor, and capital in combining other factors of production. Work is irksome and labor is relatively scarce; creation of capital involves saving, or the postponing of consumption. The entrepreneur might loan his capital and hire himself out to someone else; that is, entrepreneurship, too, has its supply price. The landlord does not create the land, but under our laws of private ownership he is in a position to command a price for the release of his holdings for the use of others. Because workers must sell and are eager to sell their labor power, because savers are eager to loan out their capital or use it themselves, and because land owners want to have their land utilized and entrepreneurs want to employ their talents in making a living, these factors of production tend, under a freely competitive system, to become utilized in the productive process. Thus each unit of the factors comes to have a price attached to it. This price tends to be the one which will absorb into industry the entire supply of each factor. The price for labor is wages; for capital, the price is the interest rate; for land it is rent, and for entrepreneurship it is profits. The essential idea of the productivity theory of distribution is that the earning power of the factors of production derives from the demand for products and services of these factors. Demand for pork imputes a value to corn; the value for corn in turn imputes a value to land and other factors aiding in production of corn. Thus for economic society as a whole, it is not cost of production (the prices of the factors used in production) which imputes value to the consumer products, but rather it is the relative scarcity of the finished product, which drives up its value and thereby places a value on the factors of production that create that product.

> If you'd know why
> The land is high
> Consider this: its price is big
> Because it pays
> Thereon to raise
> The costly corn, the high-priced pig.[8]

Causal sequence is relative scarcity of factor of production to relative scarcity of product, thence to relatively high price of product, and thence to relatively high remuneration of factor.

This brief analysis of the relation between cost of production and value of output, be the output commodities or services, indicates that problems of production and consumption are not separate but intimately intertwined. Production and consumption are opposite sides of the same shield. The amateur interpreter of economics frequently says, "We have solved the production problem, but the problem of consumption remains a mystery." This view indicates a superficial understanding of the relations between the two.

---

[8] Davenport, *op. cit.*, p. 108.

THE MARGINAL PRODUCTIVITY OF LABOR

The price of labor is subject to the law of supply and demand. To illustrate the operation of the law, let us suppose that a resident of a primitive community conceives the idea of gathering sticks of wood for fuel in a nearby woodland that is claimed by no one. He carries bundles of wood in his hands to the community and sells them for what they will bring. In this simple case it is quite clear that the wages of the wood carrier are identical with the value of the wood to the consumer who buys it. If the bundles of wood are worth twenty cents each and the carrier can deliver ten bundles a day, his wages will be two dollars a day. Should the demand for fuel rise and the value of bundles of wood go to twenty-five cents, then wages would be $2.50 a day. This leads us to a productivity theory of wages—the laborer is *worth* what he *produces*.

If, however, one carrier sees this money-making opportunity, others are likely to see it also. If no one has a monopoly of the supply of wood and a goodly number of other carriers bring wood to the community, the enlarged supply probably cannot be sold at the old price of twenty cents, because lower levels of demand must be tapped. People who have less intense demands for wood will buy only at lower prices. Let us assume that when the supply is increased to two hundred bundles a day with twenty laborers working in the field, no additional workers are attracted to this occupation, and this volume of wood can be sold for ten cents a bundle. This is called a state of equilibrium—there is no tendency toward further change.

These are the essentials of the "marginal-productivity

theory of wages," which is accepted by practically all economists as the best explanation of the facts.

The idea of productivity emphasizes the fact that labor gets what it produces, that is, it is paid according to the value of the commodity or service produced. The concept of *marginal* is necessary because it shows that the value of the wood, and in turn the value of labor, is determined at the margin of demand for the wood. Some persons might be willing to pay more than ten cents a bundle, but under competition these more intense demands are satisfied at the same price as the marginal demands—those worth just ten cents a bundle. The persons who will pay just ten cents a bundle are said to be marginal; they are price sensitive. Should the price rise, such marginal buyers would buy less of it or cease buying entirely. Accordingly economists say that the value of any commodity is equal to its marginal utility. The value of the commodity imputes a value back to the person or other factor producing it. This explains why labor unions frequently oppose immigration; the more laborers who come to this country, the greater the competition for jobs.

The above wood-bundles illustration is, of course, a great over-simplification of reality. Labor works with machines, tools, and land, and there are many kinds of labor. The economic forces determining wages in this real world have, however, a strong similarity to all the forces noted in the illustration. Machines and factories are purchased with savings. Savings have their price, namely, interest. Land too has its price, namely, rent. As every laborer tries to get a job, so every saver tries to get his capital employed and every landlord endeavors to rent his land or use it himself productively. Hence the rent of land is determined by the forces of supply and demand. The same holds true for physical capital.[9]

When all available capital, land, and labor are fully employed, each will tend to be remunerated according to its marginal productivity or, we might say, according to its marginal importance in the world of buying and selling. True, some of each of these factors of production are always unemployed. Thus, men walk the streets; some factories and stores are idle; some farms and building lots are at all times unused. This unemployment of services and capital is due to numerous dynamic forces in society, and to friction; but there is, nevertheless, a tendency to employ these factors. Prolonged non-use of land tends to lower its price; and at a sufficiently lower price it becomes profitable to use it. Factories and stores after standing idle for some weeks or months are put to use after their prices or rentals have declined sufficiently. This combined effort of each owner to get his labor, capital, or land utilized in the economic system causes a definite supply price to be attached to it. This supply price constitutes its earnings.

If wages should come to be established in the restaurant business at two dollars a day, employers would be inclined to add laborers until the last laborer just pays for himself. That is, if by adding another waitress the employer secured ten dollars' worth of additional business daily, and the added costs of food, fuel, and wear and tear were eight dollars, then whether this extra waitress would be employed would be a matter of indifference. If she produced the

---

[9] Interest theory is the most complex and most controversial part of economic theory, and the foregoing statement is so brief as to be almost wholly inadequate. The student who wants a firmer grasp of the nature of capital and interest should read Fisher, Irving, *Theory of Interest* (The Macmillan Company, New York, 1930).

same gross receipts ($10) but her wages were only $1.50 a day, she would be eminently worth employing. Or, if she produced more than ten dollars' worth of business and her wages were two dollars, she would also be worth employing. Now, if at this rate of two dollars a number of waitresses in the community are unemployed, their attempts to secure work will gradually force the wage rate down until all can secure work. On the contrary, if the employer finds that the last waitress employed seems to add more than ten dollars a day gross receipts (costs other than wages being eight dollars) and the going rate for labor is two dollars, he will be inclined to add another waitress or perhaps to add several more. Thus, if the wage rate in the community comes to be established at a level below the marginal productivity, this competition on the part of employers to profit by adding more labor gradually lifts the wage rate until the marginal productivity and the wage rates are identical. Thus, for the individual employer the current rate of pay seems to determine the number of employees he will hire; but for the whole community the supply of labor in the light of the demand for labor determines wage rates. What this restaurant owner does, all employers do. The combined effects of the demand for labor and the supply determine the wage.

Actually, of course, there are many kinds of labor from the unskilled to the skilled and professional. At times there is considerable immobility in the supply of labor; carpenters in one city may secure several cents per hour more than in another simply because of lack of knowledge in regard to better opportunities or because of unwillingness to leave home and friends for the higher pay. Yet the enormous immigration of labor from Europe to America in the nineteenth and twentieth centuries was an expression of the working of this law. We have assumed that laborers compete with laborers and employers with employers. However, at times employers agree secretly on certain wage rates, and laborers unite in labor unions and insist on union rates. The marginal-productivity law of wages is just as true under these realistic conditions, but the results of the law may be different.

It is sometimes asserted that the employer cannot know what a laborer is worth to him, and that he knows only that he must pay the going rate of wages. But to assert that he cannot know whether he has too much or too little labor leads to the absurd conclusion that any number of workers might just as well be employed with a given quantity of land and capital. Yet we see that grocery stores or filling stations do have a definite number of laborers in attendance. How did the particular owner in each case settle on the exact number of workers? The number of workers to be employed is often determined by trial and error. The device by which he discovers the productivity of labor is the usual one of hiring or firing a little labor and then noting the result. If an increase in the wage bill is accompanied by an equal increase in the net value of the product, then the extra laborer is worth hiring; if the increase is greater than the wages paid then still more labor will be employed.

Some employers by virtue of technical considerations are not in a position to add or subtract laborers. In a machine shop there must be at least one man to a lathe; an insurance agent may be inclined to keep one stenographer in his office. But even in such cases where the "technical coefficient" seems to prescribe once and for all the number of workers which must be employed, the principle operates nevertheless. The insurance agent might, if his employee fails "to produce" her salary, close his office and do his business from his residence. Or he might share his office with another agent and thus virtually "divide up" a unit of labor to make it fit his demand. Again he might hire a public stenographer for a given number of hours a day. The owner of the machine likewise would be forced by competition to discover the correct combination of his agents of production. If his machines and plant layout indicated a wrong combination (that is, one which is inferior to that of his competitors) he might go bankrupt or he might, by appraising the situation, scrap some of his machinery and purchase the type which will enable him to compete in the market for the sale of his goods. Here again we encounter the operation of the law of substitution, with all employers adjusting and readjusting their combinations of the factors so as to discover the optimum arrangement.

This brief analysis of wage determination indicates that neither laborers alone nor employers alone can dictate wages. Combined demand for labor and combined supply determine the wage rate.

THE SUPPLY OF LABOR

The number of laborers is one of the forces determining marginal productivity of labor; the others are: (1) amounts and quality of other factors, including machines, tools, natural resources, climate, and the entrepreneurial ability; (2) ability and capacity of laborers. The quality of labor depends on education, health, habits, and morale. Quality and quantity of other factors depends on the bountifulness of nature, state of industrial arts, and the mentality and other characteristics of entrepreneurs. Here we will discuss only the supply of labor.

Labor supply responds to demand. But the response is

very complex. Malthus believed the biological law of population growth was such that the future of labor was very dark. Any improvement in the standard of living would lead to earlier marriages and lower infant mortality, and thus the gains in real wages would be lost. Increased pressure of population on food supply, he argued, would lead to overcrowding, war, and disease. Then, owing to decreased supply of labor, the standard of living might rise again, only to repeat the same cycle. But labor could never be raised above this low natural level of subsistence.

There is much truth in the essentials of this analysis. Travelers in China and India have noted this tendency of population to increase. The high standard of living in our own land brought millions of immigrants, and many of them had large families. However, forces other than those listed by Malthus operate. Since the time of Malthus, the theory of the supply of labor has been modified to include emphasis on voluntary limitation of births and on certain other non-economic factors. Parents desire their children to have a better economic status than they themselves have. To achieve this, children must be carefully nurtured in infancy so that they will enter the competitive world with better physiques; they must be educated through trade and professional training so as to lift them above the dead level of the most severe competition. They must be provided with capital when starting out on a career. The entrance of women on an increasing scale into the economic world has enabled many of them to secure a satisfactory livelihood without marrying. The average age of women at marriage has a tendency to rise, thus reducing the potential supply of labor in the subsequent generation. The rising standard of living has stimulated wants so intensively that young people postpone marriage, and a large proportion of

married couples limit the size of their families. These
limitations have been most effective in the middle and
upper classes, but they are becoming pronounced in the
lower income classes as well. The Harvard University
graduate has an average of "three quarters of a child." A
recent study indicates the following:[10]

Employment status	Births per 1,000 married women	
Unskilled labor	182	
Unemployed workers		234
Part-time workers		166
Full-time workers		169
Skilled workers	150	
Unemployed workers		188
Part-time workers		152
Full-time workers		134
Salaried workers	134	
Unemployed workers		167
Part-time workers		153
Full-time workers		120

This differential birth rate shows that the groups least
able to care for children properly have the largest number
of them. The same study showed that families under $1,200
annual income had 176 births per 1,000 married women; 145
births for families with $1,200 to $1,999; 124 births for
families with incomes of $2,000 to $2,499; and 115 births
for families with more than $2,500 income.

Possibly supply of labor responds to the demand for it.
Among the high-income classes, however, larger incomes
seem to indicate an actual decrease in the supply. But
among the lower classes the Malthusian principle appears

---

[10] *New York Times,* March 10, 1935.

to be still in operation, although the relation between sustenance and population development has been modified by technological advances which Malthus could not foresee.

That supply of labor does not correlate perfectly with amount of population has been recognized from the earliest economic writings. In the United States, due to immigration, there has been an unusually high proportion of adult males, whereas in Ireland average age has been higher and proportion of females larger. Thus the relative supply of labor in the United States has been higher. Again, customs and standard of living of a people determine whether or not a large or small proportion of females will engage in gainful occupations. In Great Britain a larger proportion of women are employed than in the United States; this augments the British supply of labor. Supply of labor is a function of the number of working hours per day and per week. Should the working day be cut from eight to six hours, this would be equivalent to cutting the supply of labor by 25 per cent, and hours vary widely in different countries. In some countries children begin working early in life and continue to be employed until old age forces their retirement. Elsewhere the standard of living may be so high that the majority of children spend twelve years in school, and others spend more; the average age at retirement may be much lower for the same reason.

In our time if a father is earning a high wage, his children do not have to work, and may continue their education. Thus again high wages may reduce the supply of labor— that is, the number of work hours available. Obviously this influences the supply of labor. Clearly a mere examination of census figures for population will reveal only an approximate conception of the "supply of labor."

If we start with a given population, there is some evidence that the supply curve of available labor is actually negatively inclined. In the previous chapter we noted that a rise in price of commodities usually brought forth a larger supply of them; but for labor the supply curve seems to have a slope somewhat similar to that of a demand curve for commodities. The Mercantilists, who wrote on economics nearly two hundred years ago, insisted that the wage rates must be kept low; otherwise the supply of labor would decrease. That is, the workers aimed at a certain standard of living; a rise in wages therefore required fewer working hours to maintain it.

Thus when economists report that the supply and demand of labor determine wages, the concept of *supply* has an entirely different meaning from what it has when used in popular discussion. The real meaning of the concept in any given situation can be grasped only by thorough research and careful thought. Wage determination is much more complex than is commonly supposed.

CAUSES OF INEQUALITIES

Earlier in this chapter statistical evidence was presented which confirms the popular view that enormous inequalities of income prevail. What are the causes of these inequalities? Complete explanation would involve an analysis of social institutions, particularly the analysis of the laws of property and inheritance, psychology and the natural distribution of abilities in society, monopoly, labor unions, and the desires and tastes of the masses.

For example, painters and poets may have great ability and yet have low incomes because they produce a product or service which is not highly prized by purchasers. Electricians may secure substantial incomes because of the limitation of their numbers. Other monopolists may enrich themselves because they create an artificial scarcity of their product. Some individuals inherit wealth; others by a fortunate stroke produce something highly prized by society. Clearly the forces responsible for inequalities of income are as inclusive as society itself.

Of wage workers there are several fairly distinct groups. The lowest-income group includes those who perform common labor in factories, stores, railroads, and highways. In the semi-skilled group are such workers as streetcar men, truck operators, and many clerical employees. Above this group are skilled artisans: carpenters, bricklayers, locomotive engineers, the upper group of clerical workers, and salesmen. The highest group is composed of professional and business people, self-employed or employees. Although by good fortune, hard work, and ability a person may move up from one group to another, these four classes are more or less independent and do not compete with one another.

Differences in the incomes of these groups are more apparent than real, for the following reasons: (1) The age at which the worker can command the average wage of his group is higher in each succeeding group. The common laborer attains his maximum wage almost as soon as he reaches physical maturity. (2) The higher the group the greater is the expense involved in training and apprenticeship. Physicians and other professional people, for example, are put to much expense in acquiring an education. (3) Risk of failure increases from lower- to higher-paid groups. (4) Many occupations such as teaching and nursing have non-monetary values. All these factors must be taken into account in ascertaining net earnings in a lifetime work.

The differences in incomes of these four groups are traceable to variations in relative supplies of labor for the different types of work. The wages of common labor are low because the supply is large relative to the demand, and because the supply is large the marginal productivity is low. Even where common labor, skilled labor, and professional labor are employed on a single project, as in planning and constructing a skyscraper, the marginal contribution of common labor is low. That is, the price that must be paid to secure the services of the unskilled labor is much less than that paid for the skilled or professional labor.

The incomes of professional people and of business managers are sometimes said to be high because of the heavy responsibilities which they accept. The manager of a large railway, it is said, receives a large salary because on the outcome of his decisions depends the fate of a half-billion-dollar corporation, and the safety of the trainmen and passengers. But there is no necessary correlation between responsibility and income. The most common reason why a plant superintendent or railway manager commands a high salary is because few people are competent to carry on such operations. Railroads compete with each other for the services of competent executives, and this competition drives their salaries up. These same corporations do not have to bid up the wage scales in a similar way in order to secure competent maintenance-of-way workers. At times, it is true, business executives are in a position to dictate their own salaries.

It is also asserted that great hazards to life and limb go with high rewards to the persons undergoing such hazards. But this is true only if the hazard is so great that extra rewards have to be offered to bring forth the necessary labor supply. It is well known that woodsmen, building razers, miners, and bridge painters ordinarily secure low incomes, and yet these occupations are among the most dangerous. We must conclude that there is no necessary correlation between the degree of hazard and the wages paid. At times a very hazardous occupation such as that of a steeplejack may require great skill. In so far as this skill is scarce, the occupation may be well rewarded, but the reward is for the skill and not for the hazard.

Differences in wages are said to be due also to differences in the efficiency of the workers (ratio between input and output). This is usually a correct explanation for wage differences within the same trade or group, but it does not explain the variations between groups. If the efficiency of common labor should double overnight, other things remaining the same, the wages would actually decline. Doubling the efficiency is equivalent to doubling the supply; larger supply lowers marginal productivity. This follows from the law of diminishing returns. So we must conclude that between groups differences in efficiency are not the causes of wage differences. Whether a rise in efficiency in practice will lower wages depends on what happens to the other factors of production. If the supply of capital and natural resources also increases in quality or quantity, an increase in labor efficiency may be accompanied by a rise in wages. In fact, our increased supply and efficiency of labor has been matched by improvements in the industrial arts through the years, so that the standard of living (real wages) has actually risen.

Such differences in incomes of physicians or attorneys as were noticed earlier in this chapter must be explained largely in terms of variations of ability, efficiency, temperament, social graces, and education. In the same city one doctor may virtually starve to death while a colleague makes $50,000 annually. Both doctors may be graduates of the same medical school and have virtually identical opportunities so far as the law, citizenship, and personal freedom are concerned. In other cases early opportunities, race, education, physical appearance, and personality, as well as ability, may vary greatly and lead to inequality of income. We must conclude, therefore, that variations in efficiency may account for the inequalities of income among members of a group, but do not account for the variations in income between groups. The latter variations are traceable to variations in supply for the different groups. But what causes these variations in supply? Why are doctors and attorneys few in number and unskilled laborers plentiful?

The fundamental forces regulating the supplies of the different grades of labor may be analyzed in terms of variations in (1) ability, and (2) opportunity and training. Students are thoroughly familiar with the normal distribution curve of natural phenomena. If 1,000 leaves are picked at random from a tree the average length of leaf may be found to be seven inches. Possibly 70 per cent of the leaves will be within an inch of the same length. Fifteen per cent may be considerably longer and another 15 per cent considerably shorter. Very few will be excessively short and very few excessively long. Similarly, psychologists have discovered that human abilities (capacity to learn, remember, and apply) conform to this same distribution curve.[11] In the economic world a few individuals are able to excel in any kind of competition; a much larger number can attain to moderate proficiency, and a small number cannot get beyond the poorest sort of achievement. Three or four per cent are so incompetent that they cannot complete success-

---

[11] See Figure 1 on p. 232.

fully a grade school education; others are eliminated in high school, and still others in college. Some cannot learn a trade because of defective mentality or unwillingness to apply themselves properly. Even among those who complete a formal education or acquire a trade, great differences obtain, from mere "passing" to graduation with honors and *magna cum laude*. We conclude, therefore, that differences in native ability are in part responsible for differences in earning power. It is well known, however, that a curve of income distribution among all members of society does not conform strictly to the curve of normal distribution of ability. There must be other reasons for inequalities.

Opportunity and training play considerable roles in determining incomes. The son of a widow, however brilliant he is, may be forced to quit formal education early and earn a living for the family. Sons and daughters of farmers and laborers, as well as those reared in isolated villages and towns, may not have the same opportunity to enter college or learn a trade as those who are born under more fortunate stars. The child of a professional man is from youth surrounded with books, magazines, and conversation which stimulate his mind and lead to self-improvement. It is true that many children born in humble circumstances rise above their environment, but the struggle to lift themselves above their comrades is more arduous than that of children born in more comfortable circumstances.

Thus differential-income groups tend to be self-perpetuating. Unskilled laborers have large families, and their children usually tend to remain in that class. On the average they inherit a relatively low capacity which fits them for only routine work. Early training and formal education usually fit them for nothing else. Their more limited opportunities also tend to keep them in the lower walks of life.

On the other hand, the birth rate among the skilled and professional workers is lower. Their contacts are of the types which lead to advancement. Each child has a better opportunity, and probably his native abilities are somewhat higher than the average.

In many instances inequalities between groups may be largely explained in terms of institutional organizations. Trade unions and medical societies, for example, restrict free entrance into the occupation. As a rule highly organized labor unions are able to demand better pay for their members than that secured by unorganized workers. This leads to the popular view that unions can raise wages, and the unskilled are urged to unite in unions also to demand similar rewards. This is obviously a superficial view of the matter. In the first place, labor unionism has been essentially a skilled-trade phenomenon. As a rule the lowest workers do not organize. As we noticed earlier, the skilled men secure higher pay because of the relatively limited supply of such skill; their high pay is not necessarily due to the union. Furthermore, in most cases the union attempts to raise wages by limiting the supply of labor permitted to learn a given trade. Numerous techniques to accomplish this end have been utilized.

Many unions have adopted an elaborate system of apprentice training which may run from half a year to several years. The young apprentice, who as a rule must not be over twenty years of age, may start at a very low rate of pay and not receive the regular journeyman's wage until he has served his full training period. This hurdle operates as a bar to the trade, thereby limiting the number of men who acquire the skill. The marginal productivity of this type of labor is thereby raised. Many unions have a fixed limit on the number of apprentices permitted to learn the trade, and others resort to high initiation fees. At one time in Chicago the electrical workers' union required each applicant for membership to pay a $750 initiation fee. This eliminated many. In New York the electricians' union permitted several thousand workers to join the union, but when a building boom called for even more electricians, the union issued temporary permits, which were withdrawn after the boom. In this way the union limited the supply of labor to a predetermined quantity, and by this monopoly control was able to dictate wages. Where closed-shop conditions prevail no worker may be employed unless he carries the union card. A glass-workers' union actually closed its doors to all future workers. Thus, both the natural limitation on the supply of skilled labor and the artificial control exercised by the union may help to account for the relatively high pay of skilled workers.

If unions spread to the mass-production industries and unskilled workers become organized, demanding higher wages and shorter hours by means of collective bargaining, sit-down strikes, and other techniques, their money wages may go up. This tends to drive upward the cost of goods. For example, in March 1937 collective bargaining in the steel industry boosted wages about 10 per cent. Quickly the price of steel products went up by a similar amount, and this reflected itself in higher prices for hardware, steel products, and other commodities. If a rise in wage rates is offset by an increase in the cost of living, there is no gain to labor. Thus one cannot be sure that widespread unionism can raise wages for labor *as a whole*. The unions which have been most successful in raising wages are those which have limited the supply of labor in a given trade. Such limitations injure laborers outside of the trade. Such gains in the standard of living of laborers as those experienced in the last century came from higher productivity. Unions, by raising the cost of labor, stimulate technical efficiency of industry and thus make higher wages possible. Unduly aggressive unionism, however, may place a premium on labor-saving techniques and result in technological unemployment, and then labor as a whole may suffer; that is, those workers who cannot sell their labor power at this higher price may remain unemployed.

Recently there has been much criticism of the high cost of medical care. Unquestionably physicians' incomes have been driven upward through the practices of the medical societies and the medical schools. In 1905 there were a hundred and sixty medical schools in the country and today there are only seventy-seven, most or all of them limiting enrollment. Today there are actually 3,500 fewer medical students in the schools than in 1905, although the population has increased by 45 per cent. In 1931 there were fifty fewer physicians per 100,000 of population in the United States than in 1900. The elimination of many of the medical schools and the limitation on medical-school enrollment has been done partially in the public interest; many of the schools were of the "diploma mill" type, and it was necessary to limit enrollment to the more competent students. But it may be surmised that the medical fraternity also understood the laws of supply and demand.

Law schools and bar-examination agencies also have followed a policy of restricting the free flow of professional talent into legal work. Supply of nurses, on the contrary, is unrestricted, because hospitals find that nurses-in-training are a source of cheap labor; the attractiveness of the occupation also leads to over-crowding. Public-school teachers have not benefited by natural or artificial restriction of supply. The standards of normal schools and other institutions where teachers are trained have not been conspicuously high. In many of our large universities the schools of education are among the most populous on the campuses. No serious attempt has been made to raise standards or to limit the supply of teachers in order that the "marginal productivity" of this type of labor might be raised. Nearly anyone with average ability or less can complete the requirements. School boards in many areas have been able to secure all the teachers they needed at their own price. In one of our large middle-western states average incomes of public-school teachers in 1935 was $750, a figure exceeded five- or six-fold by lawyers and physicians.

Thus differences in income between occupational groups may be explained by (1) differences in the ability required to learn the trade or occupation; (2) differences in the amount of time and effort it takes to master the occupation; (3) the attractiveness of the occupation; and (4) artificial control of the number of persons permitted to learn the trade or profession.

THE CORRECTION OF INEQUALITIES

Nearly everyone is agreed that great inequalities of income and excessively low standards of living for some of the people have many disastrous effects. Health, teeth, education, and comforts are sacrificed. Not everyone is agreed that a mere rise in incomes will necessarily result in greater happiness or improvements in health and status. The teeth of Eskimo removed from civilization show virtually no defects. Higher incomes would in many cases go into greater consumption of spirits, tobacco, and low-grade amusements. The more enduring improvements in the standard of living may be neglected. Those who take this view argue that mere rise in incomes would not necessarily lead to an improvement in the quality of civilization. This type of reasoning, however, involves the valuation of the different elements that go to make up a civilization, and it is not for the economist to set up his criteria in this respect.

Others who criticize the attempts to create greater equality point out that the present system of distribution rewards different persons (factors of production) according to their respective contributions to society. They point out that "we the people" actually made Mr. Henry Ford's fortune for him. Our demands for motor cars enriched him. Similarly the enormous income of a very successful physician constitutes society's expression of satisfaction with the services of that physician.   These critics point out that if we destroyed these large incomes or took them from their recipients, these individuals would lose their motivation. They would cease to put forth their best efforts, and would thereby be prevented from making their greatest contribution to society.   High fees, salaries, bonuses, piece rates, wage differentials, and profits are the economic techniques for inducing efficiency, great efforts, and hard work.   It is of some significance that in Russia a reversion to some of these bourgeois methods of payments has taken place. Piece rates, bonuses, and wages graded according to efficiency and output are being increasingly employed there.

Had Mr. Ford from the beginning reduced the selling price of his car to cost, or had he paid out all his profits in the form of higher wages, he would not have been able to engage in elaborate experimentation and research; he would not have been able to make and purchase new and improved machinery, and it is quite conceivable that we would still be buying a motor model of 1905 and paying $2,000 for it. Had the workmen secured the extra incomes they would merely have dissipated the income in personal consumption for the most part, with no enduring improvements for society as a whole.

That the foregoing argument has much truth in it must be admitted. As previously indicated, the benefits of accumulated wealth under a competitive system are broadly shared by the community. However, most students of these problems are also agreed that many professional people, including artists and also business executives, would put forth nearly as great efforts to make a living and thereby enrich society if their economic returns were greatly decreased. Thus a great pianist drawing $3,000 for each appearance might play just as beautifully and as often for $500 per appearance.

The star pianist can draw the $3,000, however, because of the demand for his services. If the fee were fixed by law at $500 and there were three hundred communities demanding one appearance yearly, but the star insisted that his energy would permit only a hundred and fifty appearances a year, we should have to contrive some scheme to ration his service among those who demand it. Under the price system his service is given to those who voluntarily pay for it.

That many salaries and bonuses in industry are fixed arbitrarily by "insiders" should be pointed out. Frequently the chief executives, such as the chairman of the board of directors, the president, the vice-presidents (one of our railways has thirteen vice-presidents and one bank has over sixty), the treasurer, and the secretary, are also large stockholders of the corporation. Possibly the company has a monopoly of some patent or trade name, or through product differentiation has gained a partial monopoly. These stockholders, who are also officers, vote each other high salaries, and may in many instances be said not to be earning their salaries; they have enriched themselves through their preferred positions.

Similarly many corporations return fabulous profits to their stockholders by virtue of superior management and the absence of perfect competition. A person who purchased one share of stock for $50 in Sears, Roebuck and Company in 1906 would now be the owner of about sixteen shares (because of stock dividends) without additional investment on his part, and these would be worth about $1,500, representing an appreciation of 3,000 per cent. Meantime the cash dividends would have amounted to an additional $482. Thousands of other such illustrations might be given.

Economists would agree that in so far as huge incomes are the result of monopoly or preferred positions, society would in most instances gain by the dissolution of such artificial controls. The enthusiastic reformer, however, must be curbed for fear that he "kill the goose that lays the golden eggs." Impetuous legislation such as the NRA of 1933, designed to remedy an evil, may create an economic impasse and paralyze the business community to such a degree that those in whose behalf the legislation is passed do not have their status improved by the new laws. The student of economics wants to know the long-time effect of a proposed law as well as the immediate effect.

Eliminating monopolies

Both the common law and statutes have been hostile to artificial restrictions on production. In 1890 Congress passed the Sherman Anti-Trust Act, which prohibited monopolies, attempts to monopolize and restrain trade. In 1914 this statute was strengthened by the passage of the

Clayton Act, and the creation of the Federal Trade Commission. Since 1890 hundreds of business combinations have been found in contravention of the laws. Numerous large monopolies have been broken up, including those in water pipe, sugar, oil, and tobacco. This type of monopoly has been important in the building up of vast fortunes, and much of the inequalities are traceable to it. Protective tariffs have fostered some monopolies. Economists would agree that the elimination of these combinations is a legitimate function of government.

Of greater importance as a source of inequality of income is the growth of partial monopoly through trade marks, trade names, slogans, patents, copyrights, and all the advertising techniques employed to bring about "product differentiation." Nearly every article bought by the reader is sold under some form of designation to make it stand apart from its competitors. The producer in each case thereby creates for himself a partial monopoly. (See preceding chapter, p. 580.) In the successful cases the owners and managers of the enterprise enrich themselves at the expense of the consumer.

In the assignment of one of the duties to the Federal Trade Commission, Congress, perhaps unwittingly, fostered and made secure this type of monopoly. The Act declared, "Unfair methods of competition in commerce are . . . declared unlawful." Pursuant to this clause the Commission has issued hundreds of "cease and desist" orders in cases where business concerns attempted to copy the trade name, shape, size, color, odor, or package of their successful competitors. Many cases have been cited to the courts for action. "Hygrade Knitting Company, Inc.," was found to infringe "Hygrade Knitting Mills"; "Duraleather" infringed

"Duro." It was found that "Juvenile Shoe Company, Inc." would infringe "Juvenile Shoe Corp." The list could be extended indefinitely.

In all of these cases the law is encouraging and perpetuating monopoly. If a manufacturer were permitted to imitate the slogan, trade name, size, shape, or product of another producer the result would be greater standardization of the product with the inevitable effect of a reduction in large incomes of the competitors. If soap manufacturers were permitted to copy each other's techniques for differentiating their output, the consumers would buy indiscriminately from all sellers, and no one producer could secure a larger sale volume than another, and larger profits would disappear. Larger profits are traceable to individuality of products (imagined or otherwise), and therefore must be explained in terms of monopoly elements.[12]

Why, then, does the law foster monopolies? The answer is, to protect producer and consumer. Under our law a producer has no right to exclude others from manufacturing and selling the same product (unless covered by a patent), no matter how similar the products are. He can claim legal aid only in protecting himself against the use of his name. The courts have held that the purpose of a trade name is to aid in the identification of the owner or producer. But where does identification cease and differentiation begin? If each producer were permitted to imitate the products of others in every way (again excluding patented articles), and the producer of a given commodity were to place only his name or trade mark in some inconspicuous place in fine print to aid in identification, the whole purpose of product

---

[12] See Chamberlin, Edward, *The Theory of Monopolistic Competition,* especially pp. 204–208 (Harvard University Press, Cambridge, Mass., 1936). This is perhaps the most important book in economic theory since 1900.

differentiation would be defeated. Buyers would then select indiscriminately, and profits would drop to a minimum. But under present rules the name or trade marks stand for certain qualifications of the product in the mind of the consumer, and to permit only one manufacturer to use the name is to grant him a monopoly of the product. The law thus goes much farther than merely to permit identification. It fosters monopoly.

Trade marks are necessary to protect the consumer against counterfeit, deceptions, and fraud, it may be argued. If all soap makers might freely imitate the outward appearances of the "Lux" package, none would have any incentive to keep up the quality.

We might substitute for trade marks a requirement that when imitation takes place it must be perfect imitation, in order to avoid deterioration. Or the law might define standards of quality.

It is argued that trade marks stimulate variety and so offer the consumer a greater range of choices. There are several hundred varieties of soap on the market. What for? Within limits, variety is desirable, but in so far as our legal build-up of trade marks has stimulated the multiplication of brands, varieties without a difference, and so on, the system is not producing a maximum of economic output. In the absence of trade marks, these monopolies could not be created, and less attention would be devoted to trying to create them and more would be devoted to physical production. Needless differentiation would be largely eliminated. In order to encourage research, discovery, and new products, patents might be granted, as now, for limited periods, and in certain cases trade marks might be permitted also for limited periods, instead of in perpetuity, as now. More nearly equal returns would accrue to all businessmen; exceptionally large incomes would disappear, and inequalities would be reduced. Whether the suggestions made in this section are feasible may be problematical, but certainly without some such change as herein contained, extremely large profits are destined to continue, and the economic system will not be organized as efficiently as it might be.

Taxation

For hundreds of years states or local political subdivisions have had an obligation to take care of their paupers. In recent years the arm of the law has been utilized increasingly to take from the successful rich in order to give to the unsuccessful poor. As long as public revenues were raised chiefly through the general property tax, little thought was given to the problem of bringing about a redistribution of income through taxation. With growth of the income, inheritance, and gift taxes a new theory of taxation emerged, the theory of taxation according to ability to pay. By this principle each resident will contribute to the support of the government and its multifarious enterprises and wards according to his own success. The higher the income the greater the responsibility of the individual for the ills of his fellow residents. This has been defined as charity by compulsion. It required an amendment to the federal Constitution to permit Congress to legislate on this theory.

At present, in addition to the federal income-tax law, in more than thirty states a state income-tax law applies to corporations and individuals, or both. Incomes below one or two thousand dollars a year are usually exempt from the tax, and the tax rate rises with the amount of income. For example, the federal income tax on individual annual incomes of $10,000 is $700; for incomes of $50,000 the tax is about $10,000; and for incomes of $5,000,000 the tax is nearly $3,600,000. The maximum rate is 75 per cent on that portion of incomes in excess of $5,000,000 for the year.

Corporations are subject to a special income tax as well as to a tax on undivided profits, that is, profits which are earned but not distributed to the stockholders.

In addition to the income-tax collections of the federal government, every state except Nevada collects considerable sums through estate and inheritance taxes. Federal law levies a tax of 2 per cent on a net estate of $10,000 after deducting certain exemptions; the rate is graduated upward until it reaches 29 per cent on that portion of an estate in excess of $1,000,000, and the rate for the portion of the estate in excess of $50,000,000 is 70 per cent. For example, the tax on an estate of $5,000,000 is about $2,000,000, and on an estate of $10,000,000 the tax is about $5,000,000.

In addition to death duties and income taxes the federal government and a number of states have gift taxes. Frequently rich persons, in anticipation of death, make gifts to their children or other people. The federal gift tax begins with a rate of 1½ per cent on the first $10,000 of gift (after certain exemptions) and the rate is graduated upward until it reaches 52½ per cent on that portion of gifts in excess of $50,000,000.

In 1929 the federal government raised $2,331,000,000 under the income-tax law, and the state of New York raised $150,000,000. Whether this type of taxation constitutes redistribution of income depends on how the funds are spent. If they are spent in furnishing services which will benefit the people in proportion to the amount of taxes they paid, it does not mean redistribution. Actually, the funds expended benefit all classes—in roads, weather reporting, health, education, law enforcement, and civil and criminal courts. However, it is generally agreed that the expenditure of the funds under modern democracies yields benefits to the poorer classes (non-income-tax payers) considerably in excess of the benefits which accrue to the rich. The latter may send their children to private schools and at the same time contribute heavily to the maintenance of the public schools. Similarly, funds spent for relief, public works, health, old-age pensions, and the administration of labor and public-utility laws redound to the benefit of the poorer classes to a greater extent than to other groups.

Whether the proceeds from these taxes are given to people in the form of cash or in the form of government services, the incomes of recipients are thereby augmented. Old-age assistance, poor relief, mothers' allowances, and veterans' pensions may take the form of cash. When the government uses the proceeds from taxation to build libraries, schools, roads, bridges, hospitals, and recreational facilities, the flow of services (income) to the people is increased. In short, what governments do for the people, they, the people, do not need to do for themselves. Tax spending is coöperative spending. It appears that taxation is destined to be employed on a larger scale to effect a redistribution of income from the more fortunate or more successful classes to those less fortunate and less successful.

Education

Free, compulsory, and universal education has been an American tradition for one hundred years. Every child, rich or poor, must be given an equal opportunity. If such a universal system of education had the capacity to bring about equality or greater equality of income, it should have accomplished this end in the course of a century. The very fact that it has failed to achieve this goal leads to the suspicion that education, however useful for other purposes, is no solution to the problem of inequalities. In fact, there is abundant evidence that education, instead of bringing about greater equality, actually causes greater inequality.

Numerous controlled experiments have been conducted to test the effect of education. For example, in one case 1,500 pupils in a certain city were divided by the teachers into two groups, bright and dull. These pupils were then divided into small groups of forty pupils—there being twenty bright ones and twenty dull ones in a room under the direction of a teacher. All pupils were given the same series of arithmetic problems to solve, beginning with problems so simple that even the bulk of the dull pupils had no difficulties. Gradually more difficult problems were given; in case of inability to solve a problem the child was given aid and instruction. After several hundred problems were given under this guidance all the pupils were asked to take an examination in arithmetic.

The examination showed that all pupils profited by the training. The bright ones, however, profited so much more by it than the dull ones that at the end of the experiment the discrepancy in solving arithmetic problems between the dull and bright pupils was even greater than it was before the experiment began. Similar experiments with other subjects and groups have been performed, and the general conclusion to be drawn from this type of scientific experiment is that education, while benefiting all, benefits the brighter child relatively much more. For this reason we must conclude that the solution to the problem of inequalities of income does not lie in the direction of more education for all.

The earning of a living requires qualities and competence in many respects. Education, by refining and sharpening these qualities, benefits those most who are best able to profit by the training. This does not condemn universal education, however. Unquestionably, education does improve general well-being.

An educational system which educates an increasing proportion of people for the artisan positions and for the professions will increase the supply of these higher-grade workers and perforce lower the supply of the unskilled classes. This will correct some of the inequality of incomes according to the law of the marginal productivity of labor. Possibly, therefore, some of the group monopolies among labor unions and professional societies must be broken down. Any such threat to these groups is likely to be resisted.

Other attempts to correct inequality might be analyzed. Much reliance is being placed in some circles in consumers' coöperation. Excessively large salaries are eliminated and profits are returned to the consumers in the form of patronage rebates. Others believe that consumer education, such as that attempted by Consumers' Research, Inc., will make the buyer's dollar go farther and thereby enable those in the lower income brackets to raise their incomes effectively.

According to some popular opinion a change in the social order would solve this problem. As the Russian experiment shows, the problem of distribution of income is much more complicated than is usually supposed. In spite of the fact that private ownership of the means of production has been abolished, capital accumulation, which means a current decline of present income, has gone on at an accelerated rate. The state has taken over the function of saving, and workers are not paid the full value of current production.

On the other hand, the differences in income of skilled, unskilled, educated, and uneducated workers is very great.[13] Enormous salaries are being paid to engineers and plant managers in some cases. If the supplies of competent workers and managers are scarce, salaries adequate to attract and produce sufficient high-grade personnel must be paid. Possibly these departures from the communist standard are transitional, but it is significant that they persist and are becoming more pronounced at this date, twenty years after the experiment was launched. The abolition of private property, monopoly, and other institutions causing inequality of incomes will tend to bring about greater equality. But the change wrought in income distribution by such a radical shift in institutions would not be as far-reaching as is commonly assumed because the functions of managing, planning, saving, and risk-taking would have to be carried on by the state through its public personnel.

BIBLIOGRAPHY

Garver, F. B., and Hansen, A. H., *Principles of Economics* (Ginn & Company, Boston, 1928).

Chamberlin, Edward, *Theory of Monopolistic Competition* (Harvard University Press, Cambridge, Mass., 1936).

Douglas, Paul, *The Theory of Wages* (The Macmillan Company, New York, 1934).

Moulton, Harold G., *Income and Economic Progress* (Brookings Institution, Washington, 1935).

Leven, Maurice, *et al.*, *America's Capacity to Consume* (Brookings Institution, Washington, 1934).

Clark, J. B., *The Distribution of Wealth* (The Macmillan Company, New York, 1899).

---

[13] Eastman, Max, *The End of Socialism in Russia* (Little, Brown & Company, Boston, 1937).

CHAPTER XIV

Economic Security

EMERSON P. SCHMIDT

University of Minnesota

INTRODUCTION

THE two preceding chapters have described the operations of the economic system under conditions relatively free from regulation. No economist believes that the maximum welfare can be achieved in the complete absence of regulation or control of the economic process. Yet it is significant that periods of maximum government regulation are periods of relative stagnation, that is, lack of progress. After the break-up of medieval controls, guilds, and mercantilism, progress began.

The nineteenth century is noted for its enormous progress and its rise in the standard of living for both the higher and the lower classes. This was also the period of minimum regulation.[1] The twentieth century appears destined to see rapid growth in regulation and regimentation; whether this will be accompanied by stagnation and retrogression remains to be seen. Many students of the social sciences detect a serious conflict between progress and security. Progress has meant experimentation, trial and error, adventures in the unknown, freedom of enterprise, private initiative, and free consumer choice. Security means caution, limitation to the known, regimentation, accepting the tried and proved, regu-

---

[1] Lippmann, Walter, "The Providential State," *Atlantic Monthly*, October, 1936, pp. 403–12.

lation of enterprise, initiative, and possibly dictation to consumer. Actually, every century has been characterized by some security and some progress.

In this chapter an account will be given of attempts to improve economic well-being and to create greater economic security for specific groups. In each case of regulation the area of freedom of some individuals has been reduced, and at times the area of others, in whose behalf the regulation was designed, has been increased. In other cases the victimized group has not secured larger freedom by means of legislation, but has secured some form of protection through the arm of the state.

This chapter will be concerned with an outline of the elements of insecurity due to industrial accidents, illness, old age, and unemployment; proposed remedies will be discussed. The operation of economic laws previously discussed will be discernible in this analysis.

WORKMEN'S COMPENSATION

Industrial accidents cause about 17,000 deaths annually and injure hundreds of thousands of workmen. Formerly under the common law the worker had to bear the cost of such accidents in wages lost, medical expenses, and rehabilitation. The employer had three duties which, if performed by him, absolved him of any obligation to the injured worker. He was required to furnish reasonably competent (1) workmen, (2) tools, and (3) work place. Furthermore, the employer enjoyed three common-law defenses which he utilized to prevent the injured worker from securing a judgment in case of a damage suit. These defenses included the doctrines of (1) contributory-negligence, (2) the fellow-servant, and (3) assumption-of-risk. Under the contributory-negligence doctrine, if the employer could show that the worker was unduly careless, failed to follow orders, or violated customary shop practice, the court would decide against the injured worker. If a fellow servant was negligent, or if he failed to perform his duties, the employer could plead the fellow-servant doctrine, and the injured worker could not recover from the employer. Again, if the employer could show that a given number of workmen typically were injured or killed in that type of work he could plead the assumption-of-risk doctrine. That is, workmen, when accepting jobs, assume the ordinary risks of injury.

Under this procedure hundreds of injury and death claims were filed in the courts. Attorneys had to be paid, briefs prepared, and witnesses furnished. The cases lingered in the courts for months and years. Many workmen, or their widows, did not have the means to prosecute such cases; in other instances the workmen understood their rights only partially or not at all. Frequently the fear of discharge deterred injured workmen from filing claims. As a result families lost their source of income and had no recourse. Children were taken out of school prematurely, and mothers were forced into industry; the family was frequently disorganized by this absence of economic security.

The first attempt to furnish certain and adequate relief to the injured workmen was made in Germany in 1885. Other countries proceeded along similar lines. The first law of general application in the United States was passed by New York in 1910. Most of the other states followed in quick succession. These laws are known as workmen's compensation laws. The old common-law defenses of employers are abrogated, and the question of who was at fault is not raised in case of accident. The only question that must be settled is, did the accident or death *arise out of and in the course of employment?* If the answer is in the affirmative, the worker receives medical care and compensation during the course of the injury or for stated periods.[2]

Injuries that are due, for example, to wasp bites, frostbites, and sunstroke, although they occur *during* the working period, are not compensable as a rule, because they do not also arise *out of* the occupation. Accidents due to horseplay among the workers are compensable on the theory that workmen must be expected to be human. If the worker deviates from his work temporarily an injury received may not be compensable. For example, a truck driver who stepped into a saloon for a drink was injured by a fall and failed to receive compensation. Injuries received on the way to work or on the way home are usually not compensable. However, the great bulk of all industrial accidents, if they can be shown to rise *out of* and *in the course* of the work, are compensable. The negligence of the worker, or of a fellow worker, does not bar compensation.

The basic theory underlying this "liability without fault" is that if the employer can be made responsible for accidents he will take steps to prevent them. The main purpose of compensation laws is not to compensate the injured workmen but to prevent accidents by giving the employer a pecuniary interest in reducing them. The immediate effect of such laws has been the hiring of safety engineers, installation of protective guards wherever hazards prevailed, and the inauguration of "safety first" campaigns among workers.

The employer must pay annual premiums either to insurance companies or to a state fund from which the claims are paid. The premiums for each class of industry are deter-

---

[2] See Commons, J. R., and Andrews, J. B., *Principles of Labor Legislation,* Chapter V (Harper & Brothers, New York, 1936), for a full account of this legislation.

mined according to the degree of hazard in that class. Thus in one state, streetcar companies must pay a premium of $1.69 per $100 of payroll; the rate for wreckers and razers is $8.01; for carpenters, $3.23; for college teachers, $.09; and for clerical help, $.04. Thus it is in the interest of the employers to reduce accidents. Noted achievements are on record, many establishments having reduced accident rates by 50 per cent or more over a period of years.

The injured workers (or the beneficiaries in fatal cases) are paid a regular weekly amount, usually about 50 per cent of their normal pay, and medical expenses. In case of death the beneficiary secures a lump-sum settlement or perhaps a compensation payment for 1,000 weeks. Some states provide rehabilitation of the person who is injured to a degree which makes it impossible for him to return to his former employment. Great variations in state laws prevail, but the foregoing is a generalized statement of the technique developed to meet one of the most serious sources of economic insecurity. While many state laws are not as adequate as might be desired, especially in regard to coverage of occupational diseases, and while the administration of the laws frequently is inefficient, economic insecurity due to industrial accidents has been met in an intelligent and, on the whole, competent way.[3]

HEALTH INSURANCE

The present system of individualist medicine has frequently been criticized because (1) it emphasizes cures rather than prevention; (2) the burden of illness falls

---

[3] Two southern states do not have compensation laws. Railway employees engaged in interstate commerce oppose compensation laws. Compensation for accidents due to highway traffic is still provided in nearly all jurisdictions by the uncertain and inequitable damage-suit method.

unevenly on families and varies from year to year; and
(3) fees based on the principle of rate discrimination create
a situation in which only the "millionaire and the pauper
can afford surgery."

1. A family which cannot afford adequate medical care
in cases of acute illness can go without, or it can try to be
satisfied with one or two visits of the physician, or it can
resort to charity. Of 17,217 cases of illness studied by the
United States Public Health Service in 1921–1924, 35 per
cent, not including colds and minor digestive disturbances,
received no medical attention. Chronic illnesses seem to
receive inadequate care. For example, of 1,176 patients
with chronic arthritis (rheumatism) studied by the Massachusetts Department of Public Health in 1930, nearly 68
per cent were either treating themselves or receiving no
treatment at all; among the well-to-do cases 50 per cent
were without care; among the poor the proportion untreated
was 76 per cent. It has been estimated that less than 25
per cent of the population see a dentist once a year for
examination and cleaning of teeth. Minor symptoms, which
may be the beginnings of serious derangement or illness,
are either neglected or treated with home remedies in the
hope that nothing serious is wrong. People follow the
practice of "not calling the doctor until the case is serious
enough so that they will get their money's worth." The
fee-for-service system of medical practice puts the emphasis
on individual cure and not on public health and prevention.
Annual health audits, required by some insurance companies
of their insured persons, are not common.

2. The burden of illness falls unevenly on families and
unevenly from year to year on a given family. One study
indicates that for a twelve-month period 47.5 per cent of
families had no illnesses calling for medical aid; 32 per cent

had one illness; 13.5 per cent had two; nearly 5 per cent had three; and over 2 per cent had four or more such illnesses. The records indicate that the higher the income the greater the number of *recognized* illnesses calling for medical care. Families vary greatly in size and therefore in exposure to illness. The amount of illness that a family will suffer in a year is not known in advance. If illnesses occurred regularly and with relatively equal expense from year to year, the family could more readily budget the costs. If the bread winner is disabled the trouble comes when the family is least able to shoulder the financial burden. We underwrite the risks of death by life insurance; similarly many students of the problem feel that we ought to pool our medical funds and provide that all risks be covered with some form of assured aid. Considerable progress has already been made in this direction with respect to hospital service. In Minneapolis all the leading hospitals have formed an association under which groups of employees in private and public enterprises are assured free hospital service for three weeks by the payment of a fee of seventy-five cents a month. Dependents of the insured secure reduced rates by the payment of one dollar annually. Similar plans are in force in hundreds of other communities.

On an increasing scale physicians and clinics, both private and public, are experimenting with fixed annual fees to cover all cases of family illnesses, or at least certain groups of ailments. Perhaps the best-known private clinic operating on a fixed annual-fee basis is the Ross-Loos clinic in Los Angeles.

Public bodies have also attempted to meet the problem of preventive medicine. Most communities now have one or more public health officers, who provide, either at cost or free, numerous services including vaccination, inoculation, and in the larger communities, public-school nursing facilities. A number of communities in western Canada have embarked on an ambitious program of tax-supported "municipal doctor" systems under which residents are entitled to an unlimited number of office calls and consultations and a limited number of free house calls; sometimes nominal fees are charged for the latter in order to discourage trivial calls. Colleges and universities have student health services of virtually unlimited character for a fixed annual fee. Public health departments and universities are also engaging in much study and research, which culminates in the publication of materials designed to stimulate better health habits. Nearly all large mercantile and industrial concerns provide either free medical service or service at a fixed annual cost to their employees, and frequently to the employee's family. Thus a very considerable attempt has been made to emphasize the sharing of risks and at the same time the preventive aspects of medicine; but both these phases of health preservation are destined to grow much more rapidly.

3. Physicians are in a position to set fees according to the principle of "charging what the traffic will bear." For office calls this principle is seldom utilized, but it is virtually universal for surgery and chronic ailments. Persons of the middle class with moderate incomes are most adversely affected by this method because the rich can afford the fees and the poor become objects of charity. Already half of the hospital beds in New York City are publicly owned; the same holds true for many other cities. The staffs of the hospitals and the facilities are used in many communities chiefly by charity cases. In addition, all physi-

cians do a great deal of charity work. This puts the overworked physician in an embarrassing position, and the burden of charity is not shared equally by the doctors.

Nearly all European countries have adopted some form of compulsory health insurance. In 1935 the province of Alberta, Canada, enacted a health-insurance law providing elective coverage by the localities; and in 1936 British Columbia adopted a compulsory law. The laws are exceedingly diverse. Some cover only workers; others include the family of the worker as well. Some cover specified types of ailments, and others cover all illnesses. In some cases the law provides only medical and hospital expenses, while in others the benefits are extended to include money benefits to cover cases where the workers are unable to return to their work because of disability.[4]

The British Columbia system of health insurance

As an example of one type of insurance system, that in British Columbia will be described briefly.

The system applies to all employees earning less than $1,800 per year, and their dependents, with the exception of farm workers, Christian Scientists, and members of any industrial medical-service plan in operation January 1, 1936. The Health Insurance Commission set up by the act may exclude domestic servants employed in private households, casual employees, part-time employees, and employees in designated establishments, industries, or localities, whom it is considered unnecessary or inexpedient to include. Voluntary insurance is offered persons not covered by the compulsory plan.

---

[4] The Committee on the Costs of Medical Care, Washington, D. C., has studied the economics of medicine for a period of five years and has published several dozen books and reports. Those of most interest to social scientists are listed in the bibliography.

A health-insurance fund, formed from the contributions of employers and insured persons and all other moneys and incomes received by the commission, is established. Contributions by employees, which will be deducted from their pay, are fixed at 2 per cent of the remuneration, with a minimum of thirty-five cents per week and a maximum of seventy cents per week. The value of payments in kind will be fixed by the Commission in establishing the amount of the contribution. The employer's contribution amounts to 1 per cent of the employee's pay, with a minimum of twenty cents per week and a maximum of thirty-five cents. The contributions of voluntarily insured persons are fixed at a rate sufficient to cover the total cost of providing all benefits, including costs of administration. Provision is made for the proper investment of the health-insurance fund.

The benefits include the services of a physician when required for preventive, diagnostic, or therapeutic treatment, prenatal and maternity treatment for women, and surgical and specialist services, as may be necessary. Hospital maintenance and care in a public ward is provided for not more than ten consecutive weeks for any one illness, unless a longer period is prescribed by the regulations, or the value of such service may be applied towards more expensive accommodations or treatment. Necessary drugs, medicines, and dressings are provided, although, subject to the provisions of the regulations, insured persons may be required to bear up to one-half of these costs, while necessary laboratory services and diagnostic aids are supplied without charge. Certain services for the diagnosis and treatment of tuberculosis, venereal diseases, and nervous and mental diseases, for which service is available in public or governmental institutions, are not covered by the insurance.

Insured persons and their dependents are eligible for benefits at the expiration of four weeks after contributions become payable, and they continue eligible to receive benefits during each succeeding contribution week for four additional calendar weeks and for such further additional period as may be determined by the Commission. Employees who have ceased to be eligible for benefits under the foregoing section, but who again become insured, are eligible together with their dependents to receive benefits after the expiration of one week after contributions have become deductible and payable, and they are eligible in each succeeding contribution week for one additional calendar week and for such further additional period as may be determined by the commission. Employees who become ineligible for benefits under both of these sections, but because of sickness or injury are unable to engage in any employment, may receive benefits for an additional twelve weeks. This provision does not now apply to the dependents, but may be made applicable to them by the regulation.

The Commission is empowered to provide benefits for insured persons in such manner as it may consider expedient, but in all cases where it considers that the circumstances do not require the exercise of such power in order to secure prompt, efficient, and economical medical service, the insured person is allowed to choose the physician or druggist, so that so far as possible all competent physicians and pharmacists may be employed and be available to insured persons.

The Commission is to make its own financial arrangements with physicians, druggists, hospitals, laboratories, and other persons or agencies providing services. Three methods of payment, or any combination or modification of these methods, may be used for the physicians: (1) a salary system, (2) a per capita system under which the physician is paid a fixed amount per annum for every insured person for whom he has agreed to provide services, and (3) a fee system under which payment is based on the extent and character of the services rendered. In the last case the total expenditures in any one year may not exceed a fixed rate per annum per insured person eligible to receive benefits. If the per capita or fee system is used, the Commission shall set aside for the payment of physicians not less than $4.50 per annum per insured person.

The act will be administered by a Health Insurance Commission consisting of a chairman and no more than four other members appointed by the government. A technical advisory council of not more than six members may be appointed to assist the Commission. On this council there will be the Provincial health officer, a representative of the workmen's compensation board, a physician, and at least one woman. The Commission will appoint and employ a physician as director of medical services and such other physicians and other employees as may be required for administration and enforcement of the act. The Commission is empowered, subject to government approval, to make all regulations, not inconsistent with the provisions of the act, that are considered necessary to its administration and enforcement.

This outline indicates that the act merely sets down broad policy and grants considerable discretion to the administrative agency to adapt the plan to conditions. Probably this plan is not final. Situations will arise calling for modifications of procedure, but it constitutes an interesting American experiment in socialized medicine affecting nearly 300,000 people.

Criticisms of public medicine

Critics of public medicine argue that it will destroy personal relations between patient and physician and substitute a bureaucracy therefor. The chronic complainer will be a daily visitor at the public clinic. Again it is argued that public medicine will destroy the motive on the part of the doctor to do his best, since he will then be merely another salaried public employee assigned so many cases. Others criticize the movement because it attempts to make the rich or the general taxpayer foot the bills of the poor.

That these criticisms have weight must be admitted, but those favoring the movement state that under most systems of public medicine the patient may choose his physician from a panel to which all competent physicians may be named. Under the "municipal doctor" system of western Canada this is not the case. They also point out that under the modern private clinic system the patient usually has little or no choice of physician. Only a small percentage of patients entering, for example, the Mayo Clinic know in advance who their diagnostician or surgeon will be, and the majority prefer to follow the recommendation of the authorities in charge. Also under a public system of medicine private practice would not be outlawed; rather, we might follow the same procedure as in the field of education, in which public and private systems thrive simultaneously.

That there will be chronic complainers who will plague the doctors under a system of public medicine is generally admitted. Similarly, arguments are advanced against unemployment insurance; some individuals will abuse the security and will not try to secure work. No doubt public medicine would be abused; techniques to meet this problem will have to be evolved. The opinion in western Canada is that on the whole abuse is not great.

Removal of the profit motive in the practice of medicine may cause some physicians to fail to exert their best efforts. The more aggressive may stay out of the system, leaving the less competent to join the public payroll. Possibly there is some real danger here. There will be advantages for the doctor both in and out of the system. Many doctors are thoroughly disgusted with the inevitable financial implications of private medicine. Frequently their best judgment forces them to suggest treatment which they know the patient cannot afford. Under public medicine this trouble is removed. Also, physicians have greater security under the public system and can devote full time and thought to the art of healing and counsel. Already a large proportion of physicians are working on a salary basis in hospitals, clinics, and public health departments, and many doctors favor the public system. In order to secure maximum results from the profession the public system, if launched, should not displace private practice, but rather should supplement it.

Whether one regards the socializing of medicine as another dangerous step toward socialism depends on one's preconceptions and philosophy of the place of government in society. That it is socialism must be admitted. But so are public education, municipal ownership of electric utilities, and the like; public employment and old-age insurance are of the same order.

OLD-AGE SECURITY

The depression, beginning in 1929, and a number of other factors have made us more conscious of the insecurity facing old people under present conditions. Among these is the growing proportion of people engaged in non-agricultural pursuits. When a farmer retired and sold his farm to his youngest child he usually reserved rooms in the homestead, as well as a cow, a few chickens, and perhaps a garden patch, for himself.

Today the situation is different; only about one-fifth of the gainfully employed are engaged in agriculture; nearly 80 per cent work in towns and cities. Under urban conditions life is for most people a struggle of balancing personal budgets. Repeated periods of unemployment drain the small savings of industrial workers. The Brookings Institution, an economic-research organization, finds that 80 per cent of the people save only 2 per cent of the total savings of the population. In the cities the temptation to spend money is much greater than in rural communities. The constant barrage of advertising, the desire to live up to the Joneses, and the ever-present stimulation of wants lead to old-age insecurity. Frequently, the old folks are no longer quite welcome to spend their declining years with their own children, because the married children live in as small quarters as possible in order to save rent. When an aged worker in the city is taken off the payroll, he is likely to become dependent. Society, then, is compelled to meet the problem of dependency.

With the development of machine industry and high-speed, mass-production methods, the older worker in industry is often both relatively inefficient and a hazard. His energy and strength depleted, the man over fifty years of age cannot keep up with the pace of the machine. If he loses his job other employers hesitate to hire him, for they prefer younger men. Indeed, as pointed out below, for some types of work some large corporations will not employ men over twenty-five years of age. The man of twenty-six is actually too old—too old to be taken on for a new job. One California company recently announced that on a given date all workers over forty-five years of age would be dropped from the payroll unless they had been with the company ten years or longer. Where will the older workers turn?

Workmen's compensation laws also encourage the discharge of the older worker because of the high cost of accident insurance which the employer must carry. The premiums for this insurance vary closely with the accident experience of the employer. The older worker, less alert and slower than the young, is less able to safeguard himself from accidents.

Another fact which makes us increasingly conscious of the insecurity of old age is the growing proportion of old people. While the birth rate was high and the immigration large our stock was replenished with young blood. Immigration to this country has virtually ceased, and the birth rate has declined from 28.1 per 1000 population in 1914 to 16.6 in 1933.

As the nation has become older, average age of population has risen. From 1820 to 1930 average age rose by more than 60 per cent. In 1900 about 13 per cent of the population of Minnesota were under five years of age, but by 1930 the proportion had dropped to 9 per cent. There are now fewer children in the first grade than in the second and fewer in the second grade than in the third. Because of the declining birth rate the common-school population is destined to drop for many decades unless some marked change in birth rate occurs.

Conversely, in 1900 only 3.8 per cent of the population of the United States were over sixty-five years of age; today 6.4 per cent are over sixty-five. This is an increase of nearly

70 per cent within a period of thirty years. Obviously we have a larger proportion of old people in our midst, making us increasingly conscious of the plight of the old people, and this trend is continuing. Besides the decline in birth rates, the increasing mean length of life contributes to this dominance of old age. For example, it is estimated that in 1800 the average person could expect to live only to age thirty-five; today the average age at death is about sixty.[5]

The problem of old age calls for an analysis of the solutions in operation and those that are proposed. In meeting this issue we have up to recently followed the traditional methods, that is, piecemeal remedies and ill-conceived plans. Until 1935 no comprehensive scheme was devised to solve the problem of old-age insecurity.

Voluntary private industrial schemes

For many years a number of companies have had in operation private pension plans, which for the most part have been of a non-contributory type. That is, employees generally did not pay premiums. By 1930 there were about 420 firms with such voluntary plans, covering perhaps three and one-half million workers, or about 15 per cent of the number that are covered by the 1935 federal old-age annuity law.

Why were profit-seeking corporations sufficiently interested in their employees to provide pensions to this extent? No doubt in numerous instances the management felt a genuine sympathy for, and interest in, the aging employee whose savings were insufficient for his old age. Another motive was the desire to clear the payroll of "old timber," that is, workers no longer able to carry their share of the

---

[5] This figure has risen steadily because of the decline in infant mortality.

work; to drop them summarily without resources would appear heartless and might cause labor unrest. Also a worker who anticipates from his employer an old-age annuity is bound economically and emotionally to him. He will hesitate to strike; he has an interest in the success and survival of his employer's firm. This relationship discourages unionism, because the employee fears the union might call a strike and force him to walk out with the others. In many instances pensions were payable only for "continuous service" of, say, twenty-five years, and a strike might be interpreted by the employer as a termination or interruption of such services. Finally, an employer who became known to the public as one who had made provision for the old age of his employees would be favorably regarded.

Many of these plans were soundly motivated and conceived from the standpoint of the worker, but defective and insincere motives often worked great hardship on employees. The turnover among industrial workers is inordinately high, and most of the pension plans required continuous service with a given company for twenty, twenty-five, or even thirty-five years. Some employers, in order to avoid paying pensions, discharged employees when they approached the minimum required service. Frequently employers set up rather rigid specifications for eligibility. Those who had gone on strike or had merely joined the union were made ineligible to receive a pension. For this reason Justice Brandeis called the private industrial pension scheme the "new peonage." A marked tendency to discriminate against older applicants for work was noted among certain companies which had industrial pension schemes. Many firms would hire no one over thirty-five years of age, and in numerous instances twenty-five years was the maximum.

Another serious defect of these plans was that in nearly all cases the right to the pension was determined wholly by the goodwill of the employer. The worker had no legal claim to a pension, which was regarded not as a deferred wage but rather as a mere gratuity. If the firm became bankrupt, went out of business, or was merged with another corporation, the pensioners already receiving pensions and the employees who had looked forward to receiving pensions in old age would be left unprovided for. This situation was strikingly illustrated in the case of the merger of the Morris Packing Company with the Armour Packing Company. The pensioners of the Morris company brought suit, claiming a right to continuance of their pensions. The court held, however, that the pension was a gift, a gratuity, and that the pensioner's claim rested entirely upon the willingness of the employer to pay the pension. The aged former employees of the Morris company were left unprovided for. In many other cases pensioners found their monthly pensions reduced or wholly stopped, especially during depression.

A few companies recognized the inequity of this procedure and provided a remedy. Notable among these was the Western Clock Company. This concern adopted a system under which every employee covered by the pension plan was given a paid-up annuity policy at the end of each year of service. This entitled him to a stated annuity upon reaching the retirement age, regardless of any subsequent relations with the company. He could strike, he could leave the company either voluntarily or by discharge, yet be entitled to a pension based on the number of annual annuity policies he held from the company. The company set up reserves with adequate safeguards to protect the interests of the annuitants so that there was virtually no doubt about the size and security of the annuity when the worker reached retirement age. Had more companies adopted this enlightened policy it is probable that the general plan of private industrial pensions would not have suffered as much attack as has been made against it.[6]

We may ask, why this extended discussion of private plans in view of the fact that in 1935 the federal government adopted a broad scheme of compulsory old-age annuities? The answer is: (1) The federal act may be declared unconstitutional. (2) The Clark amendment introduced in the Senate to exempt from the federal act all employers with private plans gained considerable support and is coming up again for consideration. Indeed, so sure were employers that the adoption of private pension plans would exempt them from the federal annuity act that the movement for such plans gained considerable impetus in 1935 and 1936. In 1930 there were about 420 private plans in operation; by 1935 the number had increased to about 750. Clearly we have not heard the last of the private pension plan, and students of the problem should know its implications.[7]

Labor-union schemes

A rather limited number of labor unions have made an attempt to meet the problem of old age among their members.[8] In some cases both the international union and some of the local branches have adopted such plans. Both cover-

[6] For a more extended analysis of this phase of the problem see Schmidt, Emerson P., "The Present Impasse of Old Age Pensions," *Social Science*, 1930, Vol. 5, pp. 157–166.

[7] For an excellent analysis of the difficulties of exempting the private plans from the federal act see Douglas, Paul, *Social Security in the United States*, pp. 278–291 (McGraw-Hill Book Company, New York, 1936).

[8] *Monthly Labor Review*, July, 1934, pp. 1–24, and January, 1936, pp. 40 f.

age and extent of aid are limited. Old-age and disability benefits are frequently handled jointly. Usually these benefits, like those under the private pension schemes provided by employers, are non-contractual and therefore the member cannot feel fully confident of ultimately receiving his expected aid.

Old-age retirement systems of public employees

Federal, state, and local governments, including school boards, have made a substantial beginning in providing retirement systems for their aged employees.[9] Although the federal government has adopted a coördinated system, in the country as a whole there are literally hundreds of uncoördinated systems, varying greatly in coverage and other matters. Police and firemen's pension plans are found in almost every city; retirement schemes for teachers, while not quite so general, are very common; and numerous other groups of public employees have their own pension plans. In 1927 six states had retirement plans applying to all employees not included in some recognized pension system. Twenty-one states and the District of Columbia had plans which included—or might include—all teachers in the public employ.

In two particulars retirement plans differ fundamentally: (1) the source of the funds by which they are maintained, and (2) the method by which provision is made for meeting the liabilities incurred. As to the first, plans may be contributory or non-contributory; as to the second, they may be managed upon either the cash-disbursement or the actuarial-reserve plan.

Under the *joint contributory system* each employee con-

[9] *Public Service Retirement Systems,* United States Bureau of Labor Statistics, 1929.

tributes regularly, usually in the form of deduction from his wages, a fixed amount or percentage, and the employing agency either makes regular fixed contributions or undertakes to appropriate sufficient funds, as needed, to keep the system in operation; under the non-contributory system the whole cost is borne by one side, usually the employer. Non-contributory plans are unusual, and seem not to be gaining favor.

Under the *cash-disbursement system* benefits are paid from whatever funds are on hand, without much reference to the future. During the early years of a system's operation the employees' contributions are often more than sufficient to meet all needs, but gradually the growing pension roll demands continually heavier annual payments, the contributions of the employees are progressively less adequate to the situation, and the employing agency is called upon for rapidly increasing annual contributions. The peak cost under this system is usually reached twenty to thirty years after its adoption.

Under the *actuarial-reserve system* a fund is established, into which employer and employee pay regular contributions. Rate of contribution by each is so calculated that the fund receives annually an amount which, put at compound interest, will be sufficient to pay each employee on retirement the share of the retirement allowance due for one year's services, and also one year's share of such other benefits as the system may provide. The employing agency usually assumes responsibility for benefits due for services given before the plan was adopted and makes regular contributions to liquidate this accrued liability. Ordinarily such plans provide for an actuarial review at stated intervals, with a stipulated provision that, if the review shows a need for it, the rate of contribution may be revised.

The retirement system applying to the employees of the federal government is a compulsory contributory system. The employees contribute a percentage of their salaries, and there is an implied assumed responsibility by the government for the difference between what the employees pay and the actual cost of the benefits, and also for the cost of benefits allowed to annuitants or pensioners for service rendered prior to the inauguration of the retirement system.

The system covers all civil-service employees and certain other specified classes of employees of the federal government and regular annual employees of the District of Columbia municipal government. Employees contribute 3.5 per cent of their basic salaries. Annuity for old-age and for disability retirement is computed by multiplying average annual basic salary (not to exceed $1,500) for the last ten years of service by the number of years of service (not to exceed thirty) and dividing the product by forty-five. The maximum annuity specified in the law is $1,000.

In 1934 about 45,000 former federal employees received pensions averaging $990 per annuitant at a total cost of about $45,000,000. The balance in the federal civil-service retirement and disability fund amounted to $263,000,000. Of the $60,000,000 added to the fund in 1934, about $29,-000,000 represented employee contributions, $11,500,000 represented interest earned, and the balance, about $21,-000,000, was appropriated by Congress.[10]

State old-age aid before 1935

Before 1935 all legislation designed to furnish aid to those other than public employees was confined to the indigent

---

[10] *Monthly Labor Review,* 1935, Vol. 40. pp. 901 f.

of the state in which the legislation applied. Many aged indigent persons were placed in public almshouses. This type of aid is of long standing but has never been favored by students of the problem because it meant the breaking up of homes, in many instances the separation of husband and wife, and at best the almshouse was not an attractive place.

Public legislation began with the Arizona law of 1914, which was declared void by the state supreme court two years later. In 1923 Montana, Nevada, and Pennsylvania adopted old-age pension laws. Wisconsin enacted a law in 1925, and by June, 1934, at least twenty-eight states had passed such laws. Most of these state laws set age of eligibility at sixty-five or seventy years. Many states limited the maximum pension to a dollar a day; others placed the benefit on a monthly basis varying from twenty to forty-five dollars. Most states provided a funeral benefit. Residence requirements, which were always stated, varied from five years in Delaware to thirty-five years in Arizona. Usually fifteen years' residence was demanded, as well as United States citizenship. Property stipulations were fairly uniform, generally allowing a pension only for those owning property worth less than $3,000. Pensions were graduated according to need, those possessing other income of one dollar a day or more being ineligible. Most states placed the larger share of the burden of furnishing funds upon the local community, although at least nine states contributed to the fund. Delaware and six other states paid all costs. Arrangements for administration varied widely. Twenty-three of the state laws were statewide and mandatory upon counties; others permitted, rather than required, the establishment of pension systems. In 1933 about 340 counties in eighteen states reported over 115,000 needy aged as receiving pensions. The total assistance granted was approximately $26,000,000, an average monthly pension of $18.75 per recipient.[11]

In August, 1935, the federal Social Security Act was passed, and in anticipation of the passage of the law or subsequent to it a number of additional states adopted old-age pension legislation, so that by 1937 practically all the states, two territories, and the District of Columbia had such laws.

Old-age assistance under federal-state laws

The federal law is broad in its coverage, including old-age assistance for the needy, old-age annuities to be built up by employer and employee contributions, an employment-insurance tax, grants-in-aid of the blind and of dependent and crippled children, and grants to promote maternal and child welfare and public health. Under the first of these the federal government will grant up to fifteen dollars a month to the state for each aged recipient of assistance, providing the state law and its administration conform with certain specifications.

Thus the state law must be mandatory throughout the entire state and not optional with the counties. The state must provide some of the funds and must either administer the law or provide for a central state supervisory agency to coördinate the policies of the counties. The methods of administration must be satisfactory to the Social Security Board at Washington, which administers the federal law,

---

[11] *Monthly Labor Review*, August, 1934, p. 257. See also the issue for August, 1935, p. 331.

and the state must make such annual and other reports to this Board as may be required. The state law must provide an adequate hearing for those whose application for assistance is rejected.

The federal Social Security Board is given wide discretion in approving state plans, but may not approve any plan in which the age requirement is placed beyond sixty-five years, except that until 1940 the requirement may be seventy years; likewise the Board may not approve any state requirement as to citizenship that excludes any United States citizen, nor any residence requirement that excludes any resident of the state who has resided therein during five of the nine years immediately preceding the application for old-age assistance and has resided therein continuously for one year immediately preceding the application.

In September, 1936, the average assistance per recipient was $18.67 in thirty-seven states and the District of Columbia, ranging from a low of $3.58 in Mississippi to a high of $31.50 in California. About 863,000 persons received aid. The average number of recipients per 1000 estimated population sixty-five years of age and over was 129, ranging from a low of nine for Kentucky to a high of 345 for Colorado. In eight states more than 20 per cent of the aged people over sixty-five received this form of aid. These figures do not measure the extent of the indigent aged, because many of them were receiving direct relief rather than old-age assistance, and others were supported by children or private charity.

Compulsory retirement pensions

Most European countries, which have advanced much further in social-security legislation than the United States, have made provision for the aged poor and also for the general working population through compulsory old-age pensions. Most of these are on a contributory basis under which the employer, the employee, and the state contribute premiums toward the building up of an adequate fund for retirement. No American state has adopted such a plan (except for its own public employees, as was noted above), but in 1935 the federal social security program included a provision under which funds are to be built up which will enable some twenty-six million workers to look forward to some provision for their old age.

State governments play no part in the administration of the compulsory scheme. Retirement benefits are to be paid by the federal government, beginning in 1942, to persons over age sixty-five, providing contributions have been paid for at least five years. These benefits are payable as a matter of right, and should be distinguished from the pensions payable by the states to aged persons on the basis of need.

An excise tax, in addition to other taxes, is imposed upon the employer. The tax is based upon the total payroll [12] paid after December 31, 1936, for services performed within the United States, Alaska, and Hawaii.

Employers of one or more persons are subject to the tax. The rate is as follows: 1937 to 1939, 1 per cent; 1940 to 1942, 1.5 per cent; 1943 to 1945, 2 per cent; 1946 to 1948, 2.5 per cent; and thereafter, 3 per cent. The taxes are to be collected by the Bureau of Internal Revenue and paid into the United States Treasury as internal revenue collec-

---

[12] With certain exceptions and exclusive of wages payable to any individual employee in excess of $3,000 in any calendar year.

tions. The collection and payment of the taxes is to be in the manner and at the times prescribed by the Commissioner of internal revenue with the approval of the Secretary of the Treasury.

In addition to other taxes, an income tax is imposed upon the employee, which is measured by the employee's wages received by him after December 31, 1936.[13] The tax is to be collected by the employer, who becomes liable therefor, by deduction from the employee's wage at the time the wages are paid. The schedule of rates is the same as that for the employer.

Contributions are not required for or from agricultural laborers, domestic servants, casual laborers not employed in the course of the employer's business, persons over sixty-five, officers or crew on vessels documented under the laws of the United States or foreign countries, federal, state, and local government employees, or employees of certain non-profit organizations. For these several classes no provision is made.

To qualify for the retirement benefits, which will begin in January, 1942, the following conditions must be met:

1. The applicant must be at least sixty-five years of age. (Benefits are reduced for an individual over sixty-five who is employed.)

2. He must have received not less than $2,000 total wages after December 31, 1936, and before reaching sixty-five.

3. Wages must have been paid to him on some day in each of five years after December 31, 1936, and before age sixty-five.

---

[13] Not counting wages in excess of $3,000 in any calendar year.

The amount of monthly retirement benefits is determined as follows:

Total wages received [14]	Percentage of total wages paid as monthly benefit [15]
First $3,000	1/2
Next $42,000	1/12
All over $45,000...................	1/24

The following table illustrates the amount of retirement benefits payable under the law:

SAMPLE OF OLD-AGE BENEFITS

Average annual earnings	Monthly payments to qualified workers who become 65 years of age					
	In 1942	After 10 years of employment	After 20 years of employment	After 30 years of employment	After 40 years of employment	After 43 years of employment
$ 400	$10.00	$15.83	$19.17	$22.50	$25.83	$26.83
600	15.00	17.50	22.50	27.50	32.50	34.00
1,200	17.50	22.50	32.50	42.50	51.25	52.75
1,800	20.00	27.50	42.50	53.75	61.25	63.50
2,400	22.50	32.50	51.25	61.25	71.25	74.25
3,000	25.00	37.50	56.25	68.75	81.25	85.00
Over $3,000	25.00	37.50	56.25	68.75	81.25	85.00

For instance, a person on a salary of $150 a month who had been employed for ten years during the required period would receive retirement benefits of $27.50 a month. If he had been employed for thirty years he would receive $53.75 a month. The lowest amount that would be received

[14] After December 31, 1936, and prior to age 65 in covered employment. Not counting wages in excess of $3,000 for any calendar year.
[15] Minimum monthly benefit, $10; maximum, $85.

in benefits would be the $10.00 a month pension paid to a person getting a salary of $400 a year and employed for five years. The largest possible payment would be $85 a month, to a person employed for forty-three years at a salary of $250 a month. Thus to get the maximum pension of $85 monthly a person would have to earn $129,000 in his lifetime. Obviously few workers will qualify for the maximum.

If a person dies before reaching age sixty-five, his estate is entitled to receive an amount equal to 3.5 per cent of the total wages paid to him after December 31, 1936.[16] If he dies after reaching sixty-five and before the benefits paid to him equal 3.5 per cent of the total wages earned by him after December 31, 1936,[17] and before he reaches sixty-five, his estate will receive a sum equal to the amount by which such 3.5 per cent exceeds the amount paid to him during his life as retirement benefits.

An old-age reserve account is to be established in the Treasury of the United States and an annual appropriation to the account, beginning with the fiscal year ending June 30, 1937, is authorized. The appropriation will be an amount sufficient to provide for the retirement benefit payments.[18]

The Secretary of the Treasury is required to invest the portion of the reserve account that is not necessary to meet the current withdrawals for benefit payments. Such investments may be made in interest-bearing obligations of the United States or in obligations guaranteed as to principal

---

[16] Not counting wages in excess of $3,000 for any calendar year.

[17] Not counting wages in excess of $3,000 for any calendar year.

[18] Determined upon a reserve basis in accordance with accepted actuarial principles, and upon the basis of an interest rate of 3 per cent per annum compounded annually.

and interest by the United States. Investments may be acquired on original issue, or by purchase of outstanding obligations, at terms not to yield less than 3 per cent, or special 3 per cent obligations may be issued exclusively for this purpose.

With the passage of time the persons now receiving old-age assistance will die, and this feature of the social security program for the indigent may become less important. For a number of reasons, however, it will never be wholly replaced by the compulsory features of the plan. First, the compulsory plan does not cover all employees. Second, a number of persons in the professional and other self-employed industries, such as shopkeepers and farmers, will not be able to qualify under the act as "employees" and will not be protected. Third, there are always some people who are unemployable. In all, about twenty-three million of those who are normally gainfully employed will not come under the compulsory retirement act. In Germany, where compulsory old-age pensions have been in effect for fifty years, shopkeepers, independent professional classes, and small peasants were omitted from this protection, and it is probably no accident that these classes furnish the main membership of the Hitler movement.

Fourth, it must be remembered that the system of com-pulsory insurance only indirectly protects wives who are not gainfully employed. Should they survive their hus-bands, the lump-sum payments given to them will in many cases fail to care for them adequately, and they will demand old-age assistance in addition. Pensions will be needed also where the annuitant does not receive enough to provide for his aged wife, mother, or dependent children. Some of such families might be supported by the annuities system and a part of the old-age assistance.[19]

Constitutionality

Under our federal system of government the protection and welfare of the citizens is to a large extent left to the state. The federal government may legislate only on such matters as are assigned to it in the Constitution. The NRA and the AAA were both declared unconstitutional because Congress had exceeded its powers. Similarly, there is some doubt among constitutional lawyers about the constitutionality of the old-age assistance and annuity system. This legislation is based on the congressional power to levy taxes and appropriate money. In the AAA decision the Supreme Court disallowed the act because the processing taxes imposed by Congress were used to promote a system of crop control, which was beyond its power. Congress has, however, made repeated grants-in-aid of highways, education, and other matters, none of which have been attacked successfully even when the state governments have been used in part in the administration of the funds, and the states have been required to match the federal funds in order to secure grants. This leads many people to suppose that the old-age assistance features of the security program, resting on the appropriating power, will be upheld.[20]

The old-age annuity system, unlike the assistance plan, rests on the taxing power, and therefore the court will have

[19] Railroad employees are covered by a separate law passed in 1935. Employers and employees each pay 3.5 per cent of the payrolls, and a maximum pension of $120 a month is provided.

[20] The cases bearing most closely on this question are: Massachusetts v. Mellon, 262 U. S. 447, and Frothingham v. Mellon, 262 U. S. 447.

to pass on the constitutionality of both the taxes (taxing power) as levied and the payment (appropriating power) of the funds to legal recipients. This would seem to make the annuity system somewhat less secure than the assistance system.

The launching of this dual program marks the first real beginning of a comprehensive system of provisions for old age in the United States. If it stands the test of constitutionality, it will mean that one important phase of social insecurity under American capitalism will be materially alleviated. That the plan is in final form no one believes. Sweden has amended its old-age system every year, with one or two exceptions, since its adoption in 1914. Many criticisms have already been directed against the congressional acts by friendly critics and many more unforeseen difficulties will arise. Also, once a country launches upon such a program, pressure is always brought to liberalize the benefits, to make the government bear an ever-larger share of the burden, and to broaden the basis for eligibility.

UNEMPLOYMENT

Unemployment has been defined as idleness on the part of the worker not due to his physical, mental, or moral incapacity. A man may fail to work because of illness, accident, old age, or incompetence. He is then "unemployable" and not to be regarded as unemployed. Long privation, low income, and poor nutrition may allow serious inroads of disease and moral degeneracy to occur which lead to an unemployable condition. The unemployed, on the other hand, are potential economic producers.

Types of unemployment

If, in a given city, a thousand men are unemployed, it will be found that the reasons therefor are not identical in all cases. Some will be unemployed because they work in *casual* occupations. Many adults have never learned a trade or profession. They secure jobs intermittently where and when they can. Apparently industry requires this kind of a floating labor supply. It must be available for a sudden demand.

A second type of unemployment is *seasonal*. The ice industry is active in summer, the fuel industry in winter. In some instances this seasonality is due to a *seasonal demand,* as in the case of fuel and woolen fabrics, and in other cases it is due to a *seasonality in supply,* for example, fruit picking or fishing.

The third type of enforced idleness is *cyclical unemployment* and is due to the fluctuations in prosperity and depression. A fourth type is *structural.* This refers to cases where labor-saving machinery is taking the place of direct labor, or where a shift in demand, as from phonographs and pianos to radios, causes a readjustment. Another example is destruction of business through tariff readjustment.

The extent of unemployment

In April, 1930, with a total population of 122,700,000 in the United States, of which 48,000,000 were gainful workers, there were 2,429,000 persons able to work and looking for a job. In addition there were 758,000 persons who had jobs but were laid off without pay, not including those who were sick or voluntarily idle. At that time the greatest business depression in the history of capitalism had barely begun.

In the course of the following months the depression became much more severe, and each month added to the

extent of unemployment. This is revealed by the increase
of unemployment as shown in the following tabulation.[21]

1930	4,775,000
1931	7,775,000
1932	11,491,000
1933	11,815,000
1934	9,967,000
1935	8,979,000
1936	9,796,000

Relieving unemployment

If human illnesses are due to different causes and germs,
different remedies must be applied. It has been pointed
out that there are various types of unemployment. Obviously a single remedy will not bring a universal cure.

A certain amount of casual unemployment is, perhaps,
necessary. In the very nature of things occasional temporary demands for labor will occur. Every city has within
its bounds a floating supply of such labor. Probably unemployment among these kinds of laborers cannot be eliminated, but it can be mitigated to a considerable extent by
the creation of employment exchanges.

These exchanges are usually located in the central part
of the city where surplus labor gathers. Here the unemployed man may file his name and address, and here the
prospective employer may come if he wants help. Also,
the exchanges should effect clearings with exchanges in
neighboring cities so that any scarcity of labor in one city
can be met with a surplus from elsewhere.

Exchanges are of two kinds, private and public. The
former charge the laborers a filing fee as a rule, and a second
fee when a job is made available. During periods of great

[21] National Industrial Conference Board.

unemployment, when jobs are hard to find, they raise their fees, working a double hardship on the unemployed. Public exchanges are supported by the government and find jobs, when possible, for the unemployed free of charge. The functions of such employment offices include the following:

1. Discovery of demands for workers in various industries and localities, throughout the nation.

2. Analysis of these demands to determine types of workers being sought.

3. Registration of those who may be out of work and seeking employment.

4. Classifications of such persons according to natural abilities, training, experience, occupational preference, and other significant characteristics.

5. Compilation and publication of timely data as to demands for and supplies of various types of labor.

6. Provision of facilities for vocational guidance, to be available to all workers, particularly those entering industry for the first time.

7. Possibly, provision of transportation facilities for bringing workers into contact with opportunities for employment.

The proposal contemplates *free, public* employment exchanges to perform these functions. Its advocates explain that these characteristics are essential. Their reasons for this belief may be summarized as follows:

1. It is to the interest of society to have workers employed. Without employment, workers and their families are likely to be dependent and costly to society. Even if they are not dependent upon public funds for support, they represent a loss in that they are not producing.

2. It is clear, moreover, that in an economic organization as complex as that of modern life, and in a society with

such vast occupational and geographic expanses, workers cannot be expected to be aware of the most advantageous and socially productive uses for their services. Society, therefore, has an obligation to render all possible assistance to willing workers in their search for jobs.

3. The unemployed worker is frequently, if not generally, unable to pay for adequate employment service, yet it is socially uneconomical to permit the use of anything but the best of such services.

4. These services must be public, or they cannot be free. Simply stated, it is the feeling of most careful students that when workers in modern society are ready and willing to work, they should be assisted in every possible manner to find the most profitable employment, that to do anything less is to exhibit a shortsighted viewpoint as far as social interests are concerned.[22]

Seasonal unemployment

The second type of unemployment, seasonal, can also be mitigated to a considerable extent through more extensive development of employment exchanges. However, something more than this must be done. Several coal companies announce discounts to consumers who buy their winter's supply of coal in summer. This helps to keep the miners and coal deliverers busy a great part of the year. In many cities the ice and coal businesses are combined by one firm, using the same set of workers for both businesses. Many seasonal industries, such as manufacture of millinery goods, have developed supplementary lines to aid in smoothing out the employment curve.[23]

---

[22] Yoder, Dale, *Labor Economics and Labor Problems,* pp. 177 f. (McGraw-Hill Book Company, New York, 1933).

[23] For many suggestions along this line see Commons, J. R., *et al., Can Business Prevent Unemployment?* (Alfred A. Knopf, New York, 1925).

Cyclical unemployment

Cyclical unemployment is, perhaps, the most baffling. Several remedies may be suggested: planning public works, credit control, and employment insurance.

Planned public works. Annually every town, city, county, and state government, besides the federal government, spends thousands and perhaps millions of dollars in building roads, schools, city halls, harbors, and other improvements. The total expended amounts to several billions of dollars. It has been suggested that if each political unit mentioned above were to save just 5 per cent of such expenditures during prosperous years and utilize the funds during depression years to set the unemployed men to work, the employment curve could be smoothed out considerably. During depression years, governments, like private businesses, actually limit expenditures, thus increasing unemployment instead of decreasing it, and during prosperity they contribute to unhealthy booms.

Under a scheme of planned public works the funds saved during prosperous years could be loaned out at interest and thus gain additional income. Also, during depression years costs are always lower because of falling prices; hence governments could build schools and roads much more cheaply than during prosperity.

A number of states and the federal government have passed laws requiring all departments and bureaus within the state to plan for several years in advance their entire building program. Schools, highways, city halls, police and fire stations, and so on, instead of being built haphazardly when some politicians make a campaign and secure the funds, would be built according to a coördinated advance plan. Under ideal circumstances tax rates will be raised

somewhat in prosperous times; then, when private industry tends to stagnate, public construction will take up the
slack. This is the ideal of planned public works.

There are difficulties in this program, however. Politicians are elected to public office after making numerous
promises of new bridges, schools, and highways. It is difficult for them to restrain themselves after the election is
over and say, "We will reserve the building program until
the next depression." Rather, they feel the need of "coming
through" with their promises.

The second practical difficulty concerns the timing of
public works. It is simple as we look back to say that the
depression began in 1929. But who in 1929 or in 1930 was
in a position to know that those years were the time to
initiate a vast public works program? In the summer of
1927 the American Federation of Labor called a special conference to discuss the problem of growing unemployment.
If there had been a vast public works fund at that time, it
seems certain that the politicians would have been urged
to release the funds for building, and then two years later
when the real depression began the funds might have been
exhausted and the effectiveness of a scheme of planned public works to meet the depression of 1929–1936 would have
been nullified. Thus the timing of a public works program
is an unsolved problem.

Perhaps the most serious question involved in this program is the problem of transferring purchasing power from
a period of prosperity to a period of depression. If public
works are to be undertaken in a depression, the funds must
be made available. Those who favor planning public works
in this way urge the building up of reserves by taxation
during prosperity. This means governments will have to
raise more money in taxes than they spend during pros-

perity. This is a difficult undertaking, but if it should prove possible the government would have to invest the funds in government bonds; that is, the investment board in charge of these funds would have to buy bonds. Then when the depression occurs the bonds would have to be sold in order that governments now ready to embark on a public works program would have the funds. The sale of these government bonds in the depression is in itself deflationary, and tends to stagnate private businesses which are still functioning. This is so because the people who now will buy the government bonds are handing over funds which they might have spent on commodities. This raises the problem of transferring purchasing power from a period of prosperity to a depression. So far economists have not been able to convince themselves that it is possible to accomplish this without setting up a train of consequences which are as evil as the problem which a planned public works program is designed to solve. The best solution of the problem is to use the tax funds to pay off government debts; then when depression comes the government can borrow under an improved credit status in order to carry out public works.[24]

Credit control. Scarcely any businessman can avoid borrowing at banks from time to time. High interest rates for such loans discourage borrowing and low interest rates encourage it. Under our banking system the bulk of the banks are affiliated with one of the twelve Federal Reserve banks. This affiliation has been established in order that there might be nationwide control of credit and currency. The twelve Federal Reserve banks are bankers' banks, and

---

[24] For a good discussion of this aspect of the problem see Stevenson, R. A., *et al.*, *A Program for Unemployment Insurance and Relief*, University of Minnesota Press; Gayer, Arthur D., *Public Works in Prosperity and Depression*, National Bureau of Economic Research.

no private individual can have a checking or savings account with them. Rather, the member banks may borrow credit or currency from the federal banks in case the customers of the member banks call for more credit or currency than they can supply. Federal Reserve banks make a charge for furnishing member banks with such accommodations. Through centralized action at Washington, D. C., the Federal Reserve banks may raise or lower the price of such loans and currency to the member banks. In this way, many economists believe, central banks may encourage or discourage borrowings.

Thus local banks and Federal Reserve banks may, by united action, encourage expansion of business or discourage excessive prosperity. Since excessive prosperity may lead to inevitable decline, power to restrict flow of credit may be as important as power to stimulate use of credit. Also, Federal Reserve banks may buy and sell government bonds, that is, engage in open market operations. If the bank buys a bond from a private citizen the latter gets the money and may spend it for commodities, thus encouraging employment and business; when the bank sells a bond the citizen gives up money that he might have spent for commodities. Hence selling bonds is designed to discourage excessive business activity just as high interest rates may discourage too great business expansion. Should Federal Reserve banks buy as much as $50,000,000 of government bonds weekly, as they have done at times, an enormous amount of currency or credit will find its way into the hands of the public. In short, low borrowing rates and purchase of bonds by Federal Reserve banks tend to expand business when business threatens to stagnate; and high interest rates and sale of government bonds tend to slow up business when the optimism of business threatens a dangerous boom. Through intelligent operations banks control the business structure. That, in short, is the theory of eliminating cyclical unemployment through bank control. Many economists are inclined to think this device of control contains the seeds of a real solution of the problem; others point out that no country has ever yet been able to eliminate cycles through this technique, and they doubt its ability to control business. The suggestion has been made that we have not yet learned how to use these tools of stabilization, and only experience can teach us the precise way in which the economic system is balanced and how to keep it in balance.

Employment insurance. The basic idea underlying employment insurance is that in prosperous times employers and employees should lay aside weekly premiums in order that a fund may be built up for a period of depression. In many respects it is similar in principle to accident or life insurance. Life insurance companies sell policies and charge premiums based on life expectancy. In case of death the beneficiary secures the face value of the policy. Life insurance companies, under efficient management, can meet all claims as they accrue because the number of deaths occurring within a year can be calculated with a high degree of accuracy. Unfortunately, the risk of unemployment is not subject to such accurate forecast. Hence some critics of employment insurance have insisted that we should speak of employment *reserves* rather than insurance. We know from European experience that this criticism has much truth in it. There employment insurance laws have been in force for many decades, and in every country the insurance fund has become insolvent. Governments have had to meet the deficit, and the funds have been thrown into politics.

Before 1932 no state in the United States had adopted any scheme of employment insurance. However, a number of trade unions had made partial provision for their members. In 1931 possibly 45,000 workers were covered by such union plans. The Deutsch-Amerikanische Typographia, an organization of German text printers, was the first trade union in the United States to pay unemployment benefits on a national scale. The benefits are six dollars a week or a maximum of ninety-six dollars a year.[25] This plan has been in operation since 1908. The international Association of Siderographers and the Diamond Workers Protective Union of America also have adopted employment insurance schemes, although the latter group discontinued the plan in 1932.

In addition to the foregoing international unions a number of local unions including the bookbinders of San Francisco and Chicago, the electrotypers of Chicago, New York, and Philadelphia, and others have adopted plans. Typically these plans are very modest in their aims, and while they mitigate the evils of unemployment somewhat, and postpone resort to public relief to some extent, they do not really meet the problem. In a few cases the local union has during the depression of 1929–1936 met the entire unemployment problem of its members. Perhaps the best example of this type is the Chicago local of the Amalgamated Association of Street and Electric Railway and Motor Coach Employees of America. This union claims that not one of its members resorted to any public relief throughout the entire period of the depression, although a goodly number of the members were laid off from time to time. Most of the union plans are not on an actuarial basis.

A number of employers in the United States have also adopted comprehensive schemes of employment insurance.

Those employers who produce commodities the demand for which is stable in depression and prosperity [26] find it easier to maintain an employment reserve fund in a solvent condition. A goodly number of the funds have not proven entirely sound, and have to be modified or discontinued. Up to 1934 some twenty-three company plans had been established, of which some covered more than one plant. In that year only sixteen were still in operation.

In some instances the employer's trade agreement with the union makes some provision for unemployment aid. Up to 1934 some twenty-six joint agreements had been concluded between employers and members of trade unions which provided for the payment of unemployment benefits or guaranteed a certain minimum of employment. The fact that of these plans only five were in existence in 1934 seems to demonstrate that this is not a satisfactory solution.

State employment insurance plans. In 1932 the State of Wisconsin launched an employment insurance plan. Owing to the severity of the depression, the legislature was induced to postpone the effective date of its beginning, and not until 1934 were premiums collected. At the beginning of 1937 a third of the states had adopted such plans, and other states are seriously considering similar action.

Special impetus was given to state action by the passage of President Roosevelt's social security program in 1935. One phase of this plan imposes a federal payroll tax on all employers with eight or more employees, with certain exceptions. This tax began in January, 1936, at the rate of one per cent of the payroll; in 1937 the rate will be 2 per cent, and thereafter it will be 3 per cent. Every employer who is subject to a *state* employment insurance tax will be given

---

[26] It must be remembered that unemployment is the most severe in the capital-goods-producing industries such as building, machinery, etc.

a credit of 90 per cent of the federal tax. The federal law was drawn in these terms in order to encourage each state to adopt an employment insurance law of its own. If a state refuses to adopt such a plan the employers within its boundaries will have to pay the federal tax and yet will receive no direct benefit from the taxes collected. The basic reason for this rather cumbersome procedure was the tardiness with which the states tackled the problem and the fear that a complete federal plan of employment insurance would be declared unconstitutional, for Congress probably has no authority to embark on this type of social legislation. Rather, such laws must be passed by the states since the promotion of the general welfare of citizens belongs to the states. There is some doubt also about the constitutionality of the federal tax law, and since the state laws are based on federal legislation, the future of employment insurance is uncertain. The issue involves the federal power to levy taxes. Since the federal law has as its basic purpose the stimulation of state action and not the raising of money, the court may say that Congress has exceeded its authority in passing the law imposing taxes on employers. The AAA was declared unconstitutional in 1936 partially for this reason.

Whether or not the federal part of the program is upheld, it seems certain that many states will desire to continue their present laws; other states will adopt legislation independently, and everywhere this method of meeting the problem of unemployment will be given wide consideration.

In a program of insurance a number of important problems press for solution. Who shall be covered? What age groups? What industries shall be excluded, and who shall pay the premiums? These and other questions call for discussion.

There are two basically divergent ideas about the function of a plan of employment insurance: (1) it is a method of relief, or (2) it is a method of preventing unemployment. Those who take the latter view, as evidenced in the Wisconsin law, hold that unemployment can be prevented if businessmen are given a sufficiently powerful incentive to induce them to offer continuous employment. Under workmen's compensation the employer or the business is held responsible for all accidents regardless of who is at fault. The only question asked is: Did the accident arise out of and in the course of employment? If the answer is affirmative, the worker secures compensation. As pointed out earlier in this chapter, the theory behind this "liability without fault" was that if the employer was made responsible for *all* accidents he would see to it that accidents were reduced. Similarly the entire burden of unemployment at a given plant should be placed on that plant or employer. The employer will then make every effort to secure steady employment for all his workers; under this plan all premiums to build up the insurance fund will be paid by the employer, and a separate account will be kept for each plant. As a reward for stable employment when the given employer's fund reaches a certain size which is regarded as safe, his premiums will be reduced or eliminated entirely. Thus under the original Wisconsin law, whenever an employer has built up a reserve fund equal to seventy-five dollars per employee, premium collections cease. When the employer has a reserve fund of fifty-five dollars per employee, the rate is reduced from 2 per cent to 1 per cent. Thus the employer is supposed to be given a considerable stimulus to keep his reserve funds intact by steady employment. The employer who fails to give his employees continued employment will encounter continuous drains on the fund, and will have to keep on paying at the 2 per cent rate. Thus it is believed that by the adoption of a scheme of individual plant reserves where every employer is induced to keep his eye on the level of his own reserve, maximum effort will be made to reduce unemployment. The beneficial effects will spread through the entire economic system.

The critics of this system hold that unemployment is beyond the control of the individual plant, and however much inducement an employer may feel to stabilize his employment, he will be able to do little in the way of controlling his own employment conditions. This is so because the forces making for unstable employment are nationwide, indeed worldwide. Break in the stock market, collapse of a house of international bankers, overproduction of an internationally traded commodity—all are disturbing forces which may precipitate a business depression, and an individual employer can do little to mitigate them. Also the most severe unemployment has usually followed prolonged wars, and over these the individual employer has no control. Those who take this view hold that the solution lies in a pooling of reserves; that is, all employment insurance premiums should be paid into a common fund. Indeed, these critics say that the very idea of *insurance* requires the pooling of funds.

Between the plant-reserve and the pooled-reserve methods is the system of merit rating. Several states have adopted the last-mentioned system, under which every employer covered by the act continues to pay into the fund, but at a reduced rate providing his employment experience indicates that he is responsible for only a limited amount of unemployment. This gives him a motive for stabilizing his employment record. This system is likely to give the workers less security than the pooled fund but somewhat more than the plant reserve.

This leads directly to the question of who should pay the premiums. Employer, employee, and state are possible sources of income for the fund. Logically, those who favor the plant reserve account method must take the view that the employer alone should contribute in order to give him the maximum motive to stabilize. Since this view rests on only partially tenable ground the argument for contributions from employers alone also is weakened. There are a number of good reasons why employees should contribute premiums likewise. Only in this way can adequate funds be built up; the employers will oppose the law if asked to contribute the whole premium. Employee contributions will help to give the worker an interest in the administration of the fund; he may more readily report false claims for unemployment benefits or inefficiency in administration. Economists are agreed that the real burden of the premiums, whether paid by the employer or the employee, will, nevertheless, rest on the worker *in the long run.* The premiums, if collected from the employer, will constitute extra costs of doing business, and he will try to pass them along to the consumer in higher prices. If this encounters resistance through decreased sales, unemployment may occur, which will be the signal for wage reductions, and so in the end the worker will bear the burden of the premiums. If the worker bears the burden anyway, why not place at least part of the cost of the premiums on him in the first instance and so let him get credit for paying?

In the United States there is a pronounced view against the state contributing to the fund. There are two reasons for this opposition: in Europe where the state usually contributes there is a constant tendency for the fund to get into politics; sometimes employer and employee unite in an attempt to impose on the state an ever larger burden. The state should not contribute, because to do so would force numerous taxpayers who receive no direct benefit from the fund to help to build it up. For example, farmers or farm laborers are seldom covered by the laws; yet if the state contributes to the funds, then farmers, being taxpayers, would have to help build up the fund.

This raises the question of who should be covered by the law. Typically small employers with five or fewer employees are not covered. Agricultural and domestic labor is not covered; and usually employees of government, charitable and religious organizations, and so on are excluded.

Small employers may be excluded for two reasons. First, employment among them is much more stable than among large employers as a rule, and second, the cost of administration would be raised unduly if all small employers were covered. These facts are supported by the findings of the University of Minnesota Employment Stabilization Research Institute, that in Minnesota about 53 per cent of the employers had in their employ only 6 per cent of the workers in the state, and that the small employer, where personal relations are close, tends to retain workers longer than is the case in the larger concerns. In the 1920–1921 depression, small concerns showed much more stable employment conditions than did large concerns, as evidenced by the accompanying tabulation.

Size of firm	Decline in hours
1–21 employees	3%
22–100 employees	14%
over 100 employees	28%

Agricultural and domestic laborers are typically excluded because of the difficulties of administration. It would be onerous to collect monthly premiums from thousands of small farmers and domestic households. These are widely scattered, and in case of refusal to pay the premiums, a multiplicity of suits would soon exhaust the time and energy of the administrative authority. Furthermore, in agricultural labor the problem of unemployment is not very serious.

Another group of questions concerns premium rate and benefit rates. Low premiums and high benefits are incompatible. Most students agree that benefits should not exceed 50 per cent of the usual wage, or ten or fifteen dollars a week. If the benefit is unduly high it may encourage malingering; if it is too low the state may be forced to supplement the benefit through ordinary poor relief. Since cost of living and normal wage rates vary widely from state to state, and even within a state, it is not possible to determine precisely the correct benefit rate. It is better to make the benefit a percentage of weekly wage rather than to specify an absolute amount.

One way to secure relatively low premium rates and fairly high benefit rates is by requiring a long waiting period before an unemployed person may secure benefits. To suggest a long waiting period may at first seem cruel, but it is in the collective interest of the workers. Several studies indicate that if the Wisconsin law had been in operation from 1929 to 1932 with its two-weeks' waiting period, the funds would have been exhausted by perhaps 1931, and thus during the major part of the depression the fund would have been insolvent. Obviously this is undesirable. With a waiting period of one or two weeks it is conceivable that seasonal unemployment alone might exhaust the funds, leaving nothing for periods of prolonged cyclical unemployment.

Hence, many students recommend a waiting period of from four to eight weeks, and perhaps sixteen weeks for seasonal workers. This may cause some hardship for a few workers; but with the relatively high American standard of living most workers should be able to save something for a rainy day and also have sufficiently good credit at the stores to tide them over. If such a long waiting period is imposed it means that a very large number of cases of unemployment running from a few days to several weeks will not exhaust the fund; the money will remain in the fund for those who are unemployed for longer periods; it is they who are in more need of aid. Also if the number of cases of unemployed who must be reimbursed is reduced, this will decrease the cost of administration of the fund. If the rate of benefit is reduced or the premium rates are increased, a somewhat shortened waiting period may obtain. But obviously low premiums, high benefits, and short waiting periods are mutually incompatible.

Most states have found it necessary to include one further feature to insure the solvency of the fund, to wit, a rule with respect to ratio of number of weekly benefits a man may receive to number of contributions he has made. Clearly if an unemployed worker could draw benefits indefinitely while jobless, a few chronically unemployed workers might get the entire benefit from the fund while the balance of the workers build up the fund, and then when they are unemployed the fund would be relatively exhausted. Hence many states have adopted the "one-in-four" rule. Under this rule an unemployed worker, after the duly designated waiting period has elapsed, may draw one week's benefit for every four weeks of contributions made by him or in his behalf. Thus if a worker has been employed in an insured industry for one year he would be entitled to thirteen weeks of benefits. After two years of employment he would be entitled to twenty-six weeks of benefits, and so on. This rule seems essential to insure solvency of the fund.

Who pays for the social security program?

American industry is confronted with new taxes under the 1935 Social Security legislation, including federal grants, of about $300,000,000 in 1936, reaching $2,000,000,000 in 1940 and $3,000,000,000 in 1949.[27] Although the law divides the burden clearly between employers and workers, as shown in the accompanying table, it is well known by businessmen and economists that the real burden of many taxes does not rest upon him who makes the actual payment to

FEDERAL SOCIAL SECURITY TAXES [28]

| Year | Old-age retirement | | Employment insurance |
	Employer's contribution	Worker's contribution	Employer's contribution *
1936	0%	0%	1%
1937	1	1	2
1938	1	1	3
1939	1	1	3
1940 1942	1.5	1.5	3
1943–1945	2	2	3
1946–1948	2.5	2.5	3
After 1948	3	3	3

* The state may require employee contributions, and several have done so.

[27] Based on estimates, *Social Security Bill*, 74th Congress, 1st Session, Report No. 628. Winthrop W. Aldrich estimates the cost at 4 billion dollars by the 1950's.

[28] Old-age assistance, aid to the blind, etc., will be financed by general taxation.

the government. For example, a state may place a tax of three cents a gallon on wholesalers of gasoline. The latter pass the tax on to retailers, and the burden finally rests on motorists. Similarly, taxes on liquors are passed on to ultimate consumers. However, contrary to popular belief, the ultimate consumer does not pay all taxes. In the case of the pork-processing taxes under the AAA the intention was to make consumers pay into the hands of farmers, but instead the taxes reacted on the price of hogs, forcing them downward or keeping them lower than they otherwise would have been. Likewise, a tax on net income of competitive industry does not bear on the consumer but on the more efficient or fortunate producer, since the price of the product tends to be high enough to cover the costs of the marginal producer.

With regard to that part of the social security tax which is placed by government directly on workers, there is virtually unanimous agreement that the real final burden rests also on the worker. True, if the proceeds from the tax were not returned to these workers in the form of benefits, and the tax were very heavy, it is possible that such a tax might lower the standard of living of labor, and after a considerable period reduce the supply of labor; this reduced supply of labor would cause wages to rise, and the real burden might actually be shifted to other factors of production. But this is not likely to be the case under the United States social security program because (1) the tax rate on labor is low, and (2) the proceeds of the taxes are returned to labor. If labor resented this tax and could migrate to industries where it is not taxed, the burden would tend to shift to capital or the consumer. But labor does not necessarily resent this tax, since it represents a form of saving; and it would be difficult for labor to find occupations free from the tax. Consequently the chief controversy turns on the incidence of the taxes levied on the employers, to which attention is now turned.

Four different viewpoints are held as to the incidence of the real burden of taxes on employers: (1) the businessman pays the taxes out of profits; employers, conscious of the first impact of forced contributions, cry out against their imposition; (2) the tax is passed on to the ultimate consumer in higher prices; (3) the tax burden rests finally on the worker in the form of wage reductions or postponements of wage increases; (4) the burden is diffused among producers, consumers, and laborers in such diverse ways under the many different situations actually found in industry that no general law can be discovered.

Under conditions as they actually exist, any one of these results may occur in specific instances (discussed below), but the unanimous view of economists is that in general the third viewpoint is correct, namely, that the burden of payroll taxes, even though levied on the employer, is ultimately borne by workers. Let us assume that there is relatively little unemployment and all plants are in full operation, and a payroll tax of 3 per cent is levied on the employer, whose chief cost of doing business is wages. This will raise his wage bill by 3 per cent and he will endeavor at first, perhaps, to raise the price of his product by the same amount in order to recoup his losses. At once, with a higher price, his sales will tend to fall off. (We assume that no other factor enters into the situation.) In order to prevent further losses he lays off some workers whose services were necessary and profitable before but who can now be dispensed with under the restricted sales. The extent to which sales will fall off will depend on the elasticity of demand, that is, on the extent to which a given rise in price will decrease sales. If the employer has a monopoly of a product or is protected by trade mark or patented product, regarded by the public as essential, sales might decrease very little or not at all.

If the leading competitors of our employer are not subject to a similar tax the employer in question obviously could not pass the tax on to the consumer without a shrinking in sales. If, for example, one state adopts such a tax while the neighboring states do not, it seems clear that it would be impossible to pass the tax on to the consumer in those industries subject to interstate competition. Now if every employer tries to raise prices, and his sales thereby fall off, hundreds and perhaps thousands of workers will find themselves jobless. They will walk the streets in search of work, and their pressure for work will lead to severe competition for jobs; this competition will tend to lower wages not only of themselves but also of all other workers who are interchangeable with those laid off. Thus even though the employer tries to pass the tax on to consumers, this will fail, and in the end the real burden will rest on the worker. In so far as workers can turn to government relief or other aid, the shifting of the incidence of the tax is delayed; nevertheless the tendency will prevail.

Suppose, on the other hand, the employer feels that he cannot pass this 3 per cent tax on to the consumer and cannot directly announce a proportionate cut in wages without causing a strike or labor unrest. In this case the final burden will, nevertheless, tend to rest on the workers after a time. It must be assumed that before the tax went into effect the employer had combined the right proportion of labor with his capital and land. That is, he added workers to his staff until the last man added just earned his wages. Let us assume that before the tax was levied the employer had a hundred workers at five dollars a day, or a daily wage bill of five hundred dollars. Now with the payroll tax his wage bill will be increased by about a hundred dollars a week. If he thinks his judgment as to the proper proportions between his labor and capital was correct before, he will now be inclined to think that his plant is over-staffed, since the wage bill has risen. So he will tend to lay off several men. If all employers are affected in this way (of course, employers whose technical requirements are such that they cannot operate with less labor will not be able to lay off anyone; for example, an insurance agent with only one stenographer may not be in a position to lay off that one—but the tendency will exist nevertheless) many employees will find themselves jobless, and their competition for jobs will force wages down so that in the end the real burden of the employer payroll tax will finally rest on the worker, although the government may have intended no such result.

A tax on gasoline or a tax on liquor will raise the price of the product to the ultimate consumer by virtually the full amount of the tax. If a tax is levied on payrolls spread broadly over all industry, why does the employer not look upon this tax just as he does on a gasoline or liquor tax, and pass the tax successfully on to the ultimate consumer? There are two reasons why he does not do so. (1) A broad tax on payrolls would amount virtually to a universal tax. With a given supply of money and credit in use, a definite price level will result, and if a universal tax is levied on all commodities through a tax on all payrolls, the given quantity of money and credit cannot support a higher price level (unless some new factor, such as increased velocity of money or the utilization of idle bank credit, has entered the situation, which we will assume does not happen). Therefore some adjustment must be made and the repeated attempts of businessmen to secure higher prices, due to the tax, will restrict sales and end in unemployment, which in turn will tend to depress wages so that labor absorbs the burden of the tax. (2) A tax on gasoline constitutes a tax on the use of a finished product of industry, while a tax on payrolls *is a tax on a certain way of doing business,* that is, doing business with labor. It is a tax on the *demand* for labor. This distinction between a sales tax and a payroll tax cannot be over-emphasized. A payroll tax operates as a penalty on those who have to hire labor. In hiring, promoting, and dismissing this tax will be carefully calculated. The smaller the payroll, the less the tax. The smaller the wages, the less the tax. The fewer the employees, the less the tax. It is in the nature of business practice to attempt to circumvent taxes. A tax on payrolls puts a premium on schemes to economize the use of labor here, there, and everywhere, thereby reducing the employer's exposure to the payroll tax. Thus the employer will attempt to substitute machinery for labor (although after a time the price of machinery would rise also, if it were impossible to shift the burden of the payroll tax to labor, since it is made with the aid of labor); he will tend to lengthen hours, to increase labor efficiency by getting more units of work out of each worker, and by other means. All this will terminate in the same result as was noted before—unemployment, wage reductions, and a gradual reabsorption of labor at lower wages, and finally the worker will bear the burden of the tax. This distinction between a sales tax such as that on gasoline and a payroll tax must be kept firmly in mind. The latter tax is a tax on a way of doing business, a tax on using labor, and the more labor the higher the tax. Economic logic and observation reveals that such a payroll tax can be shifted back to the worker even though the government may have intended, and so provided by law, that the employer or ultimate consumer should bear it.

That, in brief, is the position of economists on this matter. In general there is little dissent from this viewpoint. All agree, however, that specific conditions may alter the outcome of the operation of these economic forces and that at times considerable delay will occur before the burden is shifted to the worker. For example, it is generally agreed that in the first instance the employer will bear a considerable share of the burden until wages will have become adjusted to the new situation. The presence of strong trade unions, government fixation of wages, or the relief available through an employment insurance law itself—all may thwart the free working of the laws of supply and demand of labor, and instead of labor suffering wage decreases, the profits of employers may decline for a time. This decrease would reduce the demand for labor, and considerable prolonged unemployment would prevail without any reductions in wages being effected. However, in this case the burden might be shifted to labor not in actual wage reductions but in a postponement of wage increases which would have occurred in the absence of the payroll tax. It is well known that real wages have risen about $1\frac{1}{2}$ per cent per year on the average. If, through a strong trade-union policy, it is impossible to pass the payroll tax on to labor, the same end can be achieved by postponing these wage increases.

Economists also recognize that at times there are some prices which are more flexible than the price of labor. For example, the prices of raw materials subject to international competition may be so flexible that part of the payroll tax may be absorbed in reduced raw-material prices (just as an increase in freight rates on agricultural products may not in the long run affect adversely the net return which the farmer gets for his crops because, in the course of time, the higher freight rates may be reflected in lower land values, and thus the farmers' overhead costs are reduced by the amount of the increased freight). Again the demand for some products is so inelastic that an increase in price may be accepted by the consumer so that he pays the pay-roll tax. But even in this case the employees in this industry would now get not only their former wages, but also profit from the old-age or employment insurance benefits, and so jobs in this industry would become more attractive, and in due time competition for these jobs would at least prevent these particular workers from alone reaping the benefit of shifting the burden to the consumer. In other cases the employer may be a monopolist, or at least be protected from the rigors of competition by trade mark, patents, or uniqueness of his product, so that his profits are great and the demand for his product steady and inelastic; in this case the payroll tax may be absorbed in part by the monopolist and in part by the consumer.

Since the federal employment insurance tax does not apply to employers with less than eight employees, the law may give a slight impetus to small firms. (The annuity tax, however, does not exempt small employers.) Larger plants in direct competition with these exempted firms will be quite unable to pass the tax on to consumers. Workers in insured plants might attempt to secure jobs in uninsured firms if their wage rates are lowered as a consequence of the tax. In this way competition for jobs would tend to spread the burden even to those small-firm employees not covered by the law. Yet insured workers adversely affected by the shifting of the burden to them may not resent the lowering of wages, looking upon the tax and such wage cuts as merely a deferring of wage payments—a saving. However, of this we cannot be sure. Furthermore, some state laws apply the tax to employers with as few as one or two employees, so that this particular problem in shifting the tax burden is minimized.

However, all these cases of inelastic demand, monopoly, flexible raw-material prices, and so on, must be regarded as exceptions. The general conclusion still stands—since a payroll tax is a tax on a particular factor of production, a penalty on a particular way of doing business, it differs fundamentally from a sales tax, and the burden will tend in time to rest on that factor, namely, labor.

If labor bears the final burden of a payroll tax on the employer, is it not deceptive on the part of the law to levy the tax on the employer? Possibly so, but politically it would be virtually impossible to adopt a measure which levied all the premiums on the worker. Also, since at the first impact of the tax the burden is somewhat diffused among laborers, consumers, and entrepreneurs, to place the tax on employers in part aids in effecting a gradual shift of the burden to labor.

A thorough grasp of this line of reasoning should demonstrate that businessmen's fears of payroll taxes are scarcely warranted. Because the launching of such a tax program does entail some disturbance to business, the 1935 law specified a low beginning rate, which will not reach its maximum until about fifteen years after the first tax went into effect. Over such a period business and labor can adjust to the taxes. The ultimate rate of about nine per cent should be compared with the twenty or twenty-five per cent increase in real wages which will take place in the interval between now and 1949 if past performance is repeated. Finally, the depression beginning in 1929 has demonstrated more clearly than any heretofore that even if labor is a variable cost for the individual business unit, it is an over-head cost for society as a whole. That is, whether workers are employed or not, they do secure their maintenance by means of relief, such as WPA, PWA, CWA, and so on. An intelligent advance plan to meet this overhead cost bespeaks an ordered capitalism.

CONCLUSION

Under capitalism the standard of living has risen fairly steadily. The benefits have been broadly shared by all classes. The dynamic character of the system has meant considerable insecurity for a goodly number of people. The foregoing account of attempts to meet the problem of accidents, health, old age, and unemployment indicates a recognition of this insecurity. Many critics regard this program as inadequate, but it will probably become the basis for subsequent modification and improvement.

BIBLIOGRAPHY

General

Commons, J. R., and Andrews, J. B., *Principles of Labor Legislation* (Harper & Brothers, New York, 1936).

Douglas, Paul H., *Social Security in the United States* (McGraw-Hill Book Company, New York, 1936).

Burns, Eveline, *Toward Social Security* (McGraw-Hill Book Company, New York, 1936).

Yoder, Dale, *Labor Economics and Labor Problems* (McGraw-Hill Book Company, New York, 1933).

Public medicine

Falk, I. S., *et al.*, *Costs of Medical Care* (University of Chicago Press, Chicago, 1933).

Leven, Maurice, *The Incomes of Physicians* (University of Chicago Press, Chicago, 1932).

Committee on the Costs of Medical Care, *Medical Care for the American People,* final report (University of Chicago Press, Chicago, 1932).

Old-age pensions

Epstein, Abraham, *The Challenge of the Aged* (Vanguard Press, New York, 1928).

Schmidt, Emerson P., *Old Age Security* (University of Minnesota Press, Minneapolis, 1936).

Unemployment

Hansen, A. H., Murray, M. G., Stevenson, R. A., and Stewart, Bryce M., *A Program for Unemployment Insurance and Relief in the United States* (University of Minnesota Press, Minneapolis, 1934).

Commons, J. R., *et al.*, *Can Business Prevent Unemployment?* (Alfred A. Knopf, New York, 1925).

CHAPTER XV

Causal Relationships and Their Measurement

RICHARD L. KOZELKA

University of Minnesota

WHY? THE SEARCH FOR CAUSES

FROM the primitive man, gnawing at his knuckles in the fashion of Rodin's statue "The Thinker," to the modern child, who counters each answer to his numerous questions with another "Why?" mankind has been seeking the explanation for the events which fascinate and plague him. Before "The Thinker" sat down and wrinkled his brow in the symbolic dawn of a new human activity, man adapted himself to the dangers and discomforts of his environment. The first step toward modern science was taken as he began to ask himself "Why?" when members of his family acted queerly, or when a brilliant spot of light flashed across his midnight sky.

The incentive to search for causes is probably of less consequence than the recognition that a cause existed. Curiosity for its own sake may not be as commendable, under our modern standards, as a burning desire to alleviate the sufferings of mankind, but it may originate an investigation with quite unexpected results. Those who conduct unusual expeditions or investigations often feel that they must advance some "practical" objective for the expenditure of time and money. But the leaders of the latest attempt to scale Mount Everest did not pretend to seek something useful. When a member of the staff was asked why his party risked almost certain death in climbing the highest mountain, his reply was, "Because it is there." The bump which the legendary apple left on Newton's head only served to rouse his curiosity about the speed of falling objects.

Acute distress, physical or social, has furnished more impetus for the discovery of causal relationships than idle or even learned curiosity. The sudden loss of a member of the family has directed questions at the conditions preceding death. The threatened or actual shortage of food had caused people to search their own lives for acts displeasing to their gods, and incidentally to note the relation between water supply and crops, and to select livestock for special use. Social conflicts, such as wars and domestic uprisings, are being examined for their origins, instead of being dismissed as expressions of a noble sport, on the one hand, and the inherent ingratitude of the lowly classes, on the other.

The causes which have been proposed at various times for certain effects seem absurd at the present time, but the idea of what is or is not absurd varies with the stage of mental development and the history of the science which seeks causal relations. Whether the explanation is "obvious" or highly questionable, there is a recognition of the principle of connection between events, even though the real relationship cannot be found with the present state of knowledge. Accidents may happen, but they do not serve as a satisfactory explanation of why events occur, and the term is used only as a miscellaneous spindle on which to pin problems for later solution.

THE DEVELOPMENT OF EXPLANATIONS

Supernatural causes

The first answers to the question "Why?" were relatively simple, merely postponing the real solution as we see it today. The fairies, the evil genii, the devils, and the great spirits ruled the world; in other words, these caused things to happen. To the natives living in the valleys around Mount Everest, there is no question of accidental coincidence between the earthquake in that region and the successful flight of the British airplanes over the peak of that famous mountain a short time before. They were sure that the trembling of the earth was an expression of the wrath of the mountain deity over the intrusion of these mechanical birds into her private domain. The sick, and particularly the insane, among our forefathers were considered to be possessed of the devil, and all efforts were bent to drive out the evil one. The success or failure of crops depended on the whims of the special gods of fertility, whose will had to be propitiated with suitable offerings. Mount Pelée was personified by the natives of Hawaii in the dreaded goddess who demanded human sacrifices as the price for withholding her wrath. When she broke her implied contract and showered liquid fire on her worshipers, the natives assumed that they were to blame, and sought the renegades who must have displeased the holy one.

The complexity of causes that underlies many of our most perplexing problems was met with gratifying simplicity by the supernatural theory of causation. Unexpected variations from customary routine could be excused on the basis of the unquestionable privilege of the fairies to change their minds, since they were not restricted by man-made laws. The belief in magic made extended explanations unnecessary. Consulting the stars for omens was a necessary prelude to important undertakings, and the custom is by no means dead today.

The supernatural explanation was not reserved for what today are called natural phenomena, such as earthquakes, landslides, illness, and crop failures. The divine right of kings, the inspired origin of our Constitution, the right of free speech, the privilege of private property have been invoked to "explain" or justify past and present conditions. The goddess of luck has been credited with the difference in economic and social status between two men who began with the same environment and ostensibly with the same qualifications. Self-appraisal is the unpleasant alternative when heretics begin to doubt the supernatural premise.

The acceptance of the caprice or vengeance of the elves and the gods as the complete answer to the question "Why?" effectively retarded any advance in the solution of the problem of reducing distress, loss, and disappointment. To question the motives and methods of the supernatural beings would have been impious, to say the least. One could only accept their judgment with the best possible grace, depend on the wearing of charms, on the repetition of incantations by the tribal medicineman, and on sacrificial offerings to hasten pleasurable events and to divert unpleasant ones.

Natural causes

Scientific methods began to make progress when the answer to the question "Why?" was sought in related events within the experience of the observer. Such an association of ideas depended on the assumption of a sequence of events instead of independent, isolated "accidents" answerable only to their own magical sponsors. The chains of factors might lead through devious paths, but if the pattern was systematic, that is, if it indicated a regularity and similarity between results under like conditions, the answer to the original question could be found without resorting to exhortations and burnt offerings. The recognition of regularities, uniformities, and dependable sequences in nature was the important break between the helpless, resigned acceptance of the will of the gods and the development of scientific thought as we know it today.

The transition from the supernatural theory to the search for natural consequences did not occur overnight. The germs of the new method were present in primitive man when he learned the properties of fire, or when he used his knowledge of the habits of wild animals to avoid the dangerous beasts and trap the more toothsome specimens. The change is still in process, since varying amounts of magical thinking remain in our treatment of many modern problems, from medicine to criminology.

The essence of the naturalistic or scientific approach to the question of causation is the eternal search for a pattern or set of relationships in the problem under consideration. To admit that events are unrelated would be a confession that chaos rules the world. Such chaos is denied by those engaged in research, from those who chart the paths of heavenly bodies to those who discover the life cycle of the active agent in a dreaded disease. No one denies the imperfect state of all sciences, each of which has unsolved problems whose common characteristic seems to be a confusion of apparently unrelated events. But the development of new techniques, such as chemical methods in criminology, and of more delicate instruments, such as the photo-electric cell, permit new approaches and more exact measurements of observations, which form the basic data of a problem.

The task of the scientist is to fit the facts into a hypothetical framework which will be a satisfactory explanation
of one of the more or less complex but logical or regular patterns of events in our physical or social lives. He may have
to try many frameworks, and compare his facts in many
combinations, as in the study of inequalities of wealth, and
he may still fail to find a satisfactorily complete explanation of his problem. The balance of fats, carbohydrates,
and proteins was found to be an inadequate answer to the
question of the relation of nutrition and health, after vita-
mins were discovered. The search for relief from the common cold was based for a long time on the assumption that
a germ was the secret of nature's pattern for this form of
plague. The present direction of research is toward a filter-
able virus which does not have a life cycle. Until the
doctors discover the events and conditions and their manner
of combination, we shall continue to suffer from recurrent
attacks of weeping eyes and stuffed heads. Until we can
discover the formulae for the right combination of national
pride, freedom of exchange, and "enlightened selfishness,"
we shall have wars to plague our national health.

Once the secret of the chain of events has been discovered,
appropriate action may be taken to adjust the individual
or the group to the demands of his problem, and pestilence
and famine need no longer be considered only as acts of
God. The Kansas farmer who learns to associate cyclones
with certain seasons of the year, and with special atmos-
pheric conditions at those times, may adjust himself to the
perilous situation by keeping a wary eye on weather changes
and insistence on a clear path to his cyclone cellar. The
manufacturer who sees his budding business threatened by
long-established, government-subsidized foreign competitors
may ask his own government for tariff protection. The

orderly sequence of nature's processes may be diverted by the process of inoculation against diphtheria or vaccination against smallpox, and centers of recreation and education may be established to reduce crime and delinquency. Where preventive measures are too late, curative measures are necessary; hence we find courts established to break up monopolies, and surgery called upon to remove a ruptured appendix. Whether we build dams to control flood waters, or schools and neighborhood houses to restrain prejudice and social conflict, we are acting on the knowledge gained through study of facts as part of a logical pattern. This pattern is a part of our physical and social world, and not an unpredictable expression of human or divine will.

NATURAL CAUSES AND THE SCIENTIFIC METHOD

The scientific attitude

The terms "scientist" and "scientific methods" have been used at various times in the paragraphs above. Everyone has some idea of the meaning of these terms. We can all be scientists at times, in our approach to personal problems and in determining our attitudes on larger questions. A test tube or microscope is not the necessary badge of a scientist. Science is distinguished by the method of approach and the attitude towards problems. The faith in the essential orderliness of the world in which we live is the basis for the untiring search for the facts and relations that represent the solution of the mystery that troubles us at the time. Beginning with this faith, the maintenance of an objective attitude is the most essential element, aside from the facts themselves, in the process of attacking a problem.

The scientific attitude is marked by patience. Orderliness in nature is not necessarily accompanied by simplicity in the order and importance of observed facts. The business cycle is held responsible for many economic and social ills, and economists have devoted many years in the search for fundamental causes and how they are joined. But success still seems very far away, because the complexity of inter- acting factors, such as inventions, investments, price levels, and credit policy, has defied the efforts of the scholars of many countries. Nevertheless, they have not lost courage, and research continues.

Patience is closely associated with hard labor in the scien- tific process. Edison is quoted as defining genius as "one- tenth inspiration and nine-tenths perspiration." The burn- ing of midnight oil is accepted as a necessity by the student, but is not begrudged by the scientist who becomes immersed in his problem. The late Mme. Curie and her husband spent two years in incessant, exhausting labor, reducing a ton of pitchblende to a small amount of bismuth salts, which contained some new element that had challenged their curiosity.

A total absence of bias is another characteristic of true scientific method. Personal feelings about child labor, the income tax, the Jewish race, objective examinations, or private schools, obscure the clear vision that is necessary if the facts are to be examined in their true perspective. The scientific attitude should be cold blooded in the ap- praisal of the evidence, particularly when it concerns a problem which has reached the controversial stage in the public attention, for example, the unemployment question. The evidence offered in such a case is almost sure to be colored by those from whom information must be obtained. The scientist may hold violently partisan views in matters pertaining to his personal and civic life, but when he turns to such matters as subjects for scientific inquiry, he must forego the pleasures of strong emotions.

Fundamental stages in the scientific method

The statement of the problem. The essential steps in the scientific method of seeking the fundamental elements in a problem are six in number, although this number is subject to change if one chooses to subdivide one or more in the suggested list. The first step is a clear statement of the problem. This is particularly essential in the social sciences, where words have not yet attained the exact meaning which they have acquired in the natural sciences. A labor dispute which finds expression in a strike presents a problem which is usually clear-cut and undeniable, although its causes and settlement may be highly involved and complex. A decent standard of living is frequently mentioned as the goal for a soundly organized society, particularly during a time when starvation and destruction of foodstuffs occur simultaneously and side by side. But the concept of a decent standard of living is too vague, subject to too many personal interpretations. It must be stated in more definite terms. An inefficient police department may be a serious problem, but the problem must be limited, or restated in objective terms, so that aimless wandering may be avoided.

The working hypothesis. Once the problem is stated, be it the price of wheat, the cause of cancer, or the delinquency rate, one might assume that the next obvious step is to "get the facts." But just what is a fact, and what facts are to be gathered? In relation to the farm problem and the farm surpluses, shall we consider only the facts of reduced income during the business depression, together with the rise of intense nationalism, which has caused our former European customers to grow their own foodstuffs? Shall we consider the influence of the movie heroines on the national feminine diet and the efforts of women to acquire slim silhouettes? Shall we consider the spread of central heating in homes, shops, and offices, making it less necessary for us to stoke the human furnace to generate body warmth, and permitting us to wear fewer and thinner articles of clothing (also derived from agricultural production) to insulate the body against excessive heat loss? These are all relevant facts, which may be gathered in records of production and purchases. The list of facts might literally be extended indefinitely, but we should consider such extension absurd. The absurdity does not arise from the assumption that this infinite number of facts is wholly unrelated to the problem. Rather, we recognize that life is too short to spend in the collection of endless lists of facts. If we set up "reasonable" limitations on the scope of our fact-finding activities, the likelihood of finding solutions is increased. When rheumatism was treated by hot applications and fiery lotions, the notion that the condition of the teeth might be related to the pains in the knee probably seemed laughable. The discovery of similar remote connections of facts has greatly increased the scope of information which a doctor needs for a thorough examination of a case. Nevertheless, the sky is *not* the limit in getting the facts.

The formulation of an hypothesis is the time-saving step between the statement of the problem and the collection of data. In non-scientific terms, this is merely the hunch or guess as to the probable causes and their paths of influence on the problem under consideration. This is not an attempt to pre-judge the case, or otherwise engage in wishful thinking. When the engine begins to cough and sputter, our first hypothesis may be that the supply of gasoline is exhausted. The better the hypothesis, the greater the saving in time

which would otherwise be spent in fruitless searches. The
skill of a scientist in selecting a good working hypothesis
depends on his breadth of experience and training and the
development of a knack for sensing logical relationships.
A man may draw on his knowledge in all the fields of science
in anticipating the most fruitful line of attack. His contacts with fellow scientists, in his own and other fields, keep
him informed about successful and unsuccessful hypotheses
tried on similar problems.

The need for an unbiased attitude is particularly important at this stage. When judgment becomes distorted, there
may be an excessive number of surgical operations because
the hypothesis may rule in favor of removing some innocent
part of our equipment, such as the appendix. An unusual
case of adjustment of the ductless glands with beneficial
effects to the individual's health and social behavior may
lead to a wave of gland manipulation to solve a crime wave.
The tendency of some timid souls, who must depend for
their income on investments and property, to ascribe all
forms of social unrest to "Communism" is an example of
an over-simplified hypothesis. It resembles the celebrated
maxim which detective stories credit to the French secret
police, *cherchez la femme!* An investigator may develop
a favorite line of approach, but it should not reflect his
prejudices.

The collection of data. The third step is the collection
of data within the scope suggested by the working hypothesis. Usually the organization and analysis of these data
are included as processes within the same step. The methods by which the data may be collected are usually classified
under three heads: laboratory, case, and statistical methods.
Actually, of course, a problem may be subjected to a combination of all three, as when an applicant presents himself

for examination before an insurance company will insure his life. He must furnish detailed information about his health and habits, and submit to a physical examination which may include additional laboratory tests, depending on the medical standards of his prospective company, and the size of his policy. Finally, his condition and history are checked against the experience of the company, as revealed by their statistical records and a highly technical actuarial analysis of the company data.

Before beginning a discussion of the differences between these three methods, let us review briefly our objectives and our assumptions. The world in which we live is assumed to be governed by a system of laws of cause and effect, whose relations can be described, and therefore whose future action can be predicted. Our success in discovering these laws will vary with the degree of development of the tools and methods in the various sciences concerned with a particular event. Our problem is to untangle the maze of causes which may lie at the bottom of the mystery, and to describe and measure the strength of these causes. For this purpose we need a technique that will separate these causes and bring them into sharp relief. Failure to distinguish between the effects of closely related causes may lead to false conclusions and mistaken policies, for example, the gold-buying program of the government in 1933 as an attempt to raise our domestic price level. No economist would deny the ultimate connection between the price of gold and prices of other commodities, as long as gold is the basis for the monetary system. But to assume the simple, direct relation implied in the 1933 policy is to take a short cut which is not warranted by the facts of the case.

The laboratory method. The distinguishing characteristic of the laboratory method in the collection and analysis of facts is the degree of control of variations between causes. Under ideal conditions, all causes but one are held constant, and the result of manipulating the single cause is carefully recorded. When temperature, light, moisture, and soil composition are maintained at a pre-determined level, while the amount of fertilizer is changed from one experiment to another, the difference in yield, or size of flower, is said to result from the variation in the one element. When furnace temperature is set at a different level for each of a series of batches of steel of identical composition, any differences which appear in the toughness, hardness, or ductility of the resulting metal are attributed to the amount of heat applied. However, if the laborer on the stock pile was careless about the proportions of scrap or flux which he wheeled to the furnace feeder, or if the melting foreman paid no attention to the length of time each batch was exposed to the heat, the possibility of reproducing a particular steel might be very remote. In other words, the causal relationships have not been definitely described and measured.

The ability of the research worker in the natural sciences to hold fast all but one of his conditions makes it possible and profitable for him to develop techniques for the measurement of facts with a high degree of precision. Small variations in his product and in his causal agent—for example, purity of copper and its electrical conductivity—may be highly significant, because no other condition, such as temperature or shape of bar, was permitted to vary and thereby cause an additional change in the amount of electricity carried. In very delicate experiments even the body temperature of the experimenter must be taken into account, and steps must be taken to insulate the material under study from this outside factor. Elaborate precautions are taken to clean all the apparatus and purify all the agents used.

A basic technique in the laboratory method is the use of the control group. The very fact of the experiment may introduce changes which must be taken into account as the experiment progresses. The physicist may cut a bar of metal into identical units and subject each of these to various types of strain under a bending machine; or he may measure the resistance to electricity under varying degrees of temperature, restoring the bar to ordinary temperature after each trial. It is more difficult to preserve this identity of conditions when dealing with living organisms, such as plants and animals and man himself. A beef steer who is fed a special ration is not the same animal at the end of the feeding period that he was at the beginning. Not only is he older, but the experimental diet has probably caused changes in his structure and physical functions, which would tend to confuse the results if a second experiment were conducted with another ration on the same animal. With the development of air conditioning, it would be possible to duplicate the "weather" conditions of the first experiment, and other factors in the living conditions of the steer, but the most important handicap is the change in the animal itself.

The use of the control group avoids this difficulty. Instead of submitting the same animal to repeated experiments, changes are introduced simultaneously in only a part of a group of animals which are considered to be identical in all respects essential to the experiment being carried on. Thus, the trial ration may be fed to ten steers and the customary diet fed to ten others of the same breed, age, and general condition, and then all twenty are exposed to the same conditions of weather, exercise, and housing conditions. At the end of the feeding period, there will probably be differences in weight gained by the two groups. Even under these conditions, the scientist does not judge results by the

gains of individual animals, because he was not in control
of all conditions, and even steers have some individuality
in their habits, and reactions to food. But this lack of
identity is relatively slight, and can be eliminated largely
from the problem by considering the average gain of all the
animals in each part of the group.

The power of proof of a control group has been frequently
and sometimes sensationally demonstrated in the field of
medicine. When Pasteur was upsetting the complacency of
the French veterinarians with his germ theory, and his
claims that anthrax could be eliminated from the farmers'
livestock, he was maneuvered into a demonstration which
involved the control technique. Under the scornful eyes of
the country's leading horse doctors, and before an impressive assembly of public officials, he applied his methods to
a group of twenty-four sheep, one goat, and several cattle.
A control group of the same composition was allowed to
mingle with the vaccinated animals, no change having been
made in their blood streams. Twelve days later the vaccination was repeated, again before a crowd of skeptical
horse doctors and dignitaries. At the close of the necessary
waiting period, Pasteur introduced the deadly anthrax
germs into *all* the animals. Two days later a gathering
which dwarfed the previous assemblies in numbers and
great names appeared at the field to see Pasteur confounded
or vindicated. "His twenty-four immune sheep scampered
about among the carcasses of the same number of pitiful
dead ones." [1] The other animals which he had vaccinated
also escaped the disease.

For each dramatic demonstration of cause and effect by
means of the control group, there are thousands of similar

[1] DeKruif, Paul, *Microbe Hunters,* p. 163 (Harcourt, Brace & Company,
New York, 1926).

experiments carried on in laboratories and test plots and sheds all over the world. The goal in each case is to trace the effects of the single cause, to the exclusion of every other source of variation. Hence the special efforts of the research worker to make up his control and experimental groups with identical types. The physician who is seeking the solution of a puzzling ailment finds an almost ideal experimental situation if his case involves identical twins, only one of whom is suffering from the ailment. Because the physical make-up of an individual is a delicate balance, the duplication of such a balance is most nearly approached in pairs of identical twins.

An essential condition of the control technique is the maintenance of an independent relation between the two parts, the control and the experimental groups, with respect to the cause under study. The health of the twenty-four sheep which were not immunized by Pasteur was not affected in the least by the changes developed in the sheep which had been vaccinated. There was no attempt to give the latter better pasture or better and cleaner quarters. This is the condition which is so frequently broken down when the control idea is attempted in the social relations between individuals. New techniques are often tested in the educational field by splitting a class of students of approximately the same age, background, and mental development. If one section realizes that it is a subject of experiment, or if the two groups are kept in the same room but taught by two different methods, the changes in one section react on the other, and the experimental conditions are upset.

The "social experiments" that are attempted from time to time, whether it be a small study group or a prohibition amendment, rarely measure up to the requirements of strict scientific method. Changes which are observed and measured in the body politic after passage of a law or the establishment of a new institution cannot be ascribed exclusively to that factor, no matter how sensational the law may be. Other conditions have changed, and these may hinder or augment the variations which would have resulted from the cause in question, had other things remained equal. This is the reason for the inconclusiveness of arguments which seek to associate specific results with particular events, whether it be tariffs and prosperity or smoking habits and scholastic delinquency. The laboratory method, with absolutely controlled conditions or with a control group, does not lend itself readily to social problems and has its limitations even in the natural sciences. But where the effects of a particular change can be segregated, the basis for a scientific law can be established.

The case method. The case method is an alternative to the laboratory in those branches of knowledge where it is not feasible to control the degree and direction of change. The essence of this method is the orderly collection of minute details concerning a given social situation. This may involve a limited phase of an individual person's life, or a comprehensive study of his activities, or may include a family, a community, or a nation. All the facts which may relate to a given problem are recorded, and many that at first glance seem to have no connection are gathered as grist to the mill. It is an intensive study which avoids interfering in any way with the usual mode of life of the object of the study. To be sure, the results of the case study may result in profound changes brought on by administrative ruling or by more subtle changes through education and substitution of interests and facilities. But that is the end result, not the heart of the case method.

The case method is not a new mode of attack on a problem. Over two thousand years ago Hippocrates demonstrated the value of this approach in medicine. He recorded carefully his observations of the condition of his patients, their appearance, action, and all other details which might reveal the course of illness, from health through suffering to recovery or death. The thorough, careful, systematic examination of the history, symptoms, and appearance of a patient, and similar details, is considered axiomatic by any modern reputable physician. Many soldiers during the World War, half in jest and half in earnest, insisted that their medical officers had never heard of Hippocrates, being satisfied with an impartial administration of two simple medications: tincture of iodine for external complaints and a salts solution for internal ills. Even with due allowance for overstatement, and the soldier's privilege to "grouse" about his treatment, perhaps the military doctor knew more than his patients would admit about the real ills and correct treatment for the complaints which are inevitable in a group of men forced to live under the artificial conditions of training and concentration camps.

Almost a hundred years ago a French scholar, Le Play, gave an outstanding illustration of the case method in his study of family budgets. He spent most of his vacations as a member of the family of some European peasant or laborer, carefully selected beforehand. Once he had gained the confidence of the family, he uncovered and recorded a tremendous amount of data on family habits, standards, and distribution of expenditures, which would have been impossible to obtain by the ordinary interview or questionnaire. The work of Le Play has been held up as a pattern to students in the field of social sciences to this day.

The recognition of the individual as an individual, even

though he is a member of a community, accounts in part for the importance of the case method. Where society has found it necessary to contribute directly to the needs of some of its members, it is recognized that the application of an iron-clad rule, a rigid ration, a standardized "missionary barrel," may lead to waste and gross injustice. The flexibility which is necessary to determine whether a family needs medical care, fuel, or a job, or the removal of one of its handicapped members to an institution, cannot be attained by any average formula. The adaptation of aid to needs is the practical result of the operation of the case method. Since the family, the community, and even the individual are highly complex units, a careful examination of each situation is an obvious necessity.

The scientific use of the case method, aside from its administrative function, is the development of generalizations, laws of relationship which explain the pattern of individual and social reactions to specific conditions, such as the distribution of income over the various sections of the family budget. This assumes that there is some degree of uniformity underlying the individuality of social units. The regularities which are observed in the cycle of the seasons, and in the attack of acids on metals, also exist, albeit in more complex combinations, in the relations between individuals and their environment.

The intensity of effort, which marks the case method, precludes the possibility of its wide application on a large scale. The completeness of the record for an individual case must compensate for the limited number of cases. For this reason it is highly essential that the cases which are used as the basis for a general statement on causes and effects in social behavior be selected with great care, so that they may be representative of the sphere of social action

to which the general statement shall apply. The "ordinary"
case is usually far less interesting and sensational than the
unusual case, which may attract attention far beyond its
deserts. The selection of the typical cases for study requires
a rigid adherence to the scientific attitude, plus broad knowledge and experience in the art of observation and human
relations. The skillful collection of data may then yield
the necessary factual basis for generalization.

The laws of individual and social behavior which evolve
from the examination of case records must pass through the
same process as the first uniformities observed in the physical world. The laws must be tested, verified by what is
called the deductive process. Can the general statement
be applied to a specific case, with due allowance for individual variations? Obviously, any attempt to base generalizations on spectacular cases would fail in this test.

An extension of the case method is sometimes described
as the historical method. Many records are gathered on
similar cases in the historical past, and from the mass of
facts is developed the pattern of cause and effect that presumably explains the problem. The method suffers from
the handicap of widely varying conditions and the lack of
control in the collection of data, which can be determined
in a current study. However, within the limits of the accuracy and comparability of the data, the study of historical
parallels may yield very valuable results.

The statistical method. The statistical method has been
described by an eminent English statistician as the "science
of averages." [2] This definition reveals the essential element
in the method, the selection of a representative value in a
group of more or less varying data. The reasons for this

[2] Bowley, Arthur L., *Elements of Statistics*, p. 82 (Charles Scribner's
Sons, New York, 1926).

variation are the complexity of the causal relations and
the impossibility of controlling all conditions in a selected
problem. In the physical sciences the variation may be
due to imperfect tools or materials. The physicist cannot
make a pump that gives him a perfect vacuum; the agrono-
mist finds impurities in his seeds. In the social sciences we
are dealing with man's relations with his fellow men, and
under any conceivable form of society, we cannot control
all conditions, including man, while we study the effects
of changes in one. When the price of butter fluctuates,
changes in butter consumption take place, but in the meantime styles, fads, general employment, wages, and imports
of butter cannot be held unchanged.

Time is not an important factor under ideal scientific
conditions; that is, we can wait indefinitely for results.
But in economics, sociology, and political science, time is
important, if results are to be usable, since conditions are
changing. Any attempt to experiment with conditions
might take much time and a vast expenditure of money to
prove results, and no scientist has had the temerity to
suggest the experimental method under these conditions.
Under dictatorial governments, arbitrary changes and controls have been attempted, but hardly in the scientific spirit.
In each case, furthermore, the dictator's power does not
extend beyond the borders of his own country, and he cannot
altogether exclude outside influences in his own nation.
Therefore, we must seek to establish the relations between
causes and effects in the midst of conflicting disturbances.

The separation or isolation of particular forces is accomplished in part by a process of careful classification and
subdivision. For example, what is at the root of the terrific
auto-accident toll? Where should preventive effort be expended with the best chance of success? A division between

city and country accidents shows that the majority of serious cases occur in the country. The country accidents
classified as to place (curves, blind corners, and straightaways) show a preference for straightaways. A further
classification by two-, three-, and four-lane highways shows
the three-lane road to be the most deadly. One more classification, according to the age of the car involved, will show
that the newer cars have most accidents. But this does not
necessarily lead to the conclusion that the surviving reckless
drivers are confined to new cars. An examination of the
reports of such accidents will show that a large number
of them are actually caused by the creeping antiques whose
driving speed is far below the normal speed of the modern car. The old car may continue its halting journey
unscathed, leaving behind the tangled wreckage of an
unsuccessful attempt to pass this traffic hazard.

The objective of the process of classification is the separation of counted or measured facts, concerning a large mass
of individuals, into groups which are reasonably homogeneous in all essentials except the factor under study. Thus,
if we find that new cars and old cars, in the ratio of their
numbers on the highways, are equally prone to meet head-on
in the middle of a three-lane highway, we have done all we
can to select cases with a similarity of conditions, and the
difference in the age of the cars points to no strong tendency.
If we find that old cars are involved in much higher proportions than new cars, we may have the basis for discrimination in treating the problem.

The statistical method calls for a relatively large number
of counts or measurements in order that the proper grouping or classification may be made. This is partly owing to
the problem of measurement. The problem under study
may have to be measured indirectly. Poverty may be

studied through an examination of the numbers on poor relief, although everyone recognizes that worthy cases are overlooked and that "chiselers" slip into the relief group. Unemployment may be considered as reflected by the number of trade-union members registered for jobs. Where conditions can be measured directly, the accuracy of each quantitative statement may still be in doubt. The retail price of an article can be observed in stores, but the price may vary from shop to shop. In addition, if price changes are the objective, an apparent decrease in price may actually cover a deterioration in quality. Even the shopkeeper may be uncertain as to how much an article has suffered by the substitution of cotton for wool, because he may not know how much cotton has been used.

The counting of students who engage in specified activities is a relatively simple problem. Counting the number of deaths due to cancer may be a different matter if the cause is deep seated and beyond the diagnostic powers of physicians. Furthermore, the physician may wish to spare the feelings of relatives, so he may tell them that death was due to heart disease. Finally, unless there is a law requiring a report, there may be no record of death, and it is missed entirely in the count.

The statistical method frequently depends on facts gathered as a part of some administrative routine, rather than as a special inquiry planned to cover a given problem. The administration of the tariff law incidentally yields information on the kinds and direction of our merchandise imports. The probation of wills and estates yields some data on the personal distribution of wealth. Information gathered in this way may satisfy the administrators of the laws, but may not have the accuracy of unit, or the complete coverage, desired by the statistician; yet he may find it impossible or impractical to get adequate data from voluntary informants. The necessity for counting his cases and measuring his changes where and when he can find them, rather than under controlled conditions, forces the statistician to gather data on many persons and situations. Only in this way can he have enough cases to permit the grouping necessary to yield comparable measurements that indicate a definite tendency.

Statistical methods are by no means restricted to the social sciences. Control of conditions is limited by the advancement of the science, and by practical considerations of expense. Measurements are frequently made in physics, in geology, and in botany, under conditions that yield varying results. By the use of statistical tools these variations are ironed out, and the significant differences are brought into proper focus. However, conclusions can be drawn with more certainty with a few cases observed under such conditions in those sciences than in economics or sociology, where relations between causes are more complex and control is impossible.

Interpretation and inductive inference. The fourth step in the scientific method, after the facts have been obtained by the experimental, the case, or the statistical method, is the formation of a preliminary or tentative generalization. This may or may not resemble the working hypothesis which guided the original collection of the data. The dependable relationship that is found between the factors can now be stated in definite though perhaps not in final form. To the scientist it may be only a strong suspicion, but it should never be just an intense wish.

The facts alone, as observed in the experiment or gathered in the market place, are rarely enough to point to an obvious causal connection. Particularly in the statistical method, the broader the background of the scientist, the quicker he will arrive at a sound inference. The breadth of his experience, whether by reading, formal training, or actual practice, will determine how he will interpret the changes which he finds. Experience will sharpen his faculties in sweeping aside inconsequential results, and finding the "kernel of fact" which is essential to the solution of a problem. This is especially important for the social scientist who must face a mass of data that may suggest several solutions, even after careful sifting and classification. A knowledge of dairying problems and the psychology of the farmer will be of great assistance in determining the long-term and short-term relation between the price of butter and the amount brought to the market.

Verification and correction. The inductive inference may be quite obvious, as in the law of gravity, or it may be quite uncertain, as in the phenomenon of telepathy. The aim of the scientist is to present a generalization which will justify all the faith that he can put into it. To this end, he tests his generalization in every way which might bring out a weakness or an inconsistency. Frequently this test will be made by his colleagues, to obtain a fresh point of view, and to insure the elimination of the element of personal bias. Sometimes it is made by his rivals, or even by his enemies, whose professional standing may be threatened by a newly discovered scientific law. The tests seek to prove that alleged results will follow whenever specified conditions are fulfilled. The exceptions must be accounted for, and if they are too numerous, the law will stand under a heavy shadow of doubt. The tests may have to wait many years until more delicate instruments can be discovered or perfected, as in the case of the photo-electric cell for measuring minute changes in light. The test may have to wait for the accumulation of sufficient data, such as a series of census enumerations, for the problem of population trends.

The process of verification is sometimes described as the necessary accompaniment of deduction. This is a part of the fruitless argument on the relative merits of the inductive and deductive methods of finding scientific laws. Like so many simplifications of complex relations, it has squeezed the truth out of what might be a useful distinction. The inductive process is not an aimless, industrious, magpie search for measurements or units or cases, in the fond hope that by a wave of a wand, out of the bright collection of gewgaws, some unifying principle and universal law will appear. Nor does the deductive process consist in sitting with feet on desk in the monastic quiet of one's study, waiting for the flash of inspiration in the form of a complete general statement. Perhaps Minerva was born full grown from Zeus' head, but scientists have not been able to imitate Zeus in their search for laws of causation. Every scientific law is the result of a combination of these two approaches, in varying proportions, depending on the scientific imagination and experience of the researcher and the possibility and abundance of dependable counts and measurements. The final step is always a verification of the general statement with every available means. The result may not be a clean bill of health, particularly in the social sciences where it is difficult to duplicate conditions. Qualifying conditions and degrees of error may have to be established to prevent a naïve acceptance of the law as though it were infallible in its present form.

The scientific law. The final step in the scientific method is the statement of the causal connection which has been found between observed facts. This scientific law has been verified by the best available checks and tests, like a battleship after a "shake-down" cruise, and is now ready for action and application. The proof of the discovery now lies in the many trials made by those who accept it as the latest true word, without any doubt of its success.

Irresistible nature is implied in the final awe-inspiring truth, but the social scientist must usually be content with a statement of probabilities. He is the first to admit that the imperfections of his methods result in generalizations which vary all the way from virtual certainty to a probability that he accepts with fingers crossed. Under specified conditions, certain consequences can be expected, but seldom can the necessary conditions be completely specified in a social problem. The lack of control of the elements in a situation makes it necessary to accept the problem as it comes, not as we should like it. The failure to match the requirements as to background causes the results to be uncertain. A high score on an aptitude test does not inevitably lead to success in one's chosen vocation, but it promises a high probability of achievement.

The natural sciences themselves are not immune to uncertainty in results, although by comparison their forecasts hit much closer to the mark. The physicist may be able to state quite exactly the relation between a ten-degree increase in temperature and the length of an aluminum rod. The economist cannot duplicate such certainty in the relation between an increase of one hundred million dollars in our gold supply and a change in the price level. As a result, he states his conclusions in terms of tendencies and probabilities, rather than in certainties, making allowances for short-term and long-term effects.

The layman becomes exasperated with the social scientist, because the latter avoids being caught out on a limb with a flat statement of cause and effect. Instead, the layman gets an answer, "It depends." The careful scholar regrets this no less than the troubled inquirer, but he cannot rush the development of his young science. His task is to whittle constantly at the huge block of probability, tendency, and limitation, until he has reduced it to a virtual certainty. Not until then can he expect his discovery of the laws of human relations to be used to the greatest benefit of society.

How Much? The Statistical Measurement of Causes

FAMILIAR TOOLS RE-EXAMINED

The statistical tools used in economics, in sociology, and in related disciplines are generally not inventions of workers in those fields. The various devices are usually gratefully borrowed from mathematics and the more exact sciences, particularly physics. The adaptations of these tools, and the interpretation of the results mark the skillful statistician.

The average person who has had no training in statistical methods is nevertheless familiar with many statistical devices. They have become an important aid to administration, education, and propaganda. The real necessity is for people to examine these familiar measuring sticks, to find their logical bases, to learn the best methods of computation, and to appreciate their limitations and special uses. No statistical tool is the whole tool kit, although several tools are well nigh indispensable. The simplest and most frequently used of these is the average, which will be taken up presently.

METHODS OF COLLECTING DATA IN THE SOCIAL SCIENCES

The first step in the statistical process, after a problem has been presented, delimited, and organized, is the collec-

tion of facts. These may be gathered by personal solicitation, or by resort to an appeal by mail, or by reference to
official records.

The personal solicitation or schedule method is used
when complete coverage is necessary, as in a census of population, and information must be gathered from people of
varying levels of intelligence and who are more or less
coöperative. The method is expensive, because a large staff
is necessary if the inquiry is to be completed in a short
time. Skilled interviewers are necessary if the questions
are of a personal nature, and if they must be put to the
informant without rousing prejudice or hostility. The
schedule method has a great advantage from the statistical
point of view—that each question is interpreted by all interviewers in the same way, if proper training has been given.
This makes for greater comparability of data when results
have been gathered over a large area. The dangers of
misinformation and bias are greatly reduced.

The census of population of the United States is one of
the most extensive statistical projects in the world. Starting in 1790 as a simple listing of the names of heads of
families and the numbers of persons in the household, the
census now gathers information every ten years, from every
person, concerning such matters as age, residence, marital
condition, and occupation. In addition, the census now
covers agriculture, manufacturing, mining, and merchandis-
ing. These census reports are supplemented by special
reports on births and deaths, on financial statistics of states
and cities, on education, and on the blind population. The
census of population is still taken only once in ten years,
but a five-year census has been urged by many people,
because social and economic changes have been taking place
very rapidly in the last two decades, and because the need

for current information as a basis for private or governmental action is becoming more acute.

The census of agriculture has been taken every five years, and the census of manufactures has supplemented its detailed decennial census with a two-year survey which covers a very high percentage of total production. The citizen and businessman frequently express annoyance over the many questions asked by the census enumerator, but this is as nothing compared to the fear of heavenly wrath which led many people to oppose the first census. The sentiment is by no means dead today, because the census opponents can quote Biblical chapter and verse to defend their stand.[3] However, modern society would be greatly handicapped without a census, and many enumerations have been made since 1790 without a visitation of divine punishment.

The questionnaire and voluntary survey are the methods generally used for collecting data when time and money are limited. The questionnaire may vary from a postcard to a six- or eight-page document with a promise of a reward for completion. The difficulty has been to rouse enough interest in the informants to draw more than ten to fifteen per cent returns. A more serious difficulty is the lack of representativeness of the returns, assuming that the mailing list was a fair cross-section of the group to be tested. A carload of grain is sampled with a grain probe, which takes a handful of grain at each of eight levels, and which is thrust into the grain at five or six different locations in the car. A social group is much more complex than a carload of grain, but it is difficult in most mail inquiries to ascertain whether the returns are truly representative, or are drawn from the top or one end of the "social carload." After the failure of

[3] I Chronicles xxi; II Samuel xxiv.

a recent presidential straw ballot to forecast the election, one facetious explanation offered was that the members of one party lived closer to mail boxes than the others, hence the inaccuracy of the returns.

Personal inquiries by skilled interviewers are generally more satisfactory in terms of dependable results. Although the method is more costly in time and money, the returns can more accurately represent the group sampled, because informants are systematically selected to give each stratum or special interest its due weight. Furthermore, a skillful interviewer will allay suspicion, explain questions, and obtain information which would be regarded as too personal if asked via questionnaire.

The proper selection of a sample is a thorny problem in the social sciences. The reliability of a general statement based on a sample depends on the resemblance between that sample and the array of individuals or situations from which it is taken. There is an allowable variation of the sample around the true value, due to the multitude of small causes that contribute to the general class of chance fluctuations. Theoretically, ten perfect coins tossed in the air should come down with five heads and five tails, but a single trial may show the rare case of all heads or all tails. A lopsided coin would throw the balance in favor of more than five heads, or of an excess of tails, showing the presence of some unique disturbance rather than of a chance cause.

The most important rule in sampling is that every case or observation shall have an equal opportunity to become a member of the sample. This rule eliminates all but chance causes in the selection. An interviewer who passed by all homes bearing a plaque "Watch out for the dog," and all families where no one answered the door bell, may be eliminating two distinct and important groups in the population. A mail questionnaire sent to every fifth name in the telephone directory gives no opportunity for response from those without phones, and no incentive to the lazy and the busy people who do not mail their returns. To avoid such an unrepresentative selection, the statisticians have resorted to a stratified sample. This procedure recognizes the heterogeneous character of the population. To insure that every group gets a fair chance to be represented, each must contribute its proportionate number, no more and no less, to the final sample. Special effort is made to reach those who might otherwise slip through the net, and the results are weighted in the aggregate sample. This is not a deliberate attempt to distort the sample of the basic situation, but to prevent unconscious distortion through careless selection.

The assumption that small fluctuations tend to cancel each other in the sampling method is based on a condition which is noticeably lacking in the typical problem in the social sciences. This condition is the independence of events. When the ten coins are tossed in the air, the action of one coin is independent of the actions of the others. But the consumption habits of one family are not independent of the habits of other families in the same general class. The price of butter in one store is not independent of the prices in other stores. This places a heavy responsibility on the collector of representative data, and an equal responsibility on the analyst for a careful interpretation.

METHODS OF ANALYZING MASSES OF DATA

The central value—the average

The analysis of huge masses of data would be extremely arduous, if not impossible, without the aid of averages. These are statistical tools which reduce long series of meas-

urements to a single summarizing or typical value. They
permit the convenient comparison of periods or places, even
though the number of observations is unequal; for example,
the average test grades of graduating classes of two high
schools of widely different enrollment. The average is a
useful point of reference in setting standards by which to
judge individual performance. The average prevents the
formation of conclusions from a few striking, unusual cases
which blind the judgment of the multitude of "ordinary"
individuals, although the various averages are not equally
safe in avoiding this type of distortion.

The typical person is familiar with at least two types of
average and frequently uses them interchangeably when
only one really applies. He has used arithmetic mean since
he learned his grade-school arithmetic, while he has used
the concept of the mode whenever he wished to draw a
favorable comparison between the average American and
another average national. The very familiarity with the
arithmetic mean has led to its indiscriminate use in situations where its characteristics become a handicap instead
of an aid. Nevertheless, it is probably the most useful
average, once its disadvantages are recognized.

The arithmetic mean is simply defined as the sum of a
series of values divided by their number. If the luncheon
checks of five students at the school cafeteria are for 37,
24, 31, 16, and 22 cents, the sum is $1.30 and the average
is $1.30 divided by five, or 26 cents. None of the five actu-
ally spent 26 cents, but this conveniently summarizes the
individual expenditures and is not far from a fair representation of this small group. If the first student had been
exceptionally hungry or accepted the challenge of his companions to test his capacity with an 87-cent load on his tray,
the average would be markedly affected. The arithmetic

mean would be increased to 36 cents. This value is a correct summary of the five checks, in the sense that it takes due notice of the exact size of each check. It is not a satisfactory representative of the five lunch trays, because it has been distorted by the extreme value of one of them.

The disturbing effects of unusual values on the arithmetic mean become less serious as the number of ordinary cases is increased. Nevertheless, the presence of extreme values must always be a danger signal to the person who uses the mean as a fair representative of the mass of the data. A substantial "increase" in average earnings in a company over a period of time may be due entirely to handsome bonuses given to a few top executives. If these officers are included with the janitors, truck drivers, and junior clerks in the calculation of the average, the result is perfectly correct as an arithmetic mean, but quite misleading as an implied statement of general or typical conditions.

Statistical measurements which run into the thousands and millions are usually consolidated into groups, called a frequency distribution, to facilitate analysis. The average value of 10,503,386 non-farm homes in 1930 could be obtained by listing them individually on an adding machine tape and dividing the grand total by the number. The study of home values would be more fruitful if one could obtain some idea of the distribution of values and their relation to the average. This can be conveniently arranged by grouping the homes in classes, for example, under $1000, $1000 to $1499, $1500 to $1999, and so on.

The calculation of the arithmetic mean from a frequency distribution requires an assumption of midvalues. The ages of 757 persons who died of tuberculosis are set up in ten-year groups in the following table. For example, the third class indicates that 212 persons suffered tubercular deaths at a time when they were at least 20 years of age but not yet 30.

AGE DISTRIBUTION OF DEATHS BY TUBERCULOSIS

Age class	No. of deaths (frequency)	Midvalue of class	Frequency times midvalue
0–10 yrs.	19	5 yrs.	95
10–20 "	76	15 "	1140
20–30 "	212	25 "	5300
30–40 "	165	35 "	5775
40–50 "	132	45 "	5940
50–60 "	92	55 "	5060
60–70 "	61	65 "	3965
Totals...............	757		27,275

The computation of the arithmetic mean of a specified group of individuals calls for a value for each of them. In the table, the exact age of each case is not known, but only the limits within which it falls. If the frequency distribution has been properly constructed by the person who had access to the original data, one may make certain substitutions which will yield a satisfactory value for the calculation of the mean. If one assumes that the nineteen cases in the first age class, under 10 years, are concentrated at the mid-position, or evenly distributed over the class, the midvalue, 5 years, may be used as a satisfactory representative for each of the persons in the class. Multiplying the number of cases by the midvalue is equivalent to adding up the values of the first nineteen cases. If this process is repeated for the other classes, and the results are summed, we have the total age of the whole group, 27,275 years. Dividing this total by 757 gives us the arithmetic mean, which is 36.03 years.

Many frequency distributions of economic and social data are published with unequal or indeterminate end classes, or both. A distribution of incomes requires this, because the bulk of the incomes are below $2000, and because the frequency table would quickly become unwieldy if the classes advanced by $1000 steps until the multi-millionaire incomes are accounted for. Furthermore, the laws providing for the publication of such data may require that the table shall be presented in such a manner that the identity of an individual cannot be revealed. Thus, if one person in a community is suspected of receiving an income far above anyone else, the publication of an income table for that area, indicating one person in the class $91,000–$92,000, with no other person for twenty classes below that level, makes the identity virtually assured. For this reason, the final class in a table may read "$15,000 and over." This presents a real difficulty in the calculation of the arithmetic mean. In the table above, a final class of sixteen cases aged 70 years and over was deliberately omitted to simplify the example. If the class had been included, the assumption would have been made that the midvalue was 75, even though this very probably understated the true midvalue of the sixteen cases.

The average which many people have in mind when they use the term is the mode, rather than the arithmetic mean. If a salesman in a men's clothing store were asked to select a wardrobe for an average man, he would probably set aside a hat, size seven and one-eighth; a shirt, size fifteen; shoes, size eight, and so on. These are the sizes called for more frequently than any others, and that is precisely the concept of the mode. According to the 1930 census the average family, based on the mode, consisted of two persons, because 6,982,835 families reported this size, while only 6,226,519 families reported three persons, and 5,234,696 families

reported four persons. This average is not disturbed by
the presence of a few unusual values. The generously pro-
portioned gentleman who asks for a shirt with a size eighteen neckband might disturb the arithmetic mean of shirt
sizes, but will have no effect on the selection of the typical,
most common size.

The mode, as the most popular value, is comparatively
easy to determine when values appear only at a small number of sharply separated values, as with the number of
children in different families. When the values may appear
at any point along a scale of measurements, a rough approxi-
mation is usually made. In the table above, page 732, we
cannot say with certainty at which age the largest number
of people died of tuberculosis. Under such circumstances,
where a high degree of accuracy is not required, it is customary to select, as the mode, the midvalue of the class
containing the largest number of cases. In the example
above the modal age for tuberculosis deaths is twenty-five.
A necessary condition of this method is that the class interval shall be uniform—for example, that each class shall
cover an age interval of ten years, at least in the most
populous classes.

The median is another average that avoids some of the
difficulties arising out of extreme cases. It is defined as
the value which has an equal number of cases on either
side, assuming that the values are arranged in order of size.
In other words, half the cases exceed the median, and half
the values fall short of it. In the lunch-tray example, if
the lunch checks are arranged in order of size (16, 22, 24,
31, 37) the twenty-four-cent check satisfies the definition
of the median. It is a good representative of the group.
If the last case happened to be eighty-seven cents, the
arithmetic mean would be disturbed profoundly, but the
median would remain unaffected. This is the great advan-

tage of the median in those cases where a few unusual items are recognized as part of the record but should not be permitted to distort the representative value.

The selection of the median from a frequency distribution is somewhat more complex, because of the lack of specific information on each value. It is necessary to assume a reconstruction of the arrangement of individuals within each class. For example, in the table on tubercular deaths, if we had the original data, we would simply arrange the records in order of age and select the 379th case. This would yield an equal number above and below. We do not have the details, but we can see by the table that the 379th case falls in the 30–40 age class, because there are only 307 cases below 30 years. We are seeking the case which is the 379th from the beginning, or the 72nd position within the 30–40 age class. (Subtract 307 from 379.) If we assume that the 165 cases in this class are distributed evenly over the ten-year interval, from 30 to 40 years, the space will be divided into 165 segments, each 10/165 of a year in length. The case in the 72nd position in the class will be $72 \times 10/165$ years removed from the initial position of 30 years. This proves to be 4.46 years, and the median age is designated as 34.46 years. This compares with 36.03 for the arithmetic mean, which was affected by the people who died at an advanced age. The median is not handicapped by the use of indeterminate end classes in frequency distributions.

The principle of the median is repeated in a group of related measures which help in describing the distribution of data. In the same way that the median divides the cases at the 50 per cent point, the quartiles divide the cases at the 25 and 75 per cent level, the deciles divide at successive 10 per cent levels, and the percentiles mark the 1 per cent divisions.

The measure of dispersion

Statistical measures can be described in terms of homogeneity or uniformity as well as in terms of high or low level. The averages show the position around which the individuals tend to rally, but some groups are much more faithful or loyal to their averages than others. The statistical tool which measures the tendency for concentration or scatter of values around a central position is called a measure of dispersion, or deviation.

An example of the difference between two groups of data which have almost the same average is illustrated in the monthly normal temperatures at San Diego, California, and Oklahoma City, Oklahoma.

MONTHLY NORMAL MEAN TEMPERATURE

	San Diego			Oklahoma City		
	Monthly mean	Deviation from mean	Deviations squared	Monthly mean	Deviation from mean	Deviations squared
January	54.3°	−6.7	44.89	37.6°	−23.0	529.0
February	55.1	−5.9	34.81	40.8	−19.8	392.04
March	56.7	−4.3	18.49	51.2	− 9.4	88.36
April	58.5	−2.5	6.25	61.0	.4	.16
May	60.8	− .2	.04	68.9	8.3	68.89
June	63.9	2.9	8.41	77.2	16.6	275.56
July	67.2	6.2	38.44	81.8	21.2	449.44
August	68.7	7.7	59.29	80.9	20.3	412.09
September	67.1	6.1	37.21	74.0	13.2	174.04
October	63.7	2.7	7.29	62.7	2.1	4.41
November	59.7	−1.3	1.69	50.0	−10.6	112.36
December	56.0	−5.	25.	40.5	−20.1	404.01
Total	731.7	51.5*	281.81	726.6	165.0*	2910.36
Average	61.0	4.3	23.48	60.6	13.8	242.53
Standard Deviation.			4.8			15.6

* Values added without regard to sign.

A glance at the table indicates immediately that although both cities hover around practically the same level (the average), San Diego has a more "even" climate than Oklahoma City. The measure of dispersion makes it possible to compare this characteristic.

The simplest measure of variation is the range. In San Diego the monthly temperature fluctuates between 54.3 and 68.7 degrees, a difference of 14.4 degrees. In Oklahoma City, this difference is over three times greater, 44.2 degrees separating the high and low months. This is a fairly satisfactory measure of the difference in temperature behavior because the twelve months may be considered as integral parts of the year. The range is frequently unsatisfactory in social and economic data because extreme cases are inclined to be isolated cases. Since the range is the difference between the two extreme values, it may become quite unreliable as a measure for the group, if the unusual values are far removed from the general run of cases.

The arithmetic deviation is an average of the distances, regardless of direction, of the individual members from some common point, usually the arithmetic mean. Thus January in San Diego is normally 6.7 degrees below the average of 61 degrees, and in Oklahoma City it is 23 degrees below the average of 60.6 degrees. Similar calculations for the other months are indicated in the table in the second column under each city. The total deviations in a year are 51.5 degrees and 165.0 degrees respectively. The average deviation is 4.3 degrees in San Diego and 13.8 degrees in Oklahoma City.

The measure of dispersion most widely used in scientific work is the standard deviation. Like the average deviation, it is based on all values, rather than merely two extreme items, but it considers a more distant stray value

as a much more serious defection from the central position
(always the arithmetic mean) than a near-by value. The
extra emphasis is obtained by squaring each deviation,
which is illustrated in the last column under each city.
An average is taken of these squared deviations, and the
square root extracted. This is the standard deviation.
Thus, under San Diego, the sum of the squared deviations
of each monthly mean from 61 degrees is 281.81, the average is 23.48 and the square root is 4.8 degrees. For Oklahoma City, measured from 60.6, the standard deviation by
the same method, is 15.6 degrees. The marked difference
between standard deviations is a measure of the difference
in evenness of climate, in so far as temperature is concerned.

The range, standard deviation, and average deviation can
be measured for frequency distributions, using the same
assumptions involved for the arithmetic mean. In actual
practice, the standard deviation is most frequently used,
because it is an important tool in theoretical work involving
the fluctuations of sampling.

The measure of correlation

The tendency for the price of wheat to rise when there
is a crop shortage, and fall with bumper crops, can be
observed in our agricultural history. People with a low
income spend a higher proportion of it for food than do
people with high incomes. The accident rate for workmen
increases with their age. The burden of poor relief increases
with the percentage of illiteracy. These and many other
examples of direct relationships are measurable by statistical
means.

The technique for measuring the degree of simultaneous
or contrary fluctuation is a statistical problem, but the
interpretation of the results requires careful analysis of

the causes. A discovery that the number of marriages declines with the interest rate on government bonds may lead to the superficial conclusion that these two series are directly related. To assume that the Secretary of the Treasury could substantially increase the number of marriages by declaring a higher interest rate on Treasury bonds would be as absurd as an attempt to lower government bond yields by rejecting half the applications for marriage licenses. A careful examination of circumstances surrounding these important measurements would show that both of them are profoundly affected by the state of business in the nation. When times are prosperous, marriages promise to be successful, and capital funds need not be satisfied with low government interest rates for lack of alternative uses. The common cause affects them both, although the measure of correlation is too often considered to be the proof of direct causal connection between the two parties.

The statistical measure of correlation which is most widely used is the Pearsonian coefficient of correlation, designated by the letter "r." It recognizes the degree to which each pair of observations contributes to the general statement that one characteristic changes directly or inversely with changes in the other. It is mathematically related to the arithmetic mean, and is subject to the same qualifications when the record includes a freakish value among a comparatively small list of items. The coefficient uses another statistical measure described in this chapter, the standard deviation. In its simplest terms, the coefficient is an average of the combination relationship between the two variables. If larger values in one are always or nearly always associated with large values in the other, and small values with small, the correlation is said to be positively high. When large values in one are always associated with small values in the other, the correlation is negatively high. As the qualification "nearly" becomes more and more important, that is, as large values in one series are indiscriminately associated with large, small, and medium values of the other, the correlation approaches zero. The coefficient of correlation is a quantitative statement of a relation which would otherwise have to be described more indefinitely by qualifications such as "nearly," "just a little," and so on.

The earning power of an individual depends very definitely on his education. This axiom is quite generally accepted, but there are disturbing exceptions to the rule. The exceptions may influence some to reject the rule entirely, while others may brush them aside as inconsequential. How can we measure the efficacy of this general statement, with due regard for the exceptions? Consider the simple illustration of ten individuals whose weekly earnings and years of schooling are listed opposite.

The deviation of each individual from the average, both in earnings and schooling, are computed and listed in the third and fourth columns respectively. Note that the deviations below the average are designated with a minus sign. In the fifth and sixth columns, the deviations are squared, and each column is totaled in preparation for the computation of the standard deviation. In the last column the deviations in earnings and schooling are multiplied and the products totaled. One should bear in mind that the product of two negative quantities is positive, but a negative value multiplied by a positive yields a negative product. The fourth case in the last column is a negative value, and must be deducted from the others in arriving at the net total. If this were an example of negative correlation—for example, the relation of earnings to days lost through ill-

CORRELATION OF EARNINGS AND SCHOOL ATTENDANCE

X Earnings	Y Years of schooling	D_x	D_y	$D_x{}^2$	$D_y{}^2$	D_xD_y
$20	4	−9	−5.8	81	33.64	52.2
22	6	−7	−3.8	49	14.44	26.2
25	9	−4	− .8	16	.64	3.2
25	11	−4	1.2	16	1.44	−4.8
27	8	−2	−1.8	4	3.24	3.6
30	12	1	2.2	1	4.84	2.2
30	10	1	.2	1	.04	.2
34	12	5	2.2	25	4.84	11.0
35	14	6	4.2	36	17.64	25.2
42	12	13	2.2	169	4.84	28.6
$290*	98			398	85.6	148.0
$29**	9.8			39.8	8.56	

Average earnings $=$ $29.
Average schooling $=$ 9.8 years.
For the sake of convenience, the earnings are designated by X and the
school attendance by Y.
D_x is the deviation of each value of X from the mean of all values of X.
D_y is the deviation of each value of Y from the mean of all values of Y.
N is the number of cases in the problem.
 * Totals.
** Averages.

Standard deviation of $X = \sqrt{\dfrac{398}{10}} = 6.3 = $ S.D.$_x$

Standard deviation of $Y = \sqrt{\dfrac{85.6}{10}} = 2.9 = $ S.D.$_y$

$r = \dfrac{\text{Sum of } D_xD_y}{\text{N.S.D.}_x\text{S.D.}_y} = \dfrac{148.0}{10(6.3)(2.9)} = .81$ (the coefficient of correlation)

ness—most of the products in the last column would be
negative, and the net sum would be negative.

It is apparent that the earnings are not strictly proportional to years of schooling, but nevertheless tend to vary
with the educational experience. Perfect correlation would
be indicated by $r = 1$. A correlation of .81 is considered
a very respectable correlation. The exceptions to the gen-

eral rule, which cause the difference between .81 and 1.,
may be due to difference in age, in native intelligence, or
in habits of industry, or to several other causes. If these
exceptions become too insistent, the size of the coefficient
may be reduced materially, and search must be made for
another factor to explain variations in earnings.

Correlation techniques are intriguing because of the
brevity of statement and the power of conviction of a high
numerical value of r, but they should be used only as a
supplement to careful analysis of the logical relationships
to be expected, particularly if a causal connection is sought.
Arithmetically speaking, it is no more difficult to compute
the correlation between rainfall and divorces than the correlation between heights and weights of college freshmen,
but causal connection, if any, would be more difficult to
find in the former. The essential element in the analysis
is always the search for the logical hypothesis, first; the
techniques come later.

Index numbers and ratios

The index number is one of the most widely used statistical tools in social and economic analysis. It is a special
adaptation of the average, and its object is the compression
of a multitude of changes or differences into a single representative figure. Its original use, and its most frequent use
today, has been to measure price changes, although it is
finding increasing favor for measuring production, the flow
of trade, and the burden of relief.

The price of butter is determined by many factors, such
as the amount in storage, the condition of pastures in the
dairy regions, the cost of butter substitutes, and the economic well-being of potential purchasers. A similar list
could be drawn up for every other food product bought by
the average family. If special circumstances, such as a

heavy frost in an important citrus region, or a plague in a beef-raising state, cause a marked increase in the price of an individual food item, the thrifty housewife may try to escape the higher cost by serving substitutes on her table. However, when a widespread drought, or an inflation of currency, or a major depression visits a country, few food commodities can escape the effects, although some may not change in price as much as others. An index of food prices measures the composite change in a sample or representative group of commodities, and then additional study is necessary to estimate how much of the change is due to any single important cause.

The following table lists the average retail prices of ten foods in fifty-one American cities on about July 1, 1935 and 1936, and the percentage ratio of the 1936 prices to the 1935 prices, usually called the price relative.

Commodity	Unit	July 1, 1935	July 1, 1936	Price relative, 1935 base
Flour	lb.	4.9¢	4.5¢	92%
Bread	lb.	8.3	8.1	97
Round steak	lb.	37.5	33.6	89
Veal cutlets	lb.	38.8	40.8	105
Leg of lamb	lb.	27.3	31.4	115
Butter	lb.	31.1	37.4	120
Eggs	doz.	36.8	33.8	92
Oranges	doz.	32.6	34.9	107
Potatoes	lb.	2.2	4.8	218
Chocolate	pkge.	22.1	16.5	74
Average				110.9

Five of the foods rose in price and five declined, but the advances more than offset the drops, as the average price relative (by the arithmetic mean) was 111 per cent, a gain of 11 per cent over 1935. The sharp increase in potato prices more than offset the price declines.

The average price change just computed assumes an equality of importance among the commodities, which experience tells us is untrue. To most families, a change in the price of potatoes is much more important than a similar change in the price of chocolate. How important? Our purchases express our judgment of significance. This is the problem of weighting in index-number calculations.

Irving Fisher has popularized the "market-basket" concept of weighting commodities in an index number. After a trip to the grocers, our shopping basket contains varying quantities of commodities, not just one unit of each. Let us assume that we asked the grocer to fill the basket with a year's supply of each item on July 1, 1935, and to refill the order on July 1, 1936. What would be the ratio of the grocer's bill in 1936 to the bill in 1935? The table of commodities is repeated below, with the average annual consumption of a working-class family in a Midwestern city, as reported by the United States Bureau of Labor Statistics.

Commodity	Annual consumption	July 1, 1935	July 1, 1936	1935 Market basket	1936 Market basket
Flour	391.8 lbs	4.9¢	4.5¢	$19.20	$17.63
Bread	324.0 lbs.	8.3	8.1	26.89	26.24
Round steak	37.4 lbs..	37.5	33.6	14.02	12.57
Veal cutlets......	22.4 lbs.	38.8	40.8	8.69	9.14
Leg of lamb......	2.1 lbs.	27.3	31.4	.57	.66
Butter	68.4 lbs.	31.1	37.4	21.27	25.58
Eggs	49.9 doz.	36.8	33.8	18.36	16.87
Oranges	4.4 doz.	32.8	34.9	1.44	1.54
Potatoes	1141.1 lbs.	2.2	4.8	25.10	54.77
Chocolate	3.0 pkge.	22.2	16.5	.67	.50
Totals				$136.21	$165.50

The ratio of 1936 prices to 1935, as now weighted, is 121.5 per cent, or a 21.5 per cent increase instead of 11 per cent.

The same procedure could be used when measuring changes in wholesale prices, or prices received by farmers, or volume of manufactured products. A modified technique is used for the index of the cost of living, issued by the United States Bureau of Labor Statistics. An index is formed for each of five groups of family expenditures, and these are combined in a weighted average. The weights are the fractions of the wage earner's dollar that go to each group, according to past budget studies. For July, 1936, the separate and combined indexes, as compared to a base position of a 1923–1925 average, were as follows:

Expenditure group	July 1936 index	Weight	Weighted index
Food	84%	.32	26.88%
Clothing	78	.14	10.92
Rent	64	.20	12.80
Fuel and light......,...	87	.06	5.22
House furnishings	77	.05	3.85
Miscellaneous	97	.23	22.31
All items..............		1.00	81.98

The wage earner could live in 1936 for 18 per cent less than was necessary in 1923 to 1925, assuming that he kept the same standards of living. An individual family, or a professional man's family, which did not spend its income in the proportions indicated above, might find that the ratio of its cost to a 1923–1925 level was distinctly more or less than the 18 per cent difference.

A frequent use of cost-of-living index numbers is in wage disputes, and in measurements of real wages. The World War convinced the working population that a 50 per cent increase in wages was no advantage if the wage dollar bought only half as much as before, that is, if the cost of living had doubled. The correction of the money wages

by a measure of the purchasing power of the worker's dollar
permits a comparison of real wages which shows the status
of the worker's well-being. In the following table, the
average weekly earnings in New York State factories are
converted into 1923–1925 dollars by dividing each value
by the index of cost of living for that year.

NOMINAL AND REAL WAGES IN NEW YORK STATE, 1926–1935

Year	Average weekly earnings	Index of cost of living 1923–1925 base	Real wages
1926	$29.02	102	$28.42
1927	29.30	101	29.02
1928	29.44	99	29.75
1929	29.99	99	30.25
1930	28.81	96	30.00
1931	26.42	87	30.30
1932	22.73	78	29.15
1933	21.83	76	28.70
1934	23.19	79	29.35
1935	24.36	81	30.06

The variation in real wages is very slight compared to
the variation in money wages, because the decline in cost
of living compensated for the thinner pay envelope. During and after the World War, many trade unions in the
United States and abroad had wage agreements which provided for an automatic adjustment of wages according to
the cost of living. Most of these agreements fell into disuse
by 1926, because the worker lost his enthusiasm for the
contract when the cost of living stopped its secondary
post-war rise in 1926.

The table above gives an incomplete picture, because
unemployment became serious after 1929 and the worker
lost much of the advantage of a declining cost of living.
A much more correct picture would be obtained by apply-

ing an index of cost of living to data on annual earnings. In all purchasing-power corrections, an essential point is the selection of a proper index. The manner in which the workingman spends his dollar is not the way the professional man or the junior executive spends his, hence the workingman's index should not be used carelessly to measure purchasing power for any and all standards of living.

The index number is a ratio, because it is usually expressed as a relation of one period or place to some selected base year or base location. Ratios are a great convenience in statistical comparisons because they reduce large values to usable proportions. Per capita county debts, or per capita relief expenditures, eliminate the factor of difference in population numbers and permit comparisons with simpler values. A similar use is the ratio per thousand or per hundred thousand, which is the basis for much of the work in vital statistics. Death rates, birth rates, and crime rates are usually expressed in ratios per thousand persons. Specific death rates, for individual causes of death, are expressed in ratios per hundred thousand.

For all their simplicity, ratios should be handled with great care in drawing conclusions from statistical data. The numerator and the denominator which constitute the ratio should have some reasonably close relation to each other. Dead timber should be thrown out of the denominator, particularly. The number of marriages should be related to that part of the population which is of marriageable age, rather than to the entire population. The deaths from an infectious disease in a camp should be compared with the number of exposures, rather than to the entire camp population. It is not always possible to remove extraneous matter from the data, but the objective should always be kept in mind.

DANGERS OF STATISTICAL INDIGESTION

The beginning of a statistical inquiry is a careful examination of the objective and an understanding of the logical
premises which shall guide the collection of data. When
the study is continuous, and monthly or annual data are
currently added to an existing store, there may be a tendency to assume that the established routine will insure the
comparability of the data. Small changes frequently occur
in business practices, in government bureaus, or in welfare
administration, which seem inconsequential individually,
but may accumulate over a number of years until the data
cannot or should not be compared with earlier records.
The addition of previously non-reporting areas to the
"registration area" for statistics on deaths temporarily dis-
torts the data, although ultimately the statistics will be
more complete and more accurate. The statistician must
take every precaution that his data shall consistently apply
to his problem from start to finish.

The necessity for reducing masses of data to convenient
form may lead to a misleading simplicity. The average
working-class family may spend a third of its income for
food, but this does not mean that any wage earner, selected
at random, will spend this proportion for groceries. There
are good chances that he will not be found far from the
ratio, but the statistician can rarely predict an individual's
behavior. Prediction, with reservations, is made only for
the mass. That is why statistical laws are expressed in
probabilities rather than certainties.

An increasing use of statistics is found in the field of
propaganda or "public enlightenment." Unfortunately,
most modern propaganda cannot be dismissed as 100 per
cent falsehood, because it is frequently based on official

records and statements by persons of unquestioned integrity. The damage lies not in deliberately changing a figure, but in using half truths, treating a mixture of data as though it were pure and homogeneous. Compulsory vaccination against small pox has been opposed on the grounds that a certain number of people have died from small pox after being vaccinated. It is difficult to prove by statistics how many lives have been saved from small pox. Like an efficient police department, vaccination operates by prevention, which is much less spectacular than a cure. Comparisons of government expenditures are difficult because the functions and tax burdens are shifted back and forth between local, state, and national government units, which do not publish data on a comparable basis. Investments are hard to evaluate because accounting data are incomplete, or consolidated into useless totals. These types of propaganda are much more difficult to combat than deliberate falsifications, and the defense lies only in careful examination of the sources of data, the original purpose of their collection, the logical basis for distinctions and classifications used, and comparisons made.

Many scientific milestones have been passed with relatively simple instruments but with great patience and care in the collection of data. Noguchi discovered the spirochæte that causes locomotor ataxia with an ordinary medical microscope set in the midst of many specimen slides, books, and papers on his dining-room table. Faraday worked for seven years with simple magnets and wires to prove that electricity could be induced by magnets in a "dead" wire. Elaborate instruments can do little to compensate for carelessness in the control of conditions, or for an indiscriminate collection of facts. Nobody will deny that we lack satisfactory and sufficient data on many social and technical problems. Before we open a new investigation, mail a million questionnaires, or release a thousand interviewers, we should be reasonably sure that the possibilities of data now available have been exhausted. Library shelves are bending with volumes, and filing cases are bulging with folders containing data which have never been fully explored. Before an extra page is added to a voluminous questionnaire, or another one or two questions added to the census schedule, we should inquire whether the present questions are stated in the best form to avoid prejudice and confusion. Careful selection and adequate training of interviewers would increase the accuracy of data now being collected.

Statistical indigestion may result from an excess of faith in the magic of mountains of data. We are bewildered by the vast amount of information which has been gathered. We may try to reduce it to convenient size by means of averages and ratios, but our averages may contain many "impurities," because they cover too much territory. An average based on fewer cases, more carefully measured and selected, in the scientific sense, would yield more significant results. It is not true that there is "safety in numbers" if the classifications are too broad, and lack of ingenuity results in the oversight of significant relationships. Statistical methods are restricted to data in the mass, but the mass should be as homogeneous as possible, and this goal can be approached only by careful measurement, careful selection, and careful interpretation.

BIBLIOGRAPHY

Barry, Frederick, *The Scientific Habit of Thought* (Columbia University Press, New York, 1927).
Ogburn, William F., and Goldenweiser, Alexander, *The Social Sciences* (Houghton Mifflin Company, Boston, 1927).

Ritchie, Arthur D., *Scientific Method* (Harcourt, Brace & Company, New York, 1923).

Wolf, Abraham, *The Essentials of Scientific Method* (The Macmillan Company, New York, 1925).

Chaddock, R. E., *Principles and Methods of Statistics* (Houghton Mifflin Company, Boston, 1925).

Mills, F. C., *Statistical Methods* (Henry Holt & Company, New York, 1924).

Pearl, Raymond, *Medical Biometry and Statistics*, Second Edition (W. B. Saunders & Company, Philadelphia, 1930).

Sorensen, Herbert, *Statistics for Students of Psychology and Education* (McGraw-Hill Book Company, New York, 1936).

Whipple, G. C., *Vital Statistics*, Second Edition (John Wiley & Sons, New York, 1923).

White, R. Clyde, *Social Statistics* (Harper & Brothers, New York, 1933).

CHAPTER XVI

Social Valuation

MARY J. SHAW
University of Minnesota

INTRODUCTION

THE preceding chapters of this book have included little discussion of social values, of the good and the bad, the better and the worse. Moreover, it is clear that the omission has been deliberate. It has been pointed out in some of the chapters that questions of value are not a legitimate part of the subject matter of the social sciences. Since the social scientist draws attention to this exclusion, it is obvious that questions of good and bad, the better and the worse, must lie close to the social sciences, and yet for presumably good reasons they are excluded.

Students coming for the first time to the formal study of the social studies are often impatient with this situation, and every teacher of sociology or of economics meets this type of question, "What do you really think about this?" The one who puts the question usually means not, "What do you think the facts are?" but "What do you think about the values involved?" If the scientist answers, "That question is inappropriate," he is likely to be accused of hedging. Obviously there is confusion somewhere. A book concerned with the social sciences therefore may well include at least a postscript about social values and their place in the world of knowledge.

Value judgments and value terms

When we assign a value of any kind to an object or situation, we are making a value judgment. Illustrations may clarify the difference between such judgments and what are often called judgments of fact. When we say for instance, that a picture called "Aurora" was painted by Guido Reni, that the quantum theory accounts for certain phenomena of light, or that the Russian Revolution occurred in 1917, we are merely stating that certain situations exist, without giving them any value whatever. If we add that the "Aurora" is not a good painting, that the quantum theory is a beautiful example of scientific reasoning, or that the Russian Revolution was a disaster, then we are making judgments of value. We are affirming that some object or state of affairs is good or bad, beautiful or ugly, or better or worse than some other possible situation.

Every language has such direct value terms as we have used in these judgments. In addition, many words which were once purely descriptive have become value terms through long use. The current slang and the current situation make new, if transitory, additions. Illustrations of such indirect terms for expressing approval or disapproval are good only for limited times and places, but for the United States in 1937, we may safely list "democratic," "practical," "vulgar," "modern," "un-American," "individualism," and "politician" as examples of the kind of thing we mean. Indeed there are so many of these indirect value terms that the social scientist who is trying to state the facts of social life without a coloring of approval or disapproval is forced either to define painstakingly the common words he uses or to invent a new vocabulary.

Value judgments based on preference

The large number of value terms and the frequency of value judgments arise from the fact that preference is a fundamental human trait. Perhaps nothing about man is more conspicuous or more important than the obvious truth that he does not view the world of nature and society impartially. To him it is never a colorless and neutral scene. Some aspects of the environment interest him more than others and, among those that interest him, some attract and some repel. He pronounces them good or bad, better or worse, beautiful or ugly. He sees heroes and villains in natural forces and conceives a world nearer to his heart's desire.

These preferences are based on our own interests as biological and social individuals. All of the things which we judge to be good or desirable seem to us to make their contribution to satisfactory living. Some are more important than others, some fulfill permanent needs, some are transitory. Each person develops a pattern of living in which some goods are subordinated to others, and as many as possible are achieved. This is not easy, for the goods of life are limited, while those which can be had are not always compatible with each other. Furthermore, since no two men are the same, no two sets of values can be identical. Yet each has to take the other's evaluation as real and adjust himself to it as best he can, since all human beings are born into a society which they cannot leave and would not leave if they could.

Because nature and society do not furnish all of the good things which men's interests can suggest to their imaginations, we set up standards to which we try to make the world conform. Most men agree that this is not the best of all possible worlds and are reformers, on a small scale at least. They wish to change nature or social institutions, here a little, there a little, until a better situation is produced. A few bold souls, not content with such piecemeal improvement, hope to bring about wide-sweeping reorganizations of society. In any social group, therefore, imaginary utopias are as natural as any other social product.

Standards, like values, are constantly expressed in language. "There ought to be a better bridge over this river." "We should not allow our natural resources to be squandered." "No one should starve in the midst of plenty." "Examinations should be abolished." "Those who will not work should not eat." "The best government is a dictatorship of the proletariat." Every "ought," every "should" or "should not" in these judgments implies some ideal, some standard of values.

Judgments of value in the social sciences

So strong is this tendency to value and to set up standards, that it is only in exceptional cases, and after careful discipline, that most of us are able to view even a small area of the universe in an unprejudiced way. If the scene is very remote from our own life, we can look at it with little emotion, and perhaps abstain from passing judgment upon it. What the Chinese do, we may say, makes little difference to us. Or when we devote ourselves to the pursuit of science, we make a rigorous effort to exclude, for the time at least, all other interests except the interest in truth. The emphasis on scientific method, on scientific objectivity, in this book and elsewhere, is evidence that this is a difficult accomplishment. Even when we succeed we are still exhibiting preference, the preference for truth rather than falsehood.

Men have always valued knowledge; even those who do not rate it highly will agree that, within limits, it is a good thing. The limitation of its popularity is partly due to the fact that it is exclusive of other interests, at least for the time being. One who wishes to learn what the truth is about a subject must forget other preferences, leave out of consideration his likes and dislikes and questions of good and bad. The individual who classifies only some of the facts he is investigating to that extent defeats his own interest in truth. Hence in this book there is little discussion of what ought to be. The social scientist believes that, in order to treat social facts with impartiality, he must omit evaluations.

Values, moreover, are in some important ways quite different from matters of fact and, therefore, according to many social scientists, not suitable subject matter for scientific inquiry. A prominent sociologist says:

> The principal task of ethics in the past has been an elaboration of the prescription of *what ought to be* and *what ought not to be.* . . . So far as sociology professes that its scientific task consists in the study of social phenomena *as they have existed, do exist and will exist,* there is no direct connection between the two disciplines. . . . Natural sciences and other real sciences study the reality as it is, irrespective of whether it is "good" or "bad." [1]

This point of view has had its critics. One of them makes this comment:

> Some sociologists have banished from their program all questions of value and have sought to restrict themselves to the theory of social happenings. This effort to look upon human actions with the same ethical neutrality with which we view geometric figures, is admirable.

---

[1] Sorokin, Pitirim A., "Sociology and Ethics," in *The Social Sciences and Their Interrelations,* edited by Ogburn, William F., and Goldenweiser, Alexander, p. 311 (Houghton Mifflin Company, Boston, 1927).

But the questions of human value are inescapable, and those who banish them at the front door admit them unavowedly and therefore uncritically at the back door.[2]

Perhaps the social scientist does admit values at the back door; that is, he must take some of them for granted whether he considers them a part of his subject matter or not. But on the whole, as long as he consistently holds to his own idea of what the scientific method requires, he refuses to commit himself as to what he thinks is good or bad. Is communism worse than capitalism? Is the profit motive good for society as a whole? Should freedom of speech be curtailed? The scientist as a human being, an American, a Baptist, a Republican, or a philosopher may answer; as a scientist he has nothing to say. He will tell you what, as a matter of fact, the consequences are when freedom of speech is not allowed, how the profit motive operates in a market; he will not otherwise help you to choose between alternatives. And if anything in the presentation of his material gives the reader an inkling as to which side he is taking, his scientific colleagues are likely to bring him to book for wandering from the narrow path of scientific rectitude, and accuse him of becoming a philosopher.

There is only one way in which the social scientist believes that he can safely treat of values and retain scientific impartiality; namely, he can discuss them as facts. For example, the anthropoligist and the sociologist will necessarily include man's judgments of value, his ideals, and his standards as part of his non-material culture. The moral code of the Plains Indians is an important part of their whole culture pattern and, as such, is part of the

[2] Cohen, Morris R., "The Social Sciences and the Natural Sciences," *op. cit.,* p. 453.

subject matter of cultural anthropology. Beliefs of contemporary Americans about the desirability of divorce, about the value of going to church, or about the importance of discipline in bringing up children are all parts of the culture pattern and will be noted by the sociologist.

Another scientific ideal, as yet imperfectly attained in the biological and social sciences, but still their goal, is attainment of the kind of knowledge that can be mathematically expressed. It seems clear that this ideal excludes knowledge of values, since they are not subject to the type of measurement required. For justifiable reasons, the modern sciences have tried to limit their field to the quantitative aspects of the world. The high regard in which science is held today sometimes leads to the fallacious conclusion that whatever is not scientific in this sense cannot be knowledge. Yet there are important fields of investigation in which we have organized and verified knowledge which is not capable of mathematical treatment. In these cases we are dealing with material which either is not measurable with sufficient exactness, or is essentially qualitative. The social sciences include much descriptive material; history, literature, the other arts, and philosophy furnish other examples of non-quantitative disciplines.

Omission of evaluation from the social sciences, then, does not imply that we have no verified and organized knowledge of values. It means that they are more suitably handled by other methods than those to which the ideal sciences would restrict themselves. Specific assumptions and concepts underlie each science. Analysis of these assumptions constitutes the philosophy of the sciences. The philosophy of the social sciences would analyze, among other concepts, those of social values. And finally, the disciplines of ethics and esthetics consider the fundamental meaning of the good and of the beautiful, and their related ideas.

CRITICAL REFLECTION IN THE STUDY OF SOCIAL VALUES

Because it is undeniably difficult, if not impossible, to come to final conclusions about questions of value, there is a tendency to assume that no intelligent methods can be applied to them. Here, as we sometimes say, one man's ideas are as good as another's. Yet even those who make this claim are likely to betray the fact that it is impossible to maintain such a point of view consistently. For if no comparison of values can be made, then we should not feel the necessity of giving reasons for our preferences. And yet we constantly do give reasons, and thereby imply that there are bases for our judgments of value which should convince reflective people. If we were consistent in the denial that any reasons could be given, we should be reduced to exclamation rather than to argument. "This is good" or "that is bad" would then be the last word about the matter.

Without going into the more difficult attempt to determine what we mean ultimately by good and bad, we shall now consider how a reflective method can be applied to questions of social value. We shall begin with the fact that we do give things different values, and ask, "How can we be more intelligent in our choices among them?"

Origin of reflection in social conflict

The preferences and values of an individual depend largely upon the groups to which, as we say significantly, he *belongs*. Inasmuch as he is a member of the group and participates in its activities, the interests of the group are necessarily his interests. The member of a family, of a church, of a trade union, of a fraternity, or of a nation, in so far as he is functionally part of the group, has accepted its standards, at least in part. For those standards express interests that the members have in common—the very thing that makes them a group.

Furthermore, everyone is born into one of these groups, the family, becomes an involuntary member of others, a school or possibly a church, and is trained in childhood to accept the standards of his group, long before he is in a position to make his own choices. From his elders, who express in their judgments of approval and disapproval the values of the group, he learns what he may successfully do as a member of his family and his neighborhood. It has always been a function of education to train the younger members of society in the behavior that is acceptable to those in control. Thus, education, particularly the training given by parents, brothers, or sisters, is conservative in the original meaning of the term. It conserves or saves the values of the group. In some societies this is the only function of education; in all societies schools are limited in the amount of criticism of the prevailing tradition which they dare introduce.

We recognize the influence of education upon standards easily enough in countries where national propaganda is deliberately used to build up one set of values at the expense of others. In Soviet Russia, for example, a child is taught that individually buying articles at one price and selling them at a higher price to make a profit is an evil practice, not to be tolerated in a socialist society. For this undesirable behavior there are, of course, terms of reproach.

It is "speculation," "counter-revolutionary activity," or a "crime against the toiling masses."

Yet it is also true, although not so obvious, that even in those societies in which a unified propaganda is at a minimum, the total educational process is effective in producing individuals who agree to a large extent about values. In America few find anything undesirable in private profit, for which, accordingly, we have terms of approval. It is not "speculation" but "good business," an exhibition of "individual freedom" and "initiative." We have schools and colleges devoted to making this process of trade for profit more effective.

Because so many of our values are learned through education, with little conscious choice on our part, it is usually difficult, if not impossible, to recall how or when we learned them. They seem obvious and natural, and as a result, absolute; they seem to be good and valid for everyone. Those who do not accept them we are likely to consider ignorant, stupid, or at least perverse. Yet, of course, the fact that we feel this way about it is no guarantee that we are right. Fiji Islander, African Bushman, Russian, and Italian are like us in this respect. Each believes that there is a superior set of values and that he possesses it. It is, of course, possible that some one set of values is superior to all others and that this superiority would finally be generally recognized if there were a chance for everyone to compare values fairly, without prejudice. Meanwhile let us admit that a feeling of assurance does not imply any such superiority. It usually means only that the dogmatic individual has been effectively trained in one culture rather than in another, and is incapable of feeling the good which is inherent in systems outside of his own. Such dogmatism has frequently led to cultural oppression, the forcing of foreign values upon reluctant but helpless groups. The imperialistic expansion of European civilization into other parts of the world provides a wealth of illustrations.

As long as we stay at home, either physically or mentally, this business of taking our own code for granted, with little reflection upon it, works fairly well. But standards are sharply challenged when we move from one group into another. The student who leaves a small town to attend a university, the businessman who represents his firm abroad, the tourist who spends a summer in England or Russia—each finds himself among people whose loyalties are different from those to which he has given allegiance. The experience may be enlightening, but it is unlikely to be comfortable. If the contrast is marked, the individual feels lost, or on the defensive for the values which he holds. It is not difficult then to understand the astonishment of the South Sea islanders when they first heard from Christian missionaries that the amount of clothing one wears is an index to his moral condition.

In the face of contrasts between codes, some individuals merely laugh off the opposing standard as an amusing oddity or a bit of childishness on the part of a foreigner. Travelers return with amusing stories to illustrate how queer life is in the outskirts of their own moral world. The reaction may be more dogmatic, and then the outsider is judged to be unreasonable, or even immoral. Many a tourist comes back to the safe haven of home, reinforced in his feeling of personal righteousness and none the wiser for his excursion. He is still innocent of any reflection. There are other more fundamentally stirring experiences from which it is, in a sense, impossible to come home. Some types of contrast arise out of, and represent, conflict between group standards from which it is hopeless to try to escape. If it were not for such conflicts there would be little or no difficulty about accepting values, and thought about them would not arise.

Modern civilizations are characterized by the complexity of the groupings that make them up. The individual is not merely a member of one unit, but of many. This is true, though to a much lesser degree, of all societies, even the primitive ones. But the increase of what we call civilization has brought division of social activity among many types of groups, each of which serves a slightly different purpose from that of any other. The membership of these groups necessarily overlaps. In a democratic state, lesser organizations are largely voluntary; the state regulates relations between them only to the extent that regulation is necessary to preserve the basic social system. Consequently any adult member of society is a member, by virtue of birth or of choice, of several groups.

The individual may have the good fortune to belong to social groupings that do not conflict; but inasmuch as the purpose of every organization differs from that of every other, it is likely that at times he will be confronted with the problem of bringing into harmony his own many-sided interests, of comparing standards which are incompatible and possibly irreconcilable. A small child in school accepts the standards of the teacher or of the other pupils and returns in a missionary spirit to improve his parents. In 1936 a German merchant complained that his daughter in the fourth grade of the public school came home announcing that Wotan was the real German god, and that the Christian faith was non-Aryan and good only for outsiders. The teacher and the other pupils said so. On a slightly different level, many a college student finds an embarrassing difference between the social standards of his family and those of the fraternity to which he belongs.

The German school child illustrated one way of solving such a conflict; she allied herself on one side of the question, took the part of one group against the other. Quite obviously the matter is not always so easy. Loyalties may be deeply rooted in the personality and still in fundamental ways be in conflict. In such cases, taking sides is not enough. Sometimes it is possible to avoid the issue by compartmentalizing one's life, placing the contending interests in separate spheres. An often cited example is that of the businessman who has one ethical code for family and friends and another for business associates. The obvious objection to this so-called solution is that it resolves nothing and is therefore unstable. A third solution, and the only one which affords satisfactory results, is to give thoughtful consideration to the opposing values with either a clear-cut choice between them or a reorganization of one or both sets of values so that they are no longer in conflict. This type of solution involves working out an harmonious ethical code. It is the beginning of ethical wisdom. The questions which philosophers and laymen have debated for centuries about the highest or the ultimate good have arisen out of conflicts of loyalties and the search for ideals that make harmonious living possible.

Within a large social group, such as the nation, other conflicts arise which may, for the individual, be remote or near according to his situation. Trade unions and associations of manufacturers, farmers, and merchants have different interests and, consequently, different standards as to what ought to be done. Conflicts arise between states which lead to treaties or to war. In these large conflicts, methods similar to those used in facing personal conflicts have been employed. There have been attempts to compartmentalize the struggle, as when a government gives encouragement first to the laborer and then to the employer. Nations take sides even though their allegiance brings war. Occasionally there is an effort to find some kind of real harmony between the apparently conflicting interests. Out of such attempts have arisen important theories of social, economic, and political ethics.

Analysis of meaning—a first step in solving conflicts

To make an intelligent analysis of values, we must first consider a difficulty about words which is particularly acute in discussions of social problems. If we are to think about values we must be sure that we are *thinking* instead of merely *feeling*, and that we know what we are thinking about. A little consideration of some of the difficulties of language will show that these are not trivial points.

Words are arbitrary symbols of things, relations, and ideas. That is to say, they have meanings which can be discovered by looking in dictionaries. However, they are learned not by reading dictionaries but by hearing them used in different tones of voice suggesting approval or disapproval, and in different circumstances. Consequently, due to these associations, they have not merely an idea meaning for us but also a flavor, an emotional coloring. Sometimes their idea meaning is very obscure while nevertheless they readily suggest the pleasant or the unpleasant. And since our use of words is learned by gradual experience, it is easy to forget what experience it was which first gave them the emotional coloring which they now have. The conditioning occasion is forgotten; the flavor remains. For example, we often have strong prejudices against proper names which, as a matter of fact, are pleasant enough to the ear. The horrid little girl at school whose name was Marjorie may make that name unpleasant to her schoolmates even after they are middle-aged businessmen who have long ago forgotten her existence.

Our vocabularies of approval or disapproval thus come to contain many words which originally were merely descriptive terms. And as the value content of the word increases, the idea content becomes less important; when such words are used, feeling swamps thinking. A teacher once asked a class of forty adults how they felt about communism. Every one stated that he was strongly opposed to it. The instructor then asked them to write an explanation of the meaning of the word, communism. Not one could do so, beyond saying that communism is un-American.

The emotional coloring of words must be taken into account if speech is to be accurate or effective. The scientist creates for himself a special vocabulary in order to avoid shop-worn terms which trail emotional clouds behind them. The poet arouses the desired emotions by using words which will evoke them; the poetry of one nation will seldom arouse the same feelings in another culture, where the usage has been different. The politician, the propagandist for any cause, the rabble rouser, the advertiser, all speak to us in emotionalized words to win us to their causes.

Detaching words from their surrounding fog of feeling is only a preliminary step in analysis of their meaning. Analysis obviously requires accurate definition, but we soon discover that definition is something more than the mere matter of deciding how words are to be used. It requires careful analysis of the ideas involved. A first step in the solution of an intellectual problem, whether scientific or philosophical, is analysis of fundamental concepts or general ideas used in the discussion of that problem. This analysis is, however, in a sense provisional, a starting point. For as the study proceeds, the meaning and application of the idea becomes more precise, and at the end it is more thoroughly understood than at the beginning. The economist, for instance, must decide upon a preliminary definition of economic value. As he goes on to develop the application of the idea to a multitude of cases, its meaning becomes clearer. We may say that, in a sense, the whole science of economics is required for adequate analysis of the meaning of those terms which have been given tentative definitions at the outset of the study.

In dealing with questions of value of any kind the fundamental procedure is an analysis of what we mean by certain general ideas which are before us in at least vague form. We clarify our meanings and thereby arrive at the solution of intellectual problems about values. We shall discuss later the way in which such analysis may help us to solve practical conflicts.

Two things are required for the real understanding of a general idea: we must know what meanings it includes or excludes, and what the particular cases are to which it applies. When definition of meaning is difficult, we are tempted to fall back on illustrations, yet mere illustrations do not define. If we wish to understand, for instance, the meaning of democracy, it is not enough to be able to point to the United States and England as examples.

In one of Plato's dialogues Socrates is represented as talking about piety with a young man who is supposed to be a specialist in matters of religion and who, rather surprisingly, has charged his own father with murder on the ground that piety requires him to do so. (His excuse is that his father has offended the gods by his crime and that it is the duty of a pious son to bring accusation against him.) Socrates thinks or pretends to think that this is an excellent opportunity for him to learn what the real nature of piety is, since the young man is so certain that he has knowledge about such matters. And so he puts the question, "What is piety and what is impiety?" "Piety," replies the young man, "is doing as I am doing; that is to say, prosecuting any one who is guilty of murder, sacrilege, or any similar crime—whether he be your father or mother, or whoever he may be, that makes no difference—and not prosecuting them is impiety." Socrates, who expected this unsatisfactory type of answer, leads the conversation to the place where he can put the question again, and this time he specifies the kind of answer he is looking for. "I did not ask you to give me two or three examples of piety, but to explain the general idea which makes all pious things to be pious. . . . Tell me what you mean, and then I shall have a standard to which I may look, and by which I may measure the nature of actions, whether yours or anyone's else, and say that this action is pious, and that impious."

Socrates was trying to get at a definition of the general idea of piety, whereas the young man apparently had never considered that problem but had merely attached a high-sounding name to his own action.

Although examples are not sufficient for the understanding of a term, it is true that the meaning of a principle becomes completely clear only when applied to concrete cases. Often when we have our first contact with a new general idea, we say, "What would that mean in practice?" Certainly when we are thinking about values, it is of the greatest importance to ask that question. If we are to choose between two high-sounding principles such as freedom and social control, for example, we must consider exactly what each means in concrete cases. The general idea provides, as Socrates said, a kind of standard for meas-

uring the particular situation, whereas the concrete application enables one to see precisely what the idea includes.

Inasmuch as reflection about values is largely for the
purpose of bringing them to a greater degree of realization
in the existing world, it is important to recognize that in
human affairs we are never dealing with absolutes. Values
compete with one another in such a way that questions
about them can always be put in relative terms. We are not
called upon to decide whether we want absolute democracy;
what we do have to decide is how much democracy we want,
of what kind, for whom, and under what circumstances. Is
it, for instance, to be merely political democracy, or shall
we include economic and social? The three are not the
same. When, during the early days of the Bolshevik revolution in Russia, soldiers on the war front refused to obey
commands of their officers and insisted on settling what
should be done by a show of hands, most of the world agreed
that democracy, in that form, at that time, and under those
circumstances, was ineffectual. A bit of autocracy was
needed. When a national government controls elections in
such a way that the dictator then in power cannot fail to
receive a vote of confidence, most of the world agrees that
autocracy in that form, at that time, and under those circumstances, is a decidedly bad thing. A measure of political
democracy is needed. In practice we are always asking how
much of this good thing we want, and when and where;
seldom do we ask whether we want it all, or at all. Yet the
propagandist tries to make us believe that we are settling
an absolute question and sometimes persuades us in the
face of all of our human experience to the contrary. The
fact is that no American is wholly free and no Russian completely enslaved, no democrary is complete and no dictatorship absolute.

Instrumental and final values

It is impossible to proceed far in comparison of values without coming across a very fundamental, although not an absolute, distinction between two kinds of goods—mediate or instrumental, and immediate or final. The first type includes those goods which are valued, not chiefly for their own sake, but for the further goods to which they lead. A simple example of a mediate value is the possession of money. In most cases we want it, not for itself, but for the things that it will buy, or for the social influences or power that its possession gives us. It is not a good in itself, but it is distinctly good for something. All values that are good primarily for something beyond themselves are included in mediate goods. Immediate values are desired primarily for themselves rather than for their consequences. The pleasure one has in watching a football game is immediate or final. It does not require justification; it justifies itself.

Now although this distinction is important, it is not absolute. Almost anything which is usually only a means to an end may, for some people, under some circumstances, be a final good. The miser, for instance, considers mere possession of money a good without regard to any consequences. Where mediate goods are obtained with difficulty, so that attention is focused upon them, there is a tendency to consider them final values. The ultimate goal is lost sight of in concentration upon the means.

On the other hand, when we examine final or immediate goods more carefully, it is clear that they have, in most cases at least, consequences that are either good or bad, and they are desired or avoided partly upon this ground. In other words, they have both immediate and instrumental value. The pleasure of watching a football game may be self-justifying, but if you catch a bad cold at the same time the entire experience will be judged as a not unmixed good.

It is possible to conceive of actions or situations which would be without any consequences in the way of values beyond themselves. If such situations did exist, they would have no importance for this discussion. They would not require justification, nor lead to conflicts. If we could all enjoy the things which we think good, without suffering any loss or encroaching upon the values of anyone else, there would be no conflicts.

The fact that values lead to other values beyond themselves, that they have consequences which, in turn, are valuable, furnishes a basis for resolving conflicts by intelligence or reflection, rather than by brute force. For as long as we are discussing mediate values, there is at least the possibility of coming to some agreement. We can give reasons for faith in some particular value by pointing out its consequences in further values, and so hope to find an ultimate common ground with an opponent. Two individuals disagree, for instance, about the value of social security legislation. Each supports his position by pointing out the consequences to which he believes the legislation leads. If, however, they agree that a greater degree of security is a desirable end which should be brought about by the most expedient means, then possibly they can, if they are reasonable men, determine whether the legislation proposed is as a matter of fact the best way of bringing about the desired aim. If, however, one maintains that security is a good and the other denies this assertion, there is then a conflict which cannot be resolved by rational argument on these conflicting assumptions. Fortunately, for the reasonable solution of conflicts, there usually is, if the attempt to solve them is honestly made, a common ground, though perhaps remote, upon which disputants can stand. Their differences then resolve into differences about the most desirable means.[3]

At this point, two obvious objections suggest themselves. In the above example are we not assuming that men act from rational motives, whereas in fact they behave emotionally? Our assumption is simple and limited. True, human behavior is far from wholly rational; nevertheless, our conduct is based upon the view that we take of the situation in which we find ourselves. This fact comes out clearly in some common expressions. For instance, if we are called upon to justify our behavior, we may say, "Well, it looked to me as if this were the situation, so I did this thing to which you object." All propaganda is based upon this fact. During the World War Americans were persuaded to knit sweaters, to suspect their German neighbors, and in general to display what was called morale, by means of presenting to them a picture of the world situation which made these activities seem reasonable and desirable. It was taken for granted that if they saw the situation in any other way, they would act differently. When, then, a conflict about values arises between individuals or groups, it is possible to widen the view that each side takes of the situation, to show what the further consequences of a line of action may be and, as a result, to change the attitudes and behavior of the contestants.

A second objection might be that some conflicts are incapable of solution because the values involved are final and also in conflict with one another. There may be such con-

---

[3] For a more detailed discussion of mediate and final values, see *Introduction to Reflective Thinking,* Columbia Associates in Philosophy, Chapters IX and XII.

flicts; at least, we cannot rule them out as impossible. Even so, it is perhaps wiser to assume in particular cases that there are grounds for agreement than to conclude that these are instances of irreconcilable conflict. For if the latter is true, the human loss is great.

Desire for a rational and, therefore, a peaceful solution of conflicts between social groups lies back of movements for settlements by negotiation, mediation, and arbitration. In recent years, doubt has arisen as to the value of this method because of the frequent and conspicuous failures in its application. In Russia, Italy, and Germany the interests of particular classes have been carried through by force; in the international field, the League of Nations has not been able to prevent aggression. Such failures, however, do not demonstrate that the method of conflict is superior to the method of reflection and compromise.

This discussion has been based upon an ultimate assumption: Force is undesirable because resort to it means that some values are lost without having the opportunity to have their day in court. They are ruled out, not because they have been proved incapable of being harmonized with other goods, but on completely arbitrary grounds. The reasons for this assumption would lead far beyond the possible limits of this chapter. It has been stated here partly to illustrate the fundamental point that mediate values are judged in the light of some further good that is for the time being accepted as final.

Up to this point we have been concerned with this question: In how far can we use an intellectual or reflective method in solving conflicts between values? We shall now consider certain specific social values which illustrate some of the points previously made.

FREEDOM AS A SOCIAL VALUE

Liberty or freedom is a social value which has been highly prized in many societies, particularly in modern democratic nations. It has been conceived both as a right and as an ideal or standard for evaluating institutions and laws. So highly is it rated, in name at least, that even those governments which seem to restrict it most feel called upon to justify themselves on the ground that they are promoting "real" liberty as opposed to the supposedly spurious article to be had in nations that boast of their free institutions.

Limitations upon the meaning of freedom

When we analyze the notion of freedom as it has existed in the minds of those who have waged conflicts to gain it, two things become evident. It has usually been limited in the range of its application, and in the breadth of its meaning. Men have fought, not for the liberty of everyone, but for the liberty of a particular group, and they have had in mind, not liberty in general, but some partial aspect or particular embodiment of freedom.

It would be very difficult to say whether for the mass of the people there is more liberty today than there was, for instance, in the twelfth century. In any case, every historic struggle for freedom, no matter how wide its claims, resolved itself into the contest of a particular group to gain recognition of its own right to liberty. The Magna Charta of England, sometimes spoken of as a basic charter of English rights, as a matter of fact guaranteed protection of the barons against the encroachments of the king. The French Revolution, with its emphasis upon the rights of the common man, was at the same time a denial of most of the liberties of the nobility. The American Revolution was fought and won by the rather small part of the British Empire represented in the thirteen colonies in order to obtain relief from economic and political restrictions such as were almost universally imposed upon colonies in the eighteenth century. It did not attempt to free other colonies from those restrictions.

The appeal for greater liberty is thus usually the demand of one group for the right to compete on equal terms for the goods of life with other groups which have previously had an advantage. This motive often comes out clearly when an insurgent group gains its point, for frequently its success leads to its suppression of other helpless groups. The history of religious persecution furnishes numerous cases in which one oppressed sect gains its freedom, only to inflict persecution upon all dissenters within its own ranks.

We have stressed the fact that practical struggles for liberty have usually been carried on by groups interested in their own increased freedom. This fact is frequently overlooked and it is easy to forget, when we are promoting some form of liberty, that our aim may not be as broad as we are likely to believe. Nevertheless there has been here and there in European and American history the achievement of some types of liberty for very large groups of individuals, if not literally for everyone. In democratic nations, some kinds of freedom for almost all persons are guaranteed by law. The liberties are in fact often infringed upon, yet the theory is that any person can appeal for redress, since his rights are assured by the constitution of the state. The constitutional guarantee is designed to protect the individual or the group against aggression from others acting in behalf of their own selfish or unenlightened interests. Freedom of speech, of the press, and of religious worship, the right to trial by jury and to vote are among such liberties

in the United States and England; the right to work is
stressed in the new Russian constitution.

These illustrations bring us to the second limitation upon
liberty. The liberty for which men struggle is usually
specific, even though they state their ideal in general terms.
The particular form of freedom demanded depends upon
the circumstances and groups involved. The most conspicuous conflicts in European and American history have
been described in terms of struggle for political and civil
liberties. Sometimes, however, the more obvious struggle
undoubtedly was for economic freedom. While the liberties
which were finally guaranteed to Negroes during the American Civil War were civil and political, the underlying conflict was between two economic systems, neither of which
seemed able to succeed without encroaching upon the other.
A group which demands freedom may be thinking of the
right to vote without coercion, of the right to think independently, to write and speak without fear of imprisonment, to hire and fire laborers without outside control, to
strike against employers, of the right to work, or even
to eat.

Since the Russian Revolution and the rise of Mussolini
in Italy and of Hitler in Germany, certain of these rights,
largely political and civil, conceived in democratic societies
as belonging to all citizens, have been challenged in a
dramatic way. We may agree that these rights have been
denied in dictatorial governments partly because it suits the
convenience of small groups on their way to power, but the
matter cannot be dismissed so summarily. The opponents
of civil liberties have developed a philosophical justification
of their action and are, by education, developing attitudes
which will eventually affect the entire world. Their theories
challenge our traditional notions of social values, and that

challenge makes it imperative for those who wish to base their social ideals upon something more defensible than habit to reconsider the grounds upon which specific liberties should be defended.

In 1923 Mussolini stated the fascist attitude toward freedom in a manner which has since become familiar. "The plain truth that must stare into the eyes of anyone not blinded by dogmatism, is that men are perhaps tired of liberty. They have had an orgy of it. Today liberty is no longer the chaste stern virgin for whom the generations of the first half of last century fought and died. For the youth that is intrepid, restless and hard, that faces the dawn of the new history, there are other words of much greater power, and they are: order, hierarchy, discipline. . . . Let it be known therefore once and for all that fascism knows no idols and worships no fetishes; it has already passed over and if necessary will turn once more and quietly pass over the more or less decayed corpse of the Goddess Liberty." [4]

The liberties abolished by fascism are chiefly the rights to vote without coercion, to speak one's mind on controversial issues, and to ally oneself freely with organizations within the state. We shall consider here freedom of speech as a specific liberty which is conceived in democratic countries as, with few limitations, the right of all men.

Up to this point we have used the words "liberty" and "right" interchangeably. It would be well to consider briefly the relation between the two in order to avoid misunderstandings. First, a right is effective only in the society that guarantees it. The citizen of Germany in 1936 had, for instance, no effective right to freedom of speech, because

---

[4] Mussolini, Benito, "Forza e Consenso," *Gerarchia*, March, 1923. Quoted in Schneider, Herbert W., *Making the Fascist State*, p. 342 (Oxford University Press, New York, 1928).

the society in which he lived not only had failed to set up
machinery for protecting such freedom, but actually forbade and punished its exercise. During the World War
effective right to freedom of speech in the United States was
much less than in times of peace.

What then do we means when we say that we have the
right to freedom even if that freedom is not operative in
the society in which we live? To avoid confusion and
unprofitable debate we need to take account of one fact,
which is clear regardless of underlying ethical theory. When
we say we have a right that we are not allowed to exercise
within our existing group, we mean that the right in question is a valuable activity and that our society would be
better if it guaranteed that value. We appeal, in other
words, to an ideal situation which we think should be made
actual in society. The German, for instance, who believed
that he had a right to declare his convictions on political
questions judged the existing state in the light of a social
and ethical standard not exemplified in practice.

Freedom of speech

If the right is thus viewed as potential social value or
good, the best rational defense of it lies in an exposition
of the further social goods to which it leads. In terms of
our previous analysis, this means that we treat the particular value as a mediate or instrumental good which leads
to other goods about which agreement may exist. We shall
consider freedom of speech from this point of view. Our
question will be: What further social values does such
freedom lead to, and what social evils does it guard against?

Let us begin with one of the more superficial justifica-
tions that have been given. It is often stated that free
speech should be allowed because it furnishes a safety

valve for dissatisfied elements within society who would otherwise be more dangerous to the stability of the social order. Particularly have the English been praised for the tolerance with which Hyde Park soap-box orators are allowed to say what they please, whether they advocate new religions, new governments, or new economic systems. The argument is good within limits, but it certainly is not a very profound one. For it seems to suggest either that social discontent is trifling and may therefore be taken out in talk, or that, if there is a fundamental social disharmony and discontent, it may evaporate in words. Both assumptions are false. The validity of such defense of free speech lies in the fact that there are minor discontents which free speech renders less violent.

A more basic justification, and perhaps the one most frequently offered, is that freedom of speech is ultimately a safeguard against the tyranny of the government and of smaller groups within the state. Free speech therefore guarantees and preserves many other goods which can flourish only in the absence of tyranny. In a state which allows free criticism of the groups in power, there is at least the possibility of pointing out abuses and arousing an effective public opinion against them. The force of this argument is attested to by the fact that wherever tyrannical governments arise, freedom of speech is one of the first social values attacked. It is not to the interest of the ruler to have his action subject to criticism, however valuable such criticism might be to the citizens. Conversely, when freedom of speech is abolished, there is reason to suspect that the government recognizes its own tyrannical character, although, of course, it rationalizes its tyranny as an interest in the public welfare.

There is need for free speech not only under autocratic

governments but also in those countries in which a constitution and a long tradition guarantee many civil liberties.
Oppression of individuals and of groups by others is always
possible, and the only recourse against it may lie in public
opinion aroused by the free speaking of those who know
and resent these wrongs. Illustrations of this need for free
speech could be given at great length. In the United States,
to take an obvious example, where trial by jury is guaranteed in criminal cases, Negroes are sometimes lynched.
At the same time an active minority is engaged in arousing
general opposition to this clear case of injustice and has
had a large measure of success.

There are, however, more positive gains from free speech
in a democratic country than the ones we have so far discussed. Democracy implies a large degree of free discussion
if it is to exist as such, for democracy involves a decision of
many important questions by a majority. If the decision
is to reflect a majority opinion, there must be the widest
possible discussion of the issues involved. And since the
majority may be wrong—and undoubtedly it often is wrong
—the minority has the social value of continuing to point
out another course which might better have been followed.
This remains true in spite of the notorious faults of the
method by which a majority decision is reached. Free discussion does not insure a wise decision, but it does furnish
a basis on which it is possible to improve the character of
decisions. It has been suggested frequently that a body
of experts should present facts to the people so that they
might have a sound basis for their vote upon issues. This,
however, would not change the essential situation which
we are discussing here, for freedom must be guaranteed to
those experts if their statements are to be of use. Every
such scheme therefore includes elaborate precautions against
even indirect pressure upon such a group, as this might

prevent their giving a complete and unbiased account of their findings.

John Stuart Mill gives a classic exposition of the value of freedom of speech, which is closely allied to the argument that we have just presented: [5]

> Let us suppose, therefore, that the government is entirely at one with the people, and never thinks of exerting any power of coercion unless in agreement with what it conceives to be their voice. But I deny the right of the people to exercise such coercion, either by themselves or by their government. The power itself is illegitimate. The best governments have no more title to it than the worst. It is as noxious, or more noxious, when exerted in accordance with public opinion, than when in opposition to it. If all mankind, minus one, were of one opinion, mankind would be no more justified in silencing that one person, than he, if he had the power, would be justified in silencing mankind.

Now the reason for this is not that there is some mystic right which an individual possesses independently of all duty to society, but that any suppression of freedom of opinion and of speech is, in the long run, harmful to society and the individuals who live in it.

> The peculiar evil of silencing the expression of an opinion is, that it is robbing the human race; posterity as well as the existing generation; those who dissent from the opinion, still more than those who hold it. If the opinion is right, they are deprived of the opportunity of exchanging error for truth; if wrong, they lose, what is almost as great a benefit, the clearer perception and livelier impression of truth, produced by its collision with error.

Limitations upon freedom of speech. If freedom of speech has the social values which we have indicated, does it follow that no limitations should be set upon it? Some ardent advocates say yes. If, however, free speech is defended as a social good, as it has been throughout this discussion, then it is impossible to decide, before examining

---

[5] Mill, John Stuart, *On Liberty,* Third Edition, pp. 32–33 (Longmans, Green & Company, New York, 1912).

the facts, whether it should sometimes be subject to limitation. For although it leads to social consequences which
are undeniably good, it is after all not the only social value.
We should expect that in practice, where it must take its
chances with other social goods, it would sometimes have
to be limited.

If we examine the kinds of situations in which it is
actually limited, we discover that the other social good
with which it most frequently comes into conflict is order,
or stability. Speech is closely linked to action; those who
desire freedom in its exercise do so because they hope to
influence the behavior of other men. In practice every
society, therefore, when it feels its existence or its stability
endangered, places a ban upon free speech. War times
furnish the clearest examples, but peace times have their
illustrations as well. In Russia, for example, when pressure
from the outside world upon the Soviets appeared most
dangerous, restrictions upon thought and opinion were most
severe. Can public order and social stability in a democratic country ever be so threatened by free speech that
a ban should be placed upon it? This cannot be decided
beforehand. When war comes, most of us at least acquiesce
in restrictions which we would not tolerate in times of
peace. In England in 1936 it seemed necessary to the
authorities to prevent the free speaking of the organized
fascist group, because in parts of London it led to violence
against citizens who were entitled to protection.

While we may say that there are circumstances in which
it is necessary that one liberty must be curtailed for the
sake of other things, it is well to remember as a practical
maxim that it is unwise to give up any value lightly.
Freedom of speech will at times be subject to attack by
any selfish group which feels that its private good is en-

dangered by free criticism. The burden of proof for restriction of such freedom of speech lies upon those who attack it.

The difficulties inherent in resolving conflicts of rights suggest that, in the last analysis, the balancing of values which come into conflict is an art, not a science. Because values are not accurately measurable and consequences can be only partially foreseen, we are forced to act without complete assurance regarding the value of the outcome. And yet we are forced to act. Reflection upon values and knowledge about the social world are better guides than blind prejudice, but even when they are most complete and discriminating, there is still a large area of uncertainty. To complain about the existence of this difficulty would be to misunderstand completely our human situation. For that which is true of action in the social field is true of action of any kind. Whatever we do, we make assumptions about a future state of affairs which is in a measure unpredictable. We act upon probabilities and take risks. If we refused to do so, we should, of course, cease to live. Risk is a necessary condition of all action. Risks may be taken after much reflection or after little, but the outcome is usually favorably affected by previous thought. It is not a criticism of thinking to point out that it is never final or absolute.

The complete objectivity which the social scientist tries to achieve in his study of social facts may be necessary to discover fact and distinguish it from fiction. Outside of the scientific field, complete objectivity is an inappropriate ideal, perhaps a contradiction in terms. For objectivity means exclusion of all interests except one, the interest in truth. Yet the fact that we are living beings means that we have many interests, preferences, and aims. They must seek fulfillment in an uncertain world. We must therefore by our very nature take sides.

Throughout the argument for the value of free speech that value has been considered as an instrumental good leading to other values beyond itself. Those further values have been final for the purposes of this discussion. Nevertheless we should be clear as to the character of these final goods. Exactly what is it that has been assumed? We have taken for granted that social measures are to be judged in the light of their effects in the lives of individual members of society. For instance, we have said that free speech is a good because it protects individuals from exploitation by government or by smaller groups. Although this assumption is not so clearly stated in defense of other arguments, it is implicit in them all. In other words, we have made an assumption which lies at the basis of democratic societies. Unless we agree about this assumption, the arguments that we have stated for freedom of speech carry no weight.

When we say we assume that the life of the individual must be the final testing ground of social measures, we do not overlook the fact that the individual is what he is by virtue of the society in which he lives. His desires and aims have been conditioned by the society that is his habitat. We cannot conceive the human individual outside of some social group. The characteristics which make up human personality, as differentiated from merely animal existence, are developed only through social interaction. Society furnishes the necessary opportunity for development of latent individual capacities. How good those opportunities are in given groups is measured by results in socialized human personalities.

Other assumptions are possible and many others have been made. One, which has been stated by some philosophers and is now the formulated theory, in so far as such theory exists, of both the Italian and the German state, denies that the individual is the final touchstone of value The good of the state, which is almost completely identified with society, is conceived as the ultimate value in terms of which all action should be measured. From this point of view it would, therefore, be beside the point to object to the treatment of the Jews in Germany on the ground that discrimination against them causes extreme personal hardships. The logical answer to such objection would be, "We work on a different assumption from yours. You seem to believe that the state exists for the sake of the individuals within it. We assume that the individuals exist for the state, and that its good is always paramount."

This conflict between two views cannot be discussed in detail here. It involves the entire ethical theory of the state and is a difficult problem. One comment may, however, be made: In the most consistent philosophical expositions of this idea, the good of the state or of society seems to be justified, finally, on the ground that within the ideal society the individual would also find his own best ethical development. If this interpretation is correct, the individual remains the touchstone of the good.

CONCLUSION

This chapter has been devoted to discussion of only a few of the many questions concerning social values. The central problem is the part which intelligence may play in leading to a solution of conflicting values. We have seen that analysis of a value in the light of the further goods to which it leads furnishes a possible avenue to agreement. Yet force, rather than reflection, remains the method of solution in many social fields. If we agree that force is no solution and settles no ethical issues, but leads to needless destruction of many human values, there remains a twofold ideal: encouragement of every means, such as education, and negotiation, which may increase the number of peaceful solutions, and the endeavor to bring about a type of social organization in which fundamental conflicts are reduced to a minimum. This program, you may object, is only an ideal. True enough, but as such it has the kind of value that ideals possess. It may serve as a standard for evaluation of institutions and societies. When it does that, it serves its appropriate purpose.

A young man, with whom Socrates was discussing the nature of the ideal city, objected that such a city could not be found anywhere. Socrates assented, but added: "There is laid up a pattern of it, methinks, which he who desires may behold, and beholding, may set his own house in order." To set the world's house, or a room within it, in order, requires a standard, however remote its attainment may be. A plan is an idea; but plans stimulate and test performance. Fiction can pass into fact no less readily than fact into fiction.

BIBLIOGRAPHY

Dewey, John, *How We Think* (D. C. Heath & Company, Boston, 1910).

Columbia Associates in Philosophy, *Introduction to Reflective Thinking* (Houghton Mifflin Company, Boston, 1923).

Castell, Alburey, *A College Logic* (The Macmillan Company, New York, 1935).

Ogburn, William F., and Goldenweiser, Alexander, *The Social Sciences and Their Interrelations* (Houghton Mifflin Company, Boston, 1927).

Mill, John Stuart, *On Liberty* (Longmans, Green & Company, New York, 1912). (Also in Everyman's Library.)

Russell, Bertrand, *Political Ideals* (D. Appleton-Century Company, New York, 1917).

Wilde, Norman, *The Ethical Basis of the State* (Princeton University Press, Princeton, N. J., 1924).

Index

A

Abnormal psychology, 234
Accidents, industrial, 637-640 (see also Workmen's compensation)
Accommodation, 52
Adjustment:
  basis of personality, 228
  definition of, 228
Administration of laws, 505, 535-540
Administrative branch of government (see also Executive branch of government):
  civil service, 537-540
  control of, 535-537
  defined, 535
  merit system, 538-540
  organization, 535-540
  spoils system, 537-538
Administrative rules (see Law and Administrative branch of government)
Adrenal gland, 206
Advertising:
  productive and unproductive, 549
  psychological techniques, 252-254
  psychology of, 249-254
  scientific attitude, 249-250
  theme, 252-253
Aesthetic and expressional institutions, 80-81
Africa:
  anthropology, 104-106, 110-120, 140
  geography:
    northern, 331-333, 378
    southern, 348, 349-351, 374
    tropical, 336-339, 342, 351-354, 362

Age (see also Old-age insecurity)
  chronological, 236-238
  effect on learning, 212-213
  influence of hormones, 207
  mental, 236-238
  of foster children, 240
  social importance of, 107-110
Agriculture, 324, 325, 327-357
  map, 331
  relation to manufacturing, 360-61, 366, 371
  revolution, 349
  systems of, 345
Alcheringa, 117
Aliens, rights of resident, 447-448
Amerindian agriculture, 345-346
  map, 331
Ancestry, inheritance, 243
Animal:
  behavior, 208
  learning, 208
  psychology, 208
Anthropology, 92-143
  definition of, 92
Appalachian coal field, 368, 371
Appearances:
  physical, 226
  relation to personality, 226
Arabs, Egyptian, 137
Argentina, geography, 324, 328, 341, 376
Aristocracy, political, 406-407
Aristotle, 400
Art, 100
Arunta, 102, 107
Assimilation, 52
Associations, 66
  related to institutions, 55-91
Attention:
  applied to advertising, 250-251
  factors of, 250

Attitudes:
  relation to personality, 227
  scientific, 202
  scientific applied to advertising, 249
Australia, anthropology, 102, 107–109, 111–120, 129, 138
Automobile tire illustration, 595–597
Averages, 233–236, 729–735
  arithmetic mean, 730–733
  deviation (*see* Dispersion)
  index numbers, 742
  median, 734–735
  misuses in interpretation, 748–750
  mode, 733–734

B

Baker, O. E., cited, 361
Behavior (*see also* Culture, Psychology, Economics):
  definition of, 199
  effect of hormones upon, 207
  general laws, 231
  how original behavior is modified, 206, 209, 210, 223
  human, 199, 201
  man's, 203
  native, 203
  patterns, 203, 234
  rejection, 216
"Best friend" relationship, 105
Betrothal, infant, 132, 134
Bias in science, 2–13, 705, 749–750
Bicameral (*see* Legislature)
Binet, Alfred, 235
  test, 235–238
Birmingham, Alabama, geography, 369
Birth rate (*see also* Supply of labor):
  differential of economic groups, 612–613
Blast furnaces, 366
Bowman, Isaiah, 379
Brazil, geography, 338, 354, 358
Bull-roarer, 129–130
Burks, Barbara, 239, 240

Burma, 134
Business cycle, causes, 705

C

Cairo, customs in, 106
Camp, 102
Campaign, electoral, 477–483 (*see also* Electoral process)
Canada, geography, 334–335, 341, 350, 362, 365
Capital, role in production, 364, 550, 595–597, 607, 624
Case method, 19, 714–717
  Hippocrates, 715
  Le Play, 715
Catalonia, geography, 365
Cattell, James McKeen, 231, 235
Cattle plague illustration, 573 ff.
Causal relationship:
  and correlation, 243–244, 738
  natural, 701
  pattern of, 702
  search for, 9–13, 698–699
  supernatural, 700
Central values (*see* Averages)
Chicago, culture areas of, 34–37
Chieftainship, 141–142
Child:
  dress of primitive, 112
  primitive status of, 120–128
  punishment of, 122–124
Chile, geography, 348, 356, 376
China, geography, 346–347, 353, 355–356, 372
Chinese kinship terms, 136
Chippewa, 131–132
Chthonian, 107
Church, 79–80
Citizenship (*see* Chapters X and XI)
  duties and obligations, 451–452
  how acquired, 446–447
  rights and privileges, 448–451
Civilization, effect on preliterate cultures, 94
Civil Service (*see* Administrative branch of government)

Climate (*see also* Rainfall, Growing season)
effect on health, 336, 373
in general, 342, 343, 344, 347, 348
Coal, 356, 362, 365, 366, 367–368, 369–370, 371, 372
Coconuts, 337, 338, 352
Codes, social, 65
Coefficient of correlation (*see* Correlation)
Coffee, 352, 354
"Cold lands," 328, 330–332, 334–336
Collection of data, 708–721, 725–729, 748
case method, 714–717
census, 726–727
cumulative errors, 748–750
laboratory method, 709–714
questionnaires, 727–729
statistical method, 717–721
Collective behaviorism, 145–146 (*see also* Social psychology)
Combination of factors of production (*see* Factors)
Commerce, 334, 336, 338, 339, 341, 342, 346–347, 349, 350–351, 352, 354–359, 364
basis of trade, 356–357
Commercial grain farming, 350–351
Commercial grazing, 333–334, 341, 377–378
map, 331
Common law (*see* Law)
Communicative institutions, 78–79
Communism (*see* Russia, Dictatorship)
Community life, 81
Complexes, 220–221 (*see also* Culture)
definition of, 220
determine behavior, 221
direct and indirect expression, 221
indications of, 222–223
Comradeship, 104–105
Conditioned reflex, 209 (*see also* Pavlov)
experiment, 209–210

Conflict, 52
result of demands, 228
Consciousness, 215
Constant-cost industry, 576–577, 586
Constitution:
amendment, 502–503
as basis of government, 428–429
Bill of Rights, 506
constitutionality of social security law, 667–668, 679–680
controlling government and its branches, 506
defined, 501
rigid or flexible, 502–503
written and unwritten, 501–502
Constitutional law (*see* Law)
Control group, 711–713
Pasteur, Louis, 712–713
Convention (*see* Electoral process)
Convict-made goods:
amount of, 588–591
economics of, 582–591
effect on external prices small, 582–585
Cooley, C. H., view of human nature, 24, 166–169
Corn, 328, 337, 345–346, 348, 350, 352, 354, 357
Correlation, 243–244, 738–742
interpretation in causation, 739
Pearsonian coefficient, 739–742
positive and negative, 739–740
Cost:
of food, measurement, 743–744
relation to prices of factors, 603–604, 607
Cotton, 324, 352, 354
Cree, 121
Creek Indians, 140
Crime:
age as a factor, 266
amount and nature of, 259–264
and conformity, 258
cost, 264–265
crimes known to the police, 261–263

Crime *(Cont.)*:
  death penalty and homicide rates, 263–264
  definition and point of view, 257–259
  economic status and crime, 273–277
  endocrine glands, 271
  environment as factor, 272–276
  grand jury *(see* Prosecutor)
  heredity *(see* Environment)
  imprisonment *(see* Prisons)
  interrelation with heredity, 273
  judge, 283–286
    and politics, 283–284
    functions of, 284–285
  law, 47–48, 275–276
  Lindbergh Law *(see* Police)
  mental defectiveness as factor, 268
  mental disorders and psychopathy as factors, 269–272
  parole *(see* Probation and parole)
  penology and penal philosophy, 286–289
    classical, 287
    positive, 288
    treatment vs. punishment, 289
  physical defectiveness as a factor, 267–268
  police, 277–282
    criticisms of, 279
    salaries of, 280
    state police, 281
  prediction methods *(see* Probation and parole)
  prevention, 298–303
  prisons, 289–292
    historical background of, 290
    modern prisons, 291
    treatment as ideal, 292
  probation and parole, 292–296
    criticisms of parole, 294
    parole function, 293–294
    prediction of parole success, 295
    probation problems, 296
    relation to indeterminate sentences, 292

Crime *(Cont.)*:
  prosecutor, 282–283
    and politics, 282
    relation to grand jury, 283
  punishment *(see* Penology *and* Penal philosophy)
  recidivism, 297
    success of present penal system, 296–298
  sex as a factor, 266–267
  state police *(see* Police)
  sterilization *(see* Prevention)
  trends, 262
  visting teacher *(see* Prevention)
Crises, social, 99–100
Crow Indians, 98, 137
Cultivated lands, 342–357
  map, 331
Cultural determinism, 154–157
  limitations, 157
Cultural inheritance, 345, 348
Cultural landscapes, 323, 325, 328
  map, 331
Culture:
  area, 34–37, 96–97
  complex, 32–37
  contact, 87–88
  definition of, 29
  differential rates of change, 45–50
  diffusion, 43–45
  lag, 45–50
    reasons for, 49–50, 89–91
  maladjustment:
    personal disorganization and, 50–52
    the individual and, 50–52
  nature of, 29–37
  pattern, 32–37
  stratifications, 95–96
  trait, 30–32
Curie, Mme., 705
Customs, 64

D

Dahomey, 105, 110, 129
Dakota Indians, 99, 125
Darwin, influence on history, 317

Deciles, 735
Decreasing-cost industry, 577–579, 586
Deduction vs. induction, 721–723 (*see also* Science *and* Scientific method)
Delinquency areas, 34–37
Delinquents, 19
Demand:
  change in, 570
  definition, 562
  elasticity, 562–563
Democracy:
  as a form of government, 406–407, 412, 421–428
  attributes, 421–428
  importance of rights, 449
  popular participation under, 444–499 (*see also* Government)
Deserts, 331–332, 356, 358
Desire:
  inventory of, 252
  satisfaction of, 251
Determinism, in geography, 377–379
Deviation, standard, average (*see* Dispersion)
Dictatorships:
  one-party system, 487
  place of citizen, 449
  threat to liberty, 496–497
Dieri, 108
Differences:
  individual, 231
  racial and national, 240–241
Diffusion of culture, 97
Dispersion, 736
  average deviation, 737
  range, 737
  standard deviation, 737–738
Dissociated, 215
Distribution (*see also* Income *and* Wealth):
  curve, 232–233
  law of normal, 232
Division of labor, 557–560 (*see also* Trade)

Domestic animals, 328, 329, 332–334, 336–337, 346–347, 348, 350, 352, 377–378
Domestic institutions, 70–73
Donetz coal basin, 370
Drainage, 343, 349, 357
Dreams, 114, 217
  day, 230
  relation to personality, 227
Dress, social function of, 110–113

E

"Early start," advantage, 364
Economic geography, 327–373
  as a division of geography, 373
Economic institutions, 68–70
Economics, 545–697
  as a science, 546
  assumptions, 547
  definition, 545–546
  objectivity in, 546–547
Economic security, 636–697 (*see also* Workmen's compensation, Health insurance, Old-age insecurity, *and* Employment insurance):
  conflict with progress, 636
  health insurance, 640–649
  old age, 649–668
  unemployment, 668–697
  workmen's compensation, 637–640
Educational and scientific institutions, 76–78
Edwards family, 242–243
Elasticity of demand (*see* Demand)
Electoral process (*see also* Parties *and* Popular participation):
  election proper, 483–484
  electoral campaign, 477–483
  financing campaign, E n g l i s h, French, American, 480–483
  nominating by convention, 471–472
  nominating by petition, 475–477
  nomination procedures, 469–477
  primaries, 472–475

Electorate, as a branch of government, 505-506 (see also Electoral process and Popular participation)

Emotions:
as motivators, 221
complex adult, 205
determiners of behavior towards advertising, 251-252
example of, 204
relation to complexes, 220-221
role in altering original behavior, 223
rudimentary, 205

Employment exchanges, character and purpose of, 670-672

Employment insurance, 677-687
basic features of compulsory plan, 681-687
constitutionality of compulsory plan, 680
coverage, 684-685
extent of taxes, 687
federal-state plan, 679-680
four-in-one ratio, 686-687
incidence of social security taxes. 687-696
labor union plans, 677-678
merit rating, 682
plant reserves, 681-682
pooled reserves, 682-683
premiums, 683-684
trade agreement plans, 678-679
waiting period, 686
Wisconsin plan, 681-682

Endocrine glands (see also Crime)
in general, 206-208
relation to personality, 226

Entrepreneur:
definition, 550
differentials, 583-586
in production, 550

Environment (see also Culture and Cultural determinism)
demands of, 228
importance of, 246

Environment (Cont.):
influence on intelligence, 238-240, 243, 245
part played in personality, 224

Equality, principle of democracy, 425-427

Equity (see Law)

Eskimos:
anthropology, 103, 120-121, 132-133, 140
geography of region, 334

Ethnocentrism, 1, 52, 93-94
defined, 3

Euhalayi, 120

European manufacturing belt, 365-368, 371
map, 331

Exchange value, 557-560

Executive (see Separation of powers)

Executive branch of government:
powers and functions, 521-524
relation to legislature, 527-535
structure, 518-521

Experimental method (see Laboratory method and Scientific method)

F

Factors of production (see also Production):
combining of, 551-556
functions of, 603
income earned equals cost of production, 603-604
interchangeability of, 552-556

Factory system in agriculture, 350, 352

Fairies as supernatural causes, 700

Family:
as social institution, 70-73
Edwards, 242-243
histories, 242-243
Kallikak, 242-243

Fascism (see also Dictatorships):
as a philosophy of government, 416-421

Fear, stimulus for, 205

Federalism in government, 407–410 (*see also* Government, Constitution)
Feeble-minded, 201, 238, 245
Fertilizers, 346–347, 349
Finch, 326, 379
Fish illustration, 573 ff.
Fishing, 329, 334, 335, 337, 364
Flour mills, 359
Folkways, 37–40, 64
Ford, Henry:
contribution to society, 595
on value of history, 319
Forests, 348, 375, 377 (*see also* Taiga, Tropical forests)
Forgetting, 214
wishful, 215
Formal, discipline, theory of, 212
France, 365, 367–368
Franchise (*see* Citizenship, Popular participation in government)
Fraternities, college, 27
Freedom:
and rights, 777–778
as a social value, 774–785
limitations in meaning of, 774–778
of speech, 778–785
limitations upon, 781–783
Freeman, Frank, 239, 240
Frequency distributions, 731–733
assumptions in averages, 732–735
indeterminate classes, 733
Freud, S., 215, 217, 218, 223
Fuller utilization, 577–579
Functional distribution, 598–599 (*see also* Income *and* Wealth)
would persist under socialism or communism, 598–599, 634–635
Fundament, 326, 343, 377–379
Future developments, 339–342, 371–373

G

Garver, Frederic B., cited, 371–372
Geography, 323–379
agricultural, 327–379
definition, 324–327

Geography *(Cont.)*:
divisions of, 373–375
economic, 327–373
historical, 373
nature and purpose, 323–324, 379
of nationalities, 374
of peoples, 374
physical, 326
political, 374–375
relations to the other social sciences, 375–379
settlement, 373
social, 373–374
urban, 373 (*see also* Urban centers)
Germany, geography of, 365, 367–368
Gerontes, 107
Gilyak, 131
Glands, 206, 225 (*see also* Endocrine)
Government (*see also* Constitution, Administration, Political science, State, Legislative branch, Judicial branch, Executive branch, Administrative branch, Parties, Electoral process, *and* Popular participation in government):
classifying governments, 404–428
autocratic and democratic, 412–428
monarchy, aristocracy, and democracy, 406–407
parliamentary and presidential, 410–412
unitary and federal systems, 407–410
classifying states, 402–404
Communism, 414–416
concept of law, 393–398
constitution, 501–503
constitutional basis, 428–429
democratic, 421–428
distinguished from state, 391–393
expanding interests, 445
Fascism, 416–421

Government *(Cont.):*
  international, 428–443
  machinery of, 500–544
  machinery of state, 391–393
  political theory, 398–402
  popular participation in, 444–499
Grain trade in ancient times, 355
Grasslands, 377–378 *(see also* Steppes)
Grazing, 331–334, 338–339, 340–341, 377–378 *(see also* Steppes, Nomads, Commercial grazing)
Great Britain, geography of, 365, 367–368
Greece, ancient, 107
Group behavior, nature of, 5–6 *(see also* Groups)
Grouping, ceremonial, 103–104
Group mind, 144–146
Group plans for health insurance, 642–647
Groups:
  nature of, 24–28
  primary, 24–25
  secondary, 25
Growing season, 334, 335, 343

H

Habit, 65
  relation to personality, 227, 230
Handicraft industries, 347, 349, 359, 364
Hart, B., 215
Hartshorne, Richard, 323, 379
Hay, 348–349
Health, 373
Health institutions, 82–84
Health insurance, 640–649
  British Columbia health insurance, 644–647
  criticisms of private medicine, 640–644
  criticisms of public medicine, 648–649
  scope of public medicine, 642–644
Herodotus, 313

Hides, 339
Hippocrates and the case method, 715
Historical geography, 373
Historical method *(see* Case method)
"Historical mindedness," 320
History, 205–321
  as literature, 318
  as memory of human race, 320
  as social science, 319
  bias in, 312
  definition of, 305, 307
  Henry Ford on value of, 319
  importance of style in, 315, 316
  influence of Darwin on, 317
  influence of Marx on, 317
  material value of, 318
  reasons for writing, 313
  scientific, 316
  scope of, 306, 308
  sources for knowledge of, 309–312
  the "new," 308
  truth in, 313
  value of, 318–321
Hobbes, Thomas, quoted, 139
Hoe culture, 337–338
Homer, 138
Homogeneity:
  importance in scientific method, 719–720
  measure of *(see* Dispersion)
Hormone:
  adrenal, change with age, 207
  definition of, 206
  thyroid, pituitary, sex, 207
Hottentot, 110, 137
Household circle, 101
Human factors in manufacturing, 363–365
Human nature, 142, 166–169
Hume, David, quoted, 139
Hunting, 95–96, 329, 334, 335, 337, 377
Huntington, Ellsworth, 379
Hypothesis in scientific method, 706–708

I

Ice areas, 330–331, 358
Imitation, 172–175
    ceremonies, 116–120
Income (*see also* Wages, Inequalities):
    among people, generally, 600
    attorneys, 601
    causes of inequality, 614–623
    controlling, 602
    defined, 592–593
    distribution, 592–635
    education, effect on inequality, 632–635
    effect of labor unions, 620–621
    families, 601–602
    farmers, 600–601
    low income groups tend to be self-perpetuating, 612, 619
    measuring, 592–593
    monopolies, 626–629
    non-farm, 601
    physicians, 601
    taxation, 602, 630–635
Increasing-cost industry, 574–576, 586
Index numbers, 743
    average of relatives, 743
    market basket, 744
    measurement of real wages, 745–746
    measurement of standard of living, 745
    weighted prices, 744
India, geography of, 338, 341, 346–347, 353, 372
Indians (American), 121–133, 328, 334, 345–346, 376
Industrial revolution, 349, 359
Inequalities of income (*see also* Income, Wages):
    ability and opportunity, 617–623
    causes, 614–623
    causes, complex, 614
    corrections, 623–635
    correlation with responsibility, hazard, efficiency, 616, 617

Inequalities of income (*Cont.*):
    due to monopolies, 626–629
    due to preferred positions, 625
    education no remedy, 632–635
    effect of labor unions, 620–621
    fundamental cause is variation in supply, 617–623
    in Russia, 634–635
    more apparent than real, 615
    physicians, 622
    statistics, 600–602
    summary of causes, 623
    taxation as a remedy, 602, 630–632
    teachers, 622
Infant:
    adjustment to environment, 228
    effect of maturation upon his adaptive behavior, 208
    helplessness of, 208
    newborn, 203, 204, 205
In-group, 26
Initiative (*see* Popular participation in government)
Insects, 336, 341, 343
Insight:
    comparison with conditioning, 24
    definition of, 211
    experiment on, 211
Instincts and human behavior, 4, 147–151
Institutions, 41 (*see* Social institutions)
Intelligence, 235
    assumptions underlying its measurement, 235
    Binet test, 235–236
    influence of environment, 238
    native, its implication, 245–246
    native or acquired, 238–246
    quotient (*see* I.Q.)
    relation to desires, 229
    relation to personality, 228–229
International Labor Organization, 440
International law, 396–397, 438–439
    (*see also* International relations)

International relations, 429–442 (*see also* International law):
difficulties of coöperation, 433–437
future, 431–433
progress, 437–438
significance, 429–431
Inventions and culture, 41–43
I.Q., 236
constancy of, 239–240
distribution in a normal group, 237
formula for, 236
influence of environment on, 239
Iron and steel industry, 366–370
"Iron moves to coal," 367
Iron ore, 362, 366–372
Iroquois, 122
Irrigation, 332, 333, 340, 345, 346–347
projects in United States, 340
Isolating, 202
verification, 202
Italy, geography, 349, 365, 371

J

James, Preston E., 379
James, William, 229
formula for self-esteem, 229
Japan, geography, 324, 346–347, 353, 364–365, 369–370, 372
Java, geography, 341, 346–347
Judicial branch of government (*see also* Crime):
administrative courts, 540–541
function, 543–544
jurisdiction of courts, 542–544
ordinary courts, 540–543
unified judiciary, 541–542
Judicial function (*see* Separation of powers *and* Judicial branch of government)
Justice, machinery of, related to crime, 277–286

K

Kallikak family, 242–243
Kinship, 136

Köppen, 344
Koran, 374
Krivoi-Rog iron district, 370

L

Labor, in manufacturing, 364–369
(*see also* Wages *and* Income):
insecurity of aged, 649–652
Laboratory method, 709–714
control group, 711
use of statistics, 721
Labor unions:
effect on inequality of income, 620–621
for unemployment, 677–678
plans for old age security, 655–656
Land utilization, 327–359
map, 331
Late start, advantage of, 364–365
Law:
as a concept of political science, 393–398
defined, 503–504
psychology in, 254–255
types of law, 393–397
League of Nations, 429–442, 439–441
(*see also* International relations)
Leahy, Alice, 239, 240
Learning:
examples of, 208
factor in behavior evaluation, 208
improving, 213–215
more primitive than understanding, 209
motor, 214
overlearning, 215
why we learn, 216
Legislative:
committees (*see* Legislature)
function (*see* Separation of powers *and* Legislature)
Legislature:
bicameral vs. unicameral, 510–513
committees, 517–518
election, 513–516

Legislature *(Cont.)*:
functions, 524–526
organization, 516–518
presiding officers, 516–517
relation to executive, 527–535
single-member and general ticket
plans, 513–516
structure, 510–513
Le Play, 715
Levirate, 131
Liberty (*see also* Dictatorships, Self-
government, *and* Freedom) :
restraints on, 444, 774–785
under democracy, 421–428
under Russia and Fascism, 414–
421
Lie detector, 254–255
"Light industries," 368–369
Link, H. C., 252
Lobbying (*see* Popular participation
in government)
Location, relative, 343, 344, 357–379
Lorraine, geography of, 367
Love:
"medicines," 133
stimulus for, 205–206
Lumbering, 335–336, 360

M

Machinery, 364
McKay, H. D., 34
Magic in causal relationships, 700
Malthus, 611
Man and nature, 377–379
Manufacturing areas, 359–373
American, 368–369, 371–373
European, 365–368, 371
map, 331
others, 369–370, 371–373
Soviet Union, 370–371
Maps, 325, 327, 331, 344
Marginal productivity of labor (*see*
Wages, Labor)
Marriage, 131–135
Marx, Karl, influence on history, 317
Massim, 135

Matrimonial and domestic institu-
tions, 70–73
Maturation, definition of, 206
social implications of, 208
Maya, 109
Meaning, an analysis of, 765–769
Measurements, 201
Medicine, criticisms of private, 640–
644 (*see also* Health insur-
ance)
Medicineman, 113–116
Mediterranean agriculture, 347–348
Memory, factors affecting, 215–216
Menomini, 123–125
Mental age, 236–237
Metallurgical industries, 360, 363,
366
Method (*see also* Scientific
method):
case-study, 19
comparative, 18–19
experimental, 22–23
historical, 18
statistical, 20–22
Mexico, geography, 345–346, 362
Migratory agriculture, 337
Mill, John Stuart, 781
Mining, 330, 336 (*see also* Coal,
Iron ore):
relation to manufacturing, 361
Minnesota, geography of, 323, 324,
356–357
Mohammedanism, 374
Monarchy, 406–407
Monopoly:
costs, 581
defined, 579
inequality of income caused by,
626–630
law and, 579
methods of creating, 580–581
price, 581
profits, 581
regulating, 626–627, 629
Montreal, geography of, 365
Mores, 38–41, 64
Moron, relation to personality, 229

Motivation, 184–186, 216–220
  conscious motives, 219
  unconscious motives, 219
Motor skills, 208
Mountains, 332, 339, 358, 360
Movements, random, 204
Mussolini, Benito, on freedom, 777

N

Name, 118, 120
Narrinyeri, 108
Native, 203
  behavior, 203
  emotions, 205
  intelligence, 238–246
Natural environment, 325–326, 343–345, 377–379
Natural landscape, 325
Navigation, 355
Nationalities, 374
Negroes:
  geographical aspects of, 352–354
  intelligence of, 240–241
  tested during World War, 241
Nerve, auditory, 200
  impulse, 200
New England, geography of, 323, 335, 369
New Guinea, 135
New World:
  effect on Old World, 338, 345
  geography, 328, 349–351
Nigeria, geography of, 338, 341
Nomads, 331–333, 334, 338, 341, 373–374, 376, 377
Normal law of distribution, 232–234
North Atlantic areas, 358, 363, 365, 366

O

Oases, 332, 333, 374
Occidental agriculture, 345, 347–351, 354
  map, 331
Ogburn, William F., 42 ff.

Old-age assistance, 660–661 (see also Old-age insecurity)
Old-age insecurity, 649–668
  benefits and coverage of compulsory system, 663–666
  causes of, 649–652
  compulsory retirement pension under 1935 act, 661–668
  compulsory system not to displace old-age assistance, 666–667
  constitutionality of old-age security legislation, 667–668
  depression effect, 649
  effect of high-speed industry, 650
  effect of immigration, falling birth rate, longevity, 651–652
  effect of shift to urban life, 649–650
  financing compulsory system, 662–663
  incidence of taxes, 687–696
  industrial pension plans, 652–655
  labor union pensions, 655–656
  old-age assistance, 660–661
  provision for indigent aged before 1935, 658–660
  public employee retirement plans, 656–658
Omaha tribe, 127
Ontong Java, 103–104
Opinion, 138–141
Opposition, 52
Oriental agriculture, 345, 346–347
  map, 331
Orosius, *Seven Books of History Directed Against the Pagans*, 314
Other-group, 26
Out-group, 26

P

Pacific Coast, 365, 372
Packing plants, 359
Paddy field, 346–347
Pampas, 328, 341
Papua, 140
Parents, foster, 239

Parliamentary government, 410–412
(*see also* Government)
Parties:
basis of, 487–490
Bureaucracy, 491
defined, 486
Fascism, Conservatism, Liberalism, Socialism, Communism, as attitudes in politics, 488–490
functions, 486–487
membership voluntary, 492–493
nonpartisan, 494
organization, 478, 490–491
platform, 479
political, 477–496
purpose, 491–492
Pasteur, Louis, 712–713
Pattern of causation, 702
Pavlov, Ivan, 209, 210
Pearsonian correlation (*see* Correlation)
Peary, Robert S., 332
Pensions, (*see* Old-age insecurity)
Pepys, Samuel, quoted, 139
Percentiles, 735
Permanent Court of International Justice, 440–441
Personal income distribution, 598–599 (*see also* Income, Wealth, Wages, *and* Inequalities):
attorneys, 601
families, 601–602
farmers, 600–601
non-farm, 601
physicians, 601
population generally, 600
statistics, 599–602
Personality, 105–106, 113–116, 175–184, 201
definition of, 224
relation of attitudes to, 227
relation of glands to, 225
relation of habits to, 227
relation of health to, 225

Personality *(Cont.)*:
relation of intelligence to, 228–229
relation of physical appearances to, 226–227
result of adjustments, 228
well-adjusted, 216, 224–233
Personnel, selection, 249
Peru, geography, 345–346, 359, 362
Physical geography, 326 (*see also* Fundament, Geography, *and* Natural landscape)
Pituitary gland, 206 (*see also* Glands)
Placement, selective, 240
Planned public works, 673–675
Plantations, 345, 351–354, 360
map, 331
Plato, political speculation, 400 (*see also* Socrates)
Podzols, 335
Poland, geography of, 339, 365, 371
Police (*see* Crime)
Political geography, 374–375, 379
Political institutions, 73–76
Political organization, 337, 373–375
Political parties (*see* Parties *and* Electoral process)
Political science, scope and definition, 380–385 (*see also* Administration, State, *and* Government):
autocratic and democratic government, 412–428
classification of governments, 404–428
classification of states, 402–404
concept of law, 393–398
constitutional basis of government, 428–429
definition of state, 385–386
international government, 428–443
monarchy, aristocracy and democracy, 406–407
parliamentary and presidential government, 410–412
political theory, 398–402

Political science (Cont.):
  problems of political theory, 399–402
  state as a concept of political science, 385–389
  state sovereignty, 389–391
  unitary and federal systems, 407–410
Political stability, essential for manufacturing, 364
Political theory (see Political science)
Polybius, 314
Polynesia, 103–104
Popular participation in government, modes (see also Political science, Electoral process, and Parties):
  electoral process, 469–484
  improving, 496–498
  initiative, referendum, and recall, 465–469
  lobbying, 494–496
  nonpartisan parties, 494
  officeholding, 452–457
  parties, 477–496
  voting, 457–465
Potato, 328, 335, 345, 348
Power, 362–363 (see also Water power, Coal)
Precipitation efficiency, 344
Pre-Columbian civilizations, 345, 376
Presidential government, 410–412 (see also Government, State, and Separation of powers)
Price (see also Index numbers):
  agency of price changes, 565
  equals cost under competition, 548 ff., 579
  function of, 545, 560–562
  laws of, 564 ff.
  market, 562
  mechanism, 561
  normal or long term, 573 ff.
  of factors of production, 551

Primaries (see Electoral process)
Primary industries, 330
Prison-made goods, economics of, 582–591 (see also Convict-made goods)
Prisons (see Crime)
Probability in science, 724
Probation and parole, 292–296 (see also Crime):
  criticisms of parole, 294
  parole function, 293–294
  prediction of parole success, 295
  probation problems, 296
  relation to indeterminate sentence, 292
Product differentiation, 580–581
  cause of inequality of income, 626
Production, 548–557
  definition, 548–549
  factors of, 550–556
Progress, conflict with security, 636
Propaganda by statistical methods, 748–750 (see also Scientific method)
Psychologist, 201
  differential, 232
  interest in accuracy of testimony, 254
Psychology (see also Social psychology):
  animal, 208
  applied, 231
  definition of, 199
  differential, 231–232
  general, 199
  of advertising, 249–254
  social, 144–197
  stimulus response, 200
  subject matter of, 199
Public employee, retirement plans, 656–658 (see also Administration)
Punishment for crime (see Crime)
Purchasing power (see Index numbers)

Q

Quantitative methods, limitations in social sciences, 190–191, 194 (*see also* Scientific method)
Quartiles, 735
Questionnaire:
in statistics, 727–729
pitfalls, 189–190

R

Races, geography, 336, 343, 346, 352–354, 374, 376
Rage, stimulus for, 205
Railroads, 334, 341, 342, 349, 350, 355–356
relation to settlement, 350, 355
Rainfall, 332–334, 336–337, 338, 340, 343, 344, 346–347, 348, 374
Ranches, 333–334
Random movements, 204
Random selection:
effect on sampling, 727–729
reliability of statistical measures, 748
Ranke, Leopold von, 316
Rationalization, 221–224
definition of, 221
Ratios:
index number, 747
per capita usage, 747
vital statistics, 747
Reactions, acceptance, rejection, 215
Real wages, 745–746
Reason:
contrasted with complexes, 223
description of, 223
Recall (*see* Popular participation in government)
Recreational institutions, 81–82
Referendum (*see* Popular participation in government)
Reflexes:
conditioned, 209
examples of, 204
Reflex theory of original nature, 151–152
Region, defined, 325, 326–327

Regional geography, 326
Regulation and stagnation, 636
Relationship, joking, 136–138
Relief, geographical, 343, 344, 346, 347, 349, 357 (*see also* Mountains)
Religion, 373, 374
Religious institutions, 79–80
Rent, 551, 555
Representative values (*see* Averages)
Response, 200, 201
conditioned, 209
emotional, 205
substitute, 210
Rice, 352, 354, 436–447
Rights, 777–778 (*see also* Citizenship *and* Popular participation in government)
Roads, 334, 342, 349, 375
Robinson, Edward S., 199
Robinson, James Harvey, on scope of history, 308
Roman Empire, trade, 355
Rome, ancient, 107
Rubber, 338, 352
industry, 364
Ruger, H. A., 211
Ruhr, geography of, 367
Russia:
autocratic government, 414–416
geographical aspects, 336, 339, 341, 349, 350–351, 362, 370–371
growing inequalities of income, 634–635

S

St. Louis, geography, 365
Sampling process, 21–22
in statistics, 727–729
Sandra, 104
São Paulo, geography, 354, 358
Sauer, Carl, 379
Savannas, 338–339, 341–342
Savings, effect on society, 595–597, 602, 624

Science, nature of, 10–11, 199–203, 324, 546–547, 698–751
Scientific approach, 702–705
  induction and deduction, 721–723
  in writing history, 309–331
  method, 755–759
  method, fundamental stages, 706
  the scientific law, 723
  verification of inductions, 722
Scientific institutions, 76–78
Seas, use of, 329
Self, as viewed by G. H. Mead, 180–181
Self-government (see also Electoral process, Political parties, Popular participation in government, Democracy, and Government):
  citizenship, 446–452
  limitations on, 444
  place of individual, 444–446, 484–485
Separation of powers (see also Executive, Legislature, and Judiciary)
  administrative branch, 525–540
  election to legislature, 513–516
  judicial branch, 540–544
  organization of legislature, 516–518
  powers of executive, 521–524
  relation of executive and legislature, 527–535
  structure of executive, 518–521
  structure of legislature, 510–513
  theory of, 502–510
  union of powers, 508–510
Settlement, 327, 357, 360, 361–363, 365–366, 373
Sex (see also Glands):
  as a motivating force, 217
  effect of sex hormone on behavior, 207
  Freud's emphasis of, 217
  gland, 206
  importance of sex hormone in relation to age, 207

Sex (Cont.):
  primitive separation of, 128
  secondary sex characteristics, 207
Shaw, Clifford, 34
Shawnee, 137, 141
Sickness (see Health insurance)
Smith, Adam, on specialization and self interest, 558
Social change, 41–52
Social conduct, development of, 160
Social conflict, 759–765
Social control, 62
Social geography, 373
Social institutions, 55–91
  attributes, 63–67
  causes, 58
  changing, 85–88
  definition, 57–58
  description, 55–56
  functions, 60–63
  inflexibility, 89–91
  interrelationship, 84–85
  main groups, 67–84
  range, 59–60
  survival, 89
Social interaction, 8
Socialized medicine, 640–649 (see also Health insurance)
Sociology:
  defined, 9
  field of, 6
  methods of, 18–23
  other sciences and, 13–18
  value of, 52–54
Social psychology, 144–197
  criticism of instinct theory, 149–151
  definition, 144–147
  development, 144
  French influence, 145–156
  group setting, 154
  interested in individual development, 146
  motivation, 184–186
  personality, 175–184
  present status, 196–197
  reflex theory, 151–152

Social psychology (Cont.):
  relation to sociology and psychology, 146–147
  social interaction, 169–175
  study of conduct and personality, 186–196
  symbolic interaction theory, 152–154
  view of original nature, 147–154
Social sciences and natural sciences, 13–16
Social security (see Economic security)
Social Security Act, 660–668, 677–687 (see also Old-age insecurity, Employment insurance, Workmen's compensation, and Health insurance)
Social valuation, 752–786
  application of critical method in study of, 759–786
  exclusion from social science, 752, 755–759
Socrates, 767, 768, 786
  and the problem of definition, 767–768
  on the status of ideals, 786
Soil, 328, 335, 337, 339, 343, 344, 346, 353, 373, 377–378
Sources, historical, 309–312
South Africa, geography of, 348, 349–351, 374
South America, geography of, 341–342, 374 (see also under separate countries and Hispanic America):
  temperate, 333–334, 349–351
  tropical, 336–339, 342, 351–354, 376
South Atlantic Piedmont, 365, 369, 372
Soviet Union (see Russia)
Soy bean, 347
Spain, geography of, 349, 365, 367
Sparta, 118
Specialization of labor, 557–560 (see also Division of labor)
Standard deviation (see Dispersion)

Standardize, test, 236
Standard of living, 745–747
Starch, Daniel, 253
State (see also Political science and Government):
  classification, 402–404
  classifying governments, 404–428
  concept in political science, 385–389
  concept of law, 393–398
  definition, 385–386
  functions of, 73–76
  machinery of, 391–393
  needs, organs, and agencies, 500–501
  political theory, 398–402
  sovereignty, 389–391
  totalitarian, 389
State medicine, 640–649 (see also Health insurance)
Statistical method, 717–721, 748–750
  collection of data, 725–731
  importance of homogeneity, 718–720, 749
  need for averages, 729–735
Status, economic, 106
Stefansson, 341
Steppes, 332–334, 338, 340–341, 350–351, 373–374, 376
Stimuli:
  adequate, 209
  conditioned, 209
  definition of, 200–201
  emotional, 205
  inadequate, 209
  substitute, 210
Stimulus-response view of group behavior, 157, 209–211
  contributions, 160–162
  effect of view on research, 187
  limitations, 162, 187–191
  view of personality, 175–184
  view of social interaction, 169–171
Style, importance in writing history, 315–316
Suffrage (see Citizenship and Popular participation in government)

Sugar-cane, 337, 352, 354
Suggestion, 172–175
Sumner, William Graham, 1, 38
Supernatural causation, 700–701
Supply:
  change in, 571
  laws of, 564 ff.
  reserve, 566
Supply of labor (see also Wages)
  differential birth rates among
    classes, 610–612
  effect on wages, 610–614
  Malthus, 611
Sweden, geography of, 336, 365, 367
Switzerland, geography of, 368
Symbolic interactionist view of ori-
    ginal nature, 152–153
  attitude toward research, 191
  emphasis on inner experience, 193
  interpretation of social conduct,
    163–166
  view of group life, 158–160
  view of personality, 175–180
  view of social interaction, 171–175

T

Taboos, on food, 108, 119, 121
Taiga, 334–336, 362
  map, 331
Tanaina, 104, 141
Tariffs, 357
Tasmanians, 141
Taxation:
  incidence of social security, 687–
    696
  reducing inequality, 602, 630
Temperature 330, 332, 334, 335, 336,
    343, 344, 348 (see also Climate
    and Growing season)
Tennessee Valley Authority, 344
Terman, Lewis M., 236
Test:
  Binet's, 235–238
  laboratory field, 253
  language, 240
  non-language, 240

Test (Cont.):
  standardize, 236
  triple associates, 252–253
Testimony, accuracy of, 254
Textile industries, geography of, 360,
    366, 369, 557
Thomas, W. I., four wishes, 184
Thucydides, 314
Thyroid gland, 206–207, 226
Tire, motor car, 595–597
Tobacco factories, 369
Toda, 130–131
Topography (see Relief)
Towns (see Urban centers)
Trade (see also Commerce, Trans-
    portation, Ports, Railroads,
    and Roads):
  basis of, 356–357, 557–560
Training, transfer of, 211–212
Transportation:
  costs, in relation to location, 357–
    359
  development, 354–356
Tree belts, 340
Trewartha, Glenn T., 326
Tribal organization, 333, 337, 374
Tropical:
  areas, 328, 336–339, 341–342, 376
  forests, 336–338, 351–354
  highlands, 345–346
Truth, in history, 313 (see also Sci-
    ence)
Tundra, 330–332, 334
"Turning the child" ceremony, 125–
    126
Twins:
  fraternal, identical, 244
  relation in intelligence, 244
Tylor, Edward B., 29
Typical value (see Averages)

U

Ubiquitous industries, 330, 359, 360
Ukraine, geography of, 370
Unconscious, 215
  bias, 220
  motives, 219

Unemployment:
  casual unemployment, 670–672
  credit control, 675–677
  cyclical unemployment remedies,
    673–675
  employment exchanges, 670–672
  employment insurance, 677–697
  extent, 669–670
  planned public works, 673–675
  remedies, 670–697
  seasonal unemployment and reme-
    dies, 672
  state employment compensation
    plans, 679–697
  types, 668–669
Unicameral (see Legislature)
Uniformity, measures of (see Dispersion)
Union of governmental powers, 508–
  510 (see also Separation of
  powers)
Unitary government, 407–410
United States, geography of, 333–
  335, 340–341, 349–351, 353–354,
  362–365, 368–369, 371–372, 374,
  376
United States Bureau of Labor Statistics, index numbers, 745
Upper Silesia, geography of, 365
Urban centers, 330, 332, 334, 336,
  337–338, 342, 347, 349–350,
  353–354, 359–360, 363, 366,
  368–369, 372–375
Urban geography, 373
Uruguay, geography of, 328, 341, 378

V

Value in exchange, 557–560
Value judgments, 753–759
  based on preference, 754–755
  in the social sciences, 755–759
Values, instrumental and final, 770,
  773
Variation:
  continuity of, 234–235, 238
  measures of statistical (see Dis-
    persion)
Vidal de la Blache, P., 379

Villages, 330, 351
Vital statistics, ratios in, 747
Vocational guidance, 231, 246–249

W

Wages (see also Income, Inequalities):
  causes of inequality, 614–623
  difficulty in exploiting labor, 607–
    609
  marginal productivity theory of,
    605–610
  supply of labor, 610–614
  unemployment as a corrective to
    wage rates, 607–609
  value of labor, 605
Water power, 362–363, 368, 369
Watson, J. B., 205
Wealth:
  concentration and income distri-
    bution, 594–598
  defined, 593
  distribution of, 594–598
  in Massachusetts, 594
We-group, 26
West Africa, geography of, 352 (see
  also Nigeria)
Wheat, 335, 347–348, 356–357
Whitbeck, R. H., 379
Whites, American, 240
Wine, 347, 355
Winnebago, 128, 137
Wishram, 123
Wood bundles (illustration), 605
Workmen's compensation, 637–640
  accidents compensable, 638–639
  aim to reduce accidents, 639
  employers' liability, 637
  premiums, 639–640
Wündt, Wilhelm, 231
Wyandot, 131

Y

Yana, 133
Yoruba, 129

Z

Zimmermann, Erich W., cited, 360